MISSOURI NEWSPAPERS

MISSOURI

NEWSPAPERS

William H. Taft

UNIVERSITY OF MISSOURI PRESS
Columbia, Missouri

PUBLICATION OF THIS BOOK
HAS BEEN AIDED BY THE
MISSOURI PRESS ASSOCIATION AND THE
STATE HISTORICAL SOCIETY OF MISSOURI

PREFACE

THE STUDENT of the history of a state must draw upon newspapers for background material; few, however, go behind the scenes to study the newspapers themselves. Those who undertake such study encounter problems, for only a few of the early newspapermen were so historically minded as to arrange to save file copies of their publications. Thus, many blank walls, many voids frustrate the researcher's efforts. Too, conflicts in dates, differences in the spelling of names, irregularities in the titles of papers all add to the confusion which must be ordered before a clear picture may emerge.

This history is one of three projects concerning Missouri newspapers. It attempts to provide highlights of the state and national history from 1808 to the present, with emphasis on the newspapers and on their editors who recorded this information for use by today's historians. The second project concerns the personalities among newspapermen, those individuals who left their mark upon the profession and who carried on the highest standards despite unfavorable odds. A third, directed more precisely to the researcher, lists all papers the author has uncovered—more than five thousand—and the places where copies or microfilms may be found. This project has been published by the State Historical Society of Missouri under the title, *Missouri Newspapers: When and Where, 1808-1963*. Such a list, while incomplete, will, it is hoped, stimulate further research into the many papers that have contributed so much to the state's history.

Many "thank you's" are due. The files of the State Historical Society of Missouri in Columbia were most useful, with aid from Richard S. Brownlee and Kenneth Holmes; the work of many journalism students, especially those in the author's class in History and Principles who wrote term papers on Missouri topics; the inspiration of Dean Emeritus Frank Luther Mott, who set a pace difficult to follow; the Missouri Press Association, its general manager, William A. Bray, and the support of its member papers; Professor Earl English, Dean of the University of Missouri School of Journalism, for making the time available; the University of Missouri Research Council, for a grant to acquire photostats and to visit the Library of Congress; my colleagues who read chapters and offered useful comments, including Dean Thomas A. Brady, Dean James L. Bugg, Jr., Dr. Richard S. Brownlee, Dr. Floyd C. Shoemaker, Mitchell White, and Frank W. Rucker; and especially my wife, whose patience, continual encouragement, and reading of this copy has made all this possible, and to my children for their endurance.

Still, the author holds himself responsible for all visible errors.

W. H. T.

School of Journalism
University of Missouri
April, 1964

CONTENTS

CHAPTER   I.   BEGINNING: THE *Missouri Gazette*   1

CHAPTER   II.   MISSOURI PAPERS EXPAND WITH TERRITORY   12

CHAPTER   III.   NEW STATE, MORE PAPERS WELCOMED   24

CHAPTER   IV.   PIONEER PERIOD COMES TO END   39

CHAPTER   V.   LULL BEFORE THE STORM   50

CHAPTER   VI.   CIVIL WAR SPLITS STATE AND PRESS   70

CHAPTER   VII.   PUBLISHERS LOOK AHEAD FOLLOWING
THE WAR   93

CHAPTER   VIII.   GROWTH IN PERIOD OF TRANSITION   103

CHAPTER   IX.   EARLY YEARS OF MISSOURI PRESS
ASSOCIATION   122

CHAPTER   X.   MODERN PERIOD IN MISSOURI   139

CHAPTER   XI.   PRESS ASSOCIATION GROWS IN STRENGTH
AND SERVICE   152

CHAPTER   XII.   MISSOURI'S BIG-CITY EDITORS   168

CHAPTER   XIII.   THE COUNTRY EDITOR AS SEEN BY
HIS COLLEAGUES   179

CHAPTER   XIV.   HISTORICAL SOCIETY ESTABLISHED
BY PRESS   195

CHAPTER   XV.   NEW CENTURY REACHED: PRESS AT PEAK   202

ix

CHAPTER   XVI.   SCHOOL OF JOURNALISM ESTABLISHED   209

CHAPTER   XVII.   STATE AFFAIRS AFTER TURN OF CENTURY   220

CHAPTER   XVIII. WORLD WAR I REPORTED BY STATE PRESS   230

CHAPTER   XIX.   ROARING TWENTIES IN THE MISSOURI PRESS   247

CHAPTER   XX.   DEPRESSION, LEAN YEARS, THEN WAR   262

CHAPTER   XXI.   WAR NEWS: GROWTH DESPITE SHORTAGES   282

CHAPTER   XXII.   PRESS REBUILDS: STRONGER AT
                   MID-CENTURY   301

CHAPTER   XXIII. MISSOURI PRESS FACES THE FUTURE   322

CHAPTER   XXIV.   MISSOURI PRESS AND LEADERS TODAY   334

APPENDIX A   BLUE RIBBON PAPERS IN MISSOURI   352

APPENDIX B   MISSOURI PRESS ASSOCIATION PRESIDENTS   354

APPENDIX C   AWARDS FOR DISTINGUISHED SERVICE IN
                   JOURNALISM   357

APPENDIX D   AYER'S DIRECTORY OF MISSOURI
                   NEWSPAPERS   359

NOTES   361

INDEX   405

CHAPTER I

BEGINNING: THE *MISSOURI GAZETTE*

THE HISTORY of Missouri since before its statehood has been recorded in its press. Through newspapers that first appeared in 1808, the reader can learn of the growth and development of all the phases of life in Missouri. In addition to the newspapers' records of "history in the making," three major events that concern the development of the press in the state stand out in a study of Missouri newspapers.

The first occurred on July 12, 1808, when Joseph Charless founded the *Missouri Gazette* in St. Louis, inaugurating newspaper publishing in the territory that was to become the state of Missouri, and earning for himself, a transplanted Irishman, the title of "Father of Missouri Journalism."[1]

In May, 1867, the second key event occurred when a group of men met in convention in St. Louis and organized the Editors' and Publishers' Association of Missouri, known today as the Missouri Press Association.[2]

The third major event in this more than a century and a half of journalism in the Showme State was the establishment of the University of Missouri School of Journalism in Columbia in 1908, not long after the press association had pushed for the founding of the State Historical Society.[3]

Through such events the history of journalism in Missouri can be reviewed, together with the contributions made to the life of the state by the editors, the press association, and the historical and educational centers.

CHARLESS REACHES MISSOURI

In 1808 Missouri residents for the first time had an opportunity to read a newspaper published in their own community when Joseph Charless pulled copies of the *Missouri Gazette* from the Ramage hand-operated printing press that he had shipped from Pennsylvania to St. Louis.

What was the territory like when the first press arrived?

Historians have stressed the significance of St. Louis as a gateway to the West and as a center for refugees from Europe. The community had become a new frontier home for settlers from Virginia, the Carolinas, Tennessee, Maryland, and Kentucky, when land in those states became more difficult to obtain at low prices. Population figures indicate the rapid growth, both for the area later to become Missouri and for St. Louis.[4]

Only a month before Charless established his newspaper, St. Louis had become a town—on June 18, 1808, under an act of the territorial legislature. The new town was yet to hold its first election, on July 28, to establish its government and to elect trustees.[5]

Preparatory steps had been made for Missouri to become a state before Charless arrived in the territory. As early as October, 1803, Congress had provided a temporary form of government for the area, and President Thomas Jefferson had appointed Captain Amos Stoddard civil commandant, with headquarters in St. Louis for the Upper Louisiana area, providing for the Territory of Orleans south of the thirty-third parallel and for the District of Louisiana to the north. This latter area became a part of the Territory of Indiana, which had its seat of government at Vincennes. Considerable discontent was voiced by residents over this partition of the territory, especially after many of the Spanish land grants had been declared null and void. Further, the distance to Vincennes created problems for those having business with the government. In order to satisfy some of these objections, Congress in 1805 made the Upper Louisiana a separate territory, removing it from its association with Indiana and shifting its center of government to St. Louis. This situation continued until 1812, so that St. Louis was part of the Upper Louisiana territory when Charless started his journalistic endeavors there.[6]

THE EARLY EDITOR

In his study of *The Pioneer Editor in Missouri*, William H. Lyon, Jr., notes that the minister, physician, lawyer, merchant, and journalist were among the early settlers in any community, with the journalist among the last of the professional men to arrive. One reason for this delay might be in Lyon's explanation of the needs that must exist in a community before a newspaper can operate successfully.

> Four agents in pioneer society labored to found a newspaper press that would enhance their status as effective participants; the government, which needed to publicize its laws; politicians, who wished to crystallize public opinion; the literate citizenry, who sought information and intelligence; and the printer-editor who was motivated by an amalgam of altruism and political and economic advantages. All four of these founding agents seldom, if ever, cooperated in establishing a public journal, but a com-

bination of two or more of them constituted a requisite for setting up a pioneer press.[7]

Charless possessed many of the characteristics requisite for success as a pioneer editor. He had come to America by way of France from his native Ireland, where he had participated in the rebellion of 1795. A publishing effort in the late 1790's with the *Mifflin Gazette* of Lewistown, Pennsylvania, failed. Eventually he joined another Irish refugee, Matthew Carey, in the latter's print shop in Philadelphia and published books in the years 1800-1802. While in Philadelphia Charless became acquainted with a number of the nation's leaders, including Benjamin Franklin, Alexander Hamilton, Henry Clay, and others, and was associated briefly with Franklin's grandson, Benjamin Franklin Bache, in publishing an attack on President George Washington.[8] Like Franklin, Charless always considered himself a "printer," not an "editor."

Apparently it was from Philadelphia that Charless decided to seek success on the frontier. He sent a prospectus for a weekly newspaper to Lexington, Kentucky, but his proposed *Gettysburg Gazette and Weekly Advertiser* never materialized. In this prospectus he expressed a desire to "defume public and private character" and deter "the flagitious from crime," among other objectives. In 1803 Charless moved to Lexington, Kentucky, and to Louisville later where, on November 24, 1807, he started the *Gazette and Western Advertiser*, with only one newspaper, the *Farmer's Library*, in competition. Charless kept his Kentucky paper when he moved to St. Louis; on July 26, 1809, an item in the *Missouri Gazette* announced its sale.

Kentucky had become crowded, and the frontier beckoned to Charless, who turned his attention to the virgin Louisiana Territory, a region full of promise, yet void of printers. Charless pushed on to St. Louis, arriving during the summer of 1808. He had been encouraged to come to the territory by Governor Meriwether Lewis, who wanted his press established in time to publish the new laws to be enacted in June, 1808, when the territorial legislature was to meet. By now this "warm-hearted, generous Irish gentleman"[9] was in his mid-thirties, with considerable printing experience, including some successes and some failures; Charless was ready to meet the Governor's request. Illness, however, delayed his starting the *Missouri Gazette*.

While in Philadelphia Charless had married, and when he brought his family to St. Louis he had to provide for a stepson,

Robert McCloud—who was to print the first paper in St. Charles
—his own three sons, and two daughters. Charless encouraged
his sons to learn the printing trade, but apparently only the
eldest, Edward, followed this idea.

Charless received an advance of $225 from Governor Lewis
to help buy equipment and supplies. Soon he was to receive a
more sizable advance for printing the laws of the territory.[10] He
had already issued his prospectus several weeks prior to his
arrival in St. Louis, a customary procedure of the day. While
many printers promised the impossible, Charless does not appear
to have done so, as the following prospectus would indicate:

> It is self evident that in every country where the rays of the
> Press is not clouded by despotic power, that the people have
> arrived to the highest grade of civilization, there science holds
> her head erect, and bids her sons to call into action those talents
> which lie in a good soil inviting cultivation. The inviolation of
> the Press is co-existent with the liberties of the people, they live
> or die together, it is the vestal fire upon the preservation of
> which, the fate of nations depends; and the most pure hands
> officiating for the whole community, should be incessantly em-
> ployed in keeping it alive.
>
> It is now proposed to establish a Weekly Newspaper, to be
> published by subscription at St. Louis, to be called the

MISSOURI GAZETTE
AND LOUISIANA ADVERTISER:

BY JOSEPH CHARLESS

> For the reasons above stated, we conceive it unnecessary to
> offer anything like professions to the public, but rather let the
> columns of the GAZETTE speak for themselves, and the print
> let to live or die by the character it may acquire, but its intended
> Patrons have a right to be acquainted with the grounds upon
> which their approbation is solicited.
>
> To extinguish party animosities and foster a cordial union,
> among the people on the basis of toleration and equal govern-
> ment. To impress upon the mind, that next to the love of GOD,
> the love of our COUNTRY should be paramount in the human
> breast; to advocate that cause which placed Jefferson at the head
> of the magistracy, and in fine to infuse and keep alive those
> principles which the test of experience has so evidently por-
> trayed its merits, to these ends shall the labours of the *Gazette*
> be directed.
>
> No endeavours nor expense shall be spared in procuring the
> earliest Foreign Intelligence, which shall be impartially given, and

a particular attention paid to the detail of domestic occurrences, with extracts from the proceeding of the state and national legislature—To diversify scenes, we shall glean whatever may be most instructive and amusing in Belles Letters with historical and Poetical extracts—men of genius are invited to send their productions to the *Gazette,* which will be open for fair discussion on public subjects—it will disdain to direct its flights at smaller game —scurrility and defamation can never be admitted as auxiliaries —private character is one of the possessions of civil society which ought to be held sacred; to follow a man into the circle of private life, would be a very unfair and licentious act;—therefore, the editor will invariably exclude any and every piece which might lead to disturb our public officers, in the honest discharge of their duty, or the peaceful walk of the private citizen.

(Similar ideas were then written in French.)

CONDITIONS

I. The *Gazette* will be published once a week on handsome Type and Paper, the day of publication will be regulated by the arrival of the Mail; during the session of Congress, should their proceedings be particularly interesting, a supplementary sheet shall be occasionally issued.

II. Terms of payment will be Three Dollars payable in advance, or Four Dollars in Country Produce. Advertisements not exceeding a square will be inserted one week for one dollar, and for every continuance Fifty Cents, those of a greater length in proportion.

III. The first number of the *Gazette* will appear as soon as possible, the Types being ready at Louisville, Ky., and the press expected in the course of a month from Pennsylvania. The intended editor pledges his reputation, that there will be no unnecessary delay.[11]

PROBLEMS ARE PLENTIFUL

Charless experienced most of the problems that plagued the frontier printer. He had difficulty obtaining paper; the largest sheets available for the initial issue were twelve inches long and eight inches wide. His Ramage press, probably the best available to him at the time, was of wood, with a stone bed and iron framed tympan. The shop's quarters in a log house were quite cramped.[12] During his first two years of publishing, Charless estimated his costs to be approximately $20 weekly.

Maintaining adequate help soon became difficult when Charless' first associate, Jacob Hinkle, left after only four months in St. Louis. Hinkle had come with Charless from Kentucky and, according to two notices Charless printed in the *Gazette*

November 23-30, 1808, was a gambler. Charless cautioned other printers and the public in general about Hinkle, citing his gambling which had caused him to shift from Virginia to Kentucky to Missouri. Hinkle owed $600 around and about St. Louis at the time of his sudden departure, including $200 worth of goods and funds that Charless had advanced him to get established. Charless' cautionary notice indicated that Hinkle's earlier activities had centered around proposals to issue papers in various communities; he would collect in advance for subscriptions, then leave town. Later in his career he bought horses, watches, and other items, giving notes for their purchase, then he would sell these articles, taking part cash, and again move on. Charless' description made it easy to identify Hinkle: twenty-four years of age, five feet nine or ten in height, a shuffling walk, sallow complexion, black and curly hair, crossed eyes, very near-sighted, and "plainly stamped *The Villain* in every lineament thereof." Charless later advertised for "a man of good orderly habits" with "a wish for instruction or a knowledge of a branch of the printing business."[13]

Not only did his paper stock vary in size, but Charless frequently noted in the *Gazette* delays in obtaining shipments. In 1814 he informed readers that he had sent money to Lexington for newsprint, "but in consequence of no regular trade being carried on with that place, his paper waits for an accidental trader coming this way." On other occasions, he placed additional orders with Eastern firms to ensure deliveries.

Charless intended to provide readers with ample news, yet his concept of news did not stress timeliness; in his third issue, for example, there appeared a story from London dated April 22, 1808. This disregard of timeliness in the news was a happy circumstance, for apparently the editor failed to reckon with transportation along the frontier; irregularities in mail services were encountered frequently. Charless blamed the postmaster and his aids for the delays, yet the weather and other factors were beyond the control of these officials. Charless likewise failed to take into account the possibilities of attacks from Indians, roads that generally were nonexistent except on maps, and streams that suddenly became rivers during the rainy season. Even under the best of conditions, St. Louis was scheduled for only weekly mail deliveries, and when the cargo was heavy, bulky newspapers frequently were left behind by the postriders. Local individuals held the contracts with the federal government to carry the mail, and postal officials in the East had little contact or control over these postriders. Improvement in transportation was slow; the *Missouri Gazette* was ten years old before Charless could print an advertisement announcing the opening of a triweekly stage line to St. Charles, some twenty-five miles away.[14]

Charless' early problems with the mail handicapped his publishing efforts seriously. Early in 1809 he told his readers about sending a messenger to Vincennes to probe for the cause of the delays which frequently stretched to a month for papers from the East. When news was short or the paper stock limited, Charless reduced the *Missouri Gazette* to two pages that varied in size.[15] Once when news was extremely meager, Charless began printing "A History of Kentucky" to fill the space.

Subscribers, too, kept Charless on a tightrope. Missouri editors from 1808 on were to voice criticisms about delinquent subscribers. On November 16, 1809, Charless wrote that those who "intend to discharge the amount of their subscription in flour are requested to do so immediately." Threats were numerous about cutting off the subscribers—but not until they had paid their past accounts. Charless' delinquent accounts reached $1,200 within two years. Had it not been for his government printing, it is doubtful whether he could have maintained the paper during the early years. In later years Charless carried on the *Missouri Gazette* more from public spirit and love of the newspaper business than for any profits he expected to realize.[16]

Near the end of his publishing career the editor recalled that he had 174 subscribers the first year. This was increased to 500 by 1814 and to a thousand by 1819.[17] A thousand subscribers in a community of four thousand gave Charless a deep concentration of readers. However, it was not uncommon for printers to exaggerate their circulation figures. Charless' mentions of growing lists included comments about the slow delivery of the *Missouri Gazette* to those communities because of the mail service, indicating that transportation problems continued to trouble him.

First Two Issues Missing

The first two issues of the *Missouri Gazette* have not been located, and the earliest available copy is dated Tuesday, July 26, 1808, Volume I, Number 3. This would indicate a founding date of July 12 for the first paper in the territory. Charless recorded on page 1 that he was "Printer to the Territory." In some of the later issues of 1808, he was unable to provide readers with regular-size editions, being too busy printing the *Laws of the Territory of Louisiana,* a book containing 376 pages of laws with 60 pages of index matter.[18] In several issues of December, 1808, Charless advertised for sale copies of the regulations concerning the fiscal operation of the territory.

Charless, as did many of the other pioneer printers, found it necessary to handle varied projects to make ends meet. He "conducted a boarding house and livery stable, dealt in old brass and copper and other commodities, was in the drug business for a time, and also for a time had an office for the registry and sale of lands, town lots, and slaves."[19] All this and more. Boarders were welcomed as early as 1810, and two years later Charless had a brief partnership with Dr. Bernard Gaines Farrar in the drug business. Later he became a justice of the peace and an auctioneer.

EDITORIAL COVERAGE

Considerable material that appeared in the *Missouri Gazette* Charless obtained by the scissor system, clipped from other papers, especially those from the East, and he collected information from travelers passing through the Gateway to the West, from letters, and from other sources. The first available issue, for example, devotes practically the entire front page to a two-month-old story from London. It was not until later that Charless edited copy to fit available space and to provide a wider variety of news. In the early years he made no attempt to departmentalize news or advertisements, and apparently all items were inserted as they came in or as they might fit the page.

By 1817 the steamboat reached St. Louis.[20] Charless, at first reluctant to recognize the potential value of this mode of transportation, was probably the first editor west of the Mississippi River to be a guest of a steamship captain on a promotional tour. On June 9, 1819, Charless editorially thanked the captain of the *St. Louis* for his "polite and generous conduct" on a trip to the mouth of the Missouri and return. He then predicted great gains in traffic between St. Louis and New Orleans, since the travel time, when compared with the barges, had been cut from thirty to eight days.

The *Missouri Gazette* carried accounts about the Indians—whom Charless distrusted—settlers and their problems, traders and their business activities, judicial proceedings, Army news and rumors, as well as items on wars, earthquakes, famines, and the like. At times Charless confessed his error in accepting a rumor as a fact, but normally he would blame faulty transportation or communication facilities for such misunderstandings. Political affairs received little attention during the early years, but with the creation of the territory in 1812 and the subsequent contests for election of delegates to Congress, Charless devoted more coverage to local events. Letters from readers occupied considerable space. Charless wrote that he would print such messages as were "intelligible, printable, and pertaining to a subject of public interest." These letters generally stimulated replies from the wounded party, to be followed by rebuttals and, frequently, a continuing warfare with the pen.

Charless, as a civic responsibility, used his newspaper to promote and encourage new business firms to enter St. Louis. Such concerns won the praise of the editor for their foresight in selecting the city for their enterprise. Local items, the backbone of community papers today, occupied little space in the *Missouri Gazette*. Here, however, Charless was merely following a style of news editing prevalent throughout the country. Reports on deaths and marriages were limited to those of quite prominent persons. On the other hand, news from Europe, despite its age, was considered of greater importance than local news and as lending the paper prestige. Educational items appeared in the paper, along with the traditional assortment of poems, jokes, anecdotes, and items about agricultural developments such as the currently popular Merino sheep.[21] The lists of unclaimed letters at the postoffice were printed as a service to the readers. As the community expanded and developed, advertisements gained in importance. From two advertisements in the early issues Charless built to seventy "commercials" in 1820. By 1815 the entire first page was covered with these messages, frequently decorated with woodcuts, and by December 1, 1819, the last page was filled with advertisements as well.[22] By 1817 Charless was in a position to order a new press and supplies, as indicated by an advertisement offering his old equipment for sale.

To meet the demand for more frequent publication dates, Charless in 1819 promised a Saturday mercantile paper, primarily for the businessmen. This paper was not to be considered a part of the *Missouri Gazette*, but was to be sold separately. There is no evidence such a publication ever appeared.

Before September 13, 1820, when Charless edited his final

edition, he encountered competition in the form of the *Western Journal*, which began publication in 1815. A long series of political and personal battles had taken their toll of Charless' energy and enthusiasm and contributed toward his decision to leave the news arena. One politician had spit in his face and threatened him with a pistol; another had assaulted him in the street; still another had fired at him while he was working in his garden. Although Charless was victorious in a lawsuit against Isaac Henry which resulted from a street fight, he had to pay $20 and costs for contempt of court after Thomas Hart Benton had criticized the *Missouri Gazette's* account of the struggle before the formal court action had been instituted.[23] This conflict prompted Charless to turn to the state legislature, where he sought clarification of the law on freedom of publication, but many years were to elapse before papers achieved this freedom.

Charless had lost much of his public printing to the *Enquirer*, which appeared under this title in 1818. His refusal to go along with the majority on the slavery issue apparently cost him heavily. Some readers stopped their subscriptions over his stand on congressional restrictions. Yet it is still difficult to determine any single reason that prompted Charless to leave the editorship and sell the paper to James C. Cummins, who had come to St. Louis from Pittsburgh.[24] Charless stated he made a modest profit, but how much of this came from the paper and how much from his allied interests is not clear. He printed an advertisement on July 12, 1820, about a "new entertainment house" he was opening. This, apparently, was a combination tavern and rooming house. Some believe he had acquired adequate income from operating a drugstore with his son, from his farms, his boarding and lodginghouse, and other business endeavors. Possibly the political struggle had become too much; possibly Charless preferred to keep his friends and pursue his business affairs in more peaceful conditions. After leaving the editorship he participated more actively in civic affairs and in 1826 was elected president of the Board of Aldermen. Throughout his career Charless opposed Thomas Hart Benton and supported Jefferson, Madison, and Monroe.

The *Missouri Gazette* returned to the family when his son, Edward, repurchased it in 1822 and renamed it the *Missouri Republican*.

Lyon summarizes the career of Missouri's first printer as follows:

As the first printer-editor in the Mississippi Valley, Charless's record is not unblemished, yet withal it is a laudable one, especially in the matter of freedom of expression. He stood for liberty of the press, so much so that his zeal to promote that liberty, and what he thought was just and right, sometimes led him to bend the truth. He strove for a certain amount of impartiality (except wherever the Indians or the English were concerned), and posed as the head of an independent organ, even when he knew it would cost him the financial support of the government and raise up an opposition to wrest political ascendancy from him. As the Father of Missouri Journalism, then, he is not an unworthy master.[25]

CHAPTER II

MISSOURI PAPERS EXPAND WITH TERRITORY—1808-1820

POLITICIANS who failed to gain Charless' support found it necessary to turn elsewhere for a paper to present their views to St. Louis voters. Thus it was that after seven years Charless had aroused opposition sufficient to stir these men into action, with the result that Missouri received its second paper, the *Western Journal.*

Local politicians frequently opposed Charless and his editorial comments. Lyon recalls Charless' attacks on the military for permitting excessive gambling and drinking among the men, on the authorities concerning the handling of the War of 1812 on the frontier, and on the courts for their "lenient" handling of the Indians, a subject close to Charless, who distrusted the natives.[1] Too, there were verbal battles concerning slavery, with Charless supporting the antislavery cause against such men as Thomas Hart Benton. Benton, soon to oppose Charless editorially, was seeking Missouri's admission to the Union under a constitution that would tolerate slavery.[2]

Charless' men were overwhelmingly defeated in the territorial elections—an item to support the observation that throughout his lifetime, from his youthful years in Ireland to statehood days in Missouri, Charless was on the side of the minority. Though he said the *Gazette* columns were open to all views and opinions, it appeared that his editorial and political activities sought primarily to limit any expansion of slavery. Some even charged that he omitted news or that he colored reports about persons he disagreed with, not an unusual practice among nineteenth-century editors, who made personal journalism a trademark of the times.

Charless' quarrel with the proponents of slavery broke into the open during the summer of 1814 after a group of men called upon him. They exchanged harsh words with Charless, but apparently no blows. Later, these men placed an advertisement in the Lexington, Kentucky, *Reporter* stating that the people of St. Louis were not satisfied with their present printer and would welcome one of "correct republican principles"; even one "with moderate abilities" would satisfy them. Charless defended his position, writing that it was a well-known fact that only five or six persons opposed him, including the "*little* lawyer and *would be* Lord Mayor,*"* a reference to Thomas Hart Benton. This opposition he termed the "military junto."[3]

The advertisement brought results. In March, 1815, the proposed *Western Journal* was advertised by Joshua Norvell, who had come to St. Louis from Nashville, Tennessee, attracted by the thousand dollars that had been raised by the politicians who opposed Charless.[4] Norvell, apparently of "modern republican principles," was unsuccessful as an editor and by September, 1816, had moved to Arkansas. His paper, established to wreck the financial foundation of the *Missouri Gazette*, failed. The following year it was revived as the *Emigrant and General Advertiser* with the first issue on May 17, 1817. Its editor was Sergeant Hall, a lawyer from Cincinnati. Some sources refer to this paper as the *Western Emigrant*, but this appears to be in error, since the *Missouri Gazette* always mentions it as the *Emigrant*. This paper was transferred in August, 1818, to Isaac N. Henry and Evarist Maury,[5] after Hall found the operation unprofitable. The new owners renamed the paper the *Enquirer*, without any change in volume numbering. Charless had the last word at least for the time, when he wrote, "We mentioned some time ago that Sergeant Hall would go to Arkansas and join his prototype, Mr. Norvell. It has actually come to pass; the junto have got tired of the Sergeant and have taken the press and type from him."[6] Charless continually referred to his opposition as the "tool" or "hireling press," vicious words in any age.

The "great man," Thomas Hart Benton, served as editor of the *Enquirer* with Henry and Maury, a position he utilized to place himself before the public on issues of the day. Later, Benton, according to John Q. Adams in his memoirs, was a part owner of the paper that was changed from a weekly to a semiweekly briefly in 1819 only to revert to weekly status in 1820. In the announcement of the twice-a-week schedule Henry promised to continue to "print a clear and decent paper, devoted to the general service, and holding itself above the filth of private scandal and personal abuse."[7]

Benton termed papers "the most powerful lever which can be applied to the human mind" and "the school of public instruction," what the Forum had been in Greece and Rome.[8] Quite outspoken on major issues, Benton continually replied to charges by Charless and called the editor an "old communications maker," implying that Charless wrote many of the letters printed in the *Missouri Gazette* over various signatures. Benton's views were presented in the *Enquirer* in an editorial on "Objects of Public Interest with the People of Missouri; the Accomplishment of which requires the aid of the National Government." The title is considered significant by Perry G. McCandless in his study on Benton, since it brings into one package the action necessary by the national government to meet the needs of Missouri. This also may be considered Benton's platform as used in his bid for the Senate. The program included: (1) statehood, (2) adjustment of the Spanish land claims, (3) protection of the frontier, (4) protection of the Missouri fur trade, abolition of the factory system, and the incorporation of an American Fur Company with wide stock ownership in the West, (5) more efficient operation of the salt springs, (6) sale of all lead mines to private enterprise, (7) a national road to Washington, (8) a post road to New Orleans, (9) a post road between St. Louis and Louisville by way of Vincennes, (10) post roads throughout the territory, (11) a port of entry at St. Louis, (12) a canal between Lake Michigan and the Illinois River to open the northern seas to the Mississippi Valley, and (13) a canal to unite the Mississippi River with Lake Superior to cut off British traders, make copper deposits more available, and secure access to the fish supply.[9]

The team of Henry and Maury edited the *Enquirer* only briefly. In the issue for January 6, 1821, the following obituary appeared, signaling a change in the management of the paper. It also illustrates the style then used in reporting:

> We are called upon today to record the death of ISAAC N. HENRY, Esq., one of the editors of the St. Louis *Enquirer*, in the 24th year of his age.
>
> The demise of this truly amiable man is hardly more distressing than it was unexpected, to his family and friends. Without a moment's warning he was seized with the chilling illness which hurried him to his grave, and fell a victim to its merciless severity, before many of his most intimate acquaintances had any knowledge of his danger. . . . Although young, he was well calculated to discharge the duties of his profession, having assisted in connection with his partner, in establishing this paper, under circumstances which required prudence and much firmness to guard against. . . . He was a man of warm and generous feeling, entertaining a high sense of personal character.[10]

Maury sold the paper to Patrick H. Ford and Walter B. Alexander, who pledged themselves to "a steady adherence to the leading principles which have always characterized the paper."[11] In other words, they continued to support Benton and to back John Scott, Missouri's first congressman. The *Enquirer,* along with other papers in the state, printed the proposed state constitution in full. Several partnerships for managing the paper followed, including that of Ford and Orr—noted in the December 14, 1822, issue—and Ford and Stine in December, 1823. By January 3, 1824, both Stine and Orr had departed, and Ford was joined by Duff Green, one-time editor of the *United States Telegraph* in the nation's capital. The *Telegraph* had been helpful in Jackson's first election to the Presidency, but one of Green's lifelong ambitions was to place John C. Calhoun in the White House to succeed Jackson. Green lost his official editorial position in Washington after the President learned of the scheme.

In 1829 Ford retired, leaving Green in charge of the paper. Green, born in Kentucky in 1791, had been a teacher, a captain in the War of 1812, surveyor, and lawyer in addition to his experience as a newspaperman. He later served in both the Senate and the House of Representatives of the State of Missouri and in a private capacity laid out the towns of Chariton and Bluffton. Green continued with the *Enquirer* until August 25, 1825, when it was sold to L. E. Lawless, who became editor, and Charles Keemle, printer. Keemle, who figures in so many of the early journalistic ventures in Missouri, is said to have been present at the birth and death of more such projects than any other St. Louis editor or publisher. William Orr apparently was associated with Keemle in this transaction or later, when the name of the paper was changed to *Beacon.*[12]

First Paper Outside St. Louis

Nathaniel Patten, Jr., born in Roxbury, Massachusetts, on September 9, 1793, was to become Missouri's first publisher outside of St. Louis. He reached Franklin, then located across the Missouri River from present-day Boonville, in 1819, entering the extreme outpost of civilization in the state. Patten had learned the printing trade on the Boston *Independent Chronicle* when quite young. By 1812 he had moved to Mount Sterling, Kentucky, with his parents. In Kentucky, Patten launched his first paper, the Winchester *Advertiser,* on August 5, 1814, with a partner, William W. Martin. Charless, too, had published a paper in Kentucky; Charless and Patten were equally unsuccessful there.

Despite several changes in name and partners, Patten was able
to continue this Kentucky paper only until July 26, 1817.[13]

By February 11, 1819, Patten had issued his prospectus for the
Missouri Intelligencer and Boon's Lick Advertiser, which appeared on April 23, 1819. He arrived in the river community,
then the seat for Howard County, after becoming involved in
legal maneuvers over a promissory note for $120 he had signed
in Kentucky. This note was to plague him as late as 1830, after
he had moved to Columbia. Dangers encountered by the new
editor in Franklin, still largely an undeveloped area in 1819,
have been recorded by Scroggins.[14] Patten, a reserved and sensi-
tive individual, faced a society which "demanded to know where
a man stood and was impatient with inaction"; editorial impartiality, which was Patten's goal, was not a major characteristic of
the press during that era. Further, Patten was not physically
equipped to withstand Missouri's climate, since he was deaf and
subject to frequent attacks of sickness. Throughout the files of
the *Intelligencer* there are references to the editor's "indisposi-
tion," which was at times so severe as to necessitate missing
publishing dates. Yet, Scroggins points out, Patten "had the
tenacity and personal integrity to see him through his editorial
and personal ordeals. In addition, he was sober, prudent, indus-
trious, and modest—attributes officially subscribed to him by
some of the leading residents of Franklin within a few months
of his arrival." It takes little imagination to visualize the many
problems faced by a publisher entering Franklin in 1819, some
160 miles from his nearest source of supply, St. Louis. No doubt
he had been attracted, as had others from the East and the South,
by glowing accounts from this territory. Patten, in his turn, also
promoted the Boon's Lick territory.

His prospectus, which included promises similar to so many
such literary efforts, was signed only by Patten, thus disputing
claims made by some that Benjamin Holliday, Jr., was the first
publisher of the *Intelligencer.* Though Holliday's name does appear on the first issue as co-owner, apparently the idea and plans
for the paper originated with Patten.

Unlike Charless, Patten experienced considerable difficulty
in obtaining the government contract for printing the laws. His
letter of March 24, 1819, to Secretary of State John Q. Adams
failed to bring him any federal contracts, at the time allotted to
two papers in St. Louis and one in Jackson. He then obtained
petitions, wrote more letters, and persuaded Thomas Hart Benton,

David Barton, and John Scott to write Adams, which they did on December 16, 1820. Soon Patten was able to inform his readers of success.[15]

The *Intelligencer,* as it was better known, was the first paper west of St. Louis and north of the Missouri River. It, too, was printed on a Ramage press. Patten received congratulations on its establishment from his "editorial brethren," including Benton, who then edited the St. Louis *Enquirer.* As other pioneer papers, the *Intelligencer* was tabloid in size and consisted of four pages of five columns each. The name of Patten's partner, Holliday, misspelled in the initial issue, was corrected in the second number. The usual "To The Public" editorial appeared: "Truth, on all occasions" would be the "polar star" of the paper, so Patten wrote; a declaration of impartiality in politics was followed with a pledge to be "unshackled by the influence of any party."

Early days were rough for the *Intelligencer,* with circulation slowly rising from one hundred to about four hundred in four years. Patten, who was frequently assisted by his wife in publishing the paper, echoed the complaints voiced earlier by Charless about the irregular mail service. Since the editor depended on the papers from the East for his foreign and national news, delays upset his publishing schedule, much as they had Charless in St. Louis.

Patten, recognizing the need for revenue from advertisements, solicited these prior to his initial issue. The first copy contained sixteen varied messages, from the routine notice of unclaimed letters at the postoffice to a woman's petition for separation from her husband because of desertion. For Sale, Notice, Cheap Goods, and medical advertisements were included.

Samples of his items, typical of those in other papers across the nation, illustrate Patten's style of writing both fact and opinion. Poetry, always a good filler for an editor, included such verses as these:

"A Young Swain's Lament"
I wish I was the corset bone,
  That's to thy lovely breast;
That I might be, both night and day,
  To thy fair bosum prest.

I wish I was the china cup,
  From which you drink your tea;
For then I know at every sip,
  You'd give a kiss to me.[16]

Another style, more personal, is shown in this report of a winter scene in the Franklin area. Only the lead is given.

The chilling blasts of winter have closed upon us—the earth, the trees and their branches are bowed in icy chains of sleet, snow and frost; the sound of the horses' feet and the rumbling of drays, carts and wagons as well as the shivering, silent and melancholy move of the ox, the squeaking of the imploying swine, the clustering of the domestic fowls, and the bleating of the warm clothed sheep—all tell us that the storms of winter have visited us . . . but to cheer us in this frozen gloom we have warm fires, greasy frying pans and social evening chit-chat at our own and our neighbors' grates, occasionally the sweet vibration of the violin or the melodious cadences of the flute break upon our ears and bring to our recollection times of gaiety and mirth that are gone by, and yet to come; the gay and blooming young men are distributing Ball Tickets to our wives and daughters. . . .[17]

Many letters were used by Patten and other editors of his day; too, many letters were refused, as these comments show.

"Relief" is inadmissible. An "Observer" we do not understand, and if we did, should be unable to discern how any benefit could result from its publication. A "Voter" is postponed until next week for want of room. It will be out of our power to publish any further numbers of "A Farmer" until after the election.[18]

Brief news items appeared, generally with fewer words than might be expected in similar accounts today. The following is typical:

A BARBEQUE will be prepared in the Town of Fayette, on the 4th of July.[19]

Sometimes the items were quite sad in nature. Suicides, hangings, and other tragedies apparently were covered more completely than less dramatic events, at times with editorial comment. The following are typical:

SUICIDE [a one-line headline] A Negro man, named Michael, committed suicide, in the jail of this county, on Tuesday night last, by hanging himself.[20]

The sentence of death upon Luke, a black man belonging to Hezekiah Harris, for the murder of his master, was executed in Boonville, Cooper County, on Saturday the 2d inst. With the most fearful apprehensions of his doom, and with a countenance of sorrow and despair, the unhappy man ascended the scaffold to meet a death of ignominy and shame, and thus gave a painful illustration of inspired truth, that "the way of transgressors is hard."[21]

Within a few days past our river has risen to a height unprecedented in the memory of the oldest citizen of this county. It is now, however, slowly ebbing, and there is every reason to believe that the present rise will produce no unhappy effects.[22]

A young lady of 18 was lately killed by lightning in Lebanon, Connecticut, and her breast shattered in a shocking manner—supposed to be in consequence of her wearing a steel corset. Have a care, ladies.[23]

The *Intelligencer* grew in a somewhat more orderly fashion than other early newspapers in the state. Scroggins notes that only four persons beside Patten ever held any authoritative position on the paper. In addition to John Payne, a practicing lawyer who worked with the paper for only six weeks before his death, others included Holliday, who came from Virginia and served for three years; John T. Cleveland, a teacher and a member of the family that produced President Cleveland, who came from Massachusetts and served for two years before taking over the Fayette Academy; and John Wilson, a supporter of John Quincy Adams, who served for a year before moving to California. For more than ten of the sixteen and a half years' history of the paper, Patten was solely responsible for its operation.[24]

Patten printed his last edition in Franklin on June 16, 1826, and on June 29 resumed publication in nearby Fayette. In April, 1830, another move took him to Columbia, where he began publishing the paper on May 4. A surprise announcement in the issue of December 5, 1835, reported the sale of the paper to Sinclair Kirtley and James S. Rollins. There had been indications, however, of change in management of the paper. Patten's ill health was cited as the primary factor in his sale of the paper, but since he resumed publishing in St. Charles within a year, this can hardly have been the real reason.[25]

For some months Patten had complained about delinquent subscribers, his business difficulties that followed the loss of the United States Bank charter, and the shifting of the state printing contracts from experienced printers such as Patten to lawyer-editors with closer political connections. By October 11, 1835, he had agreed to sell the *Missouri Intelligencer*, with equipment and supplies, to Kirtley and Rollins for $800. These men no doubt represented the National Republicans, or Whigs, in Columbia and outbid other politicians. Apparently they had an eye on the 1836 election.[26] Rollins was a prominent lawyer, Kirtley a member of the state legislature.

The last edition of the paper under its title, *Missouri Intelligencer*, appeared on December 5, 1835. In a column-long valedictory Patten wrote, in part: "The editor of this paper has frequently lost friends and patrons amongst the most distinguished and ambitious political aspirants, because he could not, consistently, trim his sails to every popular breeze to waft them into office." On December 12 the paper appeared under its new title, the Columbia *Patriot*.

The successor to the *Intelligencer* was to undergo numerous changes. Thomas Miller, Rollins' law partner, apparently was with the paper along with Kirtley until after the successful campaign of William Harrison for the Presidency in 1840. Frederick A. Hamilton was said by Patten to have bought the paper, but apparently he served as the printer, with the others handling editorial tasks. Rollins later sold his interest to William T. B. Sanford, a printer, and retired, leaving Miller as half owner.

In July, 1841, William F. Switzler became editor when Miller left Columbia to go to Santa Fe, in the hope of regaining his failing health; however, Miller died en route, at the age of thirty-one, some two hundred miles short of his destination. Sanford sold Miller's interest to John B. Williams and Younger J. Williams on March 1, 1842, and on August 19 of that year sold his own interest to A. J. McKelway, who became editor, with Switzler retiring temporarily from that position. By December 16, however, Switzler had purchased McKelway's half interest, and Younger J. Williams had bought out his brother's interest. With these two as equal partners and Switzler the editor, they changed the name to the *Missouri Statesman*, which appeared on January 6, 1843. Younger Williams died on February 19, 1843, and his interest was resold to his brother, John B. Williams, who retained his share until it was sold to Switzler in 1845.

NEWSPAPERS REACH JACKSON

Among the first five papers in Missouri by 1820 was the weekly Jackson *Missouri Herald*, established on June 25, 1819, by Tubal E. Strange in a community of some three hundred per-

sons living in fifty log houses. Jackson, the growing center of
Cape Girardeau County, was one of the most thriving villages in
the territory. Laid out only five years earlier, the community was
named for the victor of the Battle of New Orleans, Andrew
Jackson.

Strange published his prospectus for the *Missouri Herald* in
the Edwardsville, Illinois, *Spectator,* on June 5, 1819. The subsequent history of the paper is one of constant change in ownership and in name. Strange encountered the typical problems
faced by pioneer editors: shortage of ink and paper, the inability or unwillingness of subscribers to heed his "pay in advance" pleas, and frustrating delays with the mail.

Strange was fortunate to receive the federal government's printing contract, so that in many issues of the *Missouri Herald* the
full front page and portions of the second were devoted to publication of laws. The paper's articles were copied, in large part,
from other papers, with the St. Louis *Enquirer* and the *National
Intelligencer* in Washington providing such materials, and
Strange published many letters relating to statehood. On September 18, 1819, he wrote, "Our columns are always open to
temperate discussions," but he had refused some recent communications he termed "childish." Zenas Priest joined Strange in
a partnership with the issue of April 8, 1820.[27]

There are conflictory opinions as to the starting date of the
Missouri Herald. Strange wrote on August 5, 1820, that he was
beginning the second year of the *Missouri Herald.* He apparently
failed to change the number on some issues, since the first avail-
able copy is dated August 13, 1819, and marked Volume I,
Number 8. Strange sold his paper shortly after the first year; it
became the *Independent Patriot* on November 25, 1820, with a
new serial number, operated by Stephen Remington and James
Russell, making the *Missouri Herald's* last issue the one for
August 26, 1820. Russell became a representative to the General
Assembly and later a state senator from Cape Girardeau County.
The *Independent Patriot* continued as the official public printer.
In their prospectus the publishers stated, "The *Patriot,* as the
name suggests, will ever be found the zealous advocate of the
rights of the people."[28]

Additional changes occurred in later years. The paper became
the *Eagle* in March, 1832, under the ownership of R. W. Renfroe
and Greer W. Davis. In 1835, the equipment was moved to
nearby Cape Girardeau, where the next owner, Dr. Patrick Henry

Davis, called his publication the *Southern Advocate and State Journal.* This change occurred in November; by the following September Dr. Davis had sold the paper to Thomas B. English and a Mr. Whittle, "two young gentlemen of talent and enterprise." Some time after this change in ownership the paper returned to Jackson as the *Southern Advocate,*[29] the name applied by H. S. McFarland, who owned the paper for a brief time. Jackson's first mayor, J. W. Limbaugh, took over in 1850, calling his paper the *Southern Democrat.* Under Limbaugh it became a strong anti-Benton paper, but after Limbaugh's death in 1852 the paper reverted to a previous owner, Robert Brown, who renamed it the *Jeffersonian.* By late 1853 it had another publisher, another name: Joel Wilkerson and the *Courier.* Wilkerson continued with the *Courier* until the outbreak of the Civil War, when the paper ceased publication. Jackson was without a paper until the *Missouri Cash-Book* began, on March 4, 1871.[30]

St. Charles Fifth in State

St. Charles had its first paper, *The Missourian,* by June 24, 1820. It was founded by Robert McCloud, a printer and the step-son of Joseph Charless. Apparently McCloud had experienced delays in his plans for publication, since as early as December 3, 1819, a prospectus for his paper had appeared in the *Missouri Intelligencer,* which later reported the new paper to be "of respectable size, and executed in a neat and elegant manner."

In the initial issue of this, the fifth paper to be established in the state, McCloud wrote that "owing to the great expense attending the establishment of a newspaper in this remote part of the country, and the difficulty of collecting subscribers, that payment in advance will always be preferred." In August he was still seeking advance payments, citing "depressure of the times" and other factors for his money needs. "Just emerging from a state of territorial imbecility, to the light and life of a free and independent state, Missouri begins to see the dawn of a new order of things," McCloud wrote in his prospectus. Within a year he became "Printer to the State" and started publishing its laws. He, too, had problems with letter writers. One letter prompted him to reply that "the communication signed 'Sidney' cannot 'see the light,' his allusions 'smell' rather personal."

Thus, by 1820, when Missouri was being groomed for statehood, five papers were being published in the area. St. Louis had the *Missouri Gazette* and the *Enquirer*, St. Charles the *Missourian*, Jackson the *Missouri Herald*, and Franklin the *Missouri Intelligencer and Boon's Lick Advertiser*. It is interesting to note the frequent appearance of "Missouri" in these titles, no doubt expressing the editors' optimism for the future of the state. It is apparent that Missourians were being prepared for future greatness by the press, which was to serve the new state as a strong unifying force, despite frequent political splits, for many years.

CHAPTER III

NEW STATE, MORE PAPERS WELCOMED
1820-1836

PEOPLE on the streets, editors in their columns, and political leaders in Washington and in Missouri vigorously debated statehood and its attendant problems, slavery and boundaries, in 1819. Some wanted the full package—Missouri with slavery; others wanted Missouri—but free. Charless, characteristically siding with the minority, approved slavery, but with restrictions. Thomas Hart Benton's *Enquirer* urged settlement of the question within the state, not at the national level. "The future of the State of Missouri—Equal in sovereignty to the original states or nothing," he wrote.[1]

No doubt indecision on the slavery dispute held up some emigration to the state, but by late 1819 there were about 100,000 persons in Missouri. The *Enquirer* noted,

> Notwithstanding the great number of persons who are held in check by the agitation of the slave question in Congress, the emigration to Missouri is astonishing. Probably, from thirty to fifty wagons daily cross the Mississippi at the different ferries and bring in an average of four to five hundred souls a day. The emigrants are principally from Kentucky, Tennessee, Virginia, and the states farther south. They bring great numbers of slaves, knowing that Congress has no power to impose the agitated restriction, and that the people of Missouri will never adopt it.[2]

When Congress passed the bill granting Missouri statehood, the "second Missouri Compromise" permitted the state to have a constitution without restriction of slavery, but slavery was to be excluded from the rest of the Louisiana Territory west and north of Missouri. The "happy intelligence that the Missouri State Bill has passed Congress without restriction" was the occasion for the first "extra" in Missouri, published by the St. Louis *Enquirer* March 25, 1820. And with its next regular edition, April 1, the *Enquirer* used headlines with more decks than perhaps were ever used before in Missouri:

GRATIFYING NEWS FROM WASHINGTON; KING AND
CLINTON DEFEATED; THE SENATE TRIUMPHANT;
FINAL PASSAGE OF THE MISSOURI STATE
BILL WITHOUT RESTRICTIONS.

But the agony is over and Missouri is born into the Union, not a seven months' baby, but a man child; his birth no secret in the family, but a proud and glorious event, proclaimed to the nation with the firing of cannon, the ringing of bells and illumination of towns and cities.[3]

The *Missouri Gazette* devoted many columns to the debates in Congress to "let the public know who have been their *real* friends" in the statehood battle. Charless, describing how the city was illuminated, wrote: "We were diverted by another [sight] representing a slave in great spirits, rejoicing at the permission granted by Congress to bring slaves into so fine a country as Missouri."[4]

In Franklin, the *Missouri Intelligencer* depended on the St. Louis papers, special correspondents, rumors, and other word-of-mouth sources for information on statehood. The paper gave prominence to the compromise story and to the Loan Office Act, which had special interest for readers in the interior. Jackson heard the news on March 21, when Thomas Hempstead passed through that community. The *Patriot*, printing the federal laws at the time, soon began carrying many letters from candidates seeking public office.

As political leaders made plans to select delegates to the first constitutional convention, the fight for seats in the convention became intense. Benton, expecting certain nomination, was defeated. Charless, describing an attack upon himself, ridiculed the opposition:

The editor of the *Missouri Gazette*, whilst on the way from his office to his home, between one and two o'clock on Wednesday, the 10th of May inst., was assailed as he ascended the hill without any previous intimidation, warning or apparent quarrel by Isaac N. Henry, one of the editors of the St. Louis *Enquirer*, and received several blows with a heavy cudgell, which blows he returned with a stick disproportionately small; the combatants closed, fell and struggled for a while. The Rev. Joseph Piggot, who was accompanying Mr. Charless and was going to dine with him, twice endeavored to part them, but was as often prevented by a certain William Rector, who drew a pistol from his bosom, and declared he would blow him through if he interfered. Mr. Piggot then called for help, being determined to part them; presently two men came up and the contest ended.[5]

The item, signed "A Spectator," but no doubt written by Charless, stressed the irony of a young man setting upon an old man and using a large weapon as compared to the small stick with which

the victim defended himself. After placing on the coeditor of the
Enquirer the blame for the attack, "Spectator" noted that the
fight developed because of Charless' "being the editor of a paper
which preserves a high character of impartiality and independence, under trials and difficulties which much enhance its value
and merit." The *Enquirer* ignored the incident. Charless' signature
did not appear under the item, a custom of the times; such letters
frequently were signed "A Citizen of Missouri," "A Missourian,"
"One of the People," and at times with Latin pseudonyms.

Even without Benton, the constitutional convention was successful, and the document was signed on July 19, 1820, "amidst
a great concourse of citizens, and under a national salute of
twenty-four guns, fired by the St. Louis Guards. The entire in-
strument is published in this day's paper," according to the
Enquirer, "to the exclusion of other matter, and we trust will be
joyfully received by the people as proof that Missouri is a
sovereign state and as a pledge she will remain so."[6]

During the struggle in Congress which preceded the official
acceptance of Missouri into the Union, the *Enquirer*'s "watchful
waiting" policy was expressed editorially:

> This paper has labored for a long time to awaken the people to
> the criminal designs of men who wish to expell Missouri from
> the Union. This audacious undertaking is now verging to a
> crisis. What shall Missouri do if rejected? Fall back into the terri-
> torial grade? We hope not. Set up for herself? We hope not. The
> former would be to succumb to the Catalines of the North; the
> latter would be to promote their views. The restrictionists wish
> to divide the Union; and if Missouri would attempt to break off,
> it would be into their hand; their object would be accomplished
> and the blame thrown upon her. But let Missouri continue her
> efforts to enter the Union; preserve all her relations with the
> general government as far as her amphibious condition will
> permit it to be done; be calm and dignified in asserting her
> rights, and a reaction may be produced which will prostrate
> those Hartford Convention men who now predominate in the
> North, and give victory to the friends of the Union and to the
> republicans of the Jeffersonian school. . . . Let Missouri preserve
> all her friends, do nothing to mortify them, or to please her
> enemies, and the sober reason of the people must ultimately
> resume its empire and consign to infamy the men who have
> sought their own aggrandizement upon the minds of their
> country.[7]

Along with David Barton, the first choice of the legislature,

Benton was named to the national Senate. His editorial policy on the *Enquirer* switched to "join the Union under any condition." Apparently it was never his purpose to remain an editor; his position on the staff of the paper served merely as a stepping-stone into the political arena. Too many historians, however, have failed to give the *Enquirer* adequate credit for the role it played in placing Benton before the voters.

When Missouri was officially welcomed into the Union as the twenty-fourth state on August 10, 1821, all the papers printed President James Monroe's proclamation. Robert McCloud in St. Charles probably summed up the feeling of the editors of the state when he wrote in his *Missourian*: "May the spirit of harmony and love, the cement of society, banish hereafter from the halls of legislation and the minds of a deluded people, those sectional jealousies and malignant feelings which have so nearly undermined the temple of our constitution."[8] And the *Enquirer* noted: "It would certainly flatter the pride and excite the satisfaction of Missouri to witness even a partial development of her resources, and to see her agricultural and navigable advantages fairly drawn out and marshalled on the same page with those of her western sisters."[9]

DEVELOPMENTS, 1821 THROUGH 1836

The pioneer press of Missouri continued to gain in strength, in numbers, and in its role of political leadership as the state gained population and some characteristics of the older states. Floyd Shoemaker has noted many highlights of the area's development during this era, including the inception and growth of the steamship traffic, the departure of the Indians, the expansion of aid and credit to local citizens suffering from the financial panics, and the introduction of additional cultural products, such as tobacco and hemp. The influences of religion and education were being felt; the Methodists, Catholics, Presbyterians, and Baptists were among the groups that had entered Missouri, establishing schools as well as centers for worship. By 1832 the Temperance Society was functioning, backed by considerable press comment, and in 1833 the group met in Columbia to "effect the entire abstinence from ardent spirits" throughout the state. The Sons of Temperance formed about 1844. This, too, was a time when the Mormons were being attacked in Jackson County and neighboring counties, and their presses and papers destroyed. Private and religious schools were founded, many through local editorial support. Charless, for example, complained that "the state of religion and the want of schools has long been lamented by the thinking part of the population of this territory."[10] The school that eventually became St. Louis University began as St. Louis College in 1828—the first institution of higher education west of the Mississippi River. Lodges were founded and notices about the Masons and Odd Fellows appeared in the press. Lyon, in a study of Charless, notes that this editor had been a charter member of a Masonic lodge in 1808. Charless also supported the St. Louis Mechanics Benevolent Society, the Erin Benevolent Society, and the Missouri Hibernian Relief Society. His love for the Irish obviously had not diminished.[11]

Although little advance was made toward a systematic banking program, Missourians were prospering by the end of this period through profits from the mining industry, the fur business, agriculture, and trade along the Santa Fe Trail; one trading group reached Franklin in 1827 with $30,000 in specie and several hundred mules from an expedition to Santa Fe. During the preceding period of stress, the Bank of St. Louis had failed in 1819, and the Bank of Missouri "Obituary" appeared in the *Missouri Gazette* August 15, 1821; for a time, citizens depended on private firms for their financial needs. Many notices such as the following appeared when men sacrificed what they had to, salvaged what they could, and moved westward.

> My creditors are hereby notified, that on Saturday the 25th inst. . . . I shall make application to James Rankin and David Bryan, Esqrs., two Justices of the Peace, in and for the county of Jefferson, at my dwelling house in the town of Herculaneum, in said county, to be permitted to take the benefit of the several laws of this territory concerning insolvent debtors, and to be released from my imprisonment, when and where you may attend if you think proper. MOSES AUSTIN, Herculaneum, March 11, 1820.[12]

Generally, however, by 1821 Missourians had begun to recover from the effects of the Panic of 1819. Mississippi River travel increased, especially to New Orleans, where Missouri tobacco, hemp, meat, lard, and other products found a ready market. Land sales climbed, too. But in the general recovery, many in the debtor class sought relief from the state government and urged it to take action quickly. Farmers had overbought land in the expectation of selling part of it to new immigrants and of thus paying off their original contract. For a while immigration declined, and investors in land failed in their hopes. "An Old Farmer" wrote the *Missouri Gazette* on April 18, 1821, that "never was there in this country a time of such pecuniary distress as the present." The next month the St. Charles *Missourian* reported nine-tenths of the people were seeking economic relief.

Duels still figured in the news, with prominent persons involved. Benton, for example, had killed Charles Lucas in a duel in 1817. Charless and other editors, with ministerial support, urged an end to this practice. By 1828 the number of duels had declined, but physical force remained one of the more common methods of settling arguments.

Slavery was not the major issue in the press at this time. Few families had more than one Negro, and thus there were not many plantation-type holdings in the state. In 1810 Missouri had a population of 19,783, including 2,875 slaves; in ten years population had increased to 66,586 with 10,282 slaves. The slave population increased at a greater pace the next decade, and by 1830 there were 25,091 Negroes in a total population of 140,455.[13]

The newspapers discussed the need for internal improvements; editors agreed that such measures as improvement of roads were needed. Patten had complained in 1820 that the roads frequently were more of a nuisance than a convenience. Many were inadequately marked, and travelers became lost. Twelve years later Patten again wrote on the subject, saying that "wagoners absolutely refuse to attempt hauling. It would fatigue six horses to pull an empty wagon through the mud and up hills."[14]

This, too, was a period of personalities and prominent names, and among these Thomas Hart Benton and Andrew Jackson stood out; upon these men the editorial light was to focus for many years. Benton was the subject as well as the source of many press stories during his thirty years in the Senate. When he was first elected, it was on the strength of his personality, not on party lines; the alignment of voters into specific parties came later. Benton had split with Jackson in Tennessee, prior to moving to Missouri. In 1824 he supported Henry Clay, who carried the state, since many voters distrusted John Quincy Adams and thought it impossible for the New Englander to care about the West. When the election went into the House, Representative John Scott cast Missouri's vote for Adams, although Benton had by this time announced himself for Jackson, who had received a plurality of the nation's votes. No doubt the circumstances surrounding the campaign in 1824 contributed to the development of the strong Jackson party that captured every Missouri county in 1828. The party candidate for governor that year, John Miller, ran without opposition.

Benton helped to defeat the once popular senator from Missouri, David Barton, in 1830, thus creating problems for Missouri editors who had previously worked for both Benton and Barton. Jackson carried Missouri and the Democratic ticket in 1832. The dominance in Missouri of the Democratic party continued uninterrupted to the Civil War. The *Missouri Intelligencer*, an anti-Jackson paper, noted, however, that support of Jackson had declined since 1828. The one-sided political situation did not prevent the formation of an opposition party, the Whigs. St. Louis, and for many years Boone County, were strong Whig centers. They were active in the early thirties; their failure to continue as a force in state politics has been ascribed to the party's efforts to be "all things to all people." Disputes between the "hard" and "soft" money groups increased regarding representation in the legislature and on other state issues.[15]

Benton lost his seat in the Senate in 1851 because he opposed the expansion of slavery to new territories, yet he retained the admiration of even his enemies for his firmness, knowledge, political integrity, and interest in the West. Loss of the election was, in part, due to his failure to keep his political fences mended, though many editors co-operated by publishing his letters dispatched from the nation's capital. He avoided party channels and was not a give-and-take politician; rather, he was one-sided and acted with the full expectation that what he said would be obeyed or believed without debate by the voters. He made trips through his Missouri constituency rarely, preferring his Washington home, to which he had moved his slaves. Many Missourians met him for the first time on his "appeal campaign" across the state in 1849.[16]

The *Missouri Intelligencer* on June 29, 1826, said Benton had a strong claim on the people's support through his extraordinary and unwearied exertions for their interests. A year before, the Jackson *Independent Patriot* observed that Benton's name was kept before the public by favorable letters to editors, but his enemies accused him of writing these messages of self-praise and of signing other names to them. The *Missouri Republican* attacked him frequently, claiming he profited from overcharges on travel pay, a customary practice of his day. The paper also claimed professional dishonesty on his part in dealing with his law clients and added some comments on fraud in connection with the Bank of Missouri. In addition to the animosity of the *Republican*, Benton's enemies found the columns of other papers open to their letters.

Jackson's political career was closely followed by Missouri editors. In 1824 he was supported only by the St. Louis *Enquirer*, then edited by Duff Green, and the St. Charles *Jeffersonian*, edited by Calvin Gunn. That year the conservative press, led by the *Missouri Intelligencer* and the St. Louis *Republican*, did its part in winning 2,042 votes for Clay, while Jackson received 1,166, and Adams 218. The Jackson *Independent Patriot* was alone in its support for Calhoun. To make up for their lack of aid from the press, Jacksonians utilized personal contacts, handbills, and many speeches. The *Missouri Republican* noted that Jackson's supporters among the editors kept his name constantly before the public by continually praising him, citing his speeches, and commending his policies in every respect. "In the end the people believed that he must be something or he would not be so continually in print. They at length set him down as a great man and a patriot, all due to the influence of some hireling paper."[17] The Jackson forces could say the same for the opposition press.

Voters evidently refused to follow the conservative press in 1828, for Jackson swept the state. Anti-Jackson papers blamed their failure to secure Clay's election on their lack of adequate funds. Missouri voters, it was clear, viewed Jackson as one of their own, trusting him to develop policies advantageous to the frontier, and to provide for more suffrage, shorter terms for officeholders, and more rapid rotation in office. By 1828 Missourians were divided politically into conservatives and liberals. The first group, centered in St. Louis, included the aristocratic element that backed Adams; the second, scattered through the state, saw Jackson as a courageous leader who would express for them their social, economic, and political ideas.[18]

Expansion Keynote for Press

In the 1820's and early 1830's papers appeared for the first time in Ste. Genevieve, Palmyra, Boonville, Jefferson City, Cape Girardeau, Fayette, Independence, Bowling Green, Columbia, and Liberty.

Ste. Genevieve, first settlement in the state, had *The Correspondent and Ste. Genevieve Record* in April, 1821, but it ceased publication in 1823.[19] St. Charles, the state capital, gained in population and had a second paper, the *Missouri Gazette,* in November, 1823, with Stephen W. Foreman as its publisher.[20] Foreman, associated with many of the state's pioneer papers, backed Henry Clay for the Presidency. Charles Keemle was with him on this paper for a brief time. A year later Foreman sold his paper to McCloud of the *Missourian.* The *Missouri Advocate* was started in St. Charles on December 29, 1824, by Keemle and Foreman, but on the following February 28 the paper moved, becoming the St. Louis *Missouri Advocate.* Keemle withdrew from the paper that year because of "motives of a private nature preparatory to ulterior views."[21]

St. Charles continued to attract publishers, and in October, 1825, the *Jeffersonian* appeared, with Calvin Gunn and William Dunnica, one of the founders of Glasgow, Missouri, in charge. Gunn was a champion of Jackson. This paper followed the state capital to its permanent home in Jefferson City in 1826, and in 1827 was renamed the *Jeffersonian Republican,* with the motto, "*E Pluribus Unum.*" Gunn, in a position to print the proceedings of the first meeting of the General Assembly, was the official state printer for eighteen years.[22]

St. Louis remained a fertile breeding center for papers. In late 1826 the *Commercial Advertiser* appeared, a paper that bore several titles during its career: a year later an item reported the marriage of Major William Orr, "one of the editors of the *Commercial Advertiser,*" to Miss Minerva Foulke; in 1828 barbs were thrown at Orr and his *Missouri Observer and St. Louis Advertiser* for advocating the election of Crawford to the Presidency. The *Missouri Republican,* on March 18, 1828, reported the death of the *Missouri Observer* "for want of patronage," terming it a Jackson paper, the "mouth-piece" of the "magnificent senator." The *Republican* added, "We have heard it intimated that Col. Benton intends, on his annual visit, to re-establish the Jackson press in this city from the proceeds of his *extra mileage* as a senator of the United States." Also in 1826 St. Louisans read the *Missouri Herald and St. Louis Public Advertiser,* started by Keemle on November 8. The *Missouri Republican* reported on November 16 the receipt of the first issue, "neatly printed on super royal paper." The paper carried the political flag of "pure republicanism." Keemle, however, was unsuccessful in his efforts to keep the paper alive.[23]

Eight years after the establishment of the first paper in Franklin, another appeared in nearby Fayette. James H. Birch, later a judge of the Supreme Court of Missouri, started his *Western Monitor* in August, 1827. Two years later Birch wrote of his problems, in his prospectus announcing the start of the third volume: "Standing alone during the most embittered period of the recent national contest, its editor was made the subject of the most unrelenting systematic and ignoble persecution ever waged against the character, person or purse of an humble citizen." Birch carried on editorial feuds with his competitor, the Fayette *Missouri Intelligencer*, which fended off one such attack and then replied in part: "We perceive . . . that Mr. Birch has *again* commenced the work of slander and vituperation. . . . We view with pity and regret this evidence of a bad heart, which not even the *cloak* of *religion* can conceal."[24] The widely-quoted *Western Monitor* became the *Missouri Monitor* in 1837, and in 1840 the *Boon's Lick Times*. By 1848 its press had been moved to Glasgow, where it remained in service until the start of the Civil War.[25]

There is some evidence that Duff Green established a St. Louis *Courier* on December 8, 1828, and published it for two weeks. It was not uncommon for politicians to start a paper to "feel out the public," seeking a favorable response—a useful device, for at times the reply was a loud negative.

The first of several papers entitled *Times* appeared in St. Louis on July 7, 1829. The Fayette *Western Monitor* a month later noted the *Times*'s appearance; it was printed on an imperial sheet by Jacob R. Stine and Thomas J. Miller, with Col. Stephen W. Foreman as editor. Birch, editor of the *Monitor*, claimed the principal object of the paper would be "the prostration of some of our most valuable public servants, with the sinister design of occupying their places, or those for which they are at present indicated—under such circumstances, it is not irrational to suppose that the editorial department will present a batch as variant in *taste* as, when taken in contrast with the *Advocate* which Foreman had been publishing it will be found inconsistent in sentiment, principles, and predilections." Foreman denied any affiliation with the paper, but Birch refused to budge from his position. The *Missouri Intelligencer* said the *Times*'s editor was "of the old Democratic School" and a decided supporter of Jackson.[26]

Elijah Lovejoy arrived in St. Louis in 1827 and later became a part-time reporter on the *Times*. Although he subsequently became editor of the paper, he eventually turned to the ministry and moved to the East. He resigned from the *Times* in 1832, but St. Louis Presbyterians recalled him in 1833 to edit the *Observer,* which appeared on November 22. This paper, later moved to Alton, Illinois, was the organ Lovejoy used to voice the antislavery sentiments that eventuated in his murder.[27]

Cape Girardeau received its first paper, the *Farmer,* in 1831, with William Johnson as editor and publisher. The *State Gazette* was started there at the same time by William Baker, becoming the *Southern Gazette* in 1833, the *Missouri Democrat* edited by Philip G. Ferguson later, and in 1850 the *Creole.* By 1851 the press and equipment had been moved to St. Louis.[28]

The establishment of new papers continued in St. Louis. S. S. Brooks appeared with Keemle as co-owner of the St. Louis *Beacon,* which Keemle started March 21, 1829, to support Benton. Keemle claimed immediate success—three hundred new subscribers in three months. However, the partnership ended in January, and on November 3, 1831, Keemle offered the paper for sale. Apparently the *Beacon* died soon after November, 1832.

There are conflicting reports about a paper called *Workingman's Advocate* in St. Louis in 1831. It is said to have been published by John Steele and sold within a few months to James B. Bowlin, who changed its name to *Missouri Argus.* Lyon cites a letter written in 1832 about a "certain John Steele" who wanted to establish a press of "orthodox doctrine" to oppose the *Beacon.* In late 1832 Steele was editor of the *Free Press* and remained in that position through most of 1833. Later that year he was in Helena, Arkansas, in a position with the post office. Apparently the *Free Press* died in late 1833. If the *Argus* did follow the *Workingman's Advocate,* it started a new series, for a copy dated May 22, 1835, is marked Volume I, Number 5. Abel Rathbone Corbin, once with the *Jeffersonian Republican,* was the publisher, with J. Angevine the printer. Corbin, who supported Benton, sold the paper in 1837 to Thomas Watson and his son John Watson.[29]

Under the Watsons' management the *Daily Argus* appeared in 1838. Andrew Jackson Davis owned the paper briefly in 1839, with William Gilpin as editor. In assuming the editorship Gilpin wrote, "The contest between the many headed, multiform, quondam Federal, *now* Whig, and *always aristocratic* party and the Democratic Republican party, differs in all respects from the controversies between the parties in the Mother country." He attacked party leaders "for stealing power from the many for the few." His attacks hit home, for Davis was beaten to death in June, 1839, as a direct result of Gilpin's writing. In reporting the crime, Gilpin wrote that "a fellow by the name of w. p. darnes [sic], a common street loafer and vagabond, and fit subject for the 'vagrant act,'" had written to Davis asking the meaning of "certain phrases" in articles in the Argus. Gilpin assumed all responsibility for the articles, referring to Darnes as "a fit toady for the little clique of Federalists." Several stories told of the "murderous and brutal outrage" committed on Davis by Darnes, who assaulted Davis with an iron cane, the head of which was loaded with lead. On June 9 the Argus reported that Davis had died, "cut off in the flower of youth," at the age of twenty-five.[30] Corbin repurchased the paper in 1840 "at the request of the Democratic Party."

In October, 1841, Shadrach Penn from Louisville, and V. P. Van Antwerp from the Iowa Territory, purchased the Argus, changing its name to Missouri Reporter. Loring Pickering and Samuel Treat, who owned the Missourian, founded in November, 1843, by Van Antwerp, bought the Missouri Reporter in 1846 and combined the two papers into the St. Louis Union, a political move to consolidate the city's Democratic organs. The Union was the direct ancestor of the Globe-Democrat.[31]

MORMONS ENTER JOURNALISM

In Independence, an important departure point for the West, the Mormons began publishing a paper in 1832. After the first log courthouse was erected, journalism soon followed. Independence then was no farther from supply centers than Franklin had been from St. Louis earlier, since a paper mill had been established near Columbia in 1834.

The first publications in Independence were started by the Mormons, members of the Church of Jesus Christ of Latter Day Saints. Joseph Smith visited the area and returned to the church headquarters in Kirtland, Ohio, to map plans for a paper in the new Zion. Thus The Evening and the Morning Star, a monthly publication, appeared in June, 1832, edited by William Wine Phelps. Its prospectus had stated, "As the forerunner of the night and the end, and the messenger of the day of redemption, the Star will borrow its light from sacred sources."[32]

This paper set the pattern for future journalistic efforts by the Latter Day Saints. The first issue, four pages with two columns each, was devoted to "church news, doctrine, and 'revelations,'" according to Lloyd Wilkie, in his study of Independence papers. Probably in the same month the church started the weekly *Upper Missouri Advertiser* to "advertise that section of Missouri as the place revealed for the center stake of Zion." During the next year the *Star* began to print articles on slavery, in consequence of which, on July 20, a mob made up of settlers who feared the Mormons' growth as a political factor razed the office as well as the editor's home. The press and type were dumped into the Missouri River and the *Star* returned to the East. It is said that two men, Robert N. Kelley and William H. David, fished the press equipment out of the river and eventually used it to start the *Upper Missouri Enquirer* in Liberty in February, 1834. Still later, in 1845, William Ridenbaugh used the same press to found the St. Joseph *Gazette*. Captain John L. Merrick later purchased the press and moved it to Colorado, where it was used to print the second paper in Denver, the *Cherry Creek Pioneer*, in 1859.[33]

Many skirmishes occurred between the Mormons and settlers in the area; rumors no doubt magnified the facts. On the pleas of neutral citizens as well as of the Mormons, the state militia was sent to the vicinity to restore peace. Some editors published inflammatory stories, only to retract them later. Mobs continued to harass the Saints even as they were leaving the state, and local courts provided little protection for the churchmen; these outrages were recorded in many Missouri papers. The St. Louis *Free Press* urged tolerance: "Had individuals of this sect, or even the whole body of it committed legal offenses, the civil tribunals . . . could have given sufficient redress, but to proceed against them as a religious body . . . must be considered persecution in the most odious sense of the word."[34]

OTHER PAPERS APPEAR

The St. Louis *Farmers' & Mechanics' Advocate* was started in late 1832 under the management of James S. Mayfield and J. B. Bowlin. By April, 1833, Mayfield withdrew from the partnership to become a land claims commissioner. In Palmyra, the *Courier*, established in 1832, was a Jackson paper with a "one-sided party complexion."

A major development in 1835 was the appearance of the first daily paper in Missouri, the *Daily Evening Herald and Commercial Advertiser* of St. Louis. The *Herald* was printed by R. M. Treadway and J. W. Albright, with a weekly edition containing material from the daily. The *Herald* was nicknamed "Little Daily" because of its size. By 1835 Albright had departed, and Treadway continued until November, when the *Missouri Argus* reported the paper "had been gathered to its fathers at the advanced age of six months. Thus passes the 'cause' away. It died for want of *sustenance and breath.*"[35]

St. Louis had a *Commercial Bulletin* in May, 1835, with the ubiquitous Charles Keemle again on the scene. A triweekly, it was owned by William Preston Clark and Samuel B. Churchill. Six months later the paper was sold to Clark, and on August 23, 1836, it was converted to a daily. Data concerning the paper after 1836 are incomplete, but it is believed that Charles G. Ramsey was associated with the paper before it ceased publication on November 22, 1842.

Patten, along with Major Alphonso Wetmore, had planned to publish the *St. Louis Memoir: A Journal of Literature, Commerce, Agriculture and the Arts* in early 1836 as a triweekly. Despite the promises in their prospectus, these men were unable to interest sufficient readers to proceed. Patten did, however, establish the St. Charles *Clarion* later that year. This paper went through many transitions, becoming the *Free Press* in 1840; *Advertiser*, and then *Missouri Patriot*, by 1846; *Western Star*, 1847; *Chronotype*, 1849; and *Reveille*, 1854. In 1867 it was consolidated with the *Sentinel* to become the *Cosmos-Sentinel*, a title that was shortened to *Cosmos* in 1868. The population of St. Charles County continued to increase, from 4,320 in 1830 to 14,313 in 1860.

Boonville, with the *Herald* starting in August, and Bowling Green, with the *Salt River Journal* appearing in October, joined the growing list of communities with papers in 1833. The *Herald's* prospectus listed James H. Middleton and William Need as publishers, but John Wilson replaced Need before the initial issue appeared. This paper was to appear under various names until the Civil War. The *Salt River Journal* was established by Adam Black Chambers and Oliver Harris. Chambers, who came to the community in 1829 with 75 cents, soon was admitted to the bar and was sent to the state legislature in 1832. In 1837 the partners sold the paper and went to St. Louis to become associated with George Knapp and the *Missouri Republican.*[36]

Fayette acquired the *Boon's Lick Democrat* in December, 1834, with William B. Napton as publisher. That same year the

Palmyra *Post* appeared on June 1, but it survived only a few months.

The *Far West* had been founded in Liberty by 1836; it was published by Peter H. Burnett, who became a district judge in Oregon, the provisional governor of California, and later served on the California Supreme Court bench. That May the Palmyra *Marion Journal* was founded by Frederick A. Wise and Lucian J. Eastin. Five months later Wise became the sole owner. The *Missouri Argus* commented on the new paper; it thought Palmyra was large enough to support two papers, the *Journal* and the *Courier*.[37]

The *Patriot* was established in 1836 in Cape Girardeau as an organ for the Whig party by Edwin White. Later owners included Robert Sturdivant, Robert Renfroe, Charles D. Cook, and John W. Morris, who changed the name of the paper to *South Missourian* before it suspended publication in 1846.[38]

By the end of 1836 many Missourians were reading papers that were published locally. These carried interesting news, providing their readers were vitally concerned about the political affairs in the new state. Editors were partisan, but readers expected them to be so. Some papers were established merely to promote specific candidates or issues. They were the pioneers, to be followed by hundreds of similar publications in the years ahead. These early papers were small, grayish in appearance. Advertisements and miscellaneous material generally occupied page 1, with the news reserved for the inside pages. Readers dug for their news, but then there was less news than there is today.

CHAPTER IV

PIONEER PERIOD COMES TO END

1836-1850

MISSOURI papers expanded, and the editorial words from their pages became louder as the pioneer days were approaching their end. The effects of the Panic of 1837 on the state were delayed, yet residents were quick in making up their minds about Texas, the war with Mexico, and the proposed new state constitution. The Platte Purchase added some two million acres to the nation's expanse, much of it long occupied by Indians. In 1836, President Jackson approved a measure to extend Missouri's boundary to the Missouri River on the west, ending several years of fighting between the Indians and the encroaching settlers. Within less than a year treaties were completed with the Indians to clear titles, thereby opening up additional land for settlement.

Although the first railroad convention was held in 1836, another year elapsed before the state granted charters to nearly a score of these companies. However, it was some time before any railroads got beyond the paper stage in Missouri, since a panic crippled the nation that same year.[1] Not all editors were enthusiastic about the railroads. The hard-money editor of the *Jeffersonian Republican* said, on March 26, 1836, "There can be no objection to chartering a group of individuals who are willing to undertake the construction of a railroad upon *their own resources* if no exclusive privileges are asked for." Some editors urged the state to subscribe to half of the entire stock issues of the companies. Abel R. Corbin, editor of the *Missouri Argus*, led the campaign, believing that St. Louis would eventually become the trade center of the Mississippi Valley and the railroads would soon go from there to St. Charles, Fulton, Columbia, and Fayette.

In 1836 the Whigs improved their press representation, gaining a few papers to augment the favorable editorial comments of the St. Louis *Missouri Republican* and the Columbia *Patriot*. Additional backing for the Whigs appeared in Boonville, Cape Girardeau, Palmyra, and elsewhere. The Democrats, too, gained support, although the editors of the state disagreed on whether to back the Whigs' candidate, Hugh Lawson White, or the Democrats' Martin Van Buren for the Presidency. The Liberty *Far West* stated that it had preferred White but would support

Van Buren as a "second choice for the sake of party harmony."
Leading Democratic papers in 1836 were the St. Louis *Missouri
Argus* and the Fayette *Boon's Lick Democrat*.[2]

Missouri voters placed Lilburn W. Boggs in the governor's
seat with 14,315 votes, to 13,059 for William H. Ashley. Van
Buren won the state's electoral votes, with a popular majority of
3,658 votes; White received 7,337. Four years later Van Buren
won again in Missouri. Boggs, once associated with the Bank of
St. Louis, had been lieutenant-governor in 1832. His term as
governor encompassed the Panic of 1837, the same year the Bank
of the State of Missouri was chartered; the Mormon War; the
boundary dispute with the Iowa Territory; the authorization of
a macadamized road from New Franklin to the Missouri River;
and participation by some Missourians in the Seminole Indian
War in Florida.[3]

Missouri papers reported in this period the institution of the
shorter work day—to 10½ hours—additional regulations on child
labor, and several attempts to establish trade unions. In addition to the establishment of the state university in 1839, the
General Assembly provided for elementary schools, academies,
colleges, a permanent school fund, and additional educational
facilities. By 1868 the Negroes of the state were provided an
educational program. Trade activities expanded, with emphasis
on the fur business. River traffic became more important, and
caravans headed more frequently to Santa Fe; hundreds of mules
were brought back to Missouri from these expeditions to the
Southwest. Tobacco and hemp cultivation was enlarged.

The effects of the Panic of 1837 were late in reaching Missouri; the full impact was not felt until 1842-1843. The new state
bank helped to fend off the worst effects of the panic which a
number of communities met by issuing scrip. Some editors remained optimistic, citing the high prices paid for land, the demand for labor, and the high wages paid to workmen, while the
Fayette *Boon's Lick Democrat* reported, "There is not an indus-
trious and prudent man in the State, who is not better off now
than he was two years ago." However, the editor did admit, "that
distress does prevail, to a certain extent, in those cities which
have been seized with the mania of wild speculation, we never
entertained any doubt."[4] When the panic did hit Missouri, hundreds of notices of bankruptcy appeared in the newspapers. The
Jeffersonian Inquirer, for example, devoted all of pages 3 and 4
and most of pages 1 and 2 in its issue of March 31, 1842, to peti-

tions for bankruptcy. The editor remarked that "bankrupt notices are no rarity at present."

Disputes concerning slavery appeared, the Elijah Lovejoy case of 1837 being the most newsworthy.

From 1830 to the start of the Civil War a change occurred in agricultural interests among Missourians. They turned in large numbers from the self-sufficient farm, planned to supply the needs of the farmer and his family, to one that would produce revenue, the accumulating of money from cash crops being placed above the providing of necessities.

The Whigs, organized in Missouri about 1833, scored gains in 1840, when they obtained some 44 per cent of the vote. Some editors considered the Whigs opportunists, organized from the lawyer caucus and, while not strong in numbers, firm in their anti-Jackson views. Other voters thought the Whigs were attempting to be all things to all people; editors attacked them frequently on this point. In 1840 the Whigs had their famed Log Cabin campaign, a period cited by some historians to mark the beginning of press agentry.

POLITICAL UNREST IN STATE

During the thirties a strong belief had grown among many voters that the legislative unit of the government had become supreme in state and national affairs. To take advantage of this popular attitude, the Jacksonians directed their campaign to the small businessmen, farmers, laborers, and others, generally marked as an opposition force to the moneyed elements. Jacksonians and Whigs were split on their views toward national and state banks, and the Democrats divided into "hard-money" and "soft-money" factions. Benton led the hard-money group, seeking gold and silver for exchange purposes, not paper money.

Campaign papers appeared more frequently during this period. A number were issued by regular papers as supplements or separate publications, to continue until the election was over. For example, in 1840 the *Log Cabin Hero* was published by the St. Louis *New Era*. The first issue, on May 7, announced that thirteen numbers would be printed, with subscriptions at 50 cents. In Fayette, the *Hickory Club* appeared briefly. These publications were merely a phase of the enthusiasm shown throughout the nation in this Van Buren-Harrison campaign. Conventions, or political rallies as one would label them today, were held in many communities, frequently continuing for several days. Processions, brilliant with banners and music, were reported by editors with considerable feeling. The "state was wild with excitement and many and interesting and graphic are the scenes which our older citizens are able to recall of the campaign of 1840." William Gilpin, secretary of the 1840 Democratic state convention, also was editor of the *Missouri Argus*. In this St. Louis paper, Gilpin voiced party views, noting that "in the ranks of industry, amongst the productive classes, we find the true aristocracy."[5]

The *Missouri Republican*, naturally, felt differently about the major issues. While Gilpin attacked what he termed the policy of applying "freedom, not fetters, to trade," distinguishing the rights of "things" from the rights of "men," the *Republican* claimed "the faithless conduct and preposterous principles of Van Buren legislators" were ruining the state and pointed out that legislative actions had driven out capital and interfered with the development of commercial projects.

Starting in 1844, the political unrest that reached its climax in the Civil War began to stir. Democrats, still winning, showed gains in the presidential campaign, cutting the Whig percentage of the vote from 44 to 42. Switzler reported that in this campaign eleven papers backed the Democrats, seven the Whigs. In St. Louis the four papers were equally divided.[6] Among the major problems were the clamor for the annexation of Texas and the fight on the extension of slavery into the territories. The views of Missourians concerning slavery depended almost unerringly on their point of origin. Immigration from the free states created new thinking among the residents of the state, and large groups of Irish and German immigrants counteracted in part the previously dominant pro-Southern element.

Missourians in 1844 elected two senators and considered a new constitution in addition to studying questions of money, Texas, slavery, and other issues. To give suitable coverage of these questions, publishers renewed their political editions; for example, the *Coon Hunter* appeared in Boonville, the *Mill Boy* in St. Louis.

Tragedy highlighted the news in mid-February, 1844, when Governor Thomas Reynolds committed suicide in the executive mansion in Jefferson City. "Our city is overshadowed with gloom and distress! Gov. Reynolds is no more! He has perished by his own hands!" So did the *Jefferson Inquirer* record the event. The report said the Governor had used his rifle to kill himself in "full vigor of manhood." Reynolds, described as one of the "best and purest men of Missouri," left a farewell note that was printed in the papers: "In every situation in which I have ever been placed, I have labored to discharge my duty faithfully to the public; but this has not protected me for the last twelve months from the slanders and abuse of my enemies, which has rendered my life a burden to me. I pray God to forgive them and teach them more charity."[7] Some papers used black rules on their pages as an indication of mourning. A public meeting was held in Jefferson City, and the resolutions and testimonies to Reynolds' memory there expressed were published in the newspapers.

A major dispute developed over the proposed constitution, drafted in 1845 and presented to the voters the next year. "An adverse reaction to the 1845 convention anti-charter bias was expressed by the *Missouri Reporter*, Democratic successor to the *Argus* in St. Louis. The *Reporter* feared that because of the individual liability and repeal provisions of the article on corporations there would be no more private investment in turnpikes, railroads, and insurance companies, and that all public improvement would be stopped," according to Dr. James N. Primm.[8] The editor of the *Reporter* believed "the work of the convention will be rejected. That body has overstepped the decisions of the people, by making innovations which they did not desire and will not approve—such indeed, as no intelligent people can sanction." Even the religious angle was noted in the *Reporter*, which pointed out the limitation on the holdings of each sect—one acre of land in any town or city and not more than ten acres in a county.

More opposition to the proposed constitution appeared in the Columbia *Missouri Statesman*, which became alarmed because "the bank-hating Democrats of the convention" had introduced the individual liability principle. "These provisions would destroy all associated enterprise—all insurance officers—and would effectually prevent any internal improvement by individual effort. No one man would ever take stock in a company if he knew his whole estate would be in jeopardy," according to a letter to the editor. The Liberty *Weekly Tribune* approved the proposed constitution in general, calling it "the least of evils."[9]

Though the majority of the papers of the state supported the proposed constitution, the people rejected it in 1846. Primm says, "Its defeat was generally ascribed to the unpopularity of the banking and corporation provisions in St. Louis and the older sections of the state, combined with rural antipathy toward the new system of legislative apportionment, which reduced the advantage of the less populous frontier counties."[10]

In another matter for public debate, many Missourians disagreed with Benton in his views concerning Texas. Benton, in the Senate, sought to maintain friendly relations with Mexico in order to maintain trade. Public meetings condemned Benton, and some of his former friends declared openly they would not support him for re-election. Some Whigs backed Benton, and their support proved to be a handicap to him. Missouri's other senator, David R. Atchison, took a view opposite to Benton's on the Texas issue when it reached the Senate. The Missouri legislature in 1844 had adopted a resolution instructing its senators to approve the annexation of Texas. Benton was able to go along with these instructions at the time, since they did not stress immediate annexation.

By early 1846 the Mexican War was under way. "News From Mexico" and "Later From Texas" headlined stories frequently copied from other papers, especially the New Orleans *Picayune*. The Liberty *Weekly Tribune* reported in an all-caps, single-column headline: "WAR! WAR!" and continued: "The War Commenced—Defeat of United States Troops." This paper, by the way, opposed the annexation of Texas because of the "conquestlike manner" of the procedure.[11] Missourians quickly raised a volunteer group of 650 which was sent home after three months without seeing any active duty. Later, 1,658 Missourians went with Colonels Stephen Kearny and A. W. Doniphan on the Santa Fe Expedition.

Although most Missouri papers reprinted accounts of the Mexican War from other papers, some—such as the *Jefferson Inquirer* in the capital city—had their own correspondents. This paper published many stories, signed "E" for Lucian J. Eastin, an officer among the volunteers and a staff member. From mid-1846 to July, 1857, Eastin provided interesting copy such as these excerpts, reproduced as originally published:

> Dr. Moore is our surgeon, and is vigilant and attentive to his duties. . . . Him and myself tent together and keep Bachelors Hall every night. This trip will satisfy us, that man to be happy and comfortable must have a wife—one that can administer to his wants and soothe his cares. (July 15, 1846.)

> This evening we reached buffalo, and the whole command feasted very sumptuously of those animals. This change of

diet will produce a very salutary effect upon the health of the army. (August 4, 1846.)

During the day we encountered a ferocious enemy in the form of gnats . . . travelled 18 miles and reached the Little Arkansas; suffered much for want of water; frequently drank out of wagon ruts. (August 11, 1846.)

In a "P.S." to one of his accounts, "E" noted, "I give some of the principal items in camp. There are ten thousand rumors afloat, but I pay no attention to them." Later he reported, "Mr. Kribben of St. Louis, belonging to the artillery, designs establishing a printing press here [Santa Fe]. It is believed a press well conducted would be liberally patronized, both here and abroad." By winter "E" wrote, "Time drags on rather heavily here—nothing much of interest among the soldiers. The variety of this city is not of that character to attract much attention." In late October he added, "Since last I wrote you nothing has occurred of much interest or importance." The novelty of life in Santa Fe was wearing thinner in November, although some interest was roused in a controversy over the pay for the volunteers. Early in 1847 Eastin reported "many deaths amongst the troops" as well as "trouble with the Navajoes."

In Eastin's dispatches there are some brief reports, telling about meeting the enemy, and on one such occasion, Eastin claimed, the opposition lost three hundred killed and three hundred wounded, while "our loss, one killed, one mortally wounded, and seven so wounded as to recover without any loss of limbs." In June he noted that "most of the volunteers are tired of service, and disgusted with this country [Santa Fe]. Our eyes are directed towards home. A good many might enlist to go to California; few, if any, to remain here." Reports in July and August, 1847, tell of barbeques held for returning soldiers from Cole County.

Editor E. S. Wilkerson reported in the Platte City *Platte Argus* on September 24, 1847, under the headline, "Glorious News," that "The City of Mexico [is] at our Mercy."[12]

Reform Measures in News

The Mexican War had created some interest in the national contest of 1848 although the campaigns lacked much of the enthusiasm of the earlier Old Hickory-Log Cabin press battles. Some writers view this period and the Wilmot Proviso's exclusion of slavery from the Mexican cession area as the beginning of hard-and-fast sectionalist views on slavery. Both parties sought candidates who would appeal to the voters in both the North and the South.

The Whigs were fortunate, possibly, in the fact that the leading generals in the Mexican conflict were members of their party—Zachary Taylor and Winfield Scott. Taylor was nominated as their candidate for the Presidency on the fourth ballot, although some Missourians had held to the hope that Henry Clay, "Harry of the West," would be a candidate. Taylor, a long-time military man who had never voted in a general election, was a Southerner and a slave owner. But the *Missouri Statesman* reported that when Taylor was asked about his political views, he said, "As an officer of the army in the public service I am neither. But when the question is plumply put to me, as now, *I am a full blooded Whig and one quarter over.*"[13]

National and state issues were similar in 1848. The state Democratic press went to some pains to explain the party's views on internal improvements, stating that the party was in favor of such projects, but opposed to creating a debt to cover the cost. This stand was in conflict with the national party's views on internal improvements. The Whigs, national and state, were in favor of such improvements, and one party editor wrote that the party was pledged "by all practical and prudent means, forever to encourage works of internal improvement."[14]

Although more agreed on political issues than the Democrats, the Whigs lost again. Austin A. King was elected governor of Missouri, defeating the Whig candidate, James S. Rollins. When the state legislature met in November, Atchison was re-elected to the United States Senate. Democrats swept all other offices, including the contests for congressional seats. The *Missouri Statesman* on September 22, 1848, conceded with "We give it up—we do candidly—this State *has* gone for the Democrats! The dark pall of Locofocoism hangs *over* Missouri." Even General Taylor failed to carry Missouri, losing by more than 7,400 votes to Cass. But with Taylor's national victory, some Missourians, especially Whigs in Columbia and St. Louis, were able to celebrate with "a grand illumination, torchlight procession, and speaking at the Courthouse," as the Columbia account read.

The next major political issue to engage the attention of the press involved a debate over the Jackson "Resolutions on the Subject of Slavery," which sought to maintain the Union at almost all hazards. These resolutions were so named because they were introduced into the State Senate by Claiborne F. Jackson on January 15, 1849. Point 5, the most strongly opposed of the resolutions, said: "That in the event of the passage of any Act of Congress conflicting with the principles herein expressed, Missouri will be found in hearty co-operation with the slave-holding states, in such measures as may be deemed necessary for our mutual protection against the encroachments of Northern fanaticism." The resolutions were approved by both houses of the General Assembly, and Governor King signed them on March 10, 1849.

The adoption of the Jackson Resolutions is another indication of the growing anti-Benton feeling in the state, since these resolutions were counter to his known stand on slavery. The resolutions declared that the people in the new states should have the right to determine the issue of slavery for themselves. Benton took his views directly to the people. He started on May 26 in Jefferson City, and in the next five months he covered the state. Shoemaker notes the fiery language Benton used, quoting from his final speech:

> In the execution of this design I cannot be an instrument, nor can I believe that the people or the mass of the general assembly are with it; and I deem it right to have a full understanding with my constituents on the whole matter. I therefore appeal from the instructions . . . because they are in conflict with instructions already received and obeyed . . . they did not emanate from any known desire or understood will of the people . . . they contain unconstitutional expositions of the Constitution which I am sworn to support . . . they require me to promote disunion . . . they are copied from resolutions hatched from great mischief . . . I appeal to the people, and the whole body of the people. It is a question above party, and should be kept above it. I mean to keep it there.[15]

Even Whigs divided into Benton and anti-Benton factions. In 1848 the Whigs elected only 35 to the General Assembly, 18 less than their representation in 1844. Most Whigs had voted against the Jackson resolutions.

By 1850 Missouri was on the threshold of becoming a state coveted by both sides of the intensifying quarrel between North and South. The state's population was 700,000, and the number of papers had increased from 17 in 1835 to more than 50, including five dailies. The state had weathered the Panic of 1837; its farm land was valued at some $87 million, although only 7 per cent of the land was then improved; the taxable wealth had reached nearly $50 million; railroads had reached at least the planning stage, to be developed during the next period.[16]

DARK SIGNS ON HORIZON

Papers took an active role in reform measures. Considerable space was devoted to discussion of the penitentiary in Jefferson City, and in the early forties attention focused on capital punishment and public executions. The *Missouri Statesman* in 1846 condemned capital punishment as "one of the remnants of barbarism still lingering in our code . . . which corrupts the moral sense, hardens the sensibilities of all who witness its execution and teaches a disregard of human life."[17]

The temperance movement made considerable headway, with hundreds of societies organized to attack this "common enemy of mankind" which was blamed for the plight of so many widows and orphans and for much of the crime, insanity, and poverty that existed in the state. Although there was no formal organization for temperance in the state until 1842, by 1847 100,000 members were claimed by temperance groups. Papers freely quoted speakers who said, "Intemperance [is] the chosen ally of guilt and crime in every form in which they had fallen under the cognizance of the courts." Thousands took the pledge to stay away from this "parent of fraud." Frequently correspondents became poetical, and one looked forward to the time

> When we shall see this village freed,
> From the monstrous tyrant—Alcohol
> And men whom Bacchus erst did lead,
> Obsequious to the Temperance call.[18]

One must remember, in reading early papers and the long stories about the temperance movement, that such items were published by request. The fact that they appeared in the papers did not necessarily mean that the editors endorsed such programs. However, after 1850 the widespread temperance movement declined. Other issues were more pressing. Persons still enjoyed the excitement of mass meetings, but when political rallies and temperance sessions conflicted, the average citizen found more thrill in listening to politicians than in learning about the fate of a drunkard. Other stories concerning temperance told about local option elections, demands for state restrictions on the sale of whiskey, and the support given the movement by slaveholders who feared that whiskey would be given to their Negroes. Among the editors who went on the speaking circuit for temperance was Col. William F. Switzler of Columbia.[19]

Interest turned to women and their rights. Some papers, such as the *Boon's Lick Times*, questioned if the benefits of civilization had been extended to women when they were denied equal justice. By early 1849 a state bill provided some protection for women, but not much. One step forward was the ruling that property owned by a woman before marriage was free from liability for her husband's debts contracted before the marriage. Missouri papers reported on meetings of the woman's rights organizations in other parts of the nation, but normally without editorial comment. Some women did not agitate for their suffrage, maintaining that their place was in the home, according to some newspaper accounts.[20]

Civic problems also were discussed. An article on "Mud," which appeared in the *Daily Jefferson Inquirer* on January 15, 1859, noted, in part, that "at every step [the pedestrian] is met with a perpetual slosh, squash, squirt, splatter, splash; he slips, slides, hops, jumps, and staggers until the mud becomes so profusely distributed over his coat, pants and boots, that it is almost impossible to distinguish a gentleman from one of Warden Hughes' 'Pets.'" The editor threatened to continue his fight with the aldermen, concluding, "We will pursue them with that which is mightier than a link of Bologna sausage—the pen."

There are many reasons why 1850 should mark the end of pioneer journalism in the state. Papers had expanded across the entire state, with the exception of the Ozark region. By 1850 voters had divided along party lines, and the papers were voicing their opinions. Benton had been defeated and no longer was a great voice in the West. The editors' political positions could be traced in the names of their papers, although changes in ownership frequently brought transfer in party loyalty without an accompanying change in the name plate. Papers were established to promote a specific campaign, and such publications frequently disappeared after the final vote had been tallied.

Although debate was active on public issues, few editors were aware in 1850 of the dark clouds gathering that would bring, among other disasters, a temporary halt to the growth of journalism in Missouri.

CHAPTER V

LULL BEFORE THE STORM

1851-1860

"WE WISH IT distinctly understood that the editor and the devil are two very different persons," wrote J. Rennie in his Liberty *Western Star* in 1841. Such a statement indicates clearly the feeling that many readers held toward the press as they split over political questions and argued their opinions toward slavery. Still, the state continued to grow and papers to expand throughout this period. Missouri had five dailies and about fifty weeklies in 1850; by 1860 there were fifteen dailies and one hundred and thirty weeklies. Kansas City's first paper, the *Ledger*, appeared in 1851, forty-three years after the establishment of the first in St. Louis.[1] There were foreign-language, religious, commercial, and other publications sufficient in number to place Missouri fifth in the nation.

Some papers wilted quickly. Name changes became common; editors sought new success with new titles. Pro- and anti-slavery publications appeared; others supported or fought Thomas Hart Benton. Editors moved from town to town, hauling their meager equipment with them. Many publications listed in directories prepared by Kennedy in 1852, Coggeshall in 1856, and Kenny in 1861, have not been located, indicating that many papers had brief careers.[2] Names conveyed editors' attitudes and political parties. Among the titles were *Messenger, Western Pioneer, Golden Era, Sentinel, Examiner, Recorder, Democratic Platform, Spectator, Furnace, Agrarian, Union, American, True American Leader, Watchman, Detector, People's Press, National American, Free State Republican*. In 1860 the first paper in the state to bear a Latin name appeared, the *Vox Populi* in Fulton.

Telegraph news became more commonplace in the dailies after the completion by 1850 of connections with the East, Chicago, and New Orleans. Some papers devoted several columns to these items and relayed political stories and election results to interior communities to be moved farther westward by the Pony Express and other means. Still, one must not think that all items labeled "By Telegraphic Sources" were equally significant. Such briefs as these appeared in one edition of the *Jefferson Examiner* in 1859:

Senator Douglas was serenaded last night.

It was still raining at dark with heavy fog.

Forty persons were killed or drowned this morning by the train from Columbus to Macon running off the track in consequence of the late injuries by great heavy rains.

Page 1 still carried advertisements and filler material, generally a short story, plus some poems clipped from other publications.

Manufacturing activities increased in Missouri, though the state remained predominantly agricultural. St. Louis firms produced or processed flour and meal and refined sugar, liquor, meat, soap and candles, etc. Corn was the principal agricultural product, followed by other grains, dairy products, hemp, tobacco, and livestock. Advertisements about these products generally listed the names of the merchants and their addresses, but stated no specific prices. Frequently these messages ran the entire year without type changes.

Transportation facilities expanded as Missouri became the crossroads for westward traffic. Thousands of settlers traversed the state to set out upon the Santa Fe and Oregon trails to help populate the newly acquired territories. River transportation continued to carry the farmers' products to faraway markets and to bring in supplies. Steamboats had not, by 1860, lost the race to the railroads, which were expanding in only a few areas. Many communities still depended on the stagecoach for transportation. A few plank roads existed, and by 1859 St. Louis had its first rapid transit—horse cars.

Banking operations expanded, with facilities in St. Louis, Kansas City, St. Joseph, Lexington, Liberty, Independence, and other communities by 1860. It is possible that some of the state's conservatism can be traced to this era, when tighter controls were placed on banks to prohibit the kinds of wildcat fiscal maneuvers encountered across the nation. James Neal Primm notes in his study that Missouri "was intimately connected with the frontier and the far west, was a border slave state, and was remote from eastern markets. All of these factors proved to be of importance in the economic development of Missouri and in determining the attitude of her people toward the proper functions of state government in relation to that development." He also feels that "One of the most important developments in the Missouri economy during the decade preceding the Civil War was the gradual shift in opinion on the subject of banking. . . . Opposition to the state bank in early years . . . had come from . . . some of the so-called 'Hard' Democrats [and] Whig friends of the United States Bank."[3]

The population climbed from 682,044 in 1850 to 1,182,012 a decade later, placing Missouri eighth among the states. Some estimate there were 115,000 slaves in 1860, when all but one of the state's 114 counties had been organized.

By 1850 the Mormons had fled from Missouri, leaving behind bitter memories and shameful recollections in the press. Missourians had served in the Army during the Mexican War, some of them from a personal interest in the Southwest, dating from Santa Fe trading expeditions. Expansionist sentiments found support in the state, for some Missourians acknowledged the "manifest destiny" philosophy and believed this nation should acquire all the land between the Atlantic and the Pacific. The most pronounced feelings, however, centered on slavery. Missourians moved with their slaves to Kansas and Nebraska after the decision of 1854 permitted settlers in the territories to decide the slavery question for themselves, but at the same time, other Missourians were helping to provide escape routes for slaves still held in the state. In late 1854 the spark that was to flame up in the Missouri-Kansas border war was lit—the conflict that made Kansas the preliminary battlefield of the Civil War. Dr. Richard S. Brownlee, II, in his study, "Guerrilla Warfare in Missouri, 1861-1865," notes that "Missouri's Civil War, and perhaps the strongest reason for her identification as an ardent Southern state, actually began in 1854 with the passage of the Kansas-Nebraska Act . . . Missourians became concerned when it was felt that the territory might be settled by abolitionists."[4]

JAYHAWKERS RAID MISSOURI

More than one thousand Missourians went into Kansas in November, 1854, to help elect a proslavery congressman. Similar events occurred in early 1855, when about 6,300 ballots were cast in a Kansas community of 2,900 eligible voters. These results stirred the antislavery element, even those in the East, to actions that eventually destroyed newspapers, businesses, and homes. John Brown's raid brought death to unarmed slave owners near Osawatomie and initiated a period marked by murder, stealing, and arson. After Missourians failed to locate Brown, they proceeded to burn Osawatomie to the ground in August, 1856. Federal troops brought an uneasy and temporary peace. Kansas became a free state in 1861, but only after the border war had caused it to be called "bleeding Kansas." It was by no means a one-sided war. "Jayhawkers" raided Missouri communities in the border counties, committing murder, arson, horse thefts, looting, and other crimes. Brown "invaded" the state, taking slaves back to freedom in Kansas. After a reward of $300 was placed on his head by Missouri's Governor Robert M. Stewart, Brown disappeared from the local scene.

Attention also focused on the continuing growth of Missouri. More church organizations were established, doctors were successful in organizing, agriculturists and teachers formed their own groups, followed by the horticulturists. Cultural activities flourished, including the theater. Private schools and colleges were established, many of which survive today; some expansion was made in the public school program.[5]

Missourians, drugged by the gold-dust fever, went West, although many stumbled home to receive "I told you so" greetings. Pike County became famous through stories by Bret Harte and others who assumed all Missourians were Pike Countians since they met so many from there. The stampede west reversed itself. The California *News* reported in 1860 that "some parties have not remained in the mountains more than two or three hours before they commenced taking the back track."[6]

Nationwide attention turned to Parkville in April, 1855, after the *Industrial Luminary* was destroyed by a group of armed horsemen who rode into the town to attack the newspaper office. The editors, having been warned of the attack, hid some type in an attic, but the rest, along with the press, ended in the Missouri River. Editor George S. Park, from Vermont, was not popular in Parkville, since most of the residents were from Southern states. When he began the *Industrial Luminary* in 1853 he supported the Free Soil policy. Now he had written in his paper that the Kansas election was a fraud and farce. "This may save the country from bloodshed, but the government is held up to ridicule and contempt, and its authority disregarded." After the raid, Park fled to Illinois, but returned after the war to become a state senator and to help establish Park College. His coeditor, W. J. Patterson, was seized by the raiders, but freed after his promise to leave the county promptly and permanently. Later events indicate this incident may have backfired, since it attracted considerable publicity in the Northern press and no doubt influenced a few individuals to move to Kansas.[7]

Thomas Hart Benton's decline highlighted the political scene, although no man appeared to dominate the party as the former senator had for more than three decades. Papers continued to serve as sounding boards for politicians, while editors sought to unite factions. The *Jefferson Inquirer* of June 21, 1851, noted that though party members might have petty differences, basically they agreed on major principles. "Party nominations . . . must be sustained; we must give up our prejudices against men and submit to the decision of our party, as expressed by its majority in convention for if men selected as our candidates fail by reason of our opposition and prejudice to them, it virtually disbands our party."[8]

Still, some editors feared party splits over the slavery issue and the question of the preservation of the Union. The Whigs, generally, preferred a conservative stand on the slavery question and, as Eula Baker pointed out, "were ready to resist what they considered illegal Northern aggression and abolition on the one hand, and to suppress Southern fanaticism and nullification on the other." The Whigs reached the peak of their power in Missouri in 1850 and 1851, with a United States senator, three congressmen, and key state positions, and, according to a study by Laurence D. Lingle, the party in 1854 "cherished an understandable hope of continued existence"; the Missouri Whigs "hoped to quiet slavery agitation by condemning, in turn, abolition and nullification." By 1855 the state organization began to disintegrate, and members turned to new affiliations. The Know-Nothing, or American party, attracted many. Eula Baker concludes that in the 1856 election "The American party had become . . . the chief opposition party in Missouri politics." Parrish believes some of this downfall came because the Whig party seldom was "able to take a united stand on any given issue."

Benton's decline continued, with editors lashing invectives at the once powerful leader. Voters split into "pro" and "anti" Benton camps. This split, as well as the Kansas-Nebraska Bill, divided the Democrats, although editors such as James Lusk of the *Jefferson Inquirer* continued to seek unity within the ranks.

The 1852 campaign was another interesting conflict. The Democratic coalition candidate, General Sterling Price, a man who was not active in either faction but who was yet considered a sound Democrat, won the gubernatorial contest over James Winston. William Switzler, disgusted by the outcome of the election, wrote in his *Missouri Statesman*, "The editor . . . accompanied by the great Whig Party of thirty-one states and several territories, will embark for the head waters of Salt River." That same year the Democrats' candidate for the Presidency, Franklin Pierce, defeated the Whigs' candidate, Winfield Scott, in Missouri, 38,353 to 29,962.[9]

NEW PARTY ORGANIZED

As has been noted, by the mid-1850's, some members of the Whig party were turning elsewhere. The American party attracted some dissatisfied Whigs, since some of the parties' beliefs were similar—a strong national union, higher tariffs to protect industry, more federally supported internal improvements, and a sound banking system. Since a few of these views were shared, too, by the Bentonites, Switzler urged them also in 1858 to join the growing American party.

Major Thomas A. Harris, editor of the Hannibal *Courier*, helped to create the new American party in Missouri in 1854. He was called a "Polk, Cass, Pierce Democrat." The party grew slowly, yet by the end of the next year it had members in most counties, and was operating openly as a political unit.[10] Among the stronger Whig papers, some of which turned to the new party, were the Boonville *Observer*, Fulton *Telegraph*, Hannibal *Journal*, Hannibal *Messenger*, Columbia *Missouri Statesman*, and St. Louis *Intelligencer*. Democrats were supported by the *Jefferson Inquirer* and the *Metropolitan* in Jefferson City, the St. Louis *Daily Argus*, which opposed everything "Whiggish," and others.

One should note the political activities of such editors as Switzler, a state leader for many decades. His comments in the *Missouri Statesman* are typical, the political opinion mingled with news. Switzler supported the Compromise of 1850, as did all Whig papers in the state, and interpreted it as "proof that the Whigs were not the abolitionists and free-soilers that the Democrats charged them with being." Switzler remained consistent in his desire to keep the people united, an extremely difficult situation in "Little Dixie." He had local opposition, in 1852 from the *Missouri Sentinel*, followed later by the more radical *Dollar Journal*. He was described by his opponents as the lawyer who presumed to be an editor. When he denied being a copperhead, the *Missouri Democrat* labeled him a muttonhead.[11]

In Missouri the excitement of the campaign of 1854 for the legislature was intensified by the circumstances that the winners would decide the next United States senator when Atchison's term expired in 1855. Voters divided between Atchison and Benton and split on the passage of the Kansas-Nebraska Act and the extension of slavery into new states. In the congressional election, Whigs won six of the seven seats, with a Benton man capturing the seventh. In the General Assembly a three-cornered contest developed, pitting Atchison and Benton against each other and against Whig A. W. Doniphan. The Whigs, too, were divided. After 41 ballots the legislators adjourned on February 11, 1855, having failed to select a senator. Thus, from March 4, 1855, to March 3, 1857, the state had only one senator in Washington.[12]

As early as 1849 several editors had urged Benton to resign from the Senate. The St. Louis *Times* questioned his "affiliation with Seward, Chase, and the whole batch of Free Soilers" in 1850; the editor gave his opinion that much of Benton's support came from sentiment rather than from reason.[13] His retirement from public life was therefore strongly recommended. Benton was destroyed in 1856 in his race for the governorship, when seventy-four. In that election, anti-Benton factors won sixty-eight counties and scored important gains in the congressional contests. Trusten Polk, a Democrat and anti-Benton man, defeated Whig Robert C. Ewing; third was Benton, whose followers had been attacked on all sides and labeled "Black Republicans" by a few. Benton died two years later of cancer.

In 1856 it was too early for the newly formed national Republican party to have much influence in Missouri. Its primary aim was to halt the extension of slavery into the territories, a policy with which Benton and many prominent Democrats concurred. This is not to say there was little interest in this 1856 campaign; quite the contrary. As free soil and slave soil leaders from other states had descended on Missouri to join in the controversy which frequently led to violence and bloodshed, the events were all fully covered by reports by the partisan press.[14]

Missourians, confused and divided, soon turned their attention to the 1860 national election, the springboard to separation. This was to be the climax after years of debates over the role of the federal government and its relations to the states. It was not unusual to see editors switching from party to party as the breech widened. Some old-line Whigs joined the Democrats; some Democrats found Douglas more than they could take and turned to the Republicans. Within each major party one also found those who went their own ways.

Truly the 1860 election was among the most significant in Missouri's history, and the role played by the press on both sides was significant. Missouri was caught in a vise between the North and the South, with the prospect (or threat) of being surrounded on three sides by states interested in freedom for the slaves, while it remained basically a slaveholding area with, in some areas, strong Southern sympathies. According to Brownlee,

> The Eastern press, goaded on by Horace Greeley, sent reporters to the border, and a barrage of anti-slavery, anti-Missouri news and editorials soon appeared in its papers. On almost any occasion Missourians were about to read of themselves as aggressive "slavocrats," whose sole interest in Kansas was based on a voracious and immoral hunger to expand slavery into the west.[15]

There was no widespread desire for secession, nor did such talk exist at this time in Missouri. The press was at this time as split on its political approach as the state was to become a year later. Even names of some papers were misleading. The *Missouri Republican* in St. Louis, a Democratic paper, supported Douglas for the Presidency "as the only man at this day who can rally the people to the polls with a hearty good will."[16] The Kansas City *Journal of Commerce* preferred Joseph Lane for the Democratic nomination, but backed Douglas later.[17] Both papers attacked William H. Seward, whom they felt would certainly be the Republican candidate. The *Missouri Republican* noted as early as February that if the Republicans failed to nominate Seward it would be a "confession of the decline and fall of this mischievous, sectional party."[18] Some Republican papers did not favor Seward, preferring instead Missouri's favorite son, Edward Bates. Lincoln was only casually mentioned as a possible nominee, although he was well known to B. Gratz Brown, editor of the pro-Republican *Missouri Democrat* in St. Louis, and himself a candidate for the Vice-Presidency in 1872. Political editors —and the majority of Missouri editors were in this category in 1860—were optimistic as convention time neared, predicting party harmony. "Harmony" soon disappeared when the Democrats convened in Charleston, South Carolina, in April. The *Missouri Republican,* in reporting on the convention, expressed concern over "the reckless and unhallowed ambition" of the Southern delegates,[19] and the *Journal of Commerce* refused to believe the "false misrepresentations" about a possible mutiny of the South.[20]

City papers received much of their convention news by telegraph. Frequently their editors or reporters attended these sessions, writing about the trip, discussing topics of all types, even
noting their accommodations and their meals. Although one correspondent was unhappy about the convention results, he took
space to recommend a particular hotel for its excellent food.

When Douglas' views on slavery were adopted by the convention, seven Southern delegations walked out. Although Douglas
maintained a lead on each of the 53 ballots taken, he failed to
gain a majority. The *Missouri Republican* referred to this as "the
seceders' convention" and to many of the leaders as "bolters." A
week later the editor stated that this convention had helped
create a still louder cry across the nation for Douglas.[21] The
break between North and South appears obvious in these two
items from the *Missouri Republican,* which distinguished the
"democracy of the North" from the Southerners:

> It is unfair to the Democracy of the North that they should
> be made to carry additional burdens. They stand as the con-
> servative party between the fanaticism of sections, and are
> willing to fight, many of them with no hope of reward, as they
> have hitherto fought, only with renewed spirit and vigor.[22]

> If there was a proper respect for the Democracy of the
> North—if a reckless and unhallowed ambition did not control
> the leading men of the South in the convention—if they really
> desire to accomplish the defeat of Seward and his Black Re-
> publicans in the election—they ought to be anxious to place
> their Northern brethren on such a platform as would ensure
> their triumph in all the debatable states.[23]

Democrats focused their attention on Chicago, where the
Republicans were to gather for their Wigwam Convention. Meanwhile, in May the newly formed Constitutional Union Party met
in Baltimore and named John Bell of Tennessee and Edward
Everett of Massachusetts to head its ticket.

The Democrats hoped the "Black Republican" convention
would result in a "long and stormy session."[24] They predicted
Seward would be nominated as the Republicans' candidate for
the Presidency, although a few editors believed there were other
candidates available. The Republican St. Joseph *Free Democrat*
noted "the harmony and enthusiasm and marked courtesy" shown
by those at the sessions, compared with the Democratic convention which was "characteristic of the orgies of demons damned."

The "Democratic Party was ruled by the slavery element," wrote the editor.[25]

Horace Greeley, now broken from Seward, early supported Bates, although the editor of the New York *Tribune* expected Seward to win. Soon the tide turned from Seward—Greeley's leadership being much in evidence—and the Lincoln bandwagon became crowded. The delegates from Missouri stayed with Bates until Lincoln's nomination became obvious. On the initial ballot Seward had 173½ votes and Lincoln 102; Bates had 48, all from Missouri. The *Missouri Republican* thought Bates was "used" by Francis P. Blair, Jr., and other Missourians and that "not a man of them ever had any desire to elevate him to the office of President."[26]

BITTER CAMPAIGN UNDER WAY

With Lincoln's selection as their candidate for the Presidency, the Republican press was quick to line up behind him. The St. Joseph *Free Democrat*'s flowery comment, typical of many, was: "At the mention of Lincoln's name the heartstrings of every true Republican vibrate with the emotions of enthusiasm, patriotism and devotion to the cause of justice, truth, and freedom. . . . We toss our cap in the air with loud huzzas for the man who can rule a nation and can 'split rails.' "[27]

Lincoln and his running mate, Hannibal Hamlin, were labeled by their opposition as "two as *Black* Republicans as can be found anywhere," and the *Missouri Republican* added: "We are glad that Mr. Lincoln is the nominee of the Black Republican convention at Chicago. That body passed by, and rejected, the representative man of the party, Gov. Seward, and by so doing made it very easy for the Democratic party to achieve victory in the election."[28] The opposition across the state, the Kansas City *Journal of Commerce*, was bitter: Lincoln "is below the mediocrity of statesmen—in fact, he does not come up to the standard of intellect and ability which entitles a politician to the rank of a statesman. He would still have been unknown to the country had it not been that Douglas had to give him notoriety because the Black Republicans of Illinois had nobody else they were willing to sacrifice." Hamlin was called an unknown, a "fossil member" of the Senate.[29]

The second Democratic convention met in June in Baltimore and split again over the slavery question. The Republican *Free Democrat* called this "A conglomeration of the most virulent and antagonistic elements that discord could desire and well have their actions portrayed their characters."[30] After the Southern delegates walked out, the Northern Democrats selected Douglas to head their ticket, and the departed group named John C. Breckinridge of Kentucky. Such action led the majority of the Democratic papers in Missouri to stand behind Douglas. Some were in rather embarrassing positions, such as the *Journal of Commerce*, which had originally supported Joseph Lane, who became Breckinridge's running mate. The editor could only admit that his earlier feelings had been changed after Douglas was nominated, and that Douglas was "by every rule known to the Democratic party . . . the nominee of the Democracy of this nation, and as such, we shall support him."[31] Some Democratic papers claimed Douglas was the only "national" candidate with a chance to win.

Missouri editors now became engulfed in a whirlpool. It was a "mighty uncertain" campaign, and as voting time approached, this uncertainty increased. Not only were the editors caught in the national political maelstrom, but state politics were confusing as well. Democrats split over their candidates, and for a time the hated "Black Republicans" were almost forgotten amidst this bitter intramural feud. The *Missouri Republican*, which had sounded praise for Lincoln in 1848 for his views on the Mexican War, forgot those remarks and asked: "What has Lincoln ever done that he should be called great or worthy of the Presidency of a great nation?" Answering his own question, the editor wrote: "Absolutely nothing."[32] The *Journal of Commerce* was confident that "Black Republicanism has committed suicide and the putrefying corpse remains only to be buried out of sight." The editor added, "Bell-Everettism is a bastard bantling that can neither level a field-piece nor sway a broad sword."[33]

Lincoln disturbed the Democratic editors, and some Republicans as well, by remaining at home in Springfield, Illinois, while Douglas took to the political stump. The *Free Democrat* in St. Joseph considered this a wise move, noting, "He believes . . . that the Presidency is neither to be sought after nor declined. While the stump candidates are inspiring disgust everywhere by their blatant self-encomiums, Ole Abe is steadily growing in the affections of the people."[34] However, the *Missouri Republican* stressed the problem created by half the states being against Lincoln: "Imagine the Chief Magistrate of the Republic seated upon the Presidential chair brooding over the thought that one half of the country looks upon him as an outlaw."[35]

Republicans, although their candidate remained at home, were not idle. Editors attacked Douglas, before and after his nomination. The *Free Press* hoped Douglas would be selected "so that we may have the pleasure of seeing him so completely used up that angel Gabriel cannot trump together, with his loudest blasts, enough of the skeleton of Democracy to cast a shadow."[36] The St. Joseph paper proclaimed itself "the sole exponent of the Republican party in Western Missouri," and its editor, Frank Tracy, was frequently attacked, verbally and physically. In closing his first volume in June, 1860, Tracy said his office had been the target of "malicious hellhounds," and he referred to the Democrats as a "horde of desperate unprincipled mobocrats."[37]

Similar attacks were made in St. Louis against the *Missouri Democrat*. Its editor, Francis P. Blair, Jr., was pelted with rotten eggs while he was making a campaign speech in Hannibal. The Bell and Douglas headquarters in St. Louis sustained damage by the Wide Awakes, "who have been making a habit of desecrating the Sabbath and disturbing the rest of the peaceably-disposed citizens," according to the *Missouri Republican*. The Wide Awakes, soon to play an important role in the Civil War, were primarily German-born citizens who followed the Republican party. One editor, in reporting about elaborate plans made in Chillicothe for a rally honoring Breckinridge backers, concluded the event had ended in a "fizzle."[38]

During the campaign Lincoln said the quarrel between the two principal St. Louis papers, the *Republican* and the *Democrat*, reminded him of a battle in the courthouse yard at Springfield, Illinois:

> Two men engaged in a rough and tumble bout. They clinched and rolled and tumbled all over the courthouse yard. It was such an evenly matched fight that the circle of bystanders could not tell which man was getting the worst of it. Finally the combatants separated when both men were completely worn out. The spectators looked them over carefully and tried to determine which one had won the honors. They were unable to decide, but they did make the astonishing discovery that each combatant had on the other's coat.[39]

A most bitter struggle developed among the Democratic papers that supported Douglas and those that supported Breckinridge. When it became apparent that Breckinridge might be gaining, the pro-Douglas organs lashed out more strongly against him. One editor blamed Breckinridge forces for "the humiliating spectacle of the organization of a Black Republican party in Missouri"; the Southerner, the editor wrote, was in the contest merely to "divide and scatter" the Democratic vote. In St. Louis, the *Missouri Republican* called Breckinridge "the voluntary leader of the rashest and most suicidal movement ever contrived for the defeat of the South."[40]

All political rallies, regardless of party, were given prominence in the papers, with many-decked headlines; the editor's political views, however, were always clear. When one read, "By far the largest political gathering ever assembled turned out for ———," he knew the editor supported this candidate.[41] In Kansas City, the *Enquirer* supported Bell, and the Westport *Border Star* backed Breckinridge. In St. Joseph, the *West* and the *Gazette* were split between Breckinridge and Douglas; this situation pleased the Republican *Free Press* there as it republished their feuds. Once it asked about this dispute: "Shall these third rate pettifoggers and tenth rate politicians be permitted to dictate to the people when they utterly fail to agree among themselves?"[42] The Liberty *Tribune*, which backed the Bell-Everett ticket and called the presidential candidate one of the "purest and most profound statesmen in the Union," listed the following papers as supporting Douglas: Kansas City *Journal*, Independence *Gazette*, Parkville *Courier*, Carrollton *Democrat*, Boonville *Observer*, Savannah *Plain Dealer*, Hudson *Republican*, and others cited previously.

Lincoln's victories in Ohio, Indiana, and Pennsylvania in October gave Republican editors in Missouri something to cheer about; Democratic editors blamed Breckinridge and Buchanan for the party's defeat. With victory more nearly assured, the Republican press stirred up the controversy over slavery. The *Free Democrat* urged the border states to reject slavery, "the evil which has so long impeded their growth."[43] The *Missouri Republican* was more moderate, saying,

> Let us not give up the Union. . . . We want to see this secession business, which has been preached so long, put a stop to; and the people of Missouri, who are more deeply affected in the result than South Carolina or Alabama, should place their earnest remonstrances against the movement. Should Lincoln succeed, let him be inaugurated peaceably; but if he assumes to divert the government to his abominable Abolitionism, and

undermine the Constitution, then, indeed, will the time have come for action, and then, no doubt, some prompt and effective measure will be introduced to punish the traitor and eradicate the treason.[44]

Missouri was the only state Douglas carried in the election, and this by the narrowest of margins; he received 58,801 votes, Bell 58,372, and Breckinridge, 31,317. Lincoln, with 17,028 votes, carried only St. Louis, Osage, and Gasconade counties, all with large German populations. Parrish concludes that

> The outcome of this election clearly indicated that the great majority of Missourians were conservative and desired no extreme solution to the slavery question. Rather, they hoped for compromise and had difficulty choosing between the popular sovereignty of Stephen A. Douglas and the vague, middle-ground assurances of John Bell. The conservative strength in Missouri as represented by the Douglas-Bell vote amounted to 70.7 per cent of the total vote cast.[45]

Democratic editors were up in arms. The *Missouri Republican*, "grieved to say that the returns give almost indutitable [*sic*] evidence of the election of Lincoln," added: "Let us hope that Providence may yet open up a way to avert the dangers which are threatened to the permanence and integrity of our institutions." In Kansas City the *Journal of Commerce* said: "All fear ... that Lincoln is elected ... if so, nothing but the interposition of an over-ruling providence in the restraining of bad men, can preserve us in peace and harmony as a united people."[46] Republican papers rejoiced at the "Glorious Event." In St. Joseph the *Free Democrat* was a bit cautious, since Democratic partisans had attempted to prevent Republicans from voting. Lincoln received only 410 votes in St. Joseph, and the non-Republican papers were threatening to publish the names of these voters. They noted, however, that "Fraud and mob-law have received a blow from which they will never recover."[47]

The Rolla *Express*, which had supported Breckinridge, had stated earlier, "One wing of the Democratic partisans makes very free of calling the other bad names, as school boys do when their wrath is excited against each other." During the campaign it had warned of name-calling and said, "This indiscriminate application of hard epithets has its effect upon only weak minds which are led by the nose by any man who is supposed to possess influence." But by mid-November its lead story carried a one-line label, "The Contest Ended." It reported on "excitement in the South" and "gloomy prospects" that faced the nation.[48]

In Missouri, as across the country, the threat of war subdued many editors. In Kansas City the *Journal of Commerce* expressed the belief that there would be no secession nor war, while across the state the *Missouri Democrat* said, "It is our firm belief that never was the country less liable to be subjected to the desolating curse of civil war." The Liberty *Tribune* urged all to "stand still and wait the sober second thought of the people," but first to give a fair trial to Lincoln. The California *News,* decidedly secessionist, said, "We are ready to fight for the rights of the South in the Union," and in late December its Tennessee-born editor wrote: "So far as we, individually, are concerned, if a secession of the Southern states is inevitable, we certainly should cast our fortunes with our brethren of the South."[49] The editor of the *Missouri Republican* had written on October 24 a statement soon to become true: The state was about to become a battleground which would "disrupt ties of kindred and fraternity, turn brother against brother, and friend against friend."

Missouri editors reacted to the 1860 campaign much as they had to other political conflicts. Impartial coverage did not exist, nor did readers expect any neutrality. Editorials were biased, and subscribers selected their papers to fit their own bias. Stories were slanted; one party received all the bouquets, the opposition all the brickbats. That the 1860 contest sank to a new depth in editorial contempt, there can be little disagreement.

The Republicans became a sectional party, representing the North; Breckinridge Democrats voiced the Southern view. Douglas and Bell held moderate views, and editors deserve some credit for swinging so many voters to the Douglas-Bell tickets. They realized the obvious result—the split between North and South should either Lincoln or Breckinridge win. Still, "despite the bitterness which existed between the Missouri press during the election campaign, it is to their credit that nearly every newspaper, regardless of their earlier allegiance, pledged their support to the president-elect and earnestly opposed any secession movement within the state," wrote Ed Neider concerning the 1860 campaign.[50]

EDITORIAL PROBLEMS, GROWTH

The period leading up to the Civil War has been termed one of awakening for Missouri journalism. Growth of the press in the state can be shown by an incident involving James Lusk and his *Jefferson Inquirer*. In 1857 Lusk was reported to have been offered $10,500 for his paper, a story denied by Lusk. He indicated this price was too low, for he had "several thousand more than that" in the plant. Earlier he had installed a steam press, one of the "Adams' improved patent" machines.[51] Lusk's, however, was not a typical case. Only two years earlier the Kansas City *Enterprise* had been sold for $500. Since equipment and circulation of newspapers in Missouri varied widely, it would be difficult to estimate the value of a paper at that time, though $500 would be more realistic than would $10,500.

Many new papers were started in this period, including the *Daily Missouri Democrat,* a forerunner to the St. Louis *Globe-Democrat*. Dr. Jim A. Hart has recorded the history of this paper. In telling of its first issue on July 1, 1852, Hart writes,

> By newspaper standards of the time it was a tiny paper with four pages, only seven columns wide. It was at once scorned by the Southerners and ridiculed by its competitors. Yet this was the paper which became the mouthpiece for the emerging Republican Party. This was the paper that instigated and led the fight to keep Missouri from seceding from the Union. Abraham Lincoln was to praise its efforts as being worth more to the North than ten regiments of soldiers.[52]

By 1853 the paper was merged with the *Union,* keeping its original name. The next year Frank Blair, Jr., and B. Gratz Brown bought an interest and took over the editorship. Brown "attacked the Know-Nothings and unjust hostility to the Catholics; fought for a transcontinental railroad through St. Louis, paved streets, new wharves, and a new municipal hall." Twice, in 1853 and 1854, the *Democrat* backed the successful candidate for mayor, John How, a free-soil advocate, and one of the founders of the paper.

Earlier the *Missouri Democrat* attacked proslavery groups. In 1855 it sent James Redpath, an opponent of slavery, to cover the Kansas uprisings. The editors wanted gradual emancipation by colonization to Liberia, with repayment to the slaveholders.[53] In 1857 Blair and Brown explained their position:

> Our party in Missouri has been conservative in every age, and yet it could not prevent the repeal of the Missouri Compromise, the Kansas outrages, and the disunion agitation last summer. We have held the balance evenly . . . but the weight of the nigger was thrown in by our enemies, and the disturbed equilibrium we were unable to restore. . . . We have wearied

of it and (speaking for ourselves) we do not trust our fortunes and our fate to this great cause of Emancipation.[54]

Before Brown resigned from the editorship in 1859 the paper "came to reflect more and more the wide social, cultural, and economic interests of St. Louis." In appearance the *Missouri Democrat* resembled many papers throughout the state. With the border feuds, the Benton debates, national disturbance over slavery, and local issues, it is little wonder that editors gained readers. The excitement in the political world whetted the reader's appetite for all the news he could get.

KANSAS CITY PAPERS STARTED

Kansas City was much later in the establishment of papers than St. Louis. Long after the *Missouri Gazette* began publication in 1808, present-day Kansas City remained a struggling community of Indians, French traders, and a few settlers engaged primarily in the fur trade. By 1839 a plat was filed for the Town of Kansas, named after the river which flowed into the Missouri there and an Indian tribe. Settlers came primarily from Virginia, Tennessee, Kentucky, and the Carolinas. Nearby towns, such as Liberty, Independence, and Westport, competed for the settlers and for the outfitting of emigrants to the West. By 1845 there was a post office, the next year a hotel. In 1852 the City of Kansas was incorporated; in 1889 it became officially known as Kansas City.

The first paper in Kansas City was the *Ledger*, established in 1851 by R. C. Kennedy two years before the city's first election. When one recalls that there were fewer than five hundred persons in the area and that it required seven days to reach the community from St. Louis, it is not surprising to learn that the paper failed to last three years. The second, the *Enterprise*, appeared on September 23, 1854. A group of citizens sent W. J. Payne to St. Louis to buy press equipment, since that used by the *Ledger* had been sold and used to start a paper in Independence. By this time Kansas City's first election had been held, with 69 votes cast; by 1860, however, the population reached 4,418. During the bitter Kansas-Missouri feuds and the Civil War, Kansas City acquired the title of "the city in the war the longest." It suffered tremendously in these years, losing half of its population.[55] Citizens who favored the South were forced to leave the area, and others, who saw their business prospects destroyed, returned East or went to the Far West.

The *Enterprise* was edited by William A. Strong, with D. K. Abeel the publisher. Strong had met Robert T. Van Horn in a St. Louis hotel and upon learning that he was a printer, invited him to Kansas City to take over this work. Van Horn arranged to buy the paper, and in October, 1855, began his long career in Kansas City affairs; Abeel later purchased a half-interest. In 1856 or 1857 it became the *Western Journal of Commerce* and shortly after that the *Kansas City Journal of Commerce*. By 1858 the owners had established the first daily edition in the city, receiving telegraph news from St. Louis and other news by stage-coach from Boonville.[56]

The *Journal* had its share of wartime troubles, as related in October 12, 1865:

> In 1861 began its reverses. The rebellion broke out. This part of Missouri was almost wholly disloyal. The *Journal of Commerce* was loyal to the core. Within a fortnight the business of the city fell from metropolitan proportions to that of a neighbor-hood, and of necessity its paper followed. Its rebel contemporary . . . went quickly by the board, its editor making his exit to Independence. But the *Journal* lived on—sometimes suspended for a few weeks as a regular issue, and again appearing small in size and lean in its business columns. But whenever a battle was fought, or the old flag victorious, the paper was issued to give cheering news to the loyal people of the city.[57]

The *Western Metropolitan* was started in June, 1858, by John M. Bates and George W. Gibson. After several changes in ownership, with John McReynolds one of the publishers, in March, 1860, the paper reappeared out "of the ashes of its predecessor" as the *Enquirer* on April 19, 1860, with a new serial number. Joseph Hodgeson and John McReynolds were publishers, with the offices on Main Street between 2nd and 3rd streets. In the prospectus the editor wrote: "All around us, and far beyond us, the whole world is working out a revolution in politics, commerce and nationalities. It is then with a due appreciation of the present difficulties and dangers which beset the path of a journalist that I enter upon by duties." Although proclaiming to be independent, the *Enquirer* became a secessionist organ and ceased publication during the war. That same year and from the same plant appeared the *Free State Republican*, started by Noble T. Doane and edited by H. M. Vaile and Theodore S. Case. It succumbed at the start of the war.[58]

It is difficult to study Kansas City journalism without mention of Westport, built where the Missouri met the Kaw (or Kansas) River. By 1857 Westport was incorporated, and before 1900 it became a part of Kansas City. The first paper at Westport apparently was the *Frontier News*.[59] By January, 1856, the *Border Times* appeared as the title for the *Frontier News*, revived as a proslavery paper by W. A. King. That same year it was renamed the *Star of the Empire*, but it suspended publication following a raid on the town. A group of Missourians, including editor Henry Clay Pate, were captured by John Brown and taken to Kansas. By late 1858 the *Star of the Empire* reappeared as the *Border Star* under the management of Col. Sam Pike. In September, 1859, it was renamed the *Weekly Border Star* and was distributed in both Westport and Kansas City. Minnie Organ notes that the *Border Star* suspended publication during the war. Revived in 1867 by H. M. McCarty, it did not survive long. The next year the move to Kansas City became complete, and the paper, consolidated with the *Enquirer*, became the *Enquirer and Star*.[60]

CHANGES ARE SLIGHT

In appearance the papers of Missouri had not changed much since 1808. Headlines did not generally exist; one-line labels such as "Awful Calamity" were typical. The first few words of many news items were printed in capital letters to indicate the beginning of new articles. Advertisements occupied most front pages and in many cases more than half of the paper. Filler material was clipped from other sources. In the heat of political campaigns much space was given to letters, generally those supporting the editor's views. Editors did, however, find time and space to comment on topics other than slavery or politics, as these items show:

> On the night of the 24th of December, 1855, the Missouri River at this place was frozen over. It is now near five weeks that the river has been a highway for teams of horses, mules, and oxen. We put this fact on record for coming years. We have now had near seven weeks of hard freezing—arctic weather. A season unparalleled in the history of this county.[61]

> Shrewd Hogs—Most every one on the Levee must have noticed every day this season more or less fat and shrewd hogs, feeding, rooting, and nesting opposite the grocery and commission houses between Main and Delaware Streets.

Among these hogs and pigs there is one black spotted and streaked that we have often seen nosing into flour sacks, cracker barrels, and everything else on the levee that he could possibly get his nose into. . . . Now we have no idea who owns these . . . but we would very politely remind their masters that we now have a hog law, and if they wish any sides, shoulders, and hams . . . next winter, they had better provide a "Keeping up" place for them at once, as it is now against the law for them to be fed on staple and fancy groceries.[62]

More Places to Hitch—Buying a town lot, expressly to erect horse racks on . . . is an idea among ideas and an idea by itself. More racks were needed for hitching purposes, and the people from the country will be glad to find Mr. Stephens' racks near his store, on University street.[63]

The California *News* printed a marriage notice about C. H. Howe, editor of the LaGrange *National American,* and Miss Fannie Slaughter, taking their vows and commented: "We are pleased to learn that Howe, the ugliest editor in Missouri, has been Slaughter-ed. May the happy couple enjoy a long and prosperous life, and may their responsibilities be without number."[64]

Advertisements were hard to distinguish from news items. The *Missouri Statesman,* on March 18, 1852, stated that George Caleb Bingham's "County Election" picture was in process of being made and that the plates would be 22 by 32 inches. The editor added that the subscription cost for this picture would be ten dollars and that Bingham still lived in St. Louis.

Papers became larger, some of the "blanket sheets" carrying ten or more columns per page. The St. Louis *Bulletin* and *Weekly Union* both had ten columns and the *Missouri Democrat* nine. Weston's *Weekly Platte Argus* was another large paper.

Publishers, with improved equipment and larger circulations, were prepared for the struggle ahead, the Civil War which was to tax their endurance and their editorial skill.

CHAPTER VI

CIVIL WAR SPLITS STATE AND PRESS
1861-1865

PRESSES were destroyed, type melted into bullets, and editors forced to flee the state during the war that divided Missouri as well as the nation. Some publishers buried their press and type and went away to fight with guns instead of words; others remained at home, determined to maintain freedom of expression amidst divided communities. Before the smoke cleared, many papers had become war casualties. Some barely survived, while a few grew in strength to lead the state on the road to recovery in the late 1860's.

Missouri's politics became so chaotic immediately preceding and during the Civil War that it was difficult to determine the real line of division between the opponents. For a time Missouri had two governors and state governments—the elected and the wartime provisional governments. The retiring governor, Robert Stewart, opposed any secession move. Missouri should "best consult her own interests and the interests of the whole country by a timely declaration to stand by her sister slave-holding states, in whose wrong she participated and with whose institutions and people she sympathized." The Columbia *Missouri Statesman* devoted seven columns to the speech.[1] "With scarcely a disunionist, *per se*, to be found in her borders, she is still determined to demand and maintain her rights at every hazard," Stewart said. He cited economic factors to justify preservation of the Union, claiming "the wheels of commerce would rust upon the rails" should the states divide.

The incoming governor, Claiborne Jackson, favored the South. Reporting his inaugural address, the St. Louis *Daily Democrat* said, "Although the address was couched in some instances in cautious language, yet it is perfectly plain that his views and sympathies are entirely with the extreme South."[2]

Legislators opposed any step toward immediate secession, although the door to such action was left ajar. After Jackson's election a convention was called to study the position of Missouri and the stand it should take in case of any secessionist action. In the selection of the ninety-nine delegates, Parrish reports, "Better than half were of Virginia or Kentucky descent; all but seventeen were natives of slave states." The great majority of Missourians were not abolitionists, but many considered South Carolina's withdrawal from the Union hasty and ill-advised. According to Parrish, three political groups were represented in the convention: (1) the Unconditional Unionists, (2) States' Rights or Anti-Submission men, and (3) Conditional Unionists. Debate on two amendments to the state constitution highlighted the convention. One, which pledged Missouri to join the South in case of separation, was defeated, 70 to 23; the other, which favored the withdrawal of federal troops from southern forts, was passed, 54 to 39. Thus again it was clearly shown that Missourians were for compromise and union.[3]

It is not the intent here to retell the story of the Civil War, battle by battle, in Missouri; rather, it is to point to the role played by the press and the problems encountered as editors sought to continue to publish their papers and to voice their views. The federal government placed some censorship on papers, especially in the material sent by telegraph. Correspondents, or "specials" as they were called, were subjected to censorship as they traveled with the armies. Soon the post office placed a ban on mailing papers with anti-Union sentiments—a necessary measure since a Copperhead press existed throughout the North, with a few editors openly advocating support for the South. However, federal authorities were never fully able to curtail this opposition.

Missouri newsmen had difficulties, plenty of them. The prewar disturbances along the Kansas-Missouri border had resulted in the death of several papers, as recorded by William F. Swindler in his study of the Southern press in war years. Missouri editors remained politically orientated. The St. Louis *Democrat,* for example, was Republican in politics; the *Jefferson Examiner,* organ of Governor Jackson in the capital city, expressed his views; the Troy *States Rights Gazette,* first to be founded in Lincoln County, was among the extremists of the Southern-minded papers and was forced out of business during the first year of the conflict. The Columbia *Missouri Statesman* was more moderate, as were the Democratic St. Louis *News* and *Missouri Republican,* and the *Jefferson Inquirer.*[4]

No paper could long remain neutral. One of the most widely read papers, the St. Louis *Republican,* for a time attempted to appease all readers. It was jointly edited by a pro-Unionist, Nathaniel Paschell, and a prosecessionist, George Knapp; daily their conflicting views appeared side by side. Even this presentation of opposite opinions failed to satisfy all, as Anderson reports in *The Story of a Border City During the Civil War*: "The general public, deeming it a weakness and a sign of duplicity to receive and publish all sorts of articles, advocating the most diverse and contradictory views with more force than elegance, dubbed this great paper 'The swill-tub.'"[5] Objective journalism still was not desired by most readers. War news attracted more readers, and a few papers added evening editions, although one reader said he believed the later edition was published "to contradict the lies that they tell in the morning."

EDITORS SELECT SIDES

Lincoln's election brought added problems. Moderates who had earlier supported Douglas or Bell were reluctant to climb on the Republican bandwagon, so they urged calmness and loyalty to the Union; editors who had supported Breckinridge urged secession. These changes were not sudden. The *Jefferson Inquirer* noted as late as January 23, 1861:

> Every paper in the state, so far as our knowledge extends, with the exception of four: the *Examiner, Bulletin, States Rights Gazette,* and Milan *Farmer,* denounces *secession* as *treason,* and if the Disunionists had carried out their program—to pass the bill calling a convention without a clause submitting the action of the convention to the people—civil war would have been made upon those who labored to perpetrate the outrage.[6]

However, other papers, such as the Osceola *Osage Valley Star,* established in 1859 as the *Democrat,* joined the radical group. In 1861, the same year that a band of Kansans destroyed his plant, editor E. D. Murphy "pledged to maintain the rights of Missouri and the South, in the Union, until all hope is gone, then pledged to join the border states in whatever course they may follow."[7]

After Lincoln issued his call for troops, some previously undecided editors were no longer undecided. The Huntsville *Randolph Citizen* said:

> This call for troops will tend to alienate the affections of the people of the border slave states from the Union, and turn them southward. They can now see unmistakably what is expected of them by the Black Republican Administration, and that is, to take up arms to shed the blood of their Southern Brethren. Rather than do that, we KNOW they will choose

secession. If fight we must, we prefer to fight the Black Republicans. It is already evident that it will give a most severe shock to the Union sentiment in those states.[8]

Switzler, who wanted to preserve the Union, stressed economic arguments advanced by other editors as well as by state officials, noting talk about a possible ban on Confederate shipments to the North, the expenses involved in operating functions presently handled by Federal authorities, and other factors. The California *News* said, "We are unalterable with the South . . . and today declare that we are *first last and all the time* for our brethren of the South — COME WEAL, COME WOE OR DEATH."[9] Such feeling was not shared by the St. Louis *Republican*, which noted on April 14 that "no matter what may be the expenditure . . . a more unrighteous and unpopular war was never inaugurated." Two days later the *Missouri Statesman* declared that Missourians would never go to war against the South. "Let them [the border states] stand as a wall of fire between the belligerent extremes, and with their strong arms and political counsel keep them apart." Its neighbor, the Fulton *Missouri Telegraph*, wanted moderation, peace, and the *status quo* for Callaway County. While papers publicized mass meetings and the organization of military companies by the secession leaders, even the California *News* pointed to such problems as an empty treasury and the high costs of secession. The editor urged delay "unless forced to, until prepared to do so." In Glasgow the *Weekly Times* of May 9 reported a "Great Mass Meeting" in Fayette at which a vote showed 642 for Union and Peace, 520 for Secession and War. Another item told about the raising of a secession flag at Boonsborough.[10]

Approximately one hundred papers with Southern sympathies were forced to halt by Federal troops and authorities during the war; nearly twenty, scattered across the state, were suppressed in the first year. In July, 1861, the St. Louis *State Journal* was suppressed by General Nathaniel Lyon, and three emergency sheets that followed soon were also halted. The *Bulletin*, dated July 12 and printed on one side, reported: "The *State Journal* having been suppressed this morning, the compositors have determined to issue this extra containing the latest telegraphic dispatches of the afternoon. W. H. Swift, foreman."[11] The next day the *Bulletin* quoted the *Missouri Republican*, which said freedom of the press had been "crushed" by the Home Guards, who lacked any authority for such action. The *Bulletin* continued publication until at least August. The editor of the *State Journal*, Joseph W. Tucker, was arraigned for treason, and the *Missouri Statesman* noted on June 28 that several Southern religious publications also had felt the censor's whip.[12] The next month Tucker spoke in Columbia on his "Theory of the Constitution," and Switzler devoted two columns to his comments. Switzler approved of "that portion . . . devoted to a denunciation of the unconstitutional and diabolical acts of this Black Republican Administration and of the detestable tyrannies of the military despots who arrested him for treason, rifled his private desks and drawers, and finally capped the climax of wickedness by seizing his printing office."[13] However, when Tucker leaned too far toward Calhoun's "heresy of states' rights," Switzler objected.

The Cape Girardeau *Eagle*, founded as the *Western Eagle* in 1847, was destroyed by Federal troops; the *Eagle*, supporting Bell in 1860, advocated secession. The Hannibal *Evening News* was closed after a Confederate flag had been raised above the office; its editor, J. M. Appler, was imprisoned. In Savannah the closing of newspapers was an even trade: Union forces seized the *Northwest Democrat*, and the Confederates took the *Plain Dealer*. In Lexington, the *Citizens Daily Advocate*'s equipment was dumped into the Missouri River by Southern sympathizers after the 1860 election, and the Lexington *Expositor* lost its press to the 1st Kansas Volunteers in 1861. Union authorities took over the *Platte County Conservator* in Platte City, sending the owners into Iowa. Later they returned under bond and continued the paper through 1864. Confederates broke up the Marshfield *Sentinel* and the *Platte County Sentinel*.[14]

General John Charles Frémont, commander of the Department of the West, with headquarters in St. Louis, who bitterly resented criticism, had his provost marshal arrest Charles G. Ramsey and close the St. Louis *Evening News*, an unpardonable blunder on the General's part. This incident widened the gap between Frémont and Blair; after Frémont was removed from Missouri, the paper resumed. Frémont used Military Order No. 96 to close other papers. The document declared, "All publications uttering or publishing words calculated to produce disaffection or insubordination in militia ranks, or to bring into contempt the military authorities, may be suppressed." In addition, some Eastern papers with proslavery views were denied circulation in St. Louis.[15]

Southern Opposition Curtailed

But papers in Missouri whose editors were Southern sympathizers were difficult to close down. The California *News* reported on July 6, 1861, that it had been closed for two weeks, but it now urged subscribers to come forth with money, or even some wood, to keep the plant open. Troops, aroused by C. P. Anderson's secessionist views, had wrecked the plant. The paper carried an advertisement for a St. Louis firm selling Colt's revolvers with the added comment that it might be wise for many to purchase these weapons.

Some editors fled. The Platte City *Missouri Army Argus* followed Price and his troops south as the organ of the Missouri Confederacy. Tucker, who had escaped imprisonment in St. Louis, became editor of the paper. A Methodist minister as well as an editor, Tucker wrote, "This little newspaper is paid for by the state, expressly for the use of the army." The paper published the proceedings of the government-in-exile until its final edition at Camp Churchill near Corinth, Mississippi.[16] Also in Platte City was the *Tenth Legion*, which denounced "the war against the South as a crusade of robbers and plunderers" and kept a Confederate flag floating over the office. It, too, was later suppressed.

In Edina, the *Rebel and Copperhead Ventilator* appeared briefly. Earlier publishers of the *Herald* had joined the Confederate Army, and their equipment was used for the *Rebel.* The Confederates took the equipment to Arkansas, and the *Herald,* earlier called the *Chief,* disappeared. The Palmyra *Spectator* of November 6, 1863, reported that A. K. Abeel, editor of the St. Joseph *Tribune,* was arrested "in consequence of articles published in violation of Order No. 96." Earlier, the St. Joseph *Journal* had been suspended by the provost marshal because of "secesh" articles. Military pressure increased. Early in 1862 all papers were required to send copies to the provost marshal in St. Louis for inspection.[17] While still not supporting the cause 100 per cent, the St. Louis *Missouri Republican* listed arguments against any efforts to spread emancipation sentiments. It opposed the "General Emancipation Society," saying it was composed mostly of the German element in St. Louis.[18]

Other papers silenced included the Carrollton *Democrat,* first paper there under that title; *Franklin County Weekly Advertiser* in Washington, established in 1858, suppressed in 1862, later restarted as a Republican paper; *Shelby County Weekly* in

Shelbyville, established in 1861 with the motto, "Free as the wind, pure and firm as the voice of nature," and termed a "treasonable sheet"; and the Columbia *Standard,* founded in 1862, later seized and sold by Federal authorities and its editor, Edmund J. Ellis, expelled from Missouri.

By the end of 1862 the opposition by Southern sympathizers among the editors had been cut to a handful. Among these were the *Caldwell County Beacon* in Kingston, established in 1860 to advocate secession, but halted in 1864; the Alexandria *Delta,* founded in 1856 as a Free-Soil paper and the first in Clark County; and the Harrisonville *Cass County Gazette,* started in 1854 as an organ of the American party, but destroyed by Federal soldiers in 1863. Another paper in Plattsburg failed to survive long enough for its name to get into the records. Some continued under new titles, such as the *Caldwell County Beacon,* which became the *Banner of Liberty.* The Louisiana *Journal* noted on May 16, 1863, that a *Weekly Union* was to appear there under James Monaghan, but the provost marshal had shut down the plant. The paper was to be printed in the office formerly used by the *Democratic Herald.* The *Journal* commented, "We cannot help regretting the circumstances. If the real objects of the paper were to break down the efficiency of the Union party of this county, already too much distracted and divided, and to build up a semidisloyal party, to oppose the Government, we regard the suppression as perfectly right."[19] The *Missouri Democrat* was critical of the arrest of Howard S. Harbaugh, editor of the Chillicothe *Constitution,* in 1863. Harbaugh, who supported Lincoln in 1860, had served in the Union forces for thirteen months.[20]

The conflict between editors and the military was not entirely one-sided, though in Missouri it was generally so. Confederates were successful in forcing some papers to move to Iowa, although the editors returned as Federal troops moved southward. In 1862 the Confederates took the equipment of the Neosho *Herald* with them to Arkansas. Union publishers at times had problems within their own ranks. William McKee, senior editor of the *Missouri Democrat,* was arrested in July, 1863, under orders of General John A. Schofield for publishing in the June 27 edition a private letter from Lincoln to the officer. McKee denied anything surreptitious in his action, and his paper termed the arrest "foolish and unwarrantable." Many St. Louis civic leaders protested the arrest in letters to Lincoln.[21]

Thus the majority of the Confederate-oriented press of Missouri disappeared. Some moderates survived, and the pro-Southern voice might be recognized in an editorial or so in such papers as the Lexington *Union,* established in 1862. While supporting the Union, the editor was critical of "the unhallowed party prejudice, and political ambition that seem to hold such despotic sway over the minds and hearts of so many of our people . . . to the radical, revolutionary spirit that prevails in our midst." With foresight shared by few, the editor said the threat to the South would be the "new radicalism of the victors, about to introduce reconstruction into Missouri."[22]

ST. LOUIS VOTERS CAST SHADOW

St. Louis voters on April 1, 1861, selected officials in an election that one paper said was to determine which was the stronger party, the Republican Unionists or the Democratic group composed of Southern sympathizers and neutralists. The Democratic candidate for mayor, Dan Taylor, won. "The result . . . conveys a very gloomy lesson," reported the *Democrat.*[23] "To us, it seems that those who wished to stay in St. Louis and in the Union at the same time, will have no alternative but to appeal to arms, in defense of their position." The *Missouri Republican,* which supported Taylor, argued that all hope of maintaining the Union should not be abandoned.[24] The *Missouri Democrat* continued the fight, maintaining that if the Union government allowed the South to seize government property, Fort Sumter, what would stop them from seizing Washington and other territories? Taylor's administration would demoralize public sentiment in the city on the Union question as it did on the slavery question, according to the *Missouri Democrat.* "Disloyalty to the Union is henceforth no stigma on political character here."[25]

A week before the attack on Fort Sumter, the *Missouri Republican* criticized Lincoln. The editor asked: "Will any thinking man say that force should be inaugurated now, after it has been delayed so long?" There was no reason to resort to force, in fact really less now than earlier, according to the editorial, which declared that it was still possible for the states to adjust their problems. "Who's at fault? If it's the South, the coercion could be considered. But if the fault lies with the North, then any reasonable man would agree that a peaceable arrangement for separation by mutual consent on fair terms is the answer." In discussing what might be the consequences of the Lincoln administration, the paper said that the policy would be "probably war on a large scale of the most baleful character."[26]

In an edition which devoted ten of eleven columns on page 3 to speeches by Douglas, the *Republican* continued to advocate peaceful settlement by the border states. Major problems were traced to two classes of men pictured by the average American; both classes agreed that separation was inevitable. The first class was "the abolitionists and abolitionized Republicans" who wanted separation *now*. They felt the Southerners were barbarians with whom a political union would be detrimental in all points of view to the North. "Let the South go, we'll be well rid of her," they said. The other class was the secessionist element in the South. "This class believes a union of North and South is not desirable nor possible for the Northern class calls the Southern class ruffians, the other calls the North cheats." However, the writer could not believe that "vast numbers of Americans hate each other and treat them as enemies."[27]

CIVIL WAR UNDER WAY

The *Missouri Republican* of April 13, on page 3, reported in the "Latest by Telegraph" column, "Hostilities Commenced! The Attack Upon Fort Sumter!" The paper blamed the Administration for the outbreak of war.

> This is the first fruit of the election of Mr. Lincoln and of the war policy inaugurated by him upon the suggestion of as reckless a set of political desperadoes ever afflicting any country. Nothing was better understood weeks ago than that Fort Sumter was to be evacuated and abandoned to the possession of the Confederate States. General Scott expressed the opinion that it could not be maintained except with a very large military force, and he advised its surrender as a military necessity.

This coverage was typical—the one-column label headlines, the opinionated writing. The Glasgow *Weekly Times* began its account: "This the startling announcement! Yet it is true. Civil War! Does the reader understand the meaning of those two words? They are horrible, fearful words, when used as we now use them: Civil War begun! . . . No one can portray the horrors of civil war."[28]

In defending Lincoln, the St. Louis *Democrat* sought to disprove the *Republican's* statement, claiming the Southerners had planned to secede before Lincoln was elected. "The United flag has been hauled down under circumstances to carry deep disgrace with it," noted the *Republican*. The *Democrat* objected to the *Republican*'s "keep cool" policy:

> Yes, keep cool, and let the rebels have their way. Keep cool, and let the liberties of the best government in the world be crushed by a band of black hearted traitors. Keep cool, and let the fires they have kindled at Sumter spread and devour the nation. Keep cool, you cowardly Yankees of the free states. ... Jeff Davis and his cohorts have prepared an asylum for you.[29]

The bitterly fought city election and the outbreak of hostilities in South Carolina set the stage for the "Fort Sumter of Missouri." Governor Jackson sought control of the Federal arsenal in St. Louis, but this was prevented by Francis P. Blair, Jr., who used the available breathing spell to organize the pro-Union Wide Awakes and to arouse the German population against the probable actions of the pro-South state government. After Jackson refused Lincoln's request for troops as being "unconstitutional and diabolical," Blair offered the War Department his Wide Awakes, who were renamed the Home Guards. Blair was commissioned a colonel of the volunteers, and some 10,591 men were furnished to the Federal government. On May 10, 1861, Camp Jackson, more a bivouac area in St. Louis than an Army camp, was captured by Captain Nathaniel Lyon and his troops. This incident and acts that followed have been compared to the Boston massacre. The camp was occupied by the Minute Men, young conservative Democrats and Southerners. Their leader, General D. M. Frost, reportedly in contact with Jefferson Davis, possibly was planning an attack on the Federal arsenal, and Lyon's action was undoubtedly well timed. However, a mob demonstrated against Lyon's men as they moved their prisoners away, and after the people had hurled rocks at the troops, some soldiers fired into the crowd, killing about twenty persons. In reporting this incident, the *Missouri Republican* concluded:

> It is almost impossible to describe the intense exhibition of feeling which was manifested last evening in the city. All the most frequented streets and avenues were thronged with citizens in the highest state of excitement, and loud huzzas and occasional shots were heard in various localities. . . . There was very little congregating on the street corners. Everybody was on the move, and rapid pedestrianism was turned into account. Thousands upon thousands of restless human beings could be seen from almost every point of Fourth Street, all in search of the

latest news. Imprecations, loud and long, were hurled into the darkening air, and the most unanimous resentment was expressed on all sides at the manner of firing into the harmless crowds near Camp Jackson. . . . All the drinking saloons, restaurants, and other public resorts of similar character, were closed by their proprietors almost simultaneously at dark; and the windows of private dwellings were fastened, in fear of a general riot. Theatres and other public places of amusements were entirely out of the question, and nobody went near them. Matters of graver import were occupying the minds of our citizens, and everything but the present excitement was banished from their thoughts. . . . Squads of armed policemen were stationed at several of the most public corners, and the offices of the *Missouri Democrat* and the *Anzeiger des Westens* were placed under guard for protection.[30]

The *Democrat* office was threatened by the mob, but friends of the editor helped to keep the crowd away. One result of the incident was the determination of Sterling Price to join Jackson and the secessionists, and Price, named commander of the militia, influenced hundreds of men to join his forces.

The *Missouri Republican* noted after the fall of Camp Jackson, "We are bound hand and foot; chained down by a merciless tyranny; are subjugated and shackled." Some editors said war had been declared on Missouri and feared Union troops had been charged with instituting a reign of terror in St. Louis. Anti-Blair editors blamed Blair and his "demagogues" for precipitating the crisis."[31]

St. Louis, one of the most important cities in the West, had a population in 1860 of 151,780. Many residents were anti-Lincoln, possibly influenced by *Harper's Weekly,* which circulated widely there. The magazine depicted the President as "uncouth, drunk, horrible," and called him an "idiot, buffoon, Illinois ape and gorilla." St. Louis editors faced more problems than some of their colleagues throughout the state. Some advocated, others apologized for secession. Some remained "on the fence," others changed sides from time to time. Much of the news they received, from telegraphic dispatches by way of the Western Associated Press and through exchange papers in the East and South, was reprinted in outstate publications. Some was based on rumors; the bulk concerned war and politics.

When General Lyon moved on Frost's force in Camp Jackson, the General Assembly was in session in Jefferson City. When news reached there telling of the fall of the camp, of the terrible

aftermath, and rumors about a march by Lyon and Blair on the
capital, the legislators quickly passed bills appropriating more
than two million dollars to repel the invasion. Soon there were
two state governments, a situation thoroughly explored by Arthur
Roy Kirkpatrick in *Missouri, The Twelfth Confederate State.*[32]
The secessionist California *News* copied the Camp Jackson story
from the *Missouri Republican,* using six columns of a seven-
column page 1 for the account. C. P. Anderson termed the
incident a declaration of war forced upon the state: "Our sacred
homes have been invaded—our people ruthlessly butchered by
soldiers in the service of the U. S. Government . . . 'to arms, to
arms' should now be the watchword."[33] Even the *Missouri
Statesman* feared the psychological effect would be to drive
many undecided individuals into the secessionist camp.

Although there had already been military action in the state
on April 20, when the Federal arsenal at Liberty had been captured by secessionists from Clay and Jackson counties, the stroke
at Camp Jackson ignited men's emotions. "From May 10, 1861, to
April 9, 1865, Missouri was an armed camp. Men formerly divided
in their allegiance to the Union or the state now became partisans."[34] One study indicates that more than 1,100 skirmishes
and "battles" were fought in Missouri, but not a single one
affected the outcome of the conflict. One estimate states that
nearly 110,000 Missourians fought for the Union, 30,000 for
the Confederacy.[35]

Lyon was on his way to Jefferson City by June 11, and the
next day Jackson issued a proclamation urging Missourians to
turn to the Confederacy. "We can hope nothing from the moderation or justice of the agents of the Federal government in
this state . . . they intend to exert their whole powers to sub-
jugate you, if possible, to the military despotism which has
usurped the powers of the Federal government," he claimed, in
calling for 50,000 men to form the troops of the northern district
at Boonville.[36]

The first real battle of the Civil War in Missouri broke out
on June 17 and lasted for less than one hour. In this action Lyon
defeated Col. John S. Marmaduke at Boonville. Each side reported light casualties, but Shoemaker cites the psychological
result, "a stunning blow to the Southern sympathizers . . . and
the position of Jackson." The encounter was reported in the
Missouri Statesman of June 21 with a single-line top headline—
"Battle at Boonville." In the second deck were these details:

"Great Gallantry of the State Troops—They are repulsed by Gen.
Disorder, Not by Gen. Lyons—Boonville in Possession of the
Federal Army?—Where is the Governor of this state?" The opinionated story reported Marmaduke's men as "badly armed, and
many of them not armed at all; without officers, training or
organization, and with but a single piece of artillery, a six
pounder." Retreat was "inevitable."

Missouri's other battles, at Wilson's Creek, Lexington, Westport, and through the next four years were recorded by the press
in similar fashion.

MISSOURI'S GOVERNMENTS

During the struggle Missouri had two governing groups, one
Southern, one Union, and some believe one might include another
governing unit, the Federal Army, which played a considerable
role in the internal affairs of the state. In July, 1861, Jackson
went to Richmond, Virginia, seeking financial and military assistance to place Missouri in the Confederacy. He conferred with
Confederate leaders, received assurance of help and, in turn,
promised Missouri to the South. Jackson then issued a proclamation in New Madrid, declaring Missouri an independent and
sovereign state. Following the passage of an ordinance of secession by the rump session then sitting in Neosho, the state was
recognized by Jefferson Davis, President of the Confederate
States of America. The "Giant of the West" was officially made
a part of the Confederacy on November 28, 1861. Davis considered Jackson's government "the legally elected and regularly
constituted government . . . of Missouri."[37]

Jackson, who died December 7, 1862, was succeeded as governor by Thomas C. Reynolds, who issued his first message on
February 14, 1863. This government-in-exile had "capitols" in
Neosho and Cassville, Missouri, and in Little Rock, Arkansas, before ending its career in Marshall, Texas. Still, this Southern
group never actually governed in the state. Reynolds was with
General Price on the latter's campaign in 1864 and hoped to
be inaugurated officially in Jefferson City. Reynolds, however,
was destined to keep his exiled group in Texas, and an article
in the Louisiana *True Flag* of October 28, 1865, reported, "The
following Confederates are stopping in the Mexican Capital: Gen.
Sterling Price, Ex-Gov. Reynolds of Missouri; Ex-Gov. Allen of
Louisiana; Ex-Gov. Clark of Texas; Gen. Magruder; Gen. Jo
Shelby and twelve other defunct rebel officers." Reynolds re-

turned to Missouri in 1868, resuming his law practice in St. Louis. The next year he returned the Great Seal of the State, which had accompanied Missouri's government-in-exile in its wanderings since 1861.

Missouri's provisional government, loyal to the Union, maintained the official business of the state. The state convention, which had met earlier in 1861, reconvened in Jefferson City on July 22, 1861, to declare all state offices vacant. One was that of doorkeeper, held by C. P. Anderson, editor of the California *News*. Anderson, elected as a Union man, later had joined the secessionists. Hamilton R. Gamble was elected governor and Willard P. Hall lieutenant governor. This provisional government was to serve until November, but the general elections were postponed until late 1864. One might wonder about the legality of such action as taken by this convention, as did Switzler, but in his *Missouri Statesman* the editor reported that the state was fortunate such a fine man as Judge Gamble had accepted the position. Those who opposed secession had little choice but to aid Gamble. To establish a loyal government, the convention required all officeholders to pledge themselves not to take up arms against the Federal or the provisional government, nor to give comfort or aid to the enemy. This requirement caused many removals; soon the voting privilege was granted only to a few loyal citizens. Thus, Missourians had chosen to remain in the Union and to support plans for gradual emancipation of the slaves.

Sentiment concerning public questions changed as the Civil War progressed, and by 1863 the press was embroiled in what has been described as "scurrilous and partisan journalism reminiscent of the Federalist-Republican era of United States history." Name-calling, reaching an all-time peak, gave readers some difficulty in keeping party alignment clear. The Republicans were referred to as Charcoals, Radicals, or Jacobins. Democrats were known as Copperheads, Snowflakes, Butternuts, or Rebels. Conservatives were known as the Claybank faction, with Gamble and Blair the leaders.

In late 1862 the General Assembly was reorganized in Jefferson City and, dominated by gradual emancipationists, heard Governor Gamble ask for freedom for the slaves, citing economic factors in favor of the measure. He presented the crux of the problem that created heated press debate: Should this freedom come gradually or immediately? The *Missouri Statesman* praised

his program,[38] as did the *Missouri Republican,* Lexington *Union,*
St. Joseph *Morning News,* Louisiana *Journal,* Canton *Press,* Palmyra *Spectator,* and the Macon *Gazette.* The last-named paper
noted,

> A proper regard then, to the future welfare of the state,
> demands that such a policy should be adopted as will bring
> into the state the labor necessary to meet the wants of our
> agricultural, mining, and manufacturing interests. This can be
> done by encouraging emigration from the free states, and as
> we are aware that a prejudice exists among the inhabitants of
> such states against removing to slave states, it is necessary that
> such prejudice be removed by adopting some measure that
> will give the assurance that this will certainly be a free state.[39]

The *Missouri Republican* presented this program for the free-
ing of slaves:

1. Every child of ten, and under, to be free at twenty-five.
2. All slaves between twenty-one and forty to be free after
a service of ten years.
3. All slaves over forty to be cared for, as now, by their
masters.[40]

"We are for yielding nothing, but for standing by our rights,
and for fighting the battle from principle . . . looking to the
rights of the slaveholders, under our Constitution, to the good of
the state or to the welfare and happiness of the Negro," wrote
the Liberty *Tribune.* Robert H. Miller, editor, attacked in detail
the five beliefs presented by the emancipationists: (1) the
slaveholding states of the South had seceded from the Union;
(2) Lincoln offered some compensation for the slaves freed; (3)
Missourians had favored emancipation in the 1862 election of
legislators; (4) it was necessary to assure the future prosperity
of the state, and (5) the welfare and happiness of the Negro
race required it.[41]

The Radical press increased, urging emancipation now, con-
fiscation of land owned by the Confederate sympathizers, more
rigid enforcement of the loyalty oath, and control over the
militia. The Jefferson City *Missouri State Times,* established as
an emancipation organ, advocated on January 3, 1863, immediate
freedom for slaves. Gamble warned about any sudden loss of a
large unit of the labor force, but the *Times* claimed much of
this labor force had already been lost in the war. The *Missouri
Democrat* thought the slaves in Missouri were "far better pre-

pared for hired laborers" than those farther South.[42]

The Louisiana *Journal,* whose editor, A. J. Reid, has been given much credit for keeping Missouri in the Union, said:

> Let the form of government be what it will, the terms of social equality will always be regulated by society to suit itself, according to its own standard of virtue, religion, and morals. The color and physical attributes of the race prove that they were not intended for social or political equality with the white race, nor do I believe they ever can or will be made so, except by the consent of the whole race.[43]

Lincoln's Emancipation Proclamation was compared to the Magna Charta of England by the *Missouri State Times,* which called the act "wise and desirable."

The Conservative element controlled the legislature, followed by the radical Republicans. A third party, known as the Claybanks, was composed of political odds and ends. At one time the Republicans split between the Claybanks and the "Black Republicans," as their editorial opponents labeled them. The Charcoals were the "blackest of the black Republicans." The *Missouri Democrat* defended this title:

> Charcoal, the substance, is one of the most indispensable articles we possess. It is a great purifier, and in this respect a fit representative of what is greatly needed in politics. When ignited it gives a fervent heat, which is indicative of zeal and honesty in support of principle. Says Webster, "it is inodorous, and can not be decomposable by water or air, will endure for ages without alteration." What better qualities could a political party possess?[44]

Among the Charcoals were Charles D. Drake and B. Gratz Brown. Drake was called a turncoat by the *Missouri Republican,* since he once said that "if he had a drop of emancipation blood in his veins, he would open an artery and let it out."[45] Drake turned against Lincoln after the President rejected the views offered by seventy Missourians who visited him to seek immediate freedom for the slaves. In November, John B. Henderson, an antislavery conservative, and Brown were named to the Senate. By 1863 Brown had split with Lincoln, opposing the gradual emancipation proposal. Both Brown and Drake appear to have been opportunists in their political careers.

While most legislators felt the Negro should be freed, some believed compensation ought to be given the owners. The General Assembly had resolved that $25,000,000 would be needed for this program and had sought funds from Washington for this, but failed to get the money. The *Missouri Republican* noted on February 3, 1863, "The great outlay of money required for the scheme; the perplexity in regard to the precise number of millions necessary; the unwillingness of the radicals to put their professed philanthropy to the cash test; and the differences in regard to the details of any plan" were obstacles too difficult to surmount.[46]

CONVENTION CREATES STRUGGLE

Governor Gamble again sought freedom for the Negroes and in April, 1863, called a state convention of representatives from each county. Editors felt freedom was the ultimate goal for the slaves, but many, including Switzler, wanted a gradual program. The St. Joseph *Morning Herald*, however, opposed delay, saying on June 11: "Slavery is doomed; and those who talk of gradual emancipation may as well understand at once that the old-fashioned meaning of the term is totally inapplicable. No system of emancipation must be sufficiently gradual to legalize slavery long."[47] Gradual emancipation was favored by the convention; the press was divided. Editors even disagreed among themselves as to which papers were for, which against the plan.[48] The campaign was a most vigorous one. Radicals recorded victories in St. Louis, St. Joseph, Hannibal, Macon, and Jefferson City. The *Missouri Republican* complained of "apathy among the Conservative and Union-loving citizens which is amazing."[49]

Attention turned to the 1864 campaign. The *Missouri Democrat* complained in April that the convention, set for June 7, was too early to organize any opposition to Lincoln and urged an August or September date. A five-month campaign was thought too long, considering that the nation was at war. In reporting the gathering of a group of Republicans led by such men as Frank P. Blair, James S. Rollins, and others, the *Missouri Republican* noted, "A majority, nearly all, in fact, have, at least during the war, been identified with the moderate or conservative Republicans as distinguished from the Radicals, and all are supporters of the administration of President Lincoln, of whose re-election they are understood to be unanimously in favor."[50]

One Missouri delegation went to the Frémont convention in Cleveland, an event ignored by many papers. The St. Joseph *Morning Herald* called this gathering "one of the most unwise political moves yet made" and later said all who favored Frémont as President preferred the election of a Copperhead.[51] Frémont was named by acclamation by the Radical Democracy, a combination of the Radical Union and the War Democratic elements. The *Missouri Democrat* said the selection was received with "tremendous cheering by the Germans and others."

More attention was given by the press to the Republican convention in Baltimore which drew two Missouri delegations. One, led by Blair, was instructed to back Lincoln; the other, led by Drake, was for Grant. Lincoln is said to have urged the seating of the Radical group, which voted for Grant but later turned to work for Lincoln. The *Missouri Republican* of June 7 indicated the Radicals gained federal patronage role in the state by later promising to support Lincoln if he would include some of their proposals in the party's platform.

Drake, a delegate to the meeting in Baltimore, did not attend. He later wrote that he could not afford the expense, although this appears to have been untrue. The fact that Drake made only three campaign speeches—in Chicago, Cincinnati, and Nashville —caused the *Missouri Republican* to wonder why Drake, fond of public speaking and usually "anxious to display his undoubted talents, in season and out," had been so quiet.[52]

Pro-Lincoln papers such as the Kansas City *Journal of Commerce* greeted the President's nomination with praise. "There is a strong popular sentiment that 'Old Abe' should 'see this thing through.'" Editors faced problems in dealing with the news about the convention. The St. Joseph *Tribune* wrote, "Mr. Lincoln will not be our next president," but after the convention, the paper carried his name on its masthead. The *Missouri Democrat,* which supported Lincoln, called it the "National Radical Convention" rather than the "Union National Convention" and claimed the Radical elements gained entry on their own terms. "The many Copperheads in the city follow the *Republican* in its views that the Baltimore platform is more Radical than the Cleveland one," said the editor. The *Missouri Democrat* continued to attack the conservatives, calling a group of Democrats that met in St. Louis in June "copperheads, soreheads, Whigs, Conservatives, rebel sympathizers, and 'brushy' gentlemen."[53] A number of the papers of Missouri backed Lincoln, while Democratic editors did their best to split Republicans, both on the national and the local levels.[54]

Frémont's withdrawal from the campaign in September prompted the *Western Journal of Commerce* to say, "This removes the only real stumbling block which lay in the path of success to the Union party."[55]

Drake well summarized the Radicals' position in a letter to General W. S. Rosecrans when the latter assumed command of the Department of Missouri. According to David March, Drake informed the General, "The Radicals were all unconditional Union men; they were determined to destroy the institution of slavery, and they favored arming negroes to the farthest extent necessary for the suppression of the rebellion."[56]

Lincoln carried the state by some 40,000 votes, and the Radicals elected Thomas C. Fletcher governor. The *Missouri Democrat* summarized the election as follows:

> Before winning it, the Radical party . . . had to pass through a most imminent peril, and but for the resolute handling of some of its pilots, would have suffered inevitable shipwreck. The danger grew out of the presidential question. . . . There were those in its ranks who were desirous of separating it from the great Union party of the nation—who, in fact, wanted to convert it into a national organization, going entirely beyond the original and appropriate sphere of its operations. Had they been successful, the Radicals of Missouri . . . would have encountered the opposition of the national administration— could not have been otherwise than divided at home, and must have been reduced to a hopeless minority to suffer a defeat which would have greatly strengthened, had it not permanently re-established slavery.[57]

Missourians turned their attention to ending the war, the continuing debate over immediate or gradual freedom for slaves, and the adoption of a new state constitution.

State leaders recognized the need to bring more residents into Missouri. The state had lost approximately one-third of its population during the war, so editors undertook to stimulate immigration. The St. Joseph *Herald & Tribune* emphasized in its discussions of the need for greater population that many residents of Eastern states were waiting for Missouri to destroy slavery. One item told about fifteen Illinois farmers visiting the area to look over farms; the men said "their families would never consent to remove to Missouri whilst it was a slave state." The Canton *Press* asserted that the state should open "every avenue, remove every obstacle, and offer every proper inducement to immigration."[58]

These suggestions and others were made as the state prepared for a constitutional convention that was to reopen old wounds.

HATED IRON-CLAD CODE

"Drake's Constitution," known also as the Draconian code, was approved by Missourians 43,670 to 41,808 and became law on July 4, 1865. It required the soldiers' vote to carry, since 39,675 civilians approved the measure, 40,640 objected. This constitution prolonged the bitterness and strife in Missouri, since under it many residents were denied the right to vote. Thus, adoption of the constitution could be considered a victory by a minority group.

Drake, a St. Louis lawyer since 1834, became involved early in politics. The Germans in St. Louis did not trust him, claiming he sought to curb their rights and activities through his proposals. Previously labeled a turncoat, Drake made the transition from proslavery to antislavery, eventually pushing for quick and unconditional freedom for the slaves. In his person as well as in his politics Drake roused antipathies. Several colleagues objected to Drake's "overbearing and egotistical manner," and the St. Louis *Dispatch* noted on March 4, 1865, "He is dogmatical and not infrequently overbearing; and these traits have arrayed against him enemies in a body in which at the outset he was the admitted leader and teacher."[59]

As to the constitution he devised for the state, "We intend to erect a wall and a barrier," Drake was quoted as saying in the *Missouri Democrat*. This was to be a constitution "that shall be high as the eternal heavens, deep down as the very center of the earth, so that they [Conservatives] shall neither climb over it nor dig under it, and as thick as the whole territory of Missouri so that they shall never batter it down nor pierce through it; and never shall put upon the colored race the disqualifications which have borne them down in times past."[60]

The *Missouri State Times* observed, "The outside world is attentively and anxiously observing our progress. With a free state constitution, and the adoption of a policy that will speedily and effectively eradicate the disloyal element from amongst us, Missouri will be regarded as the emigrants' haven of rest."[61] The "kucklebur" or "Oath of Loyalty" created the most bitter reaction to the new constitution. Copied after the new constitution of Maryland, it required that all voters, officeholders, teachers, attorneys, clergymen, and jurors take an oath that they had never been guilty of any of a long list of unfriendly acts toward the Union. This list eventually included any expression or thoughts of sympathy for the Southern cause. And it helped to split the party.

The *Missouri Democrat* considered the primary functions of the constitutional convention to be "the abolishment of slavery and the disfranchisement of traitors." In discussing the results, the editor thought people would say of Missouri, "She is regenerated and born again, beyond the liability of backsliding. Ballots have confirmed the verdict of bayonets, and that verdict is against slavery and rebellion." St. Louis, however, voted 2 to 1 against the measure.[62]

Throughout the campaign there had been debates and rumors about the Negro's role, especially in voting. Brown wanted to give them full voting rights to aid immigration; others feared this might attract too many undesirable Negroes to the state. Drake thought a Negro could be free, yet not have the right to vote; he opposed voting rights for women, saying men defended the state and thus should control it.[63]

Other difficulties developed when men who had served in the Confederate Army returned home. The *Missouri State Times* of July 14, 1865, said, "Radical men, who hate rebels worse than they do the devil, will not let them stay." According to the *Missouri Statesman,* the hatchet was buried, and men shook hands "regardless of past differences." However, in some communities the postwar adjustment was not so peaceful.

ASSASSINATION OF LINCOLN

Missouri papers recorded Lincoln's death in 1865 in the same fashion as did Eastern papers. The stories were in chronological style, reporting the shooting, then late flashes from telegraph services, until Lincoln's death was recorded—well down on the page. Many editors received the news too late for that week's edition, too early for next week's. Some posted the news on store fronts for all to read. Smaller papers copied accounts from exchanges, combining items from city publications.

Some papers editorialized in their news accounts. The *Missouri Democrat* reported on "The Nation's Loss": "Public mind is stunned . . . the holy cause of the Union will only be holier and dearer because Mr. Lincoln has crowned his labors for it with his blood." It urged that "the patriotic press everywhere should exert its influence against the baneful distrust which the unwise or malicious may now seek to create against the new president."[64]
The assassination appeared on page 1 in many papers. Headlines,

still labels, occupied single column space, such as this in the *Missouri Democrat:*

HORRIBLE

THE PRESIDENT

SHOT ! ! !

HIS SPEEDY DEATH EXPECTED!

SECRETARY SEWARD ASSASSINATED!

FEARFUL DETAILS!

The *Missouri Statesman* reported, "For the first time in the history of the American government a president has fallen by the hand of the fell spirit of assassination, which could have been instituted to a committal of this brutal, cowardly crime only by motives mingled to an extraordinary degree with low, damning malice. To perpetrate such must require the most fiendish and malevolent qualities of depraved human nature."[65]

"Our paper this week is draped in mourning on account of the base murder by a fiend incarnate of Abraham Lincoln," reported the Palmyra *Spectator.*

The Kansas City *Journal of Commerce* noted, "President Lincoln, the people's choice, the poor man's friend, the liberator of the oppressed, the honest, merciful, good-natured, noble, good man is dead! The prop upon which the nation leaned has been suddenly stricken down. What language can picture the magnitude of the nation's loss, or fitly express its grief!"[66]

"No event that has happened since the beginning of the rebellion has produced half the consternation and dismay, nor filled the public mind with half as much bitter anguish as this, and surely none has been half so terrible a national calamity," said the Lexington *Union.*[67]

Other papers praised the President, in style similar to the *Missouri Statesman's* account: "Mr. Lincoln was a man of noble instincts and generous nature, who always meant to do well; and now at the end of his mortal career burying with him all his past differences as to the policy of some of his measures, we express the conviction that no other motives than those of Christian patriotism ever actuated him in the discharge of his official duties."[68]

Missouri editors struggled through a most difficult period between 1861 and 1865. That their papers survived at all is indicative of their perseverance in the face of terrific obstacles. Many, of course, disappeared from the publishing scene, but newcomers appeared each year.

Next a closer look will be taken of the press in the mid-sixties and its prospects for the decades ahead.

CHAPTER VII

PUBLISHERS LOOK AHEAD
FOLLOWING THE WAR

ONLY THE fittest papers survived the Civil War. Years of conflict exacted a heavy toll, yet failed to destroy the spirit of the
editors. Historians now turn these yellowed pages of bygone
days to see how Missourians rebuilt their state, mended their
wounds, started again with the aid of the press. Many characteristics that distinguish papers of the twentieth century from those
of the nineteenth have their roots in these publications of the
war years. News became more timely, advertising more plentiful,
and the need for organization more obvious. In early 1863, for
example, the Richmond *Northwest Conservator* said,

> The deep interest . . . in the news is evidenced by the large
> crowds that throng around the postoffice at every arrival of
> the mail from the East. . . . Three times a week, when the
> rattling of the stage over our McAdamized streets notifies the
> people of the town of its arrival, an eager crowd fills the
> postoffice. . . . And what disappointment is depicted on the
> countenance of all when it is announced that the *Missouri
> Republican* has failed to come.[1]

The telegraph gained in importance as a transmitter of news,
but no editor of a small paper could afford much of this expensive
copy. He turned to city papers, selecting those that agreed with
his political philosophy, for his solid copy—speeches, details of
debates, human interest items, Washington political maneuvers,
and other items. Some literature would also be copied, such as
short stories and poems.

Too frequently present-day readers overlook the number of
sources of information they enjoy—papers, radio, magazines, television, motion pictures, etc. For the average Missourian in 1865
his paper was his primary, generally his only, source of information. During the war, papers varied in size, depending on the
publisher's ability or funds to obtain a regular supply. It was too
early for wood-pulp paper to be widely used, and many editions
appeared on rag-content stock. Many were of the "blanket size,"
from nine to twelve columns on a page. A number of these large
papers used only one sheet, printed on both sides, but the news
content would equal that of many four-page papers. Besides

difficulties in obtaining supplies during the war, paper costs climbed. The Louisiana *Journal* in late 1864 complained of the price of paper rising from 9 cents a pound at the start of the war to 28 cents near the end and "still looking up."[2]

Circulation figures varied. Yet even if the publisher revealed his figure, one should view it with caution; the majority were well below the thousand mark. Annual subscription rates varied, with some as low as a dollar. Most papers charged two dollars or more, while dailies were much higher. Publishers still complained of "the delinquent subscriber," especially in communities evenly split between Southern and Northern views. The Columbia *Statesman* remarked: "How any intelligent citizen can content himself with doing without newspapers now is past our comprehension."[3]

"Probably there is no kind of business so sensibly affected by the blighting effects of war as that of the country press," wrote the Macon *Gazette* in 1863.

> Absolute necessity compels people to patronize the merchant and the grocer; but it is a voluntary matter to make an outlay for the labor of the printer. A general retrenchment is forced upon them, and it becomes an easy and convenient matter for the large majority of them to believe that the money withheld from the printer is that much wisely saved.[4]

An analysis of news content in the 1860's reveals items similar to those today, although the handling of the facts might differ. Many items were similar to that style made famous by the New York *Sun* in the 1830's. "Sarah Smith, a noisy and drunken woman, was fined $5 for being drunk and disturbing the peace," from the *Missouri Republican* of January 7, 1863, was typical. After reporting a penitentiary term for a girl in a grand larceny case, the editor said: "Lizzie is a young girl of good appearance." Long before the keyhole journalism of the 1920's, Missourians read, "There is a romantic story of love and crime connected with the parties, but the details are not fit for publication. Mrs. B—— is a half-witted old German woman, and manifested great indifference in being acquitted [on a stealing charge]." Sunday blue laws had their victims; Sabbath day billiard players were frequently arrested.

City papers covered the financial centers, both here and abroad. Frequently these accounts would be printed in the weeklies.

The medical profession lacked any ethical code on advertising, and papers were full of testimonials of the miraculous drugs of so-called doctors, dentists, quacks, etc. If all the doctors who advertised could have cured as they claimed, cancer would be an unknown word today.

Dieting problems existed even then. The *Missouri Statesman* published an ad in 1863 which claimed that a Dr. Lewis had "personally known scores of young women whose health had been ruined by drinking vinegar, or eating chalk and other indigestible things, all to take away their fat. And I have known a still greater number to ruin themselves with corsets in the hope of keeping themselves comely and in shape."[5] The reader finds it difficult to distinguish between news and advertising, since many items were in the same size type, under headings of identical style.

Religious news was important and when involved in political issues was accorded special attention. Revivals were widely reported. City papers told of musical programs, operas, balls, and other events. A few carried book reviews, probably "puffs" in return for advertisements.

WIDELY USED BY HISTORIANS

Papers have been used by historians to supply background material. Such an example is Elbert R. Bowen's dissertation at the University of Missouri, "A Study of Theatrical Entertainments in Rural Missouri Before the Civil War." He rewrote a section for the *Missouri Historical Review*, "The Circus in Early Rural Missouri." Telling about the circus tours in the 1830's, Dr. Bowen adds details about their acceptance or rejection in the communities. Advance notices appeared in the press, with elaborate praise for the daredevils, lion trainers, etc. All readers, it was understood, were not fond of the circus. Some ads promised that the clown's jokes would not disturb "even the most fastidious." In Columbia, the *Missouri Statesman* published a letter from a person shocked by the reaction of the crowd, when "virtuous, orderly and sober minded" persons attended such "traveling abominations."[6] Failures were recorded. The Liberty *Tribune* in 1858 told about a circus disbanding in Huntsville and retreating to St. Louis. "The bad roads, &c. made the country trip a dead loss and worse." Later the equipment was sold at a sheriff's sale.

Some circus men became involved in the slavery problem. The Brunswick *Brunswicker*, for example, associated one circus with an "abolition concern," claiming that the elephant trainer had sought to free a slave near Westport.[7] Dr. Bowen's conclusion is of interest to newsmen:

> Probably no newspaper editor ever succeeded in putting into print what the ordinary person feels when he sees a circus performance. Human thrill is rarely described adequately. The pre-Civil War newspapers sometimes did say complimentary things about circus exhibitions, but the general absence of comment on any form of entertainment in the columns of the old newspapers can be attributed to two things: the inadequacy of words to express the feelings of the observer and the common attitude among Americans that entertainment is fine but hardly an essential factor in life. Complimentary press notices usually stated only that the show was worth seeing. Adverse criticism was even rarer, possibly because the editors wished to hold on to advertising accounts . . . neither newspaper editorials, letters to newspapers, nor city laws can tell us what the circus of one hundred years ago meant to its audience.[8]

Editors were not bashful in offering readers their views, regardless of the topic. "A woman runs the risk of being spoiled by the flattering period that precedes marriage," wrote Switzler in 1863. "The sooner that a woman can divest herself of any unreasonable expectations which the lover may have excited, the greater probability of her securing permanent attachment. Courtship is a dream from which it is better to awake, voluntarily, than to be reluctantly roused."[9]

Unusual, human interest accounts were published. Local events received more coverage, but still were not of prime concern to editors. Under "Local News" or "City News" one might find items from police headquarters, City Hall, churches, etc. Between these items would be reader ads. Wedding and death notices were similar in style to today's classified ads; full-length descriptions of what the bride wore had to wait many decades. Speeches, letters, laws, official accounts, and proceedings of political groups were plentiful.

Freedom of the press had a different meaning to the writer in the St. Joseph *Gazette* of August 31, 1853, than it has to most writers today. His poém, "A Printer's Freaks," went as follows:

> Around her waist I put my arms—
>   It felt as soft as cake;
> "Oh, dear!" says she, "what liberty
>   You printer men do take!"

> Why yes, My Sal, my charming gal—
> (I squeezed her some I guess,)
> Can you say aught, my chick, against
> The Freedom of the Press.

Faster presses appeared first in St. Louis and then were shifted through the rural communities as replacements were made. The *Missouri Republican* switched from its Ramage press to a lever press in 1822 and had its first power press fifteen years later. By 1858 the best Hoe press in operation in the city could produce some 1,200 sheets hourly, but within five years the *Missouri Republican* had a press with a capacity of 20,000 sheets an hour. It was not until after the Civil War that publishers began using paper in rolls. Prior to that, the newspapers were printed from single sheets, usually with pages 1 and 4 on one press run, then pages 2 and 3 together. Long after the perfecting presses were in operation, publishers used separate machines for folding. Even in the mid-1960's one paper in Missouri was printed with hand-set type.[10]

Illustrations remained scarce, although merchants frequently dressed up their notices with woodcuts. In the *Missouri States-man*, one Civil War edition devoted nearly 60 per cent of page 1 to a map of "The Seat of War in Virginia."[11] The rest of the page included a story about a "desperate conflict" in Carthage and filler items. The shifting of ads from page 1 to inside pages was noticeable during the war years, although many dailies continued to keep page 1 solid with ads even after 1865.

Foreign news no longer dominated the papers. Too, there was a trend away from the vicious personal journalism of earlier years, but this did not disappear completely. Mottoes displayed on the mastheads were frequent and long; the California *News* in 1858 declared it was "Independent in all things, neutral in nothing—Devoted to Agriculture, Literature, Commerce, Science and Arts, and the Current News of the Day."

While news earned better positioning, the headlines remained actual labels a single column in width. Some city papers published items from the Western Associated Press, although many stories were not identified as to their origin. Probably typical of the smaller papers would be the *Missouri State Times* in Jefferson City. In a typical 1865 issue, page 1 was devoted primarily to the proceedings of the Supreme Court, with a Nasby letter copied from the Toledo, Ohio, *Blade*. Page 2 was all copy, including letters, editorials, city briefs, and other stories. Page 3

was divided between news and editorials and advertisements,
while the back page was devoted chiefly to advertisements.[12]

Some of the typical headlines, generally set in all-cap letters
or caps and small caps, were these: Important Discovery, Indian
Hostilities, River Items, Arrival at Hotels, Horse Thief Caught,
A Sad Accident, Murders Near Union Mills, etc.[13]

STATE ORGANIZATION FAVORED

Editors gave some consideration to an organization to promote
their interests. Abel Rathbone Corbin wrote in his *Missouri
Argus* that editors and publishers from Illinois, Wisconsin, and
Missouri should get together, since "we have been clawing each
other's eyes out quite long enough." He added, "The two papers
at Palmyra, the two at Cape Girardeau, the two at Fayette, &c.
&c. are particularly severe upon one another. Is this necessary?
Is it right? Is it creditable to the profession?"[14] In 1840, Corbin
said editors were too liberal and accommodating toward their
friends, thereby losing considerable money. In Columbia William
F. Switzler urged support of a move to meet with other editors
and publishers, as did F. M. Caldwell in Boonville. These men
also urged more uniform advertising rates.

Regional meetings were inaugurated. Lucian J. Eastin of the
St. Joseph *Gazette* presided at such a gathering in Savannah in
1853 at which William Ridenbaugh of the *Gazette* discussed
the "Profession of Printing." A. W. Simpson of the Boonville
Observer in 1854 complained of the competition for the subscriber's money, noting that a dollar-a-year rate did not cover
increased costs. Editors held informal meetings at the state fair
and in regional get-togethers. However, in 1859 the first successful meeting of editors was held in Jefferson City with Switzler
in charge. The Louisiana *Herald*, in an advance notice of the
session, asked some questions:

1. Did you ever know a prompt-paying patent pill peddler?
2. An honest Eastern advertising agent?
3. A truthful traveling agent?
4. A menagerie man without mutilated money?
5. An office-seeker that wouldn't lie?[15]

The Liberty *Tribune* reported that one objective of this meeting
was "to cause the press to become a more effective agent in the
promotion of the general welfare of our common country." Most
of the discussion concerned the business phases of publishing.

For example, all job printing was to be paid for on delivery, all transient advertisements to be paid for in advance. Publishers also voted to charge 10 per cent interest on "all accounts after due."[16] It is interesting to note that during this time the Liberty editor told his readers, "There is no book so instructive as the newspaper; no knowledge so necessary to be acquired as that which may be gleaned from its columns."

The publishers needed to establish regular business practices, for many editors gave valuable space away; others bargained with advertising agents; some let subscribers continue for years without paying. The policy of keeping a delinquent subscriber until he had paid in full was costly to editors. Accepting merchandise in lieu of subscription money was a common practice so that settling with the grocer each six months or annually was a routine practice. The grocer took his advertising, the publisher his food. Both hoped for a favorable balance of trade when the accounting day arrived.

The advertiser then provided less revenue than the subscriber, but his business was necessary for any publisher to survive. While news forced many advertisers off the front page, this did not curtail their elaborate claims nor the wordy messages. There was little emphasis on specific items for sale at specific prices. Most advertisers presented copy such as this, in 1862:

> In this department, we are well stocked with the very best and most fashionable goods to be found in the eastern markets.
> To our citizens, merchants and strangers visiting our city, we would simply say: to buy your supplies before visiting our extensive salesroom and examining our mammoth stock is doing yourself a great injustice, as we always exhibit a larger, better and cheaper stock than any house on the Missouri River.[17]

Advertisers resorted to ornate cuts and borders to decorate their messages. Since most papers limited them to single-width advertisements, some merchants found success in repeating their messages again and again. Headlines were slow to take hold in advertising, and messages were labeled, "To The Farmers" or "Ladies Read This." At times flowery words attracted readers, such as this from the Canton *Press* in 1864:

> The times are too critical to be dispensing jokes of such magnificent proportions or that our old practical yeomanry should be sold in the purchase of shoddy merchandise, suffice it to say, that "honesty is the best policy, and the nimble sixpence is better than a slow shilling" and furthermore, that A. L.

Richart is just receiving a large additional supply of spring and summer goods from eastern manufacturers and late importations from Europe; embracing great varieties of dry goods.[18]

Patent medicine advertisements continued to appear, promising wide and sure cures. From the Richmond *Northwest Conservator* in Civil War days one could read:

Scrofula or King's Evil is a constitutional disease, a corruption of the blood, by which this fluid becomes vitiated, weak and poor. Being in the circulation, it pervades the whole body, and may burst out in disease on any part of it. No organ is free from its attacks, nor is there one which it may not destroy. The scrofulous taint is variously caused by mercurial disease, low living, disordered or unhealthy food, impure air, filth and filthy habits, the depressing vices and, above all, by the venereal infection. Whatever be its origin, it is hereditary in the constitution, descending from parents to children unto the third and fourth generations, indeed it seems to be the rod of him who says "I will visit the iniquities of the fathers upon their children."

Its effects commence by deposition from the blood of corrupt or ulcerous matter, which in the lungs, liver and internal organs, is termed tubercles; in the glands, swelling; and on the surface, eruptions or sores.

One quarter of all our people are scrofulous; their persons are invaded by this lurking infection and their health is undermined by it. To cleanse it from the system, we must renovate the blood by an alternative medicine and invigorate it by healthy food and exercise. Such medicine we supply in Ayers' Compound Extract of Sarsaparilla.[19]

Merchants demanded money in advance during the war years. To his advertisement of the "best FAMILY FLOUR at $2 per sack, and superfine at $1.50 per sack," a merchant added: "Take notice that the money must come before the flour leaves the mill." Advertisers learned that various appeals could be used. Slogans gained prominence, such as this "They Go Right to the Spot" message in the Columbia *Missouri Statesman* in 1862:

They Go Right to the Spot!

Instant Relief!   Stop Your Cough!

Purify Your Breath

Strengthen Your Voice!

S P A L D I N G' S

Throat Confections

ARE

Good for Clergyman
 Good for Lecturers
  Good for Public Speakers
   Good for Singers
    Good for Consumptives[20]

Although it was not uncommon to find a reader advertisement between two city items, the messages did become more organized, and in many papers they were arranged in pyramid style. Printers continued to use a variety of type faces, and some messages were placed sideways or upside down to lure the attention of readers. In the cities some advertisements appeared in foreign languages. The testimonials giving glowing accounts of hair restoratives and the like came from people in all walks of life, including the ministry. Some messages carried guarantees of "immediate and lasting" relief and "infallible" results. In the face of such claims some merchants warned: "Beware of certain lying quacks who in imitation of my advertisement, style themselves regularly educated and legitimately qualified physicians." Drunkenness and venereal diseases could be readily cured by "Dr. Zane's antidote for strong drink" and use of "Venereal Powders; warranted sure cure" for $5.

Personal messages also appeared in the newspapers' columns, such as this in the Canton *Press* in 1864:

> If you wish to marry, address the undersigned, who will send you without price, valuable information that will enable you to marry happily and speedily, irrespectively of age, wealth or beauty. This information will cost you nothing and if you wish to marry, I will cheerfully assist you.[21]

Railroads and steamboat lines published their timetables, insurance firms revealed their financial status, and other messages told about auctions. Few papers published their rate cards; apparently publishers depended on their ability to outtalk advertisers in striking a bargain. Ink, newsprint, and other supplies were obtained in trade for advertising. The papers based rates on the "square," ten lines of minion type or the equivalent, and granted frequency discounts, with special yearly rates.

Missouri publishers were ready for a new period in their history by 1865. Some called this a period of transition, a time when the papers became "news" papers. The war stimulated readership; it placed the news in its rightful place. Personal journalism still existed, but it was losing ground to the objective reporting of news; the paper that served only as a political organ lost its readers and revenue to those of more general orientation.

Publishers soon organized into a permanent association, the Missouri Press Association, in 1867, to achieve more professionalism in their work and in their attitude toward newspaper publishing. Local news became more important, blanket pages gave way to smaller sheets, presses were faster and more automatic. Missouri editors and publishers were ready for the years ahead.

CHAPTER VIII

GROWTH IN PERIOD OF TRANSITION
1865-1880

JOURNALS of opinion and bitter comment declined in number as the Civil War ended, although personal journalism did not completely disappear. Editors and citizens alike joined in an effort to reunite Missouri. Papers placed more emphasis on reporting events, less on opinions, on letter writers, and on political figures. Many editors who returned to their work after four years at the front found it necessary to serve a new apprenticeship to become reacquainted with the intricacies of publishing, for new developments continued to appear—presses were faster, paper more economical, newsmen better trained. Nearly fifty papers began publication in 1865, and by 1869 there were 182 weeklies and 19 dailies in the state. This growth continued, so that Missourians were reading 211 weeklies by 1870.[1]

Other changes occurred that affected the daily living of residents of the state. Voters went to the polls on the first Tuesday instead of the first Monday in November. In 1865 the Board of Agriculture and the office of Superintendent of Public Instruction were started, and efforts were under way to rebuild the school system, seriously interrupted by the war. Teachers' salaries even then were low, from $15 to $20 a month. Growth was reported in the higher education program; libraries, public and private, expanded, the University of Missouri claiming that its library held 5,000 volumes in 1871.

Railroads became front-page news. The North Missouri (Wabash) Railroad was authorized to issue six million dollars in bonds, a financial bonanza that inaugurated an era of confusion in property values and business throughout the state. Farmers claimed insufficient benefits from the extension of the railways, charging that the companies demanded "all that the traffic would bear." From such views the Grangers developed in 1872.

It was a period of reorganization for prewar institutions as well as of the inception of new. Church groups had been much affected by the conflict. Some denominations, such as the Methodists and the Baptists, had split into North and South factions in the decades preceding the Civil War, a few to remain so until well into the twentieth century. Veterans banded together; the

Grand Army of the Republic and Confederate and Union burial associations formed in many communities. Fraternal organizations expanded as did labor groups. Interest in music grew, and theatrical programs were well advertised in the press. Sporting events became newsworthy. Horse racing and riding tournaments were popular, and before 1870 St. Louis had a baseball club. In 1869 the city claimed to be the center of the prize fighting world. Much of this enthusiasm could be traced to St. Louis' rapid growth, from 160,773 in 1860 to 310,864 by 1870. Kansas City also grew tremendously during the same decade, from 4,418 to 32,260.

The social disorganization that is an inevitable consequence of war showed in the press's reports of crime waves and the plight of the poor. The Anti-Thief Association, a citizens' group, reorganized after the war. Vigilante groups such as the Ku Klux Klan came into action; quick hangings were routine news items. Readers were fascinated by accounts of bank robberies and train holdups. Yet business and financial reports were optimistic. During these postwar years the Bank of the State of Missouri was reorganized as a national bank. Mining activities increased in the lead- and zinc-producing areas, and more oil wells came into operation. Farmers, demanding the circulation of greenbacks, sparked a movement that was to affect the political scene for several elections. Speculation continued, especially in bonds of railroads that frequently never reached beyond the "proposed" stage; some state-sponsored railroad bonds were not fully paid off until the turn of the century. The *Missouri Republican* in 1866 reported "a fever of speculation . . . which has already become a dangerous epidemic."[2]

Missourians, having been halted in the development of their state by the war, were ready to start again; 1865 marked a good starting point.

POLITICAL WARS CONTINUE

The Radical party took control of Missouri's government after the Civil War, its primary goal being to keep pro-Southerners away from the polls and out of office. However, the Radicals began to decline by 1870, and after a brief period during which the Liberals ran the state, the Democrats assumed control. Missouri papers provided full coverage of political events, though the vicious editorial attacks on men in public affairs declined in frequency. Yet editors still let readers know how they stood on issues. When there was talk in 1866 of higher salaries for state employees, the St. Louis *Missouri Republican* said: "Well may our state financiers rack their brains to invent new modes of taxation and applying its screws." The editor attacked "the repelling, animosity-breeding and hatred-perpetuating conduct toward the South, of the domineering bigots and fanatics, the section-aggrandizing and spoils and power-seeking politicians and lunatics who lead on the Radical masses to the injury of the masses, in common with the country at large."[3]

The 1865 Constitutional Convention left bitter memories as the Radicals sought to enforce their ironclad oath and their ban on voting. Frank Blair, Jr., led a test on the voting requirement and other cases challenging sections of the Drake constitution, that reached the Supreme Court before 1870. An anti-Radical campaign was begun by the Conservatives in October, 1865, in a convention of about a thousand delegates in St. Louis. No political party as such was organized, but plans were under way for the creation of the Conservative Union party, composed of some former Benton Democrats, some Whigs, a few "Snowflake" Southerners, and Radicals who opposed sections of the 1865 constitution.[4]

Blair toured Missouri, and many editors, including W. F. Switzler, were active workers in the anti-Radical movement. Johnson clubs were formed, and the new party met in July to map the campaign. Amidst charges of an unfair election, the Conservative Unionists received a guarantee that both federal and state officials would ensure obedience to the law in the registration. Still there were charges concerning the partisan methods used in counting votes and in determining voters' loyalty. Switzler lost his chance to enter Congress through a ruling by the Radical secretary of state, and within a year the Conservative Union party was dead.

Anti-Radicals in February, 1867, held a Democratic rally in St. Louis. The Democratic *Times* became their organ, and within a year the party was firmly established, but not strong enough to scare the Radicals. After the Radical Senator John Henderson voted "not guilty" in the Johnson impeachment proceedings, some changes were made. Carl Schurz, editor of the *Westliche Post*, represented Missouri at the Radical convention in Chicago in May, 1868. The Democratic convention was held in August, and with Schurz as their leader, the Radicals held their state convention in July. An endorsement of Negro suffrage was made, and Representative Joseph W. McClurg was nominated for governor. He had long been a Union man and a partisan Radical. Democrats selected John W. Phelps, also a congressman and a party member for years, to oppose McClurg.[5] The Radicals won with ease, McClurg defeating Phelps by some 20,000 votes. With control of the state government, the Radicals reached their height; a break in the ranks soon appeared, caused, according to the Democrats, by the discontent of almost 100,000 disfranchised citizens. By early 1869 the party had to select a senator to replace Henderson and had to decide on Negro suffrage. Schurz was sent to Washington, and when word reached Missouri that Congress had passed the Fifteenth Amendment, the state legislators approved the action on March 1.

One of the more interesting papers of the time was the *Repudiator,* started in St. Louis in February, 1868. This fearless and outspoken paper advocated "the repudiation of the whole fraud falsely called a debt, except that part represented by greenbacks, which the people took in good faith."

Name-calling was present here and there as Grant carried Missouri, over Horatio Seymour, but this election failed to arouse much enthusiasm. In St. Louis, the *Missouri Republican* and the *Missouri Democrat* traded blows at a steady pace. The latter poked fun at Blair, who was running for Vice-President on the Democratic ticket. Shortly before the election the editor asked: "Is it possible that his friends found him in a deranged condition, and shunted him off on a side track to get him out of mischief? . . . We want one fair chance to show him up before the people shovel him into obscurity." The *Missouri Republican* said it was no wonder that "the Democracy was not in high glee." The editor complained, "From fifty to seventy thousand white voters were disfranchised and the Radical party maintained in power by force and fraud."[6]

Supporting Grant, the Boonville *Weekly Eagle* called the Democratic ticket one of that party's weakest. "Blair is a load that no man in America is popular enough, and no party strong enough to carry and succeed."[7] In Ironton, the *Iron County Register* opposed Grant, yet after his victory described him: "As inflexible as a rock—brave and generous, but far from possessing the abilities, as a statesman, of Seymour."[8] The New London *Ralls County Record,* supporting Seymour, complained of "Radical misrepresentations" and the hike in the public debt.[9] The Bolivar *Free Press* labeled the Democratic party "a rebel party

. . . every Radical voter warned against trading votes with the Democrats."[10] The Springfield *Missouri Weekly Patriot,* supporting Grant, backed the Negro suffrage program and termed the Democratic convention a "stormy session," composed of the leading "rebels from the South." After Ohio, Pennsylvania, Indiana, and Nebraska had gone Republican in October, the *Patriot* noted: "These elections virtually decide the presidential contest." The papers' headlines declared "Peace Come to Stay," "Justice Triumphs," and "Blairism Crushed."[11] After the election, the *Free Press* told about Blair arriving in Chicago, en route to the West, but "scarcely a member of his party called upon him."[12] "As editors, our part of the contest is over. . . . We have tried to do our part, but it rests with the Radical voters and workers to make the bright promise a grand reality," noted the *Missouri Democrat* on election day. "The Nation Safe," readers were told the next day.

By 1869 all state parties were in a confused condition. In the 1870 legislature, the Liberal Republicans marked some gains, further dividing the party. That year the Democrats decided not to enter candidates, and urged their members to support the Liberals. One of the leaders was William Hyde of the *Missouri Republican.* B. Gratz Brown was elected governor, carrying 78 counties.

The year 1870 opened an era during which Missourians lived under a new constitution. Many "third" parties formed, including the Liberal Republicans of 1870-1872, which had some Democrats in their ranks; the Grange, or People's party, in 1874, with some Republicans; and the Greenbacks, 1876-1884, also with some Republicans. Brown led the fight against the Radicals, but his Liberal party faltered and failed, since Democrats refused to give up their party identity to support the new party. From Missouri in 1872 the Liberal Republican movement spread to other states, leading the opposition to Grant. Editors had an opportunity then to join or to reject members of their own craft: Horace Greeley of the New York *Tribune* ran for President, and B. Gratz Brown, once an editor, ran for Vice-President.

NATIONAL PLANS FOR LIBERALS

Carl Schurz broke with the Republicans and helped to make the Liberal Republican party a national group. The Radical Republican press viewed Brown as a party saboteur who had alienated them while he was Missouri's governor. Missouri Democrats attempted to sell party members on Greeley, but paid only slight interest to Brown. They hated Grant, yet realized no Democrat could beat him. Some, too, approved the Liberal Republican platform. The Linn *Unterrified Democrat* fought Brown, saying that to support these pseudoliberals downgraded the entire Democratic party. The Edina *Sentinel,* backing Grant, stressed Greeley's southern philosophy.[13]

Democratic papers found it convenient to devote more space to Greeley than to Brown. For years the New Yorker had been known to thousands of readers across the nation for his pointed opinions expressed in the *Weekly Tribune.* A few German editors opposed his protectionist background, as did some Democrats, but Greeley's honesty was never questioned. The California *Democrat* compared his integrity with the corruption in Grant's administration. The editor called their Republican-Democratic combination "uniting on a common basis of love of liberty and of country."[14] The Columbia *Missouri Statesman* used the same theme, conceding Greeley to be inconsistent, but admitting he was honest. Grant, on the other hand, was "consistent in everything; consistent in his stupidity; consistent in his usurpations and despotism; consistent in his disregarding the constitution," in favoring centralized despotism, taking gifts from office seekers, pensioning his poor kin upon the taxpayers, and "his dishonesty and anxiety to obtain wealth by fleecing a tax-ridden people."[15]

Greeley's feelings of sympathy toward Jefferson Davis aroused mixed emotions. It was impossible to contest his abolitionist views, but Greeley remained a kindly old fellow to many newsmen. The Carthage *People's Press* said he was "the first man of the sanguinary party in power during the recent civil strife to withhold the drawn sword of vengeance upon a vanquished foe and exhibit that eminently Christian spirit of forgiveness."[16]

Few Missouri editors placed any special emphasis on the "favorite son" theme. The Jefferson City *Peoples Tribune* urged support for Brown "because his success is the success of Missouri, and subordinate every other consideration in this object."[17] This, however, was a minority attitude. The Butler *Bates County Record* accused Brown of expressing sympathy with the Ku Klux Klan.[18] The Carrollton *Wakanda Record* said, "Nero fiddled while Rome was burning. Gratz Brown dances while a mob spirit is loose and raging in the State of Missouri."[19] The legislation concerning railroad development in Missouri was recalled, and Brown's administration stood accused of attempting to steal a million dollars from the state treasury. The Springfield *Missouri Weekly Patriot,* citing "wasteful expenditure of the people's money," had sharp questions for Brown. The editor accused the Springfield *Leader* and the *Times* of copying false statements from the St. Louis *Republican* and the Lexington *Caucasian.*[20] On the other hand, "Glory is synonymous with Brown. We've been certain of that ever since he began to develop so prodigiously from within outwardly," the Brookfield *Gazette* reported.[21]

Republican editors were entangled in a mesh of political problems. How to support the national ticket and the Greeley-Brown combination presented a dilemma. Especially was this true since the Liberals had won in 1870 with the help of Democrats. The Springfield *Missouri Weekly Patriot* claimed that Brown, Grosvenor, Pulitzer, and Schurz "had given Missouri to the Democrats" in that campaign, but said that "any thought that Missouri was lost to the Republicans [in 1872] was not true."[22] In Lexington, the *Register* supported Grant and was strong in its attack on Brown, terming him a bitter, unrelenting, false-tongued person. Under a woodcut of a tombstone, the *Register* printed: "Here lies Democracy, and her bastard child, 'Liberal,' sometimes called 'Missouri Policy,' unwept, unhonored, and unsung."[23] Many editors accused Brown of turning his back on the Republicans after he became governor in 1870.

Editors differed concerning Greeley's place on the ticket. The Carthage *Banner,* which supported Grant, wrote: "However much we admire Horace Greeley, we cannot give him our support as long as he remained in the company of Gratz Brown." The editor thought "Brown" was a byword of reproach.[24] Greeley became a "broken idol" to the *Missouri Democrat.* Mud-slinging was made easier for editors who reviewed Greeley's political career. The *Banner* claimed Greeley once said he would vote for Grant before he would vote for a Democrat, and stated that the editor was the "grandest fraud that ever was placed at the head of a Democratic ticket."[25] Greeley's idiosyncracies were overplayed by some editors. The St. Joseph *Daily Morning Herald* called him a noble-hearted man, but a "queer compound; a man who has succeeded in spite of great follies. As a newspaper man he has made a name that shall never be tarnished by a word of disrespect of ours; but there are other men who are better qualified for the office of president."[26]

Greeley's comments on himself were quoted by the *Missouri Democrat:*

I have all my life been doing what people called vastly foolish and impolite acts; and I did not dispute their judgment. I only said that what I did seemed to me the right thing. If I should die before the election or be beaten therein, please testify for me that I do not regret having braved public opinion when I thought it wrong, and knew it to be merciless.[27]

If the Radical Republicans had problems with the Greeley-Brown ticket, the Democrats had more. But they had little choice. Even before their convention at Cincinnati opened, editors let loose their venom. Delegates were termed "soreheads" by the Brookfield *Gazette* and "the offspring of rage and disappointed ambition . . . festering all over with jealousy" by the Edina *Sentinel.* In St. Joseph they were called "Rebels in Union uniform" by the *Herald.* Others voiced fears of a second Civil War if the Democrats won. The Radical Republican press came to Grant's defense, praising his initiative in cutting taxes and the national debt.[28]

There were, however, some desertions from the Radical fold. In Springfield, the *Republican* turned with disgust from Grant to Greeley, but the Jefferson City *State Times,* which backed Brown in 1860, said, "We believe the duty of the hour is to support the Republican Party."[29] Other Radical editors chided their former colleagues for "wandering off with the Democratic herd."

No doubt the Lexington *Caucasian* was the most anti-Grant, anti-Radical paper in the state. Throughout the campaign it printed on its masthead: "State Sovereignty! White Supremacy and Repudiation—This is liberty. For 1872 opposition to the Tanyard Boor, and his Countless Horde of Hungry Kin!—Gratz Brown, Horace Greeley, Cox, Trumbull, Palmer or the Devil. Anybody to beat Ulysses the Gift Taker." However, since the paper was widely known for its one-sided views, it is doubtful if its support of a candidate was of any value. The editor said he published "Plain Facts and Plain Figures for Plain People." He did. One story was titled: "Ulysses as Beast, Bird, Vegetable, and Mineral."

A number of Democratic editors adopted a passive attitude pushed to the extreme by the *Caucasian,* which blended its "Copperhead political proposals with temporary condescendence to the Liberals." Some, such as the California *Democrat,* saw an opportunity to support Greeley and thus split the Republicans. The Carthage *People's Press* supported the Liberal ticket early and was joined by the Columbia *Missouri Statesman.*

A "Republican revolution" was cited by others, with the Greeley-Brown candidacy offering an opportunity to upset Grant. The *Missouri Republican* and St. Joseph *Daily Morning Gazette* were among these papers. The latter considered the Cincinnati group "the men who formed and molded public opinion to organize the Republican party—who fought the battle for Frémont in 1856 and Lincoln in 1860" and who were now disgusted with the Grant corruption. The *Gazette*, however, stayed with Grant.[30]

After the Republican convention, other papers joined the liberal cause, including the Jackson *Missouri Cash-Book*, Canton *Press*, Edina *Knox County Democrat*, and Jefferson City *Peoples Tribune*. The Lexington *Intelligencer* and Columbia *Herald* were more reluctant to accept the Greeley-Brown ticket. The former said the Liberals should ask concessions from Democrats, not demand them, since they were in the minority. The *Herald* wanted Democrats of the state to remain organized as such and at times called the Liberals "radicals," although supporting Greeley.

There was slight interest in the "Bourbon Convention" in Louisville. Some Republican organs reported this session, and the Kansas City *Journal of Commerce* praised the determination not to give in to the Greeley "farce." It termed the gathering the only "National convention . . . representing in any measure the Democratic sentiment of the country."[31] The Carrollton *Wakanda Record*, which backed Grant, called it the "Democratic National Convention" and thought it wise to discard Greeley. Greeleyites were called the "Possumocracy."[32] The Democratic press, in general, was quite critical and suspected some Bourbon leaders as being Grant's agents. The Linn *Unterrified Democrat* and the Holden *Democrat* were among those supporting the Kentucky group.

GREELEY CARRIES MISSOURI

With more citizens eligible to go to the polls and with a larger population, Missouri doubled its vote between 1868 and 1872. Greeley received 151,433 and Grant 119,196. Silas Woodson, Democrat, defeated John B. Henderson, Republican, 156,777 to 121,889 in the contest for the governorship.

Greeley-Brown editors differed in designating the causes of the ticket's defeat in the nation. The *Missouri Republican* said the Baltimore convention had alienated Republican support for Greeley, and it thought the New Yorker would have been more successful had he turned to the Republicans for support rather than to the Democrats.[33] The St. Joseph *Daily Morning Gazette* disagreed, saying Grant had the power and political agility to get himself re-elected, regardless of what the opposition did.[34] "Northern Democratic Traitors" were blamed by the Lexington *Caucasian*. The *Intelligencer* there predicted the day would soon come when the Liberals would unite with the Democrats.[35] The Carthage *Banner*, calling the election a "magnificent victory," urged campaign subscribers to continue their reading habits even though the election had ended. The Carrollton *Wakanda Record* termed it a "Great Victory" and reminded readers that "no man was ever yet elected by or through the defamation of his opponent."[36]

Some humor appeared, even among the defeated. The *Missouri Statesman*, under its "Democratic Roosterhead" label, noted, "This historic bird when we called for him this morning to come forth from his coop and crow was not to be found in his accustomed perch. He was in one corner of the floor, with his rich plumage terribly drabled [*sic*], not quite dead but sleeping."[37] The *Caucasian*, bitter to the end, said there is "no longer a united opposition to the Radical party" and claimed the Democratic party was dead. In an unusual summary of the results, the *Caucasian* printed the following:

> MARRIED: In this country, November 5, 1872, at the residence of the bride's father, the Devil, our Country and the Empire.

> BIRTH: In this country . . . to the Radical courtesan, Goddess of Liberty, triplets—Misrule, Anarchy, and Revolution.

> DIED: In the Northern states . . . of general debility and treason to the South, the Democratic party, in the 65th year of its life.[38]

Shortly after the election, the *Caucasian* reversed its rules and reported Greeley's death, noting his last words: "It is done." America "mourns for a great and true man has fallen," wrote the editor, terming it a nation's loss, a case of moral assassination.[39]

Probably the California *Democrat* had the best answer to the questions raised by the election. It was "useless to discuss causes that led to Grant's victory," wrote the editor. Yet he could see "no use in the thought of abandoning the Democratic organization."[40]

GRANGERS ENTER POLITICS

In 1874 the Republicans welcomed a new ally—the Grangers, officially the Order of Patrons of Husbandry. Farmers, after a few years of prosperity following the war, now faced many problems. A major panic in 1873, the railroads and their practices, and the high prices charged by grain elevators and manufacturers of farm machinery led farmers to form a united front. The overproduction of crops was not an admitted factor. When farmers sought to influence legislators to restrict railroads, they found that while farmers constituted some 80 per cent of the voters, only 20 per cent of the lawgivers came from farm areas.[41]

The farmers' national organization was established in 1867, and by 1875 Missouri led all states in membership. This, however, was the peak year of the organization's strength; a decline soon set in. The Warrensburg *Journal* in late 1874 noted, "Of all the humbugs of the day, there is none so grand, and none so sublime, so to speak, as the grange, as a purifier. . . . The action of the Grangers has shown us that they love party, better than their organization; that there are no ties in any organization outside of the Democratic party strong enough to bind them or to cause them to cut loose from old political organizations. The grange, then, as a political organization and purifier, is a failure. However, as a social organization, it has done good."[42]

Still, the farmers could readily see that to achieve any of their goals they had to enter politics. The Edina *Sentinel* reported that many granges were pledged to oppose any candidate who offered "any threat, bribe, or reward, either directly or indirectly," to obtain any nomination for office.[43] Some nongrange papers saw nothing to be gained by any third party, yet at least forty-two papers supported the reform movement.[44] One of the early Grange leaders was Norman J. Colman of St. Louis. His paper, the *Valley Farmer*, which later became *Colman's Rural World*, supported the Grange activities. Many papers carried the group's resolutions, messages from national and state leaders, and articles on its progress.

Granger stores were opened, prompting some merchants to go out of their way to attract the farmers' business. An unusual message in the Brookfield *Gazette* noted:

HORRIBLE MURDER IN LINN COUNTY!
GRANGERS OUTDONE
Barnes and Decker, of St. Catherine, The Murderers! They having been convicted of murdering Mr. High Price, and the

plot effectually carried out! If you don't believe it just look at the following.

Then a list of items followed that included such prices as: salt, $3 a barrel; calicos, best, 10c a yard, and flannel, 50c a yard; sorghum molasses, 35c, and needles, 5c per paper. The same edition carried a reader advertisement, which said:

> To the Grangers: Being thankful for past favors, we will still accommodate prompt paying customers, as before, and we will sell to them for cash, as cheap as anybody can; and to such as are disposed to go back on us, we would say that we have carried you for thousands in the past, and will expect you now to call in and settle your old account.
>
> CLARKSON AND MOORE[45]

In some respects the Granger movement was a failure, in others, a success. No doubt, as Floella Carter points out, "the greatest contribution the Grange has made in Missouri has been the building of co-operative character. The Grange bore the brunt of failures which were inevitable in the making of co-operators. Its failures were due to inexperience and immaturity."[46] And, as Colman believed, to too much mixing into politics.

Party members gathered in Jefferson City in September, 1874, to nominate Major William Gentry for the governorship and to select a full state ticket. The platform objected to any increase in the state debt, sought a strong school system as well as curbs on railroads, opposed further contraction of currency, proposed better water transportation, urged reduced tariffs and taxes, suggested that the legislature meet only once in four years, and, in general, stressed economy.

Republicans put out the first bait toward the Grangers. In late September, party leaders announced they would not enter anyone in the race but would let their followers vote as they pleased, hoping, of course, they would support Gentry. Democrats selected Charles H. Hardin to head their ticket. The Audrain County Democrat barely nosed out General Francis M. Cockrell for the position.

Republicans and Grangers were surprised at the role played by Senator Carl Schurz, who was pleased with the state reform movement. In a bitter attack on the Democrats, Schurz voiced his criticism of what they had termed "good government" and said: "What has become of the reputation of the state under your rule, when the newspapers of the East and West, as well as our own, are alike with accounts of highway robbery and murder in Missouri, which the government showed itself utterly impotent to repress and punish?" Thus was started the People's party in Missouri politics. Its first outing was a failure, Hardin winning by some 37,000 votes. Shoemaker considers this campaign "a concrete expression of the dissatisfied elements of the state. As such it served as a kind of training school for the future Greenback and Populist parties."[47] Later attempts to make the Grangers a definite political unit failed.

"The Democratic party must remember that this is an age of reading, of thinking, and of *action,* and that there are too many independent journals in the country to watch the movements of politicians and of parties, and to expose their wrongs," the Warrensburg *Journal* advised party men.[48]

An analysis of Missouri papers and their treatment of the Granger movement has been reported by Alma Wilkinson in her thesis. Her informative comments cite the number of papers which gave considerable space to the movement and those which ignored it. The Savannah *Andrew County Republican* reprinted many exchange items, as did the Butler *Bates County Herald.* The Boonville *Advertiser,* later owned by L. H. Stahl and Walter Williams, ignored the Grange. The Glenwood *Criterion* threw cold water on the movement, approving the public professions of the order but opposing its secret activities. The Hannibal *Clipper* agreed with the party's agricultural aspects but not its political phase, while the Clinton *Henry County Democrat* thought better means were available to improve agricultural conditions. The Huntsville *Herald* recognized the Grange as an agricultural society, but gave little space to its political work. Others gave space to Grange reports, among them the Keytesville *Herald,* LaGrange *Democrat,* Troy *Herald,* and Tuscumbia *Miller County Vidette.* The Macon *Missouri Granger* was edited by a Granger. The Salem *Monitor* objected to their meddling in politics, a policy followed by the Memphis *Scotland County News.* The Sedalia *Weekly Democrat* provided data on their co-operative activities, such as meat packing and plans for Grange banks. Early in its history the Jefferson City *Peoples Tribune* gave good coverage to the organization, but not so much when it became involved in politics.[49]

GREENBACKS IN SLOW START

Organized nationally in 1875, the Greenback party entered Missouri's political arena in 1876, although not as strongly as the

People's party had earlier. That year Peter Cooper of New York ran for President on a ticket calling for the repeal of the act which resumed payment in specie, and which provided for redemption of greenbacks in gold. Across the nation the agrarian interests called for a movement toward inflation. Too many, apparently, had become accustomed to high wages, high prices, and the credit expansion prior to the Panic of 1873. Many, not only farmers, had acquired debts and had overexpanded. It is easy to understand this want of money. Emotional attachment to paper currency was evident in many newspaper articles.

Missouri Greenbackers selected a long-time Republican, J. P. Alexander, to run for governor. The Democrats nominated John S. Phelps, while the Republicans turned to a former congressman, Gustavus A. Finkelnburg. The state gave its electoral votes to Tilden, with 202,687 ballots; Hayes received 144,398, Cooper 3,498; for state offices voters went the same way, electing Phelps for the first four-year term a Missouri governor was to serve. Finkelnburg received 147,694 and Alexander 2,962 out of a total vote of 350,236. Greenbackers cast ballots in only sixty-six counties.[50]

The press in general showed slight interest in a third party, holding to traditional Republican-Democrat ties. Some editors discussed the money situation, commenting about the hard times evidenced by the many delinquent tax lists published in the papers. Since many individuals owed less than $10, the lists clearly indicated the severity of the panic. Democratic Senator Francis M. Cockrell was quoted in the Jefferson City *Peoples Tribune* as saying, "The Republican party has foisted upon the country a very large amount of paper currency. . . . I believe any further contraction of the currency would be disastrous."[51] The St. Louis *Missouri Republican* had, in mid-1875, pointed out the dangers of paper money, claiming "the real crime of the Republicans was in expanding the currency—in driving gold and silver out of circulation and issuing immense amounts of paper money in its place. That act added $1,500,000,000 to the national debt by adding fifty per cent to war expenditures and twenty per cent to all expenditures since the war." A month later the same Democratic paper said, "If a man wants more money he must give produce for it, this is the only way. It is a mistake to think the government printing press can do it. The laws of supply and demand must do it."[52] The St. Joseph *Bazoo* blamed Republicans for the "stupendous wrong perpetrated on the country in 1869."

The primary interest, of course, in the 1876 election was the disputed count; it was not until March that the nation knew whether Hayes or Tilden had won. The Shelbyville *Shelby County Herald,* which professed to be "Independent in all things, neutral in nothing," but was actually Republican, said that "all efforts to blacken Gov. Hayes' character have proved abortive."[53] When the Palmyra *Democrat* noted, "If the Democratic party shall be successful, then there will be no resumption of specie payment," the *Herald* asked, "Which is right: the platform or the Democrat?" After early victories in Ohio and other states, the *Herald* concluded that "the tidal wave has come and gone and left the Democratic ship badly water-logged." By November 22 it could only report, "The end is not yet," while commenting that "the Republicans don't want their candidate for President 'counted in' unless it is clearly evident that he has received a majority of all the electoral votes." When March arrived, the *Herald* said, "A feeling of relief takes the place of agonizing suspense," with Hayes elected.

That same March—1877—the Brookfield *Gazette* reported, "The country will welcome a settlement effected under the solemn sanction of law, and people will now turn with a sense of relief to other matters." The editor attacked "foolish proposals of some Democratic members of Congress to delay the count by filibustering," and noted, "The St. Louis *Republican* grumbles, and snarls, and grunts, and—advises the Democrats in Congress to 'let the count go on.' The *Republican* has a streak of sense which keeps it from making a ridiculous ass of itself, as the *Times* does, bad as it wants Tilden in."[54]

GREENBACKERS TRY AGAIN

Greenbackers convened in St. Louis in October, 1877, to map strategy. Resolutions passed there—more extreme than those in 1876—were used as the party's demands in 1878. John A. Leach has summarized them as follows:

> Repeal of the Resumption Act and the National Banking Acts was demanded. The party declared for the issue of absolute, or fiat, money equal to gold and silver and full legal tender; bonds should be redeemed in absolute money. It favored a plan by which the government was to loan absolute money at two per cent interest to states, counties, and cities to be used in paying their indebtedness. It demanded that bonds and all kinds of property be taxed; opposed the granting of public lands to corporations, favored an income tax, the reduction of salaries, an

eight-hour working day, the improvement of navigable western waters, equal pay for each sex, reform of education, arbitration to settle strikes, public lands for actual settlers, and a small standing army. It opposed internal revenue, contract prison labor and Chinese servile labor.[55]

Missouri Congressman Richard P. Bland introduced a bill to provide for more coinage of silver. State Democrats and Republicans agreed on the need for free coinage, but the Democrats became suspicious of the Greenbackers. Before the election the Democrats accused the Republicans of plotting with Greenbackers in some counties, a charge not too difficult to prove.

Missouri editors generally were in accord on the silver issue, and most blamed the East for these problems. The Linneus *Bulletin,* in February, 1878, thought it "a significant fact that all the banks and bondholders East are opposed to silver money, while all the people, especially the laboring classes, are in favor of silver."[56] The Tuscumbia *Vidette* was certain that "the free coinage of silver is so practical that it pushes its fibers into every man's pockets and sends its roots into the channels of industry." The Joplin *Globe* noted in March, "In the great silver fight that has just closed, the bondholders came out second best although backed by the President until the last." In Brunswick, the *Brunswicker* thought, "The Shylocks are organizing 'Hard Money Leagues.' When the Shylocks talk of 'hard money' they mean 'hard times for labor and free plunder for capital.' "[57]

A number of papers, such as the *Missouri Statesman* and the *Peoples Tribune,* collected comments on the silver issue and combined them into reports to their readers. The St. Louis *Republican* cited the problem of "how to prevent the speculators from juggling with silver as they have heretofore with gold." The St. Louis *Evening Post* predicted that silver men later "will be busily engaged in trying to devise some means of getting rid of it." In St. Joseph, the *Chronicle* opposed the measure, saying, "What a nation of rascals then the American taxpayers have become," while the *Herald* said the plan "will have the effect of breaking the corner in gold." The St. Louis *Dispatch* saw it as "a triumphant victory over the sordid influences of Wall Street," and the *Globe-Democrat* thought it "will neither bankrupt nor enrich the nation or individuals." The Kansas City *Times* hit at "foreign and eastern Shylocks and money changers."[58]

By 1879 good times were returning, the silver bill had passed, and party leaders thought it unwise to inject the money question into any future campaign. Democratic editors urged readers to get into the fight to prevent party members from straying away. The Liberty *Tribune* said, "Democrats should not allow themselves to be led off into any side issue," while the Nevada *Vernon County Democrat* thought, "The National Party is but a snare to catch Democratic votes." No need for a third party was seen by the Grant City *Worth County Times,* which believed the Democratic party was as strongly in favor of a greenback currency as any other group. The *Callaway Gazette* said, "There is not a Democratic paper in Missouri that is not bidding the faithful beware of the Greenback National Combination. There is not a Republican paper in Missouri that does not give it a brotherly slap on the back."[59]

Voters followed the editors. In electing state representatives, Democrats named 105, Republicans 11, and Greenbackers 26. In the state senate, Democrats had 28 members, Republicans 4, and Greenbackers 2. In Congress, Democrats won twelve of the thirteen seats, losing only in the Ninth District to the Greenbackers. Apparently party ties were too strong to be broken, and the Greenbackers' platform was too extreme to satisfy enough voters.

THREE-WAY FIGHT IN 1880

Missouri Greenbackers reached their peak in 1880, providing their national ticket with more votes than any other state. However, in state politics their strength was inadequate. The state vote for governor gave Thomas T. Crittenden, Democrat, 207,-670 votes; David P. Dyer, Republican, 153,636; and Luman A. Brown, Greenback, 36,338. For President, Winfield S. Hancock, Democrat, received 208,609 votes; James A. Garfield, Republican, 153,567; and J. B. Weaver, Greenback, 35,045.

This election again found Missouri editors split, with the Democrats in the majority. Ayer's directory for 1880, which includes information supplied in 1879 by publishers, indicates that 203 papers were Democratic, 95 Republican, 49 Independent, 26 Greenback, 10 Independent-Democratic, and one Independent-Republican. Some editors did not indicate any preference.

News coverage was typical of that for earlier elections. The Bolivar *Free Press,* Republican, reported many speeches in full and kept up an attack on Democrats about "the principles of Lee and Jackson" and the party's treatment of southern Negroes. In announcing the national Republican victory, the *Free Press* said, "The ballots have been cast, which, though they fell as lightly and as still as snowflakes upon the sod, yet executed the freeman's will as lightning does the will of God."[60] The *Globe-Democrat* said that a victory for Garfield would be a victory for Grant. The Jefferson City *Peoples Tribune,* for Hancock, offered readers "A last talk" before election and urged more interest in public questions, especially in county issues. Later, the editor said, "The election is over . . . anything but comforting to Democrats . . . some comfort . . . that our state government, which more immediately affects our person and property, is secured to us." More interest was displayed in the coming visit of P. T. Barnum's "Greatest Show on Earth" to Jefferson City that week.[61]

Both the Bloomfield *Vindicator* and the Hillsboro *Jefferson Democrat* were Democratic. The *Vindicator* gave slight coverage to the contest. At the end, it backed into the results—"Election is over and Hancock is not elected. . . . It was a canvass of personalities and abuse rather than one based on a fair discussion of principles." The Hillsboro paper said, "The fight is over. Garfield is elected, and there will be no electoral commission. Democrats are not the persons who steal office. They submit to the vote of the people."[62]

Missouri publishers moved forward in the years following the Civil War. This period of transition brought mechanical improvements, greater use of telegraph facilities, and better coverage both of the local area and of the national scene. Patents and boiler plates appeared, providing an additional two or four pages for many weeklies.

There was a tendency to move advertisements from page 1, but the larger dailies were reluctant to change. During the political campaigns there was a practice to place some hot news on page 1, but this practice, even by 1880, had not become routine. Readers perused their papers with caution, seeking to distinguish between the news and the editor's personal opinions, and between the reader advertisements selling legitimate goods and those recommending some doctor or patent medicine that would cure all ills. Advertisements were larger, with greater use of display type. At times, 72-point type was used to report sales, although it was not yet used in headlines.

Reporters became more plentiful, with some attempt at organization of news sources. A study of the papers indicates that the city hall, hotels, police stations, railroad stations, and other sources were covered regularly for news. Reports from country correspondents in nearby communities became more common.

Some growth of the papers can be seen in the yearly report from Rowell's directories, starting in 1869, and from Ayer's after 1880. These listings seldom were complete. A few papers survived a month or so and seldom were included in such lists. Some editors objected to advertising agents, such as Rowell and Ayer, and refused to submit data about their papers. Still, across the nation, the number of papers doubled between 1870 and 1880, passing the 10,000 mark.[63]

CHAPTER IX

EARLY YEARS OF THE MISSOURI
PRESS ASSOCIATION
1867-1884

EFFORTS to bring Missouri editors and publishers together prior to the Civil War proved unsuccessful. After this conflict, however, publishers gathered, first in regional meetings, to discuss mutual problems and to form permanent organizations. Apparently the first convention was that of the Publishers And Editors of North Missouri in Macon, June 12, 1866. Col. William F. Switzler of the Columbia *Missouri Statesman* became president, and A. W. Beale of the Savannah *New Era,* secretary. "Influence and Responsibilities of the Press" was the subject discussed by Judge James H. Birch of the Plattsburg *Clinton County Register.* The primary factor that prompted these newsmen to gather was their desire to increase income.[1]

To order the confusion in advertising rates, many publishers believed one uniform scale should be adopted, printed, and abided by. Publishers, realizing that profitable continuance of their papers depended on advertising, appointed a committee to suggest a scale of prices and to offer other ideas to improve business returns. Some of their recommendations are established practices today. For example, they suggested that the annual price for subscriptions be left to each publisher, but that advance payment be required in all cases. Advertising was divided into transient, regular, and local. Political candidates were to pay five dollars in advance for the announcement of their candidacies. The committee suggested that patent-medicine men and advertising agents pay regular rates, and that anyone outside the state be required to pay in advance. One resolution said: "Impress upon the public . . . the value of advertising and the dignity of the profession. Let us be independent and publish our papers on our terms." The North Missouri group met again the following June in Macon, and in 1869 Switzler suggested a merger with the state association.[2]

The Missouri Press Association developed from a meeting in St. Louis at Temperance Hall on May 16, 1867, called to order by N. T. Doane of the Trenton *Republican News.* The convention appointed a committee to report on a state publishers' association. The session was planned "for the purpose of taking into consideration matters pertaining in general to the newspaper interests," probably suggested by J. S. Williams, an advertising agent.[3] The editor of the Chillicothe *Spectator* wrote that he could see no need for such an organization, since they already had one in Macon. Switzler said, "If held and generally attended and not operated as a machine chiefly for the interest of parties who are neither printers, publishers nor editors, it may result in substantial benefits to the press of the state." Switzler, who planned to attend, but was unable to be there, later wrote that the association would "result in substantial benefits to the newspaper interests of the state."[4]

Thirty-eight papers were represented, from thirty-three towns in thirty-one counties, a representative cross-section of Missourians.[5] A committee suggested that the convention consider charges for advertising and job printing, advertising agents and their relations to the country press, the system of "dead heading," and plans for a permanent state-wide organization. They saved the first two topics for discussion in regional meetings at Macon, Springfield, and Sedalia. Williams commented on the third topic, listing advantages to publishers in having a single agent in the city to represent them.

"Dead heading," to Horace Wilcox of the Rolla *Express*, meant that every little local concern and every candidate for office expected to be noticed weekly in the papers—without pay, of course. John L. Bittenger of the St. Joseph *Herald* humorously said he understood many persons thought editors should pay their own travel and hotel costs, avoiding any obligations to the businessmen should these merchants prefer to take such costs out in advertising space.

The committee recommended the following to be the first officers of a permanent association, which was called the Editors' and Publishers' Association of Missouri: President, J. W. Barrett, Canton *Press;* vice-president, J. M. Hamilton, Cape Girardeau *Argus;* secretary, N. T. Doane, Trenton *Republican News.* For officers the next year they re-elected Barrett as president; vice-president, Daniel M. Draper, Danville *Star;* corresponding secretary, J. F. Regan, Jefferson City *Tribune;* recording secretary, N. T. Doane, Trenton *Republican News;* and treasurer, C. G. Foster, Kansas City *Journal of Commerce.*

Program assignments popular then included these: "To Deliver the annual address," C. B. Wilkinson, St. Joseph *Herald,* and "To prepare and read a poem," Col. Elwood Kirby, Jefferson City *Star Times.*[6]

Advertising Agents Thanked

The constitution of the association provided for annual meetings, a yearly membership fee of one dollar, and funds for the benefit of orphans and widows of deceased members. It stated that the association "shall not have power to regulate prices of advertising, or in any way to interfere with the business of the publishers." The role played by the advertising agents appears quite clear. One resolution thanked Williams for his "kindness and attention to providing a place for our meeting and favorable terms for our entertainment"; another recognized "the value and advantage of responsible advertising agents, and take pleasure in recommending Messrs. J. S. Williams, B. D. M. Eaton and N. M. Sheffield to the public confidence." The last two men were representatives of firms that sold auxiliary sheets, or patent insides. It is interesting to note that J. West Goodwin, who made the Sedalia *Bazoo* famous, could recall in 1916 that he was in St. Louis at the time of this convention of 1867, "but supposed it to be a scheme of the advertising agent and did not go to it." St. Louis papers apparently agreed, since they did not publish any advance stories, printing only the proceedings.[7]

H. D. B. Cutler of the Lancaster *Excelsior* told readers of his trip, citing details of the journey and sights in the city. He described Kirksville, which he thought "so called because there is no Kirk (church) in the place, being in lieu thereof, the place is filled with whiskey shops and saloons, which seem to answer the purpose to the satisfaction of the inhabitants. We took dinner at the . . . Hotel, and advise our friends visiting Kirksville to try some other house." In describing his visit to *The Black Crook,* the sensation of St. Louis, Cutler reported:

> The performers . . . changed their costumes frequently, now appearing with a bracelet on, and anon a feather. There were hundreds of them, perhaps thousands, and as each seemed bent on instructing the audience in the anatomy of the human leg divine . . . even the women on the street have caught the infection and as many legs may be seen on Fourth street as at the Varieties. That's all there is of the play, and as a result of witnessing it, for days after the air seems filled with female limbs, of every form and shape—from the broomstick to the elephantine pattern.

. . . Mrs. C. indulged herself in that acme of women's happiness —shopping in St. Louis. If our lady readers are curious as to the fashions, apply to her, as for us we only know of two things that are worn in St. Louis, and they are legs and that abomination, lousy chignons.[8]

Both city and country editors attended the second convention in St. Louis in 1868, in what the *Missouri Democrat* reported was "pre-eminently a social and fraternal reunion . . . to elevate the standard of attainment, and secure the observance of the proper amenities among the members of the editorial profession and craft."[9] Although the attendance was smaller, eight city papers were represented. Some editors were attending the National Republican Convention in Chicago. President J. W. Barrett, referring to the session as a reunion, suggested a banquet as "conducive to the fraternal feeling they ought to have in a pre-eminent degree." Four columns on page 1 of the *Missouri Republican* gave details of the convention, which included a discussion of "an editorial excursion" that could be "attended by wives and lady friends." Colonel Kirby, selected in 1867 to return and read an original poem, was absent; the *Missouri Republican* reported that "he had gone and got married."[10]

C. B. Wilkinson of the St. Louis *State Times* listed highlights in journalism history, saying, "The newspaper scatters the mists of ignorance and prejudice by flooding the pathway of man with the sunlight of truth." Barrett was re-elected president, and the following were named to serve in 1869: Vice-presidents: S. W. Smith, Warsaw *Times*, and W. C. Ebert, Hannibal *Courier;* corresponding secretary, L. Lamkin, Louisiana *Journal;* treasurer, P. M. Pinckard, St. Louis *Christian Advocate;* to deliver the address—Colonel Colman, and the poem, Thomas E. Garrett of the St. Louis *Republican*. Membership was broader then, with editors from agricultural, educational, and religious publications in the group.[11]

In reporting the third convention in St. Louis, in 1869, the *Missouri Democrat* remarked: "The advantage of these reunions can hardly be over-estimated, but none will deny that the mutual acquaintance tends to remove the asperities which unfortunately still too frequently mark the public intercourse of the press." Nearly one hundred editors attended, a record. The program featured a tour of Tower Grove Park and the lunatic asylum, followed with a trip to Carondelet Iron Mountain and Pilot

Knob in "four cars furnished free by Thomas Allen, president of the Iron Mountain Railroad."[12]

The convention opposed any attempt to classify publishers as manufacturers for tax purposes. Members selected Kansas City for the next convention, with their new president, N. J. Colman, in charge. The business sessions were arranged by Colonel Switzler of Columbia, Horace Wilcox of Jefferson City, and John T. Clements of Macon. Colman, later the nation's first secretary of agriculture, spoke on "The Power of the Press," offering some advice that eventually was to bring into existence the University of Missouri School of Journalism:

> Like all other professions, the Editorial has grave and responsible duties devolving upon it—but, unlike others, certain prescribed qualifications have not been required before entering upon the discharge of professional duty. No attendance in the lecture hall, or particular course of study, or training has been exacted. . . . The Teacher, the Physician, the Lawyer, and the Divine must each undergo a thorough preparatory course before being permitted to enter on his chosen career. Schools and colleges must be attended, lectures listened to, and thorough examinations undergone before a license will be granted. . . . An *esprit de corps* is thus cultivated, which is lasting and attended with the most beneficial results. But any particular training, or course of study, or lectures, or schools, or colleges, to prepare young men for the most important of all professions—the Editorial—has never been heard of. That institutions of this kind could be established, and would be attended with the most beneficial results can scarcely be doubted. Each member of the profession has now to learn for himself all that is to be known of the duties devolving upon him.[13]

VIVID PICTURE OF EDITOR

An interesting account of the sessions at Kansas City was written by Col. Pat Donan of the Lexington *Caucasian*. It is quoted in full to give a contemporary picture of Missouri editors —what they were like and what they believed in 1870—although written by one noted for his sarcasm and controversial style:

> Imagine two hundred and fifty *bona fide* editors, actual knights of the paste-box, quill and scissors, assembled in one vast hall— their tomahawks buried, their scalping-knives sheathed, their war-whoops hushed, or dwindled to the soft cooings of ring-doves—All arrayed, regardless of expense, in stylish slop-shop breeches and new paper collars; their ink-stains scrubbed from their phizzes and fingers—Editors of all ages, sizes, shapes, hues,

styles and characters—Genial, gentlemanly editors, like Colman of the *Rural World,* and Child of the *Conservator*—Tall, commanding editors, like Hull of the Sedalia *Democrat,* Cawling of the Shelbina *Herald,* and Tierman of the Fort Scott *Monitor*—Little, tomtit editors, like Peers of the Warrenton *Banner,* Millitt of the Kansas City *Journal,* and Holloman of the *Missouri City Herald*—Venerable, gray-hair editors, like Easton of the Glasgow *Journal,* the oldest scribbler in the state—Young, handsome editors, like Stephens of the *Boone County Journal,* Switzler of the *Statesman,* Welch of the Clarksville *Sentinel,* Stone of the Hillsboro *Democrat,* a smooth-faced boy, yet editor and proprietor of a bully paper for two years past; young and handsome—pshaw; that includes two-thirds of all who were there, present company not excepted!—Fat and jolly editors, like Naylor of the *Brunswicker,* and Southern of the Independence *Sentinel*—Slim and bony editors, like Blakey of the Pleasant Hill *Union,* McMurry of the Independence *Democrat,* and Abbott of the Atchison *Patriot*—Editors with flaming red hair, like Turner of the *Carroll County Record* and Reilley of the Kansas City *News*—Editors with dark glossy hair, like Bryan of the Wentzville *News* —and editors with no hair at all, heads slick as billiard balls, like Nesbitt of the *Clinton County Register*—Staunch Democratic editors, like Phipps of the *Randolph Citizen,* Vaughan of the Warrensburg *Journal,* and Park of the Platte City *Reveille*—straight-out nigger editors, black, kinky, stinky, peripatetic tar-barrels and wool-sacks, like Swanton of the St. Joseph *Union,* Flint of the St. Louis *Tribune,* and Wilcox of the *State Times*—and mixity-twixty, here-a-little-and-there-a-little, everything-to-everybody and nothing-to-nobody, shuttlecock "Conservative" editors, like Wilkinson of the St. Joseph *Herald*—festive and spree-ative gay boys of editors, like Goodwin of the Sedalia *Bazoo,* and Brown of the Moberly *Monitor*—and demure, austere and sanctimonious editors, like Williams of the Fulton *Telegraph,* and the *Caucasian's* religious young man!—Editors, editors, a quarter of a thousand of them, in Sunday-go-to-meeting toggery, stirring, pushing, squirming, rushing, buzzing, laughing, chatting, quaffing—everybody shaking hands with everybody—introducing and being introduced—darting out to take "gwei lager" [*sic*] or Bourbon county "lemonade," together—slapping each other on the back after three minutes' acquaintance, with all the hearty familiarity of a life-long intimacy. Graham, of the niggerite Osceola *Herald,* yelling out: "Hello! is this the big Injun of the *Caucasian?* I'm glad to meet you! I'm as strong a Red as you are a Reb! You ain't half as ferocious looking cuss as I expected to see." And we returning the compliment with the mild assurance that we had learned to act upon the scriptural principle, "Blessed

is he that expecteth little," and consequently were not at all disappointed in him. We introduced the Maynards of the Keytesville *Union* and the Glasgow *Times*, two of the wooliest little
bipeds outside of a sheep pasture or a nigger "loyal league," and
worst "seceshers" in the room. All over the capacious hall, "rebels" and radicals, democrats, conservatives, free traders and
protectionists, hobnobbing generally. Such a scene has never
before been witnessed in Missouri since the war.[14]

Politics entered into the selection of the president of the
association in 1870. Colman, later to be Missouri's lieutenant
governor and one of the founders of the College of Agriculture
at the University of Missouri, first declined the office, claiming
the ticket was one-sided. But Gen. Isaac F. Shepard of the
Missouri Democrat, a radical who admitted "he loved Colman's
politics as an angel of light loves the devil," refused to consider
Colman's excuse valid. The ticket was finally balanced with
Colman president, aided by William F. Switzler of the *Missouri
Statesman*, J. Wilder of the Kansas City *Journal of Commerce*,
D. A. Sutton of the St. Louis *Times*, Horace Wilcox of the
Jefferson City *Times*, and P. M. Pinckard of the St. Louis *Chris-
tian Advocate*.

One frequently notes the title "Colonel" used for the editors,
a practice apparently applied to everyone with a reputation and
with whiskers.

The Kansas City session was the largest the association had
held up to that time, with a sizable delegation of Kansas editors
present. This, no doubt, was the first voluntary co-operative
event to involve Missourians and Kansans since the start of the
border warfare in the 1850's. The meeting stressed "fraternity,
sociability, banquets, and excursions," with apparently little important business transacted. Barrett notes in his records of the
convention that the late "unpleasantness" between the two states
had been forgotten. P. G. Ferguson, better known to readers of
the period as "Jenks" of the *Missouri Democrat*, presented a
poem on "The Press."[15]

EDITOR AN "OLD BOOR, DISGRACE"

"Free railroads, free bills at the hotels, free busses, and *free*
was generally the order of the day" at the fifth session, held
in 1871 at St. Joseph.[16] "The tables fairly groaned under the
weight of the choice viands, every delicacy of the season being
provided" at the banquet. J. C. Moore of Kansas City discussed

history, noting "the tendency in journalism heretofore, particularly in American journalism, has been toward diffusion. Every local community had its own peculiar organ and exponent, and as men will differ, usually more than one. The tendency hereafter will inevitably be towards centralization. The great metropolitan journals will over-shadow and destroy the local and provincial press." C. B. Wilkinson of the St. Joseph *Herald* was elected president.[17]

The presence of political dignitaries highlighted the 1872 session in Sedalia. Major J. N. Edwards' poem, "The Press," was read by proxy and "received with merited applause." The major talk, by J. B. Merwin of the St. Louis *Journal of Education,* was an "able, instructive and well-timed production." Social activities predominated, with special credit to the Missouri Wine Company "whose cellars proved a point of resistless attraction to these thirsty travelers" during an excursion to Boonville. A. Y. Hull of the Sedalia *Democrat* became president.

However, all was not in harmony, at least according to R. W. McMullen of the Hillsboro *Jefferson Democrat.* He criticized one editor who "was an old boor and a disgrace to the crowd. This editor distributed circulars advertising his own 'Lightning Pain Killer,' a remedy to restore the deaf to hearing, make the lame whole, cure corns, all in ten minutes. He may be a very good corn doctor . . . but for an association of editors to admit such a nuisance as one of their members is simply ridiculous."[18]

Both "Missouri Editorial Association" and "Editorial Association of Missouri" were titles used at Louisiana in 1873. The minutes show that the excursion retained a prominent place on the program, as did the "sumptuous feast," but other more businesslike affairs were handled. In a preconvention item, the Troy *Lincoln County Herald* discussed some problems:

> Among the many problems for consideration . . . we find the Mexico *Ledger* desiring some action in regard to advertising agents. Our experience is that the less a paper has to do with them, the better. The Jefferson City *Tribune* suggests that the subject of legal advertising engage their attention. . . . The Sedalia *Democrat* looks upon the patent insides and outsides of country papers as at variance with the interests of printers, and as reflecting noncredit upon the profession. The Warrenton *Banner* also refers to this as a bar to "elevation."[19]

That some business was discussed is evident from these resolutions:

1. That a newspaper office is a business establishment by which editors and printers must make a living.

2. That a man has the same right to walk into a grocery store and order a barrel of sugar or a sack of coffee, or into a law office and demand a legal opinion from its occupant, or into an undertaker's and request a coffin without offering or expecting to pay for their respective wares or services as into a newspaper office and demand the use of its brains and muscles and type without a thought of recompense.

3. That hereafter all personal or political matters having for its object the promotion of individual fortunes or ambitions shall be treated exactly as other business matters charged at the option of publishers as editorial advertising.

4. That dead-beating political, personal and commercial, on the Missouri Press is played out.

5. That an editor or publisher who fails to carry out these resolutions in letter and in spirit shall cease to be regarded as a member of this Association.

A special train to Chicago was provided, and one editor wrote, "We demonstrated that the average editor can enjoy a good supper at some other fellow's expense, as well as the next man can. . . . The passengers did full justice to the dinner . . . and stowed away the champagne with as much familiarity as if they had been used to such things at home."[20]

Theo. D. Fisher, in his Troy *Lincoln County Herald* of June 4, 1873, provided historians important data on some of his contemporaries in these descriptions:

> Dr. A. Y. Hull, of the Sedalia *Democrat,* is a dignified gentleman, between fifty and fifty-five years of age, although his looks do not indicate it. He is of a genial nature, has a frank, open countenance and a clear head, with a subdued vein of humor permeating his being, which crops out at uncommon times. We like the doctor.
>
> Col. W. F. Switzler, of the Columbia *Statesman,* is known personally to many of our readers, and is very proud of being the handsomest (?) and oldest editor in the state, and of receiving more attention at the hands of the ladies than all the others combined. That's what it is to be handsome. The Colonel is about fifty-five, chronologically speaking, but he claims to be only twenty-five in feeling.
>
> Gen. L. J. Eastin, of the Glasgow *Journal,* with his white, flowing beard and gray head, looks the old patriarch of journalism that he is. You might travel a long distance before finding a more

perfect gentleman, or one whose kindly heart and genial smile would act more happily in gaining your confidence, love and esteem.

Col. Pat Donan, of the Lexington *Caucasian,* the man with a hundred lexicons of words unknown to Webster or Worcester, and with a vial of wrath, sarcasm and egotism, that flow from his ready pen like lava from a troubled volcano. Such is Donan the editor; but Donan in *propria persona* is another being—in fact, as dignified, clever, genial, mild and attractive a gentleman as we would desire to meet, and our heart was irresistibly drawn toward him.

Maj. J. B. Merwin, of the *American Journal of Education,* is also a very different person to that indicated by his paper, which, although it may be a paragon in that particular line of journalism, is very dry reading. The major is full of life, humor and geniality, and with two like companions, J. H. Turner, of the Carrollton *Record,* and J. G. Pangborn of the Boonville *Advertiser,* performed the funny part of the occasion, as well as a large share of the practical.

L. A. Welch, of the Clarksville *Sentinel,* the sprightliest and raciest young editor of the state, was there, looking delicate and pale, having only partly recovered from a recent illness. With a heart full of native kindness, and a brain fruitful of ideas, and language as pointed as the steel that pens it, Lem stands among the young journalists of the state.

W. S. Bryan, of the Montgomery *Standard,* with his cheerful countenance, clerical humor and dry wit, one of the cleverest young bachelors imaginable (and by way of parenthesis to the young ladies, he is good looking) was there. Bryan formerly published the St. Charles *News,* with which journal he became known to the newspaper fraternity as one of its promising members, and today he stands in the front rank of the younger journalists of Missouri.

"Altogether the editors are a motley crew, and while there are many fine looking men among them, there are also quite a number of very ordinary personages," concluded Fisher.[21]

Editors opposed a recent congressional action "in laying an embargo on the free transportation of newspapers in the counties in which they are published, and on their free interchange between publishers." The more than one hundred editors present realized that not enough solid business was being conducted and so appointed a committee to arrange the program for the meeting in 1874 at Lexington.

EUGENE FIELD RECITES POEM

At Lexington, Colonel Switzler was in charge as president. Eugene Field, then of the St. Louis *Journal of Commerce,* read his poem, "A Weird Idyl—Solomon Burch's Fighting Editor," beginning

> Solomon he sat in his office—
> His nose running blood, his eyes swelled and black
> His clothing all torn, his body all bruised,
> With great purple welts all over his back.[22]

Milo Blair of the Boonville *Eagle* said, "Apprentices to the art preservative are as thick as black birds, but hundreds of them are of far less use. . . . They are poor, miserable devils, thirsting for whisky and begging for bread." Blair said journalism had an immortal mission to perform, and "like the wand of a magician, its wing sweeps nearly every land, and shall yet penetrate the wildest haunts of the world, where the shadow and superstition of ignorance falls heavily over the people."[23]

Resolutions passed at Louisiana were repealed, and these substituted:

1. That, in the language of the holy writ, "the laborer is worthy of his hire."

2. That editors, as a class, are laborers.

3. That, in demanding compensation for our labor, we should make no class distinction.

4. That, if it is just and proper to charge a merchant, a lawyer, doctor . . . for advertising . . . it is no less right and proper to demand pay for advertising for political aspirants.

The Sedalia *Times* reported that efforts to charge churches and benevolent enterprises full prices for printing were voted down.[24] The Hillsboro *Jefferson Democrat* noted, "Judging the editors from their appearance at this meeting, a stranger would have supposed they represented the wealth of the state instead of the brass and brains."[25]

L. J. Eastin of the Glasgow *Journal* presided in 1875 at Boonville. For the first time consideration was given to recording the history of the association, and J. W. Barrett of the Canton *Press* headed a committee to write about its first decade.

Mark L. DeMotte of the Lexington *Register,* speaking on "Country Journalism as it Exists in the West," no doubt pleased many editors by saying, "So long as people continue to be born, to marry, and to die . . . in short, so long as all industries and all natural resources are not found in all localities, the local newspaper will be a necessity." Objecting to any contemptuous use of the "Partisan press" label, DeMotte said: "We do not regard the fact that a man is a Republican or a Democrat as evidence that he lacks independency."[26]

Macon was the meeting place in 1876, with Milo Blair of the Boonville *Eagle* presiding. Among the bylaws passed was this interesting one: "Any member . . . who shall, while attending any of the meetings, appear in a state of intoxication, shall be suspended from the privileges of the Association upon charge and satisfactory proof of the same." And among the toasts proposed at the banquet was one by Eugene Field to "Woman: Unhappy is he who has not such a form to press." Colonel Switzler offered a few suggestions: "Allow no temptation to secure your consent to the publication of articles, long or short, in prose or poetry, which are demoralizing in character. . . .Ask yourself the question: 'Can I read them in person to a company of virtuous and intelligent ladies?' " He called for outlawing "all personal blackguardism and abuse, all misrepresentation and unfairness, all billingsgate and ruffianism, and demonstration to the world that while we are sometimes partisans, we are always patriots— above all, that we are not only editors, but gentlemen."

One resolution urged "That at all future banquets which may be given to this Association by the citizens of the cities or towns at which we may gather, it is our request that no wine or liquor of any kind may be served."

"In Memoriam" resolutions were read honoring A. S. Kierolf of the Carrollton *Democrat;* L. J. Eastin, Glasgow *Journal;* J. N. Brooks, Mexico *Ledger;* and W. N. Hawkins, Carrollton *Journal.* This practice continued through many years. Following the sessions, about forty couples took a train excursion to Southern Colorado.[27]

T. W. Park of the Platte City *Landmark* presided in 1877, when the association met in Fredericktown. The annual fee became two dollars, and membership was limited to bona fide editors and publishers. For the first time, minutes of the convention were published. In speaking on "The Nobler Aims of the Profession," John M. London of the Macon *Examiner* noted, "The absolutely independent press is the stoutest bulwark of American liberty. And on the other hand . . . the absolutely partisan press-organ is the most dangerous instrumentality in our national economy." Additional comments were expressed by Judge S. A. Gilbert of the St. Joseph *Gazette,* who said, "There is an immense difference between the party press and the partisan press. In one may be found the highest development of journalistic power, and in the other naught but abasement and prostitution. . . . It is not the independent journals that mould opinion and controls public affairs."

Eugene Field again presented a poem.[28] An excursion to Hot Springs was extended by several days because of storms.

SENSATIONALISM DEFENDED

More than two hundred editors gathered in Springfield in 1878 to hear Governor John S. Phelps, first state leader to address the association, and to enjoy an excursion to New Orleans and Mobile. An invitation was extended to teachers to furnish papers stimulating educational news. Speakers were told, "Essays prepared for anniversaries, banquets, and special occasions are seldom worthy of the author. The humorist is not so amusing when the time, the place, and the topic are premeditated." Speakers were told to be brief and to add a little spice of variety to "tinge the whole." Speakers were instructed for the future, to "confine their efforts to matters pertaining to the newspaper and printing business."

Joseph B. McCullagh of the St. Louis *Globe-Democrat* spoke on "Modern Journalism," noting, "If the American press were not 'sensational' in the generally accepted meaning of that word, it would not be representative." After discussing the various facets of journalism, he said, "The best journalism is that which succeeds in interesting the largest number of intelligent people in the contents of a daily newspaper."[29]

President for 1879 was J. E. Hutton of the Mexico *Intelligencer.* Switzler welcomed the editors to Columbia, "the Athens of the West," and stated, "The State Press and the State University are powers with the people. Each is an important factor of their freedom and prosperity, and of their future greatness and glory. . . . Each is an educator—the Press directly—of those who now govern the country, the University primarily of those who will hereafter govern it." He expressed his thought, "There are many cogent reasons in support of this conviction, long entertained and often propounded . . . that editing newspapers is as much a profession as practicing law or medicine, and that a department of journalism ought to be established, and I have no doubt at no distant day will be established in our own and other universities."

A former editor and former governor, B. Gratz Brown, spoke on "Character in Journalism," stressing the advancements that had been made since his entry into the field many years earlier. In the first printing awards made by the association, the Warrenton *Banner* was selected as the best printed county paper and the Keytesville *Courier* the best home print to match patent insides. Honorary memberships were awarded to Brown, James S. Rollins, President Samuel S. Laws of the University of Missouri, three widows of former members, and several others. A departure from the earlier practice of the association was the presentation of a gold chain and locket to the retiring president; canes had been given before. History was made at this convention when Mrs. Julia M. Bennett of the Hannibal *Courier* became the first woman to appear on the program; Mrs. Bennett read her poem, "The Editor's Dream." A new constitution was adopted, making official the name, The Missouri Press Association. No major changes were made in the constitution, the primary goal in writing a new one being to incorporate earlier revisions.[30]

J. H. Turner of the Carrollton *Wakanda Record* presided in 1880 in Sedalia. Capt. Henry P. King, president of the Kansas Press Association, discussed "Progress and the Press; or, The Missouri Valley and its Newspapers," saying, "A town without a newspaper is a town ready to fence in and whitewash; a settlement that lacks a printing office must get one or be sold for taxes." Jacob T. Child of the Richmond *Conservator*, noted that journalism "is a stern iconoclast. It has broken down the barriers erected by years of bigotry . . . . It is a quiver to hold the stray arrows of thought." Thomas E. Garrett of the *Missouri Republican* urged all members to "elevate the dignity of our profession and truly appreciate our responsibilities."

An effort to bring about spelling changes, presented in a talk by J. B. Merwin of the *American Journal of Education,* met only partial success. Editors voted to assist in these reforms, but not as fully as Merwin sought. Merwin, claiming silent letters added about 25 per cent to the cost of printing, urged the dropping of *ue* in such words as *dialogue* and *catalogue;* the final *e* in such as *definite, infinite,* and *favorite;* the final *te* in *cigarette, quartette; me* in *programme;* and to change *ph* to *f* in words like *phantom, telegraph,* and *phase.*

"The Printer's Devil of the Future" was discussed by William

Maynard of the Moberly *Headlight,* who asked: "Would not previous schooling in all the little details of what is afterward deemed essential prove a help and a blessing to those who are to fill our places?" He opposed a degree such as the B.A. or M.A. since these "often have little more than their parchments to recommend them." Rather, he urged, "the education of our sons and other men's sons in a professional school, combining printing office and college—the practical with the theoretical. . . . Let them have enough of the ornamental branches to be sensible and competent critics."[31]

J. T. Child of the Richmond *Conservator* was president when the group met in the hall of the House of Representatives in Jefferson City in 1881. Women gained a greater role this year. Mrs. Susie Fisher, wife of the publisher of the Farmington *Times,* spoke on "Women in Journalism" and said, "The tone of a newspaper with a woman on the staff is purer and more deserving of a place in every household." She noted that some papers had been established to give the suffrage campaign a voice, since these advocates could "never find a paper which will give them space corresponding to the importance of the subject in their estimation." She admitted that "women sometimes have entered journalism from a very love of the power it gives." Two women belonged to the association that year: Miss Luelle Hudson, Lebanon *Rustic-Leader,* and Mrs. A. B. Thornton, Boonville *News.* More than fifty women were at the convention, most of them wives and daughters of editors.

"The Necessity for Political Morality" was discussed by one of Missouri's most famed politicians, Champ Clark, former editor of the Louisiana *Riverside Press.* Clark said, "Great as public opinion is, it is the plaything of that supreme power, the public press. . . . Editors are the conscience-keepers of the republic." His comments on Greeley were interesting. In noting how kind and generous the New York editor had been, Clark recalled the sudden change in attitude toward Greeley after he became a presidential candidate:

> In a short time, by a species of editorial and political legerdemain, he was transformed from an angel of light, bucolic philosopher, and friend of man, into a fiend incarnate. Every human insect buzzed him—every human viper that he had warmed into life sank its venomous fangs into his defenseless bosom—every bird and beast of prey hastened to the repast of slander. The world looked on and laughed while the jackals and hyenas worried the old lion.[32]

St. Joseph was selected for the meeting of 1882, and A. A. Lesueur of the Lexington *Intelligencer* became president. A crowded schedule of talks, essays, poems, and recitations marked this meeting. In what appears to have been a plan for frequent historical talks, J. T. Child of the Richmond *Conservator* discussed "Early Journalism in the Missouri Valley," starting with 1808. "In those days, the printer was a kind of swash-buckler, worked when he pleased, got his paper out when it suited him, frequently using the same matter twice to fill up, and running his outside pages months at a time without changing the advertisements . . . then butter, eggs, chickens, meats and vegetables were a legal tender for subscriptions."

In discussing the "Local Reporter," Phil. G. Ferguson, president of the St. Louis Press Club, said,

> Twenty years ago the most important feature of a daily paper was the "leader" of the editor. This leader was always read with avidity, as the emanation of a profound statesman and philosopher, and in times of political excitement was merely a personal tirade poured out upon the devoted head of "our idiotic contemporary." Now, not one subscriber in a thousand reads these heavy leaders. . . . For a short time the telegraphic column was the chief attraction . . . the public appetite craves news rather than instruction . . . the public taste prefers something more condensed . . . it is a notorious fact that reporters as a class are shiftless and impecunious. Their salaries are ridiculously small, and their habits expensive. Yet there is not the remotest prospect that they will ever receive better pay or become more thrifty.[33]

The convention ended with a 1,500-mile trip to Texas, following the election of J. B. Thompson of the LaPlata *Home Press* to direct the association in 1883. That year in Carthage, John A. Dillon of the St. Louis *Post-Dispatch* spoke on "The Future of Missouri," noting that while editors were not called on to take an active part in the political life of the state, "they are called on by the nature of their profession to take the most active part in shaping the course and current of political ideas. . . . Journalism and illiteracy are naturally as antagonistic as light and darkness; they cannot grow together . . . and our daily work is an unconscious service to the cause of learning." The Sedalia *Democrat,* quoted in the Carthage *Banner* of May 17, said, "The editors were there in profusion and most of them paid cash."

Opportunities in journalism were discussed by A. A. Lesueur of the Lexington *Intelligencer.* "The time is not far distant when it will be dangerous in America for a public man to oppose the confirmation to high position of a man like Richard H. Dana because he is 'One of those damned literary fellers,'" he said.

A motion that "hereafter nothing be allowed to interfere with the business of the convention, such as excursions, until after all business had been transacted" was declared out of order. After electing Richard B. Speed of the Nevada *Southwest Mail*, president for 1884 and selecting Springfield for the meeting place, members made an excursion to Joplin and Eureka Springs.[34]

The highlight of the 1884 gathering was the talk, "The Country Newspaper," by E. W. Stephens of the Columbia *Herald*. His talk covered business, news, and opinion. It was down-to-earth, specific in its suggestions.

> As a vehicle of news the country newspaper occupies a sphere peculiarly its own . . . the essential feature of the country paper is the local. It should be as far as possible comprehensive . . . the forceful feature of the newspaper is its relation to thought. Journalism—country journalism—has become a profession. The time has passed when one-horse lawyers or school teachers can hope to sustain themselves or the town paper by writing for it, or can fall back upon it as a refuge from failure in other pursuits.

In other talks the editors were told that Pulitzer's *Post-Dispatch* was netting $120,000 annually, slightly less than the $150,000 claimed for the *Globe-Democrat*. After electing R. M. White of the Mexico *Ledger* president and selecting Columbia for 1885, delegates departed, some going to Eureka Springs, others to Florida for vacation trips.

This is the era that was described by Clint H. Denman in 1940 as "the formative period, the get-acquainted period, the know-each-other period, and during these 18 years Missouri editors came to realize that they could associate with each other on friendly terms." After 1884 the emphasis at the meetings shifted, more attention being given to the seriousness of newspaper publishing and less to the "sumptuous banquets."[35]

CHAPTER X

MODERN PERIOD IN MISSOURI

1880-1900

TYPE-CASTING machines, improved stereotyping processes, faster presses, better communication facilities, and other advancements marked the modern period for Missouri papers. Advertising, circulation, and the size of papers increased. "Miscellany" occupied less space, but still appeared in some weeklies. Headlines, still generally only a column wide, did expand downward, adding decks. Advertising began to attract readers with larger type and more varied illustrations.

Sunday papers grew in numbers after the first in Missouri, the St. Louis *Reveille,* appeared in 1844. The Civil War did much to stress the value of day-by-day publication to keep readers better informed. By 1880, more than 11 per cent of the daily papers in the nation published Sunday editions, and within a decade St. Louis had nine, Kansas City six.

Papers continued to increase in numbers. Ayer, in 1891, reported 15,599 papers in the nation for 1890; ten years later 18,206 were listed. Papers followed party lines, although not so violently as in earlier years. Still, the reader had little trouble learning the editor's political views. Some gave more space than others to farm news and items about rural residents; several city papers, especially in St. Louis, published weekly, semi- and tri-weekly editions directed to this audience. In many cases, as with the Populists, papers were established to promote one such cause, since Republican and Democrat papers normally remained within deep-rooted party grooves.[1]

READYPRINTS POPULAR

Nearly half of the nation's papers used readyprints by the turn of the century; Missouri papers were no different. Normally, this meant the purchase of patent insides, pages 2 and 3 of a four-page paper, or pages 2, 3, 6, and 7 of an eight-page edition, being already printed. The editor then completed the printing with local material. Developed from necessity, the readyprints had advantages as well as weaknesses. Some printers feared that their use meant loss of employment; publishers replied that shortage of printers prompted the development and use of this process.

Wright A. Patterson, a member of the Kellogg Newspaper Company which later became part of the Western Newspaper Union, estimated that his office served more than three hundred Missouri papers about 1890. In a letter to James Lee Ashcraft, who studied the state's reform papers for 1888-1896, Patterson wrote that his firm "provided political material supporting the Republican, Democratic and Populist parties. Each editor indicated which he wanted." Such material was supplied by the political parties. Patterson wrote that after 1904 editors could indicate other material they desired in the readyprints.[2]

Missouri publishers could buy readyprints prepared in the Columbia *Herald's* office. There was a difference between those furnished by E. W. Stephens and Walter Williams and those furnished by the national distributors: *Herald* readyprints in the beginning carried no advertisements, and even later the editors could buy them with or without such messages. Started about 1893, the Missouri readyprints were going to nearly ninety weeklies in more than fifty counties by 1895. Much of this material also appeared in the *Herald*. Due to other commitments at the *Herald* plant, these readyprints declined in quality, and the firm discontinued the project about 1900. James Creighton, in a graduate project conducted at the University of Missouri, concluded: "Whether patent insides stifled the initiative of the editor who used them, contributed to the progress of the country newspaper, or had little effect, they represented a sort of family skeleton of small town journalism. Like a common workman, they shouldered the heavy burden but entered by the back door, painstakingly hidden from the reader's cognizance."[3]

Some papers continued with readyprints, purchased from the Western Newspaper Union, well into the twentieth century. The firm discontinued this project in the 1950's.

JAMES BOYS IN SPOTLIGHT

T. T. Crittenden, a strong Union man born in Kentucky, became Missouri's governor in 1881, in a period of prosperity. He was disturbed by railroad litigation, but gained some fame when the notorious James gang, headed by Jesse and Frank, was broken up. Crittenden offered a reward of $5,000 for the conviction of either man; both were charged with murder and train robberies. Crittenden's offer of a reward resulted in the betrayal

of Jesse by the Ford brothers on April 3, 1882, and the end of
Crittenden's political career. Editors followed political lines in
the James case; Republicans opposed Crittenden, and Democrats
favored his reward plan. The *Post-Dispatch* said it had

> never failed to express satisfaction with his [Jesse's] death, and
> we congratulate the state now that he is no longer alive. We
> have several times criticized our asinine governor for the lawless
> and uncivilized way in which he compassed the bandit's murder,
> and in this we have the indorsement of such journals as the New
> York *Sun*, *World*, *Telegraph*, *Graphic*, and *Tribune*, Chicago
> *Inter Ocean* and *News*, Cincinnati *Enquirer*, Louisville *Courier-
> Journal*, and a host of other intelligent and influential represen-
> tatives of public opinion.

The reference is to an apparent agreement made with the Ford
brothers and their pardon by the governor from a murder charge
"upon the grounds of public policy." One paper said, "The removal of Jesse James was not chivalrous but the method was as
creditable as any of his exploits." Another editor had "no sympathy with the maudlin sentimentality being indulged in by
certain papers over the manner of Jesse James' taking off."[4] An
excellent account of "The Development of the Jesse James Legend," written by William A. Settle, Jr., uses many newspaper
references.

The *Howell County Journal* in West Plains reported the death
of Jesse:

> We have no milk and water sentiment for Jesse James. No mat-
> ter if he was brave and fearless as a lion; no matter if he was gen-
> erous and liberal; no matter if he rewarded a kindness; no matter
> if he loved his wife and children with a tender and passionate
> love; no matter if the hand of all mankind was turned against
> him and ostracised him from society, we have no sentimental
> sympathy for a man who delighted in the blood of his fellow
> men; who struck terror to every peaceful, law abiding commu-
> nity; who made traveling on our great highways, the railroads,
> unsafe; who deterred capital from investing in, and people from
> immigrating to the grand old state of Missouri. Law, order,
> peace, justice and preservation of good society all demanded his
> LEGAL extermination. But it is the cowardly manner in which the
> deed was committed . . . the great parallel that will go down in
> history will be Crittenden and James. . . . The Ford boys should
> be tried as other criminals and Governor Crittenden with them
> as an accessory before the fact.[5]

Papers far and wide carried the story. "It would seem that the shooting of Jesse James continues to be the leading sensation of the day and the insane gush of the papers and their eager desire for sensation has caused them to convert a dead train robber into the Prince of Bandits and exalt him into a grand historical character, whose deed will be embalmed by the poets and crystalized by the historian," reported the Richmond *Conservator*.[6]

Frank James walked into the Governor's office in Jefferson City on October 5, 1882, and surrendered his pistol and belt to Crittenden. Frank, later acquitted, returned to a law-abiding life, but this incident was the subject of stories for years. The St. Louis *Missouri Republican* said James went to Crittenden and told him, "I want to hand over to you that which no living man except myself has been permitted to touch since 1861, and to say that I am your prisoner." Quite a reception followed in the Governor's office. That evening word spread about the community, and hundreds of persons, including Mrs. Crittenden, went to the hotel to see the outlaw.[7] The Kansas City *Daily Journal* reported on "The triumphal ride of Frank James from the state capital to Independence [as] ample evidence that the red-handed murderer and train and bank robber is not without friends among the Missouri mossbacks. Had the train stopped long enough he would have been given an ovation at nearly every station."[8]

Coverage of the trial was as thorough as if it were one of the leading events of the century. It would be difficult to find many impartial accounts. The St. Joseph *Gazette* reported that "at the sound of the word 'Not Guilty' the defendant embraced his devoted wife, and then one loud prolonged sound of applause marked the closing scene of the great drama."[9] Some Republican papers, such as the Kansas City *Journal* and the St. Joseph *Herald*, blamed the outcome on the exclusion of Republicans from the jury. The St. Louis *Post-Dispatch* said:

> For fifteen years it had been the burning disgrace of Missouri that the bandit chief and his gang had so many sympathizers and so much political influence that they could rob and kill and terrorize where they would, without fear of arrest in the most populous counties of the state. Yet never was this political influence displayed with such successful bravado as at this trial in the Court House which had echoed the pistol shots that killed Captain Sheets. . . . The James Boy brand has thus been burned deeper into the politics of Missouri, and she must bear the lash of her critics without a promise for the future.[10]

A week later the paper added,

> Nowhere in this Union are the people more unanimous than in
> Missouri in their absolute conviction that Frank James was guilty
> as charged. . . . If the honest sentiment of the party and of the
> state continues to be misunderstood and misrepresented abroad,
> it will be due solely to the truckling homage which candidates
> and politicians pay to the James Boy influence in the Democratic
> Party.[11]

Almost forgotten in the stir over the James brothers were the
sober facts that Crittenden's term did bring improvements in the
educational system, the penal program, care for the insane, and
an improved network of roads.

CLEVELAND CARRIES MISSOURI

Missouri voters had a wide choice in 1884, when four parties
offered candidates. On the presidential ballot were James G.
Blaine, Republican; Grover Cleveland, Democrat; Benjamin F.
Butler, Greenback; and John A. St. John, Prohibition. In the
state, the Republicans and Greenbackers worked together, selecting Nicholas Ford on a Fusion ticket for governor, while the
Democrats named James S. Marmaduke, and the Prohibitionists
ran John A. Brooks. Still other divisions within party ranks became evident, some dating to Civil War days.

Marmaduke was the last Civil War veteran to become a major
candidate in Missouri. His father, Miles M. Marmaduke, earlier
had been governor. Readers recalled the son's participation on the
Confederate side in the ill-fated skirmish at Boonville, which
some say was fought against his better judgment.

Because of the activities of the fusion party, the state vote was
closer than it might otherwise have been. Cleveland, with 235,-
988 votes, defeated Blaine and Butler, who received 202,929. St.
John polled only 2,153. For governor, the race was closer: Marmaduke received 218,885 votes; Ford, 207,939; and Brooks, 10,426.

Editorial comments on the campaign were interesting and included some rough digs now and then. The St. Louis *Post-Dispatch* presented a situation difficult for many long-time readers
to comprehend. In October it said, "The Democratic Central
Committee organized Saturday. Let us all be thankful that there
is hardly any money in the city treasury." Later it supported
Cleveland, but had reservations about Marmaduke. The editor
said the paper was "not a Democratic organ, and it does not
feel called on to support Marmaduke any further than by merely

dealing fairly with him." The *Post-Dispatch* held "the Democratic majority directly responsible for the antics, blunders, and
crimes of the Crittenden administration." On election night the
paper stretched a screen across Market Street on which returns
were flashed.[12]

The St. Louis *Missouri Republican* backed Cleveland. The
editor charged that Blaine was the candidate of "those clergymen engaged in denouncing the Democracy as the party of rum,
Romanism and rebellion." Headlines declared "Republican death
throes very distressing." The chicken cholera had seized the
Globe-Democrat, the paper noted. "Those of the crowing sex
were very sick and have not recovered in any degree whatever
yet." The next day's headline said: "Conceded. Finding it impossible to count Cleveland out."[13]

This last reference was used by other Democratic papers,
such as the Bloomfield *Vindicator,* which noted, "If certain Republicans had been one-hundredth part as anxious for a fair and
honest count in Louisiana in 1876 as they now are in New York,
the stolen presidency and the usurpation by one R. B. Hayes
would not now disgrace American history."[14]

Waiting for the New York vote delayed the display of the
victory flag on some newspapers. In Bolivar, the *Free Press,* for
Blaine, held up publication for forty-eight hours and even then
described the verdict as uncertain. Three weeks after the election, when the paper admitted defeat, it warned of possible
adverse actions from the Solid South. The Albany *Weekly Ledger,*
for Cleveland, attacked the St. Joseph *Herald,* saying that paper
believed in "the doctrine that a lie well told is as good as the
truth." On November 7, it reported, "Blaine is too sick to read
the returns."[15] The Breckenridge *Bulletin* urged all to forget
Frank James, whose "racket is becoming nauseating. Let's try
and forget that such a man is in existence and all pull together
for the advancement of the state." Coverage after the election
was slight, though space was found for such fillers as, "A sober
servant is better than his drunken lord."[16].

"Democratic triumph. Fraud rebuked. Radicalism routed all
along the line," reported the *Montgomery Standard.* "We will
paint the town a luminous red tomorrow night. Come and help
us Democrats."[17] And, "Our chicken still on top, crowing for
Cleveland and Hendricks," crowed the Troy *Free Press.* "The
conspirators are weakening and will not attempt to repeat the
fraud of 1876." It predicted "resumption of our Republic from

the rule of corruption which menaced it by the election of Blaine."[18] The *Newspaper* at California published in full, week after week, the National Greenback Labor party platform, both in English and German. However, judging from the returns, this had little influence on the voters.

Homer Clevenger's excellent study of the agrarian movement during this period cites the growth of the National Farmers' Alliance, developed to express the unrest on the farms. Other opposition groups sprang up before the 1884 election. Some Republicans, supported by the St. Louis *Globe-Democrat*, attacked the Chauncey I. Filley faction when it united with the Greenbackers in several congressional areas. Others placed the Confederate tag early on Marmaduke, hoping to split the Democrats. Some fought to drag in any of the third parties they could, to "beat the Democrats under any condition." Clevenger summarizes the situation in his statement:

> The Democratic reformers had risen in protest and elected their candidate for governor in 1884. The attempts to secure laws to regulate railroads had been circumvented by the lobby in the legislative session of 1885. The railroad strike of 1886 had aroused a still deeper hatred for the railroad companies, now personified by Jay Gould. Again in the regular session of 1887, the railroad lobby was able to block a regulation law and the governor was forced to call an extra session to secure it. In this same year, a drought increased the financial distress which had resulted from a fall in prices that began in 1885. It was also in this same year, 1887, that the Wheel and the Alliance came into the state.[19]

The St. Louis *Republican* said there were two opposing groups in that city—one for the railroads, one for the Constitution. It voiced hopes that the latter would not "be put on Jay Gould's sidetrack."[20]

During Marmaduke's administration, 1885-1887, railroad strikes occurred for the first time, organized by the Knights of Labor. Considerable destruction to property resulted, and uprisings were reported throughout Missouri.

By this time, a third of the state's revenues were earmarked for the public schools. Other improvements included a program to assist the needy, the ill, and the imprisoned. The temperance movement resulted in a vote on the local option law in 1887, when most of the state went dry. The papers supplied considerable news on the temperance movement, usually furnished by the leaders and printed without comment.

Marmaduke died on December 28, 1887, and Albert P. Morehouse became governor, serving until 1889. He had established the *Nodaway Democrat* in Maryville in 1869 and had been in politics for many years. More strikes occurred, chiefly in mining areas. Interest was displayed in expanding state libraries. Most libraries charged for their services until legislators in 1885 approved plans for making them available free after voters' approval. In 1889, the Hannibal Public Library became the first of the free tax-supported libraries. The Agricultural Experiment Station became a part of the University of Missouri College of Agriculture when federal funds became available in 1888.[21]

Francis Governor in 1889-1893

By this time, work of other parties became apparent on the political front. The Greenback party had not survived long, but similar groups appeared to support some of their principles. The Prohibition party came to the front, as did the Union Labor and United Labor parties, the latter with its single-tax program devised by Henry George. The Single Tax League, the Farmers' Alliance, and the Industrial Union were others on the scene. Four groups entered candidates in the campaign of 1888. The Democrats renamed Cleveland; Republicans ran Benjamin Harrison; the Prohibitionist-Union Labor parties nominated Clinton B. Fish and A. J. Streeter. In the state, Democrats selected David R. Francis to run for governor; Republicans named E. E. Kimball; Prohibitionists, Frank M. Lowe; and Union Laborites, Ahira Manring. Democrats captured Missouri again, providing Cleveland a plurality of 25,691. Francis, former St. Louis mayor, had a narrow call, winning by only 13,233 after considerable opposition from third parties. The total vote for the other parties was small, although Manring's 15,438 votes represented about one-eighth of the total his party received in the nation. Republicans won four seats in Congress, only to lose them two years later. "Very few of those who voted on Tuesday will live long enough to see another Democrat President elected," predicted the Butler *Bates County Record.*[22]

Southeast Missouri was the center of considerable political activity. Third-party members considered the Democrats their enemies, since they had dominated the state for so long. Some leaders hoped internal party strife would aid the third parties, and apparently the regulars felt the same, considering the frequent editorials that urged the Democrats and Republicans not

to be led astray by these newcomers. The Fordland *Journal*, a reform paper, was quoted in 1888 as follows:

> If you are a Democrat be one. Don't put your individual inter-
> ests above that of the party. . . . Yes, if you've got a collar
> branded with the name of your master, do his bidding regardless
> of whether it sends you or your children to the poor house or
> not. . . . If you adopt such a sentiment, you deserve nothing
> but bondage, and the sooner the political bosses who own you
> get you into absolute slavery, the better for your mind is too
> puerile for a free American citizen.[23]

Support your party's papers, followers were told, a policy dating to the political era dominated by Thomas Jefferson and
Alexander Hamilton. The California *Newspaper,* quoting an exchange in 1888, said, "A Union Labor voter without a Union
Labor paper in this presidential fight is like a soldier going into
battle without a gun or ammunition." Newspaper clubs were
formed, with lower rates for members and free copies for those
selling ten or more subscriptions.

Francis represented the new blood in politics, lacking any
Civil War affiliation. He had served St. Louis well as mayor and
was a strong backer of Cleveland. In 1896 Cleveland named
Francis to be secretary of the interior, and later Wilson appointed
him as ambassador to Russia. Francis was president of the Louisiana Purchase Exposition in St. Louis in 1904. His business ability
was reflected in the state's affairs; he feared "the danger in the
centralizing tendencies of business, and in the growth of monopolies and trusts." Named "the second father of the University,"
Francis helped to get that institution back on its feet after the
1892 fire.

While Crittenden had the James boys to torment him during
his term as governor, Francis was disturbed by the "Bald Knobbers," a group formed in 1885 to stop the violence aroused by
some local disputes following the Civil War and that had lingered
on and on.[24]

POPULIST MOVEMENT UNDER WAY

Discontent against economic conditions helped to create the
Populist movement near the end of the century. Money problems,
shortage of good land at cheap prices, high railroad charges, and
other factors were blamed. Problems similar to those voiced by
the Grangers and Greenbackers were attacked by the new parties.
The Anti-Monopolists appeared in 1884, the Union Laborites and

others in later years. Various agricultural units sprang up, each with its own list of complaints and demands. By 1890 the Populists arrived, and soon the People's party entered the campaigns. From a series of alliances came the People's party in Cincinnati on May 20, 1891. In July, 1892, the party entered General James B. Weaver in the presidential race. Some Missourians joined the party, but the Populist vote never became strong. A combination of various groups resulted in the Farmers' and Laborers' Union in 1890, with a membership estimated as high as 200,000. The party did not enter state contests, but supported all who backed its platform.

The first state convention of the People's party was held in Sedalia in June, 1892; Leverett Leonard was nominated to run for governor. The platform was broad, since it had to satisfy so many. Equal suffrage, the eight-hour day, union labor protection, and better coverage of workers were all endorsed. Child labor and convict labor were to be abolished under measures to be supported by the party. Women were candidates for office on some People's party tickets in 1894, but received little support. The National Populist convention in July let Miss Susan B. Anthony appear before the membership, but refused her an opportunity to speak before the Committee on Resolutions. Woman suffrage never became a political issue in Missouri.[25]

Again a four-ticket ballot faced Missourians. Cleveland, Democrat, carried the state for the Presidency with 268,400 votes; Harrison had 227,646; Weaver, 41,204; and John Bidwell, Prohibitionist, 4,333. The governor's race was closer. William J. Stone, Democrat, defeated William Warner, Republican, 265,044 to 235,383; Leonard received only 37,262 votes on the People's party ticket, and John Sobieski, Prohibitionist, had 3,393. Missourians continued to study state candidates closer than national figures.

Stone entered office at the same time the worst depression since the 1870's hit the nation. In Missouri, corn dropped to 20 cents a bushel, wheat to 43 cents. The drought of 1894 was called "unprecedented in the history of the state." Coxey's "Army" of unemployed men marched on Washington, augmented by a number of Missourians who joined the group as it crossed the state.

Republicans scored some gains in 1894, winning ten congressional seats without the Populists' support. No doubt, however, the Populists were influential in some other areas.

APPEARANCE OF REFORM PAPERS

A large number of new papers began publication at this time. One reason for this increase was the use of such publications for propaganda purposes by the third parties, or reform groups. James Lee Ashcraft, in a study of these papers during 1888-1896, has listed many. Some survived, others ended after a campaign. Much space was devoted to party messages, frequently clipped from exchanges. One of their chief problems, as cited by Ashcraft, was that all the parties and their papers "protested against much the same elements of oppression but failed to agree on remedies." Years before, the Grange, in publicizing difficulties which plagued the farmer, had served to stimulate more reading of newspapers among the rural residents.[26]

The problems of learning how many papers with Populist leanings did exist are demonstrated by Ayer's 1896 directory, which considered them to be campaign papers and thus not to be listed. It is doubtful if many editors considered their publications as campaign papers, since some continued long after the party had disappeared. Files of one of the more prominent reform papers, the California *Newspaper*, are complete from 1884 to 1896. Its editor, William C. Alldredge, was a key Populist leader. He lacked journalistic experience, so he asked his readers' "indulgence, assuring them that errors would not be intentional." He had been active in the Greenback Labor party in 1880, later in the temperance movement, on the Union Labor ticket, and then in the People's party. Frequently he was a candidate for office.

Among the leading reform editors were William O. Atkeson, Butler *Weekly Union;* Arthur Rozelle, Tarkio *Independent;* M. V. Carroll, Butler *Weekly Union;* Paul J. Dixon, Chillicothe *Crisis* and *Missouri World;* C. D. Baxter, Memphis *Farmers' Union;* J. Weller Long, *Johnson County Union;* and Phil Chew, St. Louis *Journal of Agriculture.* Several of these men were associated with other reform publications. Ashcraft lists more than one hundred papers that supported one or the other reform group between 1888 and 1896. Any such list may not be complete, since frequently papers survived too short a time to be included in directories or recorded in other historical sources.[27]

FREE SILVER AGAIN

Bland was defeated in 1894, but free silver was again a campaign issue two years later when Missourians faced their most crowded presidential ballot. William Jennings Bryan, supported by the Democrats and the People's party, carried the state with 363,667 votes; William McKinley, Republican, received 304,940; Prohibitionist Joshua Levering, 2,043; John M. Palmer, National Gold Democrat, 2,365; Charles H. Matchett, Socialist-Labor, 599; and Charles E. Bentley, National Prohibition, 292. Six parties entered state tickets. Their candidates for governor were Lon V. Stephens, Democrat, who ran behind Bryan, with 351,062 votes; Robert E. Lewis, Republican, 307,729; Herman P. Farris, Prohibitionist, 2,588; J. McD. Trimble, National Gold Democrat, 1,809; and Lewis C. Fry, Socialist Labor, 757. The Populist candidate, O. D. Jones, withdrew before the voting.

"The campaign of 1896 was a definite victory for the Populist movement. The People's party was sacrificed, but the Populists indirectly nominated the Democratic presidential candidate and also forced the Democrats to make free silver the major issue," according to Shoemaker. Democrats agreed to support Populists in seven counties; Populists backed Democrats in thirteen other counties in local contests. The Missouri Democracy "was still too strong to be defeated by a coalition of all the opposition, even if such a coalition had been attempted."[28]

Sixty Missouri Democratic editors met in July to fight for the free silver coinage at 16 to 1. Most of these men were from the county weeklies and led by H. J. Groves of the Lexington *Intelligencer* and William P. Switzler of the Boonville *Democrat*. Missouri Democrats attempted to get the presidential nomination for Bland, who led on the first three ballots.

Republicans in 1896 split, one faction for Chauncey I. Filley, one opposed to him. Lurid circulars were distributed against Filley, long a St. Louis leader, some referring to him as "a highwayman and a sandbagger in politics."[29]

Missouri papers were for Bryan about two to one, although in the cities proponents and opponents were more nearly balanced. In St. Louis, three papers supported Bryan: *Post-Dispatch, Republic,* and *Evening Journal;* for McKinley there were the *Globe-Democrat* and the *Star*. In Kansas City, the *Times* backed Bryan, the *Journal* McKinley, and the *Star* the National Gold Democrats. The *Globe-Democrat's* tactics recalled earlier campaigns and the name-calling by Missouri papers during those contests. The Democratic candidate was referred to as "a flint-lock brain and a hair-trigger mouth," "the Popocrat candidate" and "the gab-gifted galoot of the Platte." Bryan was called a Populist and "the apostle of riot and disorder" by the National Democrats. However, name-baiting tactics of this party failed to swing many votes. Reports were frequent of egg-throwing and of the heckling of candidates.[30]

The new governor, Lawrence Vest Stephens—or Lon V. as he was better known—had spent some of his younger days in the composing room of the Boonville *Advertiser*. In 1879 he became editor and took a more active role in state politics. After his term expired in 1901 he wrote a series of articles for the *Advertiser* termed "Sharps and Flats" to arouse "Missouri Democracy to a reassertion of their Jeffersonianism . . . with a continued Democratic supremacy." His term was a businesslike session, marked by many gains for the university and other state institutions. Social life became more lavish in Jefferson City. The practices of the press are reflected in Stephens' remarks during his farewell address to the legislature:

> The reckless and vituperative abuse of public officers, not only in their public but in their private lives, has become a crying evil of the times, and the passage of some law which will protect the officer and at the same time secure to the public the fullest measure of right to report the acts of public officials, comment upon such acts and fairly criticize them is peculiarly demanded.

All in all it had been an exciting era, with papers by the score rising to proclaim the platforms of the various reform movements. Many, too, fell by the wayside, following the parties they had supported.

CHAPTER XI

PRESS ASSOCIATION GROWS
IN STRENGTH AND SERVICE

EXCURSIONS and banquets began to lose priority at the meetings of the Missouri Press Association after 1885 as editors and publishers turned to more serious areas for discussion. From a desire to train better personnel and to record the history of the state, members promoted the founding of the State Historical Society and the University of Missouri School of Journalism. Today these two institutions represent the work of many Missourians, primarily those on the smaller papers, whose interest in the state's future was transformed into worth-while projects.

Indications of a new trend appeared with the election of Robert M. White of the Mexico *Ledger* in 1885 to the presidency of the organization. White sought to arrange a more practical program for the meetings which would stress operational costs and increased circulations and profits as subjects for discussion. A winter program was added—the first occurring in 1890—devoted entirely to practical topics. In February, 1894, the *Missouri Editor,* the association's semiofficial organ, was started in Columbia, with E. W. Stephens the publisher and Walter Williams editor. It was renamed the *Country Editor* three years later; it was suspended by 1900. It was of great value during its short life, especially in listing advertisers or agents who refused to pay their bills, such as:

> E. C. Howe, Chicago, is not A-1.
> Ask cash in advance from Caton Medical Company, Boston.
> When in doubt, ask cash in advance.[1]

These warnings were valuable to publishers. Suggestions for improving papers were plentiful in the association's publication. Of value to the historian are the brief references to papers "Born, Changed, Died," such as these:

> The Salem *Herald* is dead.
> T. B. McGregor has begun to print the *Miner's Journal* at Lexington. He is a strike leader.
> Rev. R. O. Harris will print at Otterville the *Cooper County Baptist* "fifty cents a year and free to poor people."[2]

Many of these papers did not survive long enough to earn a more lasting place in Ayer's or Rowell's directories.

With White in charge, the association met in "classic" Columbia. Joseph H. Turner of the Carrollton *Record* spoke on "The Duty of the Press Toward the Public School System," urging better-trained and -paid superintendents, more progressive school directors, and better newspaper support for teachers' institutes. "Write them up. Talk them up. Visit them, and if you don't like to take part in them, through lack of time for educational training in the earlier years of your history, visit them anyway," he said. J. A. Hudson of the Macon *Times* spoke on "Mechanical Management of the County Newspaper," asserting that the necessary skills were learned through years of experience, not from listening to a single lecture. Being practical, he cited dangers to rollers in cold printing offices; the numerous ways to avoid a slouchy appearance in papers, and the need for neater make-up. He warned, too, against "allowing advertisers to run your paper as it is as much of a mistake as it is to suffer prominent politicians, lawyers, or officials to dictate what you shall do." "The Story of the Printing Press" was related by Robert P. Yorkston of the *American Journalist*. "A printing press in a country office with proper care should last two hundred years and be in good order at the end of that time," he asserted.

Other changes, too, showed the growing seriousness of the association's programs. The corresponding secretary was allotted $50 as partial compensation for services, and it was decided to hire a stenographer for the meeting in 1886 "to make an exact transcript of the proceedings, to be used in the printed report." Greetings sent to General Grant expressed hope that he soon would be entirely "restored to health." A new constitution, with slight changes, was adopted. Annual meetings must "always be in a city with sufficient hotel accommodations and sufficient railroad facilities for the entertainment of this Association, unless the Association by a two-thirds vote directs otherwise." Later, a week's excursion was taken to Lake Michigan. After paying all bills, the group reported $51.05 on hand.[3]

First President Dies

J. A. Hudson of the Macon *Times* presided in 1886 at the meeting in Mexico. On the program was a twenty-one-year-old member of the Boonville *Advertiser* staff, Walter Williams, who discussed "The Profession of Journalism From a Business, Moral and Social Standpoint." He said, "There is room enough and to spare in the ranks of newspaper workers for talented young men

whose hearts are throbbing with warm affections, and in whom
the desire to be useful and noble transcends all low ambitions.
. . . The editor of a paper need not be a society man nor a kid
gloved dude, but he should be well-posted on the social movements . . . of the entire territory over which his paper circulates."
Williams placed much faith in the editorials: "Let me write the
editorials of the republic and I care not who makes the laws. If
those editorials are conservative, thoughtful and scholarly, so will
be public opinion; if they be tinged with the red of anarchism,
rapine and lawlessness will result."[4]

Although some lighter activities were scheduled, topics at
Mexico indicate a serious tone: "The Editorial Department,"
"The Advertising Department," "The Necessity of Local Organization," "The Duty of the Press During Preliminary Canvasses
Toward Candidates for Public Position," "Editorial Ethics,"
"Should Newspapers Lead or Follow Public Opinion," and others.
A resolution was passed "to appoint some discreet publisher, who
is a member of this body, whose duty it shall be, when practica-
ble, to act as arbitrator, and secure, if possible, an adjustment
of said differences, and the establishment of a satisfactory system
of prices."

Warren D. Crandall of the Brookfield *Gazette* was president
in 1887. At the annual meeting, held in Jefferson City, Crandall
urged the appointment of a historian for the organization. Joe P.
Johnston of the Plattsburg *Democrat* was first named and was
later succeeded by John W. Jacks of the Montgomery City
Standard. The editors discussed the legislature's prohibition on
free railroad passes to newsmen, but took no definite action. The
"In Memoriam" session told of the death of Jesse W. Barrett,
first president of the association, in Canton in 1886. "Lewis
County lost one of its most progressive citizens, the church . . .
was deprived of the services of one of its most earnest and un-
tiring workers, popular education, sound morality and good
government were bereft of one of their ablest champions, and
the newspaper fraternity of Missouri lost a brother indeed."[5]

Pertle Springs, near Warrensburg, was the meeting center in
1888, with Isaac H. Kinley of the Brunswick *Brunswicker* presiding. "Newspaper Legislation," "The Country Press—Its Power
and Influence," and "Relations of National and State Associations" were among topics discussed. More emphasis was placed
on legislative matters, and one resolution suggested additional
attention be given to publication of ordinances of cities of the

fourth class, of acts of the legislature, and of financial statements of counties, cities, and towns. Although no excursions were taken, members did visit the nearby springs, where "elegant refreshments were served."[6]

Nevada was the gathering place in 1889, with Walter Williams president. "Newspaper Piracy" was a new topic. Admitting it was not a pleasant subject, Sam B. Cook of the Mexico *Intelligencer* urged a curb of this practice "to protect the honor of the profession." W. L. Reid of the Monroe City *News* discussed "The Country Editor," saying he was "born into this world for the purpose of filling a long felt want." Panel leaders stressed the need for "independence of thought, independence of expression." W. O. L. Jewett of the Shelbina *Democrat* called for wider distribution of copies of the state laws, while Edwin W. Stephens, who was elected president for 1890, talked on "Practical Features of Country Journalism," concluding, "The words of the printed page do not die. The orator's voice is hushed in the tomb." The treasurer reported that "quite a large number of members of many years' connection with the Association have neglected to pay their annual dues for reasons not known." Shades of the delinquent subscriber in reverse? "Out of sympathy for the unfortunate persons" at the Nevada State Insane Asylum, the association voted to send copies of their papers there without charge. An excursion to Excelsior Springs climaxed the program.[7]

FIRST REGIONAL ASSOCIATION

First of the regional press groups to be formed was the Northeast Missouri Press Association, which met in Hannibal in November, 1889. The association had grown to nearly forty members in the early 1960's. Many of the early meetings were similar to the 1898 session in Moberly, which the president, Omar D. Gray of the Sturgeon *Leader*, wrote would be "purely informal . . . no program of papers and no entertainment is expected. No membership fee will be required and no dues will be collected." The basic objective was a gathering of publishers to share ideas on practical matters in their work. Rogers Hewitt of the Shelbyville *Shelby County Herald*, president for 1961-1962, wrote, "Unlike other retail organizations, the newspaper must, more or less, formulate its own policies. The newspapers in any association must combine their experiences and any other knowledge that each might have to constantly increase their service and usefulness to their advertisers and subscribers." He added, "Most retailers are compelled to 'keep on the ball' by competition. We don't want any newspaperman in Northeast Missouri to sit quietly by while other industry is progressing. I think that by getting together and having 'shop talk sessions,' this possibility is unlikely."[8]

During the same month the Southwest Missouri Press Association was formed in Springfield for "the furtherance of the business interests and extension of social opportunities to members." Some thirty editors joined in discussions of mutual problems. By 1911, the group became the Ozark Press Association, and five years later a typical announcement urged all to attend, since

> the citizens of Rolla and St. James will give us a cordial welcome and every minute of the trip over the Frisco through the beautiful, picturesque Ozark hills will prove interesting. And don't forget that the boss of the home needs an occasional vacation; bring her along. If you want to stay longer than the two days, you can combine rest with the invigorating sport of casting in the beautiful clear waters of the Gasconade that winds through tree-crowded hills of western Phelps County.

Robert Bowles of the Ava *Douglas County Herald,* president of the association in 1962-1963, writes that objectives today are "to exchange ideas, information and friendship, working through and with the Missouri Press Association to further the interests of the newspaper industry."[9]

WINTER SESSION IN ST. LOUIS

The first winter session of the Missouri Press Association, scheduled as a business affair, was held in January, 1890, in St. Louis with about seventy editors present. R. M. Yost of Jefferson City said, "If we could only bring ourselves to understand that, no matter what others see, think, or write, our readers are chiefly interested in what we see and think, we would thoroughly appreciate what is expected of us." Other talks concerned the advertising, subscription, and mechanical departments, as well as job work and newspaper legislation. Many questions were presented by President E. W. Stephens for group discussion.[10]

The longest meeting to date, four days, was held that August in Hannibal. Minutes of the session, set mostly in 8-point type, required 156 book-size printed pages. This session prompted many editors to join the association, so effective and informative was its program. A short history of the group was related by

William L. Thomas of the St. Louis *School and Home*. Recalling earlier emphasis on "mutual recreation," Thomas noted that many bottles of "Mumm's dry" were left untouched at a treat provided by the *Post-Dispatch* at the winter session. Advertising contracts were discussed by H. F. Childers of the Troy *Free Press*, and activities of the California and Illinois press groups were explained. After electing J. West Goodwin of the Sedalia *Bazoo* president, some sixty members and their wives went on an excursion to St. Paul and then west.

Mark Twain was invited to the Hannibal meeting. Unable to attend, the Missouri humorist wrote, "I have an honest love for the press-boys of my native state, and a most grateful appreciation of the great compliment they have paid me."[11]

In 1891 the winter meeting was held in Jefferson City. "The Personal Column" was discussed in "a witty, wise and appropriate" fashion by W. M. Bumbarger of the Nevada *Democrat*. He quoted Walter Williams as saying, "We are all Colonels, because we command a column." Advertising rates were debated again, a problem that Switzler said "the Association has been wrestling with since 1859." T. B. White of the Warsaw *Enterprise* urged publishers to co-operate in buying paper in order to obtain lower rates. E. W. Stephens said, "No man can be a journalist who does not possess the journalistic instinct. Some one has said that God Almighty puts his finger upon a man and makes him an editor. To an extent he does; but he leaves the completion of the job to the man himself."

"Is it practical to employ women in newspapers—typesetting, reporting social gatherings, and writing general articles?" This topic was "solved" about the same way as that concerning what advertising rates to charge. Other discussions revealed that some editors were paying their printers as much as $18 a week.

During the twenty-fifth meeting, held in Jefferson City, Joe P. Johnston discussed "Party Organs *vs.* Independent Journalism." The question was whether it is possible to operate an independent paper yet still make money. Johnston urged editors to firmly ingratiate themselves in the confidence of the people so that their views of public affairs will be respectfully considered and warnings of danger heeded. Others disagreed. B. F. Blanton of the Paris *Appeal* said the independent press was "like the Negro's trap, open at both ends, so it could 'catch 'em a comin' and a gwine.'"

Historian Switzler displayed files of early Missouri papers and recalled these days with this clipped poem:

> He can live without towels
> Live without soap,
> Breakfast on vowels,
> And dine upon hope;
> He can live without galluses,
> Live without shirts,
> Keep a-kicking despite
> All manner of hurts;
> He can manage to get on
> Without advertisers,
> But the editor cannot
> Survive without scissors.

Levi Chubbock, Secretary of the State Board of Agriculture, suggested that editors make an effort to interest farmers in more advertising. Association initiation fees were raised to $5 and annual dues to $3. W. O. L. Jewett of the Shelbina *Democrat* was named president for 1892. The delegation went on to Lebanon for the excursion, visiting Rolla on the way. In recording the affair, the historian noted: "Reluctantly the party left Rolla after a two hours' stay. To lessen the pain of parting, a dozen of the brightest young women were carried off to Lebanon, adding to the pleasure of the trip."[12]

Northwest Publishers Organize

Although an organizational effort was made as early as 1883, it was not until November, 1891, that the Northwest Missouri Press Association was in operation. Meeting in St. Joseph, the group discussed mutual problems and offered many toasts at their banquet, such as, "How to run a Republican newspaper in a Democratic county," "The railroads and press closely connected," "Woman, God's best blessing to man," and others that were listed in the papers. Louis Bowman of the King City *Tri-County News* wrote in 1962 that the association is now entirely a social group. However, members contributed $2,500 to the School of Journalism in 1962 to furnish a new student lounge in Neff Hall.[13]

In December, the first semiannual session of the Southeast Missouri Press Association was held in Charleston. Publishers from nearby communities discussed readyprints and the cost of a co-operative printing plant. Several years later, the group appointed one editor from each county, charged with the responsibility of preparing the history of papers in his area. Unfortunately, the project never was completed.[14] An interesting bylaw during the early day was one that stipulated, "No member shall speak twice on the same question, nor for a longer time than ten minutes, unless by suspension of this rule."

Excelsior Springs was chosen for the August, 1892, gathering of the state association. Minutes of this session were lost in the Columbia *Herald* fire, but some copies of the talks were obtained. In addition to the regular topics noted previously, there was one by Mrs. T. D. Bogie of the Richmond *Democrat* on "Some Gossip About Writers, Both Old and New, Their Labors and Characteristics."

James C. Kerby of the West Plains *Gazette* was elected president of the state group in 1893. In Columbia the next March thirty editors debated what to print and what not to print, as well as technical problems. A statistical report on national advertising rates charged by Missouri papers was made by R. M. White. For the first time, the association held its regular meeting in Clinton. Kerby, recalling highlights in the group's history, noted there were currently 782 papers in the state, including 17 in Nodaway County. White reported that he was "proud to know that in my state, journalism is fast rising to that high standard which it should always maintain." Members voted to establish a monthly journal, the *Missouri Editor*, later referred to as "worth its weight in gold." Members voiced distrust of "the formation of a trust or combine known as the American Type Founders Co." And "the patronizing of any kind of newspaper directories whatever" was opposed. White urged all papers to publish "a certified statement of their circulation" at least once a year. John A. Knott of the Hannibal *Journal* was elected president. Many editors went on an excursion to the World's Fair in Chicago.[15]

Another practical program was presented at the winter meeting in St. Louis in January, 1894. Lively discussions followed talks on everything from advertising to country correspondence, to ethics, etc. In considering costs of printing an eight-column, four-page paper some thought $703 would finance a thousand copies a year; others said between $1,200 and $1,600 would be needed. A session on ink prices showed variations from 6 to 20 cents a pound, while white paper varied from $3.10 to $5.25 a bundle.

Governor Joseph McClurg addressed members in Lebanon in September. Omar D. Gray, youthful editor of the Sturgeon

Leader, told "How to Make a Country Weekly Pay." Gray, later secretary of the World's Press Congress and a newspaper broker, said, "Journalism is a profession and demands training as severe or perhaps severer than any other." A committee was appointed to design an emblem to be used as an advertising medium. After electing John W. Jacks of the Montgomery *Standard* president for 1895, delegates went on an excursion to Atlanta.[16]

POLITICAL GROUPS FORMED

The Democratic Press Association was formed in June, 1894. When "the Democratic pencil pushers and moulders of public opinion" met in Warrensburg, they were told that their business "is the cleaning up of thought, clearing it of misery and sending it bright into the world." In 1956 a reorganization took place under the new name, "Democratic Editors of Missouri." On November 23, 1901, the Republican Editorial Association was formed in St. Joseph.[17]

Minutes of the 1895 session of the state association meeting at Pertle Springs included halftones for the first time. Of the seven new officers, headed by H. E. Robinson of the Maryville *Republican,* six sported heavy mustaches. In the group photograph, also the first published, all the men wore their hats, in wide assortment. Jacks's address recalled the aims of the association "to elevate the dignity, the honor, the purity of the press." According to Edward E. Bean of the Brookfield *Daily Argus,* the maker of a newspaper needed "Brains and backbone; conscience and common sense, not sentiment or sycophancy; honesty, not hypocrisy; truth-telling, not toadyism; firmness, fairness, fearlessness; love of humanity, a hatred of shams; public spirit, patriotism, energy, education and sound business policy." The treasury continued to increase slowly, with 159 members and nearly $600 in late 1895.[18] This year marked the end of the second phase in the history of the Missouri Press Association.

THIRD PERIOD—1896-1906

Practical discussions and social activities continued on the programs throughout the third period, but more interest was placed on the public service function of the press. This is indicated in steps taken to establish the State Historical Society, founded in 1898, and the School of Journalism, in 1908.

The steamboat *Belle of Memphis* provided the setting for the

June, 1896, meeting. As members and their guests made the round trip to Memphis, the talks were reminiscent in tone. Threats of a duel between Pat Donan of the Lexington *Caucasian* and a Mr. Nesbitt of the Platte City *Landmark* were recalled, as well as a duel between John N. Edwards of the St. Louis *Times* and Emory S. Foster of the St. Louis *Journal*. The latter encounter was fought to a bloodless conclusion in Wisconsin. A new topic appeared on the program: How to get good halftones. Details on the making of engravings were discussed. Despite efforts among the editors to expand the group, the membership dropped to 155. During the boat trip Walter Williams and E. W. Stephens published the *Daily Missouri Editor*, with young Mitchell White as head of the circulation department.

One resolution aroused considerable interest:

> This Association looks favorably upon the plan to devote a chair in our State University to Journalism, and that the president is hereby requested to appoint a committee of three to press the subject upon the attention of the curators of that institution.

The committee, enlarged to eight, included Walter Williams, who became the school's first dean.[19]

Henry W. Ewing of the Jefferson City *Tribune* was named president for 1897, and Meramec Highlands near St. Louis was chosen for the meeting place. The *Belle of Memphis* was operating that year, and members of the Mississippi Press Association came on the boat to St. Louis for a one-day joint session with the Missouri editors. Apparently June was hot in St. Louis, for the minutes record that when the president asked for discussion, "the afternoon was so excessively warm that no one . . . felt disposed to talk." B. B. Herbert, editor of the *National Printer-Journalist*, remarked, "The country press is a great educator. The idea of the modernized, of the new, metropolitan press is to make a paper that will sell. Theirs is a short-sighted policy. The sensational papers will all be dead, while those having a higher idea of their mission will be flourishing and fulfilling their missions in the education and upbuilding of the country."[20]

George W. Trigg of the Richmond *Conservator* was named president for 1898. The excursion took the editors to Nashville. During the winter session in Kansas City that year, an important resolution was approved:

> WHEREAS, it is the sense of the members of the Missouri

Press Association here assembled that this state should have a Historical Society embracing the whole state, therefore be it

Resolved, That the president of this association appoint a committee of five as an Executive Committee to prepare plans for the establishment of such a society, which shall report at the next meeting of this association.

E. W. Stephens was named chairman of the committee with Columbia the headquarters.

Eureka Springs, Arkansas, was the unusual place for the 1898 gathering later in the year. This was a combined session with the Arkansas and Texas press associations. Apparently the distance, as well as the emergencies caused by the Spanish-American War, hindered the attendance, since only fifty Missourians were there. A washout on the railway delayed the session a half day.

Stephens reported that the University of Missouri had established a chair of Journalism and approved a course of study, but lack of funds prevented further progress. He also discussed steps taken to start the historical society. Williams spoke on "The Supreme Mission of the Editor, or Education for Upliftment." The editor "is not here to gather gold, to seek the pottage, but to raise, as best he can, his people to higher life."

The year 1898 was the association's busiest, with meetings in January, May, and December. H. S. Groves of the Independence *Sentinel* was president for 1898-1899. Groves's presidency was complicated by personal crisis, for just as he was to open the December meeting in Columbia he received a telegram informing him that his office had been destroyed by fire.[21]

Editors returned to Kansas City for their meeting the following August. Williams and Stephens announced they were discontinuing the *Country Editor* because of too much other business as well as loss of money on the project. Col. B. B. Herbert of the *National Printer-Journalist* offered to provide a special Missouri department in his paper and to send members copies for one dollar annually. C. D. Morris of the Trenton *Tribune* offered to continue the magazine, but it ceased in September, 1890, having performed useful functions in its brief career. Members urged the University "to take immediate steps toward the filling of the Chair of Journalism."[22]

For 1900 the editors selected W. R. Painter of the Carrollton *Democrat* to be president. They planned early to participate in the World's Fair in St. Louis. The winter session there was highlighted by heated discussions on the paper trust, which had recently hiked costs. A representative of a paper jobber blamed the rise in prices on the tremendous consumption and on the shortage that followed the Spanish-American War. He urged publishers to raise their prices and to raise them quickly. Painter told members that the association would not accomplish its full mission "until the time comes when its members will be independent, not only in name, but in fact, will be honest and frank in their political views as they are in other departments; when editors will advocate men and measures they think are for the best good for the whole people; when smallbore politicians no longer control the policy of papers for their own selfish interests." An excursion to Niagara Falls climaxed the August meeting.

Problems concerning "Type-Setting Machines" were discussed by F. L. Wensel of the Hermann *Advertiser-Courier*. He said the estimated cost of operating a Linotype was $509.20 a year, not including labor. And at that time no Linotype operator could be hired for less than $2.75 for an eight-hour day.[23]

W. L. Robertson of the Gallatin *Democrat* became the president of the 144-member organization for 1901 and presided at the meeting in St. Louis that March. Problems of the new century were discussed. "The field of advertising is practically untouched," said F. Mitchin of the St. Louis *Ad-Writer*. "The complexity of the Twentieth Century advertising is bewildering to masters of art, science and literature." Some feared city papers would take away the smaller papers' circulation with the advent of rural free delivery, but C. D. Morris of the Trenton *Tribune* thought larger papers could not duplicate what smaller papers had to say.

William Jennings Bryan fanned himself slowly as he spoke extemporaneously on "The Weekly Newspaper" at the meeting held in St. Louis the following July. "Every editor, no matter of what political faith, should frown upon any attempt at abridgement of free speech and freedom of the press," the Nebraskan said.

Robertson called for the construction of a fireproof building for the State Historical Society as well as for more state appropriations. Routine reports, including details of the historical society and the forthcoming exposition, were given.[24] E. P. Caruthers of the Kennett *Democrat* was named president, taking over in February, 1902, at the meeting in St. Louis. There 175 editors heard I. L. Page of the Bonne Terre *Star* condemn the practice of printing personal hates and animosities. R. B. Cross-man of the Clayton *Argus* supported personal journalism, calling it the paper's duty to roast those who needed it.

Caruthers reported at the July gathering in Kansas City that he did not believe "anyone ever deliberately quits the associa-tion," although some older members were behind in their dues. He urged the association to keep "some good man, who is not an officer of the Legislature, and who is not a candidate for an office, and who is not the manager or promoter of anyone's can-didacy, who will look after the interests of the newspapermen of Missouri and keep them informed of any proposed legislation that may affect their interests."

Mark Twain, made an honorary member, accepted the honor with the remark that it was "a compliment which I hold in espe-cial value."

R. M. White read from a lithographed postcard from Paris, France, dated May 15, 1902, and signed Walter Williams: "From the heart of the Latin Quarter in remembrance of your visit there." White added,

> As we understand the matter, Williams is touring Europe to prepare lectures for his Sabbath school class, which is the largest Sabbath school class in this country. He must be preparing queer material—at least he goes to queer places and uses queer sta-tionery. We judge there must be some truth in the report that he is coming home. We are beginning to think it is time he was coming home, and if he doesn't show up before the State Press Association meeting in Kansas City on July 23-24, the writer will see to it that a committee is sent after him. It is true the writer [White] was in the Latin Quarter in Paris in 1899. At the same time we were not looking for and didn't find any of the sensa-tional features that illustrate Walter's stationery, which are not a "remembrance" to the writer, as far as he can recall. The writer did not leave any tracks in Paris that Walter could "get on to." He not only had one foot in the grave, but wore gum shoes and was chaperoned in the Latin Quarter by Miss Anne Lesueur, daughter of Hon. A. A. Lesueur, then secretary of state of Mis-souri. We begin to believe that Walter should have a lady chap-erone instead of "Jim Moss, the Kodaker." Come home, boys.[25]

The press association met in joint session with the State His-torical Society in Columbia the next January. The new president, Howard Ellis of the New Florence *Leader*, was in charge. Min-utes record that "comment is unnecessary" on Omar D. Gray's talk on "How to Induce Country Merchants to Advertise Everlastingly." Gray said, "The merchant who is not carrying an ad in his local paper now is looked upon with as much curiosity as was Barnum's white elephant in the early days of circushood." William Southern, Jr., of the Independence *Examiner* provoked "an unusual amount of discussion" on his topic: "Papers, Politics, and Patronage." He said, "A church organ is filled with wind and operated by the intelligence of the player. So is the party organ. The politician is the operator and the editor furnishes the wind."

"If a girl is well and strong and has a good grammar-school education, there is no better work than she will find in writing for newspapers," said Miss Georgina Raby of the St. Louis *Dawn*. Copies of a stylebook prepared by A. G. Tally of the Columbia *Herald* were distributed. Ellis appointed one editor in each county to compile in manuscript form a record of the papers there.

The August, 1903, meeting was the largest held to date by the Missouri Press Association. The minutes report that "the discussions were sometimes acrimonious and the debates heated," which demonstrated "a healthy activity and augurs well for the future welfare of the body." Ellis' talk was read in his absence. He hailed "the philanthropic work of Joseph Pulitzer . . . in giving of his wealth sufficient to establish and maintain a college of journalism where the editor can be made with that polish and ability as is given graduates of other professions." He also cited advances made by the State Historical Society since its incorporation in 1898. Williams noted highlights of his foreign travels, telling of the kinship among newspaper workers.[26]

T. T. Wilson of the Tarkio *Avalanche* became president and was in charge of the session held during the winter of 1904 in St. Louis. The two-day session was crowded with practical reports, including one on "How to Handle Your Competition." Williams, serving as superintendent of publicity for the Louisiana Purchase Exposition, explained this project.

A touchy problem developed when the Committee on Membership recommended the removal of three names. Two were "confessed criminals," accused of accepting bribes. Considerable debate followed, and one editor urged all "to keep politics out of the organization." One of the three was considered an honest man who had made an error, later confessing before a grand jury. A roll-call vote removed two men from membership, but not the latter editor.

The Missouri building at the World's Fair was the scene for

the May session. An entire week was devoted to meetings of press groups, the World's Press Parliament, and the National Editorial Association. Governor A. M. Dockery spoke, calling attention to two classes of newspapers:

> Sensational papers pander to their readers, delighting in the most extravagant headlines and statements concerning even trivial matters. The old style newspaper, with its single edition, embodies its findings in carefully prepared articles, setting out the news of the day, and its editorials seek to express the policies of its management in emphatic yet conservative language.

Fifty-four applications for membership, a new high for a year, raised the total to 227.

The World's Press Parliament was held at the exposition, following the sessions of the association. More than five thousand newspaper men and women attended, from every state and thirty-seven countries. Williams served as secretary of the parliament, and Sir Hugh Gilzean-Reid of London was president. Men from many of the world's leading papers spoke. John Hay, United States Secretary of State, spoke on behalf of President Theodore Roosevelt. Crosby S. Noyes of the Washington *Star* told the members, "The student of journalism should be taught, and as well in the public schools as anywhere, to write with directness, precision, and force; and there is no language in existence so capable of expressing ideas clearly, in words easily comprehended by every one, high or low, as plain, unembroidered English."

The delegate from Russia admitted the lack of freedom of the press in his native land. He said the Russians "had fewer newspapers than any other nation in the world, and therefore . . . less to read and bother our heads about things that happen in some remote part of the world."

W. D. Thomas of the Fulton *Sun* presided over the fall, 1904, session, also held at the World's Fair. This was more a social and sight-seeing reunion than a meeting for serious discussion, and members visited "the biggest show on earth." Some reports were provided, including a review of a new book by Williams, the *Missouri Book.*[27]

President Thomas moved away from Missouri during his term of office, so William Southern, Jr., presided in July, 1905, at St. Joseph. Southern jokingly called Thomas "a fugitive from justice, a defaulter," having failed to pay his dues. He urged a curb on excursions, saying, "Junkets and business do not do well together." Another Thomas was in better standing—William L. Thomas of the St. Louis *School and Home.* For his long service as treasurer he was presented a gift, but became the first retiring officer to refuse this traditional token of appreciation. In the past, rings, watch charms, gold-headed canes, and dinner sets were the customary gifts for retiring leaders of the association.[28]

Southern was elected president to serve in 1906, when the association returned to St. Louis for its meeting in February. The minutes describe this as the first *real* business meeting, a statement that is not entirely true. A reception committee composed entirely of women was indeed new. Some previous charges that a small group of publishers controlled the association were counteracted by the appointment of district representatives and a change in the constitution to provide for elections by ballot without nomination. An effort to force advance payment of subscriptions failed. One resolution recommended that "Congress pass a law granting no newspaper the privilege of the low rate of postage until it is paid for in advance." The resolution was tabled.

Hannibal was the scene for the fortieth meeting, in June. Southern said he observed "different faces at the winter working meeting and the summer play meeting" and suggested that probably it would be better to hold "one large meeting with a strong program" once a year. Although no official action was taken, few winter meetings were held after 1906. Philip Gansz of the Macon *Republican* was named president for 1907.[29]

Thus ends one of the most important periods in the growth of the Missouri Press Association. With the new era starting in 1907, the association continued to serve state publishers in many additional ways, building upon the foundations that had been established during the previous forty years.

CHAPTER XII

MISSOURI'S BIG-CITY EDITORS

COMMUNITY editors, primarily those publishing weekly papers, dominated the journalism scene before the turn of the century. These men were leaders in the affairs of the Missouri Press Association, in the growth of the State Historical Society, and later in the founding of the School of Journalism. They urged more uniform rates for advertising and job printing, met regularly to exchange ideas, warned their colleagues of misleading advertising agents, and learned the latest in technological advances

Three editors of big-city papers in Missouri earned a niche in the journalism hall of fame for achievements during the latter part of the nineteenth century. Known far beyond the borders of Missouri, their fame was earned on papers in St. Louis and Kansas City. No doubt many editors in smaller communities could have performed equally well on larger papers, but in report after report recorded in minutes of the association's conventions there is an indication that these editors were quite content to remain in smaller communities. Their independence, high status in the community, and the opportunities for political appointments were among the major reasons mentioned by editors desiring to remain in such areas as Columbia, Boonville, Mexico, Joplin, Marshall, etc. In many of these communities there are still members of the same families at the helm of the papers, the Sosey family in Palmyra, the Johnstons in Fulton, the Whites in Mexico, and others. However, to indicate some big names in the state before 1900, attention is focused on Joseph Pulitzer, William Rockhill Nelson, and Joseph B. McCullagh. No effort will be made to provide full-length biographies, since all of these men have been subjects of more complete studies.

PULITZER ARRIVES

Joseph Pulitzer, who first gained fame in St. Louis, was described by one of his literary secretaries as follows:

> Apple in one hand, open book in the other, munching, reading, bumping people on the walk—such is a St. Louis picture of the 1860's, self-drawn in his later years, of the lanky youth who was to become the founder of the *Post-Dispatch,* proprietor of the New York *World,* dominant force in American politics; destined

to leave behind him one of the greatest names in American journalism and the memory of one of the most vivid, arresting and extraordinary personalities of his time; a man whose 64 years of life contained ambition, activity, achievement—and tragedy— enough to fill a dozen ordinary lives.[1]

Pulitzer arrived in St. Louis on "some joker's assurance that it was just the place to Americanize him because he would hear only English spoken." Thus, by late 1865, Pulitzer reached the city where he first cared for sixteen mules and performed other jobs before he became a newsman. Soon he became the Jefferson City correspondent for a famed St. Louis German paper, the *Westliche Post*. While there he participated in a pistol scrape, not an uncommon affair for those days.

Long a foe of privilege, Pulitzer later labored in reform battles. He worked with Carl Schurz in fighting corruption, landgrabbing, and carpet-bagging activities associated with the Grant administration. Later he joined the Liberal Republican movement which attempted to place Horace Greeley, already famed as a New York editor, in the White House. Pulitzer made some sixty speeches in German for Greeley. In 1878 Pulitzer bought the St. Louis *Dispatch* for $2,500 plus the assumption of debts against what many termed a worthless paper. Although the presses were broken down, the sheriff's sale of the paper included one valuable item—an Associated Press franchise. John A. Dillon was operating the *Post*, a well-written and scholarly paper. Three days after the sale of the *Dispatch*, the two papers merged into the *Post and Dispatch*, with a circulation of 800. Pulitzer announced in his first edition that this paper

> . . . will serve no party, will be no organ but the organ of truth, will follow no caucuses but its own convictions, will not support the Administration, but criticize it, will oppose all frauds and shams, wherever and whatever they are; will advocate principles and ideas rather than prejudice and partisanship. These ideas and principles are precisely the same as those on which our Government was originally founded. They are the ideas of true, genuine, real democracy. They are the doctrines of hard money, home rule and revenue reform.[2]

Pulitzer drove himself hard, working from early morning until late at night. One coworker described him as "the damnedest man in the world to have in a newspaper office for an hour in the morning and for the rest of the day, the damnedest nuisance." Colonel John A. Cockerill, his assistant, objected to Pulitzer's continual changes in stories. The *Post-Dispatch* became a crusading paper, attracting thousands of new readers. One indication of Pulitzer's success was the fact that seventeen libel suits were filed during the first few years, demanding $250,000 in damages. In only one case did Pulitzer lose; that incident cost him forty dollars.

Although Pulitzer refused to permit his paper to become the organ of any one political party, the editor did engage in political activities briefly. Four years after he reached St. Louis, Pulitzer was elected to the state legislature. He learned the law and was admitted to the bar, although he never practiced the profession. While a legislator, Pulitzer retained his reporting job on the *Westliche Post*. When stories appeared about woman suffrage, Pulitzer proposed that an election be held granting them the right. He suggested, however, that the vote of the men and women be kept separate; he still believed in the 1870's that most women did not desire to vote.[3]

Pulitzer spent almost eighteen years in Missouri before he purchased the New York *World* in 1883. Still, when he went to New York he was a young man, only thirty-six.

Pulitzer's son Joseph directed the St. Louis *Post-Dispatch* after his father's death in 1911. The second Pulitzer spent his life in St. Louis and, according to the story of his death in 1955,

> . . . he personally supervised all departments of the newspaper, but said that the news and editorial pages were closest to his heart. He originated many of the campaigns which have been a distinguishing feature of the *Post-Dispatch* since its founding. Taking an active interest in the development of radio, and later television, he established the *Post-Dispatch* station, KSD, which went on the air March 7, 1922. Station KSD-TV began telecast on February 8, 1947. Each station was among the first in the United States to be operated by a newspaper. Several sons of Pulitzer Senior had remained with the *World* in New York until that paper was sold.[4]

Both Pulitzers were handicapped by poor eyesight. The senior editor became totally blind, and his son lost all vision in one eye and 80 per cent in the other.

In April, 1955, the third Joseph Pulitzer became editor and publisher of the *Post-Dispatch*. The grandson of Joseph Pulitzer, born in 1913, had been with the paper since his graduation in 1936 from Harvard.[5] Thus the tradition established by the first Pulitzer has been continued. Its independence has been displayed in its support of candidates from both major parties. For President it backed Landon in 1936, Roosevelt in 1940 and 1944, Dewey in 1948, Stevenson in 1952 and 1956, and Kennedy in 1960. For governor of Missouri it supported Republican Barrett in 1936; four years later the paper declared it had no choice, but leaned toward Forrest Donnell, Republican. The paper backed Donnelly, Democrat, in 1944 and Thompson, Republican, in 1948. Both candidates, Donnelly and Elliott, received the paper's endorsement in 1952. Lon Hocker, Republican, received it in 1956, and Democrat John Dalton in 1960.

NELSON REACHES KANSAS CITY

Fifteen years after Pulitzer invaded Missouri, William Rockhill Nelson reached the western part of the state at Kansas City to establish the *Star*. Nelson's first *Evening Star* appeared on September 18, 1880, four pages with six columns each. Nelson's paper did have considerable news, with ads limited to the last two pages. An introductory editorial, longer than a column in length, set forth Nelson's ideas. It said, in part:

> Among the most successful products of recent journalism in the United States is the cheap afternoon newspaper. Experience has demonstrated that the great morning journals printed in our large cities, admirable and enterprising as they are, do not meet the wants of the great masses of the people. Their broad pages, filled with elaborate details of all news matters, with lengthy, ponderous editorials, with long prosy sermons and other matter of the same class, which occupy a large amount of space, and demand much time for their perusal, while they make these journals invaluable to many, at the same time render them unattractive to the great majority of dwellers in cities.[6]

Nelson listed many advantages for afternoon papers. "The reader is not compelled to wade through columns of surplusage in order to get at a kernel of news . . . writers are not obliged to cover reams of white paper with words, in conveying a few ideas, which might better be stated in one-quarter of the space. Everything is told in terse, concise, direct language." Thinking Kansas City large enough then to support such a paper, he said, "[The *Star*] will labor with especial zeal and earnestness in behalf of all measures tending to advance the interests of Kansas City, and develop the resources of the great Missouri Valley. In local matters it expects to support the best men for office, utterly regardless of party considerations, and to do all that lies in its power in behalf of honest, economical and efficient government."[7]

Nelson had studied law and, turning from that, had made some $200,000 as a contractor early in his career, after a short time at Notre Dame University. He lost his fortune and later became coeditor of the *Sentinel* in his home town, Fort Wayne, Indiana. However, Nelson and his partner Samuel E. Morss decided they preferred a growing community where they might share in its growth and development. They looked about them and decided that Kansas City offered opportunities for newspapermen. By 1880, Kansas City had a population of 55,000, but was still a rough and rowdy steamboat community; to Nelson it held promise of becoming a "glorious metropolis."[8] After its first six months of operation, the success of the partners' paper, the *Star*, was assured. Eugene Field dubbed the paper "the Twilight Twinkler."

With an objective of "a greater purpose in life than merely printing news," Nelson began his crusades for reform. He urged improvements in Kansas City at a time when most residents considered themselves temporary citizens, ready to move westward when the right chance came. For years he fought the "Hammer and Padlock Club"—persons who used the hammer to beat the life out of all efforts at public improvements and the padlock to protect their pocketbooks from invasion. Yet it was said after his death that "he found the city mud and left it marble."

Public service always has been a keynote in the *Star*'s program. For years Nelson led the fight against franchise grabbers, devoting some 2,500 columns of solid type in one continuing struggle for a fair street-railway project. In 1895 his paper said, "The idea that the city ought to control its natural monopolies has been growing rapidly in favor here for the past few years." The *Star* agitated in 1893 for a public auditorium, and the first such building was completed in 1899, with John Philip Sousa's band presenting the inaugural program. The hall burned within a year, but was rebuilt by July, 1900, for the Democratic National Convention.

Nelson's dislike for the liquor business led to a ban on liquor advertisements in 1905. His reply to the fears of the business office was, "I guess we're making enough money without them." One of his ideas reappeared in public thinking in later years— that the legitimate expenses of elections should be borne by the government, rather than by large corporations, saloons, and the like. He also expressed a desire to have all lawyers on the government payroll, in the opinion that skill then would not always be on the side of money.

Nelson became famous as a journalist. William Allen White once said that the personality of the *Star* was highly reflective of its editor, but the personality of its editor was infinitely more vivid than his newspaper.[9] Like Pulitzer, Nelson varied his support for political parties, although he followed the Republicans with more regularity than he supported other parties. Readers were jolted in 1902 by the *Star's* support of Cleveland for President and of a Republican, William Warner, for governor. Later it supported Theodore Roosevelt for President and Folk, a Democrat, for governor of Missouri; in that same election the Republican candidate for governor in Kansas received the paper's backing. Although he was early a supporter of Taft, Nelson broke away to promote Roosevelt's Progressive party.[10] Unlike Pulitzer, Nelson declined public office and felt that an editor had no business with political patronage or office-holding. Both Pulitzer and Nelson devoted their lives to their editorships; both loved journalism. No doubt each looked upon his paper from the viewpoint of the reader rather than from the technical side. Nelson opposed comics as inartistic and vulgar and called them "a cheapening influence." His concern was always for the family, particularly for the women readers. Although not an active writer himself, Nelson encouraged others and was liberal with suggestions for stories and campaigns. He once said he was "always willing to overlook an error in judgment regarding news, provided it is made on the side of good taste"; he was never affected by the yellow journalism of the 1890's. Nelson preferred line drawings to halftones, believing that papers could not do justice to illustrations. He preferred handwritten copy to typewritten, in the opinion that the use of a machine destroyed creative thinking. Nelson once addressed a Journalism Week audience in Columbia by telephone from Kansas City and summarized his philosophy about journalism:

> There is just one point that I wish to emphasize to the young men who are expecting to engage in newspaper work: That is, that the reporter is the essential man on the newspaper. He is the big toad in the puddle.
>
> Young fellows looking forward to a newspaper career often have in mind an editorship of some sort. They want to guide and instruct public opinion. The trouble is that the public doesn't

yearn to have its opinion guided and instructed. It wants to get news and be entertained.[11]

He warned reporters to develop a nose for news, the instinct to recognize the big story in an event or situation, but, he said, "Never be a machine. Many reporters are ruined by allowing themselves to become messengers of the city editors."

Nelson died in 1915. He was a many-sided man, and the *Star* reflected his varied interests. While staff members remained anonymous and generally poorly paid, they benefited from the fact that the *Star* was a remarkable classroom in itself. Ernest Hemingway, after a summer as a reporter on the *Star,* could recall thirty years later the concise style practiced there.[12]

The *Star* has survived all competition. Between 1915 and 1926 it was directed by a trusteeship, and since that time it has been employe-owned. In 1961, the *Star* stated that it was the only paper in America owned 100 per cent by its employes. It continues to grow and to serve the Middle West as Nelson would have desired.[13]

GLOBE-DEMOCRAT'S NOTED EDITOR

The success of the St. Louis *Globe-Democrat* during its first twenty years has been credited to Joseph B. McCullagh by Dr. Jim Allee Hart in his history of the paper. McCullagh, born in Ireland in 1842, came to St. Louis in 1858 after serving as a printer's apprentice on the *Freeman's Journal* in New York. In St. Louis he worked first as a compositor on the *Christian Advocate* while learning shorthand from Dr. William T. Harris, Superintendent of Public Instruction there.[14] Later McCullagh became a proofreader on the *Democrat* and filled in successfully as a substitute reporter. By 1859 he was taking notes in shorthand at the state General Assembly. After a year on the Cincinnati *Daily Gazette* he returned to St. Louis to enter the Union Army, but later rejoined the *Gazette* staff. While with this paper and later while with the *Commercial* in Cincinnati, his ability to pursue news was demonstrated.[15] Additional years were spent on the Cincinnati *Enquirer* and the Chicago *Republican* before he returned to St. Louis, following the disastrous Chicago fire in 1871. He became managing editor of the *Globe*, holding that position following the merger with the *Democrat* until his death.

McCullagh realized that one of the best ways to increase a paper's circulation was to publish news that thousands of potential readers wanted to read. He, too, realized the interest controversy would incite, and for three months in 1877-1878 he published his "Great Religious Controversy," with comments from leading clergymen of many faiths and letters from hundreds of readers. McCullagh once tackled the State of Texas in a quarrel which resulted in his paper being banned from that state. The editor claimed, "If the energy that is wasted in Texas in denunciation of the *Globe-Democrat* for telling the truth about events in that state were directed to the punishment of crime and the administration of impartial justice there, the reign of lawlessness would soon be over."[16]

McCullagh utilized his crusading talent in continuous campaigns against gambling, drinking, and other crimes. He called for a better community, referring frequently to "poor old St. Louis" which let other cities, such as Chicago, pass it in population. McCullagh recognized St. Louis' opportunities to become a great rail center, a situation that had been stressed by papers before the Civil War. He opposed any violence or riots, but defended labor's right to parade. However, when the railroads were the victims of a strike, he called for "surrender first—arbitration afterwards."

Just prior to the turn of the century news-gathering was becoming more competitive. This was highlighted by the Pulitzer-Hearst struggle in New York and the reporting of the Spanish-American War. McCullagh claimed in 1884 that the *Globe-Democrat* was spending "more money for the collection and transmission of telegraphic news from all parts of the world" than was paid "by any paper in any other city of the world, New York and London not excepted."[17] McCullagh could handle men and get the most from them. Pay on his paper was good, better than on some others in the city. He gave Theodore Dreiser a job as a reporter for $20 a week and rewarded him with a $5 raise for his scoop on a train wreck. Walter B. Stevens was paid as high as $75 a week while in Washington. Expense apparently was no object—reporters knew they could spend money to secure news ahead of any competitors.

McCullagh once spoke at a meeting of the Missouri Press Association, but his speech was termed "an oratorical failure." Apparently he concurred, since he never attended another press session and practically ignored the Missouri community press, seldom noting exchanges.[18] This may have cost him many friends among state publishers, but McCullagh was not the type of man

to have intimate friends. He was described as difficult to talk
to, yet "his whole thought was in his paper—his idol, and he
cared for little else." McCullagh's policy was clear: "Spending
money is the only way to make a newspaper and I never hesitate
to lay down one dollar when I see I can thereby pick up two,"
he said. He knew how to write, learned from such experiences
as he had in the Civil War. An editorial in the *Missouri Editor*
about his death remarked that McCullagh's invective was fearful,
yet rarely did he abuse a man personally. Although he was a
Democrat, he edited a Republican paper. "Thus while as a journalist he entertained, it cannot be said that he influenced. His
paper was read for its news and sprightliness and not for its
views."[19] This is an interesting interpretation, indicative of the
way some editors felt about the functions of an editor.

When asked his view on the greatest quality of a journalist,
McCullagh said: "Knowing where hell is to break loose next."
Throughout his career, McCullagh sought new and striking material for the *Globe-Democrat*. He placed great stress on the
feature story and on the interview and recognized the effectiveness of the short, incisive editorial comment, which he proved
readers would notice. His biting language was well known, both
in and out of the profession. Some said he had a warm heart, but
many remember only his cold views of professionalism. His ideas
about politicians were clearly understood by *Globe-Democrat*
readers. He agreed with those editors who believed that newspapermen should avoid political positions, because in this opinion,
an editor was just as important as a senator.

Hart, in his account of McCullagh and his "school" wrote:
"McCullagh called the *Globe-Democrat* the best journalism
school in the country. . . . His staff believed that he delighted in
catching their errors in figures or in quotations. 'Always verify;
always verify,' he told them. Frequently he edited proof-sheets
for wordiness and called the attention of the city editor to errors
in figures, names, and statistics." McCullagh was concerned with
"all the news," not with "essays."[20]

Shortly after he wrote an article in 1896 on "The Philosophy
of Suicide," McCullagh took his own life by jumping from his
bedroom window. He had been ill for a long time, and his death
was blamed on overwork.[21] A comment in the *Missouri Editor*
said, "It is doubtful if any avocation is so wearing upon those
who engage in it as that of editing a paper." His death rated
front-page coverage in the New York *Times,* so apparently the

Missouri Editor's remarks were true about McCullagh standing "at the head of Western journalists." Truly "Little Mack" did much to give the *Globe-Democrat* a national stature.[22]

CONCLUSION: A COMPOSITE VIEW

St. Louis newsrooms were explored in an article in the *Missouri Editor* in 1895. City reporters were compared to a river—they go on forever, with few changes among the established workers and a conservatism about the heads when it comes to trying new faces that gives the regulars a grip upon their places. Salaries were of interest, with some there paid princely amounts. McCullagh received $150 weekly, plus dividends from his stock in the firm. Dr. A. Price, editor of the German-language daily *Amerika* received $4,000 annually. Among some leading writers on the *Globe-Democrat* were Maj. Henry King and Maj. Charles M. Harvey, who received $60 weekly while devoting much of their attention to the Sunday edition. The telegraph editor, O. R. Lake, earned $40 a week, the same as the city editor, Tobias Mitchell. Walter Stevens, Washington correspondent, declined the secretaryship of the Philippine Commission in 1900 although the position paid $6,000, with $2,000 more for expenses.

On the St. Louis *Republic* J. R. Graham was paid $100 a week to head the editorial staff, while the night editor, Charles Webb, was paid $50 and other editors were in the $40 bracket. Col. Charles Jones returned to the *Post-Dispatch* with a financial interest in the paper and received $150 weekly. He was said to "have a hand in everything, but his chief efforts were directed to shaping editorial policy. . . . He was a man of pronounced ideas." John Magner, guiding spirit of the *Star-Sayings*, was paid $75 weekly and his telegraph editor only $27.

On the *Chronicle*, the pioneer of penny journalism in the West, Col. George A. Shieves, editor, was paid $100 weekly, while other salaries dropped—to $35 a week for reporters. Many men were on space rates. The *Chronicle*, termed "a young men's paper," stressed brevity. One of its better-known editors was J. Bartle Parker, in charge of telegraph news. Born in Ontario in 1858, he was an apprentice when he was nine years old. Later he was elected to the Missouri legislature, but was "wedded to journalism and while he had a fancy for political life, he had no use for the objectionable necessity for scheming to get office."

One of the best known of the women writers was Mrs. Rose Walker of the *Globe-Democrat*, "a lady of silvery hair, but with a face still fresh and youthful." She received $50 a week for handling fashion and society news and for directing a group of space writers who earned from $10 to $20 a week.[23]

The composite portrait of the city newsman is somewhat more difficult to draw than that of his counterpart in the smaller areas. No doubt many community newsmen did cast an eye toward these "high" salaries, but apparently the proprietors of the small-town press preferred to remain at their own influential desks with their publications. It is primarily through these men that we will see the history of the state develop, from the grass-roots.

CHAPTER XIII

THE COUNTRY EDITOR AS SEEN
BY HIS COLLEAGUES

A TYPICAL Missouri editor? What was he like?

Some say he was an artist, others say he was a politician. Some were Southerners, a few were Yankees, still others were native Missourians. Here and there were those noted for their intellectual vigor, while a few began their careers with a handful of type and learned their profession in their own print shops. This editor was pictured in 1895 by Will M. Ledbetter of the St. Louis *Republic* as

> not an author. He writes not for posterity, but for the hard working and sometimes unapplauding present. If any of what he is pleased to call his "stuff"—that incongruous mixture of current political and social history, personal palaver, good natured chaff, unconscious and sometimes unpolished humor, unstudied pathos and unassuming merit—if anything, in short, he dashes off in the mad haste of the moment, should survive its day of circulation, there would be more surprise over that one thing than over the ninety and nine other things which are never heard of again.

Neither was he an artist, added Ledbetter. Nor was he a gloomy person.

> In words which he applied to nearly every subject except himself, he is not half bad. Nor will those of you who are acquainted with the facts doubt me when I say that he deserves a better fate than the penury and privation of which he is so prone to speak.
> But we long ago came to understand that joke. We can see the editor as he takes down the whiskered relic and prepares it for another sacrifice. At his left is a box of luscious berries, donated, which he munches as he pens the lugubrious words. A teamster drives up and is curtly told to take that load of wood (accepted on subscription) around to the house, and to be sure that it is good hickory, and not slippery elm, like the last. A farmer's wife comes in with the first spring chickens and finest vegetables of the season for which she is pleased to take pay in a notice about "Aunt Nancy Smith, the most successful housewife and market gardener in Goose Neck township." He needs new clothes. A tailor shop is around the corner, and with a neatly turned paragraph about patronizing home industries, carrying a broad reference to the metropolitan suits that are being turned

out by Snipper, the tailor, he finds the things quite easy, payable
in advertising. His other necessities and those of his family come
in the same way, and at the end of the year he has done a business whose volume, compared to the actual capital involved,
would put our real estate and railroad financiers to shame.

At the turn of the century the editor was

a pillar of the church, frequently superintendent of the Sunday
School, and almost invariably a steward or deacon . . . sometimes
he is mayor of the town, member of the fair directory and building and loan association, the prominent citizen who introduces
strangers, great or small, to the populace, often justice of the
peace in addition to his other attributes as the general municipal
Pooh-Bah, and last, but not least, the dangerous candidate for
postmaster when a change of administration occurs, and the
man whom every candidate "has to beat."

The man who recorded the history of the state on his printed
pages was "magnanimous, manly, generous to the verge of im-
providence, the friend of everyone . . . thoughtful, patient sym-
pathizer with the aged or afflicted . . . philosopher and steadfast
friend whose cheering words and hearty counsel are a constant
source of encouragement and hope."[1]

DIFFICULT TO SELECT LEADERS

It is dangerous to select for particular comment a group of
editors who served during these early, formative years of Missouri journalism without omitting some who deserve equal fame.
The beginners surely merit special emphasis. In the 1890's a
series of articles appeared in the *Missouri Editor* about editors,
as seen by their fellow writers. Some of these sketches are used
here, along with comments culled from association minutes and
other sources.

Jacob D. Allen of the Butler *Times* was one of the many who
came from Kentucky. Active in the Democratic party, Allen was
a conscientious, bright, bold, and able editor, a manly, true, and
steadfast individual.[2]

A. G. Blakey of the Pleasant Hill *Review* was a favorite with
many editors. Drifting into the business accidentally, he was
late in entering newspaper work. He was a consul in Chile, where
he became a great favorite with the *señoritas*. Blakey was "liberal
to a fault, the soul of honor, with a purse open to a friend."[3]

A big-bodied, big-hearted man who sported a Grant-type beard
was Jesse W. Barrett, first president of the association and

founder of the Canton *Press*. Born in Pennsylvania and a graduate of Dickinson College, Barrett was trained for the Methodist ministry and at one time directed a seminary. During the Civil War he started the *Press*. Barrett held several state offices. His son records that Barrett was sick nine days, died on the ninth day of the ninth month at nine minutes past nine o'clock.[4]

Many Missouri editors were associated with several papers. W. H. Balthis was with the Huntsville *Herald* and the *Vindicator* as well as the Brunswick *Brunswicker*. From Virginia, a state which provided Missouri many of its early editors, Balthis was a vigorous and able writer, an honorable, warm-hearted, and sociable friend. He, too, became a postmaster.[5]

Milo Blair, a lifelong Republican, was described by Democratic friends as "fair, honest, and generous." His papers included *Eagles* in Boonville and Sedalia. During his leadership of the state publishers in 1876, the organization adopted its present name. Public offices attracted him; he was mayor of Boonville, later postmaster in Sedalia.[6]

Benjamin Franklin Blanton was affectionately referred to as "The Old Man of the *Appeal*" in Monroe County. His paper was the envy of many colleagues since "it was on a paying basis, so its proprietor was enabled to live and maintain in comfort a large family, and out of his earnings he was enabled to put by a little for a rainy day." The *Appeal* was "the enemy of vice, immorality, and of all combinations to deceive, injure, or rob the people." Blanton possessed superior social ability, being able to mix and mingle with all.[7]

Thomas D. Bogie of the Richmond *Democrat* believed there was little need to dally with idle pastime or useless frivolity. His colleagues thought Bogie dealt with logical facts, calling things by their right names, being against deceit and hypocrisy. Although "rather a pessimist than an optimist," Bogie never hesitated in "condemnation of error in morals, or mossback ways in business."[8]

Starting as a writer of locals as a lad, I. N. Bryson caught the "editorial fire that finally burned him" on the Louisiana *Press*. He was bright, witty, thoroughly posted on matters of public moment, and fearless in fighting evil; he was an early friend of William Jennings Bryan. Bryson was a well-known deepwater "Campbellite."[9]

H. T. Burchartt, the successful operator of the Windsor *Review*, also worked on papers in Butler, Glasgow, and Fayette.

Termed a "generous, jolly, and good companion," Burchartt "had no itching palm, no grasping greed, no thirsting avarice beyond a comfortable sufficiency." The *Review* was an interesting and well-printed paper, a credit to Windsor.[10]

Ewen Cameron came to Missouri from Tennessee and after some years with the Warsaw *Independent* attempted farming. But the lure of printer's ink was too strong; Cameron returned to publishing, as editor of the Pleasant Hill *Dispatch*. Friends said he was "a quiet, unobtrusive, Christian gentleman."[11]

MANY IN OTHER PROFESSIONS

Edgar P. Caruthers worked with papers in St. Louis and Iowa as well as on both the *Conservative* and *Bee* in Fredericktown where he was born. Learning the trade when fourteen, Caruthers moved to Kansas but returned home to protest the spread of Populism there. He bought the Kennett *Clipper,* which he renamed the *Dunklin County Democrat*. He once said that never in his life had he "knowingly wronged a man politically, financially, or socially." He wanted his paper to serve the public. A nonpracticing lawyer, Caruthers was a talented printer and a born journalist who received credit for knowing equally well how to land a bass or a jack salmon.[12]

A descendant of a Quaker family, Colonel Jacob T. Child became the famed publisher of the Richmond *Conservator*. At fifteen he was an apprentice on the Richmond, Virginia, *Whig* but came to St. Joseph during the border ruffian period. Associated with several papers, he was minister to Siam during Cleveland's first term, and later consul in Hankow, China. After this tour abroad, he returned to Richmond.[13]

Norman J. Colman, editor of *Colman's Rural World*, was the second president of the press group and a leader of its work until his death in 1911. Born in New York, Colman came to Missouri in 1855 to buy an agricultural paper. Through this organ he helped to promote agriculture, especially in the Middle West. He was lieutenant governor of the state in 1874, a member of the University of Missouri Board of Curators for many years, and the nation's first secretary of agriculture. He once said, "The press of the state can confer no greater boon upon her people than by giving its hearty aid in the development of the varied resources we possess."[14]

With "a handful of type, an old Washington hand press, and

with printers who were willing to work for enough to pay for hash and drinks and take chances on getting that," E. J. Conger ran the Linneus *Bulletin* with H. J. Wigginton. From Boone County, Conger worked on papers in Mexico, becoming an all-round printer, a forcible writer, always on the right side of questions, and providing an influence for good in his community. In late 1897, Conger produced a new process engraving, similar to the line-drawing technique. He claimed these engravings could be made in fifteen minutes at a cost not to exceed ten cents.[15]

The Mexico *Intelligencer* and other Missouri papers provided the training arena for Samuel Baker Cook, a transplanted Virginian with legal training. "Though not college-bred," he was considered a student, learned in books and men, honest and truthful in politics as in business.[16]

From New York came Warren D. Crandall to serve in the Civil War and to practice law before entering journalism in 1870. He never lost his interest in politics and in 1889 became postmaster in Brookfield, where he owned the *Gazette*. Through editorials Crandall preached the doctrine of the temperance movement.[17]

In newspaper work for some forty years was Thomas R. Dodge, who died in 1891. His career was spent on the New London *Ralls County Record*, the Vandalia *Leader*, and later, the *Graphic* there.[18]

General Dan M. Draper of the Danville *Star* was a Pike County boy who served in the Union Army. Early known as a handsome and talented editor, Draper later went to Colorado for railroad work. When seen a few years later by some Missouri friends there, his "head was frosted with white."[19]

Lucian Johnson Eastin was truly a pioneer Missouri editor. Born in Kentucky in 1814, he came to Missouri twenty years later, trained as a printer. He was associated with many papers, including the Palmyra *Marion Journal*, Paris *Missouri Sentinel*, Glasgow *Pilot*, Jefferson City *Inquirer*, St. Joseph *Gazette*, Chillicothe *Chronicle*, Glasgow *Journal*, and others in Kansas and Iowa. He was so anxious to participate in the Mexican War that he walked across the plains to New Mexico and took part in three battles.[20]

Howard Ellis of the *Montgomery County Leader* was born in New Florence. A "young man of exemplary habits, careful in his calculations, and one who possessed an unusual degree of characteristics recognized among the fraternity as essential to success in practical newspaper work," Ellis was original, though not eccentric, inclined to deal with facts rather than fancy.[21]

Henry W. Ewing of the Jefferson City *Tribune* was popular with all classes of people. He mingled with governors, went on duck hunts with millionaires, and yet voiced warm sympathy for the masses. He headed his law class at the University of Missouri, where he was a classmate of Eugene Field. Ewing's work was evident in the development of journalism at the University and in the founding of the *University Missourian* in 1908. He was a "scholar, journalist, and political counselor."[22]

PRESS HIDDEN DURING WAR

Intelligence and fair treatment were characteristics that brought A. N. Evans of the Harwood *Citizen* to the attention of his colleagues. After learning to set type on the Schell City *News* when quite young, Evans developed a splendid editorial talent and combined quietness in manner with a quick sense of humor.[23]

Jacob Graf started the Hermann *Volksblatt* in 1854, and although this book is not concerned with foreign-language papers, Graf's presence among the editors was evident at association gatherings. He came to Missouri from Switzerland with a university degree. In St. Louis he learned to set type before moving up the river, where he started his one-man shop and took an active part in the antislavery movement. When Graf went to serve in the Union Army he buried his press and equipment in his yard to prevent members of the proslavery element from destroying it.[24]

M. C. Falkenburg, founder of the *Southwest Leader* at Southwest City, was a practical printer, capable of writing the news in a pithy and sharp manner. Falkenburg was a Democrat and "in all his dealings and under all circumstances he didn't forget his politics nor his courage." He was always in the background, never an office-seeker.[25]

The Sedalia *Bazoo* became one of the most widely quoted papers in the state and its editor, J. West Goodwin, one of the best known. "J. West" stood for "John Wesley," his parents being ardent Methodists. When fourteen, Goodwin learned the printer's trade in his native New York, and as a tramp printer he reached Missouri after service in the Union Army. He worked briefly in

Springfield before he established the *Bazoo* in 1869. This peculiar title typified the manner of this brisk and penetrating paper. To the point of becoming involved in several fights, Goodwin defended his principles against all comers. Although a Democrat, Goodwin defended Republican politicians when he thought they were in the right. A friend said he could not give the editor's age, "but confidentially claim that in heart and mind he is no nearer a fossil than he was at thirty." Goodwin believed in first impressions as lasting ones and claimed that "if his paper was first read by the people, he would usually defeat the candidates whom he refused to support." Briefly he published a daily, later a monthly edition. After the 1893 panic he had only hope and energy, but eventually recovered.[26]

Omar D. Gray of the Sturgeon *Leader* was born in that community and learned the trade on the Louisiana *Press*. One of the state's most handsome editors (and among the few without a beard), Gray was a frequent speaker at association meetings and wrote widely. After two years at the University of Missouri, he purchased the *Leader* with $2.40 cash, "a sack of wind, plenty of nerve, and enough gall to make the combination complete and successful." For a brief time he published the Hallsville *Herald*. Forever in love with his profession, Gray was fond of music and of women's society. He sought to treat politics and political campaigns as mere incidents.[27]

Hiram J. Groves died from wounds suffered when one of his employes shot him as the result of "real or imagined wrongs" in the office of the Kansas City *Times*. Groves formerly worked on the Lexington *Intelligencer* and later on the Independence *Sentinel*. Once he remarked that the presidency of the Missouri Press Association was the only office to which he aspired; he was elected in 1899.[28]

C. M. Harrison of the Grant City *Star* was a man with a droll humor who wrote editorials free from assumption. Yet he was a journalist who could "do about as creditable a piece of 'hide-lifting' as one will find employed on the country press."[29]

From Kentucky came T. J. Hill to the Dexter *Messenger*. He was a "quiet, scholarly-appearing fellow who wore glasses and said little." His colleagues noted that he carried his religion with him every day, yet did not believe that a fast horse, a bicycle race, or an occasional glass that cheers were things to be avoided. His interests extended to machinery, and he had a mania for investigating the workings of every piece of press equipment with which he came in contact.[30]

SEVERAL WERE "COLONELS"

Charles C. Hilton of the Appleton City *Journal* was a congenial companion and a thorough, broad-gauged newspaperman. He took great interest in the press association, and a friend wrote that "we trust that when the newspaper boys have to leave the newspaper treadmill and get off the earth and are gathered together in that great day at the golden gate, that all of them will receive a pass from St. Peter to enter the eternal city, and that Charlie Hilton will not kick on any competitor who has ever 'scooped' him."[31]

Well educated and well read, Colonel R. C. Horne of the Marshall *Democrat-News* was first a lawyer but found the practice of law neither lucrative nor lively enough, so he turned to newspaper work. There he considered it his sacred duty to "lash into line all opposition and toward them he wielded a pen inked with venom."[32]

James A. Hudson, another "colonel," was editor of the Macon *Times* on which he started as a devil in 1872. Under Hudson, the *Times* was one of the few Democratic papers to advocate the gold standard in the late 1890's. Hudson once thought he could "find gold easier and quicker than in a print shop, so went west, hustled around for a few months scratching for the yellow stuff in the sand hills of Arizona, became disgusted, and returned to his first love and bought back the *Times*." Later he acquired a telephone firm and added farming and cattle raising to his enterprises, but never lost his love for the newspaper business.[33]

A. Y. Hull of the Sedalia *Democrat* was an early leader of the state press. When he retired in 1876, the Boonville *Advertiser* referred to Hull as "a man of strong convictions, a ready and forcible writer, and a man who worked hard for what was right and just." Although he later moved to Colorado, the attraction of journalism was too much, and Hull became editor of a Pueblo paper.[34]

Twice president of the association, John E. Hutton was a doctor and a lawyer before becoming publisher of the Mexico *Intelligencer*. Always interested in politics, Hutton was a forceful and eloquent speaker and in appearance and bearing was described as "a Chesterfield of courtly grace and dignity, handsome and prepossessing appearance, faultless dress, and a peculiar grace and attractiveness of manner, and a gentleman in the most chivalrous sense of that term."[35]

An all-round newspaper man who went from roller boy to editor and proprietor was John W. Jacks of the Montgomery *Standard* and several other papers. Jacks, when fourteen, worked on the Sturgeon *Independent* with the understanding that he would receive ten dollars a month for six months. Later his venture into photography failed, and he went to Mexico. Friends found him "void of any sanctimonious assumptions, a high-minded Christian considerate of others, one who allowed no extraneous influence to divert him from what he knew to be right." His prosperous paper was the result of his effort and his willingness to work.[36]

William O. L. Jewett of the Shelbina *Democrat* "was a thorough newspaperman, an elegant gentleman, and a forcible writer." Jewett was a leader in the association and instrumental in the development of the State Historical Society, serving as president of both groups. Originally from Maine, Jewett studied law, taught school, and served in the Civil War before becoming an editor in 1872.[37]

James C. Kerby learned the craft early in his father's plant, the Carrollton *Democrat*. His career in Missouri included brief stops in St. Joseph, Milan, Memphis, and West Plains before he went to Oklahoma after the turn of the century to work on a paper with his son. Kerby, one of the first presidents of the Southwest Missouri Press Association, was "an uncompromising Democrat."[38]

I. H. Kinley, progressive editor of the Brunswick *Brunswicker*, was first an enterprising lawyer in Indiana. After the Civil War, Kinley waged a fight against the test oaths and then moved into the newspaper field. He held several civil positions, including that of mayor, before moving to Kansas City where he resumed his legal work.[39]

John A. Knott of the Hannibal *Morning Journal* had "quickness of perception, intellectual vigor, tact, restless energy, and the push necessary for such a position." He worked on papers in Chamois, Linn, Troy, and Nevada, and "made every paper he touched successful." Called "a strong man among strong men," he had "the essential qualities of a statesman." Knott loved a joke as a robin does a sunny spring day.[40]

Lewis Lamkin first set type on the Jefferson City *Inquirer* in

1854. In 1899 he was still with the profession, as editor of the Lee's Summit *Journal*.[41]

Alexander A. Lesueur, an elegant gentleman, polite and accommodating, was with the Lexington *Intelligencer*. Lesueur served the Confederacy during the war and then entered newspaper work, opposing the celebrated Pat Donan of the Lexington *Caucasian*. While secretary of state, Lesueur made the "Blue Book" the official state publication. Earlier it had been sold on a subscription basis. Later he became part owner of the Kansas City *Times* and died in California in 1924.[42]

EARLY START FOR MANY

Leonidas Luther came to Missouri from Florida after learning the printing trade in Jacksonville. Before buying the Lamonte *Record* in 1884, he worked in New Orleans, Atlanta, St. Louis, Kansas City, and Sedalia. Lon, a "pronounced Democrat," was not an aggressive man, but conservative, and strong in his friendships. What he did in this world was "not accompanied with a brass band."[43]

From Canada came Charles M. McCrae to the Rolla *Herald*, a paper noted for its local coverage. McCrae was "a big-hearted and self-sacrificing person and the confidant and champion of every youngster who needed a friend." His family rated uppermost, and McCrae had no patience with scandalmongers.[44]

R. W. McMullin of the Hillsboro *Jefferson Democrat* could detect shams of every description; "surrender or compromise were words unknown" to him. Yet there was no one who could "more skillfully slash hypocrisy with his keen-edged satire." McMullin was endowed with "the faculty of expressing his meaning in homely, graphic phraseology that precisely suits the average reader and leaves no room for doubt or uncertainty."[45]

Charles T. McFarland of the Butler *Times* was active in the press association until illness forced him to move to Colorado, where he died in 1885.[46]

Abraham G. Mason came to Missouri from Kentucky and moved from apprentice to part owner of the Paris *Mercury* before going to Shelbina where he was associated with both the *Index* and the *Torchlight*. Colleagues called him "a genial, courteous gentleman, a writer of ability, high minded and truthful, fearless in his denunciations of wrong."[47]

Harry P. Mason of the Fayette *Leader* also was with the *Mercury*, which his father owned. Then he went to Shelbina. "His honesty was unimpeachable and his life above reproach," wrote a friend. Cheerful and generous in disposition, affable in manner, and faithful in the discharge of life's manifold duties and obligations, Mason was well liked.[48]

Papers in New London and Nevada provided the area for "Little Mitch," R. W. Mitchell, to work. He was a talented descriptive writer, "a lover of scenic gardens and the sublime in nature." Still, his editorials had considerable depth. In the Presbyterian Church he was an elder and Sunday-school superintendent.[49]

Walt M. Monroe started in the printer's trade when only eleven and became editor of the Tipton *Times,* one of the most influential papers in that area. "The *Times* partakes of the character of the editor," a friend wrote. "It is bold, independent and absolutely fearless, and therefore respected." Monroe never sought public office, because he had too much appreciation of his responsibilities as a journalist.[50]

C. D. Morris of the Trenton *Tribune* was "a well-rounded man physically, a breezy and pointed writer of the local department, always in earnest, but not sentimental." Being a son of a minister and married to a minister's daughter, Morris was active in the Methodist Church. He, too, shunned public office.[51]

James I. Nichols was "the handsome and popular senior editor" of the Fulton *Gazette.* His grandfather owned the land upon which a large portion of Fulton is located. Nichols was an educator before turning to newspaper work.[52]

A prominent editor at the turn of the century was William R. Painter of the Carrollton *Democrat.* Painter, who was lieutenant governor in 1912, held other state offices, with hospitals and eleemosynary institutions occupying much of his attention. When he passed his eightieth birthday, Painter said, "Life has been my hobby and I have enjoyed it."[53]

Thomas W. Park, whose son later became a governor of Missouri, was with the Platte City *Landmark.* Earlier he had founded the *Reveille* there after service in the Confederate Army. Park was the subject of a poem by Eugene Field, "Tom Park at Fredericktown," read during the press association meeting there in 1877.[54]

J. Kelly Pool of the Centralia *Courier* and later in Jefferson City, gave up a teaching job paying $100 monthly to embark in journalism. But Pool was in love with this work and "put his whole soul into the newspaper." He was careless about his appearance, yet was noted as an orator. The fact that he did not swear, drink, nor gamble was unusual enough for other newsmen to comment.[55]

The Trenton *Republican's* W. B. Rogers was one man who spent the best years of his life standing up for Missouri, motivated by an intense love for his home and family ties. He came from Ohio, covering much of the journey on foot. Rogers worked on a farm, later taught school for $25 a month, and served in the Civil War before he took over the *Grand River Republican*, renaming it the *Republican*. A strong prohibitionist, Rogers refused liquor advertisements and apparently practiced the philosophy he preached. He served as a state senator, too.[56]

Perry Scott Rader of the Brunswick *Brunswicker* was a man of dignity and honor. A college graduate who studied law, Rader turned to journalism where "he solicited a broader and more useful field for the exercise of his capacities—one in which he could be more useful to others." He won his spurs early and became a top editorial writer.[57]

LIBRARY OF 3,500 VOLUMES

Wesley L. Robertson was identified with journalism from the time he became a printer's devil at seventeen on an Iowa paper. He was with the Princeton *Advance*, Bethany *Broadaxe*, Unionville *New Century*, Plattsburg *Jeffersonian*, and the West Plains *Gazette*, but spent more time in Gallatin, where the *Democrat* was one of the party's leading papers. In 1919 he was killed by a city official who disagreed with some of his political writings.[58]

Hamline E. Robinson came to Missouri from Vermont after war service. In 1870 he was a dentist in Maryville, but the next year he purchased the *Republican*. Robinson, who held several political jobs, had a library of 3,500 volumes, including 500 books on metaphysics. Always an omnivorous reader, Robinson was interested in genealogical studies and wrote several books about Nodaway County.[59]

W. P. Ruffel of the Glasgow *Missourian* was born in that community and grew up "just a natural boy," playing hooky with the others. He learned printing on the *Journal* and after working in other towns returned home. "A man of fine physique and popular manners, a valued friend and an enemy to be feared, an inexhaustible fund of information, and a teller of good stories" served to describe Ruffel. He was careful in his expenditures, yet was "not niggardly nor close."[60]

The editor of the Crawford *Mirror*, B. F. Russell, once served as speaker of the Missouri House of Representatives. At the age of twelve, he was a carrier on a Maine paper. Coming to Missouri, he first worked in Steelville. Russell, a Republican, was active in party affairs, being reading clerk at the 1890 and 1894 national conventions. His *Mirror* was "an aggressive, positive and well-conducted" publication.[61]

Richard B. Speed was on the Warrenton *Banner* when it won top awards in typography, and on the Nevada *Mail*. A colleague said he supposed "Speed had his faults. All of us have, but I never knew what Speed's were. To me he was always the just, generous and noble man," who acquired his knowledge of the profession on the job, his school days being limited.[62]

Colonel William F. Switzler for years was a guiding light in the state press. The Columbia editor came from Kentucky and studied law before engaging in newspaper work. Although he once edited the St. Joseph *Chronicle*, his long career is associated with Columbia, the *Patriot* and the *Statesman* published there, and the many official positions he held. It was said of Switzler that "he had such a remarkable memory that he could have written a history of Missouri without any reference books."[63]

Edwin W. Stephens, born in Columbia where he was the successful publisher of the *Herald*, later became a prominent book publisher noted for the typographical excellence of his work. His activities in the press association have been mentioned, with special credit to his name for establishing the State Historical Society and the School of Journalism. He was vice-president of the National Editorial Association and held a similar position in the World's Press Congress.[64]

James B. Thompson was an outstanding writer of business and political editorials for the LaPlata *Home Press* and Lancaster *Excelsior*. He was on several Missouri papers, in Glasgow, Huntsville, and Moberly. After serving in the Confederate Army, Thompson held a number of civic positions, and though in ill health for several years, he continued to write his widely quoted editorials.[65]

George W. Trigg of the Richmond *Conservator* was "endowed by nature with that qualification so often commended at the press association meetings—courage, a keen perception of the responsibilities of the journalist, and a purpose to elevate the profession. Wit, humor, always found on the right side of society." He was a strong, vigorous writer who entered newspaper work after engaging in several other jobs.[66]

Joseph H. Turner, publisher of the Carrollton *Record,* came to Missouri from Massachusetts by way of Iowa. Being a Northerner, he was not well received in Carrollton, where his office was burned within four months of his arrival. He rebuilt, only to lose everything in another fire ten years later. However, despite being labeled as "a Yankee who had come uninvited to the community," he stayed and acquired many friends before his death in 1888.[67]

Robert M. White of the Mexico *Ledger* was one of the best-known editors about the nation. Friends described him as "a hustler, a good fellow in the best sense of the phrase and a man of a force peculiarly his own." He was "open, blunt, and direct, physically well endowed," one who "moves like a human hurricane." A friend described White's return from the daily walk to the postoffice in this way: "He would get fifty letters. . . . On his way to his own publishing house he would dispose of all of this mail. The money and subscription memoranda would go into one pocket; the letters of inquiry into another; the orders and miscellaneous matters in another—all classified with hurried care."[68]

W. C. Van Cleve, editor of the Moberly *Democrat,* was credited with doing well in a poor newspaper town. "He cares little for dress and less for society, but he had been found guilty of having driven fifteen miles in a severe snowstorm to see a maiden he once dreamed extensively and exclusively of," wrote a friend, Omar D. Gray, who, too, was noted for such interests.[69]

T. B. White of the Warsaw *Enterprise* came up the ranks from the role of printer's devil. Born in Ohio, White served under Garfield in the Civil War. His knowledge of journalism was so broad that he was equally at home in the news room, the editorial chair, or the business office. White, always a stickler for good rates both from advertisements and job work, was considered a companionable gentleman.[70]

Charles H. Whitaker of the Clinton *Democrat* worked on Switzler's *Missouri Statesman* in 1858. In 1860 he bought the Savannah *Plaindealer* and later acquired the *Democrat.* "A keen partisan, he can give or take a sharp thrust with equal *sang froid,* but he detests and avoids undignified and vituperative controversies," according to a friend.[71]

C. B. Wilkinson of the St. Joseph *Herald* was "one of the most fertile and resourceful writers of his time, and at home in all departments of a great paper." He learned printing in his native New York before the Civil War. In that conflict he was a correspondent for New York and St. Louis papers.[72]

Volumes could be written about Walter Williams. He, too, started as a printer's devil, on the Boonville *Topic*. By the time he was nineteen, he was part owner and editor of the *Advertiser* there. Later he was with the Columbia *Herald* and the Jefferson City *State Tribune*. Williams' reputation in education is based on his early interest in a school of journalism, to the deanship of the school, and in 1930 to the presidency of the University of Missouri.[73]

CONCLUSION

What, then, was the composite editor like?

Some came directly from their apprenticeship training to the editor's chair; many turned to journalism after experiencing work in the legal and medical professions, or in teaching. A few used the papers to jump into the political arena, a situation that prompted Williams to write in 1898 about

> an unusual number of Missouri editors who held federal and state offices. . . . They have comprised very many of our brightest and best brethren, and without exception they have discharged their duties well. . . . They saved no money out of their salaries, did not add especially to their fame, had either to give up their papers or let them run down, and came back to them less fit to manage them than when they left them. The indolence of public office is very different from the industry necessary to a paper. It spoils an editor very quick, makes him inert, fat, and beefy. In the long run it will pay the editor to stick to his business, work it thoroughly and if his field is too limited, change it. He will grow more intellectually, financially, and in public confidence. Offices are a delusion and a snare. Politics is a humbug. It will do for broken-down lawyers, or people who are failures at everything else. But the live, independent, influential editor had better let it alone.[74]

Editors were not reluctant to comment about weaker members within their ranks. Press association members heard about "the little one-horse editors who are continually begging and whining for something to eat" and about "the insatiate desire to please everybody at the same time." Editors admitted some of their colleagues had left the farm and jumped into journalism too early. Such an act was compared to an uneducated man asking for the privilege of practicing law, or teaching, or compounding medicine.

Adam Rodemyre, long editor of the Centralia *Fireside Guard*, summed up his idea of the editor rather well, in a talk at the association meeting in 1889:

> The genuine editor is a man of multiplied employments and universal adaptability. . . . He who works with the silent powers of the brain, whose influence moulds the elements of society, and exalts the human race by pure and noble purpose, whose ambition is to elevate the people above the groveling instincts born in ignorance and degradation, occupies the very highest pinnacle upon the intellectual mountain that lifts its head far above the material world and his work lives forever.

Even before the turn of the century there were debates about the advantages and disadvantages of big-city versus small-town newspaper work. Williams agreed with a city newsman who commented in 1894 that he "would rather be the editor of a good country journal than to hold any other place in journalism; it is the most independent and self-satisfying of all newspaper positions." Williams admitted there were some limitations, yet concluded that the country editor "enjoys the consciousness of personal influence. He is his own master. If he is honest and true and intelligent, he moulds the thought of his constituency, and enjoys as much in their confidence and respect as though he swayed the destiny of states."[75]

Here, then, are the Missouri editors at the turn of the century, an influential, independent, and inspiring group of men.

CHAPTER XIV

HISTORICAL SOCIETY ESTABLISHED BY PRESS

THE STATE HISTORICAL SOCIETY of Missouri, containing one of the nation's largest collection of papers for any one state, received its inspiration from editors who visualized the far-reaching influence such a repository of documents would have. Four men gathered in Columbia in 1897 at the home of the editor of the *Herald*, E. W. Stephens, to map plans for this society. Others present were Walter Williams and two university professors, Isidor Loeb and F. C. Hicks. From this session developed the organization known across the nation today for its excellent file of newspapers and other historical material.[1]

The state had had such an organization in 1845, but this Missouri Historical and Philosophical Society died in 1849.[2] Nearly a half century later Williams drew upon his observations from wide travels to urge the creation of a new group. He, Stephens, and others turned to the press association for active support. During the association's winter meeting in Kansas City in 1898 the following resolution was passed:

> WHEREAS, It is the sense of the members of the Missouri Press Association . . . that this state should have a historical society embracing the whole state; therefore be it
>
> *Resolved,* That the president of this Association appoint a committee of five as an Executive Committee to prepare plans for the establishment of such a society, which shall report at the next meeting of the Association.[3]

Stephens was named to the committee, along with W. O. L. Jewett, Shelbina *Democrat;* A. A. Lesueur, Lexington *Intelligencer,* and then secretary of state; H. E. Robinson, Maryville *Republican;* and P. S. Rader, Brunswick *Brunswicker,* who also was the Supreme Court reporter. Stephens, Robinson, and Jewett later served as presidents of the society.

Editors had realized the need for such a repository to preserve papers, records, gifts, and other items of future value. When J. W. Barrett prepared his history of the first decade of the press association, he remarked about the difficulties encountered in locating material. In 1895, President John W. Jacks said, "A collection of all Missouri papers in connection with the State University would be of inestimable value and could easily be provided. No better history of the state could be made than the papers would furnish."[4] The following year Association President Robinson stressed again the need to preserve the group's archives. The minutes record with frequency historical talks given to the association, although many lacked the specific data that would make them of adequate value for research purposes today.

The meeting in Stephens' home was a natural outgrowth of years of thought concerning this project. When the committee reported in May, 1898, three editors were appointed to frame the society's constitution and bylaws in proper style: Williams, Columbia *Herald;* W. R. Painter, Carrollton *Democrat;* and W. B. Rogers, Trenton *Republican.*[5]

The University of Missouri Board of Curators agreed to provide a room in Academic Hall to house the historical documents, but lacked funds to employ any personnel. Thus, on May 26, 1898, the State Historical Society of Missouri was founded by the Missouri Press Association. The object of the society was to be

> the collection, preservation, exhibition and publication of materials for the study of history, especially the history of this State and of the Middle West; to this end, exploring the archaeology of said region, acquiring documents and manuscripts, obtaining narratives and records of pioneers, conducting a library of historical reference, maintaining a gallery of historical portraiture and an ethnological and historical museum, publishing and otherwise diffusing information relative to the history of the region, and in general encouraging and developing within this state the study of history.[6]

Stephens, the logical choice, became the first president, Dr. Loeb the first secretary. Loeb continued as a teacher in the university's history and political economy department. He trained Floyd C. Shoemaker, who followed Francis A. Sampson as secretary. Sampson, from Sedalia, was "a born bibliographer and a born collector," who assembled a library of Missouriana that became a vital part of the society's records. Taking office in May, 1902, at $125 a month, Sampson brought 16,166 books and pamphlets on Missouri history to the society. This collection has been valued at more than $100,000. When Shoemaker became secretary in 1915, after five years as assistant secretary, Sampson became the bibliographer.

After taking office, Loeb appealed to the editors for aid. In a letter to the editors, he reviewed the objectives of the society and urged them to contribute their newspapers and other periodicals. The first appeal brought 203 papers and periodicals, along with many books and pamphlets to the society.

A significant step was taken in 1899, which resulted in the society becoming the trustee for the state. Passed by the Fortieth General Assembly, this bill became law when approved by Governor Lon V. Stephens on May 4, 1899.[7]

During the society's first twenty years, Missouri publishers provided its dominant moral support, contributing their newspapers for permanent filing. By September, 1901, the society had its first paid employe, Minnie Organ, who later wrote an important contribution on the county press in the state. By the end of 1902 there were 1,136 bound volumes of papers and periodicals in the society's collection. The society was in charge of the newspaper exhibit at the Louisiana Purchase Exposition in St. Louis in 1904. When fire broke out there, Williams and his crew saved the 928 bound volumes of 764 Missouri papers and magazines that had been published during 1904.

The *Missouri Historical Review* quarterly has faithfully recorded since 1906 the state's history through the printing of many articles especially written for the publication and through the condensation of masters' and doctoral theses presented at the University of Missouri. The *Review*, too, has been valuable in calling its readers' attention to articles about Missouri and Missourians that appear in other publications. The state group has also worked with other organizations in establishing the Mississippi Valley Historical Association.

Loeb reported to the press association in 1899 that "The society was organized upon the idea that the papers would be its best allies and that their support was absolutely necessary to success." He urged editors to push for state appropriations for support of the society. Stephens suggested the incorporation of the society, and a committee was named. He reported in 1901, "On February 14, 1899, E. W. Stephens, Perry S. Rader and Isidor Loeb presented a petition to the Circuit Court of Boone County for a pro forma decree for the incorporation of the society. This decree was tendered on February 22 and the Articles of Incorporation were certified by the secretary of state on March 9, 1899."[8]

The Forty-first General Assembly in 1901 appropriated $4,500 for the work of the society, primarily for binding and preserving books and periodicals. This was the first state contribution of funds, and in 1902 Sampson said, "No work inaugurated by this association is destined to be of more value" than these files.

During the 1903 winter session of the Missouri Press Association the editors pointed "with pride to the great progress which has been achieved by the State Historical Society of Missouri, which was founded by this association." The association further recommended a state appropriation of $16,300 for the biennium. The General Assembly was asked "to make provision for the erection of a library building similar to that which has recently been completed for the joint use of the Wisconsin Historical Society and the library of Wisconsin University."[9] During the regular session that August, Association President Howard Ellis spoke of a recent $5,000 appropriation for the biennium, and urged editors to "be diligent in every work looking to its advancement and lodgment. No means should be spared to secure a permanent and commodious building for its home and in which should be the headquarters of this association and a repository for its archives."[10]

Sampson reported in 1904 that he had received more than 10,000 publications for the society's collection since early 1903. He urged all members—and all editors who sent their papers to the society were members—to donate periodicals and copies of all pamphlets printed by them such as catalogs, school board reports, minutes of religious associations, ordinances of towns, and the like.

In the first issue of the *Review* under Shoemaker in 1915 he listed 401 "Historical Articles in Missouri Newspapers, April-May 1915," showing how carefully these papers were eyed when received in Columbia. Later this list developed into a section called "Missouri History Not Found in Textbooks," a valuable reference source today. Shoemaker also began the series of the historic markers on the highways.

The press association continued its support for the society. In 1912 a resolution urged the immediate construction of a new fireproof library for the society, and three years later the move was made into the new University of Missouri Library. The society occupied quarters in that area until the Library was enlarged in 1961 when new, larger offices and file areas were provided.

Dr. Elmer Ellis, in 1949 dean of the university College of

Arts and Science, wrote about the work of the society, presenting a concise picture of its achievements:

> The contribution of the society to higher education is, also, as a collector and preserver of historical records. It has acquired in its own possession a vast accumulation of records, many of which might have been lost permanently to historical scholarship had the society not secured them and protected them. In a different way, it has preserved other records by stimulating, through its work, the organization of county historical societies to preserve local records and historical monuments, as well as to develop interesting local history.
>
> Another contribution the society has made to the field of scholarship is in the publication of historical sources, making them available for the use of scholars and teachers everywhere. Most of these have been published in the *Review*. . . .
>
> The society is also an educator of the people of the state and of the nation about Missouri history. In this aspect, there can be no question that the State Historical Society of Missouri is the most successful of all societies. Not only is the *Review* the most widely circulated, but it is the most widely read historical journal in America because of the nice balance it maintains between sound scholarship and popular interest. It is as widely diversified in the interests it serves as the library resources of the society which maintains it. "This Week in Missouri History" is a unique feature of the society's service that reaches a still higher audience than the *Review*. Not only is it an attractive feature in Missouri newspapers for which they might easily be paying a substantial sum, but it is an instrument of education which supplements the work of the scholars in making Missourians acutely conscious of their past. It and the *Review* perform a special function for higher education and scholarship. The scholar in all fields meets a serious problem in communicating his findings to the public. The society has developed by these two methods a means of translating the results of historical scholarship to a large public in an unusually effective manner.[11]

Dozens of research projects undertaken by graduate students of the University of Missouri and other educational institutions have been based on material obtained from the thousands of papers on file. Researchers of family histories have found these useful as well.

Dr. Richard S. Brownlee became director and secretary of the society in 1960 and in his first message to members said, "Its newspaper library is unique, perhaps the greatest, and certainly the most complete in the nation." He reminded all that "it is not a museum and it is not a social organization of antiquarians. It is a center for serious historical research and a heavily utilized service institution for citizens of the state." In relating highlights about 1961, Dr. Brownlee said the estimated cash value of the society's holdings exceeds by $200,000 the total appropriations the society has received since its founding in 1898.[12]

In 1937 the society became the largest in the nation and has maintained this status since. Presently, there are more than fourteen thousand members. In recent years newspaper cartoons have been added to the collections, including more than 1,300 originals by Daniel R. Fitzpatrick of the St. Louis *Post-Dispatch*, by S. J. Ray of the Kansas City *Star*, by Bill Mauldin of the St. Louis *Post-Dispatch*, and by Don Hesse of the *Globe-Democrat*.

In addition, the society also has the J. Christian Bay Collection of Middle Western Americana, the Thomas Hart Benton and George Caleb Bingham art collections, as well as special collections concerning Mark Twain, Eugene Field, and other prominent Missourians.[13]

The following facts are paraphrased from an article by Daniel H. Spies, former researcher for the society, bringing up to date the expansion of holdings since 1898:

The manuscript collections include 251,000 original manuscript pages, 1,645,598 manuscript pages on microfilm, 150,000 state archival items, and 71,000 letters. The society also has more than 17,520 newspaper articles of historical importance and more than 30,000 illustrations. In the newspaper department there are more than 24,160 bound volumes, and in the microfilm reading room there are more than ten million pages on papers. Current papers are received from all counties and important communities in the state, with approximately one million pages microfilmed annually.

The William T. League Collection, acquired in the 1920's, was a particularly valuable addition because it includes the Hannibal papers published when Orion Clemens was editor and Samuel L. Clemens was a young man.

The Missouri Newspaper Subject Index lists the contents of selected bound files of state papers. Like the "Who's Who in Missouri" biographical card index, this index is indispensable as a time-saving research device. Patterned after the *New York Times Index*, the society's subject index includes important local subjects. From the smallest want ad to the biggest story, fingertip accessibility is possible. Papers covered by the index include all Boonville files in the society's library from 1839 to 1927, the Columbia *Missourian* 1908-1929, Jefferson City papers 1831-1926, *Missouri Intelligencer* of Franklin, Fayette, and Columbia, 1819-1826, St. Louis *Missouri Gazette* 1808-1828 and *Missouri Argus* 1835-1840, and the Liberty *Tribune* 1846-1869. This complete index consists of 402,908 cards. In addition to all these source materials, the society has compiled and published nearly one hundred volumes of historical material.[14]

In his annual report in 1963 Dr. Brownlee announced the consolidation of the Manuscripts Collection of the society with that of the university's Western Historical Manuscripts Collection. In addition to the listing of Missouri newspapers noted in the Preface, the society published *Missouri Historic Sites Catalogue* by Mrs. Dorothy Caldwell in 1964.

In addition to the three presidents of the society cited earlier (Stephens, Robinson, and Jewett), other Missouri publishers and newsmen have served in this capacity. They include William N. Southern, Independence; Robert M. White and his son, L. Mitchell White, of Mexico; E. E. Swain, Kirksville; E. L. Dale, Carthage; Walter B. Stevens, St. Louis; and others who served as trustees.

Missouri publishers, who could "point with pride" at their role in the founding of the State Historical Society of Missouri, can continue to take credit for supporting its program and activities today.

CHAPTER XV

NEW CENTURY REACHED: PRESS AT PEAK

THE NUMBER of papers in Missouri reached its peak at the turn of the century, when nearly nine hundred publications appeared regularly. Even this figure, as recorded in national directories, may have been incomplete, since some publishers objected to submitting data about their circulations. The *Country Editor* in 1897 noted the omission of many prominent Missouri papers and concluded that if as many were left out of the listings for other states "the directory is a humbug."[1]

The gathering of news as a major function of the papers was gaining in importance, a trend that started during the Civil War. No longer did editors bury news to play up political sentiments. Seldom did advertisements cover the front pages. True, some papers still dragged their heels, so to speak, but these were few. Politics was still an important news area, but name-calling techniques that characterized earlier years continued to decline. In Sedalia one editor criticized another for using personal journalism techniques, saying that his story "was in thought, letter and word a devilish lie, written and printed in malice, which could only emanate from the depraved heart of a coward and a scoundrel." Such controversy was unworthy of decent papers, the editor suggested, and ought to be left to the city press.[2]

Metropolitan papers set the pace in production, adopting the latest in equipment while passing along their older items to smaller, outstate publications. During the 1880's the typewriter gained in use in St. Louis, although in Kansas City reporters on the *Star* learned that Nelson objected to their using the machine, in the opinion that the typewriter handicapped their thinking. A better stereotyping process was developed, and this, with the newer presses, permitted the publishers to produce their editions in less time. By 1898 the St. Louis papers were using halftone illustrations, replacing woodcuts.[3] Earlier, in 1872, the St. Louis *Republican* boasted of a Walter press and a Bullock perfecting press, both using rolls of paper rather than single sheets. The Linotype, first used on the New York *Tribune* in 1886, appeared in the St. Louis *Globe-Democrat* plant in 1894. This typesetting machine cost some printers their jobs, despite their earlier predictions that "you can't make a machine with brains." A few editors viewed the threat of the machine as a blessing that would force printers to maintain more regular habits and to curtail their practice of frequently moving about the country. When new equipment was purchased, the publishers held public displays. For example, in 1900 the Sosey brothers, publishers of the Palmyra *Spectator*, held an open house to show off a new folder, a new engine, and a Simplex typesetter.

There followed a decline in the use of the readyprint material that had appealed so widely to publishers after the Civil War. With newer equipment came higher publishing costs. Before 1900 it had not been difficult for one to establish a paper. Frank Luther Mott points out that the typical small plant before 1900 in which he received his early experiences usually had some old and rather well-worn equipment, such as type stands and cases, as well as presses which reflected the result of long use. The dean of journalism history remarked that he and his father frequently used type too worn to give perfect reproduction, but this was the practice of his day. Manufacturers of printing equipment frequently exchanged new items for advertisements in the papers, much as the grocer exchanged his food products for sales messages in the paper. Mott recalls that much of the "mechanical operation" of his day was old-fashioned hand- and foot-power. This method of producing a paper, however, was changing. Editors who formerly operated on a narrow margin of profit found it too costly to gamble on an expensive piece of new machinery. Some city newspapermen even predicted the weekly had become a thing of the past, its days numbered. However, even in 1963 some Missouri newspapers were still being set by hand and being published on aged presses.[5]

Newsprint costs increased, although the prices paid would appear moderate to today's publishers. Newsprint was three cents a pound in 1892, though larger users paid less; publishers of weekly papers paid the highest prices until they established co-operative buying. Some editors urged the construction of a paper mill in Missouri to break what they termed a monopoly; others turned their pleas to their congressmen, while some raised their subscription rates, generally from one dollar to one dollar and a half annually for the weeklies. Manufacturers of typesetting machines and presses suggested that publishers could save more money by purchasing newer equipment.

Changes in operation and in costs were discussed at press meetings and in articles in the journals. For example, in 1898

R. H. Lindsay, managing editor of the Kansas City *Times*, discussed "The Relation of the Metropolitan to the Country Press," concluding, "The metropolitan press may inaugurate but the country press must carry out. The ammunition is supplied by the daily newspapers but the practical uses to which it is put must come largely through the country press. The cordial cooperation of these most important forces is not only desirable but necessary if the proverbial power of the press is to be perpetuated."[6]

Other differences were remarked by Walter Williams, in discussing the earnings on the smaller paper. Williams said that it was a mistake to suppose there was no profit in a country paper, although a few did expect to live by glory alone. But

> many have accumulated money, built houses, and made investments, educated their children and lived well from the earnings of a village journal. . . . The pauper editor is a thing of the past save where he resurrects himself. Given a good paper—which every editor can make—in a good field—which not every editor has—and a fair circulation and patronage which industry secures, and a county-seat journal will pay its owner, after deducting the actual expense of getting out the paper, at least $900 a year. And $900 in the country means $1,500 in a city. This should be the minimum and from this amount to $2,000 and over the paper will pay if the conditions referred to are favorable.[7]

The transition from the political organ to a more news-minded paper can be seen in comments on the ideal country paper, as voiced by the Salisbury *Democrat* in 1897. This paper called for more editorial backbone, more spirit, more vigor, more fire, more individuality.

> The country newspaper cannot take its proper place in a community unless it takes upon itself the duty and, without it, it is merely a commercial adventure. It must learn to interest itself in all public affairs. If it discovers an effort to loot its constituency, it must not hesitate to expose it, and it cannot afford to count the enemies that it will make by such exposition. It must guard public interests and declare for progress. Indeed, the ideal country paper should be the keeper of the conscience of the town in which it is published. But how few publications approach this standard! You can almost count them on your fingers. . . . Few men admire cowards, and a cowardly newspaper is as repulsive as a cowardly man.[8]

This change from personal journalism to more objective journalism is detected in an article in the *Missouri Editor* in 1895.

"The news columns should be equally as free from prejudice as the editorial. They should be truthful to the last degree. . . . It requires a high journalistic sense to divest a paper of prejudice, for editors are human, but no paper will get there until it eliminates every vestige of it."[9]

CORRESPONDENT COPY STRESSED

Some family papers continued, with the duties handled by members of the group. However, with the emphasis on more complete reporting, use of photographs, better presses, more complex typesetting machines and the like, the publishers found it necessary to employ more trained workers.

Slight change appeared, however, in the role of the country correspondent. Successful papers continued to follow Williams' advice to have every postoffice or section of the county represented by an active, wide-awake, reliable correspondent who would send each week the personals, stock news, marriages, deaths, and other local items. "These small items often seem trivial to the editor but they attract and hold the country subscriber without whom the newspaper would not exist." Edit to avoid free advertising, he warned, but use caution in removing an item just because it appeared unimportant. "Correspondents can usually be secured by an expenditure of stamps and stationery, but if necessary pay for them and pay well. They are worth it."[10]

How to make money, and how to spend it wisely? Those were topics discussed by the editors. Some talked about libel, at the association sessions, but Williams thought time so spent was wasted, since "not one country editor in a thousand is ever sued for libel. Sometimes he ought to be and isn't."[11] However, Williams changed his mind on this matter and later ran a series of articles in the *Country Editor* on libel.

Circulation continued to increase, although many weeklies were in the 300 to 600 class. The smallest circulation reported for 1900 was 264 for the Rutledge *Record*, printed in a community of 292, followed by the Creighton *News*, with 275 in a community of 360. The smaller dailies, led by the Charleston *Enterprise*, with 250 subscribers, had their problems. The Charleston *News* noted that one editor in 1897 was losing ten dollars a week on his daily, which prompted the Cape Girardeau *Press* to remark, "There is not a town in Southeast Missouri sufficiently advanced to sustain a daily paper."[12] In St. Louis, the *Post-Dis-*

patch led with 94,000 for the week-day edition, while Sunday editions frequently went as high as 140,000.

Better Advertising Urged

An indication of the interest editors expressed in the wise use of their space can be seen in this exchange of comments by Missouri papers. The Columbia *Herald* noted in 1898:

> Boone County had 270 marriages last year. This is $270 for marriage license fees. Then the preacher was paid $5, which amounts to $1,350. The trousseau of the brides averaged $50 and the groom probably expended $50 more in getting slicked up. This would foot up to $27,000. At least $25 was paid out for wedding presents, or a total of $6,750. Adding these amounts, we find that the weddings in Boone County last year cost $35,370.

The Moberly *Monitor* was quick with a suggestion:

> We are surprised that the *Herald* did not call attention to the fact that each of the above marriages cost the papers $5, at least. Five dollars would be a low estimate of the cost of printing the marriage notices and afterwards a long, well written and frequently flattering report of the wedding. In other words, the papers, the public pack horses, donated $1,350 toward the union of loving hearts in Boone County last year. Why the newspaperman should donate $5 for every wedding in Boone County is not apparent. Sometimes, not often, he gets a microscopical and indigestible piece of wedding cake, and is expected to invest a few more dollars in a neat acknowledgment of the same. If the report of the marriage is made very flattering, and Mary Ann is made "a vision of loveliness" some of the family may come in and buy fifteen cents worth of papers. This occurs once in a while.[13]

Truly this was a period of transition to more evening papers. Missouri followed the trend, with sixty-one afternoon dailies and only ten morning dailies in 1900, including the foreign-language papers in the cities. Twenty-two published Sunday editions. Dependence upon the wire services and news agencies for stories increased, although this applied to city papers more than community publications. In 1895, fifteen Missouri dailies used the Associated Press, six the old United Press. These papers were in St. Louis, Kansas City, St. Joseph, Springfield, and Sedalia, and included four German-language dailies.

Missouri Press Association convention minutes record a continual struggle to improve advertising in order to bring in additional income. Editors were instructed in ways to solicit more merchants. Walter Williams urged greater attention to the appearance of the ads, making sure that they were set properly. "Study your exchanges and trade journals and catch new ideas and set them in such way as to attract the eye and please the advertiser," he advised. He also suggested that ads be edited carefully, since "the average man cannot write an advertisement." He urged more adaptation

> of the advertisement to the business as well as to the idiosyncracies of the advertiser. . . . Keep it alive and keep it moving about. Change its wording and its style. Make your advertising columns as fresh as your news columns. . . . They should sparkle with originality and glitter with taste. Only half the work is done when they are obtained; the more important half remains in preparing and setting and printing them well.[14]

Suggestions were made that more efforts be exerted to get church advertisements, classifieds from farmers, and legal copy. The *Missouri Editor* and the *Country Editor*, as it was later named, published lists of firms that failed to pay their national advertising accounts. Accounts that paid well were mentioned. Some editors wanted a uniform rate schedule, but this was never agreed upon at association conventions.

Conclusion

The press of Missouri in 1900 was in a strong position, well organized, and shifting the character of its papers from purely personal mouthpieces for the political parties to stronger publications that emphasized news, not only from the local scene, but from wider areas.

There was a growth in the independent press. Among the weeklies party lines still prevailed; Democratic papers led the Republicans, 46 per cent to 26 per cent of the totals. But independent papers were on the rise. Both dailies and weeklies increased; there was, however, a noticeable trend to fewer communities with competing papers. Subscribers still heard pleas to pay in advance; publishers offered prompt payers rates slightly lower than those charged the delinquents. Some problems continued, as indicated in a reply by the Lexington *Intelligencer* to an article in the Platte City *Landmark* in 1898 on "What Is Heaven?" Defined by the Lexington editor, it is

> to edit a well paying country paper with a large circulation and influence, the subscribers all pay in advance, and you don't have

to bid on every $3 job that comes in. If this is not heaven, it is
so much above the average newspaperman's lot that he would
think it heaven if he could attain it.[15]

Nevertheless, the position of the press in Missouri was good.
The papers were presenting the state's history and activities to
its people in a more informed, less biased manner. Problems
were ahead, however, and the press was to encounter wars in
the twentieth century, depressions, a continual decline in numbers of papers, and an increase in mechanization.

CHAPTER XVI

SCHOOL OF JOURNALISM ESTABLISHED

NEITHER debate nor opposition developed in the Missouri Press Association's support for the State Historical Society, but some editors professed doubts when the establishment of a "chair of journalism" at the University of Missouri was proposed. Along with the creation of the press association had come suggestions for some type of educational program to train journalists. In 1869 Norman J. Colman suggested at least "a course of study" in the field, and did not exclude the idea of a school or college.[1] In 1873, as part of the regular course in the College of Arts and Science, there was a series of lectures on journalism. Floyd Shoemaker in his unpublished history says,

> Colman was a Democrat, a man of influence, a patron of education, and a friend of James S. Rollins, a Democrat in 1873, who was the guiding hand behind University politics for nearly half a century. Moreover, in 1870-71, two Missouri editors were appointed to the Board of Curators—J. W. Barrett and Colman, the first two presidents of the association. These men were on the board for years and were close friends of the institution. That they all exerted an influence in the inception of this course of lectures in 1873 is probable.[2]

The following year Milo Blair of the Boonville *Eagle* spoke on the need for more education for editors. "The destiny of our country depends greatly on the influence which the press henceforward shall exert, and that influence will rest immeasurably on the kind of education and training which the editor has had and may still receive . . . journalism has a high and immortal mission to perform," he said.[3]

Joseph B. McCullagh of the St. Louis *Globe-Democrat* spoke on "Modern Journalism" in 1878 at the press association's meeting. "A few years ago it was proposed to establish a chair of journalism in one of the Eastern colleges," he said. "The idea received the hearty endorsement of many otherwise practical and sensible editors, but it was never carried into effect. Journalism can be learned by experience reinforced by natural aptitude, but it cannot be taught by theories or courses of study."[4]

Professor David R. McAnally, Jr., came to the University of Missouri in 1877 to teach English, history, elocution, and other courses. His appointment was called "a flattering and well deserved distinction" in the St. Louis *Republican*, although he was then on the *Globe-Democrat* staff. At a salary of $2,000 annually he became one of the twenty-seven teachers at the university. McAnally was listed in the 1878-1879 catalog as teaching a course described as "History of Journalism—Lectures with practical explanations of daily newspaper life. *The Spectator, The London Times,* and *New York Herald."* He remained at the university for eight years before returning to St. Louis to continue his newspaper work until his death in 1909. Speaking later about McAnally's career at the university, Casper S. Yost, editor of the *Globe-Democrat,* asserted that McAnally created this course "to promote vigorous and clear English, rather than to demonstrate practical journalism."[5]

Shortly before the turn of the century, pressure increased, especially within the Missouri Press Association, for a journalism program at the university. In 1895, an effort to establish a "chair of journalism" and to authorize a "bachelor of journalism degree" was defeated in the state Senate. This setback prompted the Missouri Press Association to work harder for the project, especially such members as E. W. Stephens of the Columbia *Herald.*

Late in 1895 the *Missouri Editor* reported on schools of journalism. Stephens and Williams wrote:

> Forty years ago schools to educate lawyers and doctors were laughed at; now, no lawyer or doctor can practice . . . without having passed through a technical school. So, there are now those who foolishly ridicule a school of journalism. Mark it. Within the present generation, they will be as prevalent and essential as schools of law or medicine. Why not? Journalism is as important and dignified, and is as much a profession as either law or medicine. . . . A school of journalism means elevation to our profession, better prices for what we sell, and larger prosperity and greater influence to all who belong to it. Every feature of the business can be taught in a school—from handling rollers to writing editorials, from setting type to keeping books, from buying material to clipping exchanges and giving the news. The newspapermen of Missouri who oppose the school of journalism stand in the way of progress and of their own best interests, for as surely as the new civilization is to be higher than the old it is coming.[6]

While Association members were enjoying a steamboat excursion down the Mississippi River in 1896, Stephens spoke about a school of journalism. "You will say that the place to educate a journalist is in the printing office, and that the only place for a man to learn to be a newspaper man is to be in a newspaper office." Stephens and Williams here repeated one of the most widely voiced opinions of those who opposed the school. Remarking the backgrounds of the medical and legal professions, they said journalists should be as well qualified.

> The modern idea of an education is to equip a man for his profession—a practical blacksmith, a practical farmer or a practical anything. . . . A school of this kind ought to be presided over by a thorough, practical journalist, a man who can write editorials, and teach a man how to select a subject for an editorial. A man who runs a school of journalism should teach reporting; it is more important than the editorial department. So in order to run a school of journalism we should have a man in charge who can give a thorough knowledge of this practical work. One of the most important things for a newspaper man to learn is how to write an advertisement himself. Very few men ever practice the art of writing an advertisement.

The editors claimed such a school would require no additional money, merely "the appointment of a teacher in the University and all we would have to do would be to establish a chair of journalism and the students would have the benefit of this journalistic education." They expressed confidence in Missouri newsmen, but admitted "there are men in this state who are positively unfit for the place they fill, and we need this school for our own protection; and I believe the time will come in the history of journalism when no man will be allowed to publish a newspaper who has not a license to publish it and who has not a moral character fitted for that profession." In urging the association to act, the article promised, "In ten years it will do more to elevate the young man of this state than anything that has ever been set on foot." The association did act, approving this statement:

> *Resolved,* That this Association looks favorably upon the plan to devote a chair in our State University to Journalism, and that the president is hereby requested to appoint a committee of three to press the subject upon the attention of the curators of that institution.

However, nine editors were named to the committee, which included A. A. Lesueur, Jefferson City; W. O. L. Jewett, Shelbina *Democrat;* Walter Williams, Columbia *Herald;* Joseph Flynn, DeSoto *Gazette;* W. J. Powell, Rolla *New Era;* W. L. Thomas, St. Louis *School and Home;* George W. Trigg, Richmond *Con-*

servator; Henry W. Ewing, Jefferson City *Tribune,* and Stephens.[7]

Apparently this pressure was felt both in Jefferson City and in Columbia. Within two years the Board of Curators, "in response to a request from the executive committee of the Missouri Press Association," directed that as soon as funds should become available a chair of journalism would be established. Appointed to map out a program of study were President R. H. Jesse, Dean H. J. Waters of the College of Agriculture, and Stephens. This phase of the project was completed, but the legislature refused to appropriate funds. Thus the fight for the school continued.[8]

In discussing their project, the state press offered many comments on the proposed school. The following are representative of the differing views:

> There is no profession where knowledge of all sorts is more immediately available than to that of journalism. Each professor who adds some grains of knowledge to the student's store adds something to his equipment as a possible journalist. . . . It is not believed that, however this branch of literary manufacture may be pushed at Columbia, the establishment will ever receive an order from any newspaper office for one complete journalist ready to work. The University should devote itself to the preparation of young people for immediate and practical use in this working world, leaving them to choose their own professions.— *Kansas City Star*
>
> Your local journalist . . . who dictates, at least in some degree, the class of matter your children and your neighbors may read and by which their moral, physical, mental and spiritual natures are either bettered or impaired, is turned loose without the restraint of proven fitness and may, like an unmuzzled swine in a garden of flowers, do great and lasting injury. . . . Then, in justice to humanity, the field of journalism should be safely guarded against ruthless invasion and stand open only to those whose fitness shall be proven before a competent board of examiners.— *Linneus Bulletin*
>
> The success of the proposed college of journalism will depend entirely upon the men who are given professorships. If hack newspapermen are chosen, or if the curators employ as lecturers "journalists" whose experience has been confined to small towns or agricultural journals in the cities, failure must inevitably follow. It is a question whether suitable men can be found for the positions. The truth is that a newspaper man who is competent to instruct students in journalism can command better wages than the University could probably afford to pay.—*Kansas City Times*
>
> A journalist ought by all means to have a college education,

and every other sort of education, but our fear is that the candidate may miss this in his anxiety to get close to the chair of journalism. However, President Jesse usually knows what he is about, and we shall await with interest the development of this department.—*Kansas City Journal*

The country needs more patriotic, informed journalists and the school will assist in furnishing them.—*Independence Sentinel*

So long as men can embark in the newspaper business without education, character, brains or money, there is very little inducement to take higher courses in journalism.—*Moberly Democrat*

Journalism must be learned by actual experience in a printing office instead of being imparted to students by men who, themselves, know nothing about it.—*Paris Appeal*[9]

Meanwhile, the Missouri Press Association continued its drive for the school. Robert M. White phrased his resolution presented at the 1903 meeting: "It is the sense of the Missouri Press Association that Mr. Pulitzer has wisely chosen a means of advancing the interest of the newspaper profession . . . in endowing an institution which promises not only to afford an opportunity to young men to prepare themselves thoroughly for the labor and responsibilities of newspaper work, but to raise the standard of ethics and excellence in American journalism."[10]

More Missouri newspapermen became impressed with the need for such a school when they met with visiting editors from over the world at the fair in St. Louis in 1904. Here the work of Walter Williams, as he talked with these editors, cannot be overpraised. By 1906, the university curators authorized the establishment of the School of Journalism, and some historians feel the delay permitted the school to open on a stronger foundation, the opposition having spent itself.[11]

Association members heard Williams report about their "child" after the school reached its first birthday in 1909.

> The school was to meet doubt and mistrust from some, misapprehension from others, and destructive criticism from a few. The needs of the first year compelled the adoption of a plan which was unfortunately seized upon as the "state competing with private enterprise." It was not regarded as proper for the state in training for journalism to permit the business men of Columbia to pay for the support of such public enterprise. The competition was not large if it really was competition.[12]

Williams wrote in the first edition of the school's paper, the *University Missourian,* "Its one purpose is well defined—that of affording on advanced educational lines training for journalism.

The laboratory is a necessity for this training." Some opposition appeared in the university campus paper, but according to Frank Rucker, in his biography of Williams, "The sputterings of the *Oven* were so ridiculous that the Board of Curators, the State Legislature and the alumni paid little attention to them." Here, and in other attacks, the opposition appeared at times aimed as much at Williams as toward the school.[13]

Williams, chairman of the Board of Curators' executive committee from 1898 to 1908, deserves credit for insisting on full school status, refusing to settle for a chair in the Department of English. No doubt he held up the action until much of the opposition had exhausted itself. For example, the Kansas City *Journal* in 1903 considered it as "absurd to expect a college professor to make a newspaper man as to expect a metaphysician to turn out a proficient carpenter." Five years later this same paper considered the appointment of Williams as the first dean of the school "one of the most fortunate things that could have happened to the University as well as to the State of Missouri."

Thus 1908 was the year. On March 31, the Board of Curators declared "If thirty students sign a petition asking that a School of Journalism be equipped with a laboratory and instructors, the new department will begin operation next September." Offers of assistance were received from the Associated Press and from press machinery firms. In April the legislature appropriated the necessary funds, and on July 1 Williams began his duties as dean. With more than seventy students enrolled, classes began on September 14. The next day these students prepared the first *University Missourian*. Assisting Williams on the faculty were Silas Bent, formerly with the St. Louis *Post-Dispatch*, and Charles G. Ross from the St. Louis *Republic*. Before the academic year was over, Frank L. Martin from the Kansas City *Star* replaced Bent. The catalog that year listed ten professional courses, and in many respects the basic requirements for entrance were similar to those today.

COMMENTS QUITE VARIED

Comments by Missouri newsmen in reviewing the founding of the school are interesting. The Columbia *Daily Tribune* said:

> The College of Journalism . . . will prove an addition to Missouri University's efficiency as a trainer of practical men. Experience in gathering facts and writing them out in readable style will be of value to every student who takes the work . . . its success will

be advertised and if the department achieves the degree of success it promises the good results will be felt by the whole University.[14]

"The *Missourian* is creditable in each department, neatly printed and full of life," said the Columbia *Statesman*. The dean's former paper, the *Missouri Herald*, declared that the supply of trained journalists failed to meet the demands and "There is no profession that calls for a higher standard of service and there is none so far reaching and beneficial . . . the School of Journalism will be . . . a power for the greatest good not only for publishers and writers, but for the reading public everywhere."[15]

The Hallsville *News* considered the newspaper a typographical beauty. "As a newspaper it excels the productions of many cities of twenty thousand population. It prints several feature columns that are peculiarly adapted to its columns alone, and in any others would be misfits." However, the *News* objected to the solicitation of advertising. In nearby Ashland, the *Bugle* said, "The paper is published to give students a breath of the real atmosphere of a newspaper office, let them sniff the odor of printer's ink, and experience the thrill of newspaper excitement." Later the *Bugle* said, "It may be true that journalism cannot be taught, but it is true that some journalists could be 'showed.' "[16] Bitter in its opposition to the school, the Centralia *Courier* asked:

> Why should the taxpayers of Missouri buy a printing outfit and employ newspaper men and printers to make experts in that line of business, any more than it should buy a blacksmith shop and then turn out smiths, or a dry goods store and make merchants, or a broom factory and educate broom makers? Are we not requiring the state to do too much when we undertake to have it teach the favored ones a trade? . . . There are things we must learn in the school of experience, and how to make a country newspaper a success is one of them. . . . We believe that the college of journalism is not only carrying the matter of education at the expense of the state far beyond the point of common justice to the taxpayers, but that it is thoroughly impracticable and will not make a successful journalist in a hundred years.[17]

Other interesting comments appeared across the state. The Rich Hill *Mining Review* objected to founding the school, saying, the school "seems to be all right as an advertising asset for that institution, but in practical results it will be a monumental failure." There is no marked line of procedure for a newspaper

writer, said the Lexington *News:* "He must strike boldly out for
his own particular goal and if he's got enough grey matter and
sand to overcome the buffetings of ignorance, selfishness and
superstition, he'll finally triumph . . . but a diploma won't cut
any ice in the newspaper profession because it's one line of work
where you 'can't hide the shells.'" However, the Sedalia *Ruralist*
said,

> The pioneers among our inhabitants can look back over the
> state's history for the past one or two decades and derive much
> pleasure from an observance of the great progress in all lines of
> activity. In none of these is greater advance apparent than that
> of journalism, but the latter has been dependent upon individual
> effort . . . now they are to have the inspiration imparted by the
> State School of Journalism.

"Bright prospects are before the new department," according
to the Independence *Examiner;* it had "full faith in its immediate
and abiding success." The St. Joseph *Gazette* observed, "Theo-
retically, the college idea is a very good one, but it remains to
be seen how favorably the work of the new reporter, who is sent
forth sheepskin in hand, will compare with the copy of another
who was raised on printer's ink." But the *Gazette* did concede
that "the paper now being issued by the University of Missouri
is one of unusual merit."[18]

Two days after the school opened, the St. Louis *Post-Dispatch*
made the following observations in its story:

> Dash and Class in the First Issue of the
> *University Missourian,* Daily Newspaper
> From the School of Journalism Presses
>
> Almost anyone, picking up almost anywhere the first issue of
> the *University Missourian,* published at Columbia, would read
> it through.
>
> This does not mean that the students of the new College of
> Journalism at the University have learned all, or anything, about
> newspaper work. It does mean that the men who have under-
> taken to teach them that work know how it should be done, and
> that if a student does not learn most of the essentials, it will be
> his own fault.
>
> The daily *University Missourian* is to be the "laboratory" prod-
> uct of the School of Journalism. The first issue necessarily was
> the work of the teachers. No amateur could have written the
> story of the Audrain County farmer's two leap year proposals,
> which held the place of honor in the right-hand column of the
> first page. This shorter "feature" story of the jailer who com-

plains of dull times since Columbia went dry, of the Egyptian "prince" who stayed in this country to sell real estate instead of going home to drive out the British, and of the new rule at the Christian Church, that college girls must not sit in the balcony, were also, obviously the work of trained writers.

It does not appear that anything of much moment happened at the University, or in or around Columbia, on the day of publication . . . the issue, so far as an outsider can see, was practically errorless. . . . Students are to be "broken in" at once as reporters. . . . [19]

Editorially, the St. Louis *Times* reported,

Dean Williams and his staff of able editors have begun publication of the first school journal of its kind. . . . The paper is surprisingly good in appearance, in technique and in the general character of its text. There is not a hint of amateur journalism in it. . . . There has been a feeling in interested circles that a school of journalism may be of some value to teach the theory of the art, but there has never been much enthusiasm over its worth in impressing the idea of practice upon the students. Mr. Williams and his confreres at Columbia have introduced not only theory but what seems to be very proper practice. Not many papers of any class in this country are handsomer in the general way than the *University Missourian*. In fact, the notable weak point, if one is to be found, lies in the paper's prettiness. It seems to bear a note of commercial impracticability.[20]

It was a "cleanly edited and printed journal" to the St. Louis *Republic*. Since the paper would cover the entire field, and not be limited to University news, the *Republic* considered such training "sufficiently broad to be valuable."[21] The St. Louis *Globe-Democrat* remarked, "The minutes cannot be lengthened, so the worker must be trained to adjust himself to their limitations. . . . The Columbia daily will be a positive record of both effort and restraint. It must fill its field according to the sweep of events that chooses its own hours and cannot be governed by schedule . . . the new Missouri idea in the collegiate study of newspaper work seems to open the right road."[22]

The Eighth Congressional District Editorial Association, in a session at Jefferson City, said the members "believe that the work of our University should be a pattern for all other schools of the kind and that it will prove of inestimable value to the profession in the state and the state itself."[23]

Captain Henry King, editor of the *Globe-Democrat*, wrote,

One of the things in my career that I regard with some pride is that I had the honor of delivering the initial address in the School of Journalism series at Columbia and you may remember that I then expressed the hope that journalism would be taught there by the practical method of publishing a daily newspaper. My belief is that this is the best, if not the only way to reach useful and satisfactory results.[24]

Another St. Louis newsman, Charles W. Knapp of the *Republic,* wrote he would be

much gratified if the Missouri University School of Journalism can be brought to a position which will justify it in taking rank with the schools of law and medicine now conducted at the University. There are very great differences . . . but in some measure, at least, specific direction to the line of instruction sought by a young man during his college course can rapidly fit him for more rapid progress in practical newspaper work . . . no diploma has ever put a lawyer or a doctor in the full tide of success as soon as he came out of school, and journalistic graduates must not be expected to escape the hard knocks of practical experience.[25]

Horatio W. Seymour, editor of the *Post-Dispatch,* was "confident that it will make a success. Education is a fine thing and really is necessary, but training, after all, is more to the point."[26]

"The Commoner," William Jennings Bryan, in the state at this time, was asked to comment on the experiment. He said, "I think that men can be taught to be journalists, just as men can be taught to be lawyers, doctors, or engineers. But I do think that the journalist in writing editorials should be taught to write only their honest convictions, and only what they are firmly convinced is true. I think the *University Missourian* is a newsy and well-edited newspaper."[27]

The next major step was the founding of Journalism Week. In 1910 "Editors' Week" was held, designed to serve the Missouri Press Association. Faculty members lectured, and journalists from other areas spoke on topics of concern to editors. Such a program was the first ever presented by an American university. Stressing the practical side, the program resembled, in part, the winter sessions held earlier by the association. The name was later changed to Journalism Week and more journalists from outside Missouri came to participate in the activities.[28] The variety of topics presented in 1910 has been continued during subsequent weeks. Publishers at this initial gathering heard talks on "The News as the City Editor Sees It," with seven metropolitan editors participating; "The Near City Daily," "The Country Daily," "Getting of Advertising," "The Newspaper's Obligation to the Farmer," etc.

Starting in 1912, the school published its Journalism Series Bulletin. The first, by Williams, was on "Missouri Laws Affecting Newspapers." Many Journalism Week talks were printed. In 1912 the press association amended its constitution to provide that one meeting of the group be held each year in Columbia during Journalism Week, "where lectures, displays, and other advantages can be had for a business session that cannot be had in any other town in the state."

A five-point program, set forth during Journalism Week in 1915, serves to indicate how the school, the editors, and publishers have united to promote the profession. These points include:

1. To provide the instruction necessary to a well-rounded education.

2. To train for newspaper work through professional instruction both in regular and summer terms at Columbia.

3. To publish a series of bulletins dealing with various phases of newspaper work.

4. To hold annually a Journalism Week to bring together newspaper men and women . . . for helpful interchange of opinion.

5. To serve the press of the state, and thereby serve the whole citizenship of the state in any way at its command.[29]

CHAPTER XVII

STATE AFFAIRS AFTER TURN OF CENTURY

MISSOURI, normally, has been a Democratic state and a conservative one. The role of the Democratic editors is reflected in a study of how many of the state's papers promoted their political beliefs. The growth of the Republican party can be assessed by its role in giving the state some semblance of a two-party system. However, one needs to use caution to avoid making any one-sided statements. A study of *Political Trends in Missouri, 1900-1954* by Morran D. Harris concludes that "The trend for the state as a whole has been Democratic. This . . . has not been uniform over the state. It would appear that the trend in rural Missouri has been slightly Republican, but this has been more than offset by the Democratic trend in the large metropolitan areas."[1]

Democrats captured control again in 1900 when Bryan carried the state with 351,922 votes to 314,092 for McKinley. Four other presidential candidates polled a combined total of less than 18,000. Alexander M. Dockery, Democratic candidate for the governorship, trailed his ticket slightly, but won the office with 350,045 votes, while the Republican candidate, Joseph Flory, received 317,905. Although they lost the contests, the Republicans did gain in votes. Urbanization had increased; that year only 36.3 per cent of Missourians lived in rural areas. This trend continued until 1950, when manufacturing replaced agriculture as the major source of employment in the state.

After 1904 Missouri no longer was a state that Democrats might safely place with the Solid South. That year the state favored Theodore Roosevelt over Alton B. Parker, Democrat, by more than 25,000 votes. Democrats continued to control the state, however, with Joseph W. Folk defeating Cyrus P. Walbridge, Republican, for the governorship. This Folk campaign attracted wide interest, both in and out of Missouri, and has been well recorded by Frances Patton Landen in a thesis. Folk was associated with the "tidal wave of reform that swept over the United States at the turn of the century." His drive against corruption in St. Louis while he was circuit attorney resulted in the indictment of thirteen Republican members of the House of Representatives, as well as six Democratic members. This pleased some of the Democratic press. The Kennett *Dunklin*

County Democrat coined the word "Folkacitis," a "new and alarming malady accompanied by colds, chills, loss of appetite, forgetfulness and inability to retain solid money." However, this political housecleaning evoked considerable response from outside the state; Folk became one of the prominent men in the national Democratic party organization.[2]

After Folk's star began to shine brightly on the political horizon, several papers claimed the honor of discovering him and urging his promotion to the governor's position. The St. Louis *Wetmore's Weekly*, LaGrange *Indicator*, and Sturgeon *Leader* were among the papers that recalled their early support for Folk.[3] Some editors backed Folk in 1904 after they failed to receive any state business in publishing the constitutional amendments of 1902. Omar D. Gray of the Sturgeon *Leader* carried on a running feud with J. Kelly Pool, then of the Centralia *Courier*, charging Pool supported the secretary of state, Sam B. Cook, for the governorship because Cook had arranged for printing business that aided the *Courier*. The Rich Hill *Western Enterprise*, on May 15, 1903, agreed with Gray, commenting that "Because Uncle Sam Cook has doled out backbones and spareribs to weaklings does not make him the logical candidate for governor. Two swallows (of Cardwell liquor) don't make a summer."[4]

Walter Williams, then editor of the Columbia *Herald*, supported Folk in his drive for good government but omitted his name from the potential candidates he listed early in 1903. Williams wanted to avoid any break within party ranks. "If Folk is nominated . . . the Democracy of Missouri will need all the votes it can muster in order to win."[5] Forty column inches were devoted to Folk by the Paris *Mercury*, which declared,

> No other man would be more acceptable to the Bryan wing of the party and at the same time excite so little opposition on the part of those conscientiously antagonistic to the double money standard. . . . No other man in the nation today is more fully incarnate with the growing idea of revolt against the commercialized ideals of government and certainly none stands out more thoroughly antagonistic to the slimy assertion of private graft in public places.

However, the *Mercury* later reversed itself, "accepting the rumor that Lon Stephens was on the reform slate to succeed Senator Francis Marion Cockrell and former Governor David R. Francis was to have the state delegation for President, but to be advanced under cover of Folk's boom for governor." Such party maneuverings stirred the *Mercury*, which said,

> Politics is hell. The *Mercury* had a few ideals, but they are tottering to a fall. . . . Time alone will develop whether or not Mr. Folk, prompted by ambition and seduced by the representations of designing politicians, has allowed himself to be used and his office prostituted by the most corrupt cabal that ever infested a political party in this country. If he has, the swift and sure condemnation of the party will overtake him.[6]

The Platte City *Landmark* defended Folk, but observed the same element that had disturbed the *Mercury*:

> Mr. Folk had a golden opportunity to deny the many reports that the Republican papers are putting out about the corrupt Democratic state administration. But he did not say one word about this matter or deny a single report that the Republican party has been putting out about the corruption of the Democratic party. . . . If he is ashamed of the party he had better quit it.[7]

The Republican press continued to portray Folk as "an ambitious and selfish aspirant unworthy of public office," but failed to convince the voters. The Columbia *Herald* said Folk ran on a single issue, The Missouri Idea, and on this he was qualified because of his courage and honesty.[8] In Gallatin, the *Democrat* noted,

> The common people—great, honest yeomanry of Missouri—are getting mighty tired of technicalities. They don't understand the subtle legal complexities and circumlocutions that are pulling open the doors of our penitentiary to convicted boodlers. They want fewer decisions based upon hair-spun theories and brain-bewildering subtleties and more based upon justice.[9]

Before Folk was nominated, some Republican papers, such as the St. Louis *Globe-Democrat*, defended his actions as a prosecutor. The Gallatin *Democrat* compared the platforms:

> Democratic: There is no room in the Democratic party for boodlers. We repudiate their support and do not want their votes. We invite such as are masquerading under the cloak of the Democratic party to bolt, and propose to make them bolt, not only the party, but the state.
>
> Republicans: We declare against bribe-givers and bribe-takers alike. Both are criminals, and we demand of each the punishment without regard to station in life or political affiliations. We neither solicit nor desire their support.

> One is positive; the other negative. One is the bugle challenge
> of uncompromising battle, and war to the death; the other a
> boyish dare, made merely for a bluff, and in the hopes that the
> boodlers will not call the boast.[10]

Some papers split their support between the parties, the Kansas City *Star* and Kirksville *Graphic*, traditionally Republican, backing Roosevelt on the national ticket and Folk on the local. The *Graphic* attacked the *Globe-Democrat* after it deserted Folk, commenting, "Papers that will unblushingly acknowledge that their editorial expressions have been falsehoods, and their pretensions hypocritical will hardly command the respect or confidence of men of either party."[11]

An appropriate summary was applied to the campaign by the Kirksville paper: "The Democrats won Missouri for Roosevelt, and the Republicans elected Folk. The Democrats, by remaining at home on election day, permitted Roosevelt to carry the state. The Republicans, who voted, by scratching their tickets, elected Folk."[12]

CLOSE REPUBLICAN VICTORY IN 1908

Republicans swept both key elections in 1908, Taft defeating Bryan, though by only 629 votes, and Herbert S. Hadley, first Republican governor after thirty-six years, winning over William S. Cowherd of the Old Guard Democrats by more than 15,000 votes. Partisan papers had urged all to follow their editorial counsel, although in language calmer than a few decades earlier. Republican papers gave their first page to Taft and his acceptance speech. Democrat papers ran sketches of Bryan, "Our Next President." One such paper, the Poplar Bluff *Citizen*, asked: "Isn't Taft's 'enthusiasm' about the lamest thing ever witnessed in American political history?"[13] But in Savannah the *Reporter* said, Taft "looks good to the people around here . . . a vote for protection is a vote to continue prosperity for another four years."[14]

The Gallatin *North Missourian* was happy to report, "Missouri Is Republican! Taft Sweeps the Country."[15] During the campaign another Republican paper, the Butler *Bates County Record*, cut its subscription price. "We don't expect to make a dollar on this deal. We are very much interested in the election of Taft and Hadley this fall and know of no better means we can use to this end than to place the issues of the campaign plainly and truthfully before a large number of intelligent voters in an interesting manner."[16]

"A fairer cause, championed by a purer patriot, never went down to defeat than this country experienced. . . . There is pride as well as consolation to the thought that a different result was deserved," reported the Ironton *Register*.[17] "Republican principles have received a triumphant vindication at the hands of the American people," declared the Kansas City *Journal*.[18] The Poplar Bluff *Citizen-Democrat*, merged that October, concluded, "The newspapers were the greatest factor . . . and their influence in shaping sentiment grows each year."[19]

Republicans could see early in 1910 that trouble was ahead. Issues such as the Payne-Aldrich tariff, the Ballinger-Pinchot dispute, and the attack on Joseph Cannon widened the division within the party. The Democrats won thirteen of sixteen congressional races. And Republicans lost across the nation, too.

WILSON WINS ON PARTY SPLIT

The progressive movement was the big news in 1912. This divided the Republicans into two camps, one led by Taft and the other by Theodore Roosevelt, which permitted Woodrow Wilson to capture Missouri by 122,925 votes. Still, Wilson received only 49.9 per cent of the total vote.

Among the fine studies made of this campaign are Thomas R. Yancey's *The Election of 1912 in Missouri* and William T. Miller's thesis, *The Progressive Movement in Missouri*. Both drew much source material from the papers. Miller notes a difference between the Progressive party and the movement. "The one came into being in a day, lived a short strenuous life, lingered, and died. The other developed gradually, spread its influence throughout a broad land, and in its permanent results lived on."[20]

William Rockhill Nelson, publisher of the Kansas City *Star*, supported Taft in 1908 but, being a close friend of Theodore Roosevelt, turned to the Progressive party in 1912. When Roosevelt was nominated, Nelson's *Times* noted:

> The people won their first great victory within the Republican party when they forced the nomination of a revision candidate and made the party embody a revision plank in the platform.
> They were deceived in Mr. Taft and they were disappointed in many of their senators and representatives, but the insurgent members . . . were loyal to them. . . . The Republican insurgents are the patriots of their time. They are the men to whom the

country must look for leadership in the great battle for tariff reform, for the solution of the great moral and economic issues now pressing for immediate settlement.[21]

Missourians, early in 1912, hoped to place Champ Clark on the presidential ticket, after Folk withdrew. When the smoke of convention battles had cleared, all the Democrats could say was that Clark came closer to the nomination than any other Missourian had, up to this time. Clark, according to the Kansas City *Times*, said he "lost the nomination solely through the vile and malicious slanders of Col. William Jennings Bryan of Nebraska. True, those slanders were innuendo and insinuation, but they were no less deadly for that reason."[22]

Democrats turned to Wilson, who was backed by the St. Louis *Post-Dispatch* and the *Republic*, Springfield *Leader*, Hannibal *Journal*, and others. The *Republic* gained some reputation during this campaign as being "especially good for developments that tended to create dissension in the Republican ranks."[23]

Regular Republicans were backed by the St. Louis *Globe-Democrat*, Kansas City *Journal*, St. Joseph *Gazette*, Springfield *Republican*, Joplin *News Herald*, and others. Leading organs for the Roosevelt party were the Kansas City *Star* and the *Times*. Yancey concludes that "it was through his [Nelson's] papers that the third party in Missouri was built up and enabled to put a full ticket in the field against the Republicans and Democrats."[24]

City papers led in political coverage. Smaller papers lacked adequate coverage in many areas, yet were too biased in their reporting in other instances. They tended to concentrate more on local issues.

Among the newspapers the 1912 campaign was an interesting word battle, reminiscent of some conflicts of the last century. The *Globe-Democrat* declared the Democratic ticket, led by Elliot W. Major for governor, the weakest that party had ever presented. Major inherited the reformer role set previously by Folk and Hadley. The editor of the *Globe-Democrat* was correct when he said the Democrats "can't expect to win on their merits, but only by a landslide. It is up to the Republicans and independent voters to see that Missouri takes no backward steps to Bourbonism. The only way this can be done is by voting the regular Republican ticket."[25]

Republicans, like their Democratic counterparts, had visions of success for a compromise candidate, Herbert S. Hadley, Missouri's governor. The St. Louis *Republic* and *Globe-Democrat* reported frequently that Hadley's name was mentioned in this role, even before the Republicans opened their convention that split Taft and Roosevelt. The *Globe-Democrat* reported, "A large number of Taft delegates, while believing that Taft could be nominated by keeping the 'steam roller' in high gear, were willing to support some progressive Republicans, other than Roosevelt, to save the party from disruption." Once, during a heated debate, the delegates were reported in pandemonium, with cries of "Give us Hadley for President!"[26]

Roosevelt visited St. Louis, Joplin, Springfield, and other communities during the campaign. Regular party members worked hard, too. But when the final count came, Wilson had 330,746 votes; Taft, 207,821; and Roosevelt, 124,371. Major led the Democratic ticket to victory in Missouri, winning 337,019 against the vote of 217,819 for John C. McKinley. This count indicates considerable ballot scratching. The Progressive party died quickly, running its course as third parties in the United States tend to do. As with demands presented by such groups in the 1880-1890 era, the party leaders could see their proposals gradually appear in the platforms of the Democrats and Republicans. In Missouri, the Progressive movement was not limited to one party, since two of the leaders were Folk, a Democrat, and Hadley, a Republican. The vote in 1912 for the party in part represented a protest against the regulars. In the off-year election in 1914, the Progressives lost about 75 per cent of the voting strength shown in 1912.

Missouri Republicans concurred with party leaders across the nation, blaming their setback on Roosevelt. The *Globe-Democrat* said, "When it [the party] refused to nominate him for a third term, he turned upon it in a perfidious and revengeful spirit, resolved to prevent its success as a penalty for not making him its candidate. In all the history of American politics, there is no parallel for this case of amazing egotism and flagrant ingratitude, and certainly no true Republican can ever forget or condone it."[27]

PRESS ASSOCIATION IN NEW APPROACH

A new era began for the Missouri Press Association in 1907. After the founding of the School of Journalism the next year, the editors joined each spring in the school's Journalism Week. Topics of a practical nature dominated the programs—postal rates, advertising, production costs, libel, staff training, etc. Philip Gansz of the Macon *Republican* was elected president in 1907 when the association met in St. Louis in June. A proposal was made that papers limit advertising to no more than two-thirds of their space and prohibit mailing samples to more than 10 per cent of their paid circulation. J. West Goodwin and W. L. Thomas, long-time association leaders, became honorary life members.[28]

Excelsior Springs provided facilities for the May, 1908, meeting. Printed minutes required more than 150 pages to record the talks and debates. Members heard Williams discuss the School of Journalism and W. O. L. Jewett describe the growth of the State Historical Society. Omar D. Gray, president, urged the creation of strong local press associations on a county, congressional district, and sectional level. H. F. Childers of the Troy *Free Press* presided in Fulton at the meeting in 1909, when eighty-six questions concerning business were open for discussion. Still, the fraternity spirit existed as Lee Shippey of the Higginsville *Jeffersonian* discussed "The Grip of Fellowship," half in prose, half in poetry.[29]

After attending Editors' Week in May, 1910, the association members took a boat ride from St. Louis to Cape Girardeau in June. Williams spoke on "The Practice of Journalism," reminding the editors that "books are reservoirs, newspapers are the running streams."[30]

More than two hundred editors attended the second program of Editors' Week in Columbia in April, 1911. The press association was in charge the first two days, the Association of Past Presidents met on Wednesday, and city papers were discussed on Thursday. Journalism teachers from many institutions met on Friday, when Henry Wallace, editor of *Wallace's Farmer*, spoke. The excursion session was held the next month in Joplin. The next year woman suffrage was a topic of special interest, and Mitchell White of the Mexico *Ledger* spoke on "A Look Ahead in the Profession." The Kansas City *Star* observed, "No where else is such an effort made to bring together men in every department of newspaper work from every part of the land. Interchange of ideas from various viewpoints cannot fail to be helpful to all those who are so fortunate as to be able to attend." Members gathered in Hannibal that August for a boat excursion to Keokuk Dam.[31]

Past presidents began a practice in 1913 of meeting annually during Journalism Week. Regional associations, too, used this opportunity for sessions, frequently presenting a portion of the program.

Fred Naeter of the Cape Girardeau *Republican* presided in 1913 when resolutions voiced the fears of the day about armament, the railroad problems, and the need for appropriations for the waterways. In October a dozen men met in St. Louis to organize the Missouri Association of Daily Newspapers. Mitchell White of the Mexico *Ledger* was elected chairman of the new group. Later he wrote, "The purpose at that time was to band together one paper (the strongest daily) in each of the towns having dailies for the purpose of discussing our mutual problems from a competitive basis as well as to work toward an organization that would develop our national advertising."[32]

Journalism Week in 1914 was highlighted by a telephone presentation by Nelson of the Kansas City *Star*, speaking from his office to a crowd in Neff Hall. "Dorothy Dix," Mrs. Elizabeth Gilmer, spoke on "How the Press Views the Feminist Movement."[33] A special Made-in-Missouri theme highlighted the week in 1915. Champ Clark spoke on "The State of Missouri" at a banquet in Rothwell Gymnasium. St. Joseph and Kansas City provided meeting places for a two-day session in September, with President H. S. Sturgis of the Neosho *Times* presiding. He noted that while earlier meetings had discussed truth in news and editorials, "we now hear pleas of truth in advertising."[34] An allied group of forty writers met during Journalism Week in 1915 and organized the Missouri Writers' Guild, which has held its annual spring meeting at the School of Journalism ever since.[35]

Some six hundred newspaper people and their associates met in Columbia in 1916; ten associations were represented. The theme of the preceding year was expanded to Made-in-America, and the program included such speakers as William Jennings Bryan, Arthur Brisbane, and Billy Sunday. This year was the Golden Jubilee for the press group, whose members "looked backward, but looked forward, too." In recalling the early days of the group, J. Kelly Pool of the Centralia *Courier* as president reminded publishers, "When the Missouri Press Association came on the job there was not a country office in Missouri lighted with electricity, equipped with motor power, perfecting presses, type-setting or type-casting machines, power cutters, feeders, stitchers, folders, mailers or any of the many other devices and appliances which go to make the print shop of today a thing of beauty and a joy forever." Kelly said members considered that "the better equipped newspaper plants, better qualified newspaper men, and the better edited newspapers trace their origin to the Missouri Press Association and its offspring, the School of Journalism." He added, "The School of Journalism has almost abolished the reprobate and relegated to the rear the pestiferous specimen who imagined the chief end of a newspaper man was to be jealous of his competitor and abuse him in his dirty sheet."[36]

Recollections of the first half century highlighted this convention. E. W. Stephens remarked that his father "put him in the newspaper business because he thought I was too lazy for anything else." Jewett recalled that during the early years editors "were creatures of the railroads. We traveled at their expense and helped them to keep up their high-handed tyranny." A few even professed they missed the poems. George W. Hendley, of Kansas City, who had started five papers in different areas, told of the old "Smith press, the kind you had to pull the 'devil's tail' every time a paper was printed." For fifty-three years he was a member of the Typographical Union. These looks into the past demonstrated how far Missouri publishers had advanced within a half century. More gains were in the future.

CHAPTER XVIII

WORLD WAR I REPORTED
BY STATE PRESS

BETWEEN 1914 and 1920 Missouri editors encountered many problems and controversies, some of them results of the first World War. In this period of transition Missourians shared in the newer concept of America's role in the world family. Missourians were involved in the word battles of the 1916 and 1918 elections, but these campaigns were surpassed in the public mind by the struggles over other issues, such as prohibition and the country's entrance into the League of Nations.

Missouri and the World War, 1914-1917: A Study of Public Opinion is an excellent study of the period by John Clark Crighton, who turned primarily to the metropolitan press for source material to set the stage for the state's position in the struggle. It is important in assessing public opinion of the time to note that in 1910 St. Louis had a German-American population of more than 186,000 out of a total population of 687,000. Included in this general figure were 54,482 Irish-Americans. Kansas City, with a population under 250,000, reported 5,354 German-Americans and 3,266 Irish-Americans.[1]

Missouri, by 1914, was the dominant industrial center west of the Mississippi River. Meat-packing companies were adding millions of dollars to the state's economy. The 1910 census listed other important industries, with millions of dollars invested in boot-and-shoe plants, flour mills and grist mills, printing and publishing companies, liquor and malt distilleries, foundry and machine-shop factories, bakeries, lumber yards and timber lands, clothing workrooms, etc. Agriculture remained important in the state's economy, with corn, wheat, hay and forage, and oats the top crops. Although horses outnumbered mules and cows, hogs led the count of farm animals. Mining was significant, especially lead, zinc, and coal. St. Louis, the leading industrial city, was followed by Kansas City. The role of these two cities as financial centers became clearer when the Federal Reserve system placed a bank in each; Missouri alone among all the states has more than one Federal Reserve bank. These cities neither overlap in their services to Missourians nor does the readership of their papers overlap.[2]

JOURNALISM IN 1914

On the eve of World War I, Missouri journalism was nearing the end of one of its greatest periods. Some big names disappeared from the mastheads: Joseph Pulitzer died in 1911, William Rockhill Nelson in 1915, followed by Robert T. Van Horn of the Kansas City *Journal*; Charles W. Knapp, formerly of the St. Louis *Republic*; Daniel M. Houser, publisher, and Henry King, retired editor, of the St. Louis *Globe-Democrat*; Edward L. Preetorius, president of the German-American Press Association in St. Louis, and others known far beyond the state borders.

St. Louis publishers faced complications in reporting war news. Crighton reports,

> The editorial comments of the *Globe-Democrat* regarding European questions were characterized by realism and objectivity. Its interpretations of the developments leading up to the World War were expressed in terms of power politics rather than of moral issues. . . . The *Globe-Democrat* made no concealment of the fact that it had the largest German-American constituency of any paper in the English language.

Casper S. Yost took over direction of the editorial page early in 1915, following the death of King, and gave the paper a more pro-Allies tone.[3] On the *Post-Dispatch* was George S. Jones, a classmate of Woodrow Wilson at Princeton, where he had succeeded Wilson as editor of the *Princetonian*. After war broke out in Europe in 1914 the *Post-Dispatch* declared itself "against autocracy, imperialism, and militarism. We are for liberty and justice. We are for the rule of the people everywhere."[4] Also in St. Louis was the *Republic*, which traced its ancestry to the *Missouri Gazette*, founded in 1808. The *Republic* was Democratic, but was approaching the end of its effectiveness; it was sold in 1919 to the *Globe-Democrat*. Also there were the *Star* and the *Times*.

Across the state, the Kansas City *Star* and the *Journal* were the leaders among the city's papers. Nelson gave the *Star* a strong local outlook, in contrast with the international approach of the *Post-Dispatch*. Long a friend of Theodore Roosevelt, the *Star* carried many of his editorials during the war years. There also was the *Post* in Kansas City, under Fred G. Bonfils and H. H. Tammen, who owned the Denver *Post* too. Whatever sensational journalism existed in Kansas City in 1914 appeared in the *Journal*, which, according to Crighton, "maintained a better balance be-

tween quantities of foreign, national, and local news than its
rival."[5]

These papers, and others as well, provide historians with
much information concerning Missouri during the war, but other
publications must not be overlooked, such as the St. Joseph
News-Press, Springfield *Leader,* Joplin *Globe,* etc. Smaller papers
in Missouri and across the nation gave slight attention to the
international conflict. The reporting of international politics was
not considered by their editors to be a primary function.

Other organizations issued publications in Missouri, especially
those concerned with agriculture, labor, and religion. In St. Louis
there were several German-language papers, including two dailies,
the *Westliche Post* and *Amerika.* Readers of these German-
language papers were obviously more aroused than others in the
community when Germany became involved in the conflict. The
Globe-Democrat reported in 1914, "In every foreign quarter of
St. Louis, in the clubs, on the street corners and in the homes"
the war was uppermost in the people's thoughts.[6] In Hermann,
another strongly German community, residents went to the railroad station early each morning to get the metropolitan papers
for the latest news from Europe. The Springfield *Leader* told of
meetings of German-American club members who "over beer
and pretzels" discussed the master plan of the German general
staff and "moved colored pins about on their maps to record the
progress of the Armies of the Reich."[7]

The Missouri press reported the outbreak of the war, some
papers showing clearer insight of the causes and ultimate results
than others. As early as June 30, 1914, the *Post-Dispatch* viewed
the murder of the Archduke Ferdinand as a possible cause of a
world war. Still, the paper noted, "Among the privileges of being
an American, freedom from European's haunting fear of war is
not the least." Many causes for this conflict were cited, the
variety no doubt influenced by consciousness of the readers'
viewpoints, by the political views of the editor, and by the understanding of the international situation on the part of each writer.
Some, such as the *Post-Dispatch,* saw the threat of "a steady
expansion of Russian influence in the small countries of south-
eastern Europe"; the Kansas City *Journal* urged aid for Austria
against the Russians. "Autocracy is in a death struggle with
democracy in Europe and democracy must win," stressed the
Post-Dispatch. In a large cartoon captioned, "He Should Worry,"
the paper showed Uncle Sam drinking grape juice and reading

European war news in a paper. On September 1 the paper said, "Primarily it is not a war of principles, but of politics—a war of nationalities, of flags, insignia, and the paraphernalia of armaments. It is a war of ambitions, vanities, prejudices, resentments, a letting of bad blood; and there are Czars and imperialists upon both sides of it." The *Globe-Democrat* considered the possibility of a "thunderbolt" campaign against France.

Some editors thought racial conflicts to be at the root of the problem; others refuted this theory. A few agreed that the Balkan question was the most serious. The St. Louis *Republic*, for example, editorialized on "Bird's Eye View of Causes," "With the exception of the Alsace-Lorraine question, every line of international distrust and disagreement in Western Europe runs to the Balkans and the Golden Horn."[8] Other papers, such as the *Globe-Democrat* and the Kansas City *Star*, thought a commercial war was developing, with several nations seeking to expand their own commerce. In St. Joseph the *News-Press* of July 31 called the declaration of war "the crime of the age." The *Star* visualized Austria as a "bully." The St. Louis *Republic* thought the war would "fan the prosperity of the United States," although it might be an ill wind to Europe.[9] However, in the same line of thought the *Post-Dispatch* warned of the loss in years to come if European markets were too impoverished to buy from America. The *Globe-Democrat* summarized the causes of the conflict:

> The intelligence of mankind has about reached the conclusion that more than one of the nations of Europe is responsible. France has been crying "revanche" for a full generation, and more. Germany has been preparing to hold, with the "mailed fist," those provinces, the loss of which had aroused the French Fury. Russia has persistently and of late without concealment, sought to fan a flame of resentment in the Slavic states of the Balkans against Austrian aggression—a movement not so bad in itself as viewed from these distant shores, but something not likely to be relished by those at whom it was directed—while Great Britain, although not building great land armaments, has made herself no less a menace to the peace of the world through a vast increase of her naval armaments, such as she has not hesitated to justify with the boast of her intention to remain "the mistress of the seas." Half a generation of such mutual preparing for and challenging of war could be seen to be leading inevitably toward it. A great wonder is that it was delayed so long. This plain truth is steadily sinking deeper into world consciousness, and must, if possible, be overcome, if any plan of selecting a

scapegoat in the peace conferences can be carried out without
offense to the conscience of mankind.[10]

After business and agricultural interests marked gains from
the European conflict, several papers said prosperity had arrived, with farmers reporting higher revenues. In 1916 the value
of Missouri crops was placed at $261,269,000; a year later it had
more than doubled. Many Missouri firms received contracts
from British sources for the building of aircraft, manufacturing
munitions, and producing other war supplies. Horses and mules
were among the major war-stimulated exports; some 750,000
were sent from Missouri to Europe. Lead and zinc-mining and
-processing gave the state an economic boost.

How to pay for these purchases posed international questions;
suggestions were plentiful in the editorial pages of Missouri
papers. When the first Anglo-French mission arrived in the
United States in 1915 to seek a loan, many papers of the state
approved the idea. The Nevada *Post* said such a loan "would
not be a breach of American neutrality." The editor cited a
similar action by the German government in the sale of its treasury notes in this country in April. Too, with an approach now
familiar to readers of the newspapers of the 1960's, the *Post*
editor said such credit would be necessary "to avoid the stoppage
of export trade and consequent economic disaster." Agricultural
publications saw value in the loan because it would help to
continue prosperity for farmers, and the approval by the mining
interests was voiced by the Joplin *Globe* and other papers of
the region.[11]

But dissent appeared. The *Globe-Democrat* and the Kansas
City *Star* opposed the loan, as did the *Westliche Post*. The *Globe-
Democrat* called these not *appeals* but *demands* in the character
of an ultimatum and expressed the thought that this nation's
involvement would become too great through the loan to maintain our neutrality. It, too, questioned the security and the payment plans for the loans.[12]

After Germany announced unrestricted submarine warfare in
early 1915, the press of Missouri realized the seriousness of the
struggle. The *Globe-Democrat's* view of this German act as "a
reprisal in kind" against the British strangulation policy was not
exceptional among newspapers. The Germans planned "to pit
one form of sea power against another," wrote the editor, still
viewing submarine warfare as of no special danger against
American ships. In Joplin the *News-Herald* urged the nation to

avoid "a pro-British as well as pro-German partisanship."[13] Germany received no support from either the St. Louis *Republic* or the *Post-Dispatch*. The former said the sinking of any ship "would be an unthinkable piece of barbarism involving the destruction of the lives of non-combatants and neutrals." The *Post-Dispatch* asserted that should any American vessel be destroyed without search and without rescue of passengers and crew, it "would be equivalent to an act of war."[14]

The sinking of the *Lusitania* resulted in what Crighton terms "widespread indignation and resentment" in the English-language press. Bitter words appeared in Missouri papers. In Jackson the *Missouri Cash-Book* called the sinking "murder . . . [an act] which for downright fiendishness has never been eclipsed by savages in any age of the world." The St. Joseph *News-Press* was violent about an act it termed "wanton, wholesale murder." The Columbia *Tribune* called it a "barbaric atrocity," while the St. Louis *Republic* saw it as evidence of all previous reports about German atrocities. Some papers blamed the British for carelessness, since the Germans had warned of their intent to carry on submarine warfare. The Nevada *Post* said the Cunard Line, which owned the vessel, had to share the blame with the British Admiralty and the United States Government. Caution was the watchword; some Missouri papers urged suspension of judgment in the matter. "Wait until all the facts are in," advised the *Globe-Democrat*. The *Post-Dispatch* asked whether the *Lusitania* carried any munitions of war.[15]

These debates raised other questions. Should Americans refrain from traveling in the war zones? Some papers thought citizens of the United States should not be permitted in such areas, especially if any of the ships carried munitions. The *Globe-Democrat*, reminding its readers that "the *Lusitania* is not another *Maine*," remarked that Germany was at war with England, not with the United States, a view that no doubt pleased many St. Louis readers. In its lead editorial of May 11, the paper said, "Reason should rule. . . . We do not want war. We have before us now, and have had for months, an illustration of the unparalleled horrors of war . . . the United States is happily outside that maelstrom of murder. We will not be drawn into it if we can, with honor, avoid it." The Kansas City *Journal* saw our entry into war as "unthinkable." The Joplin *News-Herald* recognized the possibility of war after the sinking of the *Lusitania*, but expressed the opinion that since this nation has "no racial prejudices and no geographical issues at stake" it should refrain from battle.

The *Globe-Democrat* noted on May 16 that the press across the nation had not clamored for war; in fact, "a few have opposed war under any conceivable circumstances." Citing the fact that many papers in the central, middlewestern, and western states expressed confidence in the President's ability to handle the situation, the editor declared, "It is equally clear that if the dreaded alternative happens (war) the nation will stand as one man back of the administration." Some papers opposed any armament race, fearing the possibility of our involvement. The St. Joseph *News-Press* said, "The possession of the finest arms and equipment is always a temptation to use them under very slight provocation." Nine months later the paper said that "the simple desire on our part for peace would by no means insure peace."[16] The Kansas City *Star* warned:

> Jealously and suspiciously regarded by all, broker in war material to the side that has command of all the sea, money lender, carrying its commerce on a belligerent country's ships, its citizens travelling under belligerent flags, exposed daily to crises involving peace and the national honor, piling up Europe's gold, coined from its spilled blood and wasted cities—in such circumstances of danger and reprisal live 100 million people on a rich, envied and unprotected continent, fair prize of war.[17]

Preparedness became a key word. Early in 1916 some editors of papers such as the Chillicothe *Constitution*, Carthage *Press*, Columbia *Tribune*, Jackson *Missouri Cash-Book*, Nevada *Post*, and Warrensburg *Standard-Herald* thought it unwise to sit back and wait. In March the *Literary Digest* conducted a poll of editors, asking for their views about the size of the Army. The *Post-Dispatch* urged that the Army build its forces to 200,000 regulars and a million trained reserves; other papers were not so demanding, although some called for a larger regular force; still others recommended universal military training. The St. Louis *Republic* declared that universal military training was within our heritage, noting the citizen soldiery of the past. The *Post-Dispatch* called such a program "efficient, democratic, and anti-militaristic; besides it would provide excellent schooling in patriotism and good citizenship." It added that the "volunteer system spells cost, failure, danger."[18]

As the United States was drawn more closely into the international net, the papers turned to support of the President. The

St. Louis *Republic* said, "There are worse things than war. It is far from the chief evil. . . . France today is a nation reborn in strength, in spirit, in devotion, and the war has done the work. What may not the soul of our nation need that only struggle will give us?"[19] Retaliation was urged by the St. Joseph *News-Press.* The lack of understanding of international diplomacy was made clear by such statements as the following in the Warrensburg *Star-Journal:* "If Germany declares a 'zone' around England and warns Americans to stay out or take their chances of getting hurt, the average American would keep out and let 'em fight. That's our idea of neutrality."[20]

Missouri newsmen approved breaking diplomatic ties with Germany. Editors assured Wilson of their support, although the Kansas City *Journal* feared "The American people will profoundly regret the severance of diplomatic relations between the United States and the German Government." In some communities "Loyalty Day" mass meetings were held. Any idea of a small-scale engagement in the European conflict was eliminated. The St. Louis *Republic* presented a view shared by other Missouri papers: "Every resource of the country, financial, industrial, physical and spiritual, mental and moral, must be brought to bear, if need be, to win this war."[21] To the *Post-Dispatch* "complete victory" was the goal, and the Nevada *Post* declared that the end would come only when the Stars and Stripes were planted at the gates of Berlin.

Crighton concludes that in Missouri there was a core of opposition to participation in the war, "the social phenomenon known as Middle Western isolationism. . . . The core of the opposition to Wilson's foreign policies was furnished by the German-Americans through their newspapers and pressure groups. They were assisted by a portion of the Irish-Americans. The strong socialist movement in Missouri took a doctrinaire anti-war stand. . . . The Missouri State Grange and the Patrons of Husbandry also took issue with the administration regarding the matter of preparedness." However, when war was declared Missourians were prepared, through their papers, for the role they were to play.[22]

WILSON RETURNED TO WHITE HOUSE

Missouri, in 1916, was a state nearly evenly divided between the major parties as the presidential election neared. The Republicans had more or less reunited following the dismal showing of the Progressive party in 1914. Republicans looked for a heavy vote from the German-Americans and Irish-Americans who opposed Wilson's actions in the European conflict; some Roosevelt Republicans knew not where to turn after their leader declined to run again.

The *Post-Dispatch* led the Democratic drive for Wilson's re-election, saying,

> It is humanly impossible that any president could work effectively with all the motley following that Mr. Hughes has rallied to his support. To satisfy Mr. Roosevelt, he must quarrel with the pro-British, who demand war with Germany. To satisfy Wall Street, he must quarrel with the Western radicals. To satisfy the jingoes and the Munitions Trust, he must quarrel with most of the country. To satisfy privilege and plutocracy, he must quarrel with the people. Even as a candidate, Mr. Hughes dare not have a policy, because to have a policy is to antagonize one element or another of his followers.

The paper thought the defeat of Wilson would certainly make war unavoidable. It saw Germany as a "keen and interested partisan," watching the outcome, feeling "the president's defeat will imply the utter rejection of his foreign policy."[23] The Nevada *Post* thought success of the Roosevelt-Hughes campaign would certainly bring war.

The *Globe-Democrat* supported Hughes and was bitter toward those who thought it impossible for this nation to stay out of the conflict.[24] The Kansas City *Journal* feared the key to Wilson's character was found in his readiness to surrender "the rights of the American people to threats of force."[25]

Papers reported other events as well as those centering on the war and national politics. The Kansas City *Post* featured a photo of Billy Sunday and Jess Willard on its front page entitled "The World's Greatest Fighters." It was difficult to escape the election issues. The *Globe-Democrat* asked if we were "a nation of poltroons":

> Is the America of the future to be a spineless creature that jumps at every shadow, and takes refuge behind a barricade of woods at every alarm? Are we to become the China of the Occident, supine, without pride, without honor, and condemned by the rest of the world? Or does the old spirit, the spirit of '76 and of '64, the spirit that holds right above safety, still inspire and control us? . . . Shall our emblem continue to be the Stars and Stripes, or shall we erase those emblems of glory won and glory

held, and leave but a pale sheet to wave over us, a flag, whose rustle is a whimper, a flag that waves only in retreat? For the first time in American history cowardice has become a national issue.[26]

Missourians answered. Wilson received 398,032 votes, Hughes 369,339; in four years Wilson had increased his vote total by more than 66,000. Frederick D. Gardner, Democrat, became the governor with only a 2,263-vote plurality over Henry Lamm. Gardner, a successful businessman, won against a Republican campaign which was critical of the Democrats as reckless spendthrifts. Six days after war was declared, the Governor called a state-wide meeting to plan defense measures. More than a million Missourians signed the Hoover food pledge, giving this state first place in proportion to its population in this economy effort.

Wilson took an active role in the state's off-year election in 1918 with a "Support-the-President" slogan. The *Globe-Democrat*, who opposed Wilson because of his refusal to consider a coalition of Democrats and Republicans in his inner circle, counted the close vote a rebuke of the President's intervention.[27]

WAR OPENS FOR UNITED STATES

When the nation entered the international conflict, Missouri papers were ready. The *Post-Dispatch*, for example, had sent its own correspondent, Clair Kenamore, to Mexico to cover Pershing's movements in 1916. Later Kenamore became the paper's correspondent-at-large on the European front. In 1918 Charles G. Ross headed the paper's Washington bureau, joined later by Paul Y. Anderson. Campaigning for freedom of thought, the *Post-Dispatch* sought the liberation of fifty-one pacifists and other political prisoners during the war. Although the paper disagreed with their views, and certainly with those of one of the prisoners (Eugene V. Debs), it considered imprisonment of such persons to be unconstitutional.

The *Globe-Democrat* urged all to "treat every German citizen residing here as we would have Germany treat Americans residing there." The paper warned of "Patriotism and Paytriotism," urging close check on shoddy products and exorbitant prices.[28] "This is a war to the finish, no mere giving of moral sympathy. This is a war for peace—to end all wars so men may live unmenaced," said the Kansas City *Post* on April 3. The American flag appeared frequently, as did the pledge of allegiance. Kansas

City residents were told about "War Preparedness in the Garden," and cigarets were sent to the men in the services under the "Smokes for the Sammies" fund. The *Post* urged a ban on the teaching of German in public schools. The editors mistrusted the Germans, urging caution, on October 14, 1918, for "Peace with a people who have chosen such brutality and lack of honor is possible only when they surrender their weapons, only when they are powerless for evil, only when they place themselves where never again can they destroy and murder and ravage."

Streamer headlines appeared frequently as the declaration of war became inevitable. On April 3, the *Globe-Democrat* bore a two-line streamer:

> President Urges State of War
> And Universal Army of 500,000

The *Post-Dispatch* banner declared:

> President Proclaims War; German Ships Seized

The St. Joseph *Gazette* remarked, "It is not a course to be entered on with joy. . . . We must look to the future to justify our course."[29]

Considerable attention was given in the *Post-Dispatch* to a St. Louis congressman who voted against war. It printed a map of his district and concluded that apparently the area had a heavy Irish-American population. Editorially, the paper said: "May we not show in the conflict upon us at this moment that efficiency under German military autocracy may be equaled by a right-directed efficiency under the republic?"[30]

Some of the smaller papers gave the declaration of war routine coverage, especially weeklies that appeared after the dailies had announced the news. In Marshall, for example, the *Weekly Democrat-News* carried such items as one concerning high school boys cultivating vacant lots and giving 10 per cent of the products to the government. The paper listed all men called in the draft and their classifications, a practice followed by many other papers. In Neosho, the *Daily Democrat* bore a one-column head: WAR. The story occupied one column of a five-column tabloid, with the other four columns filled with advertisements. Local news occupied most of the other space. Other papers followed this major story with news of Liberty Loan sales, patriotic food shows, quilt auctions, celebrations for men leaving for the front, and similar accounts of patriotic activities.

A rumor which reported too early that the war had ended

created problems for many papers. The United Press announced that the war was over several days before it had officially halted. The *Post-Dispatch* reprinted on its front page the stories from the St. Louis *Star* and the *Times* that carried this false report. A six-column headline read, "How the *Star* and *Times* Duped the City—The *Star's* Confession." Another story told that "the Mayor expresses deep regret that the people of St. Louis were duped." The *Globe-Democrat,* which used Associated Press coverage, attacked the United Press story as "an unpardonable fake" and called it "cold-blooded, deliberate persistence in a falsehood after it had been officially exposed . . . never before has the caution of the Associated Press, which would rather be right than first, been so strikingly vindicated." The paper's extra edition on November 11 headlined, "Germany Has Surrendered" and with considerable artwork noted, "Peace has come to the world."[31]

A *Post-Dispatch* extra announced terms of the armistice and editorially said, "Free civilization triumphs over despotism." Looking ahead, the paper warned its readers, "the first task is to feed the starving, clothe the naked and strengthen the peoples, exhausted by the war, among our enemies as well as our friends." A Daniel R. Fitzpatrick cartoon portrayed the world in the upper left corner with the Kaiser's helmet and sword dropping off into space. No words were used; the message was clear.

In Marshall the *Democrat-News* played up the news of the armistice in a half-column story on page 1, "End of War Is Celebrated." Some of the smaller papers that had carried the United Press report did not carry retractions.

PROHIBITION, LEAGUE OF NATIONS

Two other significant topics concerned Missouri papers in this period. Congress passed the Eighteenth Amendment in 1917, and for two years the press waged a verbal war, pro and con, on prohibition. In Missouri opposing views were publicized by the Kansas City *Star* and the *Post-Dispatch*. The *Star* favored the amendment, claiming that "whiskey drinking belongs to the stagecoach days and can't survive the modern times."[32] The paper added, "Booze and business won't mix." For the next two years the *Star* attacked "Old John Barleycorn," who was able to "disorganize industry, wreck lives, demoralize politics and lead to sedition and un-Americanism." When the proponents of the amendment won their victory a few days later, the *Star,* having predicted "Booze Gets Knockout," proclaimed: "The country grabbed prohibition when it was off its guard and led it dazed and half-unbelieving to the altar . . . when we brought our new bride home, we lit a fresh fire and decked the place with flowers and groceries beyond the dream of avarice."[33]

The *Post-Dispatch*, which approved prohibition on the state level, opposed the decision for prohibition on the national level, claiming it would stir up disunity at a time when all should be waging the war effort together.[34] When the amendment was ratified, the *Post-Dispatch*'s cartoonist Daniel Fitzpatrick sketched the Statue of Liberty diving into the ocean. An editorial that day, January 18, 1919, was one of sarcasm and anger and expressed the hope that the amendment "will achieve much good so as to compensate for the great loss of liberty which it symbolizes." Prohibitionists were branching into wider fields with their "special brand of bigotry." When the Volstead Act was passed the following October, the *Post-Dispatch* termed it an example of "the madness which drives prohibition fanatics to override all rights and interests to gain their ends."[35]

Wilson's League of Nations created its furor, too. Most Americans, no doubt, recognized a need for some such organization although they disagreed about the role America should play in its operation. The *Star* advocated an emasculated League, with only perfunctory American participation. The *Post-Dispatch* stayed with Wilson, and together they fought the losing battle. The *Star* opened its blast against the League in early 1917. Wilson's "peace without victory" speech bore "a sense of detachment from the real world," according to the *Star*. "Woe to any nation that is persuaded to put its confidence in the millennium instead of in its ability to defend itself," it warned.[36] The *Post-Dispatch* headline said: "Wilson Proposed World Concert to Preserve Peace." His plan was a "tremendous proposal . . . addressed less to the selfishness in governments than to the sense of right impulses of the people."[37] Attention was devoted primarily to the war front during the rest of 1917 and 1918, but by early 1919, the League fight again entered the news. "The League program does not assume that the world can be remade overnight—it does assume the capacity of man to redeem the world from the rule of might in international dealings, and that nations, like individuals, can be subject to the rules of law and equity," noted the *Post-Dispatch* on November 25, 1918.

The *Star* attacked what it termed Wilson's secrecy in forming the League's program, his plans for disarmament, his "freedom of the seas" proposal, and his attempt to grant independence to Germany's former colonies.[38] Many of the *Star's* views were similar to those held by Senator Henry Cabot Lodge, who led the anti-League fight on the national level. The *Post-Dispatch* opposed Lodge who, according to an editorial on March 3, 1919, was sunk in "a turmoil of partisan politics and personal jealousies in picking flaws in Wilson's peace plan." When Wilson visited Missouri to promote his peace plan, the *Post-Dispatch* gave him strong editorial support, while the *Star* ignored him editorially, even when he spoke in Kansas City. When the League was defeated in the Senate in 1920, the *Post-Dispatch* concluded, "The American people are left in the wilderness without a Moses" and blamed the setback on "the battalion of death" whose main objective was to defeat everything that Americans had fought to achieve in the war.[39] The *Star* was glad to forget it all, believing the League to be "as dead as squatter sovereignty."[40]

MISSOURI PRESS IN WAR YEARS

Problems other than editorial faced Missouri publishers.

A Made-in-Japan banquet highlighted the Journalism Week program in 1917 during which two days were devoted to association sessions. Members discussed ways to increase advertising, hearing that "copy written in short, honest, and straight-forward terms brought the best results"; and to increasing circulation by letting subscribers pay at a bank rather than by coming to the newspaper office. Resolutions echoed the war theme with such slogans as "A Liberty Bond in Every Home," to be promoted in the papers. The resolutions added,

> Members of the Missouri Press Association tender the United States Government a reasonable use of their columns, to be used in a Missouri campaign, to be conducted in such a manner as the Government . . . might direct, in building sentiment for a greater food production and conservation, in the sale of Liberty Bonds, in the increasing of the strength of the army and the navy, or any other publicity service that the members might be able to render, through the medium of the Missouri press, under the direction of that department of the government as the President might direct. . . .

"A deep patriotism, the stirring sense of war times, the new unity of spirit fostered by the combination against the paper pirates—these made themselves felt as undercurrents." So recorded the secretary at the St. Louis meeting in September. President H. J. Blanton of the Paris *Monroe County Appeal* said, "In this crisis there has ceased to be a North, a South, an East, a West. There are no Democrats, no Republicans, no Bull Moosers."

Blanton met with print paper representatives in St. Louis in 1917 "to arrive at some amicable settlement" in the rapidly increasing cost of paper. He claimed that one-fifth of Missouri papers had been forced to increase their subscription prices as a result of the hike in paper prices from $2.75 to $7 a hundred pounds in less than a year. A committee studying the situation urged an investigation of every paper house in Missouri "to ascertain whether a combination exists relative to print paper prices." A state-owned paper mill to be operated by prison labor was suggested by J. M. Sosey of Palmyra.

Testimony was offered by publishers on the dollars saved through a MPA mass-purchasing plan. Clint Denman of Sikeston told of paying $140 for a ton of paper from one mill and $115 from another, yet he later was able to buy 4,800 pounds through the association for only $198.35. Edward E. Swain of Kirksville estimated he saved more than a thousand dollars by purchasing paper through the association, and Fred Naeter of Cape Girardeau figured he saved some two thousand dollars. Naeter urged closer co-operation between city and county papers in an effort to publicize Missouri more widely. Blanton cited, as an interesting case of Missouri's need for better publicity, the front-page story in a city paper of a 56-pound pumpkin raised in Kansas when an 112-pounder had been presented to him in Paris with nothing but local mention.

Patriotism could go too far, according to W. G. Naylor of the Hannibal *Journal,* who "warned the editors that while they were giving great service to the government's war publicity work, and while they should not halt in this, they were putting the government in a position of a recipient of charity. . . . Space is the newspaper man's stock in trade, and the public should be taxed to pay for such space when used for government publicity campaigns."

Talk continued about the need for a permanent headquarters for the press association, directed by a full-time field secretary. A committee was appointed to study the matter, and a recommendation was made to proceed. Membership in the MPA in

1917 included 35 small dailies and 225 weekly papers. Membership by persons, however, was 412, with 128 added within the year.

Editors threshed out their problems in informal shop talks on advertising, circulation, and news coverage. Employment of some local town boys in military service as correspondents for the papers was discussed. Some editors sent complimentary copies to all local boys in service; others added a pen, a flag, or a Bible.[41]

J. P. Tucker of the Parkville *Gazette* became the president for 1918, and in a January meeting more plans were formulated for the buying of paper through the association and the selection of a field secretary. Greetings were sent to President Wilson, "coming from the towns and villages of the state, and knowing the people intimately, we assure you that Missouri is loyal to the nation, to you and your advisers, and to the principles for which our country is fighting." Among the bills approved was one for $9.50 for cigars for the Association.

During the regular Journalism Week sessions, the publishers changed their constitution to provide that only editors and publishers of publications that appeared at least weekly were eligible for membership. Associate membership was available for other newspapermen, such as employes, supply salesmen, etc. H. J. Blanton was presented a loving cup for "the best record of constructive service during the past year." An oil portrait of Dean Walter Williams was presented to the State Historical Society.

Publishers felt the effect of the war on the labor supply, some being forced to return to the back room or shop to resume their mechanical chores when they lost their help.

Other meetings in 1918 were canceled on account of the influenza epidemic ranging over the state and nation.[42] Association members returned to Columbia in May, 1919, and made plans to observe the state's centennial. J. N. Stonebreaker of the Carrollton *Republican-Record* became president. In September the members held their annual meeting, this time in Springfield, with a Victory dinner. E. R. Childers, earlier placed in charge of a bureau in Columbia to handle association paper-buying activities, reported on the shipments to the group.

Truly the historian or the interested reader can turn the pages of Missouri papers of the war years to learn the role this state played in that international conflict. Some of the attitudes the publishers exhibited were personal, all were patriotic, yet the disagreements over national issues which were debated in Missouri as well as elsewhere in the nation were clearly stated.

CHAPTER XIX

ROARING TWENTIES IN THE MISSOURI PRESS

"I'D RATHER praise it with faint damns than damn it with faint praise."

This opinion, voiced by Jesse W. Barrett, Missouri's attorney general in 1923, in part summarizes public attitudes toward the press in the twenties. Publishers faced many problems, from wages and hours of employes to the stock market crash.[1] Elections were still newsworthy, additional press organizations appeared, and advances were made in journalism training. Papers continued to decline in number, a nationwide trend. In 1920 Missouri had 73 dailies, 1 triweekly, 15 semiweeklies, and 632 weeklies. A decade later there were eight fewer dailies, an additional triweekly and semiweekly, but 141 less weeklies. The trend in Missouri, too, was toward the one-paper community. *Editor & Publisher*, noting that each year since 1915 more than 310 weekly papers had died, listed 544 in Missouri for 1890, 688 for 1915, and 544 for 1924. By 1928 Missouri had 28 communities with only one daily paper. Cities served by more than one paper declined to 12.[2] Highlights were adequately reported in the city press, although smaller papers continued to stress their primary role, featuring day-by-day happenings in the communities.

Washington politicians in 1921 said the news was mightier than the editors as they debated the merits of the League of Nations. In St. Louis, George S. Johns, editorial chief of the *Post-Dispatch*, told journalism teachers that the editorial had to have sincerity, justice, accuracy, humanity, courage, and brevity to be successful.

With two publishers, James M. Cox and Warren G. Harding, campaigning for the Presidency, the press had an interesting task recording the battle in 1920. In later years the debates on such events as the Washington Armament Conference, the Dawes Plan, World Court, Geneva Conference, and the London Naval Conference and problems in Mexico and Nicaragua occupied many columns. There was a business recession in 1921, and by the end of the decade signs of a serious depression began to appear. With more newspaper exposure of the Ku Klux Klan, membership in this secret organization declined to 9,000 by 1930. The death of Harding and the inauguration of Coolidge were followed by the Teapot Dome scandals, providing the partisan press with some meat to chew on.

"The queerest story of the generation, weird as a nightmare, side-splittingly funny, darkly tragic, a huge joke, a sinister threat, running the whole gamut of politics, religion, science, and sociology, all about everything and all about nothing, and by all odds the most difficult newspaper assignment for many years." That, according to *Editor & Publisher,* summed up the decade's most fascinating trial, the Scopes case in Tennessee. In Kansas City the *Star* reported that news of "the monkey trial" was widely read and discussed, but there was "no appreciable increase in circulation due to it."[3] Other trials were newsworthy, especially those of Col. Billy Mitchell and of Sacco and Vanzetti, but all gave way in the daily press to the unprecedented speculation on Wall Street.

NEW DECADE FOR MPA

Will H. Zorn of the West Plains *Howell County Gazette* became the Missouri Press Association president in 1920 when meetings were held in Columbia and St. Louis. Women took more share in the convention program. In St. Louis, Lily Frost of the Vandalia *Leader* and Adalyn Faris of the *Globe-Democrat* spoke. After an automobile tour of the city and a cruise on the Mississippi River, members elected Mitchell White of the Mexico *Ledger* president for 1921.

During White's presidency additional talks were held concerning the selection of a full-time executive secretary. To implement the plan and explain it to all members, many county and district meetings were held. A seldom discussed topic was on the 1921 program when D. P. Dobyns of the Oregon *Holt County Sentinel* explained how he built a morgue which contained data on practically every person in the county.[4]

J. S. Hubbard became the association's first full-time executive secretary in February, 1922. He formerly was connected with the Wisconsin State Printing Board and had held a similar position in Pittsburgh. His duties included visits with the smaller papers to promote a uniform standard of ethics and business policy. Hubbard's first report in May, 1922, concerned advertising and subscription rates charged by Missouri papers. A state charter was granted to the Missouri Press Association on August 8, 1922, the incorporators being J. F. Hull, Marguerite L. Reid, F. M. Harrison, John C. Stapel, and H. R. Spencer.

"The Seven Lights of Journalism" were listed by Walter Williams in September to include truth, righteousness, sympathy, interest, leadership, power, and sacrifice. Association members were dinner guests of the *Star* in the new Kansas City Club, and the paper's radio station, WDAF, designed its program that night to honor the visitors. Dwight H. Brown of the Poplar Bluff *American* became president in 1923.[5]

The Missouri Association, which included a selected list of papers organized to sell Missouri to the nation, was founded in April, 1923. The next month the Missouri Interscholastic Press Association was organized in Columbia, with representatives of eleven high school papers present.[6] That same year it could be said that Missouri newsmen almost determined the University of Missouri policies. The three-man executive board included all editors: P. E. Burton, one-time owner of the Joplin *News-Herald;* E. Lansing Ray, of the St. Louis *Globe-Democrat,* and H. J. Blanton, of the Paris *Monroe County Appeal.*[7]

During the Journalism Week session in May, the association had three days for its program. A talk on "What the Farmer Wants in the Newspaper" stressed the need to give more coverage to agricultural news and to "get behind the co-operative marketing movements, which are coming here to stay." Publishers joined in co-operative buying and saved about $2,000 that year on newsprint purchases through the association. Asa W. Butler of the Albany *Capital* was elected president for 1924 at the fall session, at which publishers suggested hiking subscription rates to help offset rising costs of other items.[8]

Missouri publishers continued to share the spotlight during Journalism Week. Of interest today is the fair division of newspaper content offered by W. Clyde Fuller of the Lebanon *Rustic,* who suggested that 30 per cent of the space be given to news, 10 to special features, 5 to editorials, 5 to miscellaneous, and 50 to advertising. Miss Sara L. Lockwood spoke on opportunities for women in journalism. Eugene B. Roach of the Carthage *Democrat* became president for 1925 and had charge of the session during Journalism Week in May and of the October gathering in St. Louis. Diversity of topics continued to mark the programs. Publishers discussed their legal rights, tendencies in cartooning, significance of radio, the crossword puzzle as a circulation factor, training of county correspondents, and other items. In the fall the association renewed a complaint voiced previously, condemning "governmental competition with private industry in the printing of envelopes as unfair and unjust since tax funds are used to cover the government's loss." During February, forty-seven editors met in Jefferson City and organized the Central Missouri Press Association. Edgar C. Nelson of the Boonville *Advertiser* was elected the first president of the group. Governor Sam A. Baker spoke to their meeting.[9]

E. H. Winter of the Warrenton *Banner* directed the Missouri Press Association's sixtieth anniversary program in Cape Girardeau the next year. Newsmen were told in Columbia in 1926 they had to consider the automobile more seriously and also the movement of farmers into cities. Still more agricultural news was suggested. "In writing my editorials I feel as though I am talking to thousands of people personally and that I must do what is right by them," Winter later told *Editor & Publisher.* "I do not believe it wholesome for the public welfare for a number of leading papers to be in the hands of a few men whose only interest is that of giving to the public the news."[10]

C. L. Hobart of the Holden *Progress* became president for 1927. An unusual aspect of the fall program was a symposium with nine news men and women of the state giving impressions from their recent trips to Europe. Henry Denman of the Farmington *News* presided in 1928 when Walter Williams told editors he feared "Journalism in Missouri and elsewhere is becoming contented to be a 'yes' man to the whims of other influences. . . . The new journalism must be courageous physically, intellectually, morally." After recommending changes in the state's libel laws, the association named Charles L. Woods of the Rolla *Herald* to preside in 1929. The May meeting held special significance for the association, which helped the School of Journalism observe its twentieth annual Journalism Week. A number of newsmen were on the program, including Woods; Mrs. Carrie Clark, Trenton *Republican;* J. G. Morgan, Unionville *Republican;* Eugene B. Roach, Carthage *Democrat;* H. S. Sturgis, Neosho *Times;* Will H. Zorn, West Plains *Howell County Gazette;* and W. R. Dutton, Seneca *News-Dispatch.*

The Kansas City *Star* and the *Journal-Post* provided special dinners for members attending the association's meeting there in November, 1929. Of interest was a statement by J. B. Jeffries of the Hannibal *Courier-Post* that "the newspaper should be regarded as a sort of barometer of the community in which it is published." Credit for such work was given to Fred and George Naeter, publishers of the Cape Girardeau *Southeast Missourian,* in a full-page feature in *Editor & Publisher* that month. These brothers were recognized far beyond Missouri's borders, and the article noted, "With their ambition to build up a better paper, they have striven constantly to quicken public spirit and develop both a better and bigger city. Friendly character has featured their policy and endeavors."[11]

Henry P. Childers, for years publisher of the Troy paper, was quoted as saying, at the end of a half century in the profession: "I have preferred to give the best I had to my neighbors and friends who have been so loyal to me when I needed friends. . . . While I am sure that I could have made more money elsewhere, there are so many things I have found that are far more worthwhile than wealth. These things I have enjoyed and the years that remain to me will still afford me enjoyment along the same lines."[12]

E. E. Swain of the Kirksville *Express and News* became the president for 1930.

PROFESSIONAL GROWTH, WAGES

"The profession of Journalism is entitled to stand side by side with the other learned professions and is, far more than any other, interwoven with the lines of public service," said William Southern, Jr., editor of the Independence *Examiner*, during Journalism Week in 1921. Southern voiced views to be heard for years, when he said, "The journalist cannot consider his profession rightly unless he recognizes his obligation to the public."

By 1921 printers generally were working a 48-hour week, though no such limits applied in the editorial department. Even then, the International Typographical Union was conducting a drive for a shorter week, apparently to help care for the many unemployed. Wages varied across the state. Printers in Kansas City earned $40.50 in 1921-1922 for a 48-hour week, while a 44-hour week in Kirksville paid $25. In St. Louis printers received $51 for a 46-hour week in 1926. That November about 600 attended a banquet celebrating the seventieth anniversary of the St. Louis Typographical Union. The city's oldest printer, Philip F. Coghlan, 94, had been a member of the national group for 75 years. His 72-year-old son worked with him in the *Post-Dispatch* composing room.

Cost of newsprint was a disturbing factor to publishers at this time. The American Newspaper Publishers Association early in

1921 decided that $60 to $65 would be a fair price per ton of paper, although most firms charged more. Prices did fall from the peak of $130 in 1920 to about $62 in 1929. Papers received a boost from a state source in 1923 when Jesse W. Barrett made his statement quoted at the start of this chapter. Speaking at Journalism Week he expressed his view of the editor as a public officer and advocated canons for reporters similar to those for editors. Charles A. Lee, State Superintendent of Schools, called the daily paper "the great vehicle of worldwide communication" and urged that it be placed in every school, with at least one daily paper receiving "proper emphasis before the student body."[13]

CHANGES HIGHLIGHT DECADE

Missouri publishers adopted new ideas and equipment in the twenties, first in the city papers and then in the smaller communities. For example, in 1921 the *Post-Dispatch* used a wireless telephone or radiophone to broadcast golf tournament scores on a hole-to-hole basis. However, the equipment was inoperative on rainy days. In 1922, with its two major-league baseball teams doing quite well, St. Louis went baseball crazy. Afternoon papers issued sports extras on colored paper, the *Times* on pink, the *Star* on green, and the *Post-Dispatch* on salmon. The morning *Globe-Democrat* featured sports in its early edition. The *Post-Dispatch* experimented with a Sunday evening edition to capture this baseball-conscious audience. The display and classified advertisements that appeared in the Saturday edition were reprinted in this special edition. At the same time, the *Star* abolished its Sunday edition, stating the management's belief that the city could not support three Sunday papers.[14]

In Fayette, the *Democrat Leader* claimed in mid-1924 that it was the first Missouri weekly paper—and perhaps one of the first in the nation—to establish its own radio station.[15]

Names continued to be important; the *Post-Dispatch* valued its title so much that it sought legal action to prohibit the Houston, Texas, Printing Company from using *Post-Dispatch* as the name for its paper. The petition stated that

> from 1878 until August 1, 1924, the complainant was the only paper in the United States using this name or any similar name, and in consequence thereof, although the words St. Louis were sometimes printed on the paper in connection with the words *Post-Dispatch* to indicate the place of publication . . . these

words formed no part of its trade name, and said paper was ordinarily handled by dealers called for and bought and sold by the
name *Post-Dispatch.*

However, the paper lost; the Houston *Post-Dispatch* appeared
for a brief time.[16]

In Columbia the School of Journalism added courses as needed.
For example, The Country Newspaper was started in 1924, its
primary object to let students gain experience in publishing a
weekly, the *Herald-Statesman,* a private enterprise of long standing which was acquired for this project.[17]

Circulation men sought new ways to make subscribers pay.
In Holden, the *Progress* began a practice now in common use—
printing a box which said: "If you find this paragraph marked,
you will know that your subscription is about to expire. The rule
among the best country papers is to stop at expiration of subscription."[18]

Speed became a dominant factor; presses turned out more
copies faster and faster. The rapidity of transmission of news
was demonstrated at the Journalism Week banquet in 1927 when
a message was flashed from Columbia around the world, via the
United Press, in eight minutes. The event proved quite exciting
as four hundred editors and students witnessed the event. The
airplane entered the scene, too. In St. Louis, papers used planes
to return pictures and stories from political conventions. Although some pilots were killed, the practice continued to expand.
One of the top pictures of 1929 was that taken by a *Post-Dispatch* photographer of a mechanic working on a plane that was
setting an endurance record at 3,000 feet over the city.

PLANT EXPANSION, SALES

Papers added presses, declared dividends, upped their advertising rates, and increased their circulations. In St. Louis a 100
per cent stock dividend was declared by the *Globe-Democrat* in
1922; in 1925 another stock dividend of a million dollars was
announced. The Kansas City *Journal-Post* moved into "one of
the West's finest plants" in 1923. The pressroom was termed
outstanding, with a bank of Hoe superspeed presses 90 feet in
length, driven by four 80-horsepower motors. The *Journal-Post*
added color presses to handle the comic pages. Space also was
provided for a rotogravure firm, and all the major wire services.
Some twenty-five type-casting machines were in the composing

room. At the same time, the Kansas City *Star* spent a million dollars expanding its facilities. Additional Goss color presses costing $250,000 were purchased. In 1927 the *Star* purchased 30 Goss presses costing $800,000, said to be the largest order Goss had received up to that time.

The Springfield *Leader* expanded in 1926 into a new three-story building. Another Linotype, additional stereotype equipment, and an improved conveyor system built to carry papers from the basement to the newsboys were added. Two years later the *Leader* and *News* merged, the *Leader* reportedly paying $400,000 for the *News*.

When the Hannibal *Courier-Post* moved into its new building in 1925 it published a 70-page special edition and held open house for some 5,000 visitors.

Numerous sales of papers occurred. In Joplin the *News-Herald* was sold to the *Globe* in 1922. In one week that year three sales were reported, involving the Newton *Chronicle*, Green City *Press*, and the Leeton *Times*. The St. Louis *Star* did an about-face in early 1924, printing a "Denying a Rumor" box story on page 1. The editor wrote, "Ordinarily the St. Louis *Star* would not dignify with a reply the circulation of baseless rumor that . . . the *Star* has been or is about to be sold or consolidated with another newspaper." The rumor was blamed on the Klu Klux Klan.[19] The *Globe-Democrat* was purchased in 1925 by E. Lansing Ray, who acquired stock from the McKee estate in a transaction involving $1,350,000, according to *Editor & Publisher*. Elzey Roberts acquired the interest owned by Frank P. Glass in the *Star*, later that year.

The largest sale of the decade was that of the Kansas City *Star* to its employes for $11,000,000 in 1926. This was said to have been the second highest price paid for a paper up to that time, being surpassed by the $13,000,000 paid for the Chicago *Daily News* in 1925. W. B. Dickey of the *Journal-Post* fought the sale, carrying his campaign to obtain the paper to the Supreme Court. I. E. Kirkwood, the *Star's* editor who assisted employes in completing the transaction, died a year after the sale, leaving an insurance policy of $625,000 to the firm.

In Poplar Bluff Dwight H. Brown, who was campaigning for the office of secretary of state, sold his *Daily Interstate-American* and *Weekly Citizen-Democrat* to J. H. Wolpers, who published the *Republican;* on March 12, 1928, the latter appeared as the *American-Republican*. About $100,000 was said to have been involved in the sale of the Maryville *Democrat-Forum and Tribune* in mid-1928, but figures were not quoted when it was sold again in 1929.

In October, 1928, the Kansas City *Journal* and *Post* merged. The suspension of the *Journal* brought to an end the city's oldest paper, which traced its ancestry to the *Enterprise*, established in 1854. Also in 1928, the St. Joseph *Gazette* was sold to the *News-Press* for a reported $175,000.

On the national scene there was an exposé of plans of the International Paper Company to buy interest in a number of leading papers across the nation, including the Kansas City *Star*. The *Star* announced in May, 1929,

> The ownership of a paper carries with it the responsibility for its disposition. A paper ought to be more than an individual property. It is, or should be, a community institution. It was a fortunate development, therefore, both for the papers themselves and for their readers, that attractive offers of purchase made to a group of publications by persons with the financial support of power interests were refused.[20]

ADVERTISING, PROMOTION, PRICES

Advertising gained, occupying a larger portion of the paper's space. Along with this were promotional activities of the larger papers, involving advertisers as well. Circulation men sought additional devices to reach their desired goals. With an increase in circulation came higher advertising rates, although at times ad rates rose higher than seemed logical. For example, a study by *Editor & Publisher* comparing figures for 1913 with those for 1922 showed that the circulation of papers in Kansas City, St. Louis, St. Joseph, and Joplin increased from 1,091,665 to 1,171,-000 during these years. However, the advertising rates for these papers jumped from 99 cents to $1.83 per line per million circulation. Another study by the same magazine showed variations of space devoted to advertising and to news in 1923. News occupied from 18 to 88 per cent of the space in the 144 evening papers reviewed. In Missouri, the St. Louis *Times* had 64 per cent news; Kansas City *Star*, 43; Kansas City *Post*, 35; St. Joseph *News-Press*, 34; and St. Louis *Post-Dispatch* 26.[21]

Special programs were designed to promote classified advertising. In 1923 Frank Rucker, advertising manager of the Independence *Examiner*, conducted a Want-ad Week with success. In writing *Editor & Publisher* about this project, Rucker said he spent ten days educating the public to the advantages of want ads, their opportunities, and interesting reading. Newspaper space, direct mail, and picture slides were used in the promotion. It was so successful that on the first day the *Examiner* carried twice the usual number of want ads.[22]

Missouri Press Association members mapped plans to combine their facilities to obtain more national advertising. In early 1923 more than 200 publishers, with a combined circulation of 290,000, pledged themselves to conform to a specific standard of advertising rates and to make no secret rate deals.[23]

Publishers realized the value of advertising Missouri and its resources long before official sources began this practice. Regional press groups joined in this project, urging the dissemination of data concerning Missouri's resources and advantages. The Northwest Missouri Press Association in 1927 made plans for each editor to report on civic improvements in his area. These data were summarized in booklets sent to national advertisers.

When should an organization be required to pay for notices? This question came up frequently in discussions, and one editor, R. E. Hodges of the Mokane *Missourian,* reported in 1923 that he charged for advertising when there was an admission cost to the meeting or program.

Publishers complained of canned publicity that went directly into the wastebasket unopened. A few even refused to accept outstate advertising when it concerned products manufactured locally. However, the majority of the papers believed that "the merchants would not hesitate to sell their products to persons outside their vicinity and the newspaper should have the same attitude toward advertising."[24]

This age-old problem of free versus paid space appeared at many association gatherings. Tom V. Bodine of the Paris *Mercury* reported in 1924 that he saved all the free publicity matter he had received for six weeks and it weighed eleven pounds. Later his colleagues in the northeast association passed a resolution to the effect that it "would no longer tolerate or encourage the attempts of paid agents to secure free publicity in its papers in any shape or form." Publishers agreed that their space was what they had to use, and it should be reserved "for news of importance to the subscribers and for honest advertising that pays the rate."[25]

A few metropolitan papers that owned radio stations entered a new era when the *Post-Dispatch* in 1925 for the first time sold advertisements over its station KSD. After the experiment had been in operation for several weeks, the paper said it "had proven satisfactory to the paper and to the advertisers, and, of great importance, to the public."[26]

Papers also utilized promotional plans to attract readers. In St. Louis, the *Star* entertained about eighteen thousand children in a series of picnics at an amusement resort. In Springfield, three thousand children were entertained by the *Leader* at a "tinymite" theater party. Cooking schools appeared, as well as similar activities, to interest readers. A Christmas party sponsored by the *Post-Dispatch* drew ten thousand children to the St. Louis Coliseum in 1924. Fifty-five thousand gifts were distributed, along with 3,800 baskets of food, representing $15,000. The *Times,* too, aided many through its Good Fellow program. In Kansas City the *Star* conducted an eight-day exhibition of new homes that attracted about 500,000 visitors, counting the many times they went into the homes which varied in price from $7,350 to $42,500.

To raise revenue to meet growing costs, papers frequently hiked their advertising rates. On a few occasions these efforts backfired. In early 1928 seven St. Louis retail stores halted advertising in the *Post-Dispatch* after being told rates would be increased one cent an agate line. The *Star* and *Globe-Democrat* gained advertising during the two-month boycott.[27]

Another controversy appeared over the growth of radio advertising. No doubt many editors agreed with W. L. Dickey of the Kansas City *Journal-Post* when, in 1929, he began to charge stations for printing their programs. "We found that we were giving free publicity in printing the programs of radio advertisers, both national and local, many of whom are not newspaper advertisers. These advertisers were getting from us for nothing what they were paying radio stations for. In many instances trade names and trade slogans were used," he said. The practice, however, did not become widespread.[28]

Theaters became larger advertisers, especially after the introduction of Al Jolson's *The Singing Fool*, probably one of the first movies to rate a million-dollar advertising budget.

Publishers became more conscious of their responsibilities to advertisers. In 1929 thirteen members of the Missouri Associated Dailies completed surveys in their trade territories with the assistance of University of Missouri School of Journalism advertising students. The results were sent to national firms and to agencies. Co-operating were the Chillicothe *Constitution-Tribune,* Columbia *Missourian,* Fulton *Sun-Gazette,* Hannibal *Courier-Post,* Independence *Examiner,* Jefferson City *Capital-News,* Kirksville *Express and News,* Macon *Chronicle-Herald,* Mexico *Ledger,* Moberly *Monitor-Index and Democrat,* Sedalia *Capital-Democrat,* Trenton *Republican-Times,* and Warrensburg *Star-Journal.*[29] Earlier the *Globe-Democrat* had surveyed 110,000 homes, obtaining 80,797 effective interviews to learn the subscribers' reading habits.

Prices remained reasonably constant. The Sunday edition normally sold for ten cents, while the dailies varied from two to five cents. In 1925 the Kansas City *Star* increased its subscription price from 10 to 15 cents for thirteen papers it delivered weekly. "Everything that goes into the making of a newspaper has remained at a high level," the paper said. "White paper, the heaviest single item in newspaper cost, was $40 a ton before the war. It costs $77 a ton. Uncle Sam demands more for transporting newspapers in the mails and has under way a still further increase. Wages of printers, of pressmen, of all labor, have gone up steadily."[30]

POLITICS IN THE TWENTIES

The first time Republicans carried the state in any sizable number was in 1920, when Warren G. Harding defeated James Cox in the contest for the Presidency. The Ohio publisher received nearly 56 per cent of Missouri's votes, carrying 85 counties. Both St. Louis and Jackson County went Republican. Other parties, such as the Farmer-Labor, Single Tax, and Prohibitionist, received scant support.

When Wilson left the White House, the *Post-Dispatch* saw his failure as a failure on the part of the American people. "Forces of envy, jealousy, sordid selfishness and partisan malice have done their work," an editorial said on March 3. The Kansas City *Star* had more concern with local problems, less with European.

The campaign leading up to the election of Harding had its interesting aspects. Some thought it was time to return to normal life—life as they recalled it before the war—which they could do by rejecting those associated with the war. The term "normalcy" became the password, setting a new image for a political philosophy. The *Post-Dispatch* and the *Star* in Kansas City represented the two-party system. Both warmed to their causes, attacking the opposition more than praising their own candidates. The *Post-Dispatch* thought Harding as colorless as the Republican platform, and a month before the election accused him of leading the nation into "a ditch of dishonesty" where "selfish greed and chaos run rampant."

Harding had "dignity, modesty, common sense, evident sincerity, a grasp of public questions and high conception of the presidential office," according to the *Star*. He was considered "practical, frank, patriotic, appreciative, and opposed to the League of Nations without selfish isolationism," a policy dear to the *Star's* heart at that time. The paper supported Harding for his anti-League sentiments and saw the election as an opportunity for Americans to "pass a verdict on the Wilson administration."

When the verdict was in, the *Post-Dispatch* suggested that the nation "give President Harding a fair deal. . . . In the circumstances it is peculiarly incumbent upon us to give Mr. Harding the fullest measure of friendship, trust and loyalty." The *Star* said, "Only the narrowest partisanship will want him to fail." Some papers thought Harding's career as a country editor would enable him better to understand the needs of the people.[31]

Considerable space was devoted to the naval and disarmament conferences. The *Star* predicted that "Japan, in a war with this country, would have no need to carry its operations into the Eastern Pacific. . . . It would simply seize the Philippines and Guam and wait for the United States to do something about it."[32] When President Harding died on August 2, 1923, the *Post-Dispatch* wrote: "President Harding is dead." The *Star* wrote: "A Nation today mourned the passing of its leader." In these leads political beliefs are clear. One is indifferent, the other a sorrowful chant. The *Post-Dispatch* editorially said Harding was fortunate in "the time of his passing," that he had realized the mistake of keeping America out of international affairs, but did not know what to do about it. Coolidge, to the *Star*, was "a safe and sane . . . old-fashioned Republican." In defense of Harding the Kansas City paper said, "The real defect of the Harding administration as it reacts on the people is that it does not make noise enough." The paper cited Harding's efforts in vetoing the bonus bill, in the reduction of federal expenses, and in keeping the country out of the League of Nations.[33]

The papers were at opposite poles in January, 1924, when the Teapot Dome scandals broke. A *Post-Dispatch* cartoon—a GOP

elephant running about with a teapot tied to its tail—gave the
paper's views. The *Star*, obviously embarrassed by the scandal,
still gave it adequate coverage.

"This thing has got to come to an end," wrote Will Rogers in
describing the nine-day convention of the Democratic party in
New York in 1924. "New York invited you people here as
guests, not to live." The party finally nominated John W. Davis
as its presidential candidate on the one-hundredth ballot. Among
the thousand newsmen present were reporters from the Kansas
City *Star* and the *Journal-Post*, and the St. Louis *Post-Dispatch*,
Globe-Democrat, and *Star*. They said they had to "swelter on
hard chairs."[34] The *Post-Dispatch* thought Davis was a good
compromise between "the reactionary Coolidge on one side and
the radical La Follette on the other."[35] The *Star* gave slight
coverage to the selection at this time.

Missouri went Republican. Coolidge received 49.7 per cent of
the votes; the balance was shared by Davis and Progressive
Robert M. La Follette.

Republicans were stronger in Missouri in 1928 and gave Herbert Hoover the largest GOP majority in the state's history.
Ninety-two counties went Republican, including ten that had
never before voted this ticket. However, Democrats scored victories in St. Louis, where the strongly Catholic population turned
to Alfred E. Smith. The one-sided vote caught a number of
Missouri editors by surprise. *Editor & Publisher* had conducted
a poll of editors, of whom 15 said Hoover would carry the state,
14 said Smith, and 2 were in doubt. However, the editors voted
20 to 11 that Hoover would carry the national ticket. Republicans
also won control of the state government, electing Arthur M.
Hyde to the governorship in 1920, Sam A. Baker in 1924, and
Henry S. Caulfield in 1928.

All in all, the twenties were eventful years for the Missouri
press. Papers were becoming larger, the writing more informal.
Personal journalism was gradually disappearing, yet some editors
mourned the loss of such descriptive writing as the following
from the Lathrop *Monitor* at the turn of the century:

> That degenerate son-of-a-good-father, who distributes cards and
> tells lies for that Contemptible Kirksville—Penitentiary sneak thief
> printing concern, polluted the pure atmosphere of Lathrop by
> the exhibition of his diseased carcass on our streets Saturday,
> but it makes us smile to think how flatly he was refused at every
> business house here. We have great confidence in the good sense

and business sagacity of our citizens and Mr. Cheap John Horse-thief Printshop can't catch them on the cheap racket. He wailed mournfully when he got so unceremoniously left and we are quite sure he walked out of town, as he did not buy a ticket or take a train at either depot. Businessmen, when he offers to do you honest, decent work, done by decent men; when he promises to take one half of all the bill in trade; when he employs honest help who spend their money here; when he fights for the up-building of the city and is willing to "chip in" to help along any movement; then, and not till then, will he have any claims on your consideration. Did he do it? We think not and you did right in giving him the shake.[36]

The papers, ready to record the thirties, were prepared to handle this task but in a less personal manner.

CHAPTER XX

DEPRESSION, LEAN YEARS, THEN WAR

THE THIRTIES were eventful years. Starting in the midst of a depression that became worse before it became better, the newspaper reader found himself engrossed in the New Deal and its alphabetical agencies. One act, the National Recovery Act, was especially disturbing to publishers. Papers in the larger cities became more deeply involved with unions as editorial workers and others organized the American Newspaper Guild on St. Louis papers and the Kansas City *Journal-Post*.

Technical advancements highlighted the decade. The transmission of pictures by Wirephoto was followed shortly with the sending of a three-color photograph of the King and Queen of England while they were visiting this nation. Photography advanced along other lines as the miniature camera became a regular part of the photographer's equipment. Presses were improved and attempts made to save newsprint whenever possible as publishers sought to hold operating costs to the minimum. Papers became more readable; publishers studied typography and discussed the use of upper- and lower-case headlines as more readable than all-caps labels. In 1936, for example, eight of the nine winners of the Ayer's typographical contest had headlines in the new style, though the New York *Times* maintained its all-caps style. Some Missouri papers used other efforts to dress up their appearance. The Mexico *Intelligencer* in 1937 "lightenized" its paper from eight to four columns, with the body type increased from eight to ten points. Some readers said it looked like *Capper's Weekly*, others like *Townsend Weekly*, and some thought it was like a New York paper. This pattern was continued for several months; the *Intelligencer* disappeared in a few years.[1]

Run-of-the-paper color was more widely used in city papers, but the outlying publications were not to use much color for at least another decade. Publishers urged lower wages to keep above financial ruin, while the federal agencies and the unions asked for higher pay and fewer working hours. Coverage of key news events became more thorough, while debates developed over excess coverage, such as occurred on the Lindbergh kidnaping. In these verbal battles the city papers were the victims; smaller papers maintained a closer eye on the home scene. Papers used any item that might possibly give a brighter account of the gloomy situation that followed the stock market crash in 1929.

Missourians were informed of a variety of events. State-wide, there was interest in the 100th anniversary of the birth of Mark Twain, in 1931. Feature stories became more prominent. A story about a dog wrung the hearts of St. Louis readers in 1930 when a small fox terrier was reportedly found dead with its mouth sewed shut. Rewards of three thousand dollars were raised after stories reached streamer-headline proportions. When the police entered the case, under public pressure, they were unable to confirm the story or even to ascertain if such a dog had ever existed.[2] In Springfield, a girl reporter on the *Leader* lived for ten days on 25 cents a day, and in her articles she frequently admitted the diet left her hungry. She counted calories and followed a physician's advice, yet still had nothing promising to offer the working girl who had to pinch pennies to survive.[3]

Motion picture advertising, welcomed only a brief time earlier as a source of revenue, became the center of a controversy in St. Louis after the *Star* rejected an ad for *The Love Parade*, starring Maurice Chevalier. An editorial, claiming the ad was full of sex suggestions, warned the theater interests that they would probably wreck their business if they continued producing such degrading copy.[4]

RADIO, TELEVISION ENTER SCENE

In mid-1930 *Editor & Publisher* reported that television could be an adjunct to dailies, saying, "What the powers of television will do when we can stand face to face with the peoples of other countries can easily be imagined. The newspaper will be a very important factor in standing shoulder to shoulder with radio and television as one great force impelling truth and righteousness."[5]

Each year the newspaper industry became more alarmed about gains in radio advertising, which reached twenty million dollars when the decade opened. By 1931, 37 per cent of all Missouri families owned radios. In newspaper association meetings, national and local, discussion of radio competition shared a part of the agenda with talks on economy measures. Meanwhile, in St. Louis the *Post-Dispatch* celebrated the tenth anniversary of its ownership of KSD in 1932. A major problem carried over from the twenties was whether a paper should or should not charge for printing radio programs. A national survey in 1934 indicated that 30 per cent of the papers carried regular radio columns, while 83 per cent carried the listings. Some, such as the St. Joseph *News-Press,* placed the listings in the classified ad section.

By 1935 there developed a closer relationship between the radio and the press when more and more papers acquired their own stations. That year the United Press and International News Service began to sell their news to radio stations, but it was 1939 before the Associated Press joined in this practice. "The vitality of the daily press in an era when prejudiced critics have declared it doomed by facsimile, television, and even less tangible inventions, is also evidenced by the strong gains in the number of papers published," *Editor & Publisher* said in 1936.[6]

The University of Missouri School of Journalism had entered the instructional area in radio broadcasting by 1936 with three fifteen-minute intervals broadcast daily over Columbia's KFRU. A facsimile license was granted in early 1938 to the St. Louis *Post-Dispatch* for experimental work, and by December it became the first in the world in this broadcasting area, transmitting news to the homes of fifteen station members. However, it took fifteen minutes for each small page to clear the machine.

As the decade neared its end, publishers still were concerned about the probable effects of television. Some publishers thought the medium definitely would become a threat in capturing local advertising money.

PAY, GUILD, ECONOMY MEASURES

Although most Missouri publishers were not seriously concerned with the growth of the American Newspaper Guild, they were directly affected by the government's efforts to spread employment through shorter work weeks. When pay scales went up in some communities, publishers elsewhere found it necessary to raise wages to keep their own personnel.

In 1930, a survey by Professor Thomas C. Morelock of the University of Missouri School of Journalism showed, "The country paper is on a better basis than at any other time in history. . . . Most of them are making money, most of them could make more money and enjoy more prestige by adopting better methods and rendering more valuable service to their constitutents." However, some publishers failed to concur in this optimism, as the year moved on and the depression came closer home.[7]

Papers helped to ease the unemployment picture, devoting space to "Give a Job" drives and similar projects. In LaPlata the

Home Press reported in late 1933 about a tramp printer visiting the plant. "The knees of his pants were out, his shirt clean, but worn, and he carried no baggage, not even a coat—just shirt and pants." After giving him the "usual quarter," the editor reported the printer said: "I thank you sincerely, I am hungry."[8] Some larger papers provided free want ads for any seeking help. Others contributed to the community funds; a few helped in clothing drives. In Maryville the *Forum* issued an extra in July, 1931, to stop a run on a bank, explained the situation and reported the plans under way to save the institution.

Wages were cut in many areas. Generally, the nonunion editorial workers suffered the larger slashes. In St. Louis, men in the mechanical departments agreed to more careful handling of newsprint. In 1932 engravers accepted a 10 per cent cut, but publishers failed to get the typographers to take any greater cut than 10 per cent. Even then, the printers voted that 3 per cent of their pay be withheld for the benefit of unemployed union workers. After the National Recovery Act was passed, the papers adopted the code despite increased costs, but not without some opposition. The Missouri Press Association, Missouri Associated Dailies, and several district press association leaders met in Jefferson City in August, 1933, to discuss the plan. They deliberated for some time on a resolution which would approve a forty-cent-per-hour scale and a forty-four-hour week. They approved the resolution, deliberated some more, then rejected it. Delegates went to the national meeting in Chicago with instructions to do what seemed best.

There was "strong talk among editorial men," according to *Editor & Publisher* that month. "Are editorial craftsmen ready for unionization?" the magazine asked. "A union must be prepared not only to accept the benefits of organization, but full responsibility." St. Louis Guild members opposed affiliation with another union, believing "evolution of the National Guild should be along the lines of a professional guild and that labor affiliation offers no immediate concrete advantages to offset the grave possible dangers of the future that it holds." When the national group joined the American Federation of Labor in 1936, the St. Louis chapter called this union a "crumbling institution which in its present set-up may not survive another six months."[9]

Workers sought additional benefits. Some labor groups called for a thirty to thirty-four-hour week with the same pay as they received in 1929. Newsmen, however, were content to seek a forty-hour week with generous discharge notices. Needless to say, freedom of the press became an active issue as the President and the papers feuded over New Deal codes.[10] The St. Louis *Post-Dispatch* noted, "No code can gag the press of the United States, which is as free as the air." However, the *Post-Dispatch* and the *Globe-Democrat* were among the first papers to adopt the five-day week for staff members.

Publishers were involved in heated verbal struggles over child labor, which concerned their carriers. The St. Louis *Star-Times* complained in 1935 that efforts of the American Newspaper Publishers Association had "done more . . . to destroy their [newspaper] influence with the American people than all their enemies combined. What wonder is it that radio orators usurp the leadership of the press, when papers thus parade their short-comings before the nation." The *Star-Times* complained about the demand that boys from ten to fourteen years of age be permitted to work during three-hour periods which ranged from 5 in the morning until 8 at night. "It is obvious that the demand is made for economic reasons which will not stand scrutiny," the paper added.[11]

After the NRA was declared unconstitutional in 1935, few changes were expected among the larger papers. However, *Editor & Publisher* said, "Insofar as the newspaper business is concerned, there is no doubt that majority publisher sentiment rejoices in the elimination of NRA, always a misfit in this field, a disturbing and menacing factor from the start." A survey of Missouri publishers voiced this sentiment as replies came from St. Louis, Sedalia, Jefferson City, Warrensburg, Boonville, and Springfield.[12]

Other problems still faced publishers. The Social Security program went into operation, and *Editor & Publisher* reported that "most dailies were not aware of the legislation's wide scope." They soon found out.

For several years the unions were content to hold their own in their contracts. Few new pay peaks were established in 1936 in city contracts, which served to determine pay in nearby communities. Members of the International Typographical Union turned down proposals to unite with the American Newspaper Guild. Many a reporter read a government release in early 1937 with mixed feelings. Under a new law, income tax returns of individuals earning more than $15,000 annually from a single source were published. Many newspapermen from St. Louis, Kansas City, and St. Joseph appeared on the first list, which recorded 1935 returns. Joseph Pulitzer led with $221,376, while his managing editor, O. K. Bovard, earned $55,000, and cartoonist Daniel R. Fitzpatrick received $21,997. By 1938 Bovard gave up this high-salaried job because of "irreconcilable differences as to general conduct of the paper."[13] In still another attempt at controlling pay scales, the publishers sought exemption from the wage-hour provisions of the federal laws in 1938, asserting that journalism is a profession, not a manufacturing process, and that its business is preponderantly intrastate.[14]

By the end of the decade union members and newsmen could report some financial gains. Their situation in 1930 was made clear in a survey of Missouri dailies, which showed these average salaries: Advertising managers, $48.65; ad salesmen, $29.18; circulation managers, $35.66; solicitors, $33.93; city editors, $43.26; reporters, $25.95; composing room foremen, $41.94; pressmen, $34.87; linotype operators, $35.05; and stereotypers, $25.30. All were much lower in a similar survey three years later, but by 1939 times had improved somewhat.[15]

ADVERTISING MORE INVOLVED

Publishers, concerned about their volume of advertising, became involved in debates about what they should or should not advertise. In St. Louis the *Star* of January 31, 1930, lashed out at Hollywood advertising, saying such sex-dominated messages would probably "wreck their businesses unless better judgment is followed." Opposition from merchants alarmed some publishers, but not all. In St. Joseph the *News-Press* printed a front-page story of a woman winning a $300 verdict against a local concern. The story named the concern, and the company canceled its advertising. The *News-Press* replied, in part: "This punitive action makes occasion to say here that the *News-Press* is primarily a newspaper and that its mission is to print the news; that it aims to meet this expectation of its readers as faithfully as possible, with full regard for fitness, fairness, truth and decency, and without regard for the persons, firms or interests affected."[16]

In Kansas City fourteen neighborhood theaters withdrew their advertisements from the *Journal-Post* when that paper citicized some pictures. The paper replied that it "would not be influenced by the withdrawal of advertising patronage in its policy of telling the truth, as it sees it, about any form of entertainment. This newspaper is not subject to pressure of that sort."[17]

With the resumption of the legal sale of beer, papers tapped a new source of revenue. St. Louis papers, for example, in 1933 carried their first beer ads in thirteen years. A few years later a number of papers refused to carry any beer advertisements, while some refused to carry liquor ads, but did permit beer ads.

Publishers began to censor their advertisements more carefully. The *Post-Dispatch* estimated this practice cost it at least $200,000 annually in lost revenue. In one case the paper rejected a cigar ad that showed a man and woman embracing each other and asked this question: "How does she kiss you?" The paper asked its own question: "Can you imagine anything more distasteful than associating intimate kissing with breath odors derived from the use of cigars?"[18]

Papers used their own columns to advertise their products and to assist worth-while projects. A campaign in Missouri dailies in 1930 urged readers to patronize centers operated by the blind and to purchase items they made. "Know Your Labels" suggested the Carondolet *News* in a double-page ad in 1930. Labels of various products handled by local merchants were published, and the ad was paid for by the manufacturers.

For many years there had been discussions among publishers leading to co-operation in obtaining national advertising. In early 1934 C. E. Watkins of the Chillicothe *Constitution-Tribune* urged such co-operation among small town publishers. He stressed the importance of collective bargaining with national advertisers to sell space in blocks of 50,000 or 100,000 circulation. Watkins said the advertising dollar was "a fickle coin, especially in times of economic distress and spotted markets."[19]

In 1937 the Missouri Press Association board approved a four-point program:

1. One order, one plate, one check service to national advertisers for all members of the association.

2. A central checking copy bureau to service advertising placed through the one-order system.

3. A publicity control bureau to keep the free-space moochers out of Missouri, thereby enlarging the field for paid advertising.

4. Group representation for members who pay annual assessments, which varied from about $72 to $176.

About one hundred papers were expected to participate in the program. In addition to progress made in obtaining advertising for Missouri papers, the association in 1939 returned more than eight thousand pieces of publicity to business institutions sponsoring these releases.[20]

CIRCULATION EFFORTS, GAINS

Circulation gains had been reported in 1929. Publishers turned to great efforts in promotion of stories and events to stimulate reader interest. Many used the serial story, and the St. Louis *Star* offered suggestions to other publishers. Select top stories, watch the timing, illustrate the stories, and watch their length, said the *Star*.

In 1930 there was an average of two dailies sold for every American home. Some of this greater readership was credited by *Editor & Publisher* to "the compelling running news story of the year, the country's industrial and financial condition, with unemployment estimated at from five to six millions . . . the great drought . . . racketeering, crime wave, prohibition, Russia's experiment, non-resistance crusade of Gandhi, fights with so-called communists in larger cities."[21]

Varied plans for stimulating circulation were used. T. Ballard Watters, in his Marshfield *Mail*, conducted a "Mail Hen Contest."[22] In 1932, for example, a farmer could trade a healthy five-pound hen for a year's renewal of his paper. Hens were selling for fifteen cents a pound. In 1936 the Macon *Chronicle-Herald* was repeating its successful egg contest. For one hundred eggs, subscriptions would be extended for a year. The paper collected more than 71,500 eggs in two days.[23]

Efforts were made continually to encourage Missouri weekly publishers to have their circulations audited. J. Edward Gerald of the University of Missouri School of Journalism faculty studied press groups in forty states and concluded that the best circulation campaign was as simple as A, B, C.

A. *Reader loyalty*, secured only by publishing a useful paper, is the indispensable element of all circulation exploitation.

B. *Personal solicitation* of subscribers is immeasurably better than the most glittering of circulation contests or campaigns.

C. A *sound business system* of handling expiration notices and renewals backed by the will of a publisher strong enough in character to cut off those who do not pay in goods or cash.[24]

By mid-decade, *Editor & Publisher* could state that circulation of the nation's dailies had increased 40 per cent since 1920, although advertising had decreased about 15 per cent. With the decade nearing its end and war clouds approaching, publishers faced the need to raise revenue from circulation to offset other rising expenses. Missouri publishers began to follow the warnings made in earlier years by taking the guesswork out of circulation and by giving more attention to both quantity and quality. Eggs and produce as payments for subscriptions were being replaced with cash by 1940.[25]

EXPANSION, SALES, CONSOLIDATIONS

Publishers in Missouri survived the depression as well as others across the nation. True, there were losses; some papers consolidated, and a few disappeared. The Dexter *Statesman* declared in 1933 that not a single paper in southeast Missouri had been forced out of business.

> A newspaper is like the frog that was taken out of a cornerstone when a church 50 years old was torn town. The frog hopped off to look for a lunch. If an editor can't support a wife and children on nothing, keep out of debt and keep the old Flag of Liberty flying, he would better not go into the business. Half the cheese and crackers made in the United States, if close investigations were made, will be found in the tummies of editors' families.[26]

"It takes three things to successfully run a newspaper and all are important—money, news and propaganda," the Memphis *Democrat* remarked. "Money will pay the grocerymen and printers, news will fill the paper and make it interesting and propaganda fills the waste basket—and a well-filled waste basket comes in handy these cool mornings."[27]

The *Globe-Democrat* erected a $2,500,000 plant in 1931, "built in the depression to demonstrate its faith in the city." The next year the St. Louis *Times* issued $1,250,000 in bonds for expansion needs and in 1934 celebrated its fiftieth year with a 120-page anniversary edition. The *Times,* which purchased the assets of the *Star,* "sought to produce a better paper for readers of each of the former papers and a larger and better medium for advertisers." Elzey Roberts was the publisher. Another merger united the Springfield *News-Leader* and *Press* in 1933. Local firms approved the move, which brought to an end a period of intense competition between the papers. More than a thousand persons visited the new plant of the Poplar Bluff *American Republic* in 1936.

By 1939 the Kansas City *Star* was owned by 117 employes who had paid off the $11,000,000 purchase price four and a half years ahead of schedule. They had paid five million dollars on the note in five years of the depression. The *Post-Dispatch* spent half a million dollars in 1930 for an outlying branch production unit for rotogravure and color presses. The next year the Kirksville *Daily Express and News* moved into its new fireproof building.

One sale in 1931 that brought response from many editors was that of the Kansas City *Journal-Post* to Henry L. Doherty, prominent utility leader who had long opposed the *Star* policies. The *Post-Dispatch* said, "It will make the *Journal-Post* a mouthpiece for public utility propaganda and even if this propaganda is counteracted by opposing views in adjacent columns, the effect will be to give special pleading a preferred place in a daily paper." The Springfield *Leader* predicted the *Journal-Post* would not survive: "It has bartered its birthright and it can never be regained." The Sedalia *Democrat* said that Doherty had "displayed grade-school-boy judgment in his appeals to governmental departments and the trustees of the William Rockhill Nelson Memorial to have the newspaper [*Star*] suppressed and the management retired." Doherty had made a great mistake, according to the Mexico *Ledger*, for "the day of the personal organ is gone." The St. Louis *Star* remarked, "Public utility interests over the country can be thankful there is only one Henry L. Doherty. A dozen like him would probably bring on universal public ownership." Doherty sued the *Star* time and again, until in mid-1932 the total amount involved reached $54,000,000. He never collected a cent.[28]

Although the sale of the New York *World* in 1931 did not directly affect Missourians, the transaction was of interest to other papers, especially in St. Louis, where the Pulitzers also owned the *Post-Dispatch*. The *Star* noted, "The sons of Joseph Pulitzer did what they could to obey the injunctions of their father's will but a deficit of $1,900,000 for 1930 was something the elder Pulitzer never contemplated when he left his newspaper estate." The *Globe-Democrat* blamed the increased cost factor for the *World's* difficulties, yet pointed out to its readers, "The *World* has been generally regarded as an organ of the Democratic party and every observer of newspaper life is aware that party organs, at least in the cities, are becoming obsolete." The *Times* praised the Pulitzers for setting aside 10 per cent of the sale price for bonuses for faithful employes. This action, according to the *Times,* "would become an historic model after which many future ones of a like character will be moulded."[29]

What's the News in the Thirties?

News in this decade reflected some of the most eventful years in America's history, climaxed by the beginning of the war in Europe in 1939. On the national scene the ten most important stories for the decade as ranked by the Associated Press, were:

1. Allies' declaration of war (1939)
2. Lindbergh kidnaping (1932)
3. Abdication of Edward VIII (1936)
4. Roosevelt bank holiday (1933)
5. Diplomatic victory of Hitler at Munich (1938)
6. Birth of the Dionne quintuplets (1934)
7. Repeal of prohibition (1933)
8. Death of Will Rogers and of Wiley Post (1935)
9. British royalty's tour of America (1939)
10. Assassination of Huey Long (1935)

In Missouri a number of journalists were in the news. Walter Williams became president of the University of Missouri in 1930; at the School of Journalism Frank Lee Martin, one-time member of the Kansas City *Star* staff, took over as assistant dean. In June, 1935, Williams retired, and he died the next month. A former student in Williams' History and Principles of Journalism class described the final session Williams taught, when he told them,

> As newspapermen and women you will find many defects, many entanglements in your profession. Much writing is crude and careless—haste makes errors. But as journalism is finding itself, so you will find yourselves. Journalism is a necessity; it is a part of civilization. As the demands increase, more readers, swifter means of communication, etc., so journalism must be alert and ready to fill these demands. Chiefly you will be interpreters, not mirrors.[30]

Father-son combinations that were operating newspapers across the nation were featured in a series published in *Editor & Publisher*. Missourians were well represented. Among the families pictured were Walter J. Brill and son, Larry A. Brill, on the

Sedalia *Capital*, with another son, Glenn M. Brill, on the Warrensburg *Star-Journal;* J. Kelly Pool and son, Cance A. Pool, Jefferson City *Capital News;* Mrs. A. L. Preston of the Liberty *Tribune* and *Advance*, with seven sons on various papers; Cullen Cain and son, Forrest Cain, St. Louis *County Leader;* C. L. Blanton, Sr., and son, C. L. Blanton, Jr., Sikeston *Standard;* C. M. Harrison and son, Fred M. Harrison, Gallatin *North Missourian;* R. M. White and son, Mitchell White, and grandson, Robert M. White II, Mexico *Ledger;* E. Lansing Ray, Sr., and son, E. Lansing Ray, Jr., St. Louis *Globe-Democrat;* E. E. Swain and sons, E. E. Swain, Jr., and Harrison E. Swain, Kirksville *Daily Express;* Hal M. Wise, Sr., and son, Hal M. Wise, Jr., Webb City *Daily Sentinel;* R. N. Hains and son, R. K. Hains, Marshall *Democrat-News;* and A. V. Burrowes and two brothers, a sister, and a nephew, St. Joseph *News-Press.*

Henry J. Haskell as editor helped the Kansas City *Star* observe its fiftieth anniversary in 1930. Casper S. Yost completed a half century on the *Globe-Democrat* in 1939. Yost, who helped to organize the American Association of Newspaper Editors, began his newspaper work when only eight years old, setting type on the Lebanon *Laclede County Leader.*

J. W. Vincent waged a five-year losing battle to prevent the construction of Bagnell Dam in the Ozark area. In his Linn Creek *Reveille* he called it the "Damn Dam." The 70-year-old editor's fight failed, but he never gave up his efforts to save his town and county from being covered by the backwater of the project. Vincent's father had worked as a printer on Greeley's New York *Tribune*, had fought in the Mexican war, and by 1868 had established the *Reveille*. His son took over in 1880 and carried on its crusading spirit.[31]

Deaths occurred among Missouri publishers, some being accorded special notice. In Kansas City the *Post* presses were shut down during the funeral of W. S. Dickey, who died in 1931. Herbert Hoover's wire cited Dickey's "energetic and valuable service to his community, his state and his country." Fred G. Bonfils of the Denver *Post* and one-time part owner of the Kansas City *Post*, died in 1933. He was born in Troy, Missouri. Omar D. Gray died in 1935 in Sturgeon, a community he made famous with his *Leader*. Gray was an editor, columnist, broker, politician, lecturer, and businessman, but was known best for some of his sayings which were widely reprinted. "If the devil finds you idle, he will set you to work as sure as Hell," he once

wrote, and "There is no such thing as success in a bad business."
Later he wrote, "I love newspaper work. If the time should
come when I had no readers I would still publish the *Leader*
and read it myself."[32]

One of Missouri's newspaper women who had been among the
earliest in newspaper work, Mrs. J. M. Patterson, died in Marshall
in 1933 at the age of 91. She and her husband operated a paper
in Warrensburg which was destroyed during the Civil War. They
later lived in Sedalia, and in 1879 her son established the Marshall *Daily News*. Col. Robert M. White, one of the leaders of
the press in the state, died in 1934. Tom V. Bodine of the Paris
Mercury died in 1937, and, abiding by his wish, the casket was
placed in the composing room, near the Linotype he operated
for years. His desire was that there be no music or fanfare at
his funeral. For fifty years he had directed the *Mercury*'s editorial policy.

OTHERS IN LIMELIGHT

William Southern, Jr., of the Independence *Examiner* was one
of Missouri's most widely quoted newsmen. "One of our troubles
as newspapermen has been that we are either Republican or
Democrat rather than editors . . . in our hands lies the power
to bring to others success or ruin, happiness or pain. We carry
under our control an explosive power much greater and much
more dangerous than T.N.T.," he said in 1931.[33] Frank P. Briggs,
editor of the Macon *Chronicle-Herald*, became that city's first
Democratic mayor in forty-eight years in 1930. George Olds,
managing editor of the Springfield *News* and *Leader*, wrote an
article for *Editor & Publisher* in 1932, a reprint of instructions
he gave his writers. Eliminate the "bunk," he told them, as he
complained of too much record-copying, too much surface-
scratching, and "a lack of genuinely humorous stories." He objected to "too much childlike faith in news sources."[34]

Dwight H. Brown, who served the newspaper business in
Poplar Bluff for more than twenty years before becoming Missouri's secretary of state, was the subject of an *Editor & Publisher* sketch in 1933 as "A Person Worth Knowing in Journalism."[35]

Mrs. Mary Mahnkey, Oasis correspondent of the Forsyth
Taney County Republican, received national fame in winning
the title of best country correspondent in the nation in 1934. In
addition to a silver tray and fifty dollars, she earned a trip to

New York, where "the white-haired, simple, charming lady of 58" met Governor Al Smith and many of the city's leading newsmen. She told the Eastern reporters the story of her success, similar to that of many of Missouri's small-town correspondents: "If any stranger came in or anybody moved or a body was born or somebody got married or died, then that was news. And when kinsfolk came from a long way off I'd mention all their names and things like that. If something I could write would brighten up the columns or make someone laugh or please some little child or some old, old person, I'd try to do that." Mrs. Mahnkey said she scratched out her adjectives, avoided the scandalous doings of neighbors, and read the Bible a lot, since she loved the simpleness of its style.[36]

MISSOURI PRESS ORGANIZATIONS

In late 1930 members of the Missouri Press Association met in St. Louis, elected Frank H. Sosey of the Palmyra *Spectator* their president, and were urged by their secretary-treasurer, J. S. Hubbard, to contribute more support to the development of the School of Journalism. The group suggested that a permanent press building be erected at the state fairgrounds. Hubbard, after serving the association for ten years, resigned in late 1932. The new president, Wallace Crossley, said the post would be filled later.[37]

A survey of Missouri dailies in 1933 showed they were holding their circulation well. In Springfield, members of the Ozark Press Association were advised that "one way out of lean times for the rural papers would be to form a syndicate to obtain national and other contracts and to distribute the proceeds of these according to circulation." The Ozark group urged the state legislature to take advantage of the federal government's relief program and of "the repeal of the present law fixing a limitation on the acreage the federal government may acquire in counties for reforestation purposes."[38]

During these years the Missouri Press Association represented the state publishers in contacts with the National Editorial Association and other press groups in formulating the federal codes for publishers.

How some of the association's operational costs were met became obvious at the state convention at Kansas City in 1933 when the field representative was instructed by the association to charge member papers 7 per cent and nonmembers 15 per cent commission for advertising handled through the central office.[39]

The Missouri Associated Dailies, at their 1934 session in Kansas City, learned that the new state sales tax was not intended to apply to circulation. The group, composed of twenty-two dailies representing 60 per cent of the small daily circulation, opposed the Tugwell bill as "an extreme regulatory measure [which] would further hamper many concerns that have long demonstrated their responsibility to the people."[40]

President Franklin D. Roosevelt sent a message to the audience at the University of Missouri Journalism Week in 1934, in which he said that talk about any curb of the free press was silly and unjustified. Roosevelt wrote the Missouri publishers and students, "Freedom of the press means freedom of expression, both in news columns and editorial columns. Judging by both these columns in papers in every part of the country, this freedom is freer than it ever has been in our history."[41]

When the School of Journalism named the fifteen leading Missouri papers that year, the verdict aroused mixed feelings in some publishers. One, apparently not among the selected few, wrote, "We could name fifty and not half try. And we could name 50 Missouri editors who have forgotten more about the newspaper game than the School of Journalism professor will ever know."[42] There were 275 members of the Missouri Press Association then; during the November meeting in St. Louis more than 325 persons attended. Among the new projects of the association was reporting on the state legislature to member papers. One proposal would provide five hundred dollars to distribute a book on Missouri advertising rates to members; a like amount would be spent for a book listing the state's publication laws.

Missouri dailies were well represented among the 761 papers with a lifespan of fifty or more years listed by *Editor & Publisher* in 1934. Included were the Brookfield *Argus,* Carrollton *Democrat,* Carthage *Democrat,* Carthage *Press,* Chillicothe *Constitution-Tribune,* Clinton *Democrat,* Hannibal *Courier-Post,* Joplin *News-Herald,* Kansas City *Journal-Post,* Kansas City *Star,* Marshall *Democrat-News,* Mexico *Intelligencer,* Moberly *Monitor Index* and *Democrat,* St. Joseph *Gazette,* St. Joseph *News-Press,* St. Louis *Globe-Democrat,* St. Louis *Post-Dispatch,* Springfield *Leader* and *Press,* and Trenton *Republican-Times.*[43]

Charles W. Keller, named the association's field representative to replace Hubbard, was re-elected in 1935. He had been a member of the School of Journalism faculty. In the fall the association "urged laws be enacted looking toward the accomplishment of safety and saneness on the highways of Missouri and of the nation. We urge the enactment of the statewide drivers' license law to accomplish this purpose, and we commend all agencies that are at present furnishing material to the newspapers in an endeavor to eliminate fatalities on the highways."[44]

During Journalism Week in 1935 Chester Krause of the Maryville *Democratic Forum* told editors, "I believe the smalltown paper should be the community's watchdog in local government." Roy Roberts of the Kansas City *Star* said, "The news columns of the paper belong to its readers" as he scoffed at protests about too many press agents in Washington.[45]

Promotion of the Missouri market and the selling of the newspapers as the leading advertising medium of the state were goals of the press association for 1936. Ground was broken that January for the Walter Williams Hall at the School of Journalism. At the ground-breaking ceremony Governor Guy B. Park said, "The great memorials to Dr. Walter Williams are not any physical monuments, but they are the thousands of newspaper men and women imbued with his ideas, thoughts, and principles that are scattered over the entire world in the profession of journalism." Missouri Press Association members received special automobile tags in 1936, which were handled through the office of the secretary of state.[46]

Publishers expressed varied opinions about their fellow newsmen in the thirties. Jewell Mayes of the Richmond *Missourian* said he had studied a number of Missouri weeklies and "no two are alike. To me, each is well worth reading and studying. No two weekly newspapers are any degree similar when you analyze them. If you want to find individuality, study the country press of Missouri." These same publishers were having their problems, though. There was a shortage of apprentices, and some even wondered if "the printer's devil is on the way out?"[47]

Publishers recorded advertising gains, and the Missouri Press Association reported a large increase in membership, with 391 members in 1936 and 323 the previous year. This included 293 weekly, semi- and triweeklies, 48 dailies, 11 magazines and miscellaneous, and 39 associate members.

During Journalism Week in 1937, Williams Hall, which cost $150,000, was dedicated. Publishers heard predictions at the

annual session that within a few years the modern daily paper
would be 50 per cent pictorial. Special sessions were held for
the small daily and weekly papers at which the trend was noted
toward consolidations in these communities.[48] In the fall of 1937
about four hundred persons attended the association sessions.
Regularly audited circulation reports and fair advertising rates
were recommended as the best means to obtain more revenue.
The Missouri Women's Press Club, now the Missouri Press
Women, was organized that May, and in the fall the group
elected Mrs. B. J. Bless, Jr., of Weston, as the first president. The
group is a charter member of the National Federation of Press
Women, founded in 1938, and has about one hundred members.

Journalism education came under the explosive attack of Dr.
Robert M. Hutchins of the University of Chicago in a talk he
made before the Inland Daily Press Association in 1938. "The
shadiest educational ventures under respectable auspices are the
schools of journalism. They exist in defiance of the obvious fact
that the best preparation for journalism is a good education.
Journalism itself can be learned, if at all, only by being a journalist," he said. Dean Frank L. Martin, quick to reply, said,
"The present accepted method of teaching journalism needs no
defense. I, for one, am willing to leave the decision to the publishers of this country, a decision based upon their contact and
experience with graduates from the better schools." The Dean
admitted there were some weak departments in the "lesser institutions," as in the colleges of law, medicine, and other professions. "Because this may be true, would he [Hutchins]
abandon all schools of journalism or special training in the other
professions?"[49]

Only a month before, *Editor & Publisher* had asked, How
much education does a newspaperman need? "Partly due to the
wide influence of Walter Williams, partly for other reasons, the
average of journalism instruction has been nearer the line set by
Missouri than that laid down for Columbia University by Pulitzer."[50] Thus many of Missouri's older editors heard pros and
cons on the education for journalism restated, much as they had
been presented at the turn of the century when the foundations
were being set for the state's School of Journalism.

During the meeting of the press association in Columbia in
May, 1938, George B. Harlan, president, praised the work of the
group. "Some of the greatest men in our state have been presidents of the Missouri Press Association, where in a position of

humble service they encouraged papers to develop themselves always for greater usefulness to the people who read them." During this Journalism Week program editors had an opportunity to hear Damon Runyon and George McManus, but Governor Lloyd C. Stark came closer to their problems when he called on them for aid in halting "the assault upon the sanctity of Missouri's Supreme Court" by the Pendergast organization of Kansas City. Journalism graduates heard discouraging words from Roy Roberts of the Kansas City *Star*, who told them "This will be the toughest year for job-hunters since 1932 . . . take any job you can get."[51] Practicality marked the state meeting in St. Louis that fall. Publishers were advised that page 1 "should contain all the vitamins of modern business from A to Z." Among the resolutions passed was a vigorous condemnation of religious and racial persecution by militaristic powers, commendation of an enlarged national defense program by the United States, and promotion of closer bonds between North and South America.

As the decade neared its end Missouri publishers prepared for the war years ahead. Although fifty-one dailies over the nation had disappeared in 1939, only one Missouri paper had ceased daily publication; the Webb City *Leader* left the daily field to become a weekly.[52]

POLITICAL NEWS OF DECADE

President Herbert Hoover praised the press in 1930 for "The splendid cooperation . . . in the measures taken to stabilize the economic situation of the country. . . . They can most usefully forward this work by continuing to express the justified optimism of American business, industry and agriculture over the outlook for steadily increasing employment and prosperity." The press reacted; headlines proclaimed good news whenever any was available. Soon, however, politics took over, and although the majority of the papers opposed him, Franklin D. Roosevelt was elected president.[53]

This election has been described as the granddaddy of all political landslides in Missouri; Roosevelt received 1,025,406 votes—a plurality of 460,693, the largest ever given a presidential candidate in the state. He ran well ahead of Guy B. Park, Democratic victor in the race for the governorship.

Papers discussed the tariff issues. Some papers approved higher rates and praised the Republicans for their efforts to increase them while others thought lower tariffs would stimulate trade. The *Post-Dispatch* believed there might be enough members of both parties disgusted with the Smoot-Hawley Tariff Act that a third party could be formed. The Kansas City *Star*, though supporting Hoover for re-election, opposed the Republican stand on the high tariff. The Springfield *Leader* approved both Hoover's candidacy and the tariff measure.[54]

Elzey Roberts wrote in the St. Louis *Star-Times* in March, 1933: "I believe President Roosevelt's progress toward solving the nation's problems is the most encouraging development of the past few years. His clear recognition of the root of the trouble, his fearless exposure of true causes and decisive action toward removing them, are bound to result in lifting the United States out of the ditch."[55] When discussions began about regulating working conditions, hours, and pay, the press and Roosevelt drew further apart. In early 1935, W. L. Dickey of the Kansas City *Journal-Post* discussed the nation's programs and concluded, "The so-called 'forgotten man' has been led a bit astray by vague promises of better times that have not materialized and of an impossible redistribution of 'wealth.' "[56]

News of the national political conventions grew in importance. A number of Missouri papers sent their reporters to be among the eight hundred newsmen who covered the Republican convention in Cleveland in 1936. "The press was powerful at Cleveland," came the report. Not since 1872, when Horace Greeley ran for nomination to the Presidency, had newspapermen so ruled a political convention. Roy Roberts of the Kansas City *Star* spearheaded the Landon campaign. Shortly after this convention the Democrats met in Philadelphia, from whence millions of words and thousands of pictures flowed forth.

Missouri newspapers were predominantly Independent in 1936. *Editor & Publisher Yearbook* listed sixteen dailies as being Democratic, four Republican, three each Independent-Republican and Independent-Democrat, and thirty-six Independent. The *Post-Dispatch* opposed Roosevelt, saying, "In simplest possible terms, the over-shadowing issue in the coming national election is whether or not we shall set up in America, in defiance of the American tradition and in defiance of the plain intent of the Constitution as it now stands, a government with vast and centralized authority over the economic life of the nation."[57]

In Missouri, the results of the election of 1936 were about the same as they had been in 1932. Alfred Landon received 133,178 more votes than Hoover had received. This vote total of 697,891 for the Kansas governor was one of the strongest he received across the nation. Roosevelt, however, carried the state with 61 per cent of the total, 1,111,403 votes. Democrats increased their gains in the big cities, but declined outstate. Lloyd C. Stark became governor, but trailed the ticket with 1,037,133 votes to 772,934 for Jesse W. Barrett. In the 1938 off-year election all incumbents, Democrats, were returned to Congress.

ATTENTION TURNED TO EUROPE

Roosevelt's declining support from the nation's press was clearly evident in a survey conducted in 1938 by the New York *Mirror*. At that time only 35 per cent of the papers favored the President; 51 per cent had approved him in 1932, 44 per cent in 1936.[58]

Newspaper readers saw dark days ahead as the decade neared its end. The most significant stories of 1938 included those on the Munich pact, the persecution of the Jews in Germany, and the fall of Chinese cities to Japan, as well as Orson Welles's Martian broadcast, Republican off-year gains, and Douglas Corrigan's "wrong-way" trip to Ireland. Editors encountered more competition from radio, which was able to provide on-the-spot coverage of the Munich crisis. However, impact of the competition from radio lessened as more papers became owners of stations. Economic news was important in 1939, but much of this was tempered by war reports from abroad and by the increasing activity among American manufacturers of armament.

The press was geared for coverage of the war by late 1939. When Germany invaded Poland, some dailies published extras. In St. Louis the *Globe-Democrat* noted considerable increase in city sales, although the afternoon extras did not sell well. The Kansas City *Star* carried a streamer headline in 96-point type for the first time since World War I days. More than 140,000 extras were sold.

Circulations climbed more than 3 per cent over the 1938 figure, with morning and Sunday papers recording the largest gains. Certainly, readers were becoming more involved in the news of the day.

The next decade was to be for the press in Missouri a test of ability to survive.

CHAPTER XXI

WAR NEWS: GROWTH DESPITE
SHORTAGES

FOR publishers as well as for other citizens, 1940 began with war clouds hanging over the American scene and bearing special problems; the decade ended with shortages of newsprint, machinery, and trained personnel. Despite these publishing problems, Missouri papers survived. The war overshadowed all other events; wide reader interest in the European conflict and its effect on this nation brought higher circulations. At the start of the decade the American dailies were approaching the forty-million mark, while Sunday editions had passed the thirty-one-million circulation figure, higher than the so-called lush days of 1929. Although offset facilities for printing papers had to wait for expansion until the 1950's, publishers turned their attention to this more economical method of producing their papers. Editors meeting in New York in 1940 were advised that offset could save 25 per cent in publishing costs.[1]

City papers quickly felt the impact of the European war, as wire associations hiked assessments and other news-gathering costs increased. Newsprint prices remained more steady than they had during World War I. Stabilized at fifty dollars a ton in 1941 by the International Paper Company, they later came under the control of federal agencies.

War news brought sudden spurts in street sales; for example, the St. Louis *Globe-Democrat* reported a one-third rise in street sales when the draft lottery was announced. Similar gains were recorded as war broke out, major battles occurred, and the conflict came to its end, first in Europe and later in the Pacific. A review of the most important stories of the decade indicates how much emphasis publishers gave to the international struggle. In 1940 these included Roosevelt's victory at the polls, the draft, surrender of France and the Battle of Britain, Italy repulsed, the evacuation at Dunkerque, the fifth column in Norway, and the acquisition of more territory by Russia. One significant controversy was the transfer of United States destroyers to England in return for use of certain bases.

In mid-1941 Missouri publishers took a closer look at the prospect of the war involving the United States. In response to a nationwide survey, eight Missouri daily publishers said they favored our immediate military participation in the war, while twenty-one opposed our becoming a belligerent; seventeen thought the best interest of the United States would be to avoid the conflict, while twelve opposed this view; twenty-one favored the seizure of strategic bases owned by foreign powers in the interest of the United States defense, eight disapproved such action; seventeen favored laws regulating prices, ten objected; in the handling of labor disputes, twenty-five preferred some law compelling arbitration, four opposed the passage of such a law. Missourians were on the side of the majority in all these categories so far as the nation's publishers were concerned.[2]

When Pearl Harbor was attacked, Missouri publishers quickly placed the details before the public. In St. Louis the *Globe-Democrat* put its first extra on the street by 5:30 Sunday afternoon, December 7, 1941, and during the first twenty-four hours after the attack, 319,000 extra copies were sold in St. Louis by the three papers. Both the Kansas City *Star* and the *Journal* published extras that Sunday. The next day, with the declaration of war, Brewster P. Campbell, executive editor of the *Journal*, used a zinc headline he had kept in his desk for several months. It read: *U. S. Declares War.*[3] This event led all other news stories in 1941, followed by other war accounts that involved the Nazis, Russia, lend-lease, mobilization of "fighting billions" of dollars, the Atlantic Charter, and strikes. The Rudolph Hess mystery was considered newsworthy, as well as Brooklyn's victory in the baseball world. But the war dominated the news; it was destined to do so for some time.

Circulation records climbed on a steady, annual basis; higher prices followed. A few dailies charged two or three cents a copy in 1942; before the war ended, a nickel a copy was more common. For weeklies, the trend also was upward. Some papers, such as the *Perry County Sun* and the *Perry County Republican*, raised their annual rates from $1 to $1.50; others went from $1.50 to $1.75, as did the Braymer *Bee*. A few, including the Lee's Summit *Journal*, went to $2 a year. More papers moved to the $2 figure when their publishers realized that circulation profits would have to carry the papers through the war years.

To conserve paper, St. Louis' dailies adopted a "no-return" policy for their distributors. This measure saved about two thousand tons of newsprint annually. By late 1942 the government had frozen the newsprint supply, limiting users to their average rate during the second and third quarters of 1942. Publishers adopted narrower rolls. The Kansas City *Star*, which also adopted the no-return policy, switched from 67- to 66-inch rolls. This paper, as did several others, curtailed its remote circulation. In St. Joseph the press-room foreman for the *Gazette* and *News-Press* designed a newsprint roll-winder to take up the small quantities of newsprint left on rolls, to be used again. As tighter rationing continued, some papers curtailed space allotted to advertisers. By 1943 St. Louis advertisers were working under quotas, and national advertisers were accepted with optional dates for their appearance. Some omitted want ads in out-city editions. Senator Harry Truman warned publishers in mid-1944 that the next year's supply of newsprint would be no greater. Publishers, unhappy about the shortage, could take some comfort in the government's efforts to peg prices. While slight increases were authorized, such as the $3 a ton increase allowed in 1945, the price then was $62 a ton, well below the $130 many had paid during World War I. Even after the end of the war, publishers had to exercise self-control; the War Production Board continued to freeze prices while in Europe Scandinavian newsprint was selling for $250 to $300 a ton.[4] The larger city dailies reduced the number of editions to save gasoline, tires, and trucks.

PAPER'S ROLE IN WAR YEARS

Despite shortages publishers in Missouri contributed their share of time and space to the victory programs. One of the first efforts concerned the USO. More than 3,500 of the nation's papers contributed space valued at $550,000 to raise over ten million dollars for this service group. Many papers joined in the sale of defense stamps through their carriers. Early on the list were the Sedalia *Capital* and *Democrat*, Kansas City *Star*, Mexico *Ledger*, Joplin *Globe* and *News-Herald*, Cape Girardeau *Southeast Missourian*, and Jefferson City *Capital* and *Post-Tribune*. The *Star's* carriers led the nation through eight drives for the sale of stamps and war bonds, collecting nearly twenty million dollars. The *Star's* achievement helped to rank Missouri second among the newspapers in the nation in respect to sale of stamps and war bonds. Missouri editors also contributed space to promote the collection of scrap. During one such drive in 1942, state dailies donated more than 1,050 columns of editorial space and 1,125 columns of display space. In 1943 these papers used more than 1,254,050 lines of space to promote a war bond drive, with space valued at $185,000 donated to the war effort.

PROBLEMS OF CENSORSHIP

President Franklin D. Roosevelt assured the nation's editors in April, 1941, that "no censorship was contemplated" in handling war news. Several months earlier an *Editor & Publisher* survey had indicated that many publishers considered rising production costs to be the greatest threat to a free press.[5] Even in February, 1941, the outlook was not reassuring, with more retrenchments feared. When censorship was discussed, a voluntary co-operative system was first proposed, but editors soon complained of the limitations of the system. Some editors wanted the Army and Navy censorship offices to work twenty-four hours a day to process stories. While the *Post-Dispatch* agreed to the censorship plan, the paper thought "it would be helpful if the government clarified the situation by issuing a list of things which it regards as of military value to the Axis powers." Yet the Kansas City *Star* believed that "rigid rules laid down by the government now would be apt to lead to difficulties in unforeseen situations. The nation can safely trust the intelligent patriotism of American editors."[6]

A survey of editors made in late 1942 revealed some public distrust over rigid censorship following a transcontinental tour by the President which was kept out of the papers. The *Post-Dispatch* called this censorship necessary for Roosevelt's safety. "There are some recent instances of censorship which might cause alarm," the paper noted, but it did not consider this one. The *Star-Times* of St. Louis thought the trip similar to any troop movement that needed to be kept secret and thought criticism of the action would be "either partisan or ill-considered." The editor added, "The fact that the press withheld the story for reasons now clear will not destroy the confidence of the people in the press as much as it will convince these people of the newspapers' sense of responsibility." The move was seen as justified by the Kansas City *Star*, which called it "spectacular" that the President could tour the nation for two weeks in secrecy.[7] The state's smaller papers received much of their war news from the Office of War Information, which supplied a weekly four- to six-page summary of the conflict. The OWI also furnished articles and mats for such drives as "Food for Freedom." A *Post-Dispatch* series on "What Are We Fighting For," written by men across the nation, was later beamed to the enemy and to both neutral and conquered countries through the OWI.

Missouri publishers figured prominently in the war news.

Leland L. Chesley, Troy *Free Press* publisher, pledged the profits from his paper to help purchase a pursuit plane. The paper printed pamphlets holding thirty ten-cent defense stamps. When these were filled by the readers, they were marked "Void" and mailed to the Treasury Department as "a present for defense."[8] L. M. White of the Mexico *Ledger* reported on the North Carolina "war games" in 1941 while visiting his son Robert, an Army public relations officer at Fort Jackson, North Carolina.[9]

Missouri's smaller papers had their newsprint problems and used various means to stay within their allotted supply. A survey by the Missouri Press Association of 15 dailies and 103 weeklies showed that more than 200 tons of newsprint had been saved yearly by dropping delinquent subscribers, cutting the exchange lists, refusing free copies over the counter, cutting back on office copies, printing fewer pages on smaller-size pages, and changing from 13- to 12-em columns.[10] Despite such efforts a few papers ceased publication, some never to reappear, although a few did resume after the war ended. In 1942 the Kansas City *Journal* came to its end, though the war could hardly be blamed for this event. Circulation had fallen to 70,000 when, on March 31, the paper closed and three hundred employes lost their jobs. In 1943 the Mexico *Intelligencer* ceased publication, and the Carthage *Daily Democrat* became a weekly. The *Intelligencer* had been in trouble and had resorted to changes of name and experiments in format in attempts to forestall the end. That same year thirty-three weeklies closed, primarily because of lack of trained workers and rising production costs. In an effort to help meet the shortage of workers, the University of Missouri School of Journalism adopted a shorter program for students who agreed to newspaper employment upon graduating. The curriculum was designed more for women than for men, because women were rapidly taking over in newspaper offices.[11] In 1944 nearly one hundred women were cited during Journalism Week for their work on Missouri's papers and for replacing men who were needed in the armed services. In journalism schools across the nation women represented more than 80 per cent of the enrollment by 1944.

According to Ayer's, Missouri's losses were chiefly among the weeklies during this decade. Starting with 1940, the state had 59 dailies, 2 triweeklies, 13 semiweeklies, and 484 weeklies, for a total of 558 newspapers, including foreign-language publications. By the end of the decade there were 3 fewer dailies, 1 less triweekly, 6 less semiweeklies, and 67 less weeklies, for a total of 481 newspapers, a loss of 77 in ten years.

ASSOCIATION IN WAR YEARS

The Missouri Press Association experienced some of its busiest years during the forties, representing state papers in dealings with the federal government and national advertisers. Early in 1940 the press group conducted a campaign seeking $2,500 to aid in a fight between the St. Louis *Post-Dispatch* and a local judge when the paper was charged with contempt of court. The press association said: "The editors and publishers of papers throughout the state have long believed, and still believe, that it is their responsibility and duty to publish information relating to the various branches of government and to the action and conduct of all public officials, and to make editorial comment thereon. . . . The Press of Missouri needs to have its rights and duties judicially defined." The paper was fined $2,000, and an editor and cartoonist Daniel Fitzpatrick fined $100 each and sentenced to ten days in jail. The paper appealed and later won the case.[12]

Seven hundred persons attended the Journalism Week banquet in 1940 to hear Lyle C. Wilson complain that Washington was a news center where correspondents had to fight the suppression of government information.[13] During that summer eighteen Missouri dailies agreed on a uniform system of merchandising assistance, market research, and frequency discounts. Working with the state association, the group employed special representatives in New York and Chicago to solicit advertising.[14] When the association met in St. Louis in November, 1940, nearly one hundred persons were on the program which attracted more than three hundred editors and publishers. Federal publicity "censors" addressed the publishers in Kansas City in 1941. George H. Scruton, editor of the Sedalia *Democrat* and *Capital*, told fellow workers that "while the government says there is no censorship these swarms of publicity men tacitly restrict information."[15] Publishers realized that "by pooling their efforts for a common cause through the facilities offered by their own organization" much could be achieved. The bitter and partisan days that marked the editorial front during Civil War years certainly had disappeared.

Missouri newsmen with more than fifty years of service were honored at the Diamond Jubilee Banquet during Journalism

Week in 1942. Nearly fifty individuals were cited. Attendance at the fall convention in St. Louis fell to 150, partially because of travel restrictions. There, publishers heard a prediction that the nation's deficit would reach 200 billion dollars by 1945.[16] Association members debated whether or not the federal government should purchase advertising space to inform civilians of what they should do to help the war efforts. A state survey in 1943 showed almost two hundred papers approving the proposal while only eighteen opposed it.

Journalism Week was omitted in 1943 because of the war. Instead, Dean Frank Luther Mott collected articles from thirty-two noted newsmen and compiled them into a book, *Journalism in Wartime*. More than one hundred publishers had a closer view of Army life in July, 1943, when they spent two days at Jefferson Barracks observing the training program and participating in question-and-answer sessions with public relations officers. Some problems editors faced could be seen in an editorial by Collins Ewing, in the Odessa *Odessan*, which said, in part: "We see by a letter from the Treasury Department that the papers had a large part in making the second war loan the big success it was, through the terrific amount of free publicity carried. We see by the papers that the President blames the unrest in the country on the papers."[17]

Newspapermen in the armed services were honored when publishers met in Kansas City in 1943. At least 1,116 state editors, publishers, and employes were in the armed forces or working for the government. A Service Honor Roll was dedicated, and Roy Roberts of the *Star* asked editors, "How does it feel to go back to work?" as he kidded them about their need to return to backroom chores to handle mechanical production duties.[18]

Journalism Week, resumed in 1944, featured practical topics, including the maintenance and repair of typesetting machines, cylinder presses, automatic jobbers, etc. Maintenance had become a more serious problem for publishers, now unable to purchase new equipment. Foreign news topics highlighted the program on which Frederic W. Goudy was a featured speaker. Another shortage was discussed at the November convention in St. Louis. After the meeting heard that few printers had been trained in the past fifteen years, the association passed a resolution which brought about the establishment of the Linotype School in 1945 at the University of Missouri. At first a three-month school, the program later was expanded to a full year with on-the-job training.[19]

During the summer of 1945 district association meetings were held across the state to circumvent the gas rationing problem. President Truman, invited to address the publishers in Kansas City in November, 1945, was unable to attend. Senator Frank P. Briggs spoke and noted the need for "a free press in a democratic society"; he pointed out that if any breakdown occurs in that freedom it will be caused by a failure within, rather than by an attack from outside. The next month, W. C. Hewitt, president of the press association, and Senator Briggs presented President Truman with a life membership in the association in ceremonies held in Washington.[20]

Jack Taylor, formerly news editor of the Sedalia *Capital*, became advertising manager for the Missouri Press Association in 1945. More attention was given to the future at the session that year. Traditional opposition to proposed increases in postal rates was expressed in discussions, and memorial services were conducted for twenty-four members and relatives of members who had died during the war. According to *Editor & Publisher*,

> Postwar plans for Missouri papers, as brought out in a discussion led by J. W. Stevenson of the Glasgow *Missourian* included the increased use of local news and pictures, the installation of new equipment and type, the remodeling and enlargement of plants, membership in the Audit Bureau of Circulations, increased purchases of office supplies, greater interest in obtaining both national and local advertising, more attention to make-up, interest in photo-engraving and offset printing equipment with continued close cooperation with the National Editorial Association and the Missouri Press Association.[21]

In mid-1946 H. R. Long resigned as manager of the press association, after serving for five years, to start work on a doctoral degree at the University of Missouri. Howard E. Palmer, acting secretary-manager of the Virginia Press Association, became the new manager in Missouri. He had been president of the National Editorial Association in 1940.

Round-table discussions of press problems featured the 1946 sessions in St. Louis, where Richard Harkness was the keynote speaker. More than 250 attended the 1947 meeting in the same city, at which time the members voted $1,000 for research in the country newspaper field to provide data on management and operation of such papers. For the first time, the best of the small daily and weekly papers were selected for Blue Ribbon awards.

The Linotype School, directed by Dr. Paul Fisher who had studied typography under Frederic Goudy, supplied state publishers with more graduates from its "corrugated campus," two tin Quonset huts on the University campus. The school joined the Missouri Press Association in sponsoring a Linotype Clinic in Columbia in May, 1948, to cover many phases of this work.[22]

Recollections of earlier years warmed the hearts of many Missourians when a cruise down the Missouri River was held for 112 editors in September, 1948. Starting in Boonville, the editors were guests of the U. S. Army Engineers on a trip to St. Charles.

Legal advertising rates were discussed at the meeting in Kansas City in 1948. Palmer Hoyt of the Denver *Post* recalled that the recent election was "embarrassing to the nation's press." Dr. Fisher presented some redesigned front pages of several Missouri papers, offering suggestions for typographical improvements.[23]

A more intensive program was outlined for the association members for 1949. H. R. Long, who had returned as manager for a time, resigned, and was replaced by John A. Hogg, who had been assistant manager during the previous eighteen months. Newspapers from seven states were represented at an Advertising Clinic that January, the second sponsored by the School of Journalism and the Missouri Newspaper Advertising Managers Association. In April a Circulation Clinic was held, and in late May a Linecasting Machine Clinic was conducted. In the summer seven regional meetings were held. More than one hundred publishers attended the press day during Journalism Week. In St. Louis the following November, Professor Cliff Edom of the University of Missouri demonstrated the Land Polaroid camera. Nearly three hundred registered for the meeting as editors and publishers looked ahead to the next decade.

Newspaper Week Effective

Missouri papers have participated in National Newspaper Week activities since the program began in 1940. Open houses, editorials, speeches before civic groups by editors, entertainment for the carriers, and other activities have sparked these observances. In 1941 Springfield papers conducted an essay contest on "Why the Constitution Guarantees the Freedom of Speech and Press." Dean Frank Luther Mott, then of the Iowa School of Journalism, wrote in *Editor & Publisher* in 1941 on "United

States Newspapers Inseparably Linked With Democracy."[24] The theme for 1942 was "The Newspapers Go All-out For Victory." The role played by the papers in aiding the defense efforts was stressed, and the loss of some 15,000 employes to the armed forces from the daily papers was noted.

In Rolla the *Daily News* gained national fame in 1947 when civic groups published the paper. One Rotarian admitted, "Never again will we gripe when we see typographical mistakes in the paper. We have learned that each day this newspaper takes 200,797 chances to make mistakes." Publisher Edward W. Sowers was pleased with his "experiment."[25]

WAR COMES TO AN END

As the war neared its close, streamer headlines and extras became common occurrences. Late in 1943 the surrender of Italy was the major event. Key stories that year were headed by the over-all blueprint for winning the war, accompanied by plans for peace. In St. Louis the *Star-Times* published a story in 1944 exposing gross negligence and inefficiency at a nearby ordnance plant, but the War Department said there was nothing to it. "Whitewash!" called the paper in a front-page editorial. The *Post-Dispatch* joined the *Star-Times* by calling the War Department's denial "Whitewash, G. I. Style." In Kansas City the *Star* felt that the general public was too little involved in the invasion of Europe by the Allies. To arouse people, the paper persuaded the Armour Packing Plant to toot its whistles on D-Day, and the *Star* used one of its rarely printed banner headlines on an extra. Other papers also heralded D-Day. The Macon *Chronicle-Herald* used a headline six inches deep, and the Galena *Stone County News-Oracle* announced in red ink, "D-Day! June 6, 1944." The Chillicothe *Constitution-Tribune* extra announced, "Invasion On." In Columbia, university students helped to sell the *Missourian* extras, and in Rolla newsboys and the publisher of the *New Era* were threatened with arrest for shouting "Extra!" and blowing whistles after the papers hit the streets. However, more than a thousand copies of the paper were sold there. Editorials in other papers described with mixed emotions the events of the day, and all urged the citizens to additional war efforts in order to bring the world-wide conflict to a close. H. D. Bradley, publisher of the St. Joseph *News-Press*, provided a light touch. After hearing the German radio's announcement of D-Day he wired the Nazi news agency: "Interested in your bulletin service. Please quote rates."

On V-E Day, too, special editions were published. The Willow Springs *News* issued its sixth extra only two and a half minutes after Truman's statement confirmed the surrender. Specials appeared across the state. A victory edition of the Flat River *Lead Belt News* contained a thousand pictures of persons of the area who had served in the armed forces. In Columbia the *Missourian* published a 24-page section on the history of the war in Europe, the Boone County Honor Roll, and similar data. The Monett *Times* carried a 56-page section. In Cabool, the *Enterprise* printed a torch, holding the Allies' flags, in red and blue on page 1.

Turmoil followed a premature announcement of the cessation of the war in Europe in May, 1945. After the war had ended, some editorials asked whether the guilty Nazis should be executed or not. Joseph Pulitzer defended the possible execution of the leaders as a "war cure," saying, "We've got to cut the cancer out of Germany." His *Post-Dispatch* prepared an exhibit of pictures displaying Nazi atrocities, which was viewed by 25,000 persons in five days.[26]

Meanwhile, with radio news gaining in importance, the *Post-Dispatch* waged a crusade in early 1945 against what it termed "Radio Plug-Uglies." The paper opposed a network practice of inserting commercials between important news items. Daniel Fitzpatrick drew an editorial cartoon, called "The Sublime and the Ridiculous," which portrayed a radio station, labeled "Radio Networks," sending out flashes: "World Crisis news, try our colic cure, Americans enter Manila, buy our pills."[27]

Preparations were made by the press to cover the birth of the United Nations in San Francisco, and on April 25, 1945, 1,800 newsmen were in that city. Within a few months two hundred newsmen hurried from a meeting with President Truman, carrying his mimeographed statement:

WAR IS OVER. JAPAN SURRENDERS. PEACE. V.

Such headlines were common in Missouri papers. The Rolla *New Era* published five extras in four days and had seventy-eight interviews with local residents. Before the month was over two papers reappeared: The Cape Girardeau *News,* closed for thirty months while its editor worked for the War Bond Division, and the Lebanon *Daily Record,* first newcomer in the state's daily field for several years. With the major conflict over, publishers turned to rebuilding. The going was not easy.

STRIKES HALT PRODUCTION

The question of salaries and wages for employes of the newspapers had become involved in government red tape the decade before, at the time the NRA codes were worked out. Even in the 1940's the debate continued as to whether newsmen were professionals or not. Employment security was granted members of the American Newspaper Guild in St. Louis in early 1945, but before the year was over, strikes by other groups halted publication. In August, the carriers tied up production. Publishers agreed to pay all the other employes for a week, but refused to go any further. The argument finally was settled after twenty-two days, during which time the printers also went on strike. The carriers' union was recognized; publishers agreed to bargain with it on wholesale prices of papers and a three-year pact signed—nearly a closed shop—by which the rights of carriers to the routes were to be maintained, and the carriers dealt with as merchants. Pressmen, too, received raises as high as $10.27 a week. Guild members shared in raises from $3 to $10 a week, which the *Post-Dispatch* said would cost an additional $24,000 weekly.[28]

Two years later International Typographical Union members walked out in St. Louis, and the papers interrupted publication for several days. Other strikes occurred from time to time. In Springfield papers were shut in 1947 when printers went out for the second year at the same time as the Ozark Empire District Fair opened; in 1949 an attack on the newspaper plant reached its climax in the beating of a nonunion printer and a dynamite blast in the pressroom. In its first shutdown since the paper was founded in 1880, the Kansas City *Star* was out sixteen days because of a strike by contract carriers in 1946. Nationwide, there were 271 strikes against newspapers between 1937 and 1948. Of these, 160 involved printers and 30 Guild members.

Although Missouri papers were not concerned at this time, there were many controversies among printers and some owners of the larger publications in the nation over the use of "cold type," the offset process which the International Typographical Union termed "the printerless product."

NEW EQUIPMENT, BUILDINGS

The *Post-Dispatch* received the first rotary web presses to be completed by R. Hoe and Company after the end of World War II when a 12-unit rotogravure press was installed by early 1946. The *Post-Dispatch* made newspaper history on September 8, 1946, when it printed a complete comic section of four colors on a rotogravure press. For many years the paper had used three-color comic pages. The next year this paper won a Pulitzer prize for a special 24-page rotogravure section recounting the story of the Centralia, Illinois, mine disaster in which 111 miners were killed. In 1948 the paper began to use its new annex, supplied with the latest mechanical items.

Plant improvements occurred across the state. By mid-1946 the Aurora *Advertiser,* St. Joseph *News-Press* and *Gazette,* Joplin *Globe* and *News-Herald,* Trenton *Grundy County Gazette,* King City *Tri-County News,* and the La Plata *Home Press* reported the purchase of new equipment or facilities. Some papers acquired new buildings or enlarged old ones, others added equipment to replace well-worn machinery aged by excessive use during the war. The Moberly *Message* finally returned home in late 1946; after his own equipment wore out during the war, L. G. Hardy had his paper printed in the Higbee *News* plant.

Several papers were damaged by fires; the most destructive was in the blaze in Springfield in 1947. All equipment of the *Leader-Press* and *Daily News* was lost, including two presses and seventeen typesetting machines. The papers were printed in Oklahoma for the three months needed to rebuild the plant. Fire destroyed the Bethany *Harrison County Times* in 1949.

H. J. Waters, Jr., moved his Columbia *Daily Tribune* in 1947 into the first new plant to be built for a daily paper in the state following the war. It was the fourth move in the paper's forty-six-year history.

St. Louis papers began using radio-telephones in cars. The *Globe-Democrat* is said to have had the first in the nation, with a phone placed beneath the dashboard of a 1946 Plymouth station wagon. When the Houston, Texas, *Post* installed similar equipment, reporters for the two papers carried on a car-to-car conversation.[29]

A nationwide survey in 1946 indicated that Missouri dailies planned to spend a half-million dollars within the next five years for plant construction, $1,858,900 for new equipment,

$1,482,500 for new presses, and $272,100 for composing machines. When one adds the needs for the state's more than four hundred weeklies, the effect of the war years becomes quite clear.[30] Other papers added new typesetting machines, presses, and additional equipment as papers prepared for the fifties.

POLITICS SHARES SPOTLIGHT

It is difficult to separate politics from the problems generated during the war years. There were times when personal journalism made a brief return to the state's editorial pages, as writers debated the decisions and events of the Roosevelt terms. When Wendell Willkie ran against Roosevelt for the Presidency in 1940 he had solid newspaper support. In the nation, 22.71 per cent of the press supported Roosevelt; 63.86 per cent backed Willkie; others were neutral. Missouri listed eighteen dailies for Willkie, sixteen for Roosevelt, with four undecided.[31]

The *Post-Dispatch* attacked "Dictator Roosevelt" in 1940 for the agreement with England which exchanged destroyers for bases. The editorial, reprinted in paid advertisements in eastern papers, said, in part:

> Today Congress is *informed* of the agreement. Note well the word "informed." Although the President referred to his undercover deal as ranking in importance with the Louisiana Purchase, he is not asking Congress—the elected representatives of the people—to ratify his deal. He is *telling* them it already has been ratified by him—America's dictator. He hands down an edict that may eventually result in the shedding of blood of millions of Americans; that may result in transforming the United States into a goose-stepping, regimented slave state.

In an editorial spread across four columns on page 1, the *Star-Times* replied: "St. Louisans, once astonished, still preplexed, are now neither surprised nor alarmed at the *Post-Dispatch's* efforts to win the Pulitzer Prize for appeasement. The prize is safe; there are no real competitors. His was not the act of a dictator, but of a servant of the people making democracy function." Later, a local resident violently protested the view held by the *Post-Dispatch*; he broke $350 worth of windows on the press building.[32]

Voters returned FDR to the White House. The Kansas City *Star*, which opposed him, was one of the first to concede defeat. The *Globe-Democrat* rushed extras by plane to Sikeston, Columbia, Jefferson City, Hannibal, and Quincy. The *Post-Dispatch* claimed a radio first with its facsimile transmitter in store windows and hotels. Opposing views in Missouri were expressed in the *Star* in Kansas City and in the *Star-Times* in St. Louis. "The nation has spoken," said the *Star*, which called for unity and warned against any split such as that which had divided France and brought about its downfall. "The nation has cause for gratitude," said the *Star-Times*. "Victory ought to end the efforts of reactionaries to repeal the great bulk of reform and regulatory laws adopted when the New Deal came to power."[33]

Missouri papers, dailies and weeklies alike, saved the state from a political tangle in 1941 when attempts were made to keep Forrest C. Donnell from taking over the governor's office which he had won the previous November by 3,613 votes. When the legislature adopted a resolution denying Donnell the right to be seated and named a partisan committee to examine the ballots, the press objected so strongly that the state Supreme Court ordered Donnell seated, forty-four days after the beginning of his term.[34]

Politics entered the back door in an issue that concerned publishers, but few of their readers, over the nation. When Marshall Field established the Chicago *Sun* in 1941, his application for membership in the Associated Press was opposed by the Chicago *Tribune*. The *Sun*, closely associated with Roosevelt, expressed views counter to those of Col. Robert McCormick of the *Tribune*. The debates continued for several years before the *Sun* won the membership, a decision that brought about revisions of the AP membership rules.

Comments on the matter by editors in Missouri tended to follow political lines. "The line that runs from the White House to the *Sun* office, back to the White House and then to the Department of Justice is clearly definite. The AP is being attacked solely because of Mr. Roosevelt's quarrel with Col. McCormick," said the *Globe-Democrat*. The Kansas City *Star* thought all efforts should be devoted to fighting the war, yet Roy A. Roberts feared that if the government won the case to force the AP to accept the *Sun's* application, all competitive wire services would end in one, which would be under government control. George H. Scruton of the Sedalia *Democrat* wrote, "The inference of the benevolently baptized New Deal newspaper that it cannot maintain reader interest and press freedom without the AP is a puerile deduction." Cowgill Blair of the Joplin *Globe* was emphatic: "By Animus, out of Revenge the pedigree of the illegitimate suit of the government against the AP to compel it to adopt any aspiring journalistic waif, is the most suspect of several administration efforts to emasculate the constitutional proviso for a free press." W. J. Sewall of the Carthage *Evening Press* compared the action to forcing a club or fraternal organization to accept any individual who applies for membership. L. M. White of the Mexico *Ledger* wrote, "You cannot have freedom of the press in this country unless you have freedom of competition in the newspaper field." According to Joseph Pulitzer, who called the suit "ill-tempered and badly-timed," the "President should get over his peeve against the press."[35]

Views of the nation's press in 1944 were summarized in a statement by Roy Roberts, then president of the American Society of Newspaper Editors. In terming it a year of crisis for papers, Roberts expressed his fear that "the free press is being crowded and pushed about. We are getting too much spoon-fed news not only from government bureaus and the military but from private industry and labor."[36]

Chicago, in 1944, attracted both political parties for their national conventions. About 1,500 newsmen reported the Republican convention first, then the Democratic. Both parties endorsed international freedom of the press. Republicans said, "All channels of news must be kept open with equality of access to information at the source. If agreement can be achieved with foreign nations to establish the same principles, it will be a valuable contribution to future peace"; Democrats said, "We believe in the world right of all men to write, send and publish news at uniform communication rates and without interference by governmental or private monopoly, and that right should be protected by treaty."[37]

Missouri dailies again backed the Republican candidate, this time, Thomas Dewey. Twenty-three were for Dewey, fourteen for Roosevelt, with six neutral. Both candidates called for a free press in messages during National Newspaper Week. Roosevelt said, "Free press . . . is a living symbol of democracy, and as such, it is in the forefront of democracy's battle for survival." Dewey recalled the practices of dictators in suppressing such freedom and said, "To the publishers and staffs of America's newspapers, our people are indebted for a great service of enlightenment."[38]

PRESIDENT IS DEAD proclaimed the nation's press in April, 1945, as newsmen recovered from the shock of the story to relay the message to the world. Missouri, whose native son became

President, felt a closer tie to Washington. In his first press conference as President of the United States, Truman spoke to 348
correspondents on April 17. One reporter noted that "the cigarette holder, 'giggle chorus' and gadgets were gone."[39]

Among the most important events of 1946 was the Republican
congressional victory. Missourians learned more about the practical aspects of politics when the Kansas City *Star* interviewed
more than five thousand residents and reported large-scale vote
frauds in the August primary. At Westminster College in Fulton
that year Winston Churchill made his famed "Iron Curtain"
talk.

During the campaign for the Presidency in 1948 many of the
nation's papers assumed that Dewey's election was inevitable.
Truman had the support of only 15 per cent of the nation's
dailies, representing 10 per cent of the circulation. In his home
state he received even less help than over the nation. Although
thirteen of the dailies in Missouri backed him, these had only
44,569 circulation; Dewey was supported by fourteen dailies
with a combined circulation of 1,326,397. When editors across
the nation reviewed 1948, Truman's election headed the list of
significant events, surpassing the Battle for Berlin, the birth of
Israel, Gandhi's assassination, the inception of the Marshall plan,
the rise in cost of living and the swelling inflation, Communist
advances in China, and the death of Babe Ruth.[40]

NAMES IN MISSOURI NEWS

A number of Missouri newspapermen reached "30" in their
careers during this decade. Among these were Edson K. Bixby
and Joel Bixby, brothers, who died in Springfield in 1940; Bart
B. Howard, *Post-Dispatch* Pulitzer Prize winner, in 1941; Casper
Yost, seventy-six, one of the founders of the American Society of
Newspaper Editors, in 1941; G. S. Johns, eighty-three, editor
emeritus of the *Post-Dispatch*, in 1941; Frank Lee Martin, dean
of the Missouri School of Journalism, in 1941; A. H. Steinbeck,
seventy-six, Union *Franklin County Tribune*, who started his
career in 1904, died in 1942; George B. Longan, president of the
Kansas City *Star*, and Wallace Crossley, Warrensburg *Star-Journal*, in 1943; Clarence E. Watkins, Chillicothe *Constitution-
Tribune*, in 1944; C. L. Hobart, Holden *Press*, in 1944; Asa W.
Butler, "dean of Northwest Missouri newspapermen," Albany
Capital, in 1945; Fred E. Kies, Jackson *Cape County Post*, in
1945; Harry S. Jewell, Springfield newspapers, who started as a

printer's apprentice when he was seventeen years old, died at the age of seventy-eight in 1945; O. K. Bovard, *Post-Dispatch*, in 1945; Ira B. Hyde, Jr., Trenton *Grundy County Gazette*, in 1946; A. J. Caywood, founder of the Laclede *Blade*, in 1946; E. Lansing Ray, Jr., *Globe-Democrat*, in 1946; Martin L. Comann, St. Charles *Cosmos-Monitor*, in 1946; and Earl McCollum, president of the Kansas City *Star;* Harry E. Booth, Lexington editor; William R. Painter, Carrollton *Daily Democrat*, and George G. Tedrick, Altamont *Times*, all in 1947.

The Missouri Senate adopted a resolution eulogizing Col. Charles L. Blanton, Sr., colorful editor of the Sikeston *Standard*, who died at the age of eighty-four in 1949. The resolution cited his "long and enviable career in the field of journalism." Mrs. Z. W. Hook, who learned to set type while a young girl in Fulton, carried on the Auxvasse *Review* until her death at the age of eighty-seven in 1948. Among other deaths were Charles W. Mulinex, LaBelle *Star*, J. Fred Hull, Maryville *Nodaway County Tribune;* John E. Dowell, Adrian *Journal;* and Wilson B. Lowry, Aurora *Advertiser*, all in 1948.

Less solemn events occurred to other Missourians during this decade. In September, 1941, Editor Tilghman R. Cloud of the Pleasant Hill *Times* won a $1,500 airplane in a radio contest, but he said he planned no flying; he would keep the plane only until "a satisfactory cash offer" was made for it. At the suggestion of Missouri Press Association President C. E. Watkins, the library at the School of Journalism became a memorial to Dean Martin. Friends contributed books, cash, research material, and other suitable items.[41]

Frank Luther Mott, head of the State University of Iowa School of Journalism, became Missouri's dean in 1942. The name of the school's first dean, Walter Williams, appeared in the war news when a Liberty ship was named in his honor in California in 1943. John B. Powell, nearly killed in a Japanese internment prison camp, endowed a Chinese-American literary prize at the School of Journalism in 1943. This $4,000 endowment was part of the money raised by the editor's friends in the Far East after he was freed. Powell dropped dead February 28, 1947, after addressing a group of University of Missouri alumni in Washington.

William Southern, Jr., of the Independence *Examiner* had a way of getting in the news frequently. In 1944 he wrote an editorial for *Editor & Publisher* about journalism education, concluding with the remark, "Pulitzer, from his great wealth, established the Columbia School of Journalism with a million dollar endowment. Williams, without wealth, established the Missouri School of Journalism, with an idea and ideal."[42] In 1948, when Frank W. Rucker became a full partner, Southern announced in the *Examiner*, "Mr. Rucker's desk is near the front and he is available. It is only fair to say that he is over 6 feet tall and weighs more than 200 pounds. If the visitor wants to say something nice and brag on the paper, my desk is toward the rear."[43]

Ensign Morton Holman, former owner of the Maitland *Herald*, wrote to the *Missouri Press News* from Leyte Island in early 1945 about his plans for a community paper when the war was over. Presenting a ten-point program, Holman, now owner of the Lawson *Review*, promised to take part in community affairs, to record all worthwhile activities, and "to use the pen in every way possible to prevent having to use the sword again soon to preserve our liberties."[44] Frank Briggs of the Macon *Chronicle-Herald* was named to succeed Truman in the Senate. J. Kelly Pool, editor of the Jefferson City *Capital News,* received birthday greetings from the Missouri Senate in 1946 when he reached the age of eighty-six. The resolution was written by a Republican— a news event of its own, since Pool was an active Democrat. In St. Joseph, *News-Press* editor Arthur Burrowes received telephone threats in 1948 after the paper published a series of stories on local gambling. The calls threatened to throw "a pineapple against your house."[45]

Mark Twain was back in the news in 1949. A story was told about the time a person found a spider in his paper and wrote Twain, then an editor, asking if this was an omen of good or bad luck. "Finding a spider in your newspaper," wrote Twain, "is neither good or bad luck. The spider was merely looking over our paper to see which merchant was not advertising so he could go to that store, spin his web across the door and lead a life of undisturbed peace ever afterwards."[46]

The decade was an eventful one in a trying era, yet successful for many Missouri papers. Changes began to appear; the papers used more photographs, more editors turned to improved typography, and the Missouri Press Association and the School of Journalism co-operated in more workshops and clinics to assist publishers. And television had arrived in St. Louis and Kansas City to add to publishers' worries, even though these early stations were operated by the *Post-Dispatch* and the *Star*.

CHAPTER XXII

PRESS REBUILDS: STRONGER AT MID-CENTURY

THE FIFTIES brought many problems for Missouri editors and publishers, from the Korean War to a recession, from newsprint shortages to higher operational costs, from "troubled and uncertain times" to the optimism that greeted the sixties.

Newsprint prices edged upward, yet in 1951 Roy A. Roberts of the Kansas City *Star* said he was "far more concerned about getting production, not just for this year but for the next five or ten years to come, than I am over any immediate price situation." Publishers, indignant the next year at the price of $126 a ton, claimed "an unsympathetic approach of the Canadian newsprint producers toward American publishers' problems of steadily increasing costs." By 1955 the price reached $130 a ton and climbed higher in later years. Despite such hikes, records were smashed in 1959 when more than 7,100,000 tons of newsprint were used by American papers.[1]

Circulation of the nation's papers climbed from fifty-four million in 1951 to more than fifty-eight million in 1960. The five-cent paper appeared doomed as publishers turned to circulation for an increase in revenues when advertisers resisted higher rates.

Income and expense continued upward. Labor costs rose higher, and strikes closed several papers. Higher pay scales in the cities forced many of the smaller publishers to raise their rates to retain trained personnel. American Newspaper Guild members voiced bitter disapproval over the sale of the St. Louis *Star-Times* to the *Post-Dispatch* in 1951, which put about 240 members out of work. For some time after this sale, union printers sought payment for unset "bogus" type on the *Star-Times* but lost in a decision by an arbitrator. In 1953 the Supreme Court ruled that bogus type demands, while "wasteful, useless and a frivolous makework exercise," did not violate the Taft-Hartley Act.[2] In the first verdict in the history of the Federal Court of Eastern Missouri against a labor union, the *Globe-Democrat* in 1957 won $20,000 damages against the typographical union in a controversy to make time records of advertising copy.[3]

The longest shutdown of the decade for any Missouri paper was that against the *Globe-Democrat* in 1959. While closed for ninety-nine days, all the paper's equipment was sold to the *Post-Dispatch,* which now prints both papers. During the strike, state legislators sought public hearings, and Joseph Pulitzer urged an end to the conflict in the public interest; he said, "No legislative investigation is going to settle this strike." The *Globe-Democrat* appeared June 1 after Guild members returned to work, only to be shut down again, along with the *Post-Dispatch,* on June 11 for fifteen days in a dispute with stereotypers. The Kansas City *Star* was closed in a printers' dispute, from June 18 to 29.[4]

A significant era in the history of the weekly papers ended in 1952 when the Western Newspaper Union quit the readyprint field. By this time, however, Missouri papers were printing all their own pages.[5]

Dr. Frank Luther Mott retired as dean of the School of Journalism in 1951, returning to full-time teaching. Replacing him as the school's fourth dean was Dr. Earl F. English, a native of Michigan who came to the faculty in 1945 from the University of Iowa. Dean English was a printer, pressman, reporter, and feature writer during his high school and college days, and for nine years taught vocational printing in a Peoria, Illinois, high school.

The Kansas City *Star* was named in an antitrust law indictment, and its trial opened in 1955. Answering charges of monopolistic practices, Roy A. Roberts said the paper's policies were "to give the public the latest news at the lowest price and to see that advertisers are served at as low rates as possible and to help build the community because the paper won't grow unless it does." The *Star* reported the case fully, giving more than two hundred columns of space on the trial over a twenty-four-day period. Later the company was fined $5,000 and its advertising director $2,500. An appeal to the Supreme Court failed to reverse the decision, and in late 1957 the firm sold both its radio and television stations for $7,600,000.[6]

Missouri publishers had other problems. They enjoyed some lighter moments, too, such as the time in 1950 when field mice invaded the pressroom of the Paris *Monroe County Appeal* and "dined and supped on a set of three new composition rollers intended for a job press."[7] Some publishers suffered heavily in fires; the Houston *Herald* lost all its files of older papers in a $100,000 blaze in 1950. Papers dating to 1886 were lost in the Clinton *Daily Democrat* fire in 1952. When the Washington *Missourian* plant was destroyed that year, millions of labels owned by the International Shoe Company were lost as well as the *Missourian* presses used to print them.

Although job printing as a revenue producer was losing its place, it still accounted for 29 per cent of gross revenue in 1954 among one hundred weeklies surveyed.[8] The importance of the weeklies was noted by the New York *Times*, which reported in 1956 that the circulation of these papers had climbed nationwide to twenty-one million. The *Times* concluded, "As long as people have names there will be—we hope—the weekly paper."[9]

Television created new difficulties for some publishers because now the advertiser's dollar was split another way. The Missouri Press Association offered statistics for publishers to use in selling ads; for example, a study made in 1957 showed how many sets were *not* on during given hours.[10]

By 1958 more than 25,000 Missourians were earning their living in the printing and publishing field, with an average pay of $2.54 hourly, highest among wage earners in the state.[11] Missouri papers, though fewer in numbers, grew in strength and stability.

Missourians in the News

State editors and publishers traveled far and wide during the 1950's. Some left the active publishing field and turned to education, as did Frank W. Rucker, who moved from the Independence *Examiner* to the School of Journalism in 1951. Others gained national recognition in *Editor & Publisher* and *Publishers' Auxiliary*. Mitchell White went to Europe in 1950 to visit the communities where copies of his Mexico *Ledger* had been distributed in a project in international relations. Ben F. Weir of the Nevada *Daily Mail* was featured by *Publishers' Auxiliary* in 1950 when Weir said, "There's no business like the newspaper business because it's twice as much fun." He admitted he "had been threatened, cursed, praised, and laughed at," but he still enjoyed the profession.[12]

Time magazine saluted Jack Blanton, famed Paris editor, who wrote a column for the *Globe-Democrat*. Blanton was quoted as saying, "City people, down underneath, are just rural folks. You run a Tom, Dick and Harry paper like I have for 60 years, and you begin to see it's the warm and simple things that make the news people hunger for most." Blanton related a story about a drunkard whose wife sewed him in a sheet, tied him to a bedpost, and called in the neighbors to look at him. "He never touched liquor again . . . he was so humiliated that he went out and hanged himself."[13]

Merrill Chilcote of the St. Joseph *News-Press* was an "Editor of the Week" in *Publishers' Auxiliary* in 1950. Chilcote confessed to a secret ambition: to be "able to fish six days a week and spend the seventh writing a column for weekly papers exclusively."[14] Along this same line was George T. Henson's practice in 1952 on his Van Buren *Current Local.* For twenty-nine years Henson had been ignoring deadlines; he maintained that his readers were accustomed to the practice. "What if I got the paper out on Thursday and something big happened on Friday. Then the news would be old before the next paper," he said.[15]

Two fine paintings were presented to the School of Journalism: in 1952 *Post-Dispatch* staff members gave a portrait of Charles G. Ross, one of the school's first teachers; in 1958 a copy of John Singer Sargent's painting of Joseph Pulitzer, founder of the *Post-Dispatch,* was placed in Neff Hall.

E. Lansing Ray was honored in 1953 for a half century's service with the *Globe-Democrat.* Two Missourians, both associated with the Mexico *Ledger,* gained prominence in the East: Herschel Schooley became the chief public information officer for the Department of Defense in Washington in 1954, and Robert M. White, II, became editor of the New York *Herald-Tribune* in 1959, a year after his father, Mitchell White, received an honorary degree from the University of Missouri. Norman Rockwell visited Paris and drew four pages of pictures for the *Saturday Evening Post* on the subject of a country editor, featuring Jack Blanton.

Publishers continued to play a prominent role in state affairs. Mitchell White became head of the State Historical Society in 1954, the eighth newspaperman to hold this position. The next year, Oliver B. Ferguson of the Fredericktown *Democrat-News* was named to the University Board of Curators. Col. William Southern, Jr., at the age of ninety, brought an end to his weekly Sunday-school lessons in 1955. During his long career on the Independence *Examiner,* Southern had written about 1,500 of these lessons, which were printed in many papers. W. J. Sewall, former publisher of the Carthage *Evening Press,* was honored by the chamber of commerce when he reached his ninetieth year in 1956. James L. Miller of the Washington *Missourian* was awarded a patent in 1957 on a newsprint rewinder and auxiliary unit designed to save newsprint and production time. Miller said the unit had saved him five hundred dollars a year.[16]

Despite all these developments and apparent advances, editorial comments by two publishers indicated that, after all, times had not changed radically. "The poor weekly newspaper is the only business in the world where if you miss out once you are through—finished—it's all over. It has to come out regularly, consecutively . . . even the neighbors will come in and help out the farmer, but nobody will come in and set type to get out a newspaper," said the Edina *Sentinel* in 1959.[17] The editor of the Linn *Unterrified Democrat* noted several months later that he had

> . . . no magic sources of information. All that he knows, he reads in the paper, hears over the radio or sees on television. If he manages to know more about a subject than some reader, it is simply because his business required him to read and listen more than the average reader . . . we have no illusion about editorial writing. No editor can please everybody and to try would only result in attempts, that rightly named, should be called foolish . . . the basic principle in our approach to the job of writing is that those who disagree with us may be right. However, we do not think they are, or we would be writing as they think. We have to express our own views, such as they are, and such as they may be.[18]

Deaths Among Publishers

Many of Missouri's leading publishers died during this decade. Some, such as Everett Pizer of the Tipton *Times*, who died at the age of eighty-eight, had given their lives to the small-town papers. Pizer spent sixty-three years in the newspaper business before his death in 1950. Frank L. Kauffman, in the printing business from the age of fourteen, died in 1950 when he was nearly seventy, in Rolla, where he was with the *Advertiser*. That December, Charles G. Ross died at his desk in Washington.

Clyde S. Smith, Sr., editor of the El Dorado Springs *Sun* since 1913, died in 1951, shortly before Thomas T. McKinney, reporter for fifty years in Hannibal, died. That year John H. Wolpers, publisher of the Poplar Bluff *American Republic* and president of the University of Missouri Board of Curators, died, followed shortly by J. Kelly Pool, who had spent his later years in Jefferson City and had reached the age of ninety. The vice-president of the Missouri Press Association, Marvin W. Pace of Mount Vernon, died at the age of thirty-nine. A publisher for many years, Harry E. Denman died in 1951 at the age of seventy-six after fifty-two years with the Farmington *News*. A trainee of William Rockhill Nelson, Henry J. Haskell, editor of the Kansas City *Star*, died in 1952.

The year 1953 took an unusually heavy toll. Included were Ronald M. Thomason, editor of the St. Charles *Banner-News* since 1905; Marvin Crawford, California *Democrat;* Robert C. Goshorn, Jefferson City; Ovid Bell, long-time Fulton publisher and printer; A. J. Martin, Braymer *Bee;* O. J. Ferguson, Fredericktown *Democrat-News;* Lon M. Burrowes, with Sedalia and St. Louis papers; Alfred Volkman, Rock Port *Atchison County Mail;* and J. W. Stevenson, Glasgow *Missourian.*

For forty-eight years Col. Charles L. Woods had edited the Rolla *Herald* before his death in 1954. Fred D. Moffett was associated with seven Missouri papers, the last being the Ashland *Bugle,* before his death that year. Arch T. Hollenbeck of West Plains died in December.

Two neighboring publishers died in early 1955: H. J. Blanton, who made the Paris *Monroe County Appeal* and *Mercury* famous, and Wirt Mitchell, known for his achievements on the Fayette *Advertiser* and *Democrat Leader.* Robert K. Wilson of the Jackson *Missouri Cash Book* died in March, and John V. Bumbarger, for fifty years publisher of the Memphis *Democrat,* in June. Joseph Pulitzer died in St. Louis. In August, E. Lansing Ray died on his seventy-first birthday. Later in 1955, H. G. Hertich, editor for forty-one years of the Clayton *Watchman-Advocate,* died, as did E. K. Lyles, eighty-nine years old, of the Houston *Herald.* James C. Jones of the Gilman City *Tribune* died on New Year's Day, 1956.

The dean of Missouri newspapermen, Col. William N. Southern, had written his own obituary when he retired from the Independence *Examiner* in 1951. It was used in February, 1956, when the Colonel died at the age of ninety-one. That same month, E. Harold Smith, ninety years old, of the Clarkton *News* died. Three more of the older members died in 1956, including John K. McMullen, seventy-five years old, Slater *News-Rustler;* George A. Naeter of the Cape Girardeau *Southeast Missourian,* at the age of eighty-seven, and Nelson Hill, Richmond *News,* who had graduated from the University of Missouri in 1915.

At the age of ninety William J. Sewall of the Carthage *Press* ended fifty-six years on that paper in 1957. In November, Bonham E. Freeman died after thirty-eight years with the Bowling Green *Times.* Charles J. L. May, with Pleasant Hill and St. Joseph papers for sixty years, died at the age of eighty-three.

Among the prominent men who died in 1958 were Eugene L. Preston, editor of the Liberty *Advance* and *Tribune;* Richard A.

Whipple, Kearney *Courier;* and Alfred Graf, Hermann *Adver-tiser-Courier.* In 1959 the profession lost Ray E. Miller, Carl Junction *Standard;* Lewis R. Taylor, Mound City *News-Inde-pendent;* James G. C. Tibbetts, *Platte County Gazette;* Ben G. Crouch, Bethany *Republican-Clipper;* E. N. Meador, Cassville *Republican;* and Raymond Lloyd, Lilbourn *Semo News.*[19]

EXPANSION, EQUIPMENT, GROWTH

Missouri publishers were quick to equip their plants with newer equipment when it became available. A number of publishers acquired teletypesetter machines, others added equipment for processing pictures, some developed their own Sunday supplements, while a number used the established weeklies. The Kansas City *Star,* which had long been averse to syndicated supplements, added *This Week* to its resources in 1959. The Poplar Bluff *American Republic* enlarged its plant at a cost of $75,000 in 1950, adding a new 24-page Duplex tubular press, six typesetting machines, and other items. Later, the Carthage *Press* held open house in its new fireproof building to display its new Goss press. E. L. Dale, who had been with the paper since his boyhood, was the editor. Some six hundred dailies across the nation adopted the Teletypesetter circuits early in 1952. At this time, the chief users were papers under the 10,000 circulation figures. That fall a course in this work was offered by the Linotype School at the University of Missouri.[20]

The Hannibal *Courier-Post* in 1952 doubled its floor space and installed a new Goss press with a 32-page capacity. Murals depicting scenes of Mark Twain's boyhood days in Hannibal were installed. The development of air conditioning provided another improvement in plants. The Kansas City *Star,* in 1952, was among the first to air-condition its plant. The United Press launched its Facsimile Pix wire service to dailies in 1954, first serving those in California. The Mergenthaler Linotype Company announced that more than eight million dollars had been spent on developing a phototypesetting machine. By 1955 the Independence *Daily News* was being published by offset, the only daily so produced in the state, although several weeklies had adopted this method.

The Trenton *Republican-Times* installed a new flatbed press in 1950, replacing one that had been in service for twenty-six years. That same year the Puxico *Press* bought a new press, a Linotype, folder, and other equipment. A new Goss press was installed in the Fredericktown *Democrat-News* plant in 1952. When the Lamar *Journal* installed teletypesetter equipment in 1954, publisher Wayne Rowland said the $4,500 cost soon would be recovered in lower labor overhead. Teletypesetters, he noted, were easier to find and train than were operators of typecasting machines.

The *Perry County Republican* in 1954 added a new Duplex press with a speed of 3,500 an hour for an eight-page paper. This cut the weekly press run from twenty-six to less than four hours. The Kahoka *Gazette-Herald* and *Courier* acquired another new Goss press in 1954, and sold its older Babcock press to the Mountain View *Standard*. In 1955 the Canton *Press-News* and *Record* replaced a 55-year-old Babcock Reliance drum cylinder press with a Miehle. A Goss automatic web-fed press was acquired by the Savannah *Reporter* in 1955, while the California *Democrat* erected a building and added a new press, and the Vandalia *Leader* obtained a new Miehle. The Mexico *Ledger* moved in 1956 into its new building, which featured a front resembling a newspaper's front page and a plant designed to permit 100 per cent expansion in all departments. The Hermitage *Index* added a new front to its building the same year.

After five years of publishing, the O'Fallon *Community News* moved into its remodeled building in 1957. The Macon *Chronicle-Herald* added a new press and remodeled its plant, and the Malden *Press-Merit* displayed its new offices and supply department that year. Additional typecasting machines were added by many papers, including the Marshall *Democrat-News*, Jefferson City *News-Tribune*, Independence *Examiner*, and others. The Marshall *Democrat-News* in 1958 went into a new building which replaced the one destroyed by fire in late 1957. The Chillicothe *Constitution-Tribune* moved from a three-floor building to a new plant where all operations were on one floor, and the Neosho *Daily News* opened a new building with up-to-date equipment in 1958. A story in 1959 concerning new equipment across the state reported that the Shelbyville *Shelby County Herald* had bought a new press, the Vandalia *Press* had redesigned its front offices, and other publishers had improved their back shops through the addition of modern Linotypes, job presses, and other equipment.[21]

This modernization by the state's papers showed they agreed closely with the comments made by the association's manager, William Bray, that small towns must either publish papers or perish. Noting the annual loss of some papers in Missouri, Bray wrote:

> In most every instance, the loss of a small newspaper means the eventual loss of a small town. Usually the bank is able to hold on a little longer . . . after the newspaper is gone, the bank's days are numbered. . . . Somebody has got to keep telling the story of the small town market over and over and if the local merchant plays his cards the manufacturer he represents will bug the junior and senior executives and the Madison Avenue whiz kids of advertising.[22]

Associated Press members have two organizations to achieve special objectives. The Missouri Associated Press Members' Association includes the editors and publishers of papers using this wire service. The working editors are included in the Associated Press Wire Editors Association, which was organized in Sedalia in 1950; Robert L. Chaplin of the Joplin *Globe* was their president in 1962. The group meets annually "to discuss problems in handling wire copy and ways to eliminate those problems." Members have conducted a continuing study of the wire services, seeking better news availability and picture coverage.

Press Association Expands

Additional services and promotional assistance featured the Missouri Press Association program during the fifties. The sponsorship, along with other groups, of workshops and conferences aided publishers across the state. Professor Cliff C. Edom of the School of Journalism faculty conducted the first workshop for photographers on smaller papers in 1950. That same year the Missouri Advertising Clinic was held for the third time. Publishers were advised that "the advertising man is a safety valve guarding against business influence over a newspaper's opinion. If the adman stands guard, he can protect editors from the influence which critics of the press say—without reason— runs newspapers today."[23]

During the association's fall convention Frank W. Rucker of the Independence *Examiner* told publishers, "If there ever can be a time when an increase in advertising rates are justified, it is now. The price of newsprint is up, labor demands higher wages, equipment and replacements are more costly than they have ever been."[24] Publishers agreed. John A. Hogg, manager of the press association, reported that the outlook for 1951 was cloudy and it would be difficult to predict which way business would turn. During the year, the association aided in surveys of readership of papers in Gallatin and King City.

Ralph Dawson, Jr., a graduate of the School of Journalism, became advertising manager for the association in 1951. In February, a group of publishers battled rain, snow, and ice to attend the Newspaper Advertising Clinic in Columbia and to share in discussions on how to sell more advertising. During Journalism Week publishers studied the Blue Ribbon papers and concluded that pictures are cheaper than type, readers' preferences decide which features are used, actual contact with the farmer is important, and street and counter sales are profitable. In Kansas City for the November sessions, the publishers asked President Truman to recall the executive security rule set up for government agencies.[25]

More than fifty advertising men attended the annual clinic in Columbia in 1952, held to analyze radio competition and double billings. They were urged to better their papers in order to meet competition and to study typography in order to make them easier to read. Salesmen were told to learn type faces and display methods. Varied topics highlighted Journalism Week in 1952, when Missouri publishers discussed planning and management, editorial policies, women's interests, correspondents, etc. Joining with the Missouri Associated Dailies and the School of Journalism, the association sponsored its first news clinic in October, 1952. During the convention in St. Louis that fall, the first award for the best editorial writing went to Robert M. White, II, of the Mexico *Ledger*.

William A. Bray, publisher of the Odessa *Odessan*, became manager of the Missouri Press Association on February 1, 1953, succeeding John A. Hogg, who became manager of the Columbia *Missourian*. Bray, a veteran of World War II in the European theater, had won the Silver Star and Purple Heart in battle. After his graduation from the School of Journalism in 1948, he purchased the *Odessan* from Collins Ewing, publisher there for more than half a century. Bray also was named to the School of Journalism faculty to teach in the community newspaper field.[26]

During the sessions of 1953, members of the Missouri Press Association heard Bob McIlvaine of the Downingtown, Pennsylvania, *Archive* speak about his book, *The Federal Snoops Are After Me*. At the October convention in Kansas City, Dr. Howard L. Cross, author of *The People's Right to Know,* spoke. Meanwhile, Missouri publishers joined with Kansas publishers in sponsoring a mechanical conference in Kansas City, Kansas. This annual affair has grown in importance and regularly attracts some four hundred publishers. At the first session that September, a short offset school was conducted for publishers and printers. Displays of the latest equipment have been features of these meetings.[27]

In 1954 publishers adopted a group insurance plan under the association's program. Tom Hammel, a veteran of the Korean War, became the association's advertising manager. During an advertising clinic in February, speakers predicted there would be no fear buying for 1954, and thus competition would be fierce for the ad dollar. That same month, three publishers went to the White House Safety Conference to represent the rural press. They were M. O. Ridings, Hamilton *Advocate-Hamiltonian;* W. M. Harrison, Gallatin *North Missourian;* and A. A. Steinbeck, Union *Franklin County Tribune.*[28]

Many Missourians shared the Journalism Week program with Turner Catledge of the New York *Times* and Louis B. Seltzer of the Cleveland *Press* in 1954. Publishers were told a month earlier by Dean Earl English, "It is time newspaper people began to glamorize the newspaper profession . . . for too long publishers have been saying what a hard grind and terrible hard job it is to publish a newspaper and it is beginning to have an effect on the enrollments of journalism schools."[29] The Missouri Circulation Managers Association and the Missouri Advertising Managers Association continued their annual meetings. More than three hundred people attended the MPA fall meeting in St. Louis, which provided round-table discussions.

Bray, writing in the *Missouri Press News* in March, 1955, expressed his belief that "smalltown papers are slipping and something should be done about it." He placed the blame partially on the papers, which, he said, had been spoiled by the lush years. "Too few papers are interested in their news and editorial columns. The big idea is to get that ad and get it in the paper, then fill 'er up with whatever we've got." Noted speakers during Journalism Week in 1955 included William Randolph Hearst, Jr., and Frank Conniff, who discussed their Russian trip, and Robert U. Brown, editor of *Editor & Publisher.* Bray joined with Dean English in urging publishers to turn their attention toward young students for help in the future. Bray's column in the association's magazine pointed out that the television industry was attracting the youth. To counteract this trend, Bray suggested better coverage of schools in the state's more than four hundred papers.[30]

Frank Heck, a graduate of the University of Missouri with newspaper experience on Nebraska and Kansas publications, became advertising manager for the association in August, 1955, replacing Hammel, who took over a weekly paper in Iowa.

One of the major decisions made by association members in this decade occurred in Kansas City during the November, 1955, convention when they agreed on the need for an office in Jefferson City to supply a news service to members while the legislature was in session. At the same time, the publishers passed a resolution asking that Fort Leonard Wood be made a permanent military training establishment.[31]

Bray in 1956 became a director of the Newspaper Association Managers, Inc., an organization of executive officers of national, regional, and state newspaper trade associations in the United States and Canada. A year later he was elected vice-president of the managers' association and was chairman of the National Newspaper Week program. He officiated at the opening ceremony in Annapolis, Maryland, where the nation's oldest newspaper, the *Maryland Gazette*, established in 1727, is published. In 1958, Bray became president of the association.

Prospects for the building of a pulp mill in the state were discussed by members of the Missouri Associated Dailies in early 1956, but studies made later by the University of Missouri forestry staff concluded that the ready supply of the right type of wood was inadequate.[32]

Papers were not doing a sufficiently aggressive and informative job of selling themselves and their product, publishers and advertising and circulation managers of newspapers of the state were told at a newspaper management clinic in Columbia in 1956. At the association's ninetieth convention in St. Louis in November a memorial scholarship plan was presented by Victor Gierke of the Louisiana *Press-Journal*. The plan suggested that $10 be deposited in the name of each deceased member of the association to provide a scholarship fund for the use of students in the School of Journalism. The Missouri Bar Association presented the press association with an illuminated plaque in recognition of the public educational program conducted for the judicial election that fall. The papers of the state had devoted considerable space to explain the nonpartisan ballot and had published editorials on the new plan for retaining or removing judges.

Some forty publishers attended the Newspaper Management Clinic in Columbia in March, 1957. With Bray in charge of the National Newspaper Week Committee that year, Missourians co-operated fully to promote the program with its theme, "Your Newspaper Serves." Bray said, "Your newspaper serves in so many ways that we can scarcely imagine our way of life without it. The American people depend more and more upon their newspaper to keep them informed as they go about their tasks. Religion, education, law enforcement—nearly every phase of this thing we call democracy is served by your newspaper."[33]

A Distinguished Professorship in Journalism was established in 1957 by the association to augment the salary of the dean of the University of Missouri School of Journalism. Earl English became the first to bear this title.

E. Clifton Daniel of the New York *Times* was guest speaker at the association's meeting in the fall of 1957. "The Role of the Publisher's Wife" was discussed by Mrs. Mark Thomason, wife of the publisher of the St. Charles *Banner-News*. "And since he, the editor, is supposedly diplomatic on Main Street all day long, we wives shouldn't mind if he comes home blowing off a little steam, or expecting us to be a sounding board for his ideas and arguments. . . . Try not to be publicity chairman of every organization of which you are a member," she said.[34]

Publishers decried the portion of the state's new juvenile code which refused publication of the names of minors in conflict with the law. In a resolution they agreed, "It violates the right of Missourians to know; it is in no way keeping with the basic strength of a free people, building a greater democracy. It helps the evil forces of secrecy and hurts our greatest strength—an informed people." Members also urged a state appropriation for a suitable shrine at Florida, Missouri, to be erected in Mark Twain Park to house and display documents, mementos, and other items concerning one of the state's most renowned citizens, and one of its early printers.[35]

Missouri newspapermen gathered in Columbia in February, 1958, for a new type of meeting. Joining with radio and television personnel, high school science teachers, and students, the newsmen were briefed on atomic science and its future role by officials of the Argonne National Laboratory. The program, sponsored by the Missouri Press Association, the School of Journalism, and Argonne officials, was intended as a pilot for possible adoption in other states. In March the Newspaper Management Clinic attracted one hundred participants to its sessions.[36]

Beginning that fall, Missouri publishers shared in the year-long fiftieth anniversary of the School of Journalism. "A Stronger Free Press for a Better Free World" was the slogan for the program, which continued through Journalism Week in 1959.

Many Missouri publishers participated in the inauguration of National Newspaper Week in Columbia in October, 1958. Secretary of the Interior Fred A. Seaton spoke. A week before, the Freedom of the Press stamp, featuring quill pen and a simplified stylization of a hand printing press, had its first-day sale in Columbia. The *Missourian* issued a Sunday edition of 32 pages on September 7, 1958, and has continued this schedule since having dropped the Saturday issue. Throughout the anniversary year of the School of Journalism Missourians shared in the activities. Some attended the Press Congress of the World in Columbia in March, 1959, at which former President Truman remarked, among other things, "I'd like to be the blue pencil man for a while in a newspaper office and cut out the things that ought to be cut out." President Eisenhower sent greetings, noting,

> Only when there is a strong free press, with an unfailing sense of responsibility, can truth flourish and man grow to his maximum capability. So the profession of journalism serves a noble cause. Indeed, it is an essential element in our free society. Its members are vital to every good country where citizens are trusted to serve the common good—when they are fully informed and alerted to the facts of the day.[37]

The Freedom of Information Center added to its operation, although any crusading role was ruled out. The advisory board limited the center's work "to collect, index, report and document the histories of pertinent cases involving freedom of information."[38] Among the early case histories collected by the center was that concerning Marion O. Ridings, publisher of the Hamilton *Advocate-Hamiltonian*, who was thrown out of a city council meeting. Several months later Arthur V. Burrowes, sixty-two-year-old editor of the St. Joseph *News-Press* and *Gazette*, was attacked by a county judge following editorial criticism of acts of the county court.[39]

During the Women in Journalism celebration in February,

1959, Mrs. Eleanor Roosevelt spoke; Inez Robb was program chairman of the meeting. From St. Louis came Clarissa Start of the *Post-Dispatch* to describe her column as "a soapbox on which I air my views and represent the average homemaker."[40]

The convention of the press association in the fall of 1958 was the largest in recent years. The new editor of the *Missouri Press News*, Russell Mann, Jr., attended. He was formerly with the Clinton *Democrat*. William Bray warned the association the next March of a trend toward creation of boards and commissions that directly or indirectly affected the publishers. "Medics, lawyers and architects have pretty well stamped out advertising by canons, codes and mutual agreement within their groups," he wrote. "While we do not like it, we respect their right to be so stupid, so long as they do not try to pass laws about it." Bray later called for more newsmen in the state legislature, remarking that while in the past many newspapermen did serve, there were none at this time in Jefferson City. "It has been said that probably no right of a free people is more important than the right to be informed. It could be added that probably no group understands this right better than the press. Scarcely a bill is introduced in the legislature that does not affect this right to some degree."[41]

Publishers participated in the third annual Church News Clinic at the University in April, 1959, which had as its keynote speaker Lillian Block, managing editor of the Religious News Service in New York. At the October convention two carriers of the Carthage *Press* were honored for saving the lives of two persons. The boys were guests of E. L. Dale, publisher of the *Press*.

Missouri publishers were acquiring a new outlook as they turned toward 1960 and anticipated better days ahead. With an optimistic look to the future, Frank Heck, association advertising chief, wrote: "Weekly newspapers, long regarded as backshop operations managed by suspender snapping, country bumpkin publishers, are coming into their own as a prime ad medium." Surveys had indicated that the management of weekly papers were generally younger men, more business minded and more advertising oriented than before. Heck admitted weeklies still faced problems: competition of dailies, magazines, radio, and television, as well as the belief of advertisers and agencies that advertisements in weeklies are too costly.[42]

Missouri papers that had survived two wars in a decade, shortages of newsprint and equipment, continually rising costs of labor, and many other problems, could look ahead to brighter opportunities.

LINOTYPE SCHOOL EXPANDS

In 1945 the University of Missouri Linotype School, a "baby" of the press association, consisted of a Model 5 Linotype, a font of matrices, a proof press, a few pounds of metal, and two students. Since then, however, it has expanded, adding typecasting machines, presses, equipment, instructors, and students. Geared to supply vocational training for veterans of World War II, the school also serves to meet the shortage of printers and machine operators on Missouri papers. By 1950 the school had trained more than 330 men and women. As the decade moved on, student enrollment declined somewhat. In 1962 the school moved into the former pressroom of the *Missourian,* where it became an integral part of the School of Journalism. Offset teaching facilities were added in 1964.

POLITICS IN THE NEWS

Though publishers became more and more independent, politics still had its place. With a Missourian, Harry S. Truman, in the White House, political news took on another aspect. Early in 1950 Truman granted an interview to the New York *Times* which prompted Raymond P. Brandt of the *Post-Dispatch* to ask if it was "an authorized, exclusive interview?" Truman quickly replied that he would talk with anyone he pleased at any time and on any subject that suited him and without answerability to the press.[43] Three years later the *Post-Dispatch* and the *Times* bought exclusive rights from *Life* magazine for the serialization of Truman's memoirs.

The Korean War brought renewed agitation over undue censorship. Before this was over the removal of General Douglas MacArthur created what Journalism Week listeners in 1951 were told by John Cowles of the Minneapolis *Star* and *Tribune* was an "orgy" that threatened to whip the public's emotionalism to an almost "psychopathic" pitch.[44]

Publishers argued whether Tass reporters should be granted press credentials in this nation. Some felt in 1951 that Tass personnel were official Soviet agents and must be barred, while Henry J. Haskell of the Kansas City *Star* said we should give these reporters the same treatment "accorded to newspaper representatives from the United States by the Soviet Union and its satellites, no more and no less."[45]

St. Louis papers were instrumental in bringing about the resignation—and in some cases jail sentences—of several key political leaders in 1951. Efforts to "fix" local tax cases were revealed by the *Post-Dispatch* and the *Globe-Democrat*.

Editor & Publisher reported in the 1952 campaign for the Presidency, twenty-six papers in Missouri with a circulation total of 1,269,176 backed Eisenhower for President, while thirteen with 441,708 circulation were for Stevenson. Only dailies were included in this accounting. The vote in the state followed this pattern by supporting Eisenhower with 959,429 votes to Stevenson's 929,830. Democrats, more successful on the state level, placed Phil M. Donnelly in the governor's mansion. Eisenhower's victory was rated the leading news story of the year.[46]

Political charges were hurled back and forth over responsibility for the recession early in the decade. "Don't expect reporters to paint a glowing picture for the future when the figures don't justify it. . . . We are fully aware that to most newsmen a forecast of a recession is a bigger story than would be a forecast of continued boom business," wrote *Editor & Publisher* in 1954. Publishers were exhorted to place "a little accent on the positive instead of the negative."[47] Meanwhile, in 1954, the Democrats regained control of Congress in the off-year elections.

The *Post-Dispatch* refused to discuss with congressmen in mid-1956 an editorial which "lamented a trend toward leaving the field of reactor development to Russia" and charged that Congress was not doing all possible to promote commercial development of atomic power. Congressman Clarence Cannon from Missouri was notified by the paper that "its sources and editorial expressions are not subject to congressional examination," and on this the inquiry ended.[48]

Television coverage highlighted the conventions of the national parties in 1956, but newsmen found the gatherings on the dull side. In Chicago with the Democrats, reporters obtained their best news in the comments made by former President Truman. The party's platform condemned secrecy concerning governmental decisions and the Eisenhower Administration "for the excesses practiced in this vital area." The Democrats promised "to press for free access to information throughout the world for our journalists and scholars." The Republicans, meeting in San Francisco, pledged their party "to overlook no opportunity that, with prudence, can be taken to bring about a progressive elimination of the barriers that interfere with the free flow of news, information and ideas, and the exchange of persons between the free peoples and the captive peoples of the world." No mention was made of secrecy. Coverage of the Eisenhower-Stevenson campaign in 1956 was watched carefully by the wire services to prevent charges of partisanship.[49]

Missouri dailies continued to support Eisenhower, but the division between parties was not so one-sided as in 1952. Sixteen papers with a circulation of 862,881 backed the President, while thirteen with a circulation of 450,429 supported Stevenson. With the exception of the *Post-Dispatch*, most of the larger city papers backed Eisenhower. This closeness in editorial support of the candidates was reflected in the voting. Stevenson carried the state, winning 918,273 votes to Eisenhower's 914,289. Democrats retained control of the governorship and placed James T. Blair, Jr., in the governor's seat.[50]

Missouri's papers, less and less politically oriented, were presenting the news of both parties in more nearly equal proportions than editors a century earlier could ever have dreamed possible.

STATE PUBLISHERS SURVEYED

The close co-operation between Missouri publishers and the University of Missouri School of Journalism became more apparent in research projects conducted by students. Many of the studies were concerned with publishers, their backgrounds, coverage of specific areas, equipment, outlook for the future, etc. One of the more informative studies was on the publishers of weekly newspapers, by John T. Kinnier in 1951.[51] A brief review of the social composition of the publishers reports their ages varying from twenty to eighty, with half between forty and fifty-nine, yet there were more publishers under forty than over sixty. While women had taken over many papers during the war years, only 7 per cent of the publishers in 1950 were women. Seventy-seven per cent of Missouri publishers were Missouri-born. The publishers' attachment to smaller communities becomes apparent when Kinnier points out that 82 per cent of the publishers were born in towns of 2,500 or less. The father-son relationship in management of the papers was not so pronounced in 1950 as it was a century earlier; however, 31 per cent of the publishers were sons of publishers. More than half had attended college from one semester to six years, ten holding advanced degrees. Many had interest in other enterprises, including farms, banks, real estate, insurance firms, etc. While there had been tendency among newspapermen in the nineteenth century to move about from paper to paper, this practice had changed; slightly more than 40 per cent of the publishers studied had spent their lifetime with the one paper.

"Considered in terms of their social composition, it can be concluded that the publishers have made a natural progress from their origins in stable, middle-class, God-fearing homes which were economically comfortable and politically conservative, to their present status as steady family men, churchgoers, political conservatives, and persons of economic stability," Kinnier concludes.

A study of the state's 340 weeklies by Harry W. Stonecipher in 1955 reviews columns and editorial comments. The staff-written personal columns led over the traditional editorial comment four to three, although forty papers published both columns and editorials.[52] D. Wayne Rowland, a former Missouri publisher who turned to teaching journalism, studied the papers in 1956 and their editorial views on politics. He noted, "The decline in number of papers . . . has been a mark of progress in many respects. The remaining papers (with few but sad exceptions) are stronger, better, have larger circulations, are more respected, and are more independent." As papers became less dependent upon political parties for bread and butter they tended to become more independent. "The day when political parties dominated Missouri papers appears to be well past," Rowland's study concludes. Al Westland, another publisher who has turned to teaching, studied the multiple newspaper plants. At the start of 1957 there were twenty-four such operations in Missouri, representing fifty-seven papers in fifty-four areas. It was not unusual to find a publisher operating both Democratic and Republican papers.[53]

In a discussion in mid-1958 on promotion, *Publishers' Auxiliary* quoted a number of Missouri publishers. James W. Price, then publisher of the Princeton *Post-Telegraph*, told about sending get-well cards and copies of his paper to patients in the hospital and flowers to business people who were hospitalized. Frequent group tours of the publishing plant were used as public relations measures by the Bethany *Republican-Clipper*. James L. Miller of the Washington *Missourian* noted, "If the paper is well written, if it does a reasonably good job of covering the news of the community it serves, plays no favorites, and is always just and fair in its dealings and, above all, it takes a strong and determined stand editorially, it will be read."[54]

C. L. Blanton, Jr., publisher of the Sikeston *Standard*, conducted a survey of his own in 1959, writing the presidents of a number of leading advertising agencies to ask, "What will be your newspaper 10 years from now?" One official replied, "Newspapers will be just as basic a medium for advertising as they are today." W. E. Freeland of the *Taney County Republican* was not so optimistic; he feared that the small weekly would continue to decline. One factor he noted was the failure of the industry to develop an economical press for this operation.[55]

School news gained in importance among state publishers, according to a study made in 1959 by Glenn E. Davis, graduate student in journalism. There were, however, some conflicts in what publishers thought was enough coverage and what an actual study of their papers indicated was enough coverage. Davis concluded that there was a need for "introduction of journalism classes, education of administrators in their responsibilities to the public, and the development of a willingness among school teachers and other school officials to become 'news hounds' and 'tipsters' for the press."[56]

The roles of the newspaperman and of the educators can best be described in this *Missouri Press News* item of July, 1956:

> The newspaperman is the historian of right now. He writes under pressure so that those who run may read. It is the newspaperman who makes the heroes and the bums. On what he hears and sees depends the future's estimate of who did what and to whom. There is no point in scoring a grand slam at golf or discovering the North and South Poles on the same day unless there is a newspaperman on hand to supply the details and let the folks back home know about it. The newspaperman is above price and unmindful of influence. He can't be bribed, nor can he be dismissed from his duty by threats or promises even though he may have holes in the seat of his pants and have no idea where last month's rent is coming from.
>
> The newspaperman is the conscience of his town, his county, his state, his nation, and his world. He wants to know the truth, and he won't quit until he finds it. The newspaperman is the difference between democracy and dictatorship. Lock the doors in his face, and human rights and liberties go out the window.

He wants nothing for himself that all can't share. But he is the spotlight that shines into dark corners and exposes the ogres of greed and double-dealing.

If there is any nobler calling than that of the newspaperman it has not yet been clearly defined. He is minister, judge, confessor, counselor, all rolled into one. He reports the facts, as he finds them without fear or favor or hope of reward. He is, to end it on a word, "Truth."

WHAT'S AHEAD FOR THE PRESS?

An idea of the future can be learned from a study of the past. An *Editor & Publisher* survey made in 1953 of the opinions of a dozen leaders in publishing on the major achievements of the past half century stressed the growth in mass communications. For example, these men valued the improvements in communications and the way the papers have harnessed them, such as the Wirephoto, Teletypewriter, and Teletypesetter. Consideration was given to the increased sense of public responsibility as well as the growth in emphasis on factual reporting, free from partisan bias. The more restrained tone of editorial comment was observed, as were advances in journalism education. These men acknowledged the need for further scientific research and development and the necessity to produce better papers more economically. More attention was focused on the background and interpretation of the news.[57]

Five years later Dean Frank Luther Mott predicted: "Electronic devices are shifting the emphasis of newspapers to interpretation and record. Television and radio have taken over the first news flashes. Daily papers must dig deeper, clarify and enlighten the facts. New processes call for new reporting in depth with strength, imagination and brilliance."[58]

Problems still existed, especially with the smaller papers. Rising costs and labor relations were among problems cited as 1960 opened, together with poor copy turned in by advertisers, difficulty in changing advertising rates, and the need for coordination of all mechanical departments with the editorial and advertising departments. Despite words of warnings, the general prediction was that the sixties would represent the papers' finest decade so far.

CHAPTER XXIII

MISSOURI PRESS FACES THE FUTURE

ACROSS the nation alarm has been voiced, rather strongly in some areas, about the gradual decline in the number of newspapers. Newspapers in Missouri have been part of this trend, though the loss in the state in recent years has been slight. No loss, however, has shown in the circulation or in the soundness of the survivors. During the last eight years, 1957-1964, the Missouri Press Association reports there has been a net loss of eighteen papers; there were 303 weeklies and semiweeklies and 53 dailies in 1964, compared with 318 weeklies and 56 dailies in 1957. These figures do not include the metropolitan papers in St. Louis and Kansas City. In circulation there has been a steady increase. From a total of 546,037, with an average of 1,717 per paper, the weeklies now reach 574,333, an average of 1,902 per paper. Dailies, too, have jumped—from 439,924 to 467,001—during this period. The average community daily reaches 8,981 readers, compared with 7,856 in 1957. In addition, circulation of the metropolitan papers continues to climb. These dailies account for nearly 1,400,000 each weekday and some 1,300,000 on Sundays.[1]

Advertising rates continue to reflect this higher circulation, as well as the higher costs of production. Many Missouri publishers have joined a trend sweeping the nation—offset. This is one of the five major trends in present-day newspaper publishing. The others include:

> Suburban journalism, growth of neighborhood papers.
> Growth of more free papers, shoppers, and the like.
> Centralization of printing plants, with two or more papers published under the same roof.
> Increased use of pictures and color.

A detailed study of the Missouri press and this trend to offset was completed in 1962 by Preston P. Clark, Jr., a graduate student in journalism at the university. Clark noted that the growth of suburban papers is taking place in St. Louis and Kansas City. For example, George I. Sandford of North Kansas City installed a web offset press for his *Press-Dispatch* in March, 1960. In addition, he is printing the *News-Dispatch*, Parkville *Platte County Dispatch*, and Gladstone *Dispatch*. In St. Louis, Lucius B. Morse publishes the *Daily Record*, Kirkwood *Advertiser*, Webster Groves *Webster Advertiser*, St. Louis *Construction*

Record, as well as about twenty papers for other publishers. For example, the Florissant *Valley Reporter* handles its own type-setting and make-up, completing the paste-up form. These pages then are photographed and printed by Morse.[2]

Another trend, centralization, finds the Pierce City *Leader Journal,* Neosho *Miner-Mechanic* and *Graphic,* and Galena *Stone County Republican* all printed in Cassville. The Van Press, or-ganized in Houston by four publishers, turns out seven papers: The Houston *Herald,* Houston *Republican,* Willow Springs *News,* Mountain View *Standard,* Mountain Grove *Tri-County News,* Licking *News,* and Summersville *Beacon.*[3] In Washington, James L. Miller prints five papers in addition to his own *Missourian* and *Citizen* in a plant that cost about $100,000 to convert to offset.[4]

Offset printing allows increased use of pictures. Readership studies have made it clear that pictures rank high on the sub-scribers' preference list. With more pictures, publishers can compete better with television and magazines. Missouri pub-lishers ranked better reproduction of pictures as the major advan-tage offered by offset, slightly ahead of its greater flexibility and versatility, easier, faster, and cheaper composition, and readers' preference for the offset "look."

Color possibilities, too, have increased with the use of new machinery. In 1963, thirty-two Missouri dailies were equipped to handle color printing, while thirty-three of the weeklies were so prepared. The Grandview *Jackson County Advocate* became, in 1960, one of twelve papers in the nation to install a Landman color unit on its press for spot color. This was one of the early weeklies in the state to offer run-of-press color.[5]

Missouri publishers have come a long way since the first offset printing operation by the Warrensburg *Star-Journal* in June, 1939. At that time, the paper published a special Photo News edition in magazine form and in 1940 its second—and last—annual edition. Probably the first paper printed by offset in the state to appear on a continuing basis was the Independence *Shopper,* in October, 1939. This was the forerunner of the *Pictorial Shop-per,* now the *Pictorial News.*[6]

The *Missouri Herald* of Hayti began with offset on January 7, 1944, and can be considered the first newspaper to use this system in the state. Since its publisher, Otis A. Popham, con-tinued to use Linotype composition on his new offset tabloid, readers were hardly aware of the change. Popham discussed the tabloid change with his readers; the changes, he said, "would

solve many mechanical and labor problems that confront us"
under wartime conditions. He was satisfied with the readers'
responses.[7] In 1956 Popham's sons switched the paper back to
letterpress.

Prior to the use of offset, pictures were not customarily used
in Missouri weeklies. In October, 1946, Glenn S. Hensley, Jr., of
the Willow Springs *News* wrote about how he had turned his
hobby, photography, to use and had increased reader interest
and advertising revenue for the paper.[8]

Since 1959 other publishers have made the change to offset.
On November 13 of that year, J. M. Fidler established the Salis-
bury *Press-Spectator* as an offset paper, with plates made in
Marceline. The next year the following publishers were among
those who answered Clark's questionnaire and indicated they
had switched to offset: North Kansas City *Press-Dispatch*, St.
Louis *Daily Record*, Jasper *Jasper County News*, West Plains
Quill, Galena *Stone County Republican*, Oak Grove *Banner*, Blue
Springs *Leader*, Buckner *Fort Osage News*, Houston *Herald*,
and Houston *Republican*. They were joined in 1961 by the
Neosho *Miner-Mechanic* and *Graphic*, Pierce City *Leader Journal*,
Camdenton *Reveille* and *Leader*, Ironton *Mountain Echo*, Shel-
bina *Democrat*, Florissant *Valley Reporter*, and Washington *Mis-
sourian* and *Citizen*. Among others listed in the MPA directory
in 1962 were the Branson *Beacon*, Diamond *Newton County
News*, Farmington *Press*, Harrisonville *Cass County Democrat
Missourian*, North Kansas City *News-Dispatch*, Parkville *Platte
County Dispatch*, and Clayton *St. Louis Countian*. By early 1963
others were the Brookfield *News-Bulletin*, DeSoto *Jefferson Re-
public* and *Press*, Eminence *Current Wave*, Licking *News*, Milan
Standard, Moberly *Message*, Mountain View *Standard*, Mountain
Grove *Tri-County News*, Neosho *Miner* and *Mechanic*, Summers-
ville *Beacon*, Waynesville *Pulaski County Democrat*, Willow
Springs *News*, Independence *News*, and St. Charles *Banner News*.
By early 1964 these papers also were being printed by offset:
Belton *Star-Herald*, Blue Springs *Jackson County Democrat*,
Boonville *Advertiser and Daily News*, Caruthersville *Journal*,
Cassville *Republican*, Greenfield *Vedette and Advocate*, Mans-
field *Mirror-Republican*, Nixa *Enterprise*, Oak Grove *Sentinel*,
Pineville *Democrat*, Pleasant Hill *Times*, Princeton *Post-Tele-
graph*, Salisbury *Press-Spectator*, and Trenton *Republican*.

This change in printing methods has not been accomplished
without problems. Some publishers considered the high cost of

conversion from letterpress to be the major disadvantage, followed by some increased costs for materials, supplies, and paper. Others thought more paper was wasted by offset, partially due to the operators' learning a new printing process. When Edgar Blanton switched his Shelbina *Democrat* to offset, he encountered problems, some expected. In recalling this experience in 1961, Blanton wrote, "For the first two issues everybody worked all night, the last run starting at 9 A.M. the day after publication ordinarily . . . it was not until the fifth issue that the pictures were worth looking at."[9]

Use of offset will expand. More attention is being given to the process at press association meetings. Phototypesetting units have been reduced in price, and other changes are directed to aiding publishers to meet increased operational costs. Some observers foresee a reversal in the number of papers, offset permitting the establishment of more publications.

EQUIPMENT, BUILDINGS IMPROVED

Despite narrow operating profits, Missouri publishers continued in the early 1960's to enlarge plants, add buildings, and trade their old equipment for newer and faster presses. Early in 1960 the Roop Printing Company in DeSoto enlarged its shop and office space for printing and stationery departments and added a new Heidelberg press. More space was provided for a new Duplex press by the St. Clair *Chronicle,* and other additions were made to overcome the "caprices of labor" in 1960.[10] That some Missouri publishers needed new equipment became clear when the *Missouri Press News* survey in mid-1960 revealed there were at least two line-casting machines still in use, despite their more than sixty years of use. Both the Lathrop *Optimist* and the Oak Grove *Banner* reported machines in use that were built before the turn of the century.[11]

In order to prepare for conversion to offset, the West Plains *Quill* added a larger building in 1960. Open house was held in August by the Eldon *Advertiser* and the *Miller County Autogram* for their new plant, which included a new Duplex press. A new press was added two months later by the Potosi *Independent-Journal.* The St. Louis *Post-Dispatch* moved its plant six blocks in September—without missing an edition—to the building formerly occupied by the *Globe-Democrat.* The Salem *News* considered 1960 one of its most eventful years. Remodeling work was started in January, and the paper announced on December 29 the purchase of the Salem *Post,* only other paper in Dent County. The new front for the plant was designed by the publisher's son, Robert L. Vickery, Jr., as his first completed architectural work.[12] Early in 1961 the Independence *Examiner* announced plans to spend $200,000 to double its floor space, renovate its building, and increase the press capacity. That same year, the St. Joseph *News-Press* and *Gazette* began a $500,000 project, which included a new six-unit Goss high-speed press to supplement other equipment.

The California *Democrat* was among the many papers that added Teletypesetter equipment. Also in 1961, the *Democrat* enlarged its building space and expanded its offset operations. In October the Flat River *St. Francois County Journal* acquired a new building, the Waynesville *Pulaski County Democrat* obtained a new home, and the Windsor *Review* remodeled its lobby, added an office, and installed TTS operations. By December the Scotland County weeklies had moved into their new plant in Memphis. Expansion continued throughout 1962. The Holden *Progress* held open house on March 30 in its new plant, which replaced one destroyed by fire. Among the features were the TTS operation, a new Ludlow typecasting machine, and Miehle press. After having used its Babcock Reliance press since 1909, the LaPlata *Home Press* took it to the junk heap and replaced it with a much newer model in 1962. Other improvements included a new press for the Edina *Sentinel,* a service office in Farmington for Flat River *Journal* subscribers, a new building for the Union *Franklin County Tribune,* remodeling for the Doniphan *Prospect-News,* a new press for the St. James *Leader-Journal,* and a new building for the Sikeston *Standard.* The Windsor *Review,* Joplin *Globe,* and others added equipment. In Kennett the *Daily Democrat* started a new weekend edition, the *Missouri Weekly.*

In 1963, when the Eminence *Current Wave* turned to offset, it retired an "old friend," an eighty-five-year-old Cranston cylinder press. In the same year, the Tipton *Times* remodeled its plant, the Vandalia *Leader* doubled its facilities, the Mountain Grove *Tri-County News* improved its facilities, and the Gainesville *Ozark County Times* erected a new plant following a fire. Preparing for its one-hundredth anniversary in 1965, the Warrensburg *Star-Journal* began a building program in 1963.

Publishers continued to expand, add presses, switch to TTS

or offset, and remodel their offices and pressrooms. The list mentioned here, while not complete, indicates the papers' growth.

DEATHS AMONG PUBLISHERS

Several prominent Missouri publishers died in the early 1960's. J. Irvin Bennett, ninety-one years of age, was the last surviving charter member of the Northwest Missouri Press Association at the time of his death on March 30, 1960; he had been associated with several papers. G. H. Miller died at the age of fifty-one on May 25 while reading proofs for his Centralia *Fireside Guard*. Amon C. Weeks, formerly co-owner of the St. Charles *Cosmos-Monitor*, died on June 5; George E. Spear of the Belton *Star-Herald* died on June 18, and L. Roy Sims, Jr., of the Fairfax *Forum*, seventy-one years old, died on December 11.

Early in January, 1961, George W. Krumsick, founder of the Washington *Citizen*, died at the age of seventy-nine; Mrs. Walter Williams, seventy-one years old, died on July 6; Walter T. Stickney of the Webb City *Sentinel* died on September 5 at the age of seventy-two, and G. R. Derby of the Gideon *News* and Clarkton *News* died on December 21, having reached the age of sixty-four.

After fifty-five years with the Doniphan *Prospect-News*, publisher William H. Beal died January 19, 1962. Charles Iden, for many of his eighty-one years publisher of the Crocker *News*, died on January 26, and Clinton H. Denman of the Sikeston *Herald* died at age eighty-two on February 17. Noah A. Gerig, seventy-seven years old, founder of the Flat River *St. Francois County Journal*, died on March 3; John T. Cooper of the Lee's Summit *Journal*, seventy-eight years old, died on May 24; Elzey Roberts, Sr., long with the St. Louis *Star-Times*, died at the age of seventy on May 14; Charles A. Knouse, seventy years old, of the Gower *Enterprise*, died on June 12; and Mark F. Denman, Sr., for more than forty years with the Farmington *News*, on August 7.

Leaving the publishing scene in 1963 were A. E. "Cap" Garvin, who had worked for many of his sixty-six years with several state papers; Earl P. Williams, owner of the Meadville *Messenger* for forty-five years; P. T. Grimes, formerly in Boonville; William S. Wiggs, former owner of the Marble Hill *Banner-Press*; Charles Richards, formerly publisher of the Wentzville *Union*; and Oliver H. Grosse, founder of the Salem *News*. The list of newspapermen who died in 1963 includes T. Norman Williams, sixty-eight, son of the founder of the West Plains *Quill;* Louis Brownlow, eighty-four, formerly of the Buffalo *Reflex* and author of two books; Howard H. Peters, eighty-six, founder of the Union Star *Herald;* James Yager, ninety-eight, publisher of the Morehouse *Messenger* from 1915 to 1934; Will Jacobi, sixty-eight, copublisher of the Martinsburg *Monitor;* Helen Purcell, daughter of the founder of the Illmo *Jimplicute;* Ira R. Franklin, eighty-seven, of the Green City *Press* and Appleton City *Journal;* Wayne B. Ennis, forty-eight, copublisher of the Cassville *Republican;* Ross D. Heifner, seventy-one, of the Diamond *News;* and Earl F. Hadden, former publisher of the Montgomery City *Standard.* Frank B. Ellinghouse, former publisher of the Greenville *Sun,* and Aldin W. Allen, former publisher of the Lexington *Intelligencer,* died in 1964.

POLITICS TOP STORY IN 1960

The election of John F. Kennedy to the Presidency in 1960 was the most important event in the news that year, ranking above the U-2 and Powers' trial, the collapse of the Summit Conference, independence for the African nations, collisions of airliners, Castro, Khrushchev, space and nuclear affairs, Eisenhower's cancellation of a trip to Japan, sit-ins, and the strife over integration of schools in New Orleans. News coverage of the conventions was extremely heavy, and both parties used television extensively. More than five thousand press personnel covered the Democratic convention at Los Angeles, where some newsmen complained that television men were given priority over representatives of other news media. Papers fared somewhat better in the facilities provided for them in Chicago to report the Republican party's activities.[13]

Editor & Publisher's survey of the nation's press revealed that 57 per cent of the dailies were for Nixon, the lightest Republican support since this survey began in 1936. Although Kennedy had the support of 16 per cent of the dailies, this was the largest support given the Democratic party since Roosevelt had more than 22 per cent in 1944. In Missouri, eleven dailies with 445,060 circulation backed Kennedy; sixteen with 1,238,260 circulation backed Nixon; six were independent.[14]

Missouri papers played a more significant role in this election than they had in elections of recent decades. However, it was a state campaign that prompted this activity, rather than the national contest. James Kirkpatrick of the Windsor *Review* ran in the Democratic primary for secretary of state. Russell A. Mann, Jr., wrote in the *Missouri Press News*, "The Country Press Flexes Muscle," adding, "Many Missouri papers came out of what can be considered virtual political retirement during the 1960 primary . . . and managed to demolish a popular political tenet of recent years that the press has little influence with the voters." Some editors pointed out to readers "the rarity of their participation in a primary election campaign." However, Kirkpatrick, who carried 95 of the 114 counties, lost the election when his opponent won by a large majority in the St. Louis area.[15]

Missourians did split their ballots. John M. Dalton, heading the Democratic ticket for governor, lead his party with 1,095,000 votes, while Kennedy defeated Nixon by less than 10,000 votes—972,201 to 962,221. At least one Missouri publisher gained personally, since the outcome placed Frank P. Briggs of the Macon *Chronicle-Herald* in Washington as assistant secretary of the interior for fish and wildlife. Another Missourian, also a Democrat, lost when his party won. Robert M. White, II, copublisher of the Mexico *Ledger* but at that time editor of the New York *Herald-Tribune*, returned to Missouri after that paper's publisher, John Hay Whitney, a Republican, resigned from his position as ambassador to the Court of St. James's in England.

State newspapers gave full coverage to the Kennedy assassination in November, 1963. The front pages of the Houston *Herald* and *Republican* have been included in a slide presentation of such pages at the University of Iowa School of Journalism in Iowa City. Other state papers, such as the Columbia *Missourian*, were complimented for their coverage of the tragedy.

MPA ACTIVITIES ENLARGED

William A. Bray, general manager of the press association, discussed "Censorship by Taxation" in 1960. He voiced opposition to the proposal by the Internal Revenue Service to rule out the deduction of costs of advertising intended "to promote or defeat legislation." Bray urged that "it is time that small newspaper publishers individually took a hand and protested the IRS action to their congressmen. It's time, too, that Congress wakes up to the fact that it had delegated so much of its authority to bureaus that we scarcely need the legislators and our government is moving in the direction of the NON-representative kind." This and other articles on legislative problems kept publishers informed of measures that might affect their business.[16] In 1961 the association began its "Operation Public Notice" project, setting out to discard the dull "Legal Advertisements" or "Legals" labels so many papers placed over these messages. The association urged as a substitute this: "Public Notices, required by law to inform citizens of matters affecting them or their property." Mats were provided to dress up this section. A series of comments on "Little Chats on Public Notice" was provided.[17]

The merits of free publicity were still debated by publishers. The association's Publicity Control Committee, headed by Paul Gould, started its campaign against the practice in 1953. The objectives of the committee, restated in 1960, were to convince publishers that free publicity was merely free advertising, and more advertising would be sold if less publicity were donated.[18]

Conferences, clinics, workshops, and other sessions have been continued during the decade, generally in co-operation with the School of Journalism and other groups. Whenever a special need to help publishers has been felt, association officials have planned a suitable solution. Thus in the 1960's Management Clinics, News-Editorial Clinics, Mechanical Conferences, and similar meetings have been conducted. Regular association meetings continue, one during the Journalism Week program and the other in the fall. Topics and discussions are geared to existing situations, such as the 1962 session in St. Louis in co-operation with the National Editorial Association and the Freedom of Information Center.

Extensive remodeling of the facilities of the press association in 1962 added more office space, an attractive conference room, new furniture, and equipment.

The old days have not been forgotten. In 1960 E. J. Melton of the Boonville *Cooper County Record* wrote: "Taking the Blame," in which he recalled his early days in publishing. He remembered the time when merchants opposed a paper's mentioning anything such as measles, chickenpox, or scarlet fever in the community for fear it might hurt business. "The average citizen should thank God daily for our freedom," Melton commented. "If the small time politicians—in big towns and crossroads—had their way, many would deal with the press as Hitler did and the Kremlin does. . . . The paper keeps informing the public, helps to stiffen the spines of honest public officials, publishes names and addresses of hangouts of criminals and goes the full way with truth, regardless of risk and sacrifice."[19]

"The business of a newspaper, at least in part, is to dispense information about what happens to people," said the Carthage *Press* in an editorial voicing ideas many papers tried to follow. "But this is more than a business. It is a public trust, a solemn responsibility and no paper worth its salt will avoid that responsibility even in the face of criticism or attack." Walter Williams had expressed similar obligations many decades earlier.[20]

Publishers were pleased in 1961 when the General Assembly affirmed Missouri's traditional policy of open public records by passing a measure guaranteeing them. Without a dissenting vote the legislators approved what was known as the "Thomas C. Hennings Jr. Memorial Statute," in honor of the Senator's long fight for freedom of information. The measure covered "all records required to be kept by law or ordinance but does not include things specifically kept secret by law, such as income tax returns, adoption records, juvenile court proceedings and the like." Earlier the press had lost a round in their battle when they sought a revision in the juvenile code which would have relaxed the provision that permitted judges to withhold names of juveniles.[21]

Publishers aided a colleague, James C. Kirkpatrick of the Windsor *Review*, in a tax promotion drive in 1961. Kirkpatrick was chairman of a committee which successfully convinced voters to approve the division of the gasoline tax among the counties, cities, and state highway department.[22]

Former presidents of the Missouri Press Association received lasting fame in early 1962 when all their portraits were placed in the entrance hall to the new School of Journalism building. Other publishers continued to be recognized for their achievements. In Troy, Joe Wells completed fifty years with the *Free Press* in 1961, and civic clubs sponsored a banquet in his honor with Congressman Clarence Cannon the speaker. He died in 1964. Mrs. J. W. Stevenson, publisher of the Glasgow *Missourian*, was named "Editor of the Week" by *Publishers' Auxiliary* in 1962, an honor given to the late Bill Stevenson of the same paper in 1953.[23]

E. L. Dale of the Carthage *Press* was named a member of the Missouri Academy of Squires in 1962, the same year he completed his presidency of the State Historical Society. During the fall session of the association J. W. Brown, Jr., of the Harrisonville *Cass County Democrat-Missourian* was named president, succeeding Harry Guth, Sr., of the Perryville *Perry County Republican*.

In mid-1963 the Missouri Senate passed a resolution of congratulations to mark the 117th year of publication of the Liberty *Tribune*. About the same time, Governor John M. Dalton was a surprise visitor in St. Joseph at the function which honored Arthur V. Burrowes for serving fifty years as an editor.[24]

Now and then sadness is part of the record. After twenty-five years as publisher of the Sedalia *Times*, Stanton Hudson wrote on April 6, 1962: "If money is the gauge, I have been a horrible failure . . . but somehow or other I don't feel like a failure is supposed to feel at all. I've been doing what I like to do." In September, C. W. Hook closed the Auxvasse *Review*, a paper founded in 1888 and in his family for sixty years. That fall William Aden French retired as publisher of the Eminence *Current Wave* and Winona *Shannon County Democrat*. Recalling the time in 1921 when he first went to work in Eminence, French wrote, "I was then a middle-aged man with lots of pep; now I am a tired old man ready to quit."[25]

John R. Jutton became editor of the *Missouri Press News* and director of the Missouri Press News Service in late 1962.

Publishers continued to fight the profit squeeze. As early as 1960 *Editor & Publisher* noted five problems faced by the smaller publishers. These included poor copy turned in by local advertisers, difficulty in changing advertising rates, problems of coordination of mechanical departments with editorial and advertising departments, rising costs, and labor relations.

WHAT'S THE FUTURE?

"Everything's Up in '62" read a headline in the *Editor & Publisher*. Missouri's population, up 40,000 over the previous year, would produce higher income by more than four hundred million dollars. Retail sales, too, were rising. A prediction of more daily papers by 1985 was made by the general manager of the American Newspaper Publishers Association, Stanford Smith, in 1961. This growth will result from techniques on which research is now under way and which will not only add papers but will raise circulations past eighty-one million. In mid-1964 the circulation of dailies was near sixty million.[26]

True, expenses continue to climb. Yet Missouri publishers are combining their know-how to combat this trend, uniting their operations, working together to save costs. A few more papers will drop by the wayside, but it is not unreasonable to expect new publications to spring up, nurtured by ever-growing populations in the suburban communities.

The Missouri press, 156 years old in 1964, can be proud of its role in placing the state on the national map and recording its history for eternity. The Missouri Press Association, on the eve of its hundredth anniversary, can be proud of its service to its member papers, its work in founding the State Historical Society and the School of Journalism, and its sponsorship of many worthwhile projects to aid the state press.

CHAPTER XXIV

MISSOURI PRESS AND LEADERS TODAY

CHANGES are constantly occurring on the Missouri newspaper scene: some are turning to offset, others are sharing production costs with papers in nearby areas, still others are being sold to newcomers, severing family ties after many decades. Space prohibits a detailed historical sketch of each paper, though some highlights are provided. Data here reflect the situation in late 1963.

In Adrian, Robert C. Gunn, after working on the paper for six years, bought the *Journal* in 1956. Since shortly after the Civil War, the Albany *Ledger* has appeared; now it is published by Jack Stapleton and Ron Morrison. The Tedrick family has owned the Altamont *Times* since 1907, when George became known as the "Oracle of Altamont," widely quoted from his column, "Heard on the Curb." Orlo Tedrick has operated the paper since 1948.

David L. Mickey has directed the Anderson *News-Review* since the early 1920's, while Norman Carlton has operated the Appleton City *Journal* since 1959. The *Journal's* history includes a long ownership by Charles C. Hilton. After starting as an apprentice in 1947, Dal Mason bought the Ash Grove *Commonwealth* in 1957. Fire destroyed some early files of the Atlanta *Express*, operated since the 1950's by Charles W. Andrews, Jr., and published by James P. Sagaser until 1963, when it was sold to Gerald D. Bloom. Wilson B. Lowry published the Aurora *Advertiser* for thirty-one years before his death in 1948. Lowry also had been a railroad telegrapher and a baseball player. A cousin, Robert G. Lowry, now runs the paper.

Since 1915, J. E. Curry has been publishing the Ava *Douglas County Herald*, and in Alton Wallace N. Jenkins publishes the *South Missourian-Democrat*. The Belle *Banner* is a member of the Tri-County Publications group, under Norman B. Gallagher, who gave up legal work, became an Associated Press correspondent, and bought the *Banner* in 1934. In 1938 he added the Bland *Courier* and the Linn *Osage County Republican*. George E. Spear, Jr., directed the Belton *Star-Herald*, a paper purchased by his father in 1933, until its sale in 1963 to J. W. Brown, Jr. Alden Pinney was with the Benton *Scott County Democrat* for thirty-three of its first thirty-five years, but Charles L. Blanton, Jr., has been running it since 1949.

Ben G. Crouch was editor of the Bethany *Republican-Clipper* for thirty years, a paper now operated by Vincent N. Conger, whose father was a former owner. S. L. Speer came from Illinois in the early 1950's to take over the Bismarck *Gazette*. The Bloomfield *Vindicator* has had several owners during the past decade, with Fred W. Koenig now directing its work. Mrs. Lois L. Wolfe is publishing the Blue Springs *Jackson County Democrat*, while Orville D. Triggs operates the *Leader*, which he started there in 1956.

The Gravely family has owned the Bolivar *Free Press* since its founding in 1868. Joseph W. Gravely learned the printing trade when he was thirteen years old. A son, Marshall, now owns the paper. In Bolivar, the *Herald* is owned by Roy E. Murphy, but for fifty-three years it was in the Stufflebam family. Bonne Terre's single paper, the *Register*, owned since 1957 by Carl Erickson, was sold in 1963 to Jack Hays. For years the Stahl family's name was associated with the Boonville *News* and *Advertiser*. Now these papers, which date to 1840, are owned by a corporation, with O. T. Maxwell directing the work. The *Cooper County Record* there has been operated by E. J. Melton since 1937. William F. Mayhall's name was long on the Bowling Green *Times*. However, since the 1930's it has been Freeman, with Bonham G. and B. Wayne in charge. In Branson, the *Beacon* has been under Leon A. Farrell since 1957. In 1945 Senator W. E. Freeland purchased the *White River Leader* there.

In 1962 the Braymer *Bee* celebrated its seventy-fifth anniversary, having as an early slogan, "The truth straight as the flight of a Bee." Mrs. Grace L. Hart has owned the paper since 1954. John H. Gilgour directs the Breckenridge *Bulletin*, owned for years by J. T. Kenower. Ira J. Williams has had the Brookfield *News Bulletin* for many years, and for three decades Joe Nichell produced the Browning *Leader-Record*, now owned by Mrs. F. N. Woodward and G. T. Woodward.

"We have worked for it, earned it, and, by the gray hairs of Gutenberg, we will have it. The ghosts of starved editors hover around us, urging us on, so hurry up, or DOWN YOU GO." Thus subscribers of the Brunswick *Brunswicker* were warned in 1869 to pay up or see their names on the Black List in the next issue. Since 1928 the Clayton family has owned the paper, with Robert H. Clayton publisher. H. H. Leach has owned an interest in both the Buffalo *Reflex* and the *Dallas County Republican* since 1950. Eugene Price has owned the Burlington Junction *Post-*

News since 1954. After the end of World War II, R. A. Ellis took over the Butler *Bates County Democrat,* owned for thirty years by Harry H. Henry. Wayne E. Turner, from Kansas, purchased the Cabool *Enterprise* in 1960. Since 1890 the McDaniel name has dominated the Cainsville *News,* published now by Glenn E. Willson. Jack P. Crawford directs both the California *Democrat* and the *Moniteau County Herald.* His father Marvin acquired the first paper in 1925, the *Herald* in 1946. For fifty-three years L. L. Carter published the *Herald.*

Gomer T. Richards bought the Camdenton *Central Missouri Leader* in 1940. His father was publisher of the *Reveille.* The two were combined, although their titles were kept; now they are published by Gomer T. and Grant T. Richards. Thomas W. McAllen publishes both the Cameron *Sun* and *News-Observer.* For years the Dorsey name was associated with journalism in Cameron. B. W. Overall and his son bought the Campbell *Citizen* in 1901 when it was less than a year old. A son, Wilson, still operates it. In Cape Girardeau, the *Southeast Missourian* is synonymous with the Naeter name, where brothers Fred and George took over in 1904. Today it is published by Fred and Harry Naeter. Mrs. Beaulah Hart publishes the *Southeast Weekly Bulletin* there.

Robert W. Miller is carrying on the family name with the Carl Junction *Standard,* earlier operated by A. W. McDowell. For more than a half century W. R. Painter was with the Carrollton *Democrat.* Earl F. Cheesman was with the paper twenty-four years before becoming editor in 1947. T. J. Clark has directed the *Republican-Record* there since the late 1930's. W. J. Sewall was with the Carthage *Press* for nearly sixty years. E. L. Dale, one of his employes, rose from printer's devil to head the firm. O. W. Chilton for years has been with the Caruthersville *Democrat-Argus,* a merger that occurred in 1921. Since the mid-1920's, J. Thomas Markey published the *Republican* there until 1963, when Allen B. Merritt bought it and renamed it the *Journal.* For three generations the name Ray was connected with the Cassville *Democrat,* starting with Dr. John Ray in 1872. Now Mrs. Kathryn Mitchell, a sister of Means Ray, and her son Bob are with the paper. Emory Melton, a Cassville attorney, and Wayne Ennis, a printer, bought the *Republican* there in 1949, after E. N. Meador had operated the paper since 1908.

Burney L. Fishback purchased the Center *Herald* in 1948. The Centralia *Fireside Guard* was for years owned by A. Rodemyre

& Son. Edgar Rodemyre was editor for more than forty years, and George H. Miller, son-in-law of Mrs. E. T. Rodemyre, ran it from 1936 until his death in 1960; John W. Rolfe is now the publisher. Started in 1910, the Chaffee *Signal* was in the C. E. Mattocks family until 1963, when it was sold to Bob Kielhofner. Since Civil War days Canton has had its *Press*. Now the *Press-News and Record*, it is published by L. L. Dimmitt, who took over in 1940. He also has the Monticello *Lewis County Journal*. Art L. Wallhausen bought the Charleston *Enterprise-Courier* in 1938 and in 1955 acquired the *Democrat*, abolishing that title. Watkins has been the name on the Chillicothe *Constitution-Tribune* masthead for decades; now it is Charles E. Watkins. H. G. Williams acquired the Clarence *Courier* in 1958, and in 1962 Ralph G. Hawkins, son of Ralph N. Hawkins of the Portageville *Southeast Missourian*, took over the Clarkton *News* and the Gideon *News*.

First printed on a Washington hand press in 1881, the Clayton *Watchman-Advocate* has been in the Essen family since 1900. The Clayton *St. Louis Countian* is published by Carl J. Teichman. The name Grady has been with the Clearmont *News* since the early 1920's, and today Dorothy V. Grady is the publisher. Van W. Davis has carried on the family name with the Clifton Hill *Rustler*. For nearly sixty years the Clinton *Democrat* was owned by the Charles Whitaker family, but since 1950 has been operated by M. N. White and his son-in-law Daniel B. Miles, and they also own the *Henry County Democrat*. For about seventy years the T. O. Smith family printed the *Eye* there until Floyd H. Pinkston and C. W. Dickgrafe took over in 1953. They also publish the Montrose *Herald-Tidings*. Edwin Wilkens resumed the Cole Camp *Courier* in 1956.

E. M. Watson made the Columbia *Tribune* noted at the start of the century, and since the 1930's the H. J. Waters family has directed its operation. Since 1908 the School of Journalism has supervised the production of the Columbia *Missourian*. For fifty-two years John J. Bredehoeft, Jr., published the Concordia *Concordian*, purchased in 1946 by Lloyd Beissenherz. Paul Langford is publishing both the Crane *Chronicle* and the Galena *Stone County News-Oracle*. L. E. Daugherty publishes the Creighton *Banner*. Bert J. Reber has published the Crystal City *Jefferson County Press-Times* since the mid-1940's, and since 1954 Dorothy O. Moore has published the Cuba *Times* and the Sullivan *Tri-County News*.

W. A. McDowell had long been with the Dearborn *Democrat*

until in 1946 G. E. Williams, who learned the printing trade
when he was twelve years old, bought the paper. In DeSoto,
Lewis W. Roop has published the *Jefferson Republic* and the
Press since 1942. The Dexter *Messenger*, then more than eighty-
five years old, was sold in 1959 to Barney Miller, who also pub-
lishes the *Statesman* there. Robert Mapes publishes the Diamond
Newton County News. Ralph W. Goforth purchased the Dixon
Pulaski County Pilot-News in 1953; his father had founded the
Pilot forty-one years earlier. Chester L. Ponder acquired the
Doniphan *Prospect-News* in 1961. James F. Forsythe bought the
Downing *News* in 1945. Forsythe also publishes the Lancaster
Excelsior, Greentop *Reporter*, and   Queen City *Monitor-Leader*.

George W. Rhea started the Drexel *Star* with a hand press, two
cases of Brevier type, one case of nonpareil, and some fonts of
job type, plus a job press and cutter. For more than fifty years
he ran the paper, until in 1954 it was acquired by Clyde W.
Thomas. Joel M. Savell is the publisher of the East Prairie *Eagle*.
In Edina the Schofield name has long been associated with the
Sentinel. R. F. Schofield first was exposed to journalism on the
Columbia *Herald* under Walter Williams. His sons have carried
on the business since his death in 1941, and today F. E. Schofield
is the publisher. In Eldon, E. H. Shepherd published the *Advertiser* for more than forty years, a paper his father had started in
1894; in 1948 it was purchased by Wallace G. Vernon. The Smith
family has for nearly seventy years been associated with the El
Dorado Springs *Sun*.

Charles L. Ellinghouse, publisher of the Piedmont *Journal-
Banner* and Greenville *Sun*, added the Ellington *Courier Press* in
1959; the Daniels family had operated the paper for fifty years. A.
V. Grady is the publisher of the Elmo *Register* and Dorothy V.
Grady of the Clearmont *News*. Gordon Crank was publisher for
forty-five years of the Elsberry *Democrat*, until his death in 1945;
Sandford Howard is editor today. The Eminence *Current Wave*
has more recently been acquired by Thomas L. Chilton; for
twenty-five years it was published by William Aden French. On
the Excelsior Springs *Standard*'s fiftieth anniversary in 1939,
W. N. "Uncle Billy" McKinney, eighty-two years of age, served
as honorary editor. Donald J. McGiffin took over in 1948, carrying on the McGiffin name, first with the paper in 1927. The
oldest business firm in Fairfax is the *Forum*, founded by W. H.
Hambaugh in 1892; L. Roy Sims took over in 1934, and it is now
operated by Roy Sims, Jr., and Earle E. Sims. Harry and Clint

Denman bought the Farmington *News* in 1900; Mack F. Denman was with the paper until his death in 1962, and Harry L. Denman is now the publisher. A more recent paper, the *Press,* founded in 1928, is published there by Jess Stewart.

Many names are associated with the long history of the Fayette *Advertiser* and the *Democrat-Leader,* including Harry P. Mason and Wirt Mitchell; since the late 1940's John Hert has published both papers. Lloyd and Harold Wright have been publishing the Festus *News-Democrat* since the early 1950's. W. L. Bouchard has made the Flat River *Lead Belt News* widely quoted for nearly fifty years. The *News* is said to be the oldest business firm in the Lead Belt and under one management longer than any other county paper. N. A. Gerig established the *St. Francois County Journal* in 1935; it was published by his son Carroll B. Gerig until 1963, when it was acquired by James A. Campbell, Frank N. Williams, and George H. Williams. Since 1950 the *Valley Reporter* has appeared in Florissant; Al F. Erdelen bought the paper in 1958 from its founder, Henry Evans. Senator W. E. Freeland publishes the Forsyth *Taney County Republican.* When honored by the School of Journalism in 1945, Freeland said, "The country weekly owes its existence to the curiosity and desire for unity of mankind." Two daughters, Mrs. Freda Ingenthron and Maude Freeland, have long been associated with state journalism.

O. B. and S. A. Ferguson are continuing the family name in Fredericktown on the *Democrat-News.* The same is true in Fulton, where V. A. Johnston and Virgil Johnston, Jr., are publishing the *Sun-Gazette.* James W. Johnston spent nearly seventy years in newspaper work before his death in 1939. One son, George, died in 1949 while in Columbia for a meeting of the directors of the press association. A more recent publisher is Fred G. Robins, who bought the Gainesville *Ozark County Times* in 1959; fire destroyed the building in early 1963. Leon Fredrick has been publishing the Galena *Stone County Republican* since the late 1950's as well as the *Table Rock Times.* W. M. Harrison and Joe R. Snyder are publishing the Gallatin *Democrat* and *North Missourian.* Long associated on Gallatin papers were Lewis Lamkin, Wes Robertson, and Fred M. Harrison. After working on several state papers, Edgar E. Coy bought the Garden City *Views* in 1939. Robert A. Edmonson is handling the Gerald *Journal.*

A paper with nearly a century of history is the Glasgow *Mis-*

sourian, published by Mrs. J. W. Stevenson. She and her husband bought the paper in 1930. He once wrote that "running a news sheet in a small town is an everlastingly hard job." Dellard Surbrugg is publishing the Golden City *Herald,* descended from the *News,* which was founded in 1881. E. P. Heckethorn has been publishing the Gorin *Argus* since 1947. James D. Turnbaugh, Jr., is publisher of the Grandview *Jackson County Advocate.* The oldest firm in Worth County is the Grant City *Times-Tribune,* operated for many years by C. L. McLaughlin and his son Chase. For the past five years John E. Ballard has published the Green City *Press.* James F. Wallace has published the Greenfield *Advertiser* since it was founded in 1954. The *Vedette and Advocate* there dates to the 1860's and for years was published by the Griffith family; Robert L. Dee has been in charge since the mid-1950's. R. A. Stark ran the Green Ridge *Local News* for thirty years, and his son J. E. now publishes this weekly. Virgil and M. F. Vaughan are publishers of the Hale *Leader,* in the family since the late 1930's. The Ridings' name has been associated with the Hamilton *Advocate-Hamiltonian* for years; the present publisher is Marion Ridings. One of the state's oldest papers, the Hannibal *Courier-Post,* is a member of the Lee Group, with E. L. Sparks, Jr., publisher. This paper is widely known as the one that Mark Twain served as a printer's devil. Started in 1954, the Hardin *Journal* is published by Lee Meador, who also has the Orrick *Sentinel,* begun in 1958.

Edgar R. Idol, Charles W. Steele, and other members of the Idol family helped to record history through the Harrisonville *Cass County Democrat-Missourian,* now published by J. W. Brown, Jr. William Tork founded the Hayti *Missouri Herald* in 1908 and operated it until his death in 1946; Wilburn Mathis is now the publisher. In Hermann, the *Advertiser-Courier* continues with the Graf family, as it has for more than a century. The Wilson family owned the Hermitage *Index* from 1919 until it was sold in 1947 to Earl Jenkins. G. Denzil Scott is carrying on that name with the Higginsville *Advance,* where George Scott was editor for thirty-five years. In recent years the Corder *Journal* and the *Jeffersonian* have been merged with the *Advance.* The Hillsboro *Jefferson County Record* continues to carry the name of Schneider on its masthead. C. L. Hobart came from Colorado and bought the Holden *Progress* in 1906. In the mid-1940's it was sold to W. L. Simpson, whose father once owned the Rolla *Times.* W. L. Moorhead edited the Hopkins

Journal for fifty years before his death in 1939. His son-in-law Joe Wright ran the paper until recent years, when Russell L. Cross became the publisher. Lane E. Davis publishes both the Houston *Herald* and the *Republican*. For fifty-seven years E. K. Lyles edited the *Herald*, with a policy "to mention everything that happens that is worth printing."

On the eve of the Humansville *Star-Leader*'s seventy-fifth birthday in 1951 it acquired a new publisher, Max E. Williams. Mrs. Bessie A. Carlton is the publisher of the Hume *Border Messenger*. Mrs. Van Davis for years published the Huntsville *Randolph County Times-Herald,* and the present publisher is Van W. Davis. Reece H. Venable is publishing the Illmo *Jimplicute;* the paper was carried on for three decades by E. L. Purcell and his daughter. Bernard F. McCarty has the Independence *Inter-City News;* William Southern, Jr., founded the *Examiner* there in 1898. In 1951 he and his partner Frank W. Rucker sold the paper to the Stauffer Publishing Company, which operates the Maryville *Forum* and the Nevada *Mail.* The *Examiner* publisher is T. Hall Collinson.

Eli D. Ake helped to establish the Ironton *Iron County Register* in the 1860's. Frank P. Ake died in 1939 after fifty years there, and today Eli P. Ake, his son, is the publisher. H. H. Hardy, who founded the Ironton *Mountain Echo* in the late 1930's, turned over its publishing to Richard L. Armfield in 1963. In May, 1962, a change occurred in Jackson when the *Missouri Cash-Book* and the *Cape County Post* were combined, given the new name *Pioneer,* and published by John W. Hoffman. L. E. Kimberling is the publisher of the Jamesport *Tri-County Weekly.* Harry Ward has been the publisher of the Jasper *Jasper County News* for the past decade. The Goshen family was long with the *Capital News* and *Post-Tribune* in Jefferson City; Mr. and Mrs. William H. Weldon are publishers today.

C. Cowgill Blair started as a school reporter on the Joplin *Globe* in 1907; in 1946 he became the publisher. Today, the *Globe* is printed in the morning and the *News-Herald* in the afternoon. Paul C. Rowe publishes both the Kahoka *Clark County Courier* and the *Gazette Herald.* He learned the printing business on the *Courier.* For many years J. L. Greenlee and his son Frank published the *Courier.* Garrett L. Smalley, Jr., is the publisher of the Kansas City *News-Press,* and Clifford B. Smith and Robert W. Smalley direct the *Record.* The Kansas City *Star* and *Times* are employe-owned, with Roy A. Roberts

president of the firm. Mrs. R. A. Whipple is publishing the
Kearney *Courier,* founded in 1932. The Kennett *Dunklin Democrat* is published by Jack Stapleton, Jr., who started a new weekend paper, the *Missouri Weekly,* there in 1962. E. P. Caruthers
founded the *Democrat* in 1888, and his son-in-law Will A. Jones
has carried on the business. Keytesville's *Chariton Courier,* with
a long record from shortly after the Civil War, is published by
Everett Kirby, Jr. Louis N. Bowman has published the King
City *Tri-County News* since it was founded in 1920. The Kirksville *Express and News* has been published by E. E. Swain since
1912; his son is associated with him today. Jack L. Thiess is
publisher of the Kirkwood *Advertiser,* founded in 1946, and the
Webster Groves *Advertiser.* The Knob Noster *Item,* which dates
from 1958, is published by Billy K. Hall. F. E. Schofield has the
Knox City *News.* In LaBelle, the *Star* was started in 1883 by
Charles W. Mulinex, noted for his "tolerance for humanity." It
is now published by William H. Bledsoe. W. L. Breuer handles
the La Grange *Indicator.* For nearly fifty years Arthur Aull was
publisher of the Lamar *Democrat,* carried on since his death in
1948 by his daughter Mrs. Madeleine Aull Van Hafften. The
LaPlata *Home Press* is the lone survivor among papers there,
now published by Gerald D. Bloom. Robert E. Cole, Jr., bought
the Lathrop *Optimist* in 1958 from E. L. Fisher, owner since
1925. Morton Holman repurchased the Lawson *Review* in 1961;
for twenty-two years it was owned by W. A. Black.

Both the Lebanon *Record* and the *Rustic-Republican* are now
published by O. R. Wright. The papers have a long association
with the city's history. Paul M. Gould, now publisher of the
Lee's Summit *Journal,* was one of three persons to buy the paper
in 1949. Others were Stanley R. Fike and Don Eck. In early
1961 the Lexington *Advertiser-News* was purchased by Jack P.
Crawford, Bill Dye, and Howard Hill, publishers of other Missouri papers. Theda and Edward Savage acquired the Liberal
News in the mid-1950's. The Liberty *Tribune,* a pre-Civil War
paper, was first owned by Robert Miller, later Irving Gilmer,
and then A. L. Preston; six sons and two daughters of the Pres-
tons entered newspaper work. Present publisher Howard Hill
was joined by Alan G. Nicholas as co-owner in 1963. In Licking,
the *News's* publisher for the past decade has been G. E. Derrickson, who also published the Summersville *Beacon* until 1963,
when it was sold to Thomas L. Chilton. Mrs. Bessie Lloyd is
the publisher of the Lilbourn *Semo News.* Urban M. Jaegers

and Harry Potts are publishers of the Linn *Osage County Observer*. Linn's *Unterrified Democrat* traces its history to 1866, when Lebbeus Zevely established the paper, bestowing this unusual title in defiance of Drake's constitution, which sought to disfranchise many voters. The paper has been in the Zevely family since, with William L. Zevely the present publisher. Fred W. Frye has published the Lockwood *Luminary* for a decade, and Victor A. Gierke has the Louisiana *Press-Journal*. The Macon *Chronicle-Herald* is published by Frank Briggs and F. M. Sagaser. R. I. Colburn and Edgar Blanton are publishers of the Madison *Times*. Since 1956 Allen Black and Miller Moll have been publishers of the Malden *Press-Merit;* they also publish the Parma *Tribune*. Chester Krause is the owner of the Mansfield *Mirror-Republican*, published for many years by Oliver B. Davis and Ralph O. Watters. For a half century W. S. Wiggs published the Marble Hill *Banner-Press*, owned later by Chester Ponder and now by Thomas and Verdell Jackson. J. V. Rockwell acquired the Marceline *News and Bucklin Herald* in 1955; the paper had been operated for a number of years by George Butts. Jack R. Thomson purchased the Marionville *Free Press* in 1962. R. N. Hains publishes both the Marshall *Saline County Citizen* and *Democrat-News*, papers with long histories. T. Ballard Watters, along with J. S. and T. W. Watters, publishes the Marshfield *Mail*, which has been in this family for more than a half century. E. C. Kehr has published the Marthasville *Record* since the early 1920's.

Byron Lord and Joe M. Roberts publish the Maysville *DeKalb County Record-Herald*. James F. Forsythe acquired both the Memphis *Democrat* and *Reveille* in 1957, now published by his son David. J. V. Bumbarger was the *Democrat* publisher for more than fifty years. In Meta, William L. Zevely has run the *Herald* since the 1940's. The third generation is publishing the Mexico *Ledger*, where Robert M. White, II, is following his father Mitchell and grandfather Robert. Dryden Baze is the Metz *Times's* publisher. The Milan *Standard*, founded in 1872, has been published by R. M. Wilson since the mid-1930's. Kenneth Friar is publishing a new paper, the Miller *Press*. L. G. and W. G. Hardy direct the Moberly *Message*, and James Todd continues to publish the *Monitor Index and Democrat*, a paper he acquired with William C. Van Cleve in 1919. Richard T. Hodges is carrying on the Mokane *Missourian*, following the death of his father in 1935. Kenneth G. Meuser acquired an interest in the Monett *Times* in 1941 and became the sole owner two years later. The Nolen family for years operated the Monroe City *News* until 1963, when Charles Hedbery bought it. Robert A. Bowling took over the Montgomery City *Standard* in 1960, a paper made famous by John W. Jacks and his family, who owned it for sixty-five years. Floyd Pinkston and C. W. Dickgrafe, publishers of the Clinton *Eye*, bought the Montrose *Tidings* in 1954. It is now the *Herald-Tidings*, consolidated with the Urich *Herald*.

Earle E. Sims and Roy Sims, Jr., bought the Mound City *News Independent* in 1959. The Ray Taylor family was long associated with this paper. W. K. Duncan bought the Mountain Grove *Journal* in 1946. George S. Townsend, who spent sixty-three years in newspaper work, was with the *Journal* thirty-eight years. Orrin Barbe is the present owner of the Mountain Grove *Tri-County News*. W. C. Park owned the Mountain View *Standard* for thirty-two years; recently Jac W. Zimmerman bought the paper from George S. Wattles. In 1960 Joseph D. Sullens bought the Mount Vernon *Lawrence Chieftain* and *Lawrence County Record*. Howard L. Bush has directed the Neosho *News* for many years. Joe Taylor published the *Miner and Mechanic* there until it was sold in the early 1960's to Andy Hall, who renamed it the *Graphic*. In Nevada, Ben F. Weir publishes both the *Mail* and *Herald*. E. H. Anderson and W. J. Lefmann bought the New Haven *Leader* in the late 1940's. J. Porter Fisher, son of John F. Fisher who was with the New London *Ralls County Record* from 1916 to 1940, bought the paper in 1940. Part interest was owned by Guiford D. Harris, who spent sixty years in newspaper work in New London.

Albert O. Allen, Jr., published the New Madrid *Record*, founded by his father in 1866, until the former's death in 1957; it is now published by L. H. Recker. Ralph W. Pogue is the publisher of the Noel *McDonald County Press*. W. D. Hill publishes the Norborne *Democrat-Leader*. George Sandford directs the *News-Dispatch* and the *Press-Dispatch* in North Kansas City, the Gladstone *Dispatch*, and the Parkville *Platte County Dispatch*. Orville D. Triggs has published the Oak Grove *Banner* since 1946 and the Buckner *Fort Osage News*. James F. Wolfe is the Oak Grove *Sentinel* publisher. William A. Bray was part-owner of the Odessa *Odessan* in 1948 with Russell Larkin; recently George Spaar acquired the paper from Joe Western. Victor A. Gierke bought the O'Fallon *Community News* in 1961.

Bob Kielhofner is the publisher of the Oran *News*. James W. Parsons bought the Oregon *Holt County Sentinel* in 1957; for many years "Dobyns and Curry" published this paper. A comparatively new paper, the Orrick *Sentinel*, is published by Lee Meador.

In Osceola, the *St. Clair County Courier* is published by Norman Carlton, while Ralph Warden and H. H. Murray directed the Owensville *Gasconade County Republican* from 1949 to 1963 when the former copublishers Mr. and Mrs. R. E. Warden purchased it. John M. Pile bought the Ozark *Christian County Republican* in 1926 and his son John L. has been running it since 1938. The Overland *Community News*, nearing its fortieth year, covers a large area of St. Louis County. B. Wayne Freeman recently acquired the *Meramec Valley Transcript* in Pacific.

The "family record" in Missouri journalism is owned by the Sosey family in Palmyra. There Jacob Sosey founded the paper now known as the *Spectator* in 1838; Don Sosey is the present publisher. Another long family association is that of the *Monroe County Appeal* in Paris; B. F. Blanton was the founder, and other Blantons have been with the paper. R. I. "Si" Colborn is the present publisher. David Edgar Blanton, one of the brothers, died in 1939. It was said that in his last hours "while in a semicoma the hands of the master printer still went through the motions of distributing type." Mrs. James C. Tibbetts runs the *Platte County Gazette*, a Parkville paper founded in 1885 by James P. Tucker, who turned the first spade of earth for the foundation of Walter Williams Hall of the School of Journalism. Gilbert Hutchinson publishes the Pattonsburg *Call*, a paper founded by Eugene A. Martin, who died in 1936. Burney L. Fishback also publishes the Perry *Enterprise*, edited for forty years by DeWitt Masters.

Harry E. Guth and P. L. Zoeller were partners since the 1920's in the Perryville *Perry County Republican* until Zoeller's death in 1964. Elmer L. Donze publishes the Perryville *Monitor*, formerly the *Sun*. Ken Bronson, now with the Independence *Examiner*, acquired the Pierce City *Leader-Journal* in 1961 from Meredith Garten, publisher for twenty-eight years; it is now published by Jack Henson. That same year John C. Wright, Jr., bought the Pineville *Democrat*, the oldest firm in McDonald County. Mrs. Max Jones is publishing the Platte City *Landmark*, the county's oldest paper, dating to 1865; Max Jones entered the *Landmark* office in 1893 as a printer. John A. Biggerstaff has published the Plattsburg *Leader* since the early 1950's and in 1963 acquired as partner Clifford McElhinney. Lois Lauer Wolfe is publisher of the Pleasant Hill *Times,* owned for more than fifty years by T. R. and F. B. Cloud. In Poplar Bluff, the Wolpers family has long been associated with the *American Republic* and the *Republican.* John H. Wolpers is believed to have been the first scoutmaster in America, organizing a troop in 1909 after reading about the movement in England. Robert M. Wolpers, a son, is now the publisher. The Portageville *Review* is published by Erwin Lloyd, whose father Raymond Lloyd bought the paper in the mid-1930's. For years the *Southeast Missourian* there was operated by Edward A. Wright, who died in 1941 while working at a job stone in his office. Ralph N. Hawkins bought the paper from Mrs. Wright and her son Erie in 1944. Hugh Richard and Lowell McFarland, brothers-in-law, bought the Potosi *Independent-Journal* from Wilson Bell, then Missouri's secretary of state, in 1945. The paper had been in the Bell family seventy-one years.

In 1901 W. C. Price established the Princeton *Post.* Later the *Telegraph* was consolidated, and in 1962 the paper was sold by James W. Price, its publisher for thirty-three years, to Donald F. Sheridan. Price, who received his journalism degree in 1925, became an advertising consultant at the School of Journalism. D. E. Russell publishes the Republic *Monitor.* A. E. Garvin and Ken Clayton are publishers of the Raytown *News,* established in 1926. The Rich Hill *Mining Review* is published by George Flexsenhar. For years the Richland *Mirror* held the distinction of being among the last of the hand-set papers in Missouri. However, in 1959 a Linotype was purchased. The paper, which has been in the family since 1937, was bought by Ralph W. Goforth from his brother Harold. Richmond has three papers, one of the few communities in the nation with so many. The *News* is published by Howard Hill, while William McCrae directs both the *Ray County Conservator* and the *Ray County Herald,* young papers. In Rock Port, John C. Stapel for years was associated with the *Atchison County Mail;* John Henry Cox now is the publisher. Edward W. Sowers, who has worked on a number of Missouri papers, is the Rolla *News* publisher; he has merged several papers, including the *New Era-Advertiser,* in 1961. At that time he said the merger was "like 'killing' one's old pet dog, but it needed to be done to 'clear the decks' for us to take on the publication of a weekly military paper, the Fort Wood *Sentinel.*"

Mark A. Thomson is continuing the family ownership of the St. Charles *Banner-News,* previously owned by his father Ronald M. Thomson, who died in 1953. The weekly edition was stopped in 1956 after ninety-two years of continuous publishing. A widely known writer and photographer, Mrs. Dorothy O. Moore, acquired the St. Clair *Chronicle* in 1952. Alvin F. Petrequin is publishing the Ste. Genevieve *Fair Play,* which was suspended for three years while its owner served in World War II. For many years three brothers were with the paper, LeClere, Felix, and Henry Janis, but all three died within a nine-month period in 1947. Another family paper is the Ste. Genevieve *Herald,* founded in 1882 by Joseph A. Ernst. After his death in 1920 a son, Frank J. A. Ernst, carried on the business until his death in 1941. Another son has worked with the paper, published now by Mrs. Katherine Ernst. Richard E. Wilson bought the St. James *Leader-Journal* in 1960. When it celebrated its centennial on April 25, 1945, the St. Joseph *Gazette* reprinted its first edition. The paper was founded by William Ridenbaugh, who rescued the Mormons' press from the Missouri River. Among former newsmen on the two papers there, now published by David R. Bradley, were Eugene Field, Walter Hines Page, Homer Croy, and Barry Farris. The papers came under local control in 1952, when Henry D. Bradley held the majority shares in the firm.

Another Pulitzer, the third in the history of the St. Louis *Post-Dispatch,* now directs that paper, while Richard Amberg is editing the Newhouse-owned *Globe-Democrat.* Both papers are printed in the *Post-Dispatch* plant.

The St. Marys *Review* continues in the Bartels family. Charles R. Bartels, long with the paper, died in 1958 at the age of eighty-three. Joseph R. Bartels is publisher today. Both the Salem *News* and the *Post* are owned by Robert L. Vickery and Charles A. Stacey, who came from Texas and acquired an interest in Salem journalism in 1950. J. M. Fidler has published the Salisbury *Press-Spectator* since the early 1950's. The paper was formerly directed by the Ritzenthaler family for nearly half a century. Bernard Finn was editor of the Sarcoxie *Record* for forty-three years before it was published by Earl A. Wright, who acquired it from Orville D. Triggs in 1945. The S. E. Lee family has long been with the Savannah *Reporter.* Howard

Sanderson is the owner of the Schell City *Ledger,* founded in 1947, and the Rockville *Leader.*

George H. Scruton, Jr., returned to the Sedalia *Democrat* in 1937 and occupied the desk used by his father from 1906 to 1925. His father had helped to merge the *Democrat* and *Capital* in 1907. Today the firm publishes the *Capital* in the morning and the *Democrat* in the evening. William E. Howsman publishes the Seneca *News-Dispatch.* Dennis Bacon owns the Senath *Dunklin County Press,* founded in 1946. J. D. Stanard operates the Seymour *Webster County Citizen.* History abounds on the Shelbina *Democrat.* For more than fifty years it was published by Col. W. O. L. Jewett; when he was residing in California, at the age of ninety, Jewett still contributed copy. He said in 1927 that in the early days "when an editor retired at night he wasn't a bit surprised to wake up the next morning to find a new rival across the street." His son Ernest W. Jewett and Edgar P. Blanton took over the paper, now published by E. P. and C. V. Blanton. W. C. and Rogers Hewitt long have been publishers of the Shelbyville *Shelby County Herald.*

Colonel C. L. Blanton bought the Sikeston *Standard* from the Naeter brothers in 1913. The "colonel" was one of the state's famed editors; at one time he declared, "I ask no one to agree with me, and don't care whether they do or not." He was noted for his sizzling phrases that caused angry responses. He was once a friend of Governor Stark, but after breaking with him, refused to capitalize his name. It always appeared in the paper in this style: lloyd c. stark. His son C. L. Blanton, Jr., is publisher today.

George A. Smith purchased the Slater *News-Rustler* in 1961; John K. McMullen and his son Lloyd had published the paper for many years. In Smithville, Charles L. Shinn has directed the *Democrat-Herald* since the early 1920's. Robert R. Orrick is the publisher of the Southwest City *Republic.* In Springfield, both the *News* and the *Leader-Press* are published by the Springfield Newspapers, Inc. Jack Stapleton, Sr., has been with the Stanberry *Headlight* since the 1920's. The Steele *Enterprise* is owned by R. C. Tennyson. Ralph E. Kehr, managing editor of the Steelville *Crawford Mirror* in 1937, soon became the publisher; the first issue of this paper was printed in 1872 in a tobacco barn. Chester W. Hoff continues the family name with the Stockton *Cedar County Republican;* his father bought the paper in 1896 and edited it until 1945. And in Stover the *Tri-County Republi-*

can, which dates from 1911, was published by H. A. Harrell to 1963, when his daughter and son-in-law, Mr. and Mrs. Mathew Washlick, took over. Harrell once said he never took a vacation in fifty years since he had "never had time to train a printer." The Sturgeon *Missouri Leader* for forty-seven years was edited by Omar D. Gray, who directed the paper with the idea, "If you can't say anything good about a person, don't say anything." Robert H. White bought the firm in 1960 and in 1963 sold it to Howard Stephens.

Frank W. Farmer began his newspaper training when only twelve years old and worked on several papers before taking over the Sweet Springs *Herald.* George H. Kaufman and his brother-in-law L. H. Sommer bought the Tarkio *Avalanche* in 1921; today Mrs. Kaufman is the publisher. R. H. Williams directs the Thayer *News,* where he has been since 1929. In Tipton, the *Times* has long been associated with the Pizer family. Everett Pizer acquired it in 1907. Following his death in 1950, E. N. Pizer became the publisher, with Mrs. Thomas W. Miller. "The *Republican* has a greater purpose in life than merely to publish the news," said W. B. Rogers, long-time newsman in Trenton. His family has carried on the *Republican-Times* for years. Ray Van Meter, foster son of Mrs. Carrie Rogers Clark, was the publisher until 1963, when it was sold to Willis Alexander and Bill Lenhart. Few names have been associated with the long history of the Troy *Free Press.* Henry F. Childers was there in 1878 at the age of nineteen, and published it until his death in 1934. Joe Wells, publisher until his death in 1964, and M. C. Foster paid $17,000 for the paper to Leland L. Chesley in 1943. Wallace G. Vernon has been publishing the Tuscumbia *Miller County Autogram-Sentinel* for nearly a decade. The paper claims a circulation seven times the population of the city.

A. A. Steinbeck took over the Union *Franklin County Tribune* in 1942, following the death of his father A. H., who began his career in Union in 1904. In 1960, Steinbeck bought the Pacific *Transcript.* Early in 1963 Wayne Freeman acquired both papers. George Choate and Aaron Stuckey recently acquired the Unionville *Republican,* long directed by the Morgan family. George T. Henson published the Van Buren *Current Local* for thirty-six years before selling to Alan Turley in 1958. Turley had learned to operate the Linotype under Henson, who was noted for his disregard for deadlines. He once said, "My only commitment is with the post office to publish and mail 52 editions a year. When

I get the paper out is strictly my affair." Henson never asked anyone to subscribe nor to pay up.

Weldon H. Steiner purchased the Vandalia *Press* and Laddonia *Herald* in 1961. The *Press-Herald* was combined with the *Leader,* which he had acquired ten years earlier, into the *Leader-Press.* Wallace G. Vernon bought the Versailles *Leader-Statesman* in 1961. Both the Vienna *Home Adviser* and the *Maries County Gazette* are published by the Tri-County Publications. Until his death in 1936, Catholic Father John Fugel edited the *Home Adviser.* He was termed an "aggressive and hard-hitting editor." One did not always agree with his plans or his methods, but there was never any question about his honesty or purpose. William C. Tucker acquired the Warrensburg *Star-Journal* in 1947 after working on Texas and Missouri papers; for forty-one years Wallace Crossley had published this paper. The Warrensburg *Standard-Herald* is owned by A. G. Taubert.

For more than twenty years Edward H. Winter, at one time the state's lieutenant-governor, was with the Warrenton *Banner;* since the 1930's the paper has been published by Frank H. Hollmann. T. B. White, who purchased the Warsaw *Benton County Enterprise* in 1883, published it for more than fifty years in the hulk of a river boat. T. B. wore a frock coat and boiled shirt in winter and summer, always with pencils and a small pair of scissors about him. His family has continued the paper, with Mahlon N. and M. K. White publishers today.

George W. Krumsick founded the Washington *Citizen* in 1905 and was with the paper until his death in 1961. His column "Pumpkin Hill News" was widely reprinted. Others associated with the paper have been Arthur Rusche, Harry W. Stonecipher, William L. Miller, and, since 1937, James L. Miller. James L. Miller acquired the *Citizen* in 1956 and merged it with the *Missourian,* which he had purchased from James N. McClure in 1937. Miller, with previous newspaper work in Kansas, Iowa, and in Kansas City, in 1961 made a $100,000 conversion to offset for his two papers and established a central printing plant there to publish other papers. R. W. Bricken took over the Galt *Tribune* in 1941, then discontinued the paper and used the equipment to start the Waverly *Times.* John H. McMullin and Joe Hanebrink purchased the Waynesville *Pulaski County Democrat* in 1950, a paper operated for thirty-six years by the Long family. John Myers is now publishing the Webb City *Sentinel,* directed for more than forty years by Hall M. Wise.

Charles T. Deiter bought the Wellsville *Optic-News* in 1944. The Jacobi family ran this paper for more than thirty years. Ralph Dummit took over the Wentzville *Union* in 1955. For years the Bless family published the Weston *Chronicle*, purchased by B. J. Bless, Jr., in 1886. His son B. J., Jr., took over in 1915, and Charles A. Bless has been the publisher since 1936.

The son of a former dean of the School of Journalism is now the publisher of the West Plains *Quill*. Frank L. Martin, Jr., took over the paper in 1946 from the Williams family; the paper was established by Mills Williams in the 1880's. James W. Fox has for many years been publishing the Wheaton *Journal*. Jac W. Zimmerman acquired the Willow Springs *News* in 1953. James C. Kirkpatrick, with several Missouri papers, purchased the Windsor *Review* in 1953, a paper edited for thirty years by Charles H. Burgess. In Winona, the *Shannon County Democrat*, founded in 1896, was combined in 1962 with the *Current Wave* of Eminence.

Still the papers continue to appear and to disappear. Three newcomers were listed in the directory for 1964 of the Missouri Press Association: Bourbon *Beacon*, Cuba *Free Press*, and Nixa *Enterprise*. No doubt there are other Missouri papers appearing today. Some are still too young to gain a place in the several directories; others may fail to satisfy certain qualifications for this study. Truly, it is a changing situation.

BLUE RIBBON PAPERS IN MISSOURI

ANNUALLY since 1948 a number of Missouri papers have been selected for outstanding work and have been designated Blue Ribbon papers. The following have been honored in the years indicated:

Albany *Ledger*, 1952, 1958–1963; Ava *Douglas County Herald*, 1955, 1958, 1962.

Bethany *Harrison County Times*, 1948–1949, 1954–1955, 1957; Bethany *Republican-Clipper*, 1948–1951, 1955–1959, 1961–1963; Blue Springs *Jackson County Democrat*, 1961, 1963; Buffalo *Reflex*, 1949; Brunswick *Brunswicker*, 1958, 1960; Butler *Bates County Democrat*, 1961–1963.

California *Democrat*, 1950–1952, 1955–1963; Canton *Press-News*, 1960; Caruthersville *Democrat-Argus*, 1960; Cassville *Democrat*, 1948, 1950, 1952; Charleston *Enterprise-Courier*, 1949–1950, 1952–1959, 1961, 1963; Centralia *Fireside Guard*, 1956–1958, 1961–1962; Clayton *Watchman-Advocate*, 1948; Clinton *Eye*, 1949–1963; Crane *Chronicle*, 1948; Crystal City *Jefferson County Press-Times*, 1959.

DeSoto *Jefferson County Republican (Republic)*, 1948-1963.

Eldon *Advertiser*, 1954–1963.

Fairmount *Inter-City News*, 1950–1953; Fairmount *Inter-City Press*, 1948; Fairfax *Forum*, 1955, 1958, 1960–1961; Farmington *News*, 1950, 1952–1954, 1957, 1962–1963; Farmington *Press*, 1952, 1954, 1957, 1960, 1962–1963; Fayette *Democrat-Leader*, 1949, 1953, 1956, 1963; Fayette *Advertiser*, 1950, 1955, 1963; Ferguson *Town Talk*, 1952; Festus *News-Democrat*, 1948–1950; Flat River *Lead Belt News*, 1948–1949, 1951–1954; Florissant *Valley Reporter*, 1960, 1962, 1963; Fredericktown *Democrat-News*, 1948–1963.

Gallatin *North Missourian*, 1948–1963; Gladstone *News*, 1960; Glasgow *Missourian*, 1951–1953; Grandview *Jackson County Advocate*, 1959; Grant City *Times-Tribune*, 1950, 1952–1958, 1962–1963.

Hamilton *Advocate-Hamiltonian*, 1948, 1955–1958, 1960–1961; Harrisonville *Cass County Democrat*, 1951–1952, 1956–1958 (*Democrat-Missourian*, 1959–1963); Hermann *Advertiser-Courier*, 1957, 1959–1962; Hillsboro *Jefferson County Record*, 1949, 1957–1963; Holden *Progress*, 1957, 1959, 1961–1963; Houston *Herald* and *Republican*, 1961–1962.

Kansas City *Dispatch*, 1962; Kansas City *News-Press*, 1960; Kennett *Dunklin Democrat*, 1952–1956; King City *Tri-County News*, 1948, 1951–1953.

LaPlata *Home Press*, 1956–1958; Lebanon *Rustic-Republican*, 1960; Lee's Summit *Journal*, 1951–1963; Liberty *Tribune*, 1956, 1959, 1961, 1963; Linn *Osage County Republican*, 1949; Louisiana *Press-Journal*, 1948–1949, 1951–1963.

Marshfield *Mail*, 1948, 1950–1952, 1954–1963; Malden *Press-Merit*, 1960–1961, 1963; Marceline *News*, 1952, 1957, 1963; Maryville *Nodaway County Tribune*, 1949; Maysville *DeKalb County Record-Herald*, 1958, 1961; Monroe City *Monroe County News*, 1949–1952; Montgomery City *Standard*, 1961; Mt. Vernon *Lawrence County Record*, 1951.

New Haven *Leader*, 1961, 1963; North Kansas City *Press-Dispatch*, 1955–1957, 1963.

Odessa *Odessan*, 1952, 1956–1957, 1959–1963; Owensville *Gasconade County Republican*, 1959–1963.

Palmyra *Spectator*, 1950, 1952; Paris *Monroe County Appeal*, 1949, 1952, 1961–1962; Pacific *Meramec Valley Transcript*, 1962–1963; Parkville *Platte County Dispatch*, 1960; Perryville *Perry County Republican*, 1951–1952, 1955–1957, 1959, 1962–1963; Pleasant Hill *Times*, 1954–1963; Portageville *Review*, 1949; Princeton *Post-Telegraph*, 1948, 1950–1963.

Raytown *News*, 1962; Richmond *News*, 1954, 1956, 1958–1963; Rockport *Atchison County Mail*, 1952, 1954–1956, 1958, 1960–1962; Rolla *Herald*, 1948.

Salem *News*, 1948, 1952–1963; Salem *Post*, 1952–1963; Salisbury *Press-Spectator*, 1959–1963; Savannah *Reporter*, 1948–1949, 1951, 1953, 1955–1958, 1960–1962; Shelbyville *Shelby County Herald*, 1949, 1951–1952, 1962; Sikeston *Herald*, 1948, 1952; Shelbina *Democrat*, 1960–1963; Stanberry *Headlight*, 1950–1963.

Trenton *Grundy County Gazette*, 1948–1949; Tuscumbia *Miller County Autogram-Sentinel*, 1959–1961, 1963.

Union *Franklin County Tribune*, 1954–1963.

Vandalia *Leader*, 1960–1963; Vandalia *Press*, 1960.

Warsaw *Benton County Guide*, 1949; Warsaw *Benton County Enterprise*, 1958–1959, 1962; Washington *Missourian*, 1948, 1950–1963; Webster Groves *News-Times*, 1948, 1951–1952; Willow Springs *News*, 1949, 1959, 1961–1962; Windsor *Review*, 1956–1963.

MISSOURI PRESS ASSOCIATION PRESIDENTS

1867—J. W. Barrett, Canton *Press*
1868—J. W. Barrett, Canton *Press*
1869—J. W. Barrett, Canton *Press*
1870—N. J. Colman, *Colman's Rural World*
1871—N. J. Colman, *Colman's Rural World*
1872—C. B. Wilkinson, St. Joseph *Herald*
1873—A. Y. Hull, Sedalia *Democrat*
1874—W. F. Switzler, Columbia *Statesman*
1875—L. J. Eastin, Glasgow *Journal*
1876—Milo Blair, Boonville *Eagle*
1877—T. W. Park, Platte City *Landmark*
1878—J. E. Hutton, Mexico *Intelligencer*
1879—J. E. Hutton, Mexico *Intelligencer*
1880—J. H. Turner, Carrollton *Record*
1881—J. T. Child, Richmond *Conservator*
1882—A. A. Lesueur, Lexington *Intelligencer*
1883—J. B. Thompson, LaPlata *Home Press*
1884—R. B. Speed, Nevada *Mail*
1885—R. M. White, Mexico *Ledger*
1886—J. A. Hudson, Macon *Times*
1887—W. D. Crandall, Brookfield *Gazette*
1888—I. H. Kinley, Brunswick *Brunswicker*
1889—Walter Williams, Boonville *Advertiser*
1890—E. W. Stephens, Columbia *Herald*
1891—J. West Goodwin, Sedalia *Bazoo*
1892—W. O. L. Jewett, Shelbina *Democrat*
1893—J. C. Kirby, West Plains *Gazette*
1894—John A. Knott, Hannibal *Journal*
1895—John W. Jacks, Montgomery *Standard*
1896—H. E. Robinson, Maryville *Republican*
1897—Henry W. Ewing, Jefferson City *Tribune*
1898—George W. Trigg, Richmond *Conservator*
1899—H. J. Groves, Independence *Sentinel*
1900—W. R. Painter, Carrollton *Democrat*
1901—Wes L. Robertson, Gallatin *Democrat*
1902—E. P. Caruthers, Kennett *Democrat*
1903—Howard Ellis, New Florence *Leader*
1904—T. T. Wilson, Tarkio *Avalanche*
1905—William Southern, Jr., *Jackson Examiner*

1906—William Southern, Jr., *Jackson Examiner*
1907—Philip Gansz, Macon *Republican*
1908—Omar D. Gray, Sturgeon *Leader*
1909—H. F. Childers, Troy *Free Press*
1910—C. M. Harrison, Gallatin *North Missourian*
1911—J. R. Lowell, Moberly *Democrat*
1912—E. L. Purcell, Fredericktown *News*
1913—Ovid Bell, Fulton *Gazette*
1914—Fred Naeter, Cape Girardeau *Republican*
1915—H. S. Sturgis, Neosho *Times*
1916—J. Kelly Pool, Centralia *Courier*
1917—H. J. Blanton, Paris *Appeal*
1918—J. P. Tucker, Parkville *Gazette*
1919—J. N. Stonebraker, Carrollton *Republican-Record*
1920—Will H. Zorn, West Plains *Gazette*
1921—Mitchell White, Mexico *Ledger*
1922—Fred Hull, Maryville *Tribune*
1923—Dwight H. Brown, Poplar Bluff *Inter-American*
1924—Asa W. Butler, Albany *Capital*
1925—Eugene B. Roach, Carthage *Democrat*
1926—E. H. Winter, Warrenton *Banner*
1927—C. L. Hobart, Holden *Progress*
1928—Harry Denman, Farmington *News*
1929—Charles L. Woods, Rolla *Herald*
1930—E. E. Swain, Kirksville *Express*
1931—Frank H. Sosey, Palmyra *Spectator*
1932—W. J. Sewall, Carthage *Press*
1933—Wallace Crossley, Warrensburg *Star-Journal*
1934—Fred M. Harrison, Gallatin *North Missourian*
1935—W. L. Bouchard, Flat River *Lead Belt News*
1936—Robert C. Goshorn, Jeffereson City *News-Tribune*
1937—John C. Stapel, Rockport *Atchison County Mail*
1938—George B. Harlan, Boonville *Cooper County Record*
1939—James Todd, Moberly *Monitor-Index*
1940—Clint H. Denman, Sikeston *Herald*
1941—C. E. Watkins, Chillicothe *Constitution-Tribune*
1942—W. E. Freeland, Forsyth *Taney County Republican*
1943—O. J. Ferguson, Fredericktown *Democrat-News*
1944—Frank H. Hollmann, Warrenton *Banner*
1945—W. C. Hewitt, Shelbyville *Shelby County Herald*
1946—T. Ballard Watters, Marshfield *Marshfield Mail*
1947—George P. Johnston, Fulton *Sun-Gazette*

1948—Meredith Garten, Pierce City *Leader-Journal*
1949—Stanley R. Fike, Fairmount *Inter-City News*
1950—T. J. Clark, Carrollton *Republican-Record*
1951—Louis N. Bowman, King City *Tri-County News*
1952—George H. Scruton, Sedalia *Democrat*
1953—Mack F. Denman, Farmington *News*
1954—A. A. Steinbeck, Union *Franklin County Tribune*
1955—C. L. Blanton, Jr., Sikeston *Standard*
1956—Joe Roberts, Maysville *DeKalb County Herald*
1957—W. L. Simpson, Holden *Progress*
1958—E. J. Melton, Boonville *Cooper County Record*
1959—James C. Kirkpatrick, Windsor *Review*
1960—E. L. Dale, Carthage *Press*
1961—Victor Gierke, Louisiana *Press-Journal*
1962—Harry Guth, Sr., Perryville *Perry County Republican*
1963—J. W. Brown, Harrisonville *Democrat Missourian*
1964—Jac W. Zimmerman, Willow Springs *News*

UNIVERSITY OF MISSOURI HONOR AWARDS FOR DISTINGUISHED SERVICE IN JOURNALISM

SINCE 1930 the University of Missouri has awarded medals for distinguished service in journalism to newspapers and to leaders in the profession. Among those from Missouri who have been cited are the following:

1930—E. W. Stephens, Columbia *Herald*

1931—Henry F. Childers, Troy *Free Press*

1932—St. Louis *Post-Dispatch;* Casper S. Yost, St. Louis *Globe-Democrat;* Frank W. Rucker, Independence *Examiner*

1933—Kansas City *Star;* Charles G. Ross, St. Louis *Post-Dispatch;* J. P. Tucker, Parkville *Gazette*

1934—Robert M. White, Mexico *Ledger*

1935—William E. Southern, Jr., Independence *Examiner*

1936—Frank W. Taylor, Jr., St. Louis *Star-Times;* William R. Painter, Carrollton *Democrat*

1937—W. J. Sewall, Carthage *Press*

1938—E. E. Swain, Kirksville *Daily Express*

1939—Raymond P. Brandt, St. Louis *Post-Dispatch;* Wallace Crossley, Warrensburg *Star-Journal;* H. J. Blanton, Paris *Monroe County Appeal*

1940—James Kelly Pool, Jefferson City *Capital-News*

1941—*Southeast Missourian,* Cape Girardeau; H. S. Jewell, Springfield Newspapers, Inc.

1943—L. Mitchell White, Mexico *Ledger*

1944—Clarence E. Watkins, Chillicothe *Constitution-Tribune*

1945—William E. Freeland, *Taney County Republican*

1946—E. Lansing Ray, St. Louis *Globe-Democrat*

1947—Joseph Pulitzer, St. Louis *Post-Dispatch*

1950—St. Louis *Star-Times;* James Todd, Moberly *Monitor-Index*

1951—George H. Scruton, Sedalia *Democrat*

1952—Charles C. Clayton, St. Louis *Globe-Democrat;* John H. Wolpers (posthumously), Poplar Bluff *American Republic*

1953—E. L. Dale, Carthage *Press*

1954—W. C. Hewitt, Shelbyville *Shelby County Herald*

1955—St. Joseph *News-Press and Gazette*

1956—Louis N. Bowman, King City *Tri-County News;* Boyd Carroll, St. Louis *Post-Dispatch*

1957—Clint H. Denman, Sikeston *Herald;* Roy A. Roberts, Kansas City *Star*

1958—Frank P. Briggs, Macon *Chronicle-Herald;* Daniel R. Fitzpatrick, St. Louis *Post-Dispatch*

1959—John W. Colt, Kansas City *Star;* Lewis Roop, DeSoto *Press* and *Jefferson Republic*

1960—Cowgill Blair, Joplin *Globe*

1961—T. Ballard Watters, Marshfield *Mail*

1962—E. L. Sparks, Jr., Hannibal *Courier-Post*

1963—Don Sosey, Palmyra *Spectator*

1964—James L. Miller, Washington *Missourian;* Arthur L. Witman, magazine photographer, St. Louis *Post-Dispatch*

N. W. AYER & SON'S DIRECTORY OF MISSOURI NEWSPAPERS

D—Daily publication
T-W—Triweekly publication
S-W—Semiweekly publication

Year	D	T-W	S-W	Weekly	Year	D	T-W	S-W	Weekly
1880	42	5	9	371	1910	91	..	10	768
1881	42	4	3	402	1911	87	..	15	750
1882	43	3	2	427	1912	82	..	14	742
1883	44	2	2	452	1913	81	..	16	733
1884	51	2	3	475	1914	80	..	16	734
1885	47	2	1	501	1915	81	..	13	752
1886	51	2	1	528	1916	87	..	13	730
1887	59	2	1	538	1917	86	..	16	735
1888	65	2	4	564	1918	81	1	18	694
1889	68	3	5	591	1919	76	1	16	656
1890	81	2	5	631	1920	75	1	15	638
1891	74	2	8	639	1921	73	1	15	632
1892	81	3	7	689	1922	74	1	14	613
1893*	78	2	9	690	1923	74	2	17	594
1894*	78	2	9	690	1924	71	2	16	589
1895	82	3	10	723	1925	73	1	17	601
1896	83	2	15	732	1926	68	1	20	587
1897	88	..	13	793	1927	69	1	20	576
1898	88	3	11	787	1928	61	2	19	512
1899	82	2	10	802	1929	66	2	18	505
1900	84	2	10	792	1930	67	2	17	498
1901	80	1	10	802	1931	65	2	16	491
1902	85	1	11	773	1932	68	2	15	489
1903	86	1	9	758	1933	60	2	15	498
1904	87	..	14	746	1934	60	2	16	493
1905	84	..	16	775	1935	58	3	13	498
1906	84	1	13	778	1936	58	3	15	493
1907	88	1	15	777	1937	59	3	15	499
1908	91	..	12	778	1938	60	2	13	483
1909	91	..	11	774	1939	61	2	12	478

* 1893-1894 editions combined

YEAR	D	T-W	S-W	WEEKLY	YEAR	D	T-W	S-W	WEEKLY
1940	59	2	13	484	1953	58	1	8	388
1941	60	3	12	473	1954	59	1	6	368
1942	58	3	10	474	1955	58	1	6	359
1943	55	3	8	448	1956	58	1	5	349
1944	53	2	10	428	1957	58	1	4	352
1945	53	2	10	426	1958	57	1	4	346
1946	54	2	9	415	1959	57	1	6	348
1947	54	1	9	441	1960	55	1	5	341
1948	54	2	7	420	1961	54	2	4	343
1949	56	1	7	417	1962	55	2	4	330
1950	56	2	7	416	1963	53	2	7	330
1951	57	2	8	412	1964	53	2	7	331
1952	57	1	8	404					

NOTES

CHAPTER I

1. William H. Lyon, Jr., "The Pioneer Editor in Missouri" (Ph.D. dissertation, University of Missouri, 1958). Dr. Lyon has developed the findings of this study into a book, *The Pioneer Editor in Missouri, 1808–1860* (Columbia: University of Missouri Press, 1964). Also, Thomas J. Scharf, *History of Saint Louis City and County* (Philadelphia: Louis H. Everts and Company, 1883), I, 902–59.

2. J. W. Barrett, *History and Transactions of the Editors' and Publishers' Association of Missouri, 1867–1876* (Canton, Mo.: Canton Press Print, 1876), pp. 1–5.

3. See Chapters XIV, XVI.

4. William Hyde and H. L. Conard, eds., *Encyclopaedia of the History of St. Louis* (St. Louis: The Southern History Company, 1899), I, 350–51. Walter B. Stevens, *St. Louis, the Fourth City, 1764–1909* (St. Louis: S. J. Clarke Publishing Company, 1909), I, 108, notes that St. Louis had a population of 1,200 in 1810 and 4,000 in 1820. Variations in figures depend on the inclusion of whites only or the addition of free mulattoes, free Negroes, and slaves.

5. Stevens, *St. Louis, the Fourth City*, I, 104.

6. Floyd C. Shoemaker, *Missouri and Missourians* (Chicago: Lewis Publishing Company, 1943), I, 104–262. Eugene M. Violette, *A History of Missouri* (Boston: D. C. Heath & Co., 1918, reprinted 1957), p. 52.

7. Lyon, "Pioneer Editor in Missouri," p. 15.

8. C. S. Brigham, *History and Bibliography of America* (Worcester, Mass.: American Antiquarian Society, 1947), I, 147, 162, 171–72; II, 877. In Lexington, Charless and Francis Peniston were partners when they established the *Independent Gazette*. The partnership quickly failed; another was equally unsuccessful, and the project was discontinued by Charless within six months. While searching for a community in which to establish a paper, Charless published more books. In Louisville another paper, Francis Peniston's *Western American*, had recently failed. Brigham has other references to Peniston, who was a partner with Charless for less than two months in Lexington. Peniston published the Bardstown *Western American* from 1803 to 1805. He then presented a proposal in the Lexington *Gazette* on October 31, 1805, to publish the *Louisiana Herald* in St. Louis, but there is no evidence this paper ever materialized.

9. Hyde and Conard, *Encyclopaedia*, I, 350.

10. William H. Lyon, "Joseph Charless, Father of Missouri Journalism," *Bulletin of the Missouri Historical Society*, XVII (January, 1961), 135. In his dissertation Lyon notes that in one year Charless was paid $1,418.75 for government printing.

11. Reprinted in centennial edition of St. Louis *Republican*, July 12, 1908. Stevens, *St. Louis, the Fourth City*, I, 147–48. Original copy in Missouri Historical Society, St. Louis.

12. Stevens, *St. Louis, the Fourth City*, I, 149–50.

13. *Missouri Gazette*, several issues between November 23, 1808, and January 4, 1809. Other such "wanted to hire" ads appeared in later years.

14. Lyon, "Joseph Charless," pp. 137–38.

15. Bailey Elston Birkhead, "A Study of the *Missouri Gazette* Through the Editorship of its Founder, Joseph Charless" (M.A. thesis, University of Missouri, 1945), p. 22. On October 2, 1813, Charless wrote about the abridged size, adding, "We dare venture to assert that our circumscribed sheet will contain as much domestic information as any paper in Kentucky or Ohio—Advertisements will be published in a supplementary page." Dorothy Brown, "Early Saint Louis Newspapers, 1808–1850" (M.A. thesis, Washington University, 1931).

16. *Missouri Gazette*, September 13, 1820. In a two-and-a-half-column farewell, Charless told about encountering "most violent hostility" and other abuses, but now he could retire "from the bustle of party strife, with moderate means for his future support."

17. *Missouri Gazette*, October 20, 1819.

18. Douglas C. McMurtrie, "Early Missouri Book and Pamphlet Imprints, 1808–1830" (Chicago: Mimeographed, 1937). From original articles in *American Book Collector*, February, March, April, 1932. McMurtrie wrote another article of interest, "The Early Career of Joseph Charless, The First Printer in Missouri," *Missouri Historical Review*, XXVI (July, 1932), 342-54. Of value is the McMurtrie Manuscript Collection, Michigan State University, under the supervision of Jackson E. Towne.

19. Lyon, "Joseph Charless," p. 143.

20. *Missouri Gazette*, November 22, 1817. The full story: "The Steam-Boat Pike, with passengers and freight, arrived here yesterday, from Louisville."

21. Birkhead, "A Study of the *Missouri Gazette*," contains a chapter on the paper's format and business policies and another about its news and politics, with many examples.

22. In an effort to attract more French readers and since the community was two-thirds French, Charless from time to time printed advertisements in both English and French. On at least two occasions he presented proposals for a French paper in St. Louis. As soon as one hundred subscribers could be obtained, Charless wrote in the December 21, 1809, *Gazette*, he would publish a weekly, *La Mouche du Ouest*. Some six months later, May 3, 1810, a similar announcement told of plans for a *Gazette de Louisiane*. Apparently his enthusiasm was not shared by the French-speaking public, for there is no evidence

Charless published either paper. McMurtrie said there were probably few Frenchmen then in St. Louis who cared to read or who could read.

23. Lyon, "Joseph Charless," pp. 140–43.

24. Stevens, *St. Louis, the Fourth City,* I, 154.

25. Lyon, "Joseph Charless," p. 145. Copies of the *Missouri Gazette* are now in more than twenty-five libraries. Several have the complete files, except for the first two issues. According to an item on "Paper Mill" in the *Missouri Historical Review,* XXVII (October, 1932), 72, a paper mill was built at Rockbridge near Columbia in 1834, probably the first west of the Mississippi. The *Missouri Intelligencer* told about plans for the mill on January 11, 1834, and said the last edition that year was printed on this home-made stock. The plant failed to make money and had a brief career.

CHAPTER II

1. Lyon, "Joseph Charless," pp. 136–38. Also, see Lyon's thesis, "Pioneer Editor in Missouri."

2. *Missouri Gazette,* November 12, 1814; January 21, 1815.

3. *Ibid.,* April 30, 1814.

4. *Ibid.,* August 18, 1819.

5. *Ibid.,* August 7, 1818. Lyon, "Pioneer Editor in Missouri," p. 10, notes, "As a profession, the editorial corps was not bound together by any tight rules of discipline or an accepted code of etiquette. Editors felt at liberty to criticize their fellow editors, even to the point of abuse, and frequently editorial relationships were marred by violence and altercation."

6. *Missouri Gazette,* August 7, 1818; May 17, 1820. From the August 18, 1817, issue we note: "The present paper called the St. Louis *Enquirer* commenced under the title of the *Western Journal.* We *predicted* the retreat of the editor to Arkansas—with his departure the *Journal* changed its name, under the auspices of a new editor, Sergeant Hall; and was called the *Emigrant.* We also *predicted* his retreat to the same place. In both these predictions we have been correct. We now *predict* the *great man* who edits the *Enquirer* will *retrograde* (to use a courtly phrase of Lord Wellington's, when he was worsted by the French generals) but we are really at a loss to know where he will *retrograde* to, as the *Arkansas* has become too civilized an asylum. But we will predict, although we are no prophets, that e'er eighteen months expire, the present editor of the *Enquirer* will leave St. Louis —as he is very assiduous in making himself master of the Spanish language, we think he will *retrograde* to South America. What will *astonished Europe* say now if the *Enquirerman* should retreat from the magnificent valley of the Mississippi and how will his majesty of all the Indies tremble on his throne when he hears of the approach of so celebrated a character."

7. St. Louis *Enquirer,* May 20, 1820.

8. William N. Chambers, "Thomas Hart Benton: Editor," *Missouri Historical Review,* XLVI (October, 1951–July, 1952), 333, from St. Louis *Enquirer,* April 21 and 28, 1819. Also, William N. Chambers, *Old Bullion Benton* (Boston: Little, Brown & Company, 1956), p. 83.

9. Perry G. McCandless, "Thomas H. Benton, His Source of Political Strength in Missouri from 1815 to 1838" (Ph.D. dissertation, University of Missouri, 1953), p. 17. Also see his articles, "The Rise of Thomas Hart Benton in Missouri Politics," *Missouri Historical Review,* L (October, 1955), and "The Political Philosophy and Political Personality of Thomas Hart Benton," *Missouri Historical Review,* L (January, 1956), 16–27; St. Louis *Enquirer,* June 16, 1819.

10. St. Louis *Enquirer,* January 6, 1821. In the same issue the editors added: "It may be necessary to state, perhaps, that the recent death of one of the editors of the St. Louis *Enquirer* and the personal absence of the other will in no wise affect the continuance or the general utility of the paper. Notwithstanding the surmises of some who appear to *cherish* evil presentments, this paper will still be published as heretofore, and remain equally steadfast in its devotion to the honor and interest of Missouri and of the Union. The handsome support which it now receives, both at home and from abroad, offers a sufficient guarantee of its future stability. We can therefore assure the people of Missouri that the paper which they have so highly distinguished by their patronage will continue to be the faithful chronicle of the times, and (we hope) a legitimate organ of public opinion."

11. St. Louis *Enquirer,* August 11, 1821.

12. Frank Luther Mott, *American Journalism* (New York: The Macmillan Company, 1962), pp. 179, 191. On June 21, 1827, the *Missouri Republican* noted the partnerships that followed Green's operating the *Enquirer* alone: Foreman and Keemle, S. W. Foreman alone, Foreman and Birch, Foreman alone, and "*now* James H. Birch and——and——and——." See Floyd C. Shoemaker, "Henry Dodge and Duff Green," in Frank Luther Mott, ed., *Missouri Reader* (Columbia: University of Missouri Press, 1964).

13. Albert T. Scroggins, Jr., "Nathaniel Patten, Jr., and the *Missouri Intelligencer and Boon's Lick Advertiser*" (Ph.D. dissertation, University of Missouri, 1961). This is the definitive study on Patten and his career. Also see Wilmoth E. Brownlee, "The Literary Editing of Nathaniel Patten, Jr., from 1822–1835 in the *Missouri Intelligencer*" (M. A. thesis, University of Missouri, 1953); Ella Johnson, "The Economic Development of the Boon's Lick Country as Reflected in the *Missouri Intelligencer*" (M. A. thesis, University of Missouri, 1931); J. Willard Ridings, "Editorial Policies of the *Missouri Intelligencer*" (M. A. thesis, University of Missouri, 1928). The Boon's Lick territory was described in the *Missouri Intelligencer* of April 1, 1820, as the area that "embraces all the settlements on the Missouri

River, and its tributary streams, west of old counties of St. Louis and St. Charles. . . . Its length on the Missouri is various, depending on . . . inducements for settlements." Scroggins adds, "It was generally felt to be an area about 50 miles wide and 150 miles long, beginning at Cedar Creek, the present boundary between Boone and Callaway counties, and extending west on both sides of the Missouri." A monument now stands across the river from Boonville indicating the original location of Franklin. Also see F. F. Stephens, "Nathaniel Patten, Pioneer Editor," *Missouri Historical Review*, IX (April, 1915), 139-55.

14. Scroggins, "Nathaniel Patten, Jr.," p. 52.

15. *Missouri Intelligencer*, January 1, 1821. By this time Patten had become postmaster at Franklin. Patten had sent his prospectus to the secretary of state. See Clarence Edwin Carter, comp. and ed., *The Territorial Papers of the United States* (Washington: Government Printing Office, 1951), XV, 530, 553-54, 641-48, 683.

16. *Missouri Intelligencer*, May 21, 1831.

17. *Ibid.*, December 21, 1827.

18. *Ibid.*, July 20, 1826.

19. *Ibid.*, June 29, 1826.

20. *Ibid.*, April 25, 1835.

21. *Ibid.*, September 7, 1826.

22. *Ibid.*, June 3, 1823.

23. *Ibid.*, October 7, 1825.

24. Scroggins, "Nathaniel Patten, Jr.," pp. 74-75.

25. *Missouri Intelligencer*, December 5, 1835. See earlier plans, October 31, 1835. Additional data from Minnie Organ's "History of the County Press in Missouri," *Missouri Historical Review*, IV (January, 1910), 114-15.

26. Scroggins, "Nathaniel Patten, Jr.," p. 348. Also, William F. Switzler, *History of Boone County Missouri* (St. Louis: Western Historical Company, 1882), pp. 136-37. Switzler relates changes after the paper reached Columbia.

27. C. S. Brigham, *History and Bibliography of America*, I, 67-68; Organ, "History of the County Press in Missouri," p. 115.

28. Remington noted on May 19, 1821, that he had joined in a partnership with James Russell, and Minor M. Whitney and William Creath would no longer be associated with the *Independent Patriot*. Later that month an advertisement announced the opening of Russell's Eagle Tavern. The paper reported on February 16, 1826, that Thomas P. Green and William Johnson were taking over from the late proprietor, Remington. Enlarged to five columns, the paper appeared on a super-royal sheet. The new editors, conscious of their responsibilities, printed "Errata" notices frequently, to correct mistakes made earlier. One source claimed the paper was sold in 1825 to William Johnson, who renamed it the *Mercury*. This is impossible, since files of the

Independent Patriot are available through 1826, naming Johnson as co-owner with Green. There are, however, copies of the *Mercury* available for 1828, 1829, and 1831. The Library of Congress has a copy of the *Jackson Mercury and Cape Girardeau Farmer*, Volume I, Number 1, December 13, 1828.

29. Files available for 1838 list English and J. Lindsay as publishers; on March 2 Robert Brown joined the firm. English sold his interest the following November to Brown and Lindsay, citing them as "young gentlemen of talent, worth and respectability, and politicians of the Jeffersonian School." English, in a signed editorial, said more than $4,000 was due him for subscriptions to Volumes I, II, and III of the *Southern Advocate*. Brown apparently became the sole owner and kept the paper until 1845, when it was sold to Nieder and McFerron, who named it the *Review*.

30. Organ, "History of the County Press in Missouri," pp. 115–16; Jefferson City *Metropolitan*, January 15, 1850.

CHAPTER III

1. William N. Chambers, "Thomas Hart Benton: Editor," p. 342, taken from the St. Louis *Enquirer* in June, 1819.

2. Walter B. Stevens, "The Travail of Missouri for Statehood," *Missouri Historical Review*, XV (October, 1920–July, 1921), 11.

3. *Ibid.*, p. 17. From *Enquirer*, March 29, 1820. Information came from *National Intelligencer* of March 4, 1820, which required three weeks to reach St. Louis.

4. *Missouri Gazette*, March 29, 1820.

5. *Ibid.*, May 17, 1820.

6. St. Louis *Enquirer*, July 22, 1820.

7. Stevens, "The Travail of Missouri for Statehood," p. 31.

8. St. Charles *Missourian*, September 5, 1821.

9. St. Louis *Enquirer*, September 29, 1821.

10. *Missouri Gazette*, January 23, 1818.

11. Floyd C. Shoemaker, "Six Periods of Missouri History," *Missouri Historical Review*, IX (July, 1915), 231–37; Lyon, "Joseph Charless," p. 144.

12. *Missouri Gazette*, March 22, 1820.

13. Shoemaker, *Missouri and Missourians*, I, 557–79.

14. See Scroggins, "Nathaniel Patten, Jr.," for many similar comments by Patten about Missouri during these years.

15. Shoemaker, *Missouri and Missourians*, I, 405–49.

16. Perry G. McCandless, "Thomas H. Benton," is useful for the early period.

17. A. Clarence Hines, "The Beginnings of the Democratic Party in Missouri, 1824–1836" (M.A. thesis, University of Missouri, 1939), pp. 33–34, quoting in part from the *Missouri Republican*, August 1, 1825.

18. *Ibid.*, p. 78.

19. Organ, "History of the County Press in Missouri," p. 117. That same year a notice appeared about a proposed *Register*, to be published by William Orr in St. Louis. There is no evidence it got beyond the prospectus stage.

20. *Missouri Intelligencer*, December 23, 1823.

21. *Missouri Republican*, August 25, 1826. The paper asked: "Who is the proprietor of the *Missouri Advocate?*" Foreman took control and published the paper until 1827, when it apparently ceased publication.

22. Gunn, on September 19, 1840, claimed his paper to be the oldest in the state; he apparently did not consider the *Missouri Republican* to be a continuation of the *Missouri Gazette*. Gunn issued a prospectus in the *Missouri Advocate*, February 12, 1825, for the *Jefferson Patriot*, but apparently failed to receive sufficient support. See Estal Earnest Sparlin, "The *Jefferson Inquirer*" (M.A. thesis, University of Missouri, 1932).

23. *Missouri Republican*, November 16, 1826. A Ste. Genevieve *Missouri Sentinel* is mentioned in the Hines study as being a Jackson paper in 1826, but there is no mention of this in other sources.

24. Fayette *Missouri Intelligencer*, October 2, 1829.

25. Organ, "History of the County Press in Missouri," pp. 120–21. A prospectus appeared in 1827 for a *Missouri Liberator* in Liberty, to be published by a Mr. Hardin, who was deaf and dumb. No record of its appearance has been found. A single reference to a *Western Monitor* in Jefferson City in April, 1829, probably can be traced to an error, since no other data have been found to indicate that the paper moved from Fayette.

26. *Western Monitor*, September 12, 1829. According to the *Missouri Intelligencer*, June 21, 1834, Foreman later was hanged in Tennessee.

27. John G. Gill, "Elijah Lovejoy's Pledge of Silence," *Missouri Historical Society Bulletin*, XIV (January, 1958), 167–71. Other sources support the 1829 founding date, saying Miller left the paper in January, 1830. Stine returned the paper to his former partner seven months later, and in August, 1830, Lovejoy became coeditor. The *Times* apparently was sold after Lovejoy left it to Keemle, who allowed it to die.

28. *Missouri Intelligencer*, September 10, 1831; Organ, "History of the County Press in Missouri," p. 121.

29. Dorothy Grace Brown, "Early Saint Louis Newspapers," p. 50.

30. *Missouri Argus*, June 1, 2, 3, and 9, and November 22, 1839.

31. Brown, "Early Saint Louis Newspapers," tells of many changes. A chart on an undated pamphlet published by the St. Louis *Globe-Democrat* traces the paper to the *Workingman's Advocate*, later the *Argus*. A prospectus was found concerning a proposed *Weekly Whig* in Fayette, to be published in 1831 by Robert N. Kelley in order to back Clay. No other mention was found of this paper.

32. *Missouri Intelligencer*, June 2, 1832; Shoemaker, *Missouri and*

Missourians, I, 450–69; Organ, "History of the County Press in Missouri," p. 129; "The Missouri Press," manuscript in the Douglas C. McMurtrie Manuscript Collection, Michigan State University.

33. David Lloyd Wilkie, "Independence, Missouri, Newspapers: 1832–1900—from Saints to Socialism" (M.A. thesis, University of Missouri, 1956).

34. Loy Otis Banks, "Latter Day Saint Journalism" (M.A. thesis, University of Missouri, 1948). See also Banks's "The *Evening and the Morning Star,*" *Missouri Historical Review,* XLIII (July, 1949), 319–33. The Bowling Green *Salt River Journal* reported: "It is with feeling of deepest regret that we learn of an encounter between a very large number of citizens of Jackson County . . . and the society of people called Mormons. If any of these people have offended against the laws, those laws are open for redress and to them the injured should look for the reparation of their wrongs . . . no circumstance, no occurrence, however aggravated, can justify the first movement of a mob, whose march is most generally, if not always, marked with disorder, cruelty, and wantonness. . . ." (Reprinted in *Missouri Republican,* November 30, 1883.)

35. *Missouri Argus,* November 27, 1835.

36. Organ, "History of the County Press in Missouri," pp. 124–25. Other papers were proposed in 1833, but apparently never appeared. Benjamin E. Perry, former editor of the *Western Monitor,* announced plans for a *Standard & Banner* at Fayette. Calvin L. Perry had plans for a *Constitutional Advocate* in Columbia, but apparently the planning stage is as far as either publisher could go.

37. Organ, "History of the County Press in Missouri," p. 128.

38. *Ibid.* Additional data from William F. Switzler, *History of Boone County, Missouri;* Shoemaker, *Missouri's Struggle for Statehood* (Jefferson City: Hugh Stephens Printing Co., 1916); James N. Primm, "State Government and the Economy: Missouri, 1820–1860" (Ph.D. dissertation, University of Missouri, 1951).

CHAPTER IV

1. Shoemaker, *Missouri and Missourians,* I, 744–86. Considerable material can be found in James Neal Primm's "State Government and the Economy." Dr. Primm made extensive use of newspapers in this study. Also of interest is an article by Marie George Windell, "Reform in the Roaring Forties and Fifties," *Missouri Historical Review,* XXXIX (April, 1945), 291–319.

2. Hines, "Beginnings of the Democratic Party in Missouri," draws from newspaper sources.

3. Shoemaker, *Missouri and Missourians,* I, 412.

4. *Jeffersonian Republican,* May 5, 1838, quoting from the *Boon's Lick Democrat.*

5. *Missouri Argus,* November 22, 1839.

6. Jefferson City *Daily Tribune,* October 30, 1891. The article noted that in 1844 Missouri had 35 papers, including 5 in German.

7. *Jefferson Inquirer,* February 15, 1844. The rules were reversed. Many resolutions appeared in later editions as public meetings were held to testify respect for his memory.

8. Primm, "State Government and the Economy," p. 95, quoting the *Missouri Reporter,* January 5, 1846. The paper predicted problems on religion, since "no sect is to be allowed to acquire and hold more than one acre of land in any town or city, or more than ten acres in a county."

9. *Missouri Statesman,* January 9 and 23, 1846; Liberty *Weekly Tribune,* April 11, 1846. Many papers copied the series of debates from the *Missouri Republican.* Additional data can be found in Priscilla Bradford's "The Missouri Constitutional Controversy of 1845" (M.A. thesis, University of Missouri, 1936). Also, Bradford, "The Missouri Constitutional Controversy of 1845," *Missouri Historical Review,* XXXII (October, 1937), 35–55.

10. Primm, "State Government and the Economy," p. 95.

11. Liberty *Weekly Tribune,* May 16, 1846. At the same time, this paper continued to give more space to local political issues.

12. Additional material on the Mexican War from Lucien Carr, *Missouri: A Bone of Contention* (New York: Houghton Mifflin Company, 1888); Justin H. Smith, *The War With Mexico,* 2 vols. (New York: The Macmillan Company, 1919); William E. Parrish, *David Rice Atchison of Missouri: Border Politician* (Columbia: University of Missouri Press, 1961); plus many others. The St. Louis *Republican,* on February 2, 1846, claimed, "This nation owes it to herself . . . not to suffer so open an insult to her representatives to pass unnoticed," in referring to the rejection of John Slidell, our minister to Mexico. See also Edwin C. McReynolds, *Missouri: A History of the Crossroads State* (Norman: University of Oklahoma Press, 1962), pp. 144–48.

13. *Missouri Statesman,* January 28, 1848.

14. *Ibid.,* April 14, 1848.

15. Shoemaker, *Missouri and Missourians,* I, 629.

16. Frederic Hudson, *Journalism in the United States From 1690 to 1872* (New York: Harper and Brothers, 1873), p. 771.

17. *Missouri Statesman,* April 3, 1846; February 28, 1851.

18. *Boon's Lick Times,* August 21, 1847, reported on the 100,000 members; Windell, "Reform in the Roaring Forties and Fifties," p. 311. Windell notes that the movement "receded rapidly after 1856." Poem from *Boon's Lick Times,* December 31, 1842; in letter from New Franklin.

19. *Missouri Statesman,* March 7, 1851.

20. Windell, "Reform in the Roaring Forties and Fifties," pp. 312–14; Fayette *Boon's Lick Times,* July 8, 1843.

CHAPTER V

1. Among the communities with papers at this time were Albany, Alexandria, Arcadia, Bethany, Bloomington, Boonville, Bowling Green, Brunswick, Buffalo, Butler, California, Canton, Cape Girardeau, Carrollton, Carthage, Cassville, Chillicothe, Clarksville, Clinton, Columbia, DeSoto, Edina, Far West, Fayette, Forest City, Franklin, Fredericktown, Fulton, Gallatin, Georgetown, Glasgow, Greenfield, Harrison Branch, Harrisonville, Huntsville, Independence, Jackson, Jefferson City, Kingston, Kirksville, Knox City, LaGrange, Lamar, Lancaster, Lebanon, Lexington, Liberty, Linneus, Louisiana, Macon, Marshall, Maryville, Memphis, Mexico, Milan, Montgomery City, Monticello, Mount Vernon, Neosho, New Madrid, Oregon, Osceola, Palmyra, Paris, Parkville, Platte City, Plattsburg, Pleasant Hill, Potosi, Princeton, Richfield, Richmond, Rock Port, Savannah, Springfield, St. Charles, Ste. Genevieve, St. Joseph, Shelbyville, Stewartsville, Sturgeon, Trenton, Troy, Unionville, Versailles, Vienna, Warrensburg, Warrenton, Warsaw, Washington, Weston, and West Point. Figures for total number of papers vary with directories and sources. Shoemaker, *Missouri and Missourians*, I, 804–5, says the state had more than 140 publications by 1860. Simon N. D. North, *History and Present Condition of the Newspaper and Periodical Press* (Washington: Government Printing Office, 1884), notes 173 publications for 1860, 61 for 1850.

Horace Greeley was asked in 1851, "At what amount of population of a town in America do they first begin the publication of a weekly newspaper, and also a daily newspaper?" He answered: "With regard to newspapers, the general rule is that each town will have one. In all the free states, if a county has a population of 20,000 it has two newspapers—one of each party. The general average is about one local journal in the agricultural counties for 10,000 inhabitants. A county containing 50,000 has five journals, which are weekly papers; and when a town grows to have as many as 15,000 inhabitants . . . then it has a daily paper. Sometimes that is the case when it has as few as 10,000. . . . At 20,000 they have two, and so on." North, *op. cit.*, p. 65.

2. See J. C. G. Kennedy, *Catalogue of the Newspapers and Periodicals Published in the United States* (New York: J. Livingston, 1852); William T. Coggeshall, *The Newspaper Record, Containing a Complete List of Newspapers and Periodicals in the United States, Canada, etc.* (Philadelphia: Lay & Brother, 1856); and Daniel J. Kenny, *The American Newspaper Directory and Record of the Press* (New York: Watson & Co., 1861).

3. Shoemaker, *Missouri and Missourians*, I, 787–819, on "Forty Years of Progress, 1820–1860"; Earl A. Collins and Felix E. Snider, *Missouri, Midland State*, rev. ed. (Cape Girardeau, Mo.: Ramfre Press, 1961), p. 364; Primm, "State Government and the Economy," Preface, ii-iii.

4. Richard S. Brownlee, II, "Guerrilla Warfare in Missouri, 1861–

1865" (Ph.D. dissertation, University of Missouri, 1955). Published in book form, *Gray Ghosts of the Confederacy* (Baton Rouge: Louisiana State University, 1958).

5. Shoemaker, "Six Periods of Missouri History," pp. 231–39; Brownlee, *op. cit.*, pp. 1–67, provides interesting data on "Social, Political, and Military Factors Leading Toward Guerrilla Warfare in 1861–1862"; Albert Castel, "Kansas Jayhawking Raids Into Western Missouri in 1861," *Missouri Historical Review*, LIV (October, 1959), 1–11.

6. California *News*, April 27, 1860; additional quotations from newspapers in Kate L. Gregg's "Missourians in the Gold Rush," *Missouri Historical Review*, XXXIX (January, 1945), 137–54.

7. Roy V. Magers, "Raid on the Parkville *Industrial Luminary*," *Missouri Historical Review*, XXX (October, 1935), 39–46.

8. *Jefferson Inquirer*, June 21, 1851.

9. *Missouri Statesman*, November 12, 1952; William E. Parrish, *Turbulent Partnership: Missouri and the Union 1861–1865* (Columbia: University of Missouri Press, 1963), p. 2; Eula Blythe Baker, "The Disintegration of the Whig Party in Missouri, 1850–1856" (M.A. thesis, University of Missouri, 1932), pp. 87–88, 157–58; Laurence D. Lingle, "Persistent Whiggery in Missouri, 1854–1890" (graduate research paper, University of Missouri Department of History, 1963), pp. 2, 5, 19, 20. These sources also used material from the *Missouri Statesman*, February 10 and 24, and March 31, 1854.

10. Among the stronger Whig papers, some of which turned to the new party, were the Boonville *Observer*, Fulton *Telegraph*, Hannibal *Messenger*, Columbia *Missouri Statesman*, and the St. Louis *Intelligencer*. Democrats were supported by the *Jefferson Inquirer* and *Metropolitan* in Jefferson City, the St. Louis *Daily Argus*, which opposed everything "Whiggish," and others. For fuller details see Frederick E. Brock, "The American Party in Missouri, 1854–1860" (M.A. thesis, University of Missouri, 1949); Columbia *Missouri Statesman*, February 29, 1856, and September 15, 1854; Baker, "The Disintegration of the Whig Party," pp. 118–62.

11. *Missouri Statesman*, March 19, 1852. Also see Elizabeth Hall, "William Franklin Switzler: Editor, Politician, and Humanitarian" (M.A. thesis, University of Missouri, 1951).

12. Shoemaker, *Missouri and Missourians*, I, 649.

13. Orlana Hensley, "The Thomas Hart Benton Faction in Missouri Politics 1850–1860" (M.A. thesis, University of Missouri, 1937), p. 9, quoting from reprinted article in Jefferson City *Metropolitan*, May 14, 1850.

14. In his study, "The American Party in Missouri," Brock says the Hannibal *Courier* was the first to advocate the American Party policies, but others soon followed, including the Chillicothe *Grand River Chronicle*, Glasgow *Times*, Richmond *Mirror*, Fulton *Telegraph*, Gallatin *Sun*, St. Joseph *Cycle*, Columbia *Missouri Statesman*, and others.

Among the new American Party papers were the Springfield *Mirror,* Greenfield *American Standard,* Lexington *American Citizen,* Louisiana *American Union,* Hannibal *National Standard,* Boonville *Patriot,* Palmyra *Southern Sentinel,* Pleasant Hill *Western Beacon,* Carrollton *Cottage Visitor,* St. Louis *American,* Harrisonville *Cass County Gazette,* Marshall *Saline County Herald,* and no doubt others whose histories have become lost. The Lexington *Express* said in early 1856 that there were 27 American papers, 17 Democratic, and 14 neutral in the state. The "phenomenal rise of the American Party is probably unequaled by that of any other political organization in the history of Missouri," according to Brock.

15. Brownlee, "Guerrilla Warfare in Missouri," pp. 10–11. Also Lloyd D. Lewis, "Propaganda and the Missouri-Kansas War," *Missouri Historical Review,* XXXIV (October, 1939), 3–17.

16. *Missouri Republican,* February 4, 1860.

17. Kansas City *Journal of Commerce,* February 22, 1860.

18. *Missouri Republican,* February 4, 1860.

19. *Ibid.,* April 28, 1860.

20. Kansas City *Journal of Commerce,* April 26, 1860.

21. *Missouri Republican,* May 12, 1860.

22. *Ibid.,* April 27, 1860.

23. *Ibid.,* April 28, 1860.

24. Kansas City *Journal of Commerce,* May 17, 1860.

25. St. Joseph *Free Democrat,* May 19, 1860.

26. *Missouri Republican,* May 19, 1860.

27. St. Joseph *Free Democrat,* May 19, 1860.

28. *Missouri Republican,* May 19, 1860.

29. Kansas City *Journal of Commerce,* May 22, 1860.

30. St. Joseph *Free Democrat,* June 23, 1860.

31. Kansas City *Journal of Commerce,* June 26, 1860.

32. *Missouri Republican,* May 30, 1860.

33. Kansas City *Journal of Commerce,* May 30, 1860.

34. St. Joseph *Free Democrat,* September 8, 1860.

35. *Missouri Republican,* August 18, 1860.

36. St. Joseph *Free Press,* May 19, 1860.

37. *Ibid.,* June 2, 1860.

38. *Missouri Republican,* September 19, 1860.

39. Stevens, *St. Louis, The Fourth City,* p. 218.

40. *Missouri Republican,* August 23, 1860.

41. Papers that indicated support for Breckenridge included the St. Louis *Bulletin, Jefferson Examiner,* Lexington *Expositor, Saline County Democrat,* Independence *Herald,* Chillocothe *Chronicle,* Stewartsville *Telegraph,* Savannah *Democrat,* Columbia *Argus,* Platte *Argus,* Bloomington *Legion,* Huntsville *Randolph Citizen,* Milan *Courier,* and others.

42. The *West* had experimented earlier with a daily edition, which

ended in May, 1860, after losing a reported $1,500 in a year, according to the California *News,* May 26, 1860.

43. St. Joseph *Free Democrat,* October 20, 1860.

44. *Missouri Republican,* October 24, 1860; November 7, 1860.

45. Parrish, *Turbulent Partnership,* pp. 5–6.

46. Kansas City *Journal of Commerce,* November 7, 1860.

47. St. Joseph *Free Democrat,* November 10, 1860.

48. Rolla *Express,* September 10, 1860.

49. California *News,* December 22, 1860.

50. Ed Nieder, "Election of 1860" (research project, University of Missouri School of Journalism, 1958).

51. Sparlin, "The *Jefferson Inquirer,*" p. 30.

52. Jim A. Hart, "The *Missouri Democrat,* 1852–1860," *Missouri Historical Review,* LV (January, 1961), 127.

53. Hart, "The *Missouri Democrat,*" p. 133.

54. *Missouri Democrat,* January 28, 1857.

55. Theodore S. Case, *History of Kansas City, Missouri* (Syracuse: D. Mason and Co., 1888), p. 10; Walter B. Stevens, *Missouri The Center State, 1821–1915* (Chicago: S. J. Clarke Publishing Company, 1915), Vol. IV; Carrie Westlake Whitney, *Kansas City, Missouri: Its History and Its People, 1808–1908* (Chicago: S. J. Clarke Publishing Company, 1908), Vol. I.

56. For example, the December 18, 1858, issue had a half column headed, "By Telegraph," with items, one sentence each, from New York, St. Louis, and Washington. An example: "Nothing has been heard of the missing steamer, *Indian Empire.*"

57. Kansas City *Journal of Commerce,* October 12, 1865.

58. Case, *History of Kansas City,* p. 52.

59. Kansas City *Enterprise,* January 5, 1856.

60. Organ, "History of the County Press in Missouri," p. 267.

61. Kansas City *Enterprise,* January 26, 1856.

62. Kansas City *Journal of Commerce,* July 17, 1858.

63. Columbia *Missouri Statesman,* May 14, 1852.

64. California *News,* April 21, 1860.

CHAPTER VI

1. Columbia *Missouri Statesman,* January 11, 1861.

2. St. Louis *Daily Democrat,* January 4, 1861.

3. Earl A. Collins and Felix E. Snider, *Missouri, Midland State,* pp. 143–44; Brownlee, "Guerrilla Warfare in Missouri," pp. 19–20; Parrish, *Turbulent Partnership,* pp. 8, 10, 13.

4. William F. Swindler, "The Southern Press in Missouri, 1861–1864," *Missouri Historical Review,* XXXV (April, 1941), 394–400.

5. Galusha Anderson, *The Story of a Border City During the Civil War* (Boston: Little, Brown & Company, 1908), pp. 144–45.

6. *Jefferson Inquirer,* January 23, 1861.

7. Osceola *Osage Valley Star*, January 31, 1861.

8. Huntsville *Randolph Citizen*, April 18, 1861.

9. California *News*, April 20, 1861.

10. Glasgow *Weekly Times*, May 9, 1861.

11. I have seen this copy, in the Library of Congress.

12. Listed were the *Western Watchman* and *Presbyterian*.

13. Columbia *Missouri Statesman*, July 19, 1861.

14. "Destruction of the Press in Missouri," *Missouri Historical Review*, XXXVI (October, 1941), 72–75.

15. Among the Eastern papers were the New York *Daily News, Day-Book, Journal of Commerce*, and *Freeman's Journal*, and the Brooklyn *Eagle*.

16. Arthur Ray Kirkpatrick, "Missouri, The Twelfth Confederate State" (Ph.D. dissertation, University of Missouri, 1954), p. 93.

17. Allen H. Carpenter, "Military Government of Southern Territory, 1861," *The Annual Report of the American Historical Association for the Year 1900*, p. 475.

18. *Missouri Republican*, May 1, 1862.

19. Louisiana *Journal*, May 16, 1863.

20. *Missouri Republican*, July 16, 1863; *Missouri Democrat*, July 17, 1863, and following issues for several weeks.

21. Arrest reported in *Tri-Weekly Missouri Democrat*, July 13, 1863; various items appeared in succeeding issues.

22. Lexington *Union*, February 27, 1864.

23. *Missouri Democrat*, April 2, 1861.

24. *Missouri Republican*, April 2, 1861.

25. *Missouri Democrat*, April 4, 1861.

26. *Missouri Republican*, April 6, 1861.

27. *Ibid.*, April 8, 1861.

28. Glasgow *Weekly Times*, April 18, 1861.

29. *Missouri Democrat*, April 15, 1860.

30. *Missouri Republican*, May 11, 1861.

31. Thomas L. Sneed, *The Fight for Missouri* (New York: Charles Scribner's Sons, 1886), p. 179.

32. Kirkpatrick, "Missouri, The Twelfth Confederate State." See also his article, "The Admission of Missouri to the Confederacy," *Missouri Historical Review*, LV (July, 1961), 366–86. Parrish, *Turbulent Partnership*, gives an excellent account of these years.

33. *Missouri Republican*, May 18, 1861.

34. Will Davis, "Tragic Brotherhood, 1860–1865," *Official Manual for 1957–1958* (Jefferson City: State of Missouri), pp. 3–32.

35. *Ibid.*, p. 3.

36. This proclamation, and others by government and military officials, were widely printed in the state press.

37. Kirkpatrick, "Missouri, The Twelfth Confederate State."

38. Columbia *Missouri Statesman*, January 9, 1863.

39. Macon *Gazette,* January 7, 1863.

40. *Missouri Republican,* February 3, 1863.

41. Liberty *Weekly Tribune,* January 30, 1863.

42. *Missouri Democrat,* January 5, 1863.

43. Louisiana *Journal,* January 22, 1863.

44. *Missouri Democrat,* April 17, 1863.

45. *Missouri Republican,* February 28, 1863.

46. *Ibid.,* February 3, 1863; Parrish, *Turbulent Partnership,* pp. 137–39.

47. St. Joseph *Morning Herald,* June 11, 1863.

48. The *Missouri Statesman* of August 14, 1863, reprinted a list from the St. Louis *Union* which named papers supporting a gradual plan: Mexico *Citizen,* Palmyra *Spectator,* St. Joseph *Herald,* St. Joseph *News, Franklin County News,* Linneus *Union,* Lexington *Union,* Paris *Mercury,* Troy *Tribune,* Louisiana *Journal,* Columbia *Missouri Statesman,* Fayette *Howard County Advertiser,* Canton *Press,* Fulton *Telegraph,* Kansas City *Journal,* Weston *Sentinel,* Cape Girardeau *Argus,* Chillicothe *Union,* and Savannah *Plaindealer.* The Canton *Press* called it "a judicious arrangement, protecting alike the interests of master and slave." For emancipation *now* were the Hannibal *Courier,* LaGrange *American,* Jefferson City *Times,* Bethany *Union,* Chillicothe *Constitution,* Springfield *Missourian,* Rolla *Express,* and Lebanon *Herald.* The Jefferson City *Missouri State Times,* not satisfied with this list, published a longer tally of papers which it said advocated immediate emancipation: St. Louis *Democrat,* St. Louis *Evening News,* St. Louis *Central Christian Advocate,* St. Joseph *Herald,* St. Charles *Democrat,* Jefferson City *Missouri State Times,* Mexico *Citizen* (which appeared on both lists), LaGrange *American,* Ironton *Radical,* Hannibal *Courier,* Kansas City *Journal,* Hannibal *Chronicle,* Edina *Herald,* Bethany *Union of States,* Chillicothe *Constitution,* Weston *Sentinel,* Springfield *Journal,* Springfield *Missourian,* Lebanon *Herald,* Lebanon *Union,* Washington *News,* Rolla *Express,* Rock Port *Atchison County Journal,* which had only recently been founded, and the St. Joseph *Tribune.* A number of the German-language papers were included from St. Louis, Hermann, and St. Joseph.

49. *Missouri Republican,* November 9, 1863. Also see Bill R. Lee, "Missouri's Fight Over Emancipation in 1863," *Missouri Historical Review,* XLV (April, 1951), 256–74.

50. See William F. Zornow, "The Missouri Radicals and the Election of 1864," *Missouri Historical Review,* XLV (July, 1951), 354-70; *Missouri Republican,* May 20, 1864.

51. St. Joseph *Morning Herald,* May 24, 1864.

52. *Missouri Republican,* July 1, 1864.

53. *Missouri Democrat,* June 13, 1864.

54. Among the papers that backed Lincoln were the *Missouri State Times,* St. Joseph *Tribune,* St. Joseph *Herald,* Hannibal *Courier,* Han-

nibal *Union,* Rock Port *Atchison County Journal,* Boonville *Monitor,*
Kingston *Banner,* Chillicothe *Constitution,* LaGrange *American,* Kan-
sas City *Journal of Commerce, Missouri Tribune,* Perryville *Union,*
Springfield *Journal,* Brunswick *Brunswicker,* Edina *Herald,* Louisiana
Pike County True Flag, Weston *Border Times,* Macon *Argus,* and
Grand River News; Missouri Democrat, June 27, 1864.

55. Kansas City *Western Journal of Commerce,* October 1, 1864.

56. David D. March, "Charles D. Drake and the Constitutional Convention of 1865," *Missouri Historical Review,* XLVII (January, 1953),
110–23.

57. *Missouri Democrat,* November 16, 1864.

58. St. Joseph *Herald & Tribune,* January 10, 1865; Canton *Press,*
January 12, 1865.

59. St. Louis *Dispatch,* March 4, 1865.

60. *Missouri Democrat,* January 20, 1865.

61. *Missouri State Times,* April 22, 1865.

62. *Missouri Democrat,* June 2, 1865.

63. *Missouri Republican,* February 10, 1865.

64. *Missouri Democrat,* April 17, 1865.

65. Columbia *Missouri Statesman,* April 21, 1865.

66. Kansas City *Journal of Commerce,* April 15, 1865.

67. Lexington *Union,* April 22, 1865.

68. Columbia *Missouri Statesman,* April 21, 1865.

CHAPTER VII

1. Richmond *Northwest Conservator,* January 22, 1863; also, Bill R.
Lee, "A View of Missouri Ideas, Society and Culture as Reflected in
the Newspapers of 1863" (M.A. thesis, University of Missouri, 1947).

2. Louisiana *Journal,* December 24, 1864.

3. Columbia *Missouri Statesman,* April 19, 1861. By July, advertisements declined in the paper to such an extent that a smaller page was
used.

4. Macon *Gazette,* January 7, 1863.

5. Columbia *Missouri Statesman,* August 28, 1863. This appeared to
be more of an essay than an advertisement.

6. *Ibid.,* August 28, 1848.

7. Brunswick *Brunswicker,* July 28, 1855.

8. Elbert R. Bowen, "The Circus in Early Rural Missouri," *Missouri
Historical Review,* XLVII (October, 1957), 1–17. Fuller details are in
his book, *Theatrical Entertainment in Rural Missouri Before the Civil
War* (University of Missouri Studies, Vol. XXXII, University of Missouri Press, 1959).

9. Columbia *Missouri Statesman,* October 23, 1863.

10. Shoemaker, *Missouri and Missourians,* II, 722–23; Charles van
Ravenswaay, "The Cover: Pioneer Presses in Missouri," *Bulletin of the*

Missouri Historical Society, VII (April, 1951), 296–301. Van Ravens-waay says that the *Missouri Gazette* used a press "made upon the Ramage screw principle," and it was later used in Franklin by the *Missouri Intelligencer.* Several other style presses are mentioned here, including a Stansbury Patent Lever and an S. Royal Press. In 1964 the Metz *Times* was handset.

11. Columbia *Missouri Statesman,* July 19, 1861.

12. Jefferson City *Missouri State Times,* October 6, 1865.

13. St. Joseph *Herald,* January 10, 1865. Typical of the headlines of the period were these: The Catholic Festival, Important Discovery, Indian Hostilities, River Items, Arrivals at Hotel, Horse Thief Caught, A Sad Accident. Later in the year this paper changed to a single-line, bold-face-type headline over the story.

14. William H. Lyon, "The First Missouri Editor's Convention 1859," *Mid-America,* XLI (October, 1959), 218–22.

15. Liberty *Weekly Tribune,* May 27, 1859.

16. Liberty *Weekly Tribune,* June 24, 1859. Among the papers that agreed to these proposals were the Columbia *Statesman,* Jefferson City *Examiner,* St. Louis *Herald,* Ste. Genevieve *Citizen,* LaGrange *American,* Warsaw *Democrat,* Palmyra *Courier,* Canton *North-East Reporter,* Kansas City *Metropolitan,* California *News,* Brunswick *Press,* Boonville *Patriot,* Chillicothe *Chronicle,* and St. Louis *Republican.*

17. Some larger ads appeared here and there. For example, the St. Joseph *Herald* early in 1864 began using two-column ads.

18. Canton *Press,* July 21, 1864.

19. Richmond *Northwest Conservator,* April 2, 1863.

20. Columbia *Missouri Statesman,* January 3, 1862.

21. Canton *Press,* October 27, 1864.

CHAPTER VIII

1. Thomas B. Hammond, "Development of Journalism in Missouri" (M.A. thesis, University of Missouri, 1922), p. 24. Hammond drew his material primarily from county histories, Organ's "History of the County Press in Missouri," and some directories.

2. Shoemaker, *Missouri and Missourians,* I, 994–1023.

3. *Ibid.*

4. *Missouri Democrat,* October 27 and 30, 1865.

5. *Missouri Republican,* for Seymour, cut its prices, offering copies from September 2 to November 13 for 25c per copy in groups of 20 or more. It claimed 1,898 new subscriptions in six days. Both this paper and the *Missouri Democrat* carried on a continuous name-calling, tongue-lashing campaign.

6. *Missouri Republican,* November 9, 1868; *Missouri Democrat,* November 2, 1868.

7. Boonville *Weekly Eagle,* November 7, 1868.

8. Ironton *Iron County Register,* November 12, 1868.

9. New London *Ralls County Record,* October 29, 1868.

10. Bolivar *Free Press,* October 22 and 29, and November 5, 1868.

11. Springfield *Missouri Weekly Patriot,* October 21 and 28, and November 5, 1868.

12. Bolivar *Free Press,* November 12, 1868.

13. Edina *Sentinel,* October 10, 1872, from the Linn *Unterrified Democrat.*

14. California *Democrat,* July 4, 1870.

15. Columbia *Missouri Statesman,* May 31, 1872.

16. Carthage *People's Press,* May 9, 1872.

17. Jefferson City *Peoples Tribune,* November 13, 1872.

18. Butler *Bates County Record,* May 18, 1872.

19. Carrollton *Wakanda Record,* November 1, 1872.

20. Springfield *Missouri Weekly Patriot,* March 7, 1872.

21. Brookfield *Gazette,* May 9, 1872.

22. Springfield *Missouri Weekly Patriot,* August 8, 1872.

23. Lexington *Register,* June 28, 1872.

24. Carthage *Banner,* May 9, 1872.

25. *Missouri Democrat,* June 21, 1872; Carthage *Banner,* October 24, 1872.

26. St. Joseph *Daily Morning Herald,* May 14, 1872.

27. *Missouri Democrat,* December 2, 1872.

28. Edina *Sentinel,* March 12, 1872; Brookfield *Gazette,* March 21, 1872; St. Joseph *Herald,* June 27, 1872.

29. Quoted in Jefferson City *Peoples Tribune,* March 13, 1872.

30. St. Joseph *Gazette,* April 28, 1872.

31. Kansas City *Journal of Commerce,* September 6, 1872.

32. Carrollton *Wakanda Record,* August 30, 1872.

33. *Missouri Republican,* November 6, 7, 1872.

34. St. Joseph *Daily Morning Gazette,* November 8, 1872.

35. Lexington *Intelligencer,* November 9, 1872.

36. Carrollton *Wakanda Record,* November 15, 1872.

37. *Missouri Statesman,* November 8, 1872.

38. Lexington *Caucasian,* November 9, 1872.

39. *Ibid.,* December 7, 1872.

40. California *Democrat,* November 21, 1872.

41. Jefferson City *Peoples Tribune,* July 3, 1873.

42. Warrensburg *Journal,* November 13, 1874.

43. Edina *Sentinel,* April 30, 1874.

44. Alma Beatrice Wilkinson, "The Granger Movement in Missouri" (M.A. thesis, University of Missouri, 1926). The study lists: Bethany *Tribune* and *Republican,* Boonville *Eagle,* Brookfield *Gazette,* Canton *Press,* Cape Girardeau *Press,* Carthage *Advance,* Chamois *Leader,* Chillicothe *Tribune,* Gallatin *North Missourian,* Glenwood *Criterion,* Granby *Miner,* Neosho *Journal,* Hamilton *News,* Jefferson City *Jour-*

nal, Kansas City *Journal,* Lebanon *Anti-Monopolist,* Lexington *Register, Linn County New Era, Macon County Granger,* Macon *Journal,* Marble City *News,* Marshfield *Democrat,* Maryville *Register,* Mexico *Leader,* Mexico *Messenger,* Osceola *Farmer's Friend,* Paris *Appeal,* Paris *Mercury,* Pittsburg *Register,* Pleasant Hill *Dispatch,* Rockport *Journal,* Rolla *Express, Southwest Missourian,* Springfield *Advertiser, State Journal,* St. Joseph *Herald,* Trenton *Republican,* Warrenton *Chronicle,* Warrensburg *Journal, Western Success.*

45. Brookfield *Gazette,* September 18, 1873.

46. Floella Kelley Carter, "The Grange in Missouri" (M.A. thesis, University of Missouri, 1940).

47. Shoemaker, *Missouri and Missourians,* II, 39–41.

48. Warrensburg *Journal,* November 13, 1874.

49. Wilkinson, "The Granger Movement in Missouri," includes informative summaries on the key papers.

50. John A. Leach, "Public Opinion and the Inflation Movement in Missouri, 1875–1879" (M.A. thesis, University of Missouri, 1923), pp. 59–60.

51. Jefferson City *Peoples Tribune,* October 13, 1875.

52. *Missouri Republican,* June 19, July 10, 1875.

53. Shelbyville *Shelby County Herald,* September 13, 1876.

54. Brookfield *Gazette,* March 1, 1877.

55. Leach, "Public Opinion and the Inflation Movement."

56. Reprinted in the Jefferson City *Peoples Tribune,* February 27, 1878.

57. Leach, as quoted from the Jefferson City *Peoples Tribune,* February–March, 1878, issues.

58. Columbia *Missouri Statesman,* March 8, 1878.

59. Jefferson City *Peoples Tribune,* April 17, 1878.

60. Bolivar *Free Press,* November 5, 1880.

61. Jefferson City *Peoples Tribune,* November 5, 1880.

62. Hillsboro *Jefferson Democrat,* November 5, 1880; Bloomfield *Vindicator,* November 6, 1880.

63. William V. Byars, "A Century of Journalism in Missouri," *Missouri Historical Review,* XV (October, 1920), 61.

CHAPTER IX

1. Floyd W. Shoemaker, "History of the First Fifty Years of the Missouri Press Association," manuscript, State Historical Society of Missouri Library. Material here has been taken from minutes of the association as well as newspaper files.

2. Lancaster *Excelsior,* June 23, 1866; Troy *Lincoln County Herald,* June 22, 1866.

3. Jefferson City *Peoples Tribune,* May 1, 1867.

4. Columbia *Missouri Statesman,* May 10, 1867.

5. J. W. Barrett, *History and Transactions of the Editors' and Publishers' Association of Missouri, 1867–1876* (Canton, Mo.: Canton Press Print, 1876), pp. 1–2. Also of value is the *History of the Missouri Press Association* (Columbia, Mo.: E. W. Stephens Publishing Co., 1931).

6. *Missouri Republican,* May 17 and 20, 1867.

7. From Barrett and Shoemaker as well as from the Proceedings of the Missouri Press Association, 1896. For many years these accounts were published in full and distributed to members.

8. Lancaster *Excelsior,* May 25, 1867.

9. *Missouri Democrat,* May 20, 1868.

10. *Missouri Republican,* May 22, 1868.

11. Wilkinson's speech is reproduced in full in Barrett, *History and Transactions,* pp. 6–17; *Missouri Democrat, Missouri Republican,* May 22, 1868.

12. *Missouri Democrat,* May 19, 1869; Barrett, *History and Transactions,* pp. 17, 19.

13. Barrett, *History and Transactions,* pp. 21–30.

14. Glenwood *Criterion,* June 15, 1870.

15. Barrett, *History and Transactions,* p. 41.

16. Kirksville *North Missouri Register,* June 1, 1871.

17. Barrett, *History and Transactions,* pp. 40–44.

18. Hillsboro *Jefferson Democrat,* May 24, 1872.

19. Troy *Lincoln County Herald,* May 7, 1873.

20. Jefferson City *Peoples Tribune,* June 4, 1873.

21. Troy *Lincoln County Herald,* June 4, 1873.

22. Poem quoted in full in Barrett, *History and Transactions,* pp. 134–37.

23. *Ibid.,* pp. 80–87.

24. Sedalia *Times,* May 28, 1874.

25. Hillsboro *Jefferson Democrat,* May 29, 1874.

26. Barrett, *History and Transactions,* pp. 93–107.

27. *Ibid.,* pp. 110–33; Boonville *Advertiser,* June 16, 1876; Jefferson City *Daily State Journal,* June 8, 1876.

28. Field's poem was titled, "Tom Park at Frederickstown."

29. *Proceedings of the Missouri Press Association,* 1878.

30. *Ibid.,* 1879.

31. *Ibid.,* 1880.

32. *Ibid.,* 1881.

33. Shoemaker, "History of Missouri Press Association."

34. Carthage *Banner,* May 10 and 17, 1883. The *Banner* reprinted many comments about the convention that appeared in other papers.

35. Columbia *Missouri Statesman,* May 30, 1884.

CHAPTER X

1. All issues of Rowell's *American Newspaper Directory* (1869–1908), and Ayer and Son's *Directory of Newspapers and Periodicals*

(1880 to present) have been consulted in this study; Shoemaker, *Missouri and Missourians*, II, 722.

2. James Lee Ashcraft, "Agrarian Reform Newspapers in Missouri, 1888–1896" (M.A. thesis, University of Missouri, 1947).

3. James Creighton, "Readyprints in Missouri Newspapers" (research project, University of Missouri, 1961).

4. Shoemaker, *Missouri and Missourians*, II, 81; an excellent account of "The Development of the Jesse James Legend" has been written by William A. Settle, Jr., as his doctoral dissertation at the University of Missouri, 1945. Settle notes that the Sedalia *Daily Democrat* was one of "the very few papers that actually upheld Jesse James," pp. 261–62.

5. Reprinted in the Sedalia *Daily Democrat*, April 19, 1882.

6. Richmond *Conservator*, April 21, 1882.

7. *Missouri Republican*, October 2, 1882; Shoemaker, *Missouri and Missourians*, II, 82.

8. Kansas City *Daily Journal*, October 30, 1882.

9. St. Joseph *Gazette*, September 7, 1883.

10. St. Louis *Post-Dispatch*, September 7, 1883.

11. *Ibid.*, September 12, 1883.

12. *Ibid.*, October 4–November 4, 1884.

13. *Missouri Republican*, November 6 and 7, 1884.

14. Bloomfield *Vindicator*, November 15, 1884.

15. St. Joseph *Herald*, September 5, November 7, 1884.

16. Breckenridge *Bulletin*, November 6 and 13, 1884.

17. Montgomery City *Montgomery Standard*, November 7, 1884.

18. Troy *Free Press*, November 14, 1884.

19. Homer Clevenger, "Agrarian Politics in Missouri, 1880–1896," (Ph.D. dissertation, University of Missouri, 1940).

20. St. Louis *Missouri Republican*, January 4, 1887.

21. Shoemaker, *Missouri and Missourians*, II, 95–116; much of the development of agriculture in Missouri is associated with the career of Norman J. Colman, publisher of *Colman's Rural World*. Colman was long active in the work of the Missouri Press Association.

22. Butler *Bates County Record*, November 10, 1888.

23. Copied from the California *Newspaper*, July 19, 1888.

24. Shoemaker, *Missouri and Missourians*, II, 125–26. The "Bald Knobbers" were organized in the Ozark area, taking their name from a bare Ozark peak. The group was similar in many ways to the Ku Klux Klan.

25. St. Louis *Globe-Democrat*, July 5, 1892; October 19, 1894.

26. Ashcraft, "Agrarian Reform Newspapers in Missouri"; Clevenger notes the Grange educational program as helping to increase the number of newspapers and farm magazines, pp. 77–78.

27. Ashcraft includes the following reform papers in his study: Anderson *Messenger*, Ash Grove *American*, Aurora *Times*, Ava *Farm Record*, Avalon *Aurora*, Bakersfield *Informer*, Barfield *Transcript*,

Bevier *Appeal*, Bloomfield *Vindicator*, Bolivar *Polk County Farmer*, Brookfield *Union*, Buffalo *People's Paper* and *Record*, Burlington Junction *Ledger*, Butler *Local News*, Cainsville *Expositor*, Calhoun *Courier*, California *Newspaper*, Callao *News*, Carthage *Labor's Tribune* and *Western Critic*, Cassville *Barry County Informer*, Centralia *Courier*, Chillicothe *Crisis* and *Missouri World*, Clarksburg *Our Home*, College Mound *North Missouri Miner*, Dexter *Enterprise-Messenger*, Edina *Independent*, El Dorado Springs *Mascot* and *Tribune*, Excelsior Springs *Banner*, Exeter *Farmers' News*, Fordland *Journal*, Greenfield *Enterprise* and *Weekly Pointers*, Hale *Hustler*, Hamilton *Farmers' Advocate*, Harrisonville *People's Record*, Humansville *Union Bee*, Jackson *Comet*, Jefferson City *Herald* and *Monitor*, Joplin *Voice*, Kahoka *Independent*, Kansas City *Appeal*, *Interstate Alliance Echo*, *The Other Side*, and *True American*, Kirksville *Adair County Farmer*, Lamar *Industrial Union*, *Leader*, and *Political Review*, Lebanon *Laclede County Sentinel*, Liberal *Enterprise*, Liberty *Searchlight*, Lincoln *Central Missouri Reflector*, Lockwood *Independent*, Lone Oak *Emancipator*, Lowry City *Independent*, Maryville *Advocate* and *Missouri Standard*, Marshall *Alliance Watchman*, *People's Record*, and *Quiz*, Memphis *Farmers' Union*, Neosho *Populist*, Nevada *Industrial Review*, *Director*, and *Daily Director*, Odessa *Moon*, Osceola *People's Advocate*, Ozark *Mail* and *Southwest Rural News* and *Stockman*, Paris *Plain-Dealer*, Parnell *Express*, Plattsburg *Critic*, Poplar Bluff *Southeast Enterprise*, Rich Hill *Bates County Populist*, Rocky Comfort *Rock o' Comfort*, Rolla *Irrepressible Vidette*, Rush Hill *Banner*, St. James *Journal* and *News*, St. Joseph *Star*, *Wasp*, and *Labor Item*, St. Louis *Rural World*, *Journal of Agriculture*, and *Monitor*, Savannah *Monitor*, Sedalia *Industrial Review* and *Truth*, Smithville *Farmers' Herald*, South Greenfield *Dade County Journal*, Springfield *New Crusade*, *People's Forum*, *The Patrick Henry*, and *Workingmen's World*, Stockton *People's Advocate*, Tarkio *Independent*, Thayer *Progress*, Tuscumbia *Eye-Opener*, Versailles *Populist*, Warrensburg *Johnson County Union*, Wellington *Monitor*, Wellsville *Club*, and West Plains *Quill*.

28. Shoemaker, *Missouri and Missourians*, II, 167.

29. Maynard Gregg Redfield, "The Political Campaign of 1896 in Missouri" (M.A. thesis, University of Missouri, 1946), pp. 70–98.

30. St. Louis *Globe-Democrat*, September 10 and 13, 1896.

31. Shoemaker, *Missouri and Missourians*, II, 169. Additional sources consulted for this chapter included Monia Cook Morris, "The History of Woman Suffrage in Missouri, 1867–1901" (M.A. thesis, University of Missouri, 1928), and Charles O. Wright, "The Populist Movement With Special Reference to Missouri" (M.A. thesis, University of Missouri, 1921).

CHAPTER XI

1. *Missouri Editor*, October, 1894, p. 1.

2. *Ibid.*, January, 1895, p. 3.

3. *Proceedings of the Missouri Press Association*, 1885.

4. Shoemaker, "History of Missouri Press Association."

5. *Proceedings of the Missouri Press Association*, 1887.

6. *Ibid.*, 1888.

7. *Ibid.*, 1889.

8. Sturgeon *Leader*, February 15, 1898; letter from Rogers Hewitt, May 21, 1962.

9. Membership today is open to publishers and newspaper personnel in the area with associate membership for journalism teachers, students, and persons in related businesses. Letter from Robert Bowles, June 2, 1962.

10. *Proceedings of the Missouri Press Association* (first winter meeting), 1890.

11. *Ibid.*

12. Proceedings of the winter and fall meetings were combined in one book of 143 pages.

13. Letter from Louis Bowman, May 22, 1962. Bowman missed only two or three of the group's latest sixty-three meetings. He was a student under Dean Walter Williams at the School of Journalism.

14. *Country Editor*, June, 1899.

15. Shoemaker, "History of the Missouri Press Association," and *Proceedings of the Missouri Press Association*, 1891.

16. Proceedings of the 1892, 1893, and 1894 meetings were combined in one book and published in 1894.

17. Material concerning the Democratic-Republican organizations may be found in the *Official Manual* of the State of Missouri, the "Blue Book," published every two years.

18. *Proceedings of the Missouri Press Association*, 1895.

19. *Ibid.*, 1896. The published minutes include a detailed map, showing the trip down the Mississippi River.

20. *Ibid.*, 1897; Shoemaker, "History of the Missouri Press Association."

21. *Proceedings of the Missouri Press Association*, 1898.

22. *Ibid.*, 1899.

23. Combined proceedings of winter meeting and fall meeting published in one book, 1900.

24. *Proceedings of the Missouri Press Association*, 1901.

25. *Ibid.*, 1902.

26. *Ibid.*, 1903; Shoemaker, "History of the Missouri Press Association."

27. *Proceedings of the Missouri Press Association*, 1904. A special book was issued by E. W. Stephens, *Proceedings of the World's Press Parliament, May 19–21, 1904*, which contains speeches in full.

28. Shoemaker, "History of the Missouri Press Association."

29. *Ibid.*

CHAPTER XII

1. St. Louis *Post-Dispatch,* April 6, 1947. A special section published on this date commemorated the one-hundredth anniversary of Pulitzer's birth and contained considerable biographical material.

2. *Ibid.,* p. 6, special section.

3. Other interesting highlights are recorded in a booklet published by the St. Louis Post-Dispatch Company, *The Story of the* Post-Dispatch, by Charles G. Ross and Carlos F. Hurd.

4. *Editor & Publisher,* April 9, 1955; *Post-Dispatch,* March 31, 1955.

5. Kansas City *Star,* September 18, 1880.

6. *Ibid.;* the Sunday edition appeared on April 29, 1894, and the *Morning Times* became a part of the *Star* on November 18, 1901. The *Weekly Star* was established March 6, 1890.

7. Mott, *American Journalism,* pp. 468–73. According to Mott, two morning and two evening English-language papers and two German-language papers were also being published in Kansas City at this time. The additional material on Nelson has been drawn from William J. Bell, "A Historical Study of the Kansas City *Star* Since the Death of William Rockhill Nelson, 1915–1949" (Ph.D. dissertation, University of Missouri, 1949); Icie F. Johnson, *William Rockhill Nelson and the Kansas City* Star (Kansas City: Burton Publishing Co., 1935); William Allen White, "The Man Who Made the *Star,*" *Collier's,* June 26, 1915; *William Rockhill Nelson: the Story of a Man, a Newspaper and a City* by members of the *Star* staff (Cambridge, Mass.: The Riverside Press, 1915); "William Rockhill Nelson," in Allen Johnson and Dumas Malone, eds., *Dictionary of American Biography,* XIII, 427–28. Nelson was not the type of person one would call "Bill."

8. White, "The Man Who Made the *Star,*" pp. 12–13. White said Nelson established "an elaborate anonymity" and was known only to a few of the *Star's* readers.

9. In Indiana, Nelson had been a Tilden supporter in 1876, but shortly after founding the *Star* he became disillusioned with the Democrats and declared that from then on the paper would be politically independent, but never neutral.

10. Talk given May 19, 1914.

11. *William Rockhill Nelson: the Story of a Man, a Newspaper and a City.* Several hundred papers in the nation eulogized him when he died, referring to him as "the man who had the most to do with the molding of the best thought in the West" and "the most powerful journal of light between the Missouri and the Pacific."

12. Nelson had asked that the paper be discontinued after the death of his wife and daughter, for he feared the destruction of the principles he held sacred if the paper fell into the hands of others.

13. Walter B. Stevens, "Joseph M. McCullagh," *Missouri Historical Review,* XXV (1930–1931), 3. This is the first of several articles by

Stevens. Also see Jim Allee Hart, *A History of the St. Louis* Globe-Democrat (Columbia: University of Missouri Press, 1961).

14. "Joseph B. McCullagh," in *Dictionary of American Biography,* XII, 5.

15. *Globe-Democrat,* July 16, 1879.

16. McCullagh was one of the founders of the new journalism, in which he sought to furnish readers the news, complete and accurate. His theory was that "a great newspaper, like a great hotel, must be conducted on the theory that tastes differ—and the best newspaper, like the best hotel, is that which prepares the largest variety in entertainment for the largest number of guests." See Stevens, "Joseph B. McCullagh," *Missouri Historical Review,* XXVI (1931–1932), 383. Shoemaker, ed., *Missouri, Day by Day,* II, 463–64, published by the State Historical Society of Missouri, 1943.

17. *Proceedings of the Missouri Press Association,* 1878; *Missouri Editor,* December, 1896. The writer said McCullagh "rarely copied an item from a Missouri exchange and practically ignored the country press. Great as were his qualities as a journalist, he made in this a mistake."

18. *Ibid.,* December, 1896.

19. Hart, *History of the* Globe-Democrat, p. 153.

20. *Ibid.,* p. 157.

21. *Missouri Editor,* December, 1896.

22. *Ibid.,* March, 1895.

CHAPTER XIII

1. *Missouri Editor,* April, 1895, pp. 8–9. Ledbetter said: "And what a galaxy of remarkable men is comprised in the newspaper history of Missouri! There is William F. Switzler, the patriarch of the state tripod, the man who never forgets anything and seldom forgets to tell about it; J. West Goodwin, of the historic hat and recent misfortunes; E. W. Stephens, the proprietor of what has been called the 'best country weekly in the United States;' Walter Williams, like Stephens, honored of late years with the presidency of the National Editorial Association and a bright particular star in the firmament of state journalism; John A. Knott, the wet nurse and chief mourner for the Dalton boom; Isaac Newton Bryson, the 'filosopher' and fulminator, like Joe Bowers, 'all the way from Pike;' White and Cook, names synonymous with Mexico and successful newspaper enterprise; Cochran and Bittinger, the more or less devoted Siamese twins from St. Joe; Perry S. Rader, perhaps the best specimen of physical manhood in Missouri Journalism and one of its brainiest exponents; the Ewings, of Jefferson City, known by the multifarious strings they pull to achieve political results; Graham, the polished and versatile; Charles H. Jones, in whose abilities as a hustler Missouri still takes pride;

George W. Trigg, sturdy and undaunted in the battle for Democracy and right; 'Buck' Kelly, of Moberly, who owns a gold mine out west and a silver paper in Missouri. All these, and scores of others, stand for the best qualities of the Missouri editor—qualities which have made him representative of the best and noblest that the state affords."

2. *Ibid.,* October, 1896.

3. *Proceedings of the Missouri Press Association,* 1896.

4. *Ibid.; Missouri Press News,* August, 1943.

5. *Missouri Editor,* November, 1896.

6. *Missouri Press News,* February, 1944.

7. *Missouri Editor,* April, 1896.

8. *Ibid.*

9. *Ibid.,* October, 1896.

10. *Ibid.,* November, 1895.

11. *Proceedings of the Missouri Press Association,* 1887.

12. *Missouri Editor,* April, 1896; *Missouri Press News,* March, 1946.

13. *Ibid.,* June, 1944.

14. *Ibid.,* September, 1943.

15. *Missouri Editor,* June, 1895.

16. *Ibid.,* February, 1896.

17. *Missouri Press News,* December, 1944.

18. *Proceedings of the Missouri Press Association,* 1891.

19. *Ibid.,* 1892, 1896.

20. *Missouri Press News,* January, 1944.

21. *Ibid.,* April, 1946; *Missouri Editor,* December, 1895.

22. *Missouri Editor,* March, 1896; *Missouri Press News,* October, 1945.

23. *Missouri Editor,* February, 1896.

24. Leonard Busen, "A History of the Newspapers of Gasconade County, Missouri, from 1843 to 1960" (M.A. thesis, University of Missouri, 1960), pp. 33–85.

25. *Missouri Editor,* July, 1895.

26. *Ibid.,* April, 1895; *Missouri Press News,* April, 1945.

27. *Missouri Editor,* July, 1896; *Missouri Press News,* August, 1946.

28. *Missouri Press News,* December, 1945.

29. *Ibid.,* October, 1946; *Missouri Editor,* February, 1896.

30. *Missouri Editor,* June, 1896.

31. *Ibid.,* May, 1896.

32. *Ibid.,* April, 1896.

33. *Ibid.,* September, 1895; *Missouri Press News,* November, 1944.

34. *Missouri Press News,* November, 1943.

35. *Ibid.,* April, 1944.

36. *Ibid.,* August, 1945; *Missouri Editor,* March, 1895.

37. *Missouri Press News,* May, 1945.

38. *Ibid.,* June, 1945.

39. *Ibid.,* January, 1945.

40. *Ibid.*, July, 1945; *Missouri Editor*, April, August, 1895; July, 1896.
41. *Missouri Press News*, October, 1939.
42. *Ibid.*, July, 1944; *Missouri Editor*, August, 1895.
43. *Missouri Editor*, December, 1895.
44. *Ibid.*, March, 1896.
45. *Ibid.*, April, 1896.
46. *Proceedings of the Missouri Press Association*, 1885.
47. *Ibid.*, 1887.
48. *Missouri Editor*, April, 1896.
49. *Ibid.*, August, 1896.
50. *Ibid.*, November, 1895.
51. *Ibid.*, February, 1896.
52. *Ibid.*, December, 1895.
53. *Missouri Press News*, January, 1946.
54. *Ibid.*, March, 1944.
55. *Ibid.*, April, 1947, and June, 1951; *Missouri Editor*, October, 1895.
56. *Missouri Editor*, May, 1895.
57. *Ibid.*, June, 1895.
58. *Missouri Press News*, February, 1946.
59. *Ibid.*, September, 1945; *Missouri Editor*, October, 1895.
60. *Missouri Editor*, October, 1896.
61. *Ibid.*, March, 1895.
62. *Ibid.*, May, 1895; *Missouri Press News*, September, 1944.
63. *Missouri Editor*, December, 1895; *Missouri Press News*, December, 1943.
64. *Missouri Press News*, March, 1945.
65. *Ibid.*, August, 1944.
66. *Ibid.*, November, 1945; *Missouri Editor*, April, 1896.
67. *Missouri Press News*, May, 1944.
68. *Ibid.*, October, 1944; *Missouri Editor*, February, 1895.
69. *Missouri Editor*, August, 1895.
70. *Ibid.*, October, 1896.
71. *Ibid.*, September, 1895.
72. *Missouri Press News*, October, 1943.
73. *Ibid.*, February, 1945.
74. *Proceedings of the Missouri Press Association*, 1898.
75. *Missouri Editor*, May and August, 1894. The careers of other editors have been described in a number of masters' theses at the University of Missouri, including these: James B. Creighton, "A Historical Study of Early Boonville Newspapers, 1831–1862"; Thomas B. Hammond, "Development of Journalism in Missouri"; Howard A. Rader, "Newspaper History of Callaway County, Missouri, from 1839 to 1960"; Dean Rea, "A History of the Springfield, Missouri, *Leader and Press*, 1867–1950"; Anthony J. Scantlen, "A History of the Mexico, Missouri, *Ledger*"; Estal E. Sparlin, "*The Jefferson Inquirer*"; David L. Wilkie, "Independence, Missouri, Newspapers 1832–1900"; Sara Lockwood

Williams, "A Study of the *Columbia Herald* from 1889 to 1908"; and Leilyn M. Young, "The *Southeast Missourian* and the Naeter Brothers —A Study of Community Service in Cape Girardeau, Missouri, by a Newspaper and Its Publishers."

CHAPTER XIV

1. Floyd C. Shoemaker, *The State Historical Society of Missouri, A Semicentennial History* (Columbia: State Historical Society of Missouri, 1948). Shoemaker has collected material from early Missouri Press Association minutes, interviews, society records, and his own experience with the society.

2. *Ibid.*, p. 16. This first historical group included editors, lawyers, state legislators and officials, judges, etc. Shoemaker points out that it "lacked sufficient support to survive."

3. *Proceedings of the Missouri Press Association*, 1898. The committee had approximately four months in which to draft the constitution and bylaws.

4. *Proceedings of the Missouri Press Association*, 1895.

5. Shoemaker, *op. cit.*, p. 24. These men primarily worked on the "style" of the material. Shoemaker adds: "Devoid of fanfare or dramatic impact, the State Historical Society of Missouri came into being that day in 1898, and the manner of its beginning set the tempo for all of the society's existence—steadfast, avoiding dramatic tangents, the society stuck to its knitting through two wars and several depressions and never retreated an inch from the progress it so steadily and surely made."

6. *Ibid.*, p. 24. He adds that the Missouri constitution was apparently copied from that of the Wisconsin Historical Society and "that of the Oklahoma society, which closely followed that of the Kansas society of 1875." Shoemaker includes the full constitution and all changes made later.

7. *Ibid.*, p. 26. "It is clear that the act . . . which governs the society and which makes it a trustee of the state, had its origin in the basic law of 1854 governing the State Historical Society of Wisconsin by way of the law of 1875 governing the Kansas State Historical Society and the law of 1895 governing the Oklahoma Historical Society."

8. *Ibid.*, pp. 25–26.

9. *Proceedings of the Missouri Press Association*, 1903.

10. *Ibid.*

11. Elmer Ellis, "The Contribution of the State Historical Society of Missouri to Higher Education," *Missouri Historical Review*, XLIII (January, 1949), 105–8.

12. Richard S. Brownlee, "Message to the Members of the State Historical Society of Missouri," *Missouri Historical Review*, LV (October, 1960), 1.

13. Shoemaker, *op. cit.*, explains more fully the contents of the major collections in the society.

14. Daniel H. Spies, "The State Historical Society of Missouri Annual Meeting and Dedication of New Quarters," *Missouri Historical Review*, LVI (January, 1962), 115–30. Spies adds valuable data on the holdings, quarters, and present-day status of the society.

CHAPTER XV

1. *Country Editor*, July, 1897. "Such newspapers as the Clinton *Democrat*, Keytesville *Courier*, Sturgeon *Leader*, Hannibal *Journal*, Boonville *Advertiser*, Jefferson City *Tribune*, Columbia *Herald*, and hundred others are omitted," Williams wrote. This was in reference to the *American Newspaper Directory*, which was discontinued in 1908.

2. *Country Editor*, August, 1897. These comments, probably written by Williams, did not identify the newspapers. In the same issue Williams reported the reorganization of the Democratic Editorial Association but added, "We do not believe in partisan editorial associations. As far as they cultivate friendly relations among editors they are all right but as far as they stir up partisanship and lower editors into politicians they are all wrong."

3. Several items appeared from time to time in the *Country Editor* about halftones, their use, costs, etc. See May, 1895; May, December, 1897, for comments.

4. Mott, *Time Enough* (Chapel Hill: University of North Carolina Press, 1962) adds interesting details of these early days.

5. Among hand-set papers in Missouri in 1963 was the Metz *Times*.

6. *Country Editor*, January, 1898.

7. *Ibid.*, March, 1897. Williams thought that if the paper did not make a living for the editor, "he ought to quit the business and go to farming or prize fighting."

8. *Ibid.*, December, 1897. In this issue Williams had an editorial on "Trash," claiming that "The rubbish that fills the daily newspapers is growing both in quantity and worthlessness . . . the most insignificant occurrences are magnified into columns and emblazoned with flaming headlines, while matters of real interest are frequently dismissed with a paragraph. . . . The average country weekly publishes more really interesting reading than the mammoth daily in its seven days."

9. *Missouri Editor*, January, 1895. Williams thought the editor "must praise his enemies and score his friends when duty requires. The public very quickly detects personal spite in a newspaper and the instant they do they lose all regard for its opinions."

10. *Ibid.*, March, 1895.

11. *Country Editor*, August, 1897.

12. Quoted in the *Country Editor*, May, 1897.

13. Reprinted in the *Country Editor*, February, 1898.

14. *Missouri Editor,* June, 1894.
15. *Country Editor,* April, 1898.

CHAPTER XVI

1. Barrett, *History and Transactions,* pp. 21–30. In this talk Colman said, "Like all other professions, the Editorial has grave and responsible duties devolving upon it—but, unlike others, certain prescribed qualifications have not been required before entering upon the discharge of professional duty."

2. Shoemaker, "History of the Missouri Press Association." For an excellent study of Colman, see George Francis Lemmer, "Norman J. Colman and *Colman's Rural World:* A Study in Agricultural Leadership" (Ph.D. dissertation, University of Missouri, 1947).

3. Barrett, *op. cit.,* p. 86. Blair added, "Journalism has a high and immortal mission to perform. Like the wand of a magician, its wing sweeps nearly every land, and shall yet penetrate the wildest haunts of the world, where the shadow and superstition of ignorance falls heavily over the people."

4. Shoemaker, "History of the Missouri Press Association."

5. From a Journalism Week talk, February 20, 1930. Reported in Leon Lindsay, "A Biography of David R. McAnally, Jr." (M.A. thesis, University of Missouri, 1956).

6. *Missouri Editor,* November, 1895.

7. *Proceedings of the Missouri Press Association,* 1896. In an account of this meeting in the *Missouri Editor,* June, 1896, Stephens is quoted as saying, "There are some persons in the newspaper profession in Missouri who are as dangerous in their communities as maddogs. The time will come when we will have licensed editors as licensed teachers and doctors. The Missouri Press Association should put itself on record as favoring a specific, technical school of journalism." Additional material on the early years can be found in Sara Lockwood Williams, *Twenty Years of Education for Journalism* (Columbia: E. W. Stephens Publishing Company, 1929).

8. A more thorough background on Walter Williams and his life has been prepared by Frank W. Rucker, of the School of Journalism faculty; several chapters were consulted for material used here. Frank W. Rucker, *Walter Williams* (Columbia: The Missourian Publishing Company, 1964).

9. *Country Editor,* March, 1898. In the *Missouri Editor,* June, 1896, J. A. Graham, editor of the St. Louis *Republic,* offered some suggestions that ran counter to those ideas voiced by Stephens. He wrote: (1) Almost any intelligent young man with a fair faculty, fairly trained, of clothing thoughts in words, can do successfully the routine of journalism after a very little instruction; (2) In the more responsible journalistic positions the difficulty of securing well qualified

men is far greater than the difficulty of finding a good lawyer or doctor; (3) Newspaper work is not a matter of systematic training within itself, but a matter of grasping, weighing, expressing all the busy activities of all masses of men each day. Graham's comparison was interesting: journalism resembles the vogue of bicycle-riding. All that one man can tell another with productive effect can be learned in a few days. In bicycle-riding it is a question of co-ordination of mental and nervous forces. Graham believed the University could teach the "duplex art of grasping the meaning of facts and expressing that meaning in clear English. . . . The general training of a college, if it were turned to the development of the faculties of seeing and writing, would produce more good newspaper men than would a special school of journalism."

10. *Proceedings of the Missouri Press Association*, 1903.

11. *Ibid.*, 1904, 1906. Also material from unpublished histories by Shoemaker and Rucker.

12. *Ibid.*, 1909. Williams was speaking of the opposition voiced by the Columbia papers, the *Statesman, Herald,* and *Tribune,* when the members of the class in advertising sales called upon local merchants for advertisements. When this protest was presented to the Board of Curators, "action was deferred to a later meeting."

13. Rucker, *Walter Williams.* Also *University Missourian,* September 14, 1908, which includes a story behind the School of Journalism development, with a mention of an address to alumni in 1879 by Leonidas M. Lawson of New York, who urged founding such an institution.

14. Columbia *Daily Tribune,* September 1, 1908.

15. Columbia *Statesman,* September 18, 1908; *Herald,* September, 1908.

16. Quoted in the *University Missourian,* October 5 and 9, 1908.

17. Reprinted in *University Missourian,* September 30, 1908.

18. *Ibid.;* for some time the *University Missourian* reprinted comments on the school, favorable and otherwise.

19. St. Louis *Post-Dispatch,* September 16, 1908.

20. St. Louis *Times,* September 17, 1908.

21. St. Louis *Republic,* September 17, 1908.

22. St. Louis *Globe-Democrat,* September 17, 1908. All were not favorable. The Springfield *Leader* noted, "Quite a number of newspaper men of big rank—Joseph Pulitzer for instance—believe that a school of journalism is practical . . . it will take time to tell, but it would seem that the best and most profitable way would be to learn the newspaper business in an office. A school of journalism would be more in place in a business college than a university."

23. Williams, *Twenty Years of Education for Journalism,* pp. 26–27.

24. Columbia *University Missourian,* September 15, 1908.

25. *Ibid.*, September 17, 1908.

26. *Ibid.*, October 12, 1908.

27. *Ibid.*, October 12, 1908.

28. Jonas Viles, *The University of Missouri: A Centennial History 1839–1939* (Columbia: E. W. Stephens Publishing Company, 1939). In addition, see Williams, *op. cit.*, which contains the full Journalism Week programs through 1928.

29. *Ibid.*, p. 54.

CHAPTER XVII

1. Morran D. Harris, "Political Trends in Missouri, 1900–1954" (M.A. thesis, University of Missouri, 1956), pp. 4–5, 99–106.

2. Frances Patton Landen, "The Joseph W. Folk Campaign for Governor in 1904 as Reflected in the Rural Press of Missouri" (M.A. thesis, University of Missouri, 1938), p. 54.

3. *Ibid.*, p. 55.

4. *Ibid.*, p. 56.

5. Columbia *Herald*, January 30, 1903.

6. Paris *Mercury*, May 29 and July 24, 1903.

7. Landen, *op. cit.*, pp. 61–64.

8. Columbia *Herald*, December 25, 1903.

9. Gallatin *Democrat*, February 11, 1904.

10. Landen, *op. cit.*, p. 140.

11. Kirksville *Graphic*, May 6, 1904.

12. Landen, *op. cit.*, p. 151. Landen quotes some titles used by the St. Louis *World* about Folk: crucifier, Holier-than-thou-gentleman, Holy Joe, Fungus Folk, Cunning political sewer rat.

13. Poplar Bluff *Citizen*, June 25 and July 2, 1908.

14. Savannah *Reporter*, October 2 and 30, 1908.

15. Gallatin *North Missourian*, November 6 and 13, 1908.

16. Butler *Bates County Record*, August 1, 1908. This paper quoted the Butler *Times*: "The Folk papers over the state are greatly agitated because their patron-saint was not made the 'big-man' at the Denver convention. Mr. Folk wasn't recognized in that capacity because he lacked a whole lot of being the big man of the delegation."

17. Ironton *Register*, November 12, 1908.

18. Kansas City *Journal*, November 4, 1908.

19. Poplar Bluff *Citizen-Democrat*, November 5, 1908. Later, the paper added, "Never before in the history of the Republican party has harmony been more perfect in the ranks than this year."

20. Thomas Ralph Yancey, "The Election of 1912 in Missouri" (M.A. thesis, University of Missouri, 1937), and William T. Miller, "The Progressive Movement in Missouri" (M.A. thesis, University of Missouri, 1927), p. 182.

21. Kansas City *Times*, September 20, 1910.

22. Kansas City *Times*, July 3, 1912.

23. Yancey, *op. cit.*, pp. 178–79. Yancey quotes the *Republic* as

noting that Roosevelt once said, "I will eat the vitals out of the old Republican party and frame up the organization to suit myself in 1918."

24. *Ibid.*, p. 149.

25. St. Louis *Globe-Democrat*, October 20, 1912.

26. *Ibid.*, September 4 and 30, 1912. Also many items in the *Republic* and *Globe-Democrat* throughout June, 1912.

27. St. Louis *Globe-Democrat*, November 6, 1912.

28. Shoemaker, "History of the Missouri Press Association"; *Proceedings of the Missouri Press Association*, 1907.

29. *Ibid.*, 1908.

30. Williams, *Twenty Years of Education for Journalism*, pp. 163–65. *Proceedings of the Missouri Press Association*, 1910.

31. Williams, *op. cit.*, pp. 166–71. *Proceedings of the Missouri Press Association*, 1911–1912.

32. Letter from Mitchell White, May 18, 1962. Represented at the first meeting were the Cape Girardeau *Republican*, Mexico *Ledger*, Independence *Examiner*, Sedalia *Democrat*, Poplar Bluff *Republican*, Jefferson City *Democrat*, Marshall *Democrat-News*, and the Columbia *Missourian*. Three editors missed the gathering because of a train wreck at Wentzville. White added, "There's no question that the discussion of comparative practices and how to meet certain problems materially helped in maintaining the leading paper in the field in the top spot."

33. Williams, *op. cit.*, pp. 174–76.

34. *Proceedings of the Missouri Press Association*, 1915.

35. Williams, *op. cit.*, pp. 284–86. The first president was William H. Hamby, a fiction writer from Chillicothe. He worked on papers in Seymour, Marceline, and Meadville before turning to magazine work. He died in 1928. Each year the Guild awards a plaque to a journalism student who has shown the most improvement in his writing and a similar award to a Missouri writer for outstanding achievements.

36. *Proceedings of the Missouri Press Association*, 1916.

CHAPTER XVIII

1. John Clark Crighton, *Missouri and the World War, 1914–1917; A Study in Public Opinion* (Columbia: University of Missouri Studies, XXI, 3, 1947). This study, based on newspapers, has been extensively used in this chapter. More background material also from Jim Allee Hart, *A History of The* St. Louis Globe-Democrat; James W. Markham, *Bovard of the* Post-Dispatch (Baton Rouge: Louisiana State University Press, 1954); and Francis Floyd Shoemaker, "The *Kansas City Post;* Its Founding, Growth and Decline" (M.A. thesis, University of Missouri, 1958).

2. Crighton, *op. cit.*, pp. 5–21.

3. *Ibid.*, pp. 22–26. King served in the Union Army, and Crighton

says it was perhaps "natural for King to view the European conflict in terms of military strategy rather than of moral or philosophical issues."

4. St. Louis *Post-Dispatch*, August 10, 1914.

5. Crighton, *op. cit.*, pp. 22–26.

6. St. Louis *Globe-Democrat*, August 3, 1914.

7. Springfield *Leader*, August 11, 1914; the Kansas City *Star*, September 27, 1914, told of the Hermann incidents.

8. St. Louis *Republic*, August 9, 1914.

9. *Ibid.*, July 29, 1914.

10. *Globe-Democrat*, September 30, 1914.

11. Nevada *Post*, September 3, 1915.

12. See *Globe-Democrat*, *Star*, and *Westliche Post*, September 15, 1915.

13. *Globe-Democrat*, February 6, 1915; Joplin *News-Herald*, February 16, 1915.

14. *Republic*, February 9, 1915; *Post-Dispatch*, February 7, 1915.

15. Quoted from Crighton, *op. cit.*, pp. 76–78. He adds many other interesting comments on the views, but space limits quotations.

16. St. Joseph *News-Press*, September 3, 1914; June 5, 1915.

17. Kansas City *Star*, February 3, 1916.

18. Crighton, *op. cit.*, adds comments to show that the press "in the early months of the war offered additional reasons why immediate rearmament was uncalled for."

19. St. Louis *Republic*, February 3, 1917.

20. Warrensburg *Star-Journal*, February 6, 1917.

21. St. Louis *Republic*, April 6, 1917.

22. Crighton, *op. cit.*, p. 186.

23. St. Louis *Post-Dispatch*, October 29, 1916.

24. St. Louis *Globe-Democrat*, on September 17, 1916, said "Germany could not reach us and we could not reach Germany," thus it would be physically impossible to engage in a war.

25. Kansas City *Journal*, November 5, 1916.

26. St. Louis *Globe-Democrat*, October 24, 1916.

27. Crighton, *op. cit.*, p. 187, notes that his study "has suggested the possibility that the pacifism and isolationism of Missouri, and of the Middle West generally, have perhaps been overestimated. It has been shown that at the time of the first World War isolationism was distinctly a minority expression in Missouri. The greater part of its newspapers and of its people had a clear knowledge of world affairs and a strong determination to uphold the rights and defend the interests of the U. S. When war seemed unavoidable in April, 1917, there was no serious division of opinion. Missouri's reaction in the crisis was thoroughly American." Edwin D. Hunter, "Presidential Participation in Off-Year Elections: The Roosevelts, Wilson, and Taft" (M.A. thesis, University of Missouri, 1939), p. 91.

28. St. Louis *Globe-Democrat*, April 6–7, 1917.

29. St. Joseph *Gazette*, April 3, 1917.
30. St. Louis *Post-Dispatch*, April 6, 1917.
31. Mott, *American Journalism*, pp. 620–21, explains this.
32. Kansas City *Star*, December 18, 1917.
33. *Ibid.*, January 17, 1919.
34. St. Louis *Post-Dispatch*, December 18, 1917.
35. *Ibid.*, October 28, 1919.
36. Kansas City *Star*, January 24, 1917.
37. St. Louis *Post-Dispatch*, January 23, 1917.
38. Kansas City *Star*, January 9, 1919.
39. St. Louis *Post-Dispatch*, March 21, 1920.
40. Kansas City *Star*, March 20, 1920.
41. *Proceedings of the Missouri Press Association*, 1917.
42. *Ibid.*, 1918.

CHAPTER XIX

1. *Editor & Publisher*, May 26, 1923. This weekly magazine, that tells the story of the nation's press, has been widely used for the 1920–1960 period. It was not until 1933 that the Missouri Press Association started its *Missouri Press News*.

2. *Ibid.*, August 18, 1928. Communities included Aurora, Boonville, Brookfield, Butler, Cameron, Cape Girardeau, Carrollton, Chillicothe, Clinton, Excelsior Springs, Fulton, Hannibal, Kirksville, Lamar, Macon, Marshall, Maryville, Moberly, Monett, Neosho, Nevada, Poplar Bluff, Rich Hill, Trenton, Warrensburg, Washington, Webb City, and West Plains.

3. *Ibid.*, July 18, 1925.

4. E. W. Stephens, *History of the Missouri Press Association, 1867–1931*, is of value here. Also see Sara L. Williams' *Twenty Years of Education for Journalism* for the complete Journalism Week programs.

5. *Editor & Publisher*, May 27, 1922.

6. Williams met with a committee of Missouri teachers. In its constitution the MIPA was "To further the interests of preparatory school journalism in Missouri; to promote co-operation among the preparatory school editors, managers and faculty advisers in the exchange of ideas for improving their publications; to take advantage of the advice and helpful co-operation offered by the School of Journalism of the University of Missouri; and to stand for the highest standards of journalistic effort and achievement among preparatory school students."

7. *Editor & Publisher*, March 24, 1923, adds more about these men.

8. *Editor & Publisher*, May 26 and October 20, 1923.

9. Members came from an area defined as "those counties embraced in the Central Missouri State Teachers College District, plus Franklin, Gasconade, Warren, Osage, Howard, Boone, Callaway, and

Chariton." In 1940 the association deplored an attack on Mark Twain's Civil War military record. A resolution said, "Since the pen is mightier than the sword we have no doubt but that the kindly philosophy of Twain in time will supplant the bitterness of strife, but we feel that the talents of our national representatives can be turned to more constructive purposes than criticism of a distinguished American and Missouri's first man of letters."

10. *Editor & Publisher*, September 21, 1929.

11. *Ibid.*, November 9, 1929.

12. *Ibid.*, August 17, 1929.

13. Scattered issues of *Editor & Publisher* used here.

14. *Editor & Publisher*, April 22, 1922.

15. *Ibid.*, July 26, 1924.

16. *Ibid.*, September 27, 1924; April 4, 1925.

17. *Ibid.*, October 11, 1924.

18. *Ibid.*, October 18, 1924.

19. *Ibid.*, January 12, 1924.

20. Scattered issues used. *Star* comments, May 25, 1929.

21. *Ibid.*, June 2, 1923.

22. *Ibid.*, January 10, 1923.

23. *Ibid.*, February 17, 1923.

24. *Ibid.*, October 20, 1923.

25. *Ibid.*, August 2, 1924.

26. *Ibid.*, May 9, 1925.

27. *Ibid.*, April 7, 14, 1928.

28. *Ibid.*, March 23, 1929.

29. *Ibid.*, April 13, 1929.

30. Quoted in *Editor & Publisher*, January 10, 1925, as the lead story of the week.

31. *Post-Dispatch, Star*, March 4, 1921.

32. *Star*, November 12, 1921.

33. Both editorials appeared August 3, 1923.

34. *Editor & Publisher*, June 28, 1924.

35. *Post-Dispatch*, July 9, 1924.

36. Reprinted in *Editor & Publisher*, December 27, 1924, from clippings sent in by a reader in Ohio.

CHAPTER XX

1. *Editor & Publisher*, July 10, 1937. On July 9 this paper ran a banner head, "No News Today," with leadout stories, "Of Hospital or Armory. . . . Of Amelia, Sought by Air and by Sea. Of Rain, Though Corn Begins to Need It."

2. *Editor & Publisher*, January 18, 1930.

3. *Ibid.*, February 8, 1930.

4. *Ibid.*, the paper called "The Gutter the Limit."

5. *Ibid.*, June 7, 1930.

6. *Ibid.*, January 25, 1936.

7. *Ibid.*, February 15, 1930. One paper reported a gross of $38,499 in a town of 2,000, with more than $12,000 from job work.

8. *Missouri Press News*, October, 1933.

9. *Editor & Publisher*, August 12 and 26, 1933.

10. *Ibid.*, February 24, 1934.

11. *Ibid.*, June 1, 7, and 15, 1935.

12. *Ibid.*, June 1 and 22, 1935.

13. *Ibid.*, January 16, 1937.

14. *Ibid.*, January 15 and February 26, 1938.

15. *Ibid.*, February 7, 1931.

16. *Ibid.*, March 8, 1930; June 6, 1931.

17. *Ibid.*, July 26, 1930.

18. *Ibid.*, April 9, 1938.

19. *Ibid.*, January 13, 1934.

20. *Missouri Press News*, September, 1937.

21. *Editor & Publisher*, January 31, 1931.

22. *Missouri Press News*, July, 1935.

23. *Ibid.*, January, 1936.

24. *Editor & Publisher*, December 2, 1933. Gerald concluded, "There exists under heaven at this time no way or means by which to insure financial success and long life to the poor newspaper."

25. *Editor & Publisher*, February 8, 1936.

26. *Missouri Press News*, August, 1933.

27. *Ibid.*, January, 1936.

28. *Editor & Publisher*, August 15, 1931; September 26, 1931.

29. Among nationwide comments in *Editor & Publisher*, March 7, 1931.

30. *Ibid.*, August 10, 1935.

31. *Ibid.*, October 4, 1930.

32. *Ibid.*, June 15, 1935.

33. *Ibid.*, April 25, 1931.

34. *Ibid.*, February 13, 1932.

35. *Ibid.*, April 8, 1933.

36. *Ibid.*, August 3, 1935.

37. *Ibid.*, December 13, 1930.

38. *Ibid.*, April 22, 1933; *Missouri Press News*, October, 1933.

39. *Missouri Press News*, December, 1933.

40. *Ibid.*, February, 1934.

41. *Editor & Publisher*, May 19, 1934.

42. *Missouri Press News*, April, 1934.

43. *Editor & Publisher*, July 21, 1934.

44. *Missouri Press News*, September, 1935.

45. *Editor & Publisher*, May 4 and 11, 1935.

46. *Missouri Press News*, January, 1936.

47. *Ibid.*, May, 1936.

48. *Editor & Publisher*, May 15, 1937.

49. *Ibid.*, February 26, 1938.

50. *Ibid.*, January 15, 1938.

51. *Missouri Press News*, May, 1938; *Editor & Publisher*, May 14, 1938. Yet by mid-year the president of the Kansas City *Star*, George B. Longan, said, "There is a decidedly better feeling over the business outlook in this section."

52. *Missouri Press News*, December, 1938; *Editor & Publisher*, November 26, 1938.

53. *Editor & Publisher*, April 19, 1930.

54. Interesting data from Morran D. Harris, "Political Trends in Missouri." Harris uses the "granddaddy" idea. Also, see Lewis Ray Robertson, "Isolationism in Missouri Via the Press, 1929–1932" (M.A. thesis, University of Missouri, 1949). Many quotations from the city press are used.

55. *Editor & Publisher*, March 25, 1933. Also, Jean Carol Sweany, "Isolationism in Missouri, 1933–1935" (M.A. thesis, University of Missouri, 1949). This continues the Robertson study, with extensive use of newspapers.

56. *Editor & Publisher*, January 12, 1935.

57. *Ibid.*, October 3, 1936. Many Missouri papers were among the 7,000 small dailies and weeklies that accepted the Democratic clipsheets and cartoons and made liberal use of them.

58. *Ibid.*, August 20, 1938.

CHAPTER XXI

1. *Editor & Publisher*, April 27, 1940.

2. *Ibid.*, August 2, 1941. In early talks about lend-lease, the *Post-Dispatch* was rather skeptical of the British. When seven billion dollars were appropriated, the paper called it "a staggering sum, as Americans will be brought to realize more actually when they make out their income tax return next winter. And seven billion dollars is only the beginning" (March 21, 1941). Passage of the bill was "a foregone conclusion" to the Kansas City *Star*. On March 10 the editor said, "It was in accordance with American tradition that the opponents of the measure did not continue a hopeless filibuster but accepted the result in good spirit."

3. *Editor & Publisher*, December 13, 1941.

4. *Ibid.*, March 14 and 21, and May 2, 1942.

5. *Ibid.*, February 15, 1941.

6. *Ibid.*, May 3 and 10, 1941.

7. *Ibid.*, October 10, 1942.

8. *Missouri Press News*, January, 1942.

9. *Ibid.*, December, 1941.

10. *Ibid.*, April, 1943.

11. *Ibid.*, January, 1943.

12. *Ibid.*, March and July, 1940.

13. *Editor & Publisher*, May 19, 1940.

14. *Ibid.*, July 20, 1940.

15. *Ibid.*, November 15, 1941.

16. *Missouri Press News*, November, 1942.

17. *Ibid.*, August, 1943.

18. *Ibid.*, November, 1943.

19. *Ibid.*, April, 1944. During this convention nearly 90 women received Molly Pitcher awards for working on Missouri papers and replacing men who were in armed services. In June, 1945, the magazine told of the need for machine operators across the state.

20. *Ibid.*, November and December, 1945.

21. *Editor & Publisher*, December 1, 1945.

22. *Missouri Press News*, November, 1947, and March, 1948. More than 200 completed the work between 1945 and 1948.

23. *Ibid.*, October, 1948.

24. *Editor & Publisher*, September 27, 1941.

25. *Ibid.*, November 1, 1947.

26. *Ibid.*, June 2, 1945.

27. St. Louis *Post-Dispatch*, February 5, 1945.

28. *Editor & Publisher*, September 15 and October 6 and 20, 1945. Prices of St. Louis dailies went from 3 to 5 cents; Sundays stayed at 10 cents.

29. All editions of *Editor & Publisher*, 1940–1949, and *Missouri Press News*, 1940–1949, reviewed for this material.

30. *Editor & Publisher*, August 17, 1946.

31. *Ibid.*, October 26, 1940.

32. *Ibid.*, September 7–28, 1940. Senator Bennett Clark of Missouri thought lend-lease was a method of authorizing the President to declare war. The Kansas City *Journal*, March 8, 1941, ridiculed his "vain effort" to preserve the peace: "If Twentieth Century civilization cannot take effective steps toward a warless world then it must confess the triumph of depravity." In explaining "Why We Aid Britain," the St. Louis *Star-Times*, March 5, commented: "The isolationists think we can secede from the world. This 'great, strong and rich country,' they say, does not 'depend for its safety on some other nation.' Such an attitude betrays both the ignorance of world organization and the astonishing provincial vanity which are hallmarks of the insular mind."

33. *Editor & Publisher*, November 9 and 16, 1940.

34. *Ibid.*, May 31, 1941.

35. *Ibid.*, November 21, 1942.

36. *Ibid.*, January 8, 1944.

37. *Ibid.*, July 1, 22, 1944.

38. *Ibid.*, September 23 and 30, 1944.

39. *Ibid.*, April 21, 1945.

40. *Ibid.*, October 30 and December 25, 1948.

41. *Missouri Press News,* August, 1941.

42. *Editor & Publisher,* July 22, 1944.

43. *Ibid.*, January 31, 1948.

44. *Missouri Press News,* February, 1945.

45. *Ibid.*, December, 1948.

46. *Ibid.*, September, 1949.

CHAPTER XXII

1. *Editor & Publisher,* June 9, 1951; May 24, 1952. *Missouri Press News,* December, 1955.

2. *Editor & Publisher,* June 23, 1951; March 24, 1953.

3. *Editor & Publisher,* December 21, 1957.

4. *Ibid.*, April 18 and June 6 and 27, 1959. When the *Globe-Democrat* reappeared, the *Post-Dispatch* welcomed it, saying, "In our view the public is well served by having a choice between editorial personalities and advertising media."

5. *Ibid.*, February 9, 1952.

6. *Ibid.*, March 12, 1955, and many later issues.

7. *Missouri Press News,* February, 1950.

8. *Ibid.*, June, 1954.

9. *Ibid.*, October, 1956.

10. *Ibid.*, January, 1957.

11. *Ibid.*, April, 1958.

12. Reprinted in *Missouri Press News,* April, 1950.

13. *Ibid.*, July, 1950.

14. *Ibid.*, November, 1950.

15. *Ibid.*, February, 1952.

16. *Ibid.*, May, 1957.

17. *Ibid.*, June, 1959.

18. *Ibid.*, September, 1959.

19. *Missouri Press News,* issues of 1950–1959 reviewed for these data.

20. *Editor & Publisher,* January 12, 1952.

21. *Missouri Press News,* August, 1959.

22. *Ibid.*, August, 1959.

23. *Ibid.*, January and June, 1950.

24. *Ibid.*, December, 1950.

25. *Ibid.*, November, 1951; *Editor & Publisher,* November 10, 1951.

26. *Missouri Press News,* January, 1953.

27. *Ibid.*, April and November, 1953.

28. *Ibid.*, February, 1954.

29. *Ibid.*, April, 1954.

30. *Ibid.*, August, 1955.

31. *Ibid.*, November, 1955; April, 1956.

32. *Ibid.*, October, 1956.

33. *Ibid.*, June, 1957.

34. *Ibid.*, November, 1957.

35. *Ibid.*

36. *Editor & Publisher*, February 22, 1958.

37. *Ibid.*, September 6 and 20, 1958; March 7, 1959.

38. *Ibid.*, December 20, 1958; *Missouri Press News*, August, 1958.

39. *Missouri Press News*, September, 1956, notes both cases.

40. *Ibid.*, March, 1959.

41. *Ibid.*, March and December, 1959.

42. *Ibid.*, December, 1959.

43. *Editor & Publisher*, February 18, 1950.

44. *Ibid.*, May 12, 1951. Statement was by John Cowles of the Minneapolis *Star* and *Tribune*.

45. *Editor & Publisher*, September 29, 1951.

46. *Ibid.*, November 1, 1952. The *Post-Dispatch* sent its own photographers to Washington, and within twenty-six hours after the transparencies were turned over to the rotogravure plant it published full-color pictures of Eisenhower's inauguration.

47. *Editor & Publisher*, January 2, 1954.

48. *Ibid.*, July 7, 1956.

49. *Ibid.*, August 18 and 25, 1956.

50. *Ibid.*, November 3, 1956.

51. John T. Kinnier, "The Publishers of Weekly Newspapers in Missouri" (M.A. thesis, University of Missouri, 1951).

52. Harry W. Stonecipher, "A Study of Editorials and Personal Columns in Missouri Weekly Newspapers" (M.A. thesis, University of Missouri, 1955), pp. 15–16, 23.

53. *Missouri Press News*, March, 1956. Also see George A. Westland, "A Study of Combined Operations of Missouri Weekly Newspapers" (M.A. thesis, University of Missouri, 1957).

54. *Missouri Press News*, July, 1958.

55. *Ibid.*, January, 1959.

56. *Ibid.*, August, 1959.

57. *Editor & Publisher*, April 18, 1953.

58. *Missouri Press News*, July, 1958, from a talk given by Dean Mott at a Kappa Tau Alpha program.

CHAPTER XXIII

1. *Missouri Newspaper Director*, published annually by the Missouri Press Service, Columbia, Missouri; *Missouri Press News*, January, 1963.

2. Preston Clark, "Missouri Newspapers and the Offset Trend,"

School of Journalism research project, May, 1962.

3. *Missouri Press News*, April, 1962.

4. *Editor & Publisher*, January 20, 1962.

5. *Missouri Press News*, January, 1960.

6. Clark, *op. cit.*, pp. 16–17. Letter from William C. Tucker, May 2, 1962.

7. Hayti *Missouri Herald*, January 7 and 21, 1944.

8. *Missouri Press News*, October, 1946.

9. *Ibid.*, October, 1961.

10. *Ibid.*, January, 1960.

11. *Ibid.*, May, 1960.

12. *Editor & Publisher*, January 7, 1961.

13. *Ibid.*, February 4, 1961.

14. *Ibid.*, November 5, 1960. The *Post-Dispatch* backed Kennedy. Since 1916 this paper has supported Democrats nine times, Republicans two (Landon and Dewey), and neither party in 1932.

15. *Missouri Press News*, October, 1960.

16. *Ibid.*, March, 1960.

17. *Ibid.*, April, 1961.

18. *Ibid.*, March, 1960.

19. *Ibid.*, January, 1960.

20. *Ibid.*, April, 1961.

21. *Ibid.*, August, 1961; *Editor & Publisher*, July 29, 1961.

22. *Missouri Press News*, January, 1962.

23. *Ibid.*, January and April, 1962.

24. *Ibid.*, July, 1963.

25. *Ibid.*, June and August, 1962.

26. *Editor & Publisher*, January 21 and July 8, 1961.

BIBLIOGRAPHICAL NOTE

IN VIEW of the exhaustive footnotes used in this book, it was thought wise not to add more bibliographical coverage. *Missouri Newspapers* is primarily a study of the papers themselves, with additional material from books, magazine articles, and theses. A study of these will provide the student with additional source materials. Masters' and doctoral theses, especially, contain extensive bibliographical listings in addition to the newspapers used. Too, the index to articles in the *Missouri Historical Review* provides the researcher with an endless source of material. The several histories of Missouri provide topics for additional probing into events in this state.

Still, the history of the Missouri press has been written in the Missouri newspapers. To them the historian should go for his source material.

INDEX

Abeel, A. K., 75
Abeel, D. K., 67
Adams, John Q., 13, 16, 17, 19, 29, 31
Adrian *Journal,* 299, 334
Advertisements, 9, 17, 38, 51, 68, 94-95, 99, 100-101, 120, 122-23, 129, 172, 202, 207, 215, 248, 255-57, 263, 267-69, 300, 309-10, 322
Agriculture, 41, 182, 234
Ake, Eli D., 341
Ake, Eli P., 341
Ake, Frank P., 341
Albany *Capital,* 249, 298
Albany *Ledger,* 144, 334, 352
Albright, J. W., 36-37
Alexander, J. P., 116
Alexander, Walter B., 14
Alexander, Willis, 349
Alexandria *Delta,* 76
Alldredge, William C., 149
Allen, Albert O., Jr., 344
Allen, Aldin W., 328
Allen, Jacob D., 180
Altamont *Times,* 299, 334
Alton, Illinois, *Observer,* 34
Alton *South Missourian-Democrat,* 334
Amberg, Richard, 347
American Journalist, 153
American Newspaper Guild, 262, 264, 265, 293, 301
American Newspaper Publishers Association, 251, 266, 332
American party, 55, 76
American Society of Newspaper Editors, 273, 297, 298
Anderson, C. P., 75, 81, 82
Anderson, E. H., 344
Anderson, Paul Y., 239
Anderson *News-Review,* 334
Andrews, Charles W., Jr., 334
Angevine, J., 34
Anti-Monopoly party, 147
Anti-thief associations, 104
Appler, J. M., 74
Appleton City *Journal,* 186, 328
Argonne National Laboratory, 313
Arkansas Press Association, 162
Armfield, Richard L., 341
Ashcraft, James Lee, 140, 149
Ash Grove *Commonwealth,* 334
Ashland *Bugle,* 215, 306

Ashley, William H., 40
Associated Press, 206, 241, 264, 272, 296, 309
Associated Press Wire Editors Association, 309
Atchison, David R., 44, 46, 56
Atkeson, William O., 149
Atlanta *Express,* 334
Aull, Arthur, 342
Aurora *Advertiser,* 294, 299, 334
Austin, Moses, 28
Auxvasse *Review,* 299, 332
Ava *Douglas County Herald,* 156, 334, 352
Ayer, Directories, 119, 121, 139, 286, 359-60

Bacon, Dennis, 348
Baker, Eula, 54
Baker, Sam A., 250, 260
Baker, William, 34
Bald Knobbers, 147
Ballard, John E., 340
Ballinger-Pinchot Dispute, 224
Balthis, W. H., 181
Bank of Missouri, 28, 104
Bank of St. Louis, 28
Banks, 51, 230
Barbe, Orrin, 344
Barrett, J. W. (ed.), 123-25, 132, 154, 180-81, 195, 209, 354
Barrett, J. W. (official), 247, 252, 281
Bartels, Charles R., 347
Bartels, Joseph R., 347
Barton, David, 17, 26-27, 30
Bates, John M., 59
Baxter, C. D., 149
Bay Collection, 200
Baze, Dryden, 343
Beal, William H., 327
Beale, A. W., 122
Bean, Edward E., 160
Beissenherz, Lloyd, 337
Bell, John, 58, 63, 72
Bell, Ovid, 306, 355
Bell, Wilson, 346
Belle *Banner,* 334
Belton *Star-Herald,* 324, 327, 334
Bennett, J. Irvin, 327
Bennett, Julia M., 135
Bent, Silas, 214
Bentley, Charles E., 150

Benton, Thomas Hart, 10, 13, 14, 16, 22, 24-25, 27, 29, 32, 34, 44, 47, 49, 53, 56; (artist), 200
Benton *Scott County Democrat,* 334
Bethany *Broadaxe,* 190
Bethany *Harrison County Times,* 295, 352
Bethany *Republican-Clipper,* 307, 319, 335, 352
Bidwell, John, 148
Biggerstaff, John A., 345
Bingham, George Caleb, 69, 200
Birch, James H., 33, 122
Bismarck *Gazette,* 335
Bittenger, John L., 123
Bixby, Edson K., 298
Bixby, Joel, 298
Black, Allen, 343
Black, W. A., 342
Blaine, James G., 144
Blair, C. Cowgill, 296, 341, 358
Blair, Francis P., Jr., 59, 61, 65, 74, 79, 86, 104
Blair, James, Jr., 318
Blair, Milo, 132, 133, 181, 209, 354
Blakey, A. G., 180
Bland, Richard P., 118, 149
Bland *Courier,* 334
Blanket sheets, 69, 93
Blanton, Benjamin F., 157, 181
Blanton, Charles L., 273, 299, 348
Blanton, Charles L., Jr., 273, 320, 334, 348, 356
Blanton, C. V., 348
Blanton, David Edgar, 345
Blanton, Edgar, 325, 343, 348
Blanton, H. J., 244-45, 249, 303-4, 306, 355, 357
Bledsoe, William H., 342
Bless, B. J., Jr., 351
Bless, Mrs. B. J., Jr., 278
Bless, Charles A., 351
Block, Lillian, 315
Bloom, Gerald D., 334, 342
Bloomfield *Vindicator,* 120, 144, 335
Blue Ribbon Papers, 310, 352-53
Blue Springs *Jackson County Democrat,* 324, 335, 352
Blue Springs *Leader,* 324, 335
Bodine, Tom V., 256, 274
Boggs, Lilburn W., 40
Bogie, Thomas D., 159, 181
Boiler plates; *see* Patent insides
Bolivar *Free Press,* 106, 107, 119, 335
Bolivar *Herald,* 335

Bonfils, Fred G., 231, 273
Bonne Terre *Register,* 335
Bonne Terre *Star,* 163
Boonville *Advertiser,* 115, 131, 151, 153, 186, 193, 250, 324, 335
Boonville *Coon Hunter,* 42
Boonville *Cooper County Record,* 330, 335
Boonville *Democrat,* 150
Boonville *Eagle,* 106, 132, 133, 181, 209
Boonville *Herald,* 37
Boonville *News,* 136, 324, 335
Boonville *Observer,* 55, 62, 98
Boonville *Topic,* 193
Booth, Harry E., 299
Boston *Independent Chronicle,* 15
Bouchard, W. L., 339, 355
Boundary disputes; *see* Civil War
Bourbon *Beacon,* 351
Bovard, O. K., 267, 299
Bowen, Elbert R., 95-96
Bowles, Robert, 156
Bowlin, James B., 34, 36
Bowling, Robert A., 344
Bowling Green *Salt River Journal,* 37
Bowling Green *Times,* 306, 335
Bowman, Louis, 158, 347, 356, 357
Bradley, David R., 347
Bradley, H. D., 291, 347
Brandt, Raymond P., 316, 357
Branson *Beacon,* 324, 335
Branson *White River Leader,* 335
Bray, William, 308-13, 315, 329-30, 344
Braymer *Bee,* 283, 306, 335
Breckinridge, John C., 60-63
Breckenridge *Bulletin,* 144, 335
Bredehoeft, John J., Jr., 337
Breuer, W. L., 342
Bricken, R. W., 350
Briggs, Frank P., 274, 289, 300, 329, 343, 358
Brill, Glenn M., 273
Brill, Larry A., 272
Brill, Walter J., 272
Brisbane, Arthur, 228
Bronson, Ken, 345
Brookfield *Daily Argus,* 160, 276
Brookfield *Gazette,* 109-10, 113, 117, 154, 183
Brookfield *News-Bulletin,* 324, 335
Brooks, John A., 143
Brooks, S. S., 34

Brown, B. Gratz, 57, 65-66, 85, 107-12, 135
Brown, Dwight H., 249, 254, 274, 355
Brown, John, 52-53, 68
Brown, J. W., Jr., 331, 334, 340, 356
Brown, Luman A., 119
Brown, Robert, 22
Brown, Robert U., 311
Browning *Leader-Record,* 335
Brownlee, Richard S., 52, 199-201
Brunswick *Brunswicker,* 95, 118, 154, 181, 187, 190, 195, 335, 352
Bryan, William J., 150, 163, 181, 218, 220, 225, 228
Bryan, W. S., 131
Bryson, I. N., 181
Buchanan, James, 62
Buckner *Fort Osage News,* 324, 344
Buffalo *Dallas County Republican,* 335
Buffalo *Reflex,* 328, 335, 352
Bumbarger, John V., 306, 343
Bumbarger, W. M., 157
Burchartt, H. T., 181
Burgess, Charles H., 351
Burlington Junction *Post-News,* 335
Burnett, Peter H., 38
Burrowes, A. V., 273, 300, 314, 332
Burrowes, Lon M., 273, 300, 314, 332
Burton, P. E., 249
Bush, Howard L., 344
Butler, Asa W., 249, 298, 355
Butler, Benjamin F., 143
Butler *Bates County Democrat,* 335, 352
Butler *Bates County Herald,* 115
Butler *Bates County Record,* 108, 146, 223
Butler *Times,* 180, 188
Butler *Weekly Union,* 149
Butternuts, 83
Butts, George, 343

Cabool *Enterprise,* 292, 336
Cain, Cullen, 273
Cain, Forrest, 273
Cainsville *News,* 53, 336
Caldwell, Mrs. Dorothy, 201
Caldwell, F. M., 98
Calhoun, John C., 15, 74
California *Democrat,* 108, 110, 112, 306, 308, 326, 336, 352
California *Moniteau County Herald,* 336

California *News,* 64, 69, 73, 75, 81, 83, 97
California *Newspaper,* 145, 146, 149
Camdenton *Central Missouri Leader,* 324, 336
Camdenton *Reveille,* 324, 336
Cameron, Ewen, 182
Cameron *News-Observer,* 336
Cameron *Sun,* 336
Camp Jackson, 79-82
Campaign papers, 41
Campbell, Brewster P., 283
Campbell, James A., 339
Campbell *Citizen,* 336
Cannon, Clarence, 317
Cannon, Joseph, 224
Canton *Press,* 84, 88, 99, 101, 111, 123, 132, 181, 337
Canton *Press-News and Record,* 308, 337, 352
Cape Girardeau *Argus,* 123
Cape Girardeau *Creole,* 34
Cape Girardeau *Eagle,* 74
Cape Girardeau *Farmer,* 34
Cape Girardeau *Missouri Democrat,* 34
Cape Girardeau *News,* 292
Cape Girardeau *Patriot,* 38
Cape Girardeau *Press,* 205
Cape Girardeau *Republican,* 228
Cape Girardeau *Southeast Missourian,* 250, 306, 336, 357
Cape Girardeau *Southeast Weekly Bulletin,* 336
Cape Girardeau *Southern Advocate and State Journal,* 22
Cape Girardeau *Southern Gazette,* 34
Cape Girardeau *State Gazette,* 34
Carey, Matthew, 3
Carl Junction *Standard,* 307, 336
Carlton, Mrs. Bessie, 341
Carlton, Norman, 334, 345
Carondolet *News,* 208
Carroll, Boyd, 357
Carroll, M. V., 149
Carrollton *Democrat,* 62, 75, 133, 162, 187, 196, 276, 299, 336, 357
Carrollton *Journal,* 133
Carrollton *Record,* 131, 192
Carrollton *Republican-Record,* 245, 336
Carrollton *Wakanda Record,* 108, 111-12, 135, 153
Carter, Floella, 114

Carter, L. L., 336
Carthage *Banner*, 109, 112, 137
Carthage *Democrat*, 249, 250, 276, 286
Carthage *Press*, 108, 110, 236, 276, 297, 304, 306-7, 315, 331, 336, 357
Caruthers, E. P., 163, 182, 342, 354
Caruthersville *Democrat-Argus*, 336, 352
Caruthersville *Journal*, 324, 336
Caruthersville *Republican*, 336
Case, Theodore S., 67
Cassville *Democrat*, 336, 352
Cassville *Republican*, 307, 324, 328, 336
Catledge, Turner, 311
Caulfield, Henry S., 260
Caywood, A. J., 299
Center *Herald*, 336
Central Missouri Press Association, 250
Centralia *Courier*, 189, 215, 221, 228
Centralia *Fireside Guard*, 194, 327, 336, 352
Chaffee *Signal*, 337
Chambers, Adam B., 37
Chaplin, Robert L., 309
Charcoals, 83, 85
Charless, Edward, 10
Charless, Joseph, 1-16, 25-26
Charleston *Democrat*, 337
Charleston *Enterprise*, 205
Charleston *Enterprise-Courier*, 337, 352
Charleston *News*, 205
Cheesman, Earl F., 336
Chesley, Leland L., 286, 349
Chew, Phil, 149
Chicago *News*, 254
Chicago *Republican*, 174
Chicago *Sun*, 296
Chicago *Tribune*, 296
Chilcote, Merrill, 304
Child, Jacob T., 135-37, 182, 354
Childers, E. R., 245
Childers, H. F., 157, 227, 251, 355, 357
Chillicothe *Chronicle*, 183
Chillicothe *Constitution*, 76, 236
Chillicothe *Constitution-Tribune*, 258, 268, 276, 298, 308, 337, 357
Chillicothe *Crisis*, 149
Chillicothe *Missouri World*, 149
Chillicothe *Spectator*, 123

Chilton, O. W., 336
Chilton, Thomas L., 338, 342
Choate, George, 349
Chubbock, Levi, 158
Churchill, Samuel B., 37
Churchill, Winston, 298
Cincinnati *Commercial*, 174
Cincinnati *Enquirer*, 174
Cincinnati *Gazette*, 174
Circulation, 94, 205, 253, 269-70, 281, 283, 301, 322
Circus in Missouri, 95-96
Civil War, 70-92
Clarence *Courier*, 337
Clark, Carrie Rogers, 250, 349
Clark, Champ, 136, 225, 228
Clark, Preston P., Jr., 322, 324
Clark, T. J., 336, 356
Clark, William P., 37
Clarksville *Sentinel*, 131
Clarkton *News*, 306, 327, 337
Clay, Henry, 29, 31, 32, 46
Claybanks, 83, 85
Clayton, Charles C., 357
Clayton, Ken, 346
Clayton, Robert H., 335
Clayton *Argus*, 164
Clayton *St. Louis Countian*, 324, 337
Clayton *Watchman-Advocate*, 306, 337, 352
Clearmont *News*, 337, 338
Clemens, Orion, 200
Clemens, Samuel; *see* Twain, Mark
Clements, John T., 19, 126
Cleveland, Grover, 19, 143-48
Cleveland *Press*, 311
Clevenger, Homer, 145
Clifton Hill *Rustler*, 337
Clinics, workshops; *see* Missouri Press Association
Clinton *Democrat*, 192, 276, 302, 337
Clinton *Eye*, 337, 344, 352
Clinton *Henry County Democrat*, 115, 337
Cloud, F. B., 346
Cloud, Tilghman R., 299, 346
Cockerill, John A., 169
Cockrell, Francis M., 114, 116, 221
Coghlan, Phillip E., 251
Colburn, R. I., 343, 345
Cole, Robert E., Jr., 342
Cole Camp *Courier*, 337
College of Agriculture, 128, 146
Collison, T. Hall, 341

Colman, Norman J., and his *Rural World*, 113, 125-26, 182
Color printing, 323
Colt, John W., 358
Columbia *Dollar Journal*, 55
Columbia *Herald*, 111, 138, 140, 159, 165, 191, 193, 196, 206, 215, 221, 222, 253, 338, 357
Columbia *Missouri Intelligencer*, 20
Columbia *Missouri Sentinel*, 55
Columbia *Missouri Statesman*, 43, 46, 48, 54-55, 69, 70-74, 81-83, 91, 94-97, 100-101, 108, 110, 112, 118, 122, 128, 130, 191-92, 215
Columbia *Missourian*, 201, 258, 291-92, 310, 314, 316, 329, 337
Columbia *Patriot*, 39, 191
Columbia *Standard*, 76
Columbia *Tribune*, 214-15, 235-36, 294, 337
Comann, Martin L., 299
Compromise of 1850, 55
Concordia *Concordian*, 337
Conger, E. J., 183
Conniff, Frank, 311
Conservatives, parties, 105
Consolidations; *see* Expansion
Constitutional conventions, 43, **104**
Cook, Charles D., 38
Cook, Samuel Baker, 155, 183, **221**
Coolidge, Calvin, 260
Cooper, John T., 327
Cooper, Peter, 116
Copperheads, 83, 87; press, 71
Corbin, Abel R., 34, 39, 98
Corder *Journal*, 340
Country correspondents, 205, 249
Country Editor, 152, 202, 207
Cowherd, William S., 223
Cowles, John, 316
Cox, James M., 247, 258
Cox, John Henry, 346
Coxey's Army, 148
Coy, Edgar E., 339
Crandall, Warren D., 154, 183, **354**
Crane *Chronicle*, 337, 352
Crank, Gordon, 338
Crawford, Jack P., 336, 342
Crawford, Marvin, 306, 336
Crawford *Mirror*, 191
Creighton, James, 140
Creighton *Banner*, 337
Creighton *News*, 205
Crighton, John Clark, 230-31, 237

Crittenden, Thomas T., 119, 140
Crocker *News*, 327
Cross, Howard L., 311
Cross, Russell L., 341
Crossley, Wallace, 275, 298, 350, 355, 357
Crossman, R. B., 164
Crouch, Ben G., 307, 335
Croy, Homer, 347
Crystal City *Jefferson County Press-Times*, 337, 352
Cuba *Times*, 337
Cummins, James C., 10
Curry, J. E., 334
Cutler, H. D. B., 124

Daily, first, 36-37
Dale, E. L., 201, 307, 315, 331, 336, 356, 357
Dalton, John M., 329, 332
Daniel, E. Clifton, 313
Daniels family, 338
Danville *Star*, 123, 183
Darnes, W. P., 35
Daugherty, L. E., 337
David, William H., 36
Davis, Andrew Jackson, 34-35
Davis, Glenn E., 320
Davis, Greer W., 21
Davis, Jefferson, 79, 108
Davis, John W., 260
Davis, Lane E., 341
Davis, Oliver B., 343
Davis, Dr. Patrick H., 22
Davis, Van W., 337, 341
Dawson, Ralph, Jr., 310
Dearborn *Democrat*, 337
Debs, Eugene V., 239
Dee, Robert L., 340
Deiter, Charles T., 351
Delinquents; *see* subscribers
Democratic Editors of Missouri, 160
Democratic Press Association, 160
De Motte, Mark L., 132-33
Denman, Clinton H., 138, 244, 327, 338, 355, 358
Denman, Harry E., 250, 305, 338, 355
Denman, Harry L., 339
Denman, Mark F., Sr., 327, 339, 356
Denver *Cherry Creek Pioneer*, 36
Denver *Post*, 231, 290
Depression, 262-81
Derby, G. R., 327
Derrickson, G. E., 342

DeSoto *Gazette*, 211
DeSoto *Jefferson Republic*, 324, 338, 352, 358
DeSoto *Press*, 324, 338, 358
Dewey, Thomas, 297-98
Dexter *Messenger*, 185, 338
Dexter *Statesman*, 270, 338
Diamond *Newton County News*, 324, 328, 338
Dickey, W. B., 254
Dickey, W. L., 257, 280
Dickgrafe, C. W., 337, 344
Dillon, John A., 137, 169
Dimmitt, L. L., 337
Dixon, Paul J., 149
Dixon *Pulaski County Pilot-News*, 338
Doane, Noble T., 67, 122, 123
Dobyns, D. P., 248
Dockery, Alexander M., 166, 220
Dodge, Thomas R., 183
Doherty, Henry L., 271
Donan, Pat, 126, 131, 161, 188
Doniphan, A. W., 44, 56
Doniphan *Prospect-News*, 326, 327, 338
Donnell, Forrest C., 296
Donnelly, Phil M., 317
Donze, Elmer L., 345
"Dorothy Dix," 228
Dorsey family, 336
Douglas, Stephen A., 56, 58, 60-64, 72, 78
Dowell, John E., 299
Downing *News*, 338
Drake, Charles D., 85-87
Drake's Constitution, 89-90, 343
Draper, Daniel M., 183
Dreiser, Theodore, 175
Drexel *Star*, 338
Duels, 29, 161
Dummit, Ralph, 351
Duncan, W. K., 344
Dunnica, William, 32
Dutton, W. R., 250
Dye, Bill, 342
Dyer, David P., 119

East Prairie *Eagle*, 338
Eastin, Lucian J., 38, 44-45, 98, 130, 132-33, 183, 354
Eaton, B. D. M., 124
Ebert, W. C., 125
Eck, Don, 342
Edina *Herald*, 75

Edina *Knox County Democrat*, 111
Edina *Rebel and Copperhead Ventilator*, 75
Edina *Sentinel*, 108, 110, 305, 326, 338
Editor & Publisher, 247-48, 250-51, 254-55, 260, 263-66, 269-70, 272, 274, 278, 280, 285, 289-90, 299, 303, 311, 317, 320, 328, 332
Editorial Association of Missouri; *see* Missouri Press Association
Editors' and Publishers' Association; *see* Missouri Press Association
Editors' Week; *see* Journalism Week
Edmonson, Robert A., 339
Edom, Cliff C., 290, 309
Educational, 27, 40, 145
Edwards, John N., 129, 161
Edwardsville, Illinois, *Spectator*, 21
Eighth Congressional District Editorial Association, 217
Eisenhower, Dwight, 314, 317-18
Eldon *Advertiser*, 325, 338, 352
Eldon *Miller County Autogram*, 325
El Dorado Springs *Sun*, 305, 338
Ellinghouse, Charles L., 338
Ellinghouse, Frank B., 328
Ellington *Courier Press*, 338
Ellis, Edmund J., 76
Ellis, Elmer, 198-99
Ellis, Howard, 164, 183, 198, 354
Ellis, R. A., 336
Elmo *Register*, 338
Elsberry *Democrat*, 338
Emancipation Proclamation, 85
Eminence *Current Wave*, 324, 326, 332, 338, 351
English, Earl F., 302, 311, 313
English, Thomas B., 22
Ennis, Wayne, 328, 336
Erdelen, Al F., 339
Erickson, Carl, 335
Ernst, Frank, 347
Ernst, Joseph A., 347
Ernst, Katherine, 347
Essen family, 337
Evans, A. N., 184
Evans, Henry, 339
Everett, Edward, 58
Ewing, Collins, 288
Ewing, Henry W., 161, 184, 212, 354
Ewing, Robert C., 56
Excelsior Springs *Standard*, 338
Expansion, sales, 253-55, 270-72, 307-9, 325-27

Facsimile, 264, 296, 307
Fairfax *Forum*, 327, 338, 352
Fairmount *Inter-City News*, 352
Fairmount *Inter-City Press*, 352
Falkenburg, M. C., 184
Faris, Adalyn, 248
Farmer, Frank W., 349
Farmers' Alliance, 146
Farmers' and Laborers' Union, 148
Farmington *News*, 250, 305, 327, 339, 352
Farmington *Press*, 324, 339, 352
Farmington *Times*, 136
Farrar, Dr. B. G., 8
Farrell, Leon A., 335
Farris, Barry, 347
Farris, Herman P., 150
Fayette Academy, 19
Fayette *Advertiser*, 306, 339, 352
Fayette *Boon's Lick Democrat*, 37, 40
Fayette *Boon's Lick Times*, 33, 49
Fayette *Democrat Leader*, 252, 306, 339, 352
Fayette Hickory Club, 41
Fayette *Leader*, 188
Fayette *Missouri Intelligencer*, 19-20
Fayette *Missouri Monitor*, 33
Fayette *Western Monitor*, 33
Federal printing, 8, 16
Ferguson, Oliver B., 304, 339
Ferguson, O. J., 306, 355
Ferguson, Phil G., 34, 128, 137
Ferguson, S. A., 339
Ferguson *Town Talk*, 352
Festus *News-Democrat*, 339, 352
Fidler, J. M., 324, 347
Field, Eugene, 132-34, 172, 184, 189, 200, 347
Field, Marshall, 296
Fike, Stanley R., 342, 356
Filley, Chauncey I., 145, 150
Finkelnburg, Gustavus A., 116
Finn, Bernard, 347
Fish, Clinton B., 146
Fishback, Burney L., 336, 345
Fisher, E. L., 342
Fisher, John F., 344
Fisher, J. Porter, 344
Fisher, Paul, 290
Fisher, Mrs. Susie, 136
Fisher, Theo. D., 130
Fitzpatrick, Daniel R., 200, 241-42, 267, 292, 358

Flat River *Lead Belt News*, 292, 339, 352
Flat River *St. Francois County Journal*, 326-27, 339
Fletcher, Thomas C., 88
Flexsenhar, George, 346
Florissant *Valley Reporter*, 323-24, 339, 352
Flory, Joseph, 220
Flynn, Joseph, 211
Folk, Joseph W., 220-23, 225
Ford, Nicholas, 143
Ford, Patrick H., 14-15
Fordland *Journal*, 147
Foreman, Stephen W., 32-33
Forsythe, David, 343
Forsythe, James F., 338, 343
Forsythe *Taney County Republican*, 274-75, 320, 339, 357
Fort Sumter, 77-78
Fort Wayne, Indiana, *Sentinel*, 172
Fort Wood *Sentinel*, 347
Foster, C. G., 123
Foster, Emory S., 161
Foster, M. C., 349
Fox, James W., 351
Francis, David R., 146, 221
Franklin, Benjamin, 5
Franklin, Ira R., 328
Franklin *Missouri Intelligencer*, 16-23, 25, 33, 201
Fredericktown *Bee*, 182
Fredericktown *Conservative*, 182
Fredericktown *Democrat-News*, 304, 306, 308, 339, 352
Fredrick, Leon, 339
Free Soil party, 53, 56
Freedom of Information Center, 314, 330
Freedom of Press stamp, 314
Freeland, Maude, 339
Freeland, W. E., 320, 335, 339, 355, 357
Freeman, Bonham E., 306, 335
Freeman, B. Wayne, 335, 345, 349
Frémont, John C., 74, 86-87
French, William Aden, 332, 338
Friar, Kenneth, 343
Frost, D. M., 79-80
Frost, Lily, 248
Fry, Lewis C., 150
Frye, Fred W., 343
Fugel, John, 350
Fuller, W. Clyde, 249

Fulton *Callaway Gazette,* 119
Fulton *Missouri Telegraph,* 73
Fulton *Sun, Sun-Gazette,* 166, 189, 258, 339
Fulton *Telegraph,* 55, 73
Fulton *Vox Populi,* 50

Gainesville *Ozark County Times,* 326, 339
Galena *Stone County News-Oracle,* 291, 337
Galena *Stone County Republican,* 323-24, 339
Galena *Table Rock Times,* 339
Gallagher, Norman B., 334
Gallatin *Democrat,* 163, 190, 222-23, 339
Gallatin *North Missourian,* 223, 273, 311, 339, 352
Galt *Tribune,* 350
Gamble, Hamilton R., 83-84, 86
Gansz, Philip, 167, 226, 355
Garden City *Views,* 339
Gardner, Frederick D., 239
Garfield, James A., 119-20
Garrett, Thomas E., 125, 135
Garten, Meredith, 345, 356
Garvin, A. E., 327, 346
General Emancipation Society, 75
Gentry, William, 114
George, Henry, 146
Gerald, J. Edward, 269
Gerald *Journal,* 339
Gerig, Carroll B., 339
Gerig, Noah A., 327, 339
German-American Press Association, 231
Gibson, George W., 67
Gideon *News,* 327, 337
Gierke, Victor, 312, 343, 344, 356
Gilbert, S. A., 134
Gilgour, John H., 335
Gilman City *Tribune,* 306
Gilmer, Irving, 342
Gilpin, William, 34-35, 32
Gilzean-Reid, Hugh, 166
Gladstone *Dispatch,* 322, 344
Gladstone *News,* 352
Glasgow *Missourian,* 190, 289, 306, 331, 339, 352
Glasgow *Pilot,* 183
Glasgow *Weekly Times,* 73, 78
Glass, Frank P., 254
Glenwood *Criterion,* 115

Goforth, Harold, 346
Goforth, Ralph W., 338, 346
Golden City *Herald,* 340
Golden City *News,* 340
Goodwin, J. West, 124, 157, 184, 227, 354
Gorin *Argus,* 340
Goshorn, Robert C., 306, 341, 355
Goudy, Frederic W., 288, 290
Gould, Paul M., 330, 342
Government-in-exile, Civil War, 82-92
Gower *Enterprise,* 327
Grady, A. V., 338
Grady, Dorothy V., 337-38
Graf, Alfred, 307
Graf, Jacob, 184, 340
Graham, J. R., 177
Grandview *Jackson County Advocate,* 323, 340, 352
Grangers, 103, 107, 113-15, 147, 237
Grant, U. S., 107-12, 153
Grant City *Star,* 185
Grant City *Times-Tribune,* 340, 352
Grant City *Worth County Times,* 119
Gravely, Joseph W., 335
Gravely, Marshall, 335
Gray, Omar D., 155, 159, 164-65, 185, 221, 227, 273, 349, 355
Greeley, Horace, 57-59, 107-12, 136, 169, 273, 280
Green, Duff, 15, 31, 33
Green City *Press,* 254, 328, 340
Greenback party, 115-21, 145, 147, 149
Greenfield *Advertiser,* 340
Greenfield *Vedette and Advocate,* 324, 340
Greenlee, Frank, 341
Greenlee, J. L., 341
Green Ridge *Local News,* 340
Greentop *Reporter,* 338
Greenville *Sun,* 328, 338
Griffith family, 340
Grimes, P. T., 327
Grosse, Oliver H., 327
Groves, Hiram J., 150, 185, 354
Groves, H. S., 162
Gunn, Calvin, 31-32
Gunn, Robert C., 334
Guth, Harry, Sr., 331, 345, 356

Hadden, Earl F., 328
Hadley, Herbert S., 223, 225-26

Hains, R. K., 273
Hains, R. N., 273, 343
Hale *Leader,* 340
Halftones, 160-61, 173
Hall, Andy, 344
Hall, Billy K., 342
Hall, Sergeant, 13
Hall, Willard P., 83
Hallsville *Herald,* 183
Hallsville *News,* 215
Hambaugh, W. H., 338
Hamilton, Alexander, 147
Hamilton, Frederick A., 20
Hamilton, J. M., 123
Hamilton *Advocate-Hamiltonian,* 311, 314, 340, 352
Hamlin, Hannibal, 59
Hammel, Tom, 311, 312
Hancock, Winfield S., 119-20
Hanebrink, Joe, 350
Hannibal *Clipper,* 115
Hannibal *Courier, Courier-Post,* 55, 125, 135, 225, 250, 254, 258, 276, 307, 340, 358
Hannibal *Evening News,* 74
Hannibal *Journal,* 55, 159, 187, 244
Hannibal *Messenger,* 55
Harbaugh, Howard S., 76
Hardin, Charles H., 114
Hardin *Journal,* 340
Harding, Warren, 247, 258-60
Hardy, H. H., 341
Hardy, L. G., 343
Hardy, W. G., 343
Harkness, Richard, 289
Harlan, George B., 278, 355
Harper's Weekly, 80
Harrell, H. A., 349
Harris, Guiford D., 344
Harris, Morran D., 220
Harris, Oliver, 37
Harris, Thomas A., 55
Harris, William T., 174
Harrison, Benjamin, 146, 148
Harrison, C. M., 185, 273, 355
Harrison, Fred M., 248, 273, 339
Harrison, William H., 20, 41
Harrison, W. M., 311, 339
Harrisonville *Cass County Democrat-Missourian,* 324, 331, 340, 352
Harrisonville *Cass County Gazette,* 76
Hart, Beaulah, 336
Hart, Grace L., 335
Hart, Jim A., 65, 176

Hartford Convention, 26
Harvey, Charles M., 177
Harwood *Citizen,* 184
Haskell, Henry J., 273, 305, 316
Hawkins, Ralph G., 337
Hawkins, Ralph N., 337, 346
Hawkins, W. N., 133
Hay, John, 166
Hayes, Rutherford B., 116, 144
Hays, Jack, 335
Hayti *Missouri Herald,* 323, 340
Headlines, 139
Hearst, W. R., Jr., 311
Heck, Frank, 312, 315
Heckethorn, E. P., 340
Hedbery, Charles, 344
Hemingway, Ernest, 175
Hempstead, Thomas, 25
Henderson, John B., 105-6, 111
Hendley, George W., 229
Hennings, Thomas C., Jr., 331
Henry, Harry H., 336
Henry, Isaac N., 13-14
Hensley, Glenn S., Jr., 324
Henson, George T., 304, 349
Henson, Jack, 345
Herbert, B. B., 161-62
Hermann *Advertiser-Courier,* 163, 307, 340, 352
Hermann *Volksblatt,* 184
Hermitage *Index,* 308, 340
Hert, John, 339
Hertich, H. G., 306
Hesse, Don, 200
Hewitt, Rogers, 155, 348
Hewitt, W. C., 289, 348, 355, 357
Hicks, F. C., 195
Higbee *News,* 294
Higginsville *Advance,* 340
Higginsville *Jeffersonian,* 227, 340
Hill, Howard, 342, 346
Hill, Nelson, 306
Hill, T. J., 185
Hill, W. D., 344
Hillsboro *Jefferson County Record,* 340, 352
Hillsboro *Jefferson Democrat,* 120, 129, 132, 188
Hilton, Charles C., 186, 334
Hinkle, Jacob, 5-6
Hobart, C. L., 250, 298, 340, 355
Hodges, R. E., 256
Hodges, Richard T., 343
Hodgeson, Joseph, 67

Hoff, Chester W., 348
Hoffman, John W., 341
Hogg, John A., 309-10
Holden *Democrat*, 111
Holden *Press*, 298
Holden *Progress*, 250, 253, 326, 340, 352
Hollenbeck, Arch T., 306
Holliday, Benjamin, Jr., 16, 19
Hollmann, Frank H., 350, 355
Holman, Morton, 300, 342
Hook, C. W., 332
Hook, Mrs. Z. W., 299
Hoover, Herbert, 273, 279
Hopkins *Journal*, 341
Horne, R. C., 186
Houser, Daniel M., 231
Houston *Herald*, 302, 306, 323-24, 329, 341, 352
Houston *Republican*, 323-24, 328, 341, 352
Houston, Texas, *Post-Dispatch*, 253
How, John, 65
Howard, Bart B., 298
Howard, Sandford, 338
Howsman, William E., 348
Hoyt, Palmer, 290
Hubbard, J. S., 248, 275
Hudson, James A., 153, 186, 354
Hudson, Luelle, 136
Hudson, Stanton, 332
Hudson *Republican*, 62
Hughes, Charles Evans, 238-39
Hull, A. Y., 129-30, 186, 354
Hull, J. Fred, 248, 299, 355
Humansville *Star-Leader*, 341
Hume *Border Messenger*, 341
Huntsville *Herald*, 115, 181
Huntsville *Randolph County Times-Herald*, 72, 341
Huntsville *Vindicator*, 181
Hutchins, Robert M., 278
Hutchinson, Gilbert, 345
Hutton, John E., 134, 186, 354
Hyde, Arthur M., 260
Hyde, Ira B., Jr., 299
Hyde, William, 107

Iden, Charles, 327
Idol, Edgar R., 340
Illmo *Jimplicute*, 328, 341
Illustrations; *see* Halftones
Immigration, 28
Independence *Evening and Morning Star*, 35

Independence *Examiner*, 165, 216, 251, 255, 258, 299-300, 303, 304, 306, 308-9, 326, 341, 345, 357
Independence *Gazette*, 62
Independence *Inter-City News*, 341
Independence *News*, 307, 324
Independence *Pictorial News*, 323
Independence *Sentinel*, 162, 185, 213
Independence *Shopper*, 323
Independence *Upper Missouri Advertiser*, 36
Indians, 6, 8, 12, 27, 39
Industrial Union, 146
Ingenthoron, Freda, 339
Inland Daily Press Association, 278
International Typographical Union, 251, 266, 293
Irish, 3, 42
Iron Curtain Talk; *see* Churchill
Ironton *Iron County Register*, 106, 224, 341
Ironton *Mountain Echo*, 324, 341

Jacks, John W., 154, 160, 187, 195, 344, 354
Jackson, Andrew, 15, 29-31, 33, 39
Jackson, Claiborne F., 46-47, 70-71
Jackson, Thomas, 343
Jackson, Verdell, 343
Jackson *Cape County Post*, 298, 341
Jackson *Courier*, 22
Jackson *Eagle*, 21
Jackson *Independent Patriot*, 21, 30-31
Jackson *Jeffersonian*, 22
Jackson *Missouri Cash-Book*, 22, 111, 235-36, 306, 341
Jackson *Missouri Herald*, 20-21, 23
Jackson *Patriot*, 25
Jackson *Pioneer*, 341
Jackson *Southern Advocate and State Journal*, 22
Jackson *Southern Democrat*, 2
Jackson's Resolutions, 47
Jacobi family, 328
Jacobins, 83
Jaegers, Urban M., 342
James, Frank and Jesse, 140-44
Jamesport *Tri-County Weekly*, 341
Janis brothers, 347
Jasper *Jasper County News*, 324, 341
Jefferson, Thomas, 2, 10, 147

Jefferson City *Capital News*, 258, 273, 283, 300, 308, 341, 357
Jefferson City *Jefferson Examiner*, 71
Jefferson City *Jefferson Inquirer*, 40, 42, 49, 53, 55, 65, 71-72, 183, 187
Jefferson City *Jeffersonian Republican*, 32, 34, 39
Jefferson City *Metropolitan*, 55
Jefferson City *Missouri State Times*, 84-85, 89-90, 97
Jefferson City *Peoples Tribune*, 108, 111, 115-16, 118, 120
Jefferson City *Post-Tribune*, 283, 308, 341
Jefferson City *State-Times*, 110, 124
Jefferson City *Times*, 124
Jefferson City *Tribune*, 123, 129, 161, 184, 193
Jeffries, J. B., 250
Jenkins, Earl, 340
Jenkins, Wallace N., 334
Jesse, R. H., 212
Jewell, Harry S., 298, 357
Jewett, Ernest W., 348
Jewett, W. O. L., 155, 158, 187, 195, 211, 227, 348, 354
Johns, George S., 247, 298
Johnson, Andrew, 105
Johnson, William, 34
Johnston, George, 339, 355
Johnston, James W., 339
Johnston, Joe P., 157
Johnston, V. A., 339
Johnston, Virgil, Jr., 339
Jones, Charles, 177
Jones, George S., 231
Jones, James C., 306
Jones, Max, 345
Jones, O. D., 150
Jones, Will A., 342
Joplin *Globe*, 118, 232, 234-35, 254, 284, 294, 296, 309, 326, 341, 358
Joplin *News-Herald*, 225, 234, 249, 254, 276, 284, 294, 341
Journalism Series bulletins, 219
Journalism Week, 173, 218-19, 226-29, 243, 245, 249, 276-79, 287-88, 310-11, 316, 331
Jutton, John R., 332

Kahoka *Clark County Courier*, 308, 341
Kahoka *Gazette Herald*, 308, 341
Kansas City *Dispatch*, 353

Kansas City *Enquirer*, 62, 68
Kansas City *Enterprise*, 65, 66
Kansas City *Free State Republican*, 67
Kansas City *Journal of Commerce*, 57, 59, 60, 63-64, 87, 91, 111, 123, 128, 150
Kansas City *Journal, Post, Journal-Post*, 62, 142, 213-14, 224-25, 231-32, 235-37, 240, 253-55, 257, 262, 267, 271, 276, 280, 283, 286
Kansas City *Ledger*, 50, 66
Kansas City *News-Press*, 341, 353
Kansas City *Star*, 150, 171-74, 200, 212, 214, 223-25, 227, 231, 233-34, 236, 241-43, 248, 254-55, 257-60, 271, 273, 276, 277, 283-85, 288, 291, 293, 295, 296, 298-300, 307, 316, 341, 357-58
Kansas City *Times*, 118, 150, 185, 188, 204, 212, 225, 341
Kansas City *Western Journal of Commerce*, 67
Kansas City *Western Metropolitan*, 67
Kansas-Missouri feuds, 66, 67
Kansas-Nebraska Bill, 54, 56
Kansas Press Association, 311
Kauffman, Frank L., 305
Kaufman, George H., 349
Kearney *Courier*, 307, 342
Keemle, Charles, 15, 32, 34, 37
Kehr, E. C., 343
Kehr, Ralph E., 348
Keller, Charles W., 276
Kelley, Robert N., 36
Kellogg Newspaper Company, 140
Kenamore, Clair, 239
Kennedy, John F., 328-29
Kennedy, R. C., 66
Kennett *Clipper*, 182
Kennett *Democrat, Dunklin County Democrat*, 163, 182, 220, 326, 342, 353
Kennett *Missouri Weekly*, 326, 342
Kenower, J. T., 335
Kentucky laws, history, 7-8
Kerby, James C., 159, 187
Keytesville *Chariton Courier*, 135, 342
Keytesville *Herald*, 115
Kielhofner, Bob, 337, 345
Kierolf, A. S., 133
Kies, Fred E., 298
Kimball, E. E., 146
Kimberling, L. E., 341

King, Austin A., 46
King, Henry P., 135, 177, 217-18, 231
King, W. A., 68
King City *Tri-County News*, 158, 294, 342, 353, 357
Kingston *Banner of Liberty*, 76
Kingston *Caldwell County Beacon*, 76
Kinley, Isaac H., 154, 187, 354
Kinnier, John T., 318
Kirby, Elwood, 124-25
Kirby, Everett, Jr., 342
Kirby, J. C., 354
Kirkpatrick, Arthur R., 81
Kirkpatrick, James, 329, 331, 351, 356
Kirksville *Express and News*, 251, 258, 271, 273, 342, 357
Kirksville *Graphic*, 223
Kirkwood, I. E., 254
Kirkwood *Advertiser*, 322, 342
Kirtley, Sinclair, 19-20
Knapp, Charles W., 218, 231
Knapp, George, 37, 71
Knights of Labor, 145
Knob Noster *Item*, 342
Knott, John A., 159, 187, 354
Knouse, Charles A., 327
Know-Nothing party, 54, 65
Knox City *News*, 342
Koenig, Fred W., 335
Korean War, 316
Krause, Chester, 277, 343
Krumsick, George W., 327, 350
Kucklebur Oath, 89
Ku Klux Klan, 104, 108, 247, 254

LaBelle *Star*, 299, 342
Laclede *Blade*, 299
Laddonia *Herald*, 350
LaFollette, Robert M., 260
LaGrange *Democrat*, 115
LaGrange *Indicator*, 221, 342
LaGrange *National American*, 69
Lake, O. R., 177
Lamar *Democrat*, 342
Lamar *Journal*, 308
Lamkin, Lewis, 125, 187, 339
Lamm, Henry, 239
Lamonte *Record*, 188
Lancaster *Excelsior*, 124, 191, 338
Landen, Frances, 220
Landon, Alfred, 280
Lane, Joseph, 57, 60
Langford, Paul, 337

LaPlata *Home Press*, 137, 191, 265, 294, 326, 342, 353
Larkin, Russell, 344
Lathrop *Monitor*, 260-61
Lathrop *Optimist*, 325, 342
Lawless, L. E., 15
Laws, Samuel, 135
Lawson *Review*, 300, 342
Leach, H. H., 335
Leach, John A., 117-18
League Collection, 200
League of Nations, 241-43, 259
Lebanon *Laclede County Leader*, 273
Lebanon *Record*, 292, 342
Lebanon *Rustic*, 249
Lebanon *Rustic-Leader*, 136
Lebanon *Rustic-Republican*, 342, 353
Ledbetter, Will M., 177-80
Lee, Charles A., 252
Lee, S. E., 347
Lee's Summit *Journal*, 188, 283, 327, 342, 353
Leeton *Times*, 254
Lefmann, W. J., 344
Lenhart, Bill, 349
Leonard, Leverett, 148
Lesueur, A. A., 137, 164, 188, 195, 211, 354
Levering, Joshua, 150
Lewis, Meriwether, 3, 4
Lewis, Robert, 150
Lewistown, Pennsylvania, *Mifflin Gazette*, 3
Lexington *Advertiser-News*, 342
Lexington *Caucasian*, 109-10, 112, 126, 131, 188
Lexington *Citizens Daily Advocate*, 74
Lexington *Expositor*, 74
Lexington *Intelligencer*, 112, 137, 150, 185, 188, 195, 207, 328
Lexington *Register*, 132
Lexington *Union*, 77, 84
Lexington, Kentucky, *Farmer's Library*, 3
Lexington, Kentucky, *Gazette and Western Advertiser*, 3
Lexington, Kentucky, *Gettysburg Gazette*, 3
Lexington, Kentucky, *Reporter*, 12
Liberal *News*, 216, 342
Liberal Republican party, 107-12, 169
Liberty *Advance*, 306
Liberty *Far West*, 38-39
Liberty *Tribune*, 43, 64, 84, 95, 98,

119, 201, 273, 306, 332, 342, 353
Liberty *Upper Missouri Enquirer,* 36
Liberty *Western Star,* 50
Libraries, 103, 146
Licking *News,* 323-24, 342
Life Magazine, 316
Lilbourn *Semo News,* 307, 342
Limbaugh, J. W., 22
Lincoln, Abraham, 59-63, 77-80, 90-91
Lindsay, R. H., 204
Lingle, Laurence D., 54
Linn *Osage County Observer,* 343
Linn *Osage County Republican,* 334, 353
Linn *Unterrified Democrat,* 108, 111, 305, 343
Linn Creek *Reveille,* 273
Linneus *Bulletin,* 118, 183, 212
Linotype, Linotype School, 288, 290, 307, 316
Literary Digest, 236
Lloyd, Bessie, 342
Lloyd, Erwin, 346
Lloyd, Raymond, 307, 346
Loan Office Act, 25
Local items, 9
Lockwood, Sara L. (Mrs. Walter Williams), 249, 327
Lockwood *Luminary,* 343
Lodge, Henry Cabot, 243
Loeb, Isidor, 195-97
London, John M., 133
Long, H. R., 289-90
Long, J. Weller, 149
Long family, 350
Longan, George B., 298
Lord, Byron, 343
Louisiana Purchase Exposition, 147, 162, 165-66, 197
Louisiana Territory, 2-3, 24
Louisiana *Democratic Herald, Herald,* 76, 98
Louisiana *Journal,* 76, 84-85, 94, 125
Louisiana *Press, Press-Journal,* 181, 185, 312, 343, 353
Louisiana *Riverside Press,* 136
Louisiana *True Flag,* 82
Lovejoy, Elijah, 33-34, 41
Lowe, Frank M., 146
Lowell, J. R., 355
Lowry, Robert G., 334
Lowry, Wilson B., 299, 334
Loyalty Oath, 89
Lucas, Charles, 29

Lusk, James, 64
Luther, Leonidas, 188
Lyles, E. K., 306, 341
Lyon, Nathaniel, 73, 79-82
Lyon, William H., Jr., 2, 10-12, 34

McAllen, Thomas W., 336
McAnally, David R., Jr., 209
MacArthur, Douglas, 316
McCandless, Perry G., 14
McCarthy, Bernard F., 341
McCarty, H. M., 68
McCloud, Robert, 4, 22, 27, 32
McClure, James N., 350
McClurg, Joseph W., 106, 159
McCollum, Earl, 299
McCormick, Robert, 296
McCrae, Charles M., 188
McCrae, William, 346
McCullagh, Joseph B., 134, 168, 174-77, 209
McDaniel family, 336
McDowell, A. W. (or W. A.), 337
McElhinney, Clifford, 346
McFarland, Charles T., 188
McFarland, H. S., 22
McFarland, Lowell, 346
McGiffin, Donald J., 338
McIlvaine, Bob, 310
McKee, William, 76
McKelway, A. J., 20
McKinley, John C., 226
McKinley, William, 150, 220
McKinney, Thomas T., 305
McKinney, W. N., 338
McLaughlin, Chase, 340
McLaughlin, C. L., 340
McManus, George, 279
McMullen, John H., 350
McMullen, John K., 306, 348
McMullen, Lloyd, 348
McMullen, R. W., 129, 188
Macon *Chronicle-Herald,* 258, 269, 274, 291, 300, 308, 329, 343, 358
Macon *Examiner,* 133
Macon *Gazette,* 84, 94
Macon *Missouri Granger,* 115
Macon *Republican,* 167, 227
Macon *Times,* 153, 186
McReynolds, John, 67
Madison, James, 10
Madison *Times,* 343
Magner, John, 177
Mahnkey, Mary, 274

Maitland *Herald,* 300
Major, Elliott W., 225-26
Malden *Press-Merit,* 308, 343, 353
Mann, Russell, Jr., 315, 329
Manring, Ahira, 146
Mansfield *Mirror-Republican,* 324, 343
Mapes, Robert, 338
Marble Hill *Banner-Press,* 343
Marceline *News and Bucklin Herald,* 343, 353
March, David, 88
Marionville *Free Press,* 343
Markey, J. Thomas, 336
Marmaduke, John S., 81, 143, 145
Marmaduke, Miles M., 143
Marshall, Texas, 82
Marshall *Democrat-News,* 186, 240-41, 273-74, 276, 308, 343
Marshall *Saline County Citizen,* 343
Marshfield *Mail,* 269, 343, 353, 358
Marshfield *Sentinel,* 74
Marthasville *Record,* 343
Martin, A. J., 306
Martin, Eugene A., 345
Martin, Frank L., 214, 272, 278, 298-99
Martin, Frank L., Jr., 351
Martin, William W., 15
Martinsburg *Monitor,* 328
Maryville *Democrat-Forum,* 255, 277
Maryville *Forum,* 265, 341
Maryville *Nodaway County Tribune,* 299, 353
Maryville *Nodaway Democrat,* 146
Maryville *Republican,* 160, 190, 195
Mason, Abraham G., 188
Mason, Dal, 334
Mason, Harry P., 188, 339
Masters, De Witt, 345
Matchett, Charles H., 150
Mathis, Wilburn, 340
Mattocks, C. E., 337
Mauldin, Bill, 200
Maury, Evarist, 13-14
Maxwell, O. T., 335
May, Charles J. L., 306
Mayes, Jewell, 277
Mayfield, James S., 36
Mayhall, William F., 335
Maynard, William, 136
Maysville *DeKalb County Record-Herald,* 343, 353
Meador, E. N., 307, 336
Meador, Lee, 340, 345

Meadville *Messenger,* 327
Melton, E. J., 330-31, 356
Melton, Emory, 335
Memphis *Democrat,* 270, 306, 343
Memphis *Farmer's Union,* 149
Memphis *Reveille,* 343
Memphis *Scotland County News,* 115
Merrick, John L., 36
Merritt, Allen B., 336
Merwin, J. B., 129, 131, 135
Meta *Herald,* 343
Metz *Times,* 343
Meuser, Kenneth G., 343
Mexican War, 39, 44-46
Mexico *Intelligencer,* 134, 155, 183, 186, 262, 276, 286
Mexico *Ledger,* 129, 133, 138, 152, 192, 228, 248, 258, 271, 273, 284, 286, 297, 303, 308, 310, 329, 343, 357
Mickey, David L., 334
Middleton, James H., 37
Milan *Farmer,* 72
Milan *Standard,* 324, 343
Miles, Daniel B., 337
Military Order No. 96, 74-75
Miller, Barney, 338
Miller, G. H., 327
Miller, James L., 304, 319, 323, 350, 358
Miller, Ray E., 307
Miller, Robert H., 84, 342
Miller, Robert W., 336
Miller, Thomas J., 33
Miller, Thomas W., 349
Miller, William L., 350
Miller, William T., 224
Miller *Press,* 343
Mississippi Press Association, 161, 196
Mississippi Valley Historical Association, 197
Missouri Advertising Managers Association, 290, 311
Missouri Associated Dailies, 257, 265, 276, 310, 312
Missouri Bar Association, 312
Missouri Circulation Managers Association, 311
Missouri Compromise, 24, 65
Missouri *Editor,* 152, 159, 176, 177, 180, 204, 207, 210
Missouri Editorial Association; *see* MPA

Missouri Gazette; see St. Louis
Missouri Historical and Philosophical Society, 195
Missouri Historical Review, 95, 197
Missouri Interscholastic Press Association, 249
Missouri Newspaper Advertising Managers Association, 290, 311
Missouri Press Association, 102, 122-38, 152-68, 175, 185, 198, 206, 209-10, 212-13, 218, 226-29, 243-45, 248-51, 256, 265, 268-69, 275-78, 286-91, 299-300, 303, 305, 309-16, 322
Missouri Press News, 300, 311, 315, 320, 325, 329, 332
Missouri Press Women, 278
Missouri Writers' Guild, 229
Mitchell, Kathryn, 336
Mitchell, R. W., 189
Mitchell, Tobias, 177
Mitchell, Wirt, 306, 339
Mitchin, F., 163
Moberly *Democrat*, 192, 213
Moberly *Headlight*, 136
Moberly *Message*, 294, 324, 343
Moberly *Monitor-Index*, 206, 258, 276, 343, 357
Moffett, Fred D., 306
Mokane *Missourian*, 256, 343
Moll, Miller, 343
Monett *Times*, 292, 344
Monroe, James, 10
Monroe, Walt M., 189
Monroe City *News*, 155, 344, 353
Montgomery City *Montgomery Standard*, 131, 144, 154, 160, 187, 323, 344, 353
Monticello *Lewis County Journal*, 337
Montrose *Tidings, Herald-Tidings*, 337, 344
Moore, Dorothy O., 337, 347
Moore, J. C., 128
Moorhead, W. L., 340
Morehouse, Albert P., 146
Morelock, Tom C., 264
Morgan family, 250
Mormons, 27, 35-36, 52, 347
Morris, C. D., 162, 163, 189
Morris, John W., 38
Morrison, Ron, 334
Morse, Lucius B., 322
Morss, Samuel E., 172

Mott, Frank Luther, 288, 290, 299, 302, 321
Mound City *News-Independent*, 307, 344
Mount Vernon *Lawrence Chieftain*, 344
Mount Vernon *Lawrence County Record*, 344, 353
Mountain Grove *Journal*, 344
Mountain Grove *Tri-County News*, 323-24, 326, 344
Mountain View *Standard*, 308, 323, 324, 344
Mulinex, Charles W., 299, 342
Murphy, E. D., 72
Murphy, Roy E., 335
Murray, H. H., 345
Myers, John, 350

Naeter, Fred, 228, 244, 250, 336, 355
Naeter, George, 250, 306, 336
Naeter, Harry, 336
Napton, William B., 37
National Editorial Association, 166, 191, 275, 289, 330
National Farmers' Alliance, 145
National Newspaper Week, 290, 297, 312, 314
National *Printer-Journalist*, 161-62
National Recovery Act, 265-66
Naylor, W. G., 244
Need, William, 37
Neider, Ed, 64
Nelson, Edgar C., 250
Nelson, William Rockhill, 168, 171-74, 224-26, 231, 305
Neosho *Democrat*, 240
Neosho *Graphic*, 323-24, 344
Neosho *Herald*, 76
Neosho *Miner-Mechanic*, 323-24, 344
Neosho *News*, 308, 344
Neosho *Times*, 228, 250
Nevada *Democrat*, 119, 157
Nevada *Herald*, 344
Nevada *Mail*, 191, 303, 341, 344
Nevada *Post*, 234-38
Nevada *Southwest Mail*, 138
Nevada *Vernon County Democrat*, 240
New Deal, 266, 275, 293
New Florence *Leader*, 164, 183
New Haven *Leader*, 344, 353
New London *Ralls County Record*, 106, 183, 344
New Madrid *Record*, 344

New Orleans *Picayune,* 44
New York *Freeman's Journal,* 174
New York *Herald Tribune,* 304, 329
New York *Mirror,* 281
New York *Sun,* 94
New York *Times,* 176, 262, 303, 311, 313, 316
New York *Tribune,* 108, 202, 273
New York *World,* 168, 170, 271
Newhouse, Samuel, 347
News, coverage, 8, 68-69, 262, 272
Newspaper Association Managers, 312
Newsprint; *see* Paper
Newton *Chronicle,* 254
Nichell, Joe, 335
Nicholas, Alan G., 342
Nichols, James I., 189
Nixa *Enterprise,* 324, 351
Nixon, Richard, 328-29
Noel *McDonald County Press,* 344
Nolen family, 344
Norborne *Democrat-Leader,* 344
North Kansas City *News-Dispatch,* 322, 324, 344
North Kansas City *Press-Dispatch,* 322, 324, 344, 353
Northeast Missouri Press Association, 155-56
Northwest Missouri Press Association, 158, 256, 327
Norvell, Joshua, 13
Noyes, Crosby S., 166

Oak Grove *Banner,* 324-25, 344
Oak Grove *Sentinel,* 324, 344
Oath of Loyalty, 89
Odessa *Odessan,* 288, 310, 344, 353
O'Fallon *Community News,* 308, 344
Office of War Information, 285
Offset (Lithography), 293, 307, 316
Olds, George, 274
Oran *News,* 345
Oregon *Holt County Sentinel,* 248, 345
Organ, Minnie, 68, 197
Orr, William, 15, 32
Orrick, Robert R., 348
Orrick *Sentinel,* 340, 345
Osceola *Democrat,* 72
Osceola *Osage Valley Star,* 72
Osceola *St. Clair County Courier,* 345
Overall, B. W., 336
Overall, Wilson, 336
Overland *Community News,* 345
Owensville *Gasconade County Republican,* 345, 353

Ozark *Christian County Republican,* 345
Ozark Press Association, 156, 275

Pace, Marvin W., 305
Pacific *Meramec Valley Transcript,* 345, 349, 353
Page, I. L., 163
Page, Walter Hines, 347
Painter, William R., 162, 189, 196, 299, 336, 354
Palmer, Howard E., 289
Palmer, John M., 150
Palmyra *Courier,* 36, 38
Palmyra *Democrat,* 117
Palmyra *Marion Journal,* 38, 183
Palmyra *Post,* 38
Palmyra *Spectator,* 75, 84, 203, 275, 345, 353, 358
Pangborn, J. G., 131
Panics, financial, 39
Paper, 5, 93, 159, 163, 203, 244-45, 251
Paris *Appeal, Monroe County Appeal,* 157, 181, 213, 244, 249, 302, 306, 345, 353, 357
Paris *Mercury,* 188, 221, 256, 274, 306
Paris *Missouri Sentinel,* 183
Park, George S., 53
Park, Guy B., 277, 279
Park, Thomas W., 133, 189, 354
Park, W. C., 344
Park College, 53
Parker, Alton B., 220
Parker, J. Bartle, 177
Parkville *Courier,* 62
Parkville *Gazette,* 245, 345
Parkville *Industrial Luminary,* 53
Parkville *Platte County Dispatch,* 322, 324, 344, 353
Parkville *Platte County Gazette,* 345
Parma *Tribune,* 343
Parrish, William, 70
Parsons, James W., 345
Paschell, Nathaniel, 71
Pate, Henry Clay, 68
Patten, Nathaniel, Jr., 15-20, 37
Patterson, Mrs. J. M., 274
Patterson, W. J., 53
Patterson, Wright, 140
Pattonsburg *Call,* 345
Pay scales, 163, 177-78, 251, 265, 267
Payne-Aldrich bill, 224

Payne, John, 19
Penn, Shadrack, 35
Peoples' party, 107, 115
Perry *Enterprise*, 345
Perryville *Monitor*, 345
Perryville *Perry County Republican*, 283, 308, 331, 345, 353
Perryville *Sun*, 283, 345
Peters, Howard H., 328
Petrequin, Alvin F., 347
Phelps, John S., 134
Phelps, John W., 106, 116
Phelps, William W., 35
Photography, 205, 262, 324, 358
Pickering, Loring, 35
Piedmont *Journal-Banner*, 338
Pierce, Franklin, 55
Pierce City *Leader-Journal*, 323-24, 345
Piggott, Joseph, 25
Pike, Sam, 68
Pile, John L., 345
Pile, John M., 345
Pinckard, P. N., 125
Pineville *Democrat*, 324, 345
Pinkston, Floyd H., 337, 344
Pinney, Alden, 334
Pizer, Everett, 305, 349
Pizer, E. N., 349
Platte Purchase, 39
Platte City *Landmark*, 133, 189, 207, 222, 345
Platte City *Missouri Army Argus*, 75
Platte City *Platte Argus*, 45
Platte City *Platte County Conservator*, 74
Platte City *Reveille*, 189
Platte City *Tenth Legion*, 75
Plattsburg *Clinton County Register*, 122
Plattsburg *Democrat*, 124
Plattsburg *Jeffersonian*, 190
Plattsburg *Leader*, 346
Pleasant Hill *Dispatch*, 182
Pleasant Hill *Review*, 180
Pleasant Hill *Times*, 299, 324, **346**, 353
Poetry, 17, 96-97, 128, 132
Pogue, Ralph W., 344
Polk, Trusten, 56
Ponder, Chester L., 338, 343
Pool, Cance A., 273
Pool, J. Kelly, 189, 221, 228, 273, **305**, 355, 357

Popham, Otis A., 323
Poplar Bluff *American-Republican*, 254, 271, 305, 307, 346
Poplar Bluff *Citizen*, 223
Poplar Bluff *Citizen-Democrat*, 224, 254
Poplar Bluff *Interstate-American*, 254
Poplar Bluff *Republican*, 254, 346
Population, 29, 47, 52, 104, 230, 332
Populist party, 148-49
Portageville *Review*, 346, 353
Portageville *Southeast Missourian*, 337, 346
Potosi *Independent-Journal*, 325, 346
Potts, Harry, 343
Powell, John B., 299
Powell, W. J., 211
Preetorius, Edward L., 231
Press, printing, 1, 5, 9, 17, 70, 97, 103, 139, 203, 262, 288, 294, 307-9
Preston, A. L., 273, 342
Preston, Eugene L., 306
Price, A., 177
Price, Eugene, 335
Price, James W., 319, 346
Price, Sterling, 54, 80, 82
Price, W. C., 346
Priest, Zenas, 21
Primm, James N., 43, 51
Princeton *Advance*, 190
Princeton *Post-Telegraph*, 319, 324, 346, 353
Princeton *Telegraph*, 346
Progressive party, 224-26, 238
Prohibition, 241-42
Prospectus, 4-5, 22, 33, 35, 37
Publishers and Editors of North Missouri, 123
Publisher's Auxiliary, 303-4, 319, 331
Pulitzer, Joseph, I, 109, 165, 168-71, 213, 231, 300, 304; Joseph, II, 267, 271, 292, 297, 302, 306, 357
Purcell, E. L., 328, 341, 355
Puxico *Press*, 307

Queen City *Monitor-Leader*, 338

Raby, Georgina, 165
Rader, Perry Scott, 190, 195, 197
Radical party, 83, 104
Radiophone, 294
Radio stations, 170, 256-57, 263-64, 315
Railroads, 39, 103, 113, 292

Ramsey, Charles G., 37, 74
Rate cards; see Advertising
Ray, Bob, 336
Ray, E. Lansing, 249, 254, 273, 304, 306, 357
Ray, E. Lansing, Jr., 273, 299
Ray, John, 336
Ray, Means, 336
Ray, S. J., 200
Raytown *News*, 346, 353
Readyprints, 139-40, 203
Reber, Bert J., 337
Recker, L. H., 344
Rector, William, 25
Redpath, James, 65
Regan, J. F., 123
Reid, A. J., 85
Reid, Marguerite L., 248
Reid, W. L., 155
Religion, 27, 95, 103
Remington, Stephen, 21
Renfroe, Robert, 38
Renfroe, R. W., 21
Rennie, J., 50
Reporters, 120, 173-74
Republic *Monitor*, 346
Republican Editorial Association, 160
Reynolds, Thomas C., 42-43, 82
Rhea, George W., 338
Rich Hill *Mining Review*, 215, 346
Rich Hill *Western Enterprise*, 221
Richard, Hugh, 346
Richards, Charles, 327
Richards, Gomer T., 336
Richards, Grant T., 336
Richland *Mirror*, 346
Richmond *Democrat*, 159, 181
Richmond *Missourian*, 277
Richmond *News*, 306, 346, 353
Richmond *Northwest Conservator*, 93, 100, 135-37, 142, 161, 182, 191, 212
Richmond *Ray County Conservator*, 346
Richmond *Ray County Herald*, 346
Ridenbaugh, William, 36, 98, 347
Ridings, Marion O., 311, 314, 340
Ritzenthaler family, 347
Roach, Eugene B., 249, 250, 355
Robb, Inez, 315
Roberts, Elzey, Sr., 254, 270, 280, 327
Roberts, Joe M., 343, 356

Roberts, Roy A., 277, 279-80, 288, 296-97, 301-2, 341, 358
Robertson, Wesley L., 163, 190, 339, 354
Robins, Fred G., 339
Robinson, Hamline E., 160, 190, 195, 354
Rock Port *Atchison County Mail*, 306, 346, 353
Rockville *Leader*, 348
Rockwell, J. V., 343
Rockwell, Norman, 304
Rodemyre, Adam, 194, 236
Rodemyre, Edgar, 337
Rogers, W. B., 190, 196, 349
Rogers, Will, 260
Rolfe, John W., 337
Rolla *Advertiser*, 305, 346
Rolla *Express*, 63, 123
Rolla *Herald*, 188, 250, 306, 353
Rolla *New Era*, 291-92, 346
Rolla *News*, 291, 346
Rolla *Times*, 340
Rollins, James S., 19, 46, 86, 135
Roop, Lewis W., 338, 358
Roosevelt, Mrs. Eleanor, 315
Roosevelt, F. D., 276, 279-81, 285, 295-97
Roosevelt, T. R., 106, 220, 224-26
Rosecrans, W. S., 88
Ross, Charles G., 214, 239, 304-5, 357
Rowe, Paul C., 341
Rowell's directories, 121
Rowland, D. Wayne, 308, 319
Rozelle, Arthur, 149
Rucker, Frank W., 255, 300, 303, 309, 341, 357
Ruffell, W. P., 190
Runyon, Damon, 279
Rusche, Arthur, 350
Russell, B. F., 191
Russell, D. E., 346
Russell, James, 21
Rutledge *Record*, 205

Sagaser, F. M., 343
Sagaser, James P., 334
St. Charles *Advertiser*, 37
St. Charles *Banner News*, 306, 313, 324, 347
St. Charles *Chronotype*, 37
St. Charles *Clarion*, 37
St. Charles *Cosmos, Cosmos-Sentinel*, 37, 299, 327

St. Charles *Free Press,* 37
St. Charles *Jeffersonian,* 32
St. Charles *Missouri Advocate,* 32
St. Charles *Missouri Gazette,* 32
St. Charles *Missouri Patriot,* 37
St. Charles *Missourian,* 22, 29
St. Charles *News,* 131
St. Charles *Reveille,* 37
St. Charles *Western Star,* 37
St. Clair *Chronicle,* 325, 347
Ste. Genevieve *Correspondent-Record,*
   31
Ste. Genevieve *Fair Play,* 347
Ste. Genevieve *Herald,* 347
St. James *Leader-Journal,* 326, 347
St. John, John A., 143
St. Joseph *Bazoo,* 116
St. Joseph *Chronicle,* 191
St. Joseph *Free Democrat,* 58-60, 63
St. Joseph *Free Press,* 62
St. Joseph *Gazette,* 62, 96, 98, 111,
   134, 142, 183, 216, 225, 240, 255,
   276, 284, 294, 314, 326, 347, 357
St. Joseph *Journal,* 75
St. Joseph *Herald,* 86, 88, 109-10,
   123-24, 129, 142, 144, 192, 357
St. Joseph *News-Press,* 232, 236, 255,
   267, 276, 284, 291, 294, 300, 304,
   314, 326
St. Joseph *Tribune,* 75, 87, 88
St. Joseph *West,* 62
St. Louis *Ad-Writer,* 163
St. Louis *Amerika,* 232
St. Louis *Anzeiger des Westens,* 80
St. Louis *Argus,* 34-35, 39-40, 42, 55,
   98
St. Louis *Beacon,* 15, 34
St. Louis *Bulletin,* 69, 73
St. Louis *Christian Advocate,* 125
St. Louis *Chronicle,* 177
St. Louis *Colman's Rural World; see*
   Colman
St. Louis *Commercial Advertiser,* 32
St. Louis *Commercial Bulletin,* 37
St. Louis *Construction Record,* 322
St. Louis *County Leader,* 273
St. Louis *Courier,* 33
St. Louis *Daily Evening Herald,* 36-37
St. Louis *Daily Record,* 322, 324
St. Louis *Dawn,* 165
St. Louis *Democrat, Missouri Demo-
   crat; see also* St. Louis *Globe-Dem-
   ocrat,* 57, 61, 64-66, 69, 70-71, 76-
   80, 84-91, 106-9, 125, 128

St. Louis *Dispatch,* 89, 118
St. Louis *Emigrant and General Advertiser,* 13
St. Louis *Enquirer,* 10, 13-15, 17, 21-
   22, 24-27
St. Louis *Evening Journal, Journal,*
   150, 161
St. Louis *Farmers' and Mechanics'
   Advocate,* 36
St. Louis *Free Press,* 34, 36
St. Louis *Globe-Democrat,* 35, 65,
   120, 123, 138, 144-45, 150, 174-77,
   200, 202, 209-10, 217, 223, 225-26,
   231-36, 238-41, 249, 252-54, 257,
   260, 266, 270-71, 273, 276, 281-83,
   294-96, 299, 301-2, 304, 317, 325,
   347, 357
St. Louis *Intelligencer,* 30, 55
St. Louis *Journal of Agriculture,* 149
St. Louis *Journal of Commerce,* 132
St. Louis *Log Cabin Hero,* 41
St. Louis *Mill Boy,* 42
St. Louis *Missouri Argus,* 34, 201
St. Louis *Missouri Gazette,* 1-22, 25,
   29, 66, 201, 231
St. Louis *Missouri Herald,* 32
St. Louis *Missouri Observer,* 32
St. Louis *Missouri Reporter,* 35, 43
St. Louis *Missouri Republican,* 30-32,
   42, 57-58, 60, 62-64, 71, 75, 77-81,
   84-87, 94, 97, 104-7, 111, 116-17,
   125, 135, 142, 144-45
St. Louis *New Era,* 41
St. Louis *Observer,* 34
St. Louis *Post, Post-Dispatch,* 118,
   137-38, 141-44, 150, 157, 168-71,
   177, 200, 206, 214, 216-18, 223,
   231-32, 235-43, 247, 251-53, 255-
   60, 264, 268, 271, 276, 280, 285,
   287, 291-95, 298-302, 304, 316-18,
   325, 347, 357, 358
St. Louis *Republic,* 214, 217-18, 225,
   231, 233, 235, 236-37
St. Louis *Republican; see also* St.
   Louis *Missouri Republican,* 31, 150,
   202, 210
St. Louis *Repudiator,* 106
St. Louis *Reveille,* 139
St. Louis *School and Home,* 157, 167,
   211
St. Louis *Star-Sayings, Star,* 150, 177,
   241, 252, 254, 257, 263, 269, 271
St. Louis *Star-Times,* 266, 280, 285,
   291, 295-96, 301, 327, 357

St. Louis *State Journal,* 73-74
St. Louis *State Times,* 125
St. Louis *Times,* 33, 56, 105, 161, 217, 241, 252, 257, 270
St. Louis *Union,* 35, 69
St. Louis University, 28
St. Louis *Western Journal,* 10, 12
St. Louis *Westliche Post,* 105, 169-70, 232, 234
St. Louis *Wetmore's Weekly,* 221
St. Louis *Workingman's Advocate,* 34
St. Marys *Review,* 347
Salaries; *see* Pay scales
Salem *Monitor,* 115
Salem *News,* 325, 327, 347, 353
Salem *Post,* 326, 347, 353
Salisbury *Democrat,* 204
Salisbury *Press-Spectator,* 324, 347, 353
Sampson, Francis A., 196, 198
Sanderson, Howard, 348
Sandford, George, 322, 344
Sanford, William T. B., 20
Santa Fe Trail, 28, 40
Sarcoxie *Record,* 347
Saturday Evening Post, 304
Savage, Edward, 342
Savannah *Andrew County Republican,* 115
Savannah *New Era,* 122
Savannah *Northwest Democrat,* 74
Savannah *Plain Dealer,* 62, 74, 192
Savannah *Reporter,* 223, 308, 347, 353
Savell, Joel M., 338
Schell City *Ledger,* 348
Schell City *News,* 184
Schneider family, 340
Schofield, F. E., 338, 342
Schofield, John A., 76
Schofield, R. F., 338
School of Journalism, 126, 152, 158, 160-61, 168, 191, 209-20, 226-29, 253, 257, 264, 269, 272, 276-77, 286, 300, 304, 310, 314, 318, 333, 346, 351
Schooley, Herschel, 304
Schurz, Carl, 105, 107, 109, 114, 169
Scott, G. Denzil, 340
Scott, George, 340
Scott, John, 15, 17, 29
Scott, Winfield, 46, 55
Scroggins, Albert T., 16, 19
Scruton, George H., 287, 296, 348
Scruton, George H., Jr., 348, 356-57

Seaton, Fred A., 314
Sedalia *Bazoo,* 124, 157, 184
Sedalia *Capital,* 258, 273, 284, 289, 348
Sedalia *Democrat,* 115, 129-30, 137, 186, 258
Sedalia *Eagle,* 181
Sedalia *Times,* 132, 332
Seltzer, Louis B., 311
Senath *Dunklin County Press,* 348
Seneca *News-Dispatch,* 250, 308
Sensationalism; *see* Yellow journalism
Settle, William A., Jr., 141
Sewall, W. J., 297, 304, 306, 336, 355, 357
Seward, William H., 57, 59
Seymour, Horatio W., 106, 218
Seymour *Webster County Citizen,* 348
Sheffield, N. M., 124
Shelbina *Democrat,* 155, 158, 187, 195, 211, 324-25, 348, 353
Shelbina *Index,* 188
Shelbina *Torchlight,* 188
Shelbyville *Shelby County Herald,* 117, 155, 308, 348, 353, 357
Shelbyville *Shelby County Weekly,* 75
Shepard, Isaac F., 128
Shepherd, E. H., 338
Sheridan, Donald F., 346
Shieves, George A., 177
Shinn, Charles L., 348
Shippey, Lee, 227
Shoemaker, Floyd, 27, 115, 150, 196, 198, 209
Sikeston *Herald,* 327, 353, 358
Sikeston *Standard,* 273, 299, 320, 326, 348
Simpson, A. W., 98
Simpson, W. L., 340, 356
Sims, Earle E., 338, 344
Sims, L. Roy, 338
Sims, L. Roy, Jr., 327, 338, 344
Single Tax League, 146
Slater *News-Rustler,* 348
Slavery, 12, 24, 29, 41-42, 52-69, 306
Smalley, Garrett L., Jr., 341
Smalley, Robert W., 341
Smith, Alfred E., 260, 275
Smith, Clifford B., 341
Smith, Clyde S., Sr., 305
Smith, E. Harold, 306
Smith, George A., 348
Smith, Joseph; *see* Mormons
Smith, Stanford, 332

Smith, S. W., 125
Smith, T. O., 337
Smithville *Democrat-Herald*, 348
Smoot-Hawley Tariff Act, 280
Snyder, Joe R., 339
Sobieski, John, 148
Sommer, L. H., 349
Sosey, Don, 345, 358
Sosey, Frank H., 275, 355
Sosey, Jacob, 244, 345
Southeast Missouri Press Association, 158
Southern, William, Jr., 165-66, 201, 251, 299, 304, 306, 341, 354-55
Southwest City *Leader*, 184
Southwest City *Republic*, 348
Southwest Missouri Press Association, 156, 187
Sowers, Edward W., 291, 346
Spaar, George, 344
Spanish-American War, 162, 175
Sparks, E. L., Jr., 340, 358
Spear, George E., 327
Spear, George E., Jr., 334
"Specials," 71
Speed, Richard B., 138, 191, 354
Speer, S. L., 335
Spencer, H. R., 248
Spies, Daniel H., 200
Springfield *Leader, Leader-Press*, 109, 225, 232, 254, 263, 270-71, 274, 276, 280, 294, 348
Springfield *Missouri Weekly Patriot*, 107, 109
Springfield *News*, 254, 270, 294, 348
Springfield *Republican*, 110, 225
Springfield *Times*, 109
Stacey, Charles A., 347
Stahl, L. H., 115, 335
Stanard, J. D., 348
Stanberry *Headlight*, 348, 353
Stapel, John C., 248, 346
Stapleton, Jack, 334, 342, 348
Stark, J. E., 340
Stark, Lloyd C., 279, 281, 348
Stark, R. A., 340
Start, Clarissa, 315
State Historical Society, 1, 152, 160, 163, 164-65, 168, 187, 191, 198-201, 209, 227, 245, 331, 333
Statehood, 24-27
Steamboat, 8, 51
Steele, Charles W., 340
Steele, John, 34

Steele *Enterprise*, 348
Steelville *Crawford Mirror*, 348
Steinbeck, A. A., 311, 349
Steinbeck, A. H., 298, 349, 356
Steiner, Weldon H., 350
Stephens, Edwin W., 138, 140, 152, 155-57, 161-62, 191, 195-98, 210, 229, 354, 357
Stephens, Howard, 349
Stephens, Lawrence Vest, 150-51, 197, 221
Stereotyping; *see* Typecasting
Stevens, Walter B., 175, 177, 201
Stevenson, Adlai, 317-18
Stevenson, J. W., 289, 306, 331, 340
Stewart, Jess, 339
Stewart, Robert, 53, 70
Stickney, Walter, 327
Stine, Jacob R., 33
Stockton *Cedar County Republican*, 348
Stoddard, Amos, 2
Stone, William J., 148
Stonebreaker, J. N., 245, 355
Stonecipher, Harry W., 319, 350
Stover *Tri-County Republican*, 348
Strange, Tubal E., 20-21
Streeter, A. J., 146
Strikes, shutdowns, 293, 301-2
Strong, William A., 67
Stuckey, Aaron, 349
Stufflebam family, 335
Sturdivant, Robert, 38
Sturgeon *Independent*, 187
Sturgeon *Leader*, 155, 184, 221, 273, 349
Sturgis, H. S., 228, 250, 355
Subscribers, subscriptions, 7, 22, 122, 207, 244, 248, 258
Sullens, Joseph D., 344
Sullivan *Tri-County News*, 337
Summersville *Beacon*, 323-24, 342
Sunday, Billy, 228, 238
Surbrugg, Dellard, 340
Sutton, D. A., 128
Swain, E. E., 201, 244, 251, 273, 342, 355
Swain, E. E., Jr., 273
Swain, Harrison E., 273, 357
Sweet Springs *Herald*, 349
Swift, W. H., 73
Swindler, William F., 71
Switzler, William F., 20, 49, 54-55, 73-74, 83, 96, 98, 105, 122, 126, 128, 130, 132-33, 150, 191, 354

Taft, William H., 223-24, 226
Taft-Hartley Act, 301
Tally, A. G., 165
Tammen, H. H., 231
Tarkio *Avalanche*, 165, 349
Tarkio *Independent*, 149
Taubert, A. G., 350
Taylor, Dan, 77
Taylor, Frank W., Jr., 357
Taylor, Jack, 289
Taylor, Joe, 344
Taylor, Lewis R., 307
Taylor, Ray, 344
Taylor, Zachary, 46
Teapot Dome scandal, 259-60
Tedrick, George G., 299, 334
Tedrick, Orlo, 334
Teichman, Carl J., 337
Telegraph, 50, 58, 67, 71, 93, 120, 175
Television, 170, 263-64, 315, 317
Temperance movement, 27, 48, 145
Tennyson, R. C., 348
Texas Press Association, 162
Thayer *News*, 349
Thiess, Jack L., 342
Thomas, Clyde W., 338
Thomas, W. D., 166
Thomas, William L., 157, 167, 211, 227
Thomason, Mrs. Mark, 313
Thomason, Ronald M., 306
Thompson, James B., 137, 191, 354
Thomson, Jack R., 343
Thomson, Mark A., 347
Thomson, Ronald M., 347
Thornton, Mrs. A. B., 136
Tibbetts, James G. C., 307, 345
Tilden, Samuel J., 116-17
Time Magazine, 303
Tipton *Times*, 189, 305, 326, 349
Todd, James, 343, 355, 357
Toledo *Blade*, 97
Tork, William, 340
Townsend, George S., 344
Treadway, R. M., 36
Treat, Samuel, 35
Trenton *Grundy County Gazette*, 294, 299, 353
Trenton *Republican*, 190, 196, 250, 324, 349
Trenton *Republican News*, 122-23
Trenton *Republican-Times*, 258, 276, 307, 349

Trenton *Tribune*, 162-63, 189
Trigg, George W., 161, 191, 211, 354
Triggs, Orville D., 335, 344, 347
Trimble, J. McD., 150
Troy *Free Press*, 144, 157, 227, 286, 331, 349, 357
Troy *Herald, Lincoln County Herald*, 115, 129-30
Troy *States Rights Gazette*, 71
Truman, Harry, 284, 289, 292, 300, 310, 314, 316
Tucker, J. P., 245, 345, 355, 357
Tucker, Joseph W., 74-75
Tucker, William C., 350
Tugwell bill, 276
Turley, Alan, 349
Turnbaugh, James D., Jr., 340
Turner, Joseph H., 131, 135, 153, 192, 350
Turner, Wayne E., 336
Tuscumbia *Miller County Autogram-Sentinel*, 349, 353
Tuscumbia *Miller County Vidette*, 115, 118
Twain, Mark, 157, 164, 200, 263, 300, 307, 313, 340
Type, typecasting machines, 139, 203, 205, 262, 288, 321

Union *Franklin County Tribune*, 298, 311, 326, 353
Union Laborites, 147, 149
Union Star *Herald*, 328
Unions, 40
Unionville *New Century*, 190
Unionville *Republican*, 250, 349
United Nations, 292
United Press, 206, 264
United States Bank, 19
University Board of Curators, 209, 212, 214, 304-5
Urich *Herald*, 344

Vaile, H. M., 67
Van Antwerp, V. P., 35
Van Buren, Martin, 39-40
Van Buren *Current Local*, 304, 349
Van Cleve, W. C., 192, 343
Vandalia *Graphic*, 183
Vandalia *Leader, Leader-Press*, 183, 248, 308, 326, 350, 353
Vandalia *Press*, 308, 350
Van Hafften, Madeleine, 342
Van Horn, Robert T., 67, 231

Van Meter, Ray, 349
Van Press, 323
Vaughan, M. F., 340
Vaughan, Virgil, 340
Venable, Reece H., 341
Vernon, Wallace G., 349-50, 338
Versailles *Leader-Statesman*, 350
Vickery, Robert L., 347
Vickery, Robert L., Jr., 326
Vienna *Home Adviser*, 350
Vienna *Maries County Gazette*, 350
Vincent, J. W., 273
Virginia (state), 70, 97
Virginia Press Association, 289
Volkman, Alfred, 306

Walbridge, Cyrus P., 220
Walker, Mrs. Rose, 177
Wallace, Henry, 227
Wallace, James F., 340
Wallhausen, Art L., 337
Ward, Harry, 341
Warden, Ralph, 345
Warden, R. E., 345
Warner, William, 148
Warrensburg *Journal*, 113, 115
Warrensburg *Standard-Herald*, 236, 350
Warrensburg *Standard-Journal*, 323
Warrensburg *Star-Journal*, 258, 273, 298, 326, 350, 357
Warrenton *Banner*, 129, 135, 191, 250, 350
Warsaw *Benton County Enterprise*, 157, 192, 350, 353
Warsaw *Benton County Guide*, 353
Warsaw *Independent*, 182
Warsaw *Times*, 125
Washington *Citizen*, 323-24, 327, 350
Washington *Franklin County Advertiser*, 75
Washington *Missourian*, 302, 304, 320, 323-24, 350, 353, 358
Washington, D. C., *National Intelligencer*, 21
Washington, D. C., *Star*, 166
Washington, D. C., *United States Telegraph*, 15
Washlick, Mathew, 349
Waters, H. J., 212, 337
Waters, H. J., Jr., 294
Watkins, C. E., 268, 298-99, 337, 355, 357
Watson, E. M., 337

Watson, John, 34
Watson, Thomas, 34
Watters, J. S., 343
Watters, Ralph O., 343
Watters, T. Ballard, 269, 343, 355, 358
Watters, T. W., 343
Wattles, George S., 344
Waverly *Times*, 350
Waynesville *Pulaski County Democrat*, 324, 326, 350
Weaver, James B., 119, 148
Webb, Charles, 177
Webb City *Leader*, 279
Webb City *Sentinel*, 273, 327, 350
Webster Groves *News-Times*, 353
Webster Groves *Webster Advertiser*, 322, 342
Weeks, Amon C., 327
Weir, Ben F., 303, 344
Welch, L. A., 131
Weldon, William H., 341
Wells, Joe, 331, 349
Wellsville *Optic-News*, 351
Wensel, F. L., 163
Wentzville *Union*, 327, 351
West Plains *Gazette*, 159, 190
West Plains *Howell County Journal*, 141, 250
West Plains *Quill*, 324-25, 328, 351
Western, Joe, 344
Western Associated Press, 97
Western Historical Manuscripts Collection, 201
Western Newspaper Union, 140, 302
Westland, Al, 319
Westminster College, 298
Weston *Chronicle*, 351
Weston *Platte Argus*, 69
Westport *Border Star*, 62, 68
Westport *Border Times*, 68
Westport *Frontier News*, 68
Westport *Star of the Empire*, 68
Wetmore, Alphonso, 37
Wheaton *Journal*, 351
Whig party, 30, 38, 41-49, 54-56
Whipple, Richard A., 307, 342
Whitaker, Charles H., 192, 337
White, Edwin, 38
White, Hugh M., 39
White, L. Mitchell, 161, 201, 227-28, 248, 273, 286, 297, 303-4, 343, 355, 357
White, M. K., 350

White, M. N., 337, 350
White, Robert H., 349
White, Robert M., 138, 152, 159, 164,
    192, 201, 213, 273, 343, 354, 357
White, Robert M., II, 273, 286, 304,
    310, 329, 343
White, T. B., 157, 192, 350
White, William Allen, 173
Whitney, John Hay, 329
Wide Awakes, 61, 79
Wigginton, H. J., 183
Wiggs, William S., 327, 343
Wilcox, Horace, 123, 126
Wilder, J., 128
Wilkens, Edwin, 337
Wilkerson, E. S., 45
Wilkerson, Joel, 22
Wilkie, Lloyd, 36
Wilkinson, C. B., 124-25, 129, 192,
    354
Willard, Jess, 238
Williams, Earl P., 327
Williams, Frank N., 339
Williams, G. E., 338
Williams, George H., 339
Williams, H. G., 337
Williams, Ira J., 335
Williams, John B., 20
Williams, J. S., 123-24
Williams, Max E., 341
Williams, Mills, 351
Williams, R. H., 349
Williams, T. Norman, 328
Williams, Walter, 115, 140, 152-55,
    161-62, 164-66, 193-96, 204-5, 207,
    210, 211, 213-14, 217, 219, 221,
    227, 245, 249-50, 272, 299, 338,
    354
Williams, Younger J., 20
Williams Hall, 277, 345
Willkie, Wendell, 295
Willow Springs News, 292, 323-24,
    353, 357
Willson, Glenn E., 336
Wilmot Proviso, 45
Wilson, John, 37
Wilson, Lyle C., 287
Wilson, Richard E., 347
Wilson, Robert K., 306
Wilson, R. M., 343

Wilson, T. T., 165, 354
Wilson, Woodrow, 224-26, 231, 238-
    39, 242, 243
Winchester, Kentucky, Advertiser, 15
Windsor Review, 181, 326, 329, 331,
    351, 353
Winona Shannon County Democrat,
    332, 351
Winter, Edward H., 250, 350, 355
Wirephoto, 262, 321
Wisconsin Historical Association, 198
Wise, Frederick A., 38
Wise, Hal M., 273, 350
Wise, Hal M., Jr., 273
Witman, Arthur L., 358
Wolfe, James F., 344
Wolfe, Lois L., 335, 346
Wolpers, J. H., 254, 305, 346
Wolpers, Robert M., 346
Women in Journalism, 314-15
Woods, Charles L., 250, 306, 355
Woodson, Silas, 111
Woodward, F. N., 335
Woodward, G. T., 335
World's Press Congress, 191, 314
World's Press Parliament, 166
World War I, 230-46
World War II, 282-93
Wright, Earl A., 347
Wright, Edward A., 346
Wright, Erie, 346
Wright, Harold, 339
Wright, Joe, 341
Wright, John C., Jr., 345
Wright, Lloyd, 339
Wright, O. R., 342

Yancey, Thomas R., 223
Yegar, James, 328
Yellow journalism, 173, 231
Yorkston, Robert P., 153
Yost, Casper S., 210, 298, 357
Yost, R. M., 156, 273

Zevely, Lebbeus, 343
Zevely, William L., 343
Zimmerman, Jac W., 344, 350, 356
Zoeller, P. L., 345
Zorn, Will H., 248, 250, 355